DEATH, SOCIETY, AND HUMAN EXPERIENCE

DEATH, SOCIETY, AND HUMAN EXPERIENCE

Fourth Edition

ROBERT J. KASTENBAUM

Arizona State University

Merrill, an imprint of
Macmillan Publishing Company
NEW YORK

Collier Macmillan Canada, Inc.
TORONTO

Maxwell Macmillan International Publishing Group
NEW YORK   OXFORD   SINGAPORE   SYDNEY

Cover photo: Courtesy Ohio State University Publications
Editor: Linda James Scharp
Production Editor: Constantina Geldis
Photo Editor: Gail Meese
Cover Designer: Brian Deep
Production Buyer: Pamela D. Bennett

This book was set in Goudy Old Style.

Photo credits: pp. ii, xiv, 28, 54, 214, 244, and 296 by H. Armstrong Roberts; pp. 76 and 106 courtesy of Hospice at Riverside, Riverside Methodist Hospital, Columbus, OH; pp. 126 and 172 by AP/Wide World Photos; p. 146 reprinted by permission from Sandra Bertman, *Facing Death: Images Insights and Interventions,* Hemisphere Publishing Corp. 1991; p. 276 by K. Strand/H. Armstrong Roberts; p. 314 by Photo Researchers, Inc.

Macmillan Publishing Company
866 Third Avenue, New York, NY 10022

Collier Macmillan Canada, Inc.

Library of Congress Cataloging-in-Publication Data
Kastenbaum, Robert.
    Death, society, and human experience / Robert J. Kastenbaum. —
4th ed.
       p.   cm.
    Includes bibliographical references and index.
    ISBN 0-675-21189-1
    1. Death—Psychological aspects. 2. Death—Social aspects.
I. Title.
BF789.D4K36   1991
306.9—dc20   90-22254
                                                         CIP

Printing: 1 2 3 4 5 6 7 8 9   Year: 1 2 3 4

For Cynthia

Sometimes you just listen.

- *The subject is AIDS.* "If you don't catch AIDS, you'll live forever. That's what I think. No, wait! If you eat low cholesterol stuff and do the Jane Fonda work-out *and* you don't catch AIDS, *then* you'll live forever!" (Class reaction bubbles up; the social work student continues.) "Hey, I'm just kidding! What I mean is that AIDS is getting so much attention lately, you'd think that if we watch the seven warning signs— (Interruption: "That's cancer!")—whatever—I mean, *they* act like we never had death before there was AIDS, and who gets AIDS? Not us, right? Worrying about *their* AIDS is a lot easier than really worrying about *our* death, and how it's going to happen even if we never eat another doughnut either. How we love to kid ourselves!"

- *The subject is denial.* A young man in the second row recalls one of his experiences in Vietnam. He speaks softly, but nobody misses a word. A quiet night—so far. Suddenly the daily mortar barrage began—right on time. The first round was closer than usual. He turned to speak to his buddy. "Only his boots were left, and they were steaming. A minute ago he was there, and then . . . only his boots." The student remembered his immediate reaction: "I said to myself, 'It can be dangerous here.' It's amazing to think about it now, but I went about for a couple of weeks before it struck me that my buddy was dead. I guess that's some kind of denial, huh?"

- *The subject is funerals.* A woman has returned to class after a week's absence. Her father's sudden death had brought family members together from around the nation. The funeral director rejected one of the family's requests. "He insisted that Dad wear a suit and a tie. We knew that Dad wouldn't want that. He used to joke that he wouldn't be caught dead in a suit and a tie!" Family members agreed among themselves that Dad would have preferred to be buried in his red jogger's outfit, topped off with his favorite bolo tie. The funeral director wouldn't hear of such an impropriety and pressured the family to withdraw the request. "But we didn't cave in. I had learned enough in this class that I felt strong about insisting that our Dad still belonged to us, and that our rights were more important than the funeral director's stuffy old habits." It was the funeral director who capitulated. Later the funeral director apologized to the family for his resistance and said that he had learned something valuable from this experience.

- *The subject is suicide.* A new and angry voice is heard in class. It belongs to a woman who has attended every session but has never said a word. "I hear everybody feeling sorry for people who kill themselves. They have it easy. It's all over for them. Do you ever think about their children?" Her own father, it turns out, had committed suicide more than 40 years ago. "They all said it wasn't suicide, but we all knew it was. I kept wondering what I did wrong, or what Mother did wrong that my father would kill himself. I spent years being scared, being guilty, being angry. And the being angry is still there, as you can hear!"

A class on death, society, and human experience provides an exceptional opportunity for students and instructor alike. Generalities become specifics as strangers become part of each other's lives. Perhaps it is not surprising that many students later report that this has been the most compelling and valuable academic experience they have ever had. The topic is certainly both powerful and of universal provenance. When a course focusing on death proves useful, it is through the contributions of the students themselves, as well as the instructor, readings, videos, and other materials. Each component offers something distinctive. The instructor's knowledge and teaching skills and the personal experiences of everybody in the classroom together comprise the foundation for significant learning. The quality, scope, and pertinence of the readings, however, also have an important role. It is time, then, to say something about what the fourth edition of *Death, Society, and Human Experience* tries to accomplish and how it differs from previous editions.

GOALS

1. *To provide accurate and up-to-date knowledge on a wide variety of death-related topics.* The importance of such knowledge can be illustrated by a few very brief examples:
   - Parents and caregivers experience enormous stress when a child is dying. Naturally, the dying child becomes the focus of concern. But what of the brothers and sisters? What do they feel? What help do they need?
   - As we move through the 1990s, should we pause to feel grateful for the major advances in disease control that have extended the average life expectancy—or should we feel alarmed by the massive waves of violence that people have been inflicting on each other through this bloody, bloody century? How can our race devote itself so fervently both to the prevention and the infliction of death?
   - Is the real question, "Do we have the right to die?" Or is it perhaps, "Who has the right to make this decision—and on what basis?" The right-to-die issue is no longer only a matter for philosophical discussion: decisions are being made every day, and they are not necessarily consistent or to everybody's liking.

2. *To provide guidance to caregivers, whether professionals, volunteers, or family members.* Among the many examples:
   - Suicide continues to take a significant toll, not only on those who end their own lives, but also on their survivors who may be left with a sense of loss, guilt, anger, regret, and confusion. Clearing up some misunderstandings about suicide and becoming more aware of warning signs can help reduce the chances of a lethal suicide attempt.
   - What should caregivers for terminally ill people and their families expect of themselves? And know about themselves? Precisely what do hospice volunteers do? What are the legitimate responsibilities of the death educator? These are among the questions that have arisen in recent years and for which answers are starting to become available.
   - Why do people sometimes become so attached to an object that seems to be of little value, say, an old guitar? By recognizing that personal possessions may be cherished as a link with lost loved ones, we may become more sensitive in our interactions with others, and also more aware of our own attachments.

3. *To help the reader understand how the life and death of the individual are connected to sociocultural processes and events.* For example:
   - How a society behaves toward the dead may tell us something important about both its values and its viability. We see how ethnic/racial life-styles carry over to the place of the cemetery in the lives of various peoples.
   - Rights of the individual are highly valued in American society. Precisely how far these rights extend and how much claim society can place on the individual are questions that may take on life-and-death urgency in some situations, as expressed, for example, in the views of the Hemlock Society, and in a continuing series of court decisions regarding both terminally ill and disabled-but-not-dying individuals.

- The work activities of many Americans are under the rule of schedules, deadlines, and our culture's intense time-consciousness. What happens when these routines and obligations are interrupted by the death of a loved one? In particular, how does big business attempt to accommodate itself to the needs of the individual? "Grief by negotiation" explores this interface between the individual and society.

NEW FOR THE FOURTH EDITION

Several important changes have been made for the fourth edition of *Death, Society, and Human Experience*. These changes include:

1. A new chapter focused on AIDS, Society, and Human Experience (Chapter 6). Acquired Immune Deficiency Syndrome has already taken many lives throughout the world; a still larger number of people have been infected with the virus. On the individual level, there are survivors who grieve over the deaths of friends and family members, and others who worry about their own health— not to mention caregivers faced with the many challenges of the AIDS-related syndrome. On the societal level, there are complex and divisive political, economic, and attitudinal issues to consider. I have tried to do justice to both the individual and societal aspects of the AIDS menace.

2. Ethical issues are frequently encountered by those who provide care to terminally ill people and their families, and in a number of other death-related situations. This topic obviously deserves a chapter of its own, and the need has been met with the fourth edition (Chapter 11).

3. "How Can We Help? The Promise of Death Education and Counseling" is another topic that has become ripe for more extensive treatment, and so we have a new Chapter 12.

4. *Death, Society, and Human Experience* has always attempted to encourage readers' explorations of their own experiences, thoughts, feelings, and values. Chapter 1 begins with a fairly extensive set of self-inventory measures that readers are invited to complete. The self-exploration exercises are closely linked with major findings and concepts from the death and dying literature. They make the most effective and useful introduction we have ever been able to offer students and instructors.

5. Suicide has always been given substantial attention in this text. The new edition adds significant coverage to murder and terrorism (Chapter 8). I have often discussed violence and death in my own courses, and I welcomed the suggestions from several reviewers that this topic also receive attention in the book.

There are many other changes, including both the deletion of some older material and the addition of new coverage on such topics as the Buddhist stage theory of dying, and the paramedic's encounter with life and death situations. I am grateful to my editors at Merrill for their willingness to expand the length of this book in order to accommodate the new material. I also appreciate suggestions made by a number of students, other readers, and the following reviewers: Ronald Barrett, Loyola Marymount, Los Angeles; Allan Parelius, Indiana University, South Bend; Arthur Dell Orto, Boston University; Natalie Duany, Castleton State College, Vermont; and Stan Scobie, State University of New York, Binghamton.

MORE PERSONALLY . . .

In prefacing the third edition I confessed to a curious habit: "wanting to apologize in advance to those readers who have a strong need to find THE ANSWERS. This apology might begin by saying that I can draw upon a large reservoir of experience and research from many sources: psychology, nursing, medicine, sociology, philosophy, anthropology, religion, history, and what have I forgotten? I can draw as well upon a quarter of a century of my own clinical and research efforts. The apology might continue by admitting that none of these suffice. For THE ANSWERS, I am afraid we will still have to depend upon either our deepest caverns of faith (somehow immune to the shocks and calamities that any moment can thrust upon us) or to enlightened common sense. But this is my last such apology. I must tell you that I would be providing no service if I presented the uncertain as certain, the dangerous as docile, the complex as simple." There is definitely a market for the "quick fix," the follow-the-dots approach to understanding death in human experience. But as in many another superficial project (e.g., "The All-the-Okra-You-Can-Eat Diet"), one tends to end up as both victim and coperpetrator of an assault on reason. We still must depend upon our own common sense and faith as well as the knowledge that has been laboriously distilled from research and clinical experience.

Death was fresh in my mind as I wrote the preface to the third edition. I think now more about Cynthia's life than her death; she would now have completed her college education (with who knows what adventures along the way). Cynthia was still exploring so many of her own possibilities that there's no telling what she might have decided to do with her life. That option was taken away forever by a motorist's inattention to a young woman whose mind was probably full of graduation plans as she started to cross the street. You be careful, please—at the wheel, on the street, in all those situations that can in an instant so amazingly demonstrate that death is not just a word.

I think you will find in this book what limited truth there is at the moment and, in the oddly contorted way that a textbook must do such things, perhaps a little love as well.

Robert J. Kastenbaum

CONTENTS

chapter 1

AS WE THINK ABOUT DEATH

experiences, attitudes, beliefs, feelings

Before all this happened, it was just a word to me, death. I could hear death. I could say death. Really though, it was just a word. Now it's like something under my own skin, if you know what I mean.

I was an A-1 bastard for about ten years after finishing medical school. I became human again just in time to save my marriage. I won't say that I'm ever comfortable with death, but now I am more comfortable with letting God play God and not taking every death as though it were a personal insult.

Will the next test be Wednesday?

Let's begin with the "next test" question. A young man had been told by a young woman that she did not want to continue their relationship. He left, but returned with a can of gasoline. He doused himself, lit a match, and became a living torch. The first report from the hospital indicated that he was in critical condition with burns covering about 90 percent of his body. I heard this report on the morning news as I drove to the university. I thought this horrifying incident might lead to an illuminating discussion in my Introduction to Human Communication course (a general studies section with nearly 500 students enrolled). Here were two young people in our own metropolitan area who were having difficulties in their relationship, and one of them

had so despaired that he had chosen excruciating pain and probable death. Surely there were more effective ways to communicate, and we could explore these together. I described the incident to the class and invited their response. Silence. Uncomfortable silence. After a long moment, one young woman raised her hand and spoke up: "Will the next test be Wednesday?"

There are a number of terms that could be used to describe this response. Perhaps she had used the strategy of *compartmentalizing*, placing a painful subject into a little mental box so it would not arouse anxiety or interfere with her other interests. Perhaps she was "in denial," acting as though the incident had never happened or as if she had not just heard about it. Perhaps, instead, she was more perplexed and annoyed than anything else: "What does this have to do with *me*? A guy I don't know has just set himself on fire—it's not in the book, and it's not in the syllabus. Let's get back to the course material!" Whatever the explanation, it is obvious that this student was not ready to discuss this incident, nor was the class in general. Like that ill-fated relationship reported on the morning news, the class and I were having our own difficulties in communicating.

Our "A-1 bastard" is a distinguished professor of medicine who is appreciated for his humane approach as well as for his store of technical knowledge. He recognizes a major shift in his personal attitude since the days when he believed that a physician had to be relentlessly aggressive, victorious, and invulnerable. Death had always been the unwelcome reminder that his goals were illusory and his quest misguided. He smiles about this now: "Even a doctor can grow up!"

Death stopped being just a word to a graduate student of social work when both her parents were killed in an automobile accident. She could not go on with her own life until she fully *realized* their deaths as well as her own mortality. Simply knowing intellectually that people die is not enough; she now had to connect death with life in a very personal way.

This challenge is ours as well. Psychiatrist Avery D. Weisman (1974) introduced the concept of *realization* with these words:

> Realization has two meanings: to perceive a reality, and to make real. Neither occurs without the other. In the instance of death and dying, although they are by no means identical, we are always haunted by our awareness of our time-limited existence. Nevertheless, we readily postpone, put aside, disavow, and deny its relevance for us. . . . As a rule, we perpetuate self-deception through comfortable platitudes, assigning the task of confronting death to certain professionals in our society. Few people are willing to accept death as a topic to be directly and dispassionately investigated. Most people concede that death is inevitable, a fact of nature. But they

are not prepared to *realize*, in the double sense I indicated, that death can be systematically explored, and thereby, much of its inherent dread can be attenuated (pp. 1–2).

The person who chooses to take (or teach) a course on the meaning of death in human experience has shown some willingness to confront issues that many of us prefer to avoid. This willingness, however, does not guarantee success. We must find within ourselves the intellectual, emotional, and spiritual resources to accomplish both tasks mentioned by Weisman: perceiving reality and making reality real to us. The woman whose parents were killed in an automobile accident still half-expected to hear from them and still had the urge to call them to share a bit of news or ask for advice. It would be some time before she could fully acknowledge the basic fact that her parents were dead *and* integrate this loss into her total life view (i.e., "Who am I, now that I am no longer a daughter?").

Our challenge becomes intensified as we encounter problems that resist quick, definitive, and stable solutions. Consider the following situations:

• An infant is born without a functional brain. There is zero possibility that this infant can ever become a person in the usual sense, or survive for even a brief time without special care. Should this infant be kept alive long enough to allow its organs to be harvested to help another infant in its battle for life?

• A physician enters the room of Debbie, a young woman who is said to be dying of ovarian cancer. He has never seen this woman before. She is suffering "from what was obviously severe air hunger" (very effortful breathing) and tells the doctor, "Let's get this over with" (Anonymous, 1988). He administers a lethal injection and within four minutes, Debbie is dead. Was this a humane action—or murder?

• The parents of a critically ill child refuse to authorize medical treatment because blood transfusions violate their religious beliefs. Does society have the right to intervene, or must the parents' beliefs be respected even if they deprive the child of potentially life-saving care?

In all of these instances we need to consult our own values and beliefs—but also our knowledge base. It is not sufficient to be knowledgeable about neonatal development, air hunger, or religious doctrines and their legal status. This kind of information will not necessarily make our decisions for us. But it would be less than responsible to participate in making life-and-death decisions while ignoring the many relevant facts of the situation. A lazy mind becomes a dangerous weapon in many death-related situations. All too often, even the most alert and open mind cannot keep up with all of the developments. Things may be happening very quickly at many levels at the same time. But the lazy or closed mind is a definite menace.

It is useful to keep an open mind, even about the assumptions that often govern our studies of death, society, and human experience. Two such assumptions were offered by Weisman: (1) that death should be "dispassionately investigated" and (2) that by doing so, "much of its inherent dread can be attenuated." Well, maybe yes, maybe no. Certain aspects of our relationship to death can be investigated in an objective manner, leaving our own beliefs and preferences aside. This approach often can be used in formal research studies in which many variables are controlled or manipulated.

The objective approach works especially well in studies that draw upon statistical information. Suppose, for example, that we want to know whether or not "grief kills." Many of us have known situations in which it seems as though a survivor died soon after the death of a loved one *because* of the death of the loved one. This question cannot be answered adequately by any one study, and when several studies are conducted, their findings may not agree. As Levav (1989–1990) has recently shown, some studies have found increased mortality among those who have experienced the death of a person significant to them, but some studies have not found this re-

lationship. Furthermore, when there is evidence of increased mortality or morbidity (illness), there may be other causes than grief as such.

The lazy mind will quickly give up in the presence of complex and discordant findings, and the closed mind will stick to whatever feelings and beliefs it has already developed for whatever reason. The rest of us will continue to grapple with the issue and to take the results of well-crafted studies into account in forming our own judgments.

Sometimes, however, the dispassionate, objective approach just will not work very well. This is likely to be true when we have a personal stake in the situation, when our own feelings and actions are intimately involved. It is also likely to be true when we are concerned with particular people in the midst of unique circumstances. For physicians, nurses, emergency medical technicians, paramedics, and certain other caregivers, these situations may arise regularly as a part of their responsibilities. Arriving at the scene of an accident, for example, paramedics often must make a very quick assessment of status and need. The paramedics will be intensely task-oriented as they follow the guidelines that have been set for their actions. It all seems—and is—skilled, professional, and objective. But let one of the victims be a young child, and the paramedics may suddenly experience an upsurge of personal feeling. "It was as if I could see Eddie lying there, my Eddie." From that moment onward, the paramedics will continue to move through their investigatory and interventive program, but the adjectives *dispassionate* or *objective* will no longer apply.

In many other death-related situations there is also the need for careful perception and evaluation of the circumstances before we decide upon our response. It is not realistic to pretend objectivity if we are the child, parent, spouse, or friend of the person who is dying, grieving, or suicidal. Instead, our challenge is to call upon both our strong emotional involvement and our ability to examine the facts of the situation with the care they deserve.

The other assumption is that by studying death we will somehow reduce our fears and anxiety. There is research literature on this question that is surveyed in Chapter 12. For the moment, however, let's just bear in mind that there are important individual differences among us. Why are we interested in studying death at this time? What fears and concerns are uppermost in our own minds? Can a book and a teacher meet our needs, or are we seeking something that goes well beyond the academic? Furthermore, is it even appropriate to expect that a class *should* reduce our anxieties? Many people do come away from readings, lectures, and discussions with a greater sense of security, and often with more tolerance for their own and other people's fears. However, students often experience some distress along the way as painful memories are rekindled and suppressed fears come to the surface. "Death education" (as it is sometimes called) is not always pain-free and does not necessarily result in a "what—me worry?" state of mind.

YOUR SELF-INVENTORY OF ATTITUDES, BELIEFS, AND FEELINGS

Perhaps you have noticed that some of your own attitudes, beliefs, and feelings have already come to mind. This would be quite natural. It is difficult to think about death without also thinking about particular people and experiences, and all filtered through our own unique perspectives.

But what *is* your perspective on death? Now would be a good time to find out. It is possible—in fact, it is probable—that your perspective will change to some extent as you continue to read, listen, and discuss. I invite you to take stock of your present experiences, attitudes, beliefs, and feelings. This will not only give you a personal data baseline but will also contribute to your appreciation of the ways in which other people view death. After exploring your own configuration of experiences, attitudes, beliefs,

and feelings, you will also be in a better position to understand the general relationships that have been observed between what we think and what we do in death-related situations.

Before reading further, begin sampling your personal experiences with death by completing Self-Inventories 1, 2, and 3. These exercises deal with several realms of knowledge, attitude, belief, and feeling. It is in your own interest to complete these exercises in a frank and serious manner. As a personal bonus, try to notice what thoughts and feelings come to mind as you answer these questions. Which questions make you angry? Which questions would you prefer not to answer? Which questions seem foolish or make you want to laugh? This is also part of the self-monitoring process that has been found invaluable by many of the people who work systematically with death-related issues. Take a few moments to complete Self-Inventories 1, 2, and 3 now.

By completing Self-Inventories 1, 2, and 3 you have now sampled your own knowledge base, personal experiences, attitudes, and beliefs. Many other questions might have been included, but enough is enough! We still have another set of questions to consider. In Self-Inventory 4 the emphasis is less on what we know (or hope we know) than on what we *feel*. The answers you choose today may or may not be the answers you would choose at another time, but try to get in touch with your feelings at this moment and allow them to guide your responses. Please complete Self-Inventory 4 before reading further.

OUR DEATH ATTITUDES IN REVIEW

In a moment we will review the self-inventory questions and provide the answers—where there are answers to provide. First, however, it will be useful to take a few examples of the many ways in which attitudes, beliefs, and feelings influence our death-related actions.

SELF-INVENTORY 1
MY KNOWLEDGE BASE

Fill in the blanks or select alternative answers as accurately as you can. If you are not sure of the answer, offer your best guess.

1. Each year, about _____ Americans die.

2. In recent years, the mortality rate (deaths per 100,000) in the United States population has _____ .
   (a) Increased (b) Decreased (c) Remained the same

3. The leading cause of death in the United States is _____ .

4. Among American youth (ages 14–24), the leading cause of death is _____ .

5. In recent years, the death rate from lung disease in the United States has _____ .
   (a) Increased (b) Decreased (c) Remained the same

6. In third-world nations a leading cause of death is _____ .
   (a) AIDS (b) Cancer (c) Heart disease (d) Measles

7. Capital punishment (the death penalty) is _____ .
   (a) Legal throughout the U.S.A. (b) Legal in some, but not all states (c) Not legal in the U.S.A.

8. Cryonic suspension attempts to _____ by a procedure that involves _____ .

9. The Living Will is a document that instructs _____ .
   (a) Doctors to do everything they can to keep this person alive (b) Doctors not to keep a dying person alive by artificial means (c) Lawyers to sue medical personnel who disobey the patient's request

10. Cremation is more likely to be the preferred means of body disposal for _____ .
    (a) Elderly men (b) Elderly women (c) Young men (d) Young women
    (e) No age or sex differences in preference

11. Which of these factors has been shown to have an important influence on how a person grieves a death: _____ .
    (a) How this person reacted to previous deaths (b) How this person expresses his/her emotions generally (c) The nature of his/her social support system (d) None of the above (e) All of the above

12. There are about _____ hospice organizations in the United States. _____ provide 24-hour service and are accredited under the National Hospice Reimbursement Act.
    (a) All (b) Some (c) None

13. There are approximately _____ suicide prevention centers in the United States. _____ are certified by the American Association of Suicidology.
    (a) All (b) Some (c) None

14. Among ethnic/racial subpopulations of the United States, the highest suicide rate appears among _____ .
    (a) African-Americans (b) Asian-Americans (c) Hispanic-Americans (d) Native Americans

15. A Gallup poll finds that about _____ percent of the American population believes in life after death.

Answers to self-inventory questions are found later in this chapter. Please don't peek!

SELF-INVENTORY 2
MY EXPERIENCES WITH DEATH

Fill in the blanks or select the most accurate alternative answers.

1. a. I (have/have not) had an animal companion who died.
   b. How I felt when my pet died can be described by words such as _____ , _____ , and _____ .

2. The following people in my life have died.
   Person _____ How long ago? _____
   a.
   b.
   c.
   d.
   e.

3. The death that affected me the most at the time was _____ .

4. How I felt when this person died can be described by words such as _____ , _____ , and _____ .

5. This death was especially significant to me because _____
   _____
   _____ .

6. In all the circumstances surrounding this person's death, including what happened afterward, my most positive memory is of _____
   _____ .

7. My most disturbing memory is of _____
   _____ .

8. I have conversed with dying people.
   Never _____ One person _____ Several people _____ Many people _____

9. I have provided care for a dying person.
   Never _____ One person _____ Several people _____ Many people _____

10. I have known a person who attempted suicide.
    Not to my knowledge _____ One person _____ Several people _____

11. I have known a person who committed suicide.
    Not to my knowledge _____ One person _____ Several people _____

12. I have known a person who died in an accident.
    Not to my knowledge _____ One person _____ Several people _____

13. I have known a person who was murdered.
    Not to my knowledge _____ One person _____ Several people _____

14. I have known a person who died of AIDS-related disease.
    Not to my knowledge _____ One person _____ Several people _____

15. I know a person who has tested positive for the AIDS virus.
    Not to my knowledge _____ One person _____ Several people _____

SELF-INVENTORY 3
MY ATTITUDES AND BELIEFS

Select the most accurate alternative answer. If you are not sure of the answer, offer your best guess.

1. I believe in some form of life after death.
   Yes, definitely _____ Yes, but not quite sure _____
   No, but not quite sure _____ No, definitely _____

2. I believe that you die when your number comes up—it's in the hands of fate.
   Yes, definitely _____ Yes, but not quite sure _____
   No, but not quite sure _____ No, definitely _____

3. I believe that taking one's own life is _____ .
   (a) Never justified (b) Justified when terminally ill
   (c) Justified whenever life no longer seems worth living

4. I believe that taking another person's life is _____ .
   (a) Never justified (b) Justified in defense of your own life
   (c) Justified when that person has committed a terrible crime

5. I believe that dying people should be _____ .
   (a) Told the truth about their condition (b) Kept hopeful by sparing them the facts
   (c) Depends upon the person and the circumstances

6. In thinking about my own old age, I would prefer _____ .
   (a) To die before I grow old (b) To live as long as I can
   (c) To discover what challenges and opportunities old age will bring

7. The possibility of nuclear warfare or accident that might destroy much of life on earth has been of _____ to me.
   (a) No concern (b) Little concern (c) Some concern (d) Major concern

8. The possibility of environmental catastrophes that might destroy much of life on earth has been of _____ to me.
   (a) No concern (b) Little concern (c) Some concern (d) Major concern

9. Drivers and passengers should be required to wear seat belts.
   Yes, agree _____ Tend to agree _____
   Tend to disagree _____ No, disagree _____

10. The availability of handguns should be more tightly controlled to reduce accidental and impulsive shootings.
    Yes, agree _____ Tend to agree _____
    Tend to disagree _____ No, disagree _____

SELF-INVENTORY 4
MY FEELINGS*

Select the most accurate alternative answer. If you are not sure of the answer, offer your best guess.

1. I would feel comfortable developing an intimate conversation with a dying person.
   Yes, agree _____ Tend to agree _____ Tend to disagree _____ No, disagree _____

2. I would hesitate to touch someone who was dying.
   Yes, agree _____ Tend to agree _____ Tend to disagree _____ No, disagree _____

3. My hands would tremble when I was talking to a dying person.
   Yes, agree _____ Tend to agree _____ Tend to disagree _____ No, disagree _____

4. I would have more difficulty talking if the dying person was about my age.
   Yes, agree _____ Tend to agree _____ Tend to disagree _____ No, disagree _____

5. I would avoid talking about death and dying with a person who was terminally ill.
   Yes, agree _____ Tend to agree _____ Tend to disagree _____ No, disagree _____

6. I would avoid talking with a dying person if possible.
   Yes, agree _____ Tend to agree _____ Tend to disagree _____ No, disagree _____

7. I have had moments of anxiety in which I think of my own death.
   Never _____ Once _____ Several times _____ Often _____

8. I fear that I will die too soon.
   Yes, agree _____ Tend to agree _____ Tend to disagree _____ No, disagree _____

9. I have no fear of death as such.
   Yes, agree _____ Tend to agree _____ Tend to disagree _____ No, disagree _____

10. I have no fears associated with dying.
    Yes, agree _____ Tend to agree _____ Tend to disagree _____ No, disagree _____

11. I feel good when I think about life after death.
    Yes, agree _____ Tend to agree _____ Tend to disagree _____ No, disagree _____

12. I am anxious about the possible death of somebody I love.
    Yes, definitely _____ Tend to agree _____ Tend to disagree _____ No, disagree _____

13. I am grieving over somebody who has already died.
    Yes, definitely _____ Tend to agree _____ Tend to disagree _____ No, disagree _____

14. I have a hard time taking death seriously. It feels remote to me, not really connected to my own life.
    Yes, definitely _____ Tend to agree _____ Tend to disagree _____ No, disagree _____

15. I have some strong, even urgent feelings regarding death these days.
    Yes, definitely _____ Tend to agree _____ Tend to disagree _____ No, disagree _____

*Questions 1–6 are part of a scale introduced by Hayslip (1986–1987).

Stepping Off the Curb:
An Observational Study

A few years ago Laura Briscoe and I did a little study of the possible relationships between state of mind and actual risk-taking behavior. After watching people cross a busy street, we developed five categories that differed in the extent of risk involved. The *Type A* pedestrian

- Stood on the curb until the light changed in his or her favor
- Glanced briefly at the oncoming traffic in the nearest lanes
- Immediately entered the crosswalk
- Moved across at a moderate-to-brisk pace
- Checked out traffic from the opposite direction lanes before reaching the half-way point
- Exhibited no erratic or hesitational behavior

At the other extreme was the *Type E* pedestrian, who

- Stepped out from some location other than the corner (i.e., middle of the block)
- Stepped out from between parked cars
- Crossed with the traffic light against him or her
- Crossed without looking in either direction

We interviewed 125 street-crossers, equally divided among the five categories. There was a strong relationship between what the observers saw and what the pedestrians reported about themselves. People who had crossed the street carefully (*Type A* or *B*) were much more aware of the fact that they had, indeed, just crossed the street. The low risk-taking crossers saw themselves as low risk-takers, and the high risk-taking crossers saw themselves as having taken a high risk. Their observed street-crossing behavior was closely linked with their general attitudes toward risk-taking. For example, the high-risk pedestrians also classified themselves as high-risk drivers. Furthermore, the *Type E* crossers judged that they were placing their lives in jeopardy about 16% of the time in an average week, as compared

with only 2% of the time as judged by *Type A* crossers. It was even possible to predict (actually, postdict) people's suicidal tendencies by observing how they crossed this busy street: the *Type E* crossers were four times more likely than the *Type A* crossers to have contemplated or attempted suicide. They also reported a higher level of frustration with life. Within the limits of this study (Kastenbaum & Briscoe, 1975) it was clear that a person's general attitudes and feelings can be expressed in behavior choices that either reduce or increase the probability of injury or death.

Sex Discrimination after Death?

A society's general attitudes and beliefs can influence behaviors toward the dead as well as the living. This concept was illustrated in a study that essentially involved reading through two sets of newspapers (Kastenbaum, Peyton, & Kastenbaum, 1977). We recognized that the United States and many other western societies have often treated women as being less important or valuable than men. This discriminatory attitude tends to follow women throughout their lives. We wondered if it follows women into death as well. A simple and inexpensive method of inquiry was established: we read all the death notices and obituaries that appeared in a month's publication run of two major metropolitan newspapers, the *Boston Globe* and the *New York Times*. There were approximately equal numbers of male and female deaths reported in the brief notices. However, both newspapers provided significantly more obituaries (the longer, more personal articles) for males. A woman had only about one-fourth the chance of receiving an obituary as a man. "Elite obituaries," including a photograph of the deceased, were even more unequally distributed: ten men were pictured for every woman. A subsequent study (Spilka, Lacey, & Gelb, 1979) found a similar, though less marked, pattern of sex discrimination after death in two newspapers in the Rocky Mountain

area, while Onu (1978) found male preferential-
ity in mortuary advertisements in African newspapers. Habits of thought, including entrenched
stereotypes and biases, are likely to influence the
ways we behave toward the dying, the grieving,
and even the dead.

I Give My Heart Away: Attitudes of Organ Donors and Nondonors

Should I sign an organ donor card? Should I allow
one or more of my organs to be removed from my
body at death for use by another person? This is
a significant decision. All of the states, as well as
the District of Columbia, have enacted some version of the Uniform Anatomical Gift Act. Despite the widespread availability of this option,
relatively few people sign and carry organ donor
cards. There is reason to think that personal attitudes and fears play a major role in the decision.
Several studies reviewed by Robbins (1990) have
found that nondonors tend to be more anxious
about death. Furthermore, there was a specific
fear about being declared dead prematurely. In her
own study, Robbins also found more anxiety
among the nondonors—not only direct death-
related anxiety, but also uneasiness about their
physical condition in general. There also seems to
be a relationship between willingness to donate
organs and the sense of self-efficacy: people who
think of themselves as effective and self-reliant
copers are more likely to sign the donation cards.
Although there is much more to learn on this
subject, the pattern of evidence suggests that this
consequential death-related behavior is closely related to the individual's general attitude and his
or her fears and anxieties.

We have chosen three very different settings in
which attitudes and feelings show a close relationship to death-relevant behaviors: (1) the degree of risk-taking in crossing a busy street, (2)
sex-biased media attention to recently deceased
people, and (3) personal attitudes and fears that
influence people either to agree or decline to
become organ donors. Each of these situations is
a good deal more complicated than the research

findings have demonstrated. Studies usually are
most helpful in calling our attention to factors
that are likely to be important—but it is still up
to us to perceive and understand the total reality
of the particular people we see attempting to
cope with particular situations. We also want to
keep in mind that our knowledge, experience,
attitudes, beliefs and feelings are likely to influence *every* encounter we have with death. These
encounters range from the distant (e.g., do you
want to watch that bloody horror film on the
late, late show?) to the "up close and personal"
(e.g., will you make and keep that appointment
for a thorough physical examination, or will you
assume that the symptoms are nothing serious?).
As we explore death-related topics throughout
this book we will come upon many other examples of the attitude-behavior interaction, and it is
highly probable that you will also find many examples in your own life and in the lives of your
family, friends, and colleagues. But now it is time
to review your own self-inventories.

Knowledge Base

Here are the answers to the first self-inventory
you answered earlier in this chapter:

1. Each year, about *two million* Americans die
   (*Information Please Almanac 1990* [Johnson,
   1990]).
2. The United States mortality rate has *decreased* in recent years (Gee, 1989b). The
   overall death rate has decreased by about 8%
   in the most recent seven-year period available for analysis.
3. The leading cause of death in the United
   States is *heart disease,* usually classified as
   cardiovascular disease in statistical reports
   (Gee, 1989a). However, heart or cardiovascular disease has been declining as a cause of
   death in recent years.
4. Among American youth ages 14–24 the
   leading cause of death is *accident* (Gee,
   1989a). Three of every ten deaths under the
   age of 25 are attributable to accidents, and
   two-thirds of these involve motor vehicles.

Among youth, white males have the highest rate of death by accident.

5. The death rate from lung disease in the United States has *increased* in recent years (Centers for Disease Control, 1990; Gee, 1989a). The mortality rate for lung cancer has risen by 15%, while two other smoking-related lung disorders, emphysema and bronchitis, have risen by 33% during the same seven-year period.

6. In third-world nations, *measles* kills more people than AIDS, cancer, or heart disease (World Health Organization, 1990). An effective inoculation against measles has been available for years; but it is not administered universally, and each year many thousands of children and young people die from this preventable disease.

7. Capital punishment is *legal in some, but not all states.* At the time of this writing, the death penalty is not legal in 13 states, as well as Puerto Rico, the Virgin Islands, and the District of Columbia (Kastenbaum, 1989c).

8. Cryonic suspension attempts to *preserve the body of a deceased person for possible future restoration and reanimation* by a procedure that involves *maintenance at a low (hypothermic) temperature* (Kastenbaum, 1989d). The bodies of several people have been placed in hypothermic chambers; there have been no known attempts at restoration and reanimation.

9. The Living Will is a document that instructs *doctors not to keep a person alive by artificial means* (Scofield, 1989). Legislation supportive of the Living Will has been passed in 38 states and the District of Columbia (see Chapter 11 for further information and discussion).

10. Cremation is more likely to be the preferred means of body disposal for: actually, *there are no age or sex differences in preference* (Kastenbaum, 1989b). It is usually the deceased person whose expressed preference has guided the choice of cremation.

11. *All* of the factors mentioned have been shown to have important influences on how a person grieves a death: reaction to previous deaths, characteristic way of expressing emotions, and the nature of his/her social support system (Doka, 1989). And these are only a few of the factors that influence our grief reactions (Chapter 10).

12. There are about *1,700* hospice organizations in the United States. However, no precise number is available, and new hospices are still coming into existence, while some existing hospices have become inactive (Kastenbaum, 1989a). Hospice care is examined in Chapter 5.

13. There are approximately *170* suicide prevention centers in the United States, of which *37* have been certified by the American Association of Suicidology (Farberow, 1989). Like hospices, suicide prevention centers differ significantly in their operations. Furthermore, some new centers appear, while some existing centers disappear or take on different functions. Suicide is explored in Chapter 8.

14. Among ethnic and racial subpopulations of the United States, the highest suicide rate appears among *Native Americans* (McIntosh, 1989). The young male Native American is at especially high risk for suicide. There are significant differences in suicide rates among various tribes.

15. A Gallup poll finds that about *70%* of the American population believes in life after death (Gallup, 1982). Other surveys have also found that a majority of the population holds this belief. Questions related to survival of death are explored in Chapter 13.

How do your answers match up? If you had accurate responses to 13 or more of these questions, you bring an unusually broad range of knowledge to your continuing study of death-related phenomena. Most students beginning a formal class in death education score within the 8–12 range. Lower scores usually are associated with a lack of exposure to accurate information on these topics and some overexposure to popular assumptions and stereotypes. Of course, these 15 questions only sample a person's total knowledge base of death-related phenomena, and some of these phenomena are themselves subject to change over time.

Experiences, Attitudes, Beliefs, and Feelings

The facts that have just been reviewed are closely interrelated with many experiences, attitudes, beliefs, and feelings. Why do so many children continue to die of measles and other diseases that can be prevented? What experiences and what alterations in attitudes, beliefs, and feelings have contributed to the life-style changes that have reduced mortality from cardiovascular disease in the United States? And what configuration of attitudes and feelings can explain the fact that smoking-related deaths continue to increase, despite overwhelming evidence of the danger?

As we now briefly review your responses to the other self-inventories, it will not be appropriate to say "this is right" or "this is mistaken." It is natural that we all have somewhat different experiences, and it is reasonable to expect a variety of attitudes, beliefs, and feelings as well. Therefore, we will not be counting up correct answers. Instead, we will be exploring some implications of your own distinctive configuration of experiences, attitudes, beliefs, and feelings.

Experiences

The most significant experiential difference is between people who have had a personally significant death and those (like the social work student mentioned earlier) for whom death has remained essentially a distant topic or even just a word. If you have experienced a death that "got" to you—whether a death of a person or an animal companion—then you are also more likely to *realize* what other people have been going through as well. This is one of the most powerful dynamics at work in community support groups.

Organizations such as Compassionate Friends (Klass, 1988) provide people who have experienced loss the opportunity to offer understanding and emotional support for others who have had similar bereavements. In recent years there has been a tendency to develop peer support groups that are increasingly specialized. Groups have formed, for example, for parents who have had a child killed by a drunk driver, or for persons with AIDS.

The experiential factor is important, but not all-important. Just because a person has had a particular kind of loss experience does not necessarily mean that this person has the ability to support others. Furthermore, some people have proven helpful to the dying, the grieving, and the suicidal even if they have not had very similar experiences in their own lives. The basic point to consider is whether at this point in your life you are "part of the club" that has experienced death in an undeniably personal and significant way, or whether you still have something of an outsider's perspective. In other words, you must consider whether you have had occasion to *realize* death in Weisman's sense, or whether death remains an intriguing, but somewhat external and distant topic.

Some people have an inner relationship with death that goes beyond basic realization. A person's thoughts, attitudes, and feelings may be *dominated* by experiences they have had with death. The sense of being dominated, controlled, or haunted by death can emerge from having had one critical experience with death or from a cluster of experiences. Perhaps you have mourned the deaths of so many people that you could not even list them all in the space provided. Perhaps several people died unexpectedly at the same time. Or perhaps you are still responding strongly to the death of one person who had been at the very center of your life. The question of whether or not your life is presently being highly influenced, even dominated, by death-related experiences cannot be answered by examining a simple list. We would need to appreciate what these people meant to you, and what remains in your mind regarding the deaths themselves, the funeral, and memorialization processes. Furthermore, we would need to examine what you yourself did or did not do in connection with your attitudes and feelings. For example, people who have provided direct personal care for a dying friend or relative have a different set of experiences than those who did not. Perhaps you have a clear and powerful memory of your last visits with a person who was a very important part of your life. On the other hand, perhaps you were thousands of miles away when this person died and had no opportunity to be with your loved one.

We may be much influenced by how a person has died as well as by the death itself. Consider, for example, suicide and AIDS-related deaths, explored further in Chapters 8 and 6, respectively. It may be that your experience does not include having known a person who took his or her own life nor a person who died of AIDS-related complications. If this is the case, then you might regard suicide and AIDS as obscure or tainted kinds of death that befall people who are different and who perhaps in some unspoken way even deserved these fates. If, however, it is one of your favorite neighbors who took his life after his job disappeared and he could no longer make the mortgage payments, your perception of suicide would be altered. Then it would be this particular family's tragedy that would come to mind when you think of suicide: suicide would no longer be a distant abstraction. Similarly, if a person who has always had a word of encouragement for you and who was one of the more entertaining people you have met should die of AIDS-related complications, it again may be the loss of a cherished person and not the name of the disease that will most remain in your memory.

These are but a few of the ways in which our past experiences with death are likely to influence us in the future. It is helpful to keep in mind that people differ markedly in the kinds of experiences they have had with death. Therefore, if we behave differently when we encounter

a situation, the answer can be found in the fact that it is not really the "same" situation for each of us.

Attitudes, Beliefs, Feelings

When we have challenges in everyday life, our attitudes, beliefs, and feelings all come into play. It is not easy to separate out their differing contributions. However, when we are in an analytical mood, we can recognize that attitudes refer to our action tendencies. I am ready to act or I am not ready to act. I am ready to approach this situation or I am ready to avoid this situation. Beliefs refer to our relatively stable and broad interpretations of the world and our place in it. Fatalism, for example, is the broad, generalized belief that what's going to happen will happen. If I were a fatalist, I would have answered Self-Inventory 3, Question 2 as, "Yes, definitely . . . I believe that you die when your number comes up. . . ." If this belief actually influences my behavior, then I would have answered Question 9, "No, drivers and passengers should not be required to wear seat belts." If it's all a matter of predetermined fate (a belief), then why bother to wear seat belts (an attitude)? Broad beliefs and specific action tendencies (attitudes) do not always have such a consistent relationship. It is not unusual for us to be self-contradictory. Nevertheless, identifying beliefs and attitudes is a useful starting point for understanding ourselves and others.

Feelings are qualitatively different from beliefs and attitudes. I feel safe or endangered. I feel happy or sorrowful. I feel aroused or lethargic. Two people may hold identical beliefs and attitudes, but differ greatly in their feelings. On Inventory 3, Question 10, for example, these two people may answer, "Yes, agree: the availability of handguns should be more tightly controlled to reduce accidental and impulsive shootings." However, one of these people may have relatively little feeling attached to this view. Perhaps he or she thinks that it is risky to have a lot of handguns around on general principles. The other person might be the widow of a physician who was shot to death by an emotionally disturbed individual who did not even know him. Her feelings could hardly be more intense. (This is a real person, the former owner of a home my wife and I purchased. Incredible as it may seem, the young widow herself became the recipient of death threats because she spoke up in favor of gun control.)

Review your own answers to Self-Inventory 3. Ask yourself the following questions:

1. What is my knowledge base for each of these attitudes and beliefs? Is this knowledge base adequate and up-to-date, or do I need to check my facts and assumptions?
2. How much does each of these attitudes and beliefs reflect my current state of knowledge? How much does each reflect needs and wishes I have been carrying about with me for some time?
3. How do these various separate attitudes and beliefs add up together? Try to select just a few words to summarize your present configuration of death-related attitudes and beliefs. For example, "I do not believe in rocking the boat . . . let things take their own course." Or, "I oppose death wherever and however I can." Or . . . ?

Nuclear Holocaust

We will explore one area of attitude, belief, and feeling in a little more detail to provide a richer illustration of our orientations toward death-related issues. For half a century now, all of humankind (all of life on Planet Earth, actually) has been threatened by the possibility of a nuclear holocaust. *Megadeath* has become a familiar concept, and we have been exposed to a number of scenarios about precisely how we will perish if nuclear weapons are put to use. Although there have been some areas of controversy, there has long been consensus on the main point: there are more than enough existing nuclear weapons to destroy life on earth many times over.

Naturally there has been much discussion regarding our response to this situation. What

should we think? What should we do? What could we do? To gain perspective on your own attitude toward nuclear holocaust and megadeath, we will examine some surveys. (These studies were conducted before the recent massive political changes in the Soviet bloc that have contributed to a lessening of military tensions among major powers. We will touch upon the attitudinal response to this reduction of nuclear threat.)

The attitudes of young men and women toward the possibility of nuclear war has been studied repeatedly over more than four decades. In reviewing these studies, Chivian, et al. (1988) conclude that "nuclear war is one of the greatest concerns of American children and adolescents." This concern was already evident soon after the conclusion of World War II, although the United States and the Soviet Union had been allies and the Russians had not yet tested their first nuclear weapon. As the United States and the Soviet Union continued to develop and stockpile nuclear weapons, young people in many other nations also expressed fear of an eventual holocaust. International researchers had reason to believe that several generations of children had grown up with anxiety not only about their own future, but about the future of life on earth (Solantaus, et al., 1985).

In their own study, Chivian, et al. compared the attitudes of teenagers in the Soviet Union and the United States. Among American youth, age, sex, race, religion, social class, and political preference had no relationship to worries about nuclear war. This finding (confirmed by other research teams) indicates that fears of nuclear megadeath have not been limited to any one subpopulation: concern was widespread. The youth of both nations had been "inundated with imagery of nuclear explosions and, until very recently, warned frequently that the other superpower might attack them at any moment" (p. 412). Although American and Soviet youth feared nuclear war, there were some differences in their assessment of the risk. Almost all the Russians (94%) responded that they were "very worried" about nuclear war, but only 1 in 11 (9%) expected this to happen in their lifetimes. By contrast, more than half the Americans (54%) expected nuclear war to occur during their lifetimes.

This finding is even more curious because only 42% responded that they were "very worried." In other words, almost all Russian youth reported themselves intensely concerned about a nuclear holocaust that they did not really expect to happen—while about half the American youth expected to see the world destroyed in a nuclear holocaust, yet fewer actually worried about it! This peculiar-seeming pattern seems related to differences in the general attitudes toward life held by American and Soviet youth. The Russians appeared to be more aware of global problems and attuned to political issues; the Americans appeared to be more focused on their own individual hopes and goals. But what might be even more important for our understanding of attitudes toward megadeath is the reminder that there is not a simple relationship among expectation, feeling, and action tendencies. I might be preoccupied with the fear of nuclear war, even though I don't think it's really going to happen. You might be convinced that doomsday is just around the corner, but that it's not worth worrying about! (It is worth keeping this variability in mind as we encounter other types of death-related situations as well. For example, the heavy smoker may know the statistics and the pathophysiology, but not allow this information to connect with lighting up the next cigarette.)

We learn to be curious, then, about how people *feel*, as well as how they think when dealing with death-related issues. One approach is to determine the priority that people assign to a particular concern. A national survey conducted by the *Los Angeles Times* (1982) did just that. The majority of respondents (men and women 18 and older) believed that a nuclear war would result in the end of civilization, or at least the total destruction of the United States and the Soviet Union. But how many people paid more attention to the possibility of nuclear war than other

news item topics? Only 3%! Furthermore, most people (72%) "seldom" or "hardly ever" worried about the possibility of nuclear war, and only 14% considered their presidential candidate's position on nuclear weapons to be an important consideration in deciding their vote.

What does all this tell us about attitudes and feelings regarding megadeath? Can the possibility of nuclear war somehow be important and unimportant at the same time? This question comes into sharper focus when we consult the results of two other studies. Millions of Americans watched the nationwide (ABC, November 20, 1983) telecast of *The Day After*. This film attempted to make a visual reality of the incredible devastation that would be brought by nuclear war. It was perhaps the most graphic and realistic film of its type, as well as the one viewed by the most people. Researchers French and Van Hoorn (1988) asked 1,239 high school and college students to complete questionnaires before and after they saw the movie. What were the attitudinal effects of this film? "Despite the surprising magnitude of the film's audience . . . little discernible change occurred. . . . The lack of appreciable change on most of the items is striking" (p. 280). There was some increased respect for the destructiveness of nuclear war, but expectations and attitudes showed little change. After careful consideration of the results, the authors suggest that "public apathy, fostered by selective inattention" may be the greatest obstacle to the prevention of nuclear war. This selective inattention seems to be related to a "sense of remoteness, helplessness, anxiety, or uncertainty. . . ." Fundamentally, people resist changing their attitudes toward a threat unless they can also envision a way of taking effective action, of being empowered to do something about it.

There is a link between these studies and a survey I conducted of more than a thousand Arizona State University undergraduates. The survey questions covered a broad variety of preferences and concerns, including many death-related items (some are identical with questions included in the Self-Inventories). For our present purposes, we will just compare two of the items. "I worry about how well I will do in my college studies" was a major concern for almost all the respondents (92%). "I worry about the possibility of nuclear war" was a major concern for very few (7.6%). Although nuclear megadeath might well be considered the most powerful source of potential catastrophe, it did not even approach the priority of concerns more pertinent to the students' daily lives (e.g., it was also well below "I worry about whether or not people will like me").

In short, most of us are more attuned to challenges in our everyday lives than more global or philosophical concerns. The prospect of a poor grade on an exam or having to pay an unexpected bill may arouse more feeling in us than such remote-seeming catastrophes as nuclear war or accident, the loss of the world's forests, or the mounting AIDS death toll (if we suppose ourselves not to be at risk). Why? There are at least two significant elements to be examined in any thorough analysis: (1) our perceived sense of efficacy vs. helplessness, and (2) our ability or inability to *realize* that the world is larger than the dimensions of our own lives and our own immediate concerns.

Further clues could be gained by observing what has happened since the Soviet bloc has become disrupted by its own internal problems, leading to a marked reduction in the risk of nuclear confrontation by the superpowers. Formal studies of possible attitude change will probably appear before long. Let me just share what I have noticed and ask you to reflect upon your own observations. The news media regularly featured stories about the lessening of nuclear threat as the United States and the Soviet Union agreed to significant arms reductions. A person who paid attention to the news could not escape noticing that the sword of nuclear catastrophe that had so long hovered over the human race was now being placed back in the scabbard. The Soviet Union had a desperate need to contend with its pressing internal problems, and nations previously constrained within the Russian orbit were achieving significant measures of independence and political freedom.

So there was dancing in the street, right? So students—and faculty—could talk of nothing but the relief, the liberation from megadeath anxieties, the renewed hope for humanity! But there was barely a whisper. For years, psychiatrists had spoken of the nuclear cloud of doom that was oppressing young people, depressing and distorting their lives, shaping the dismal prospect of a futureless future. Now the clouds were drifting away—but nobody seemed to notice. Most students did not seem to connect the change in the global military-political climate with their own lives. The evaporation of megadeath was a big non-event. Furthermore, many people who had lived with the cold war/megadeath threat through all four decades also seemed to be unaffected by the change. Individual exceptions aside, spirits did not rise, the quality of life did not transform itself as the prospect of nuclear megadeath continued to diminish. By contrast, many people do seem vitally concerned with the confrontation in the Middle East (at the time of this writing it was not known whether or not it would develop into a "shooting war"). Nuclear megadeath might have been too enormous an idea to be emotionally realized by many people—but individual and family lives have been disrupted in a concrete way by the departure of loved ones, and the prospect of having one's own studies interrupted by a call to service. Perhaps we need to feel a very direct connection with a source of danger before we are ready to take it seriously.

How did you feel? What did you observe in the response of others? And what do you make of our society's overall response or nonresponse? We cannot pursue these questions any further here. However, the odd, complex, and unpredictable ways our minds work when confronted with death-related issues is well illustrated by the nuclear catastrophe issue. It also serves as a useful contrast to our more personal encounters with death. Perhaps for many of us, nuclear war seems too remote to earn our attention and stir our feelings. But what about our close friend who has just learned that he has a life-threatening illness? Are we comfortable being with him? Do our hands tremble? Do our eyes avoid contact? We turn now to some of the attitudinal and emotional challenges that are encountered when dying and death become intimate issues in our lives.

MAN IS MORTAL: BUT WHAT DOES THAT HAVE TO DO WITH ME?

Our own attitudes toward life and death are challenged when a person close to us dies. In *The Death of Ivan Ilych* (1886/1960) Tolstoy provides an insightful portrait of the complexities, confusions, and urgencies that may afflict a survivor. Consider just one passage from the novel:

> The thought of the sufferings of the man he had known so intimately, first as a schoolmate, and later as a grown-up colleague, suddenly struck Peter Ivanovich with horror. . . . "Three days of frightful suffering and then death! Why, that might suddenly, at any moment, happen to me," he thought, and for a moment felt terrified. But—he himself did not know how—the customary reflection at once occurred to him, that this *had* happened to Ivan Ilych and not to him. . . . After which reflection Peter Ivanovich felt reassured, and began to ask with interest about the details of Ivan Ilych's death, as though death were an accident natural to Ivan Ilych but certainly not to himself (pp. 101–102).

Peter Ivanovich is a responsible adult who presumably knows that death is both inevitable and universal, sparing nobody. Yet we catch him, with Tolstoy's help, playing a desperate game of evasion. Consider some of the elements in Peter Ivanovich's response:

1. He already knows of Ivan Ilych's death; otherwise he would not have been at the widow's home participating in an obligatory paying of respects. But it is only on viewing the corpse that the realization of death strikes him. There is obviously a difference between the intellectual knowledge and the emotional impact. For one alarming moment he himself feels vulnerable.
2. Peter Ivanovich immediately becomes concerned for Peter Ivanovich. His feelings do not center on the man who has lost his life or the woman who has lost her husband.
3. Yet he cannot admit that his outer line of defenses has been penetrated, that his personal anxieties have been touched off. He is supposed to show concern for others, not let them see his own distress. Furthermore, he wants to leave this house of death with the confidence that death had, in fact, been left behind.
4. Peter Ivanovich's basic evasive technique in this passage is the effort to *differentiate* himself from Ivan Ilych. Yes, people really do die; no, the kind of person that Peter Ivanovich is does not die. The proof was in the fact that he was the vertical man who could walk around, while Ivan (that luckless, inferior specimen) was horizontal and immobile. We witness Peter Ivanovich, then, stretching and tormenting his logic in the hope of arriving at an anxiety-reducing conclusion.
5. Once Peter Ivanovich has quelled his momentary panic, he is able to discuss Ivan Ilych's death. Even so, he is more interested in factual details than in feelings and meanings. He has started to rebuild the barriers between himself and death. Whatever he learns about how his friend died will strengthen this barrier—all that was true of Ivan is manifestly not applicable to him.

ANXIETY, DENIAL, AND ACCEPTANCE: CORE CONCEPTS

Three concepts central to research and theory on death attitudes are interwoven through this excerpt from Tolstoy's masterpiece. Peter Ivanovich felt tense, distressed, and apprehensive. *Death anxiety* is the term most often applied to such responses. (In the literature, this term is used in a number of ways, and is subject to criticism. We use it here in the most general and descriptive sense.) Anxiety is a condition that seeks its own relief. To reduce the painful tension, a person might try many different actions—taking drugs or alcohol, for example, or fleeing from the situation. One form of avoiding death anxiety has received most of the attention: *denial*. This is a response that rejects certain key features of reality in the attempt to avoid or reduce anxiety. Peter Ivanovich denies the mortal humanity he shares with Ivan Ilych in order to distance himself from the death.

Many writers have urged that we should *accept* rather than deny death. We are urged to work our way through the anxiety that death arouses without calling on the denial mechanism. Precisely what we should accept and why this is considered the most desirable response are questions that are often neglected. Despite its many hidden problems, the concept of *acceptance* receives serious attention here both because of its intrinsic importance and because it has been so highly featured in both the popular media and the professional literature. In Tolstoy's novel, Ivan Ilych eventually achieves a sense of acceptance, but Peter Ivanovich seems to be as self-deceived and befuddled as ever.

Anxiety, denial, and acceptance are not the only death attitudes that we encounter, although most of the research explored below does concentrate on this trio of concepts. To take one example of a more neglected phenomenon: some people attempt to reduce their own death anxieties by killing others, whether in reality or in games and fantasies. Perhaps researchers will give more attention to a wider spectrum of death attitudes in the future.

STUDIES OF DEATH ANXIETY AND RELATED VARIABLES

Although denial and acceptance are the most frequently discussed attitudes toward death, it is anxiety (or fear) that has attracted most of the research efforts. A brief description of the research methods will be followed by a review of the major findings.

How Death Anxiety Is Usually Studied

Most studies of death anxiety use self-report questionnaires. An early review of the research literature (Lester, 1967) noted that the questionnaires available at that time fell short of the established standards for psychometric techniques. This criticism has been overcome to some extent, especially in the most popular scales. However, it has remained difficult to establish the external validity of death anxiety scales. This reflects the difficulty in finding definitive criteria against which the scales can be tested. One of the more useful validation studies is Templer's finding concerning his own *Death Anxiety Scale* (*DAS*), in which psychiatric patients who had spontaneously expressed urgent fears of death scored higher than matched controls (Templer, et al., 1971). Even here, though, the validation was limited to two different types of self-report. The *DAS* has been subjected to the most extensive development and evaluation and is widely used in research. The 15 true/false items are all rather direct—for example:

"I am very much afraid to die."
"The sight of a dead body is horrifying to me."

Another often-used questionnaire was developed by Lester (1966). This scale has the advantage of providing separate scores for "death of self," "death of others," "dying of self," and "dying of others." A questionnaire designed by Shneidman (1970) is also interesting because it was published in *Psychology Today* and attracted about 30,000 responses. A *Threat Index* developed by Krieger, Eptin, and Leitner (1974) takes a more complex approach. Going beyond the true/false format, the *Threat Index* attempts to elicit the respondents' organizing ideas (constructs) about death. Perhaps because of its relative complexity, the *Threat Index* has not become as popular as the *DAS*.

The typical studies of death anxiety and related variables remain subject to criticisms, such as the following (Handal, et al., 1984–1985; Kastenbaum, 1987–1988; Kastenbaum & Costa, 1977):

1. Little is learned about the respondent's overall attitude structure or belief system, therefore *death anxiety* is taken out of context.

(This criticism does not apply to the *Threat Index.*)

2. Low scores on death anxiety scales are difficult to interpret. Do they mean low anxiety or high denial? The scales themselves provide no way to make the distinction.

3. How high is high anxiety, and what is a normal level? Many assumptions have been made, but the scales themselves have not clarified these questions.

4. The respondents are too often selected on opportunistic and conveniency grounds, rather than for sound theoretical or applied reasons. College students are overrepresented, for example (why does that not surprise us?), and members of ethnic and racial minorities tend to be underrepresented.

5. The typical study is a one-shot affair. How the same respondents might express their attitudes at another time or in another situation is seldom explored.

6. No link is established between attitude and behavior. The fact that people may differ in scores on a death anxiety questionnaire does not prove that they would behave differently in any particular situation.

Despite the flaws and limitations of most death anxiety studies, there have been some findings that are worth our attention. At the least, these studies provide some information on how people respond to direct questions about their death attitudes.

Gender, Age, and Death Anxiety

Women tend to express higher levels of death anxiety. This is a fairly consistent finding. What might account for this difference? DaSilva and Schork (1984–1985) used selected items from the *Psychology Today* survey and were able to construct profiles of the typical female and male respondent. (All were graduate students in a public health program, so the findings may or may not generalize to the population in general.) These were young men and women who identified themselves with the Christian religious tradition.

The typical female respondent

. . . recalls that death was talked about openly in her family during her childhood. Presently, she thinks occasionally about her own death, but quite a bit more frequently than her male counterparts. Given a choice, she would opt to die in her old age. She believes that religion played a very significant role in the development of her attitude toward death. Possibly as a consequence, she strongly believes in life after death. Her reaction when she thinks of her own death is a feeling of pleasure at being alive (p. 82).

The typical male respondent

. . . recalls that death was not only not talked about openly in his family during childhood, but when it was mentioned it was with some sense of discomfort. Although he thinks occasionally of his own death, he would be quite comfortable avoiding such thoughts and thinking about death not more than once a year. Given the choice he would opt to die in old age. He does not believe that religion had a very significant role in the development of his attitude to death. Possibly as a consequence he tends to doubt life after death and would rather believe in death as the end. . . . He feels motivated to achieve more in life when he thinks of his own mortality (p. 82).

This study suggests that what appears to be women's higher anxiety might be better understood as a greater comfort in thinking about death. Less emotional energy is devoted to reducing the impact of death-related topics as compared with males. This conclusion is consistent with the observation that American women tend to be more open in expressing a variety of feelings, not only those associated with death. It is also worth noting that women almost always outnumber men in seminars and workshops that deal with dying, death, and grief. In hospice and other caregiving situations as well, I almost always find more women than men. If this is anxiety, then perhaps we should be grateful for it, since relatively few low death anxiety men respond to this challenge.

What about age and death anxiety? Some studies reveal little or no difference within the adult age range. When differences are found, however, elderly adults express lower levels of death anxiety than their juniors, a finding first made by Munnichs (1966), in his pioneering study in the Netherlands and since replicated by others in the United States. There is no research basis for the fairly common view that people become more anxious about death with advancing age (Lonetto & Templer, 1986). Our thoughts and feelings do change as we move through life, but these subtle and idiosyncratic developments do not necessarily show up as death anxiety scale scores.

In reviewing the available research findings, it appears to me that death anxiety tends to rise in adolescence and early adulthood, then diminish somewhat as one's life becomes more settled and predictable. Death anxiety is apt to rise again in later middle age, perhaps occasioned by the death of friends and family and signs of one's own aging. After this rise, there tends to be a decline to a new low in death anxiety for people in their 70s. It should be noted, however, that all the studies have been cross-sectional. We need systematic studies of large numbers of people as they move through their entire lives and cope with the challenges of life and death.

Occupation, Personality, and Mental Health: Related to Death Anxiety?

Studies of death anxiety have attempted to establish correlations with the usual range of demographic and mental health variables. Pollak's (1979–1980) review of the literature concluded that no clear association had emerged between occupation and death anxiety (leaving aside those who choose to work with the terminally ill, grieving, or suicidal, as explored in Chapter 12). In preparing another review of the literature a decade later (Kastenbaum, 1987–1988) I could find no basis for altering Pollak's conclusion.

The personality findings are more complex. We might guess that people with a strong need to achieve would be more threatened by the prospect of death, but this hypothesis has not been confirmed by research. However another line of exploration has yielded some positive findings. Higher levels of death anxiety are reported by people who lack a sense of personal effectiveness, mastery, and power. The relationship between religiosity and death anxiety has not really been clarified. This is an important topic that still awaits the type of research that might help us to understand how religious beliefs and participation in religious rituals influence and are influenced by death anxiety.

People experiencing mental or emotional problems do tend to express higher levels of death anxiety. The usual interpretation is that death anxiety rushes to the surface when a person's "ego defenses" are weakened and can no longer inhibit the impulses, fears, and fantasies that are ordinarily suppressed. It should be emphasized, however, that "death concern is not limited to certain personality types, certainly not only to 'neurotic' people. . . . Rather, these concerns seem to be present in different forms, or on different levels, in all of us" (Rosenheim & Muchnik, 1984–1985, p. 21). This study attempted to assess the respondents' attitudes toward death on more than one level of awareness. People who reported a low level of death anxiety in response to direct questions often had a higher level of implicit death anxiety in the stories they constructed to Thematic Apperception Test pictures. The research of Feifel and Branscomb (1973) also suggests that we have several levels of death concern that can be assessed if the researcher goes beyond direct self-report questions.

How Death-Anxious Are Most People?

The death awareness movement has stimulated the development of hospices, grief counseling, death education courses, and other important developments. However, some of its guiding assumptions have not been fully tested. One set of guiding assumptions centers on death anxiety. It is assumed that death does make us feel anxious, and that most of us are too anxious. Therefore, we should "face" death more openly—this will lead to reduced anxiety and more effective coping. For some people, these assumptions have become articles of faith. What does the research literature have to say about them?

The guiding assumptions would lead us to expect that death anxiety scores are generally rather high. But this is not the case. Most people score in the low-to-moderate range. Only "high death anxiety psychiatric patients" exceed the midpoint to any appreciable extent. The average score is usually below the scale's theoretical midpoint.

The fact, then, is that generally self-report studies show only low-to-moderate manifest death anxiety. This pattern of results does not support the assumption that most American adults carry a burden of excessive anxiety. As Kastenbaum and Costa (1977) note, researchers have been tempted to hold on to their theories despite the facts by maintaining that the relatively low scores prove not low anxiety but high denial. But this is not a persuasive explanation since the typical study neither defines nor includes an independent measure of denial.

The focus now will turn from the mainstream of death attitude research to the clinical or applied perspective.

DENYING AND ACCEPTING DEATH

> Sitting in his favorite chair after dinner, the man suddenly went pale. He felt severe pain in his chest, and had to gasp for breath. His wife was by his side in a moment. "What's wrong? Oh! I'll get the doctor, the hospital. . . ." The man struggled for control and waved one hand feebly in a dismissive gesture. "It's nothing—really. . . . I'll just lie down till it goes away."

This scene, with variations, has been repeated often enough to become well recognized by professional caregivers. The concept of *denial* may come to mind when a person has delayed in seeking diagnosis and treatment for a life-threatening condition. *Accepting* the reality of serious illness might help to save that person's life. Both denial

and acceptance show their true power in real-life situations such as the one just sketched rather than in self-report questionnaires.

Facing or Evading the Bad News

If our anxiety level increases, are we more likely to face or evade the prospect of death? One study included nearly 1,000 men who ranged in age from 25 to 90 years (McCrae, et al., 1976). At every age there were some men with high, moderate, and low levels of expressed anxiety. An interesting difference showed up when highly anxious men of various ages were compared with each other on their reporting of physical complaints. Young and middle-aged anxious men reported more physical symptoms than adjusted men of the same age. But anxious elderly men reported *fewer* physical symptoms than adjusted men of the same age. What was going on?

The investigators constructed a discrepancy index that compared the number of expressed complaints with the actual findings of thorough medical examinations. The pattern of age and anxiety again showed a reversal. Young and middle-aged men with high anxiety reported more illnesses than their physicians could find. But in old age, the less anxious men reported more illnesses, and the anxious young men were more likely to overestimate the severity of their problems. So it was the well-adjusted—not the highly anxious—old man who was concerned about his health. The anxious elderly person underestimated the severity of his physical problems. It was as though the anxious old man must protect himself from recognizing an actual threat to life, whereas the anxious young person can afford to focus on symptoms because he does not really think his life is in danger.

The well-adjusted old men seemed to be actively monitoring their own physical status. This is a realistic policy to follow in the advanced years of life. It is not like the anxious younger man's constant preoccupation with the state of his body. Does this mean that the adjusted old men had a greater fear of death than their anxious peers, or less denial? We might expect men who are more anxious in general to be more anxious about death as well. Yet the better adjusted elders could face the prospect of serious illness more openly. Their concern did not have to be disguised or denied. People who express direct concern about the state of their health might be acting in their own enlightened self-interest. By contrast, a high level of anxiety seems to be associated with evading actual medical problems. The men with less defensive life-styles were better able to confront their physical condition realistically. (The participants were all male veterans of the United States armed forces; a parallel study with women would be most useful.)

Another interesting link between anxiety and denial was suggested in a study by Schulz and Aderman (1978). They reasoned that physicians who themselves had different levels of death anxiety might have different outcomes in their work with terminally ill patients. They received surprisingly good cooperation (no refusals) from 24 physicians in a community hospital who completed a brief death anxiety self-report measure. Hospital records were then examined to determine the following for a 12-month period: (1) the percentage of total patients treated who died under the physicians' care, (2) the average length of their terminally ill patients' final stays in the hospital, and (3) the average length of their nondying patients' stays in the hospital. The physicians were classified into high, moderate, and low death anxiety groups on the basis of their questionnaire responses.

There were no significant differences in the length of stay of the nondying patients nor the percentage of terminally ill patients among physicians with varying degrees of anxiety. But "the length of final hospitalization for patients who died varied directly as a function of the physicians' death anxiety. Patients of physicians with high death anxiety were in the hospital an average of five days longer before dying than patients treated by physicians of medium and low death anxiety" (p. 331). We can only speculate on specific ways in which the physicians' death anxiety might have been translated into behaviors that influenced

survival. This is, nevertheless, a provocative study that emphasizes the intimate relationship between how people feel about death and what actually happens. And it also leaves us with an unanswered question concerning values: Is it better to have a physician with a lower death anxiety who seems to allow a dying person to slip away a little sooner, or one with a higher death anxiety who seems able to prolong life a little longer?

Types and Contexts of Acceptance and Denial

Like many other important words, "acceptance" and "denial" are used in a variety of ways, and sometimes their meanings become so blurred that they mislead more than they help. From a psychiatric standpoint, denial is regarded as a *primitive* defense, perhaps the most primitive of all. Denial rejects the existence of unpleasant or threatening reality. This kind of defense is available to the infant long before it has developed more adequate ways to cope with stress and threat. Basic denial is a strategy that may be somewhat effective for a short period of time, and for situations in which there is one particular overwhelming threat. It becomes increasingly ineffective when prolonged or used repeatedly: we do not survive long in this world when we ignore crucial aspects of reality. Denial is most often found among people suffering from a psychotic reaction or as a fleeting response to crisis and catastrophe.

Denial in this basic sense is not usually part of our everyday repertoire of coping strategies. But we do engage in a number of behaviors that look more or less like denial. There has been a widespread tendency to speak of all forms of resistance or evasive action as though they were denial. By using this term as a buzz word ("Oh, she's just in denial") we often come to glib and premature conclusions. Usually, the person is not "denying" in the basic psychiatric sense of the term (a primitive and ineffective mechanism). Rather, the person is more likely to be coping with a difficult situation in the most resourceful way he or she can discover at the moment. This will become clearer when several processes—all of which can look like denial—are distinguished.

1. *Selective attention.* Imagine a situation in which many things that compete for attention are happening. To focus on one or two of the events necessarily means that others will be given less attention. A person who has never been in a hospital before, for example, might find many new, interesting, and challenging things to notice and think about. These may seem more vivid and perceptually real than something as abstract as the diagnosis that will be made eventually. At the moment other, more immediate perceptual and interpersonal phenomena exert a greater claim for attention. This often happens with children.

2. *Selective response.* In this instance the person may have death-relevant thoughts well in mind. However, he or she has judged that this is not the time or place to express them. The person may think, "I'm not going to open up to this young doctor who looks more scared than I am," or "There is nothing effective I can do about the situation at this moment, so I will do something else (or nothing in particular) even though I know all too well what's up." Or he or she may decide, "There is something very important I must accomplish while I have the opportunity, and it must take priority over words and actions that center on my impending death."

3. *Compartmentalizing.* This process involves some awareness and some response to death-salient aspects of the situation. But something is missing: the connection between one aspect of the situation and another. For example, the individual may know that he or she has a poor prognosis. This is an accurate perception; there is no denial involved. He or she may also be cooperating with treatment and discussing the condition rationally (adaptive response, and still no denial). Yet the same person may be making future plans that involve travel, vigorous exercise, etc., just as though he or she were going to be around in good health for years to come. In compartmentalizing, much of the dying and death reality is acknowledged, but the person stops just short of *realizing*

the situation. All the pieces are there, but the individual resists adding them up.

4. *Deception.* People sometimes deliberately give false information to others. This takes place in dying and death situations, too. When people are telling each other lies (for whatever purpose), it makes sense to acknowledge this deceptive action for what it is and not confuse the issue with the buzz word, "denial."

5. *Denial* (the real thing). This is the basic defensive process defined earlier. The individual is not just selecting among possible perceptions and responses, limiting the logical connections between one phenomenon and the other, or engaging in conscious deception. Rather, the self appears to be totally organized against recognizing death-laden reality. Such an orientation can be bizarre and may accompany a psychotic reaction. It does not have to be quite that extreme, however, and we can sometimes detect the existence of a true denial process that weaves in and out of other, more sophisticated ways of coping.

Each individual in a dying and death situation influences others and is being influenced by others. The process of acceptance and denial therefore is *interpersonal* as well as *intrapsychic*. Change the interpersonal dynamics, and the dynamics of acceptance/denial are also likely to change. Furthermore, both the immediate situation and the historical background must be considered. One man may come from an ethnic background that treats dying and death in a straightforward manner: the Amish, for example. But suppose he finds himself in a medical establishment where death is still a taboo and high-anxiety topic: here is a potential death accepter trapped among the denyers. The reverse also takes place. Consider a woman who grew up learning how to deny death, especially the deeper emotions associated with death. Suppose she becomes a patient in a more liberated health-care establishment where the staff is relentless in its belief that we must be open and sharing with each other. Here, then, is the denyer confronted by the accepters. To understand how a particular person is coping with the acceptance-denial dynamics requires some attention to the past and to the current interpersonal field as well as to the individual's own momentary thoughts and feelings.

Fortunately, there are now a number of sensitive observers who have recognized the complexity of acceptance-denial dynamics. For example, a clinical study by Daniel A. Dansak and Rosemary S. Cordes (1979), a psychiatrist-nurse team, points out that when terminally ill cancer patients speak little about their death fears, this silence is often construed as denial. However, they found that often "such patients are not truly 'denying' cancer and its consequences, but have merely decided, more or less voluntarily, to 'suppress' these thoughts as a method of coping with their illness." This conclusion was reached after working closely with more than 100 cancer patients. Sometimes they found that staff made the "in denial" interpretation when, in fact, the patient knew his or her situation very well. It was common for people to make the best of a bad situation, to cultivate whatever hope still remained, and continue to make realistic or semirealistic plans with their families. Essentially, denial was in the eye of the beholder.

Weisman (1972) has called attention to two points that are particularly important here. He has observed that a person does not usually deny everything about death to everybody. More often, a selective process is involved. We must then go beyond the question, "Is this person denying death?" It is more useful to ask instead, "What aspects of dying or death are being shared with what other people, under what circumstances, and why?" (Parallel questions could be asked about acceptance.) Apparent denial on the part of the patient may derive from a lack of responsive people in the environment.

The related point has to do with the *function* of so-called denial. "The purpose of denial," writes Weisman, "is not simply to avoid a danger, but to prevent loss of a significant relationship." All of the adaptive processes that have been described here might be used, then, in an effort to make the other person feel comfortable enough to maintain a vitally needed relationship. The

individual faced with death may have to struggle as much with the other person's anxiety as with his or her own. Instead of placing the negative judgment of denial upon these adaptive efforts, we might appreciate the care and sensitivity with which they are carried out.

Anxiety, Denial, and Acceptance: How Should We Respond?

Anxiety is an uncomfortable, at times almost unbearable condition. It would be a mistake, however, to consider anxiety either completely negative or completely useful. Small doses of anxiety can alert us to danger ("Something's wrong here—what?") or prepare us for action ("I've been on stage a thousand times, and been a bundle of nerves a thousand times—but that's just how I want to feel before the curtain goes up!"). Within limits we do have some choices about how we make use of the anxieties aroused in us by death-related situations.

The response strategies of acceptance and denial likewise are not necessarily good or bad in themselves. We must examine the contexts in which these processes are used and the purposes they seem to be serving. If what we are calling denial really *is* denial, then we may be dealing with a person who is making a desperate stand against catastrophe. He or she has been forced to fall back on a primitive defense process that involves rejecting important aspects of reality. This person needs psychological help and, quite possibly, other types of help as well. On the other hand, the person may not be denying so much as selectively perceiving, linking, and responding to what is taking place. This pattern of coping with difficult reality may have its evasive aspects at certain times with certain people, but there is method, judgment, and purpose at work. Even flashes of pure denial may contribute to overall adaptation, as when challenges come too swiftly, last too long, or are too overwhelming to meet in other ways (Breznitz, 1983). A little later the individual may have found another way to deal with the same challenge, once the first impact has been partially warded off and partially absorbed.

I suggest that we proceed with the following set of premises:

1. Most of the time most people probably have both acceptance and denial-type dynamics in process at different levels within their personalities, with different degrees of dominance.
2. States of total acceptance and total denial of death do occur, but these usually occur in extreme circumstances: when the individual is letting go of life after achieving a sense of completion and having struggled as long as struggling seemed worthwhile, or when the individual is resisting catastrophic reality when it first bursts in on him or her.
3. Much of what is loosely spoken of as denial can be understood more adequately as adaptive processes through which the person responds selectively to various aspects of a difficult situation.
4. The individual's pattern of adaptation should be considered within the context of the acceptance and denial that characterizes the larger interpersonal network around him or her.
5. Acceptance and denial can be evaluated only when we are in a position to understand what the person is trying to accomplish and what he or she is up against.

And, yes, the test was Wednesday and almost all the students showed their understanding of the terrible failure in communication that transformed a man into a suicidal torch.

REFERENCES

Anon. (1988). It's over, Debbie. *Journal of the American Medical Association, 259*(2), 272.

Breznitz, S. (1983). Anticipatory stress and denial. In S. Breznitz (Ed.), *The denial of death* (pp. 225–256). New York: International Universities Press Inc.

Centers for Disease Control (Atlanta) (1990). Mortality statistics.

Chivian, E., Robinson, J. P., Tudge, J. R. H., Popov, N. P., & Andreyenkov, V. G. (1988). American and Soviet teenagers' concerns about nuclear war and the future. *New England Journal of Medicine, 19,* 407–413.

Dansak, D. A., & Cordes, R. S. (1979). Cancer: Denial or suppression? *International Journal of Psychiatry in Medicine, 9,* 257–262.

Da Silva, A., & Schork, M. S. (1984–1985). Gender differences in attitudes to death among a group of public health students. *Omega, Journal of Death and Dying, 15,* 77–84.

Doka, K. J. (1989). Grief. In R. Kastenbaum & B. Kastenbaum (Eds.), *Encyclopedia of death* (pp. 227–230). Phoenix: The Oryx Press.

Farberow, N. L. (1989). Suicide. In R. Kastenbaum & B. Kastenbaum (Eds.), *Encyclopedia of death* (pp. 227–230). Phoenix: The Oryx Press.

Feifel, H., & Branscomb, A. B. (1973). Who's afraid of death? *Journal of Abnormal and Social Psychology, 81,* 282–288.

French, P. L., & Van Hoorn, J. (1988). Half a nation saw nuclear war and nobody blinked? *Journal of Orthopsychiatry, 58,* 276–297.

Gallup, G., Jr. (1982). *Adventures in immortality.* New York: McGraw-Hill.

Gee, E. (1989a). Causes of death. In R. Kastenbaum & B. Kastenbaum (Eds.), *Encyclopedia of death* (pp. 38–40). Phoenix: The Oryx Press.

Gee, E. (1989b). Mortality rate. In R. Kastenbaum & B. Kastenbaum (Eds.), *Encyclopedia of death* (pp. 183–185). Phoenix: The Oryx Press.

Goodfriend, M., & Wolpoert, E. A. (1976). Death from fright: Report of a case and literature review. *Psychosomatic Medicine, 38,* 348–356.

Handal, P. J., Peal, R. L., Napoli, J. C., & Austrin, H. R. (1984–1985). The relationship between direct and indirect measures of death anxiety. *Omega, Journal of Death and Dying, 15,* 245–262.

Hayslip, B. (1986–1987). The measurement of communication apprehension regarding the terminally ill. *Omega, Journal of Death and Dying, 17,* 251–261.

Johnson, O. (Ed.) (1990). *Information please almanac 1990.* New York: Houghton Mifflin Company.

Kastenbaum, R. (1987–1988). Theory, research, and application: Some critical issues for thanatology. *Omega, Journal of Death and Dying, 18,* 397–410.

Kastenbaum, R. (1989a). Hospice: Philosophy and practice. In R. Kastenbaum & B. Kastenbaum (Eds.), *Encyclopedia of death* (pp. 143–147). Phoenix: The Oryx Press.

Kastenbaum, R. (1989b). Cremation. In R. Kastenbaum & B. Kastenbaum (Eds.), *Encyclopedia of death* (pp. 57–60). Phoenix: The Oryx Press.

Kastenbaum, R. (1989c). Death penalty. In R. Kastenbaum & B. Kastenbaum (Eds.), *Encyclopedia of death* (pp. 85–89). Phoenix: The Oryx Press.

Kastenbaum, R. (1989d). Cryonic suspension. In R. Kastenbaum & B. Kastenbaum (Eds.), *Encyclopedia of death* (pp. 61–66). Phoenix: The Oryx Press.

Kastenbaum, R., & Briscoe, L. (1975). The street corner: A laboratory for the study of life-threatening behavior. *Omega, Journal of Death and Dying, 6,* 33–44.

Kastenbaum, R., & Costa, P. T., Jr. (1977). Psychological perspectives on death. In M. R. Rosenzweig & L. W. Porter, (Eds.), *Annual Review of Psychology* Vol. 28 (pp. 225–250). Palo Alto: Stanford University Press.

Kastenbaum, R., Peyton, S., & Kastenbaum, B. (1977). Sex discrimination after death. *Omega, Journal of Death and Dying, 7,* 351–359.

Klass, D. (1988). *Parental grief.* New York: Springer.

Krieger, S. R., Epting, R. R., & Leitner, L. M. (1974). Personal constructs, threat, and attitudes toward death. *Omega, Journal of Death and Dying, 5,* 299–310.

Lester, D. (1966). A scale measuring the fear of death: Its construction and consistency. *ADI Auxiliary Publications Project document no. 9449.* Washington, D.C.: Library of Congress.

Lester, D. (1967). Experimental and correlational studies of the fear of death. *Psychological Bulletin, 67,* 26–36.

Levav, I. (1989–1990). Second thoughts on the lethal aftermath of a loss. *Omega, Journal of Death and Dying, 20,* 81–90.

Lonetto, R., & Templer, D. I. (1986). *Death anxiety.* Washington: Hemisphere Publishing Corporation.

Los Angeles Times (1982). *Nuclear weapons.* (Study No. 51). *Los Angeles Times Poll,* 14–17 March. Los Angeles: Los Angeles Times.

McCrae, R. R., Bartone, P. T., & Costa, P. T., Jr. (1976). Age, personality, and self-reported health. *International Journal of Aging & Human Development, 6,* 49–58.

McIntosh, J. (1989). Suicide: Native Americans. In R. Kastenbaum & B. Kastenbaum (Eds.), *Encyclopedia of death* (pp. 238–239). Phoenix: The Oryx Press.

Munnichs, J. M. A. (1966). *Old age and finitude.* New York: Karger.

Onu, P. E. (1978). *Sex discrimination after death: A study of mortuary advertisements in African newspapers.* Unpublished manuscript. Simon Fraser University, Burnaby, British Columbia.

Pollak, J. M. (1979–1980). Correlates of death anxiety: A review of empirical studies. *Omega, Journal of Death and Dying, 10,* 97–122.

Robbins, R. A. (1990). Signing an organ donor card: Psychological factors. *Death Studies, 14,* 219–230.

Rosenheim, E., & Muchnik, B. (1984–1985). Death concerns in differential levels of consciousness as functions of defense strategy and religious belief. *Omega, Journal of Death and Dying, 15,* 15–24.

Schulz, R., & Aderman, D. (1978). Physician's death anxiety and patient outcomes. *Omega, Journal of Death and Dying, 9:* 327–332.

Scofield, G. (1989). (The) living will. In R. Kastenbaum & B. Kastenbaum (Eds.), *Encyclopedia of death* (pp. 175–176). Phoenix: The Oryx Press.

Shneidman, E. S. (1970). Death attitudes questionnaire. *Psychology Today, 4,* 43–47.

Solantaus, T., Chivian, E., Vartanyan, M., & Chivian, S. (Eds.) (1984). *Impact of the threat of nuclear war on children and adolescents: Proceedings of an international research symposium.* Helsinki-Espoo, Finland: International Physicians for the Prevention of Nuclear War.

Spilka, B., Lacey, G., & Gelb. B. (1979). Sex discrimination after death: A replication, an extension, and a difference. *Omega, Journal of Death and Dying, 10,* 227–333.

Templer, D. I. (1970). The construction and validation of a Death Anxiety Scale. *Journal of General Psychology, 82,* 165–177.

Templer, D. I., Ruff, C. F., & Franks, C. M. (1971). Death anxiety: Age, sex, and parental resemblances in diverse populations. *Developmental Psychology, 4,* 108.

Tolstoy, L. (1960). *The death of Ivan Ilych.* New York: The New American Library, Inc. (Original work 1886).

Weisman, A. D. (1972). *On dying and denying.* New York: Behavioral Publications, Inc.

Weisman, A. D. (1974). *The realization of death.* New York, London: Jason Aronson.

World Health Organization (1990). Statistical report.

chapter 2

WHAT IS DEATH?

What does death mean?

BIOMEDICAL APPROACHES TO THE DEFINITION OF DEATH

Death is "certified" thousands of times every day by physicians. In this practical usage the question shifts from "What is death?" to "Under what conditions should a person be considered dead?" The physician meets society's need for verifying that one of its members has been lost. The concept of *nonreversible cessation of life processes* provides a general criterion for classifying a person as dead. This is a satisfactory definition for some people, yet others have a more complex view that is not addressed by the physician's ritual. Death may be conceived variously as a transition, a splitting of spirit from body, or some otherwise altered state of being. To the physician, *dead* means the body no longer supports or can support life processes. To many people, however, *death* implies something that continues or begins when the last breath is released. After the biomedical approach has been explored, some of the major philosophical, religious, and social conceptions of death also must be considered.

Traditional Determination of Death

Recent developments in biomedical science have created new pressures on decision makers and produced new criteria for the determination of death. Not everything is new, however. Physi-

cians have already had a set of criteria to employ and have sometimes been faced with difficult circumstances.

The most commonly relied on indices of death have been lack of respiration; lack of pulse (or heartbeat); and failure to respond to stimuli such as light, movement, and pain. Lowered body temperature and stiffness were other characteristics expected to appear after a period, followed still later by bloating and signs of decomposition. A competent physician did not generally have reason to miss the more advanced equipment available today. Simple tests, carefully performed, usually would make it clear whether or not life had fled. In many instances the physician or family could also take the time to wait before burial arrangements were made, thereby allowing more opportunity for a possible spontaneous revival of function.

Nevertheless, life-threatening errors could be made. Victims of drowning and lightning, for example, would sometimes be taken for dead, when in fact their vital functions had only been suspended (Royal Humane Society, 1820; Whiter, 1819). Those who suffered a stroke, epileptic seizure, or diabetic coma might also be pronounced dead instead of receiving treatment. The same fate could befall a person gifted in the once popular art of hysterical fainting (Kastenbaum & Aisenberg, 1972). More than a century and a half ago a Transylvanian physician carefully pointed out how almost all the signs of death could be mistaken in particular instances—his own uncle had narrowly escaped just such an error (Shrock, 1835).

The prudent physician, as well as the informed public, had sufficient opportunity to learn that the possibility of survival could still exist under the appearance of death. How often this situation actually existed is impossible to determine, but enough such circumstances arose for a tradition to establish itself—a tradition of second-guessing the physician, seeking protection against premature determinations, and looking for ways to revive the apparently dead. Indeed, the fear of being buried alive held much the same morbid fascination for people of the 19th century as the fear of being kept indefinitely in a vegetative state somewhere between life and death does today. Mark Twain (1883/1972) reported with appalled fascination on his visit to a municipal "dead house" in Munich:

> Around a finger of each of these fifty still forms, both great and small, was a ring; and from the ring a wire led to the ceiling, and thence to a bell in a watch-room yonder, where, day and night, a watchman sits always alert and ready to spring to the aid of any of that pallid company who, waking out of death, shall make a movement—for any, even the slightest movement will twitch the wire and ring that fearful bell. I imagined myself a death-sentinel drowsing there alone, far in the dragging watches of some wailing, gusty night, and having in a twinkling all my body stricken to quivering jelly by the sudden clamor of that awful summons! (p. 189)

This tradition of concern remains with us today, taking new forms such as the cryonic movement that attempts to preserve dead bodies at lowered temperatures for subsequent rejuvenation (Mollaret & Boulon, 1959). Although the municipal death watch has vanished, its place is gradually being taken by medicolegal regulations buttressed by the technique of electroencephalography (EEG). The challenge to both concept and method will now be exemplified.

Ways of "Being Dead"

The question "When is a person dead?" has gained increasing practical significance in the past twenty years. This is a direct consequence of advances in clinical medicine. A patient who would have lapsed into coma and died in a short period can now be maintained by a life-support system for months or even years. Traditional approaches to defining death no longer seem adequate. The heartbeat, the respiratory system exchanging its gases, and reflex responses may also occur.

We hesitate to say "dead." We also hesitate to say "alive." The body retains some of its functions, but the *person* appears to have departed. There is no speech, no clear signs of understanding, no complex actions. Theoretically, even one such instance should challenge casual, overly familiar conceptions of death. How can we say a person is dead when the chest rises and falls and deep reflexes can be elicited? Yet how can we say the person is not dead when there are no words or actions indicative of a functioning human being? Practical decisions must be made. Following are a few of them, each dependent on a firm definition of death:

1. Family members and the attending physician agree that the life-support system should be withdrawn because the patient is unresponsive and has no apparent chance to recover. Would "pulling the plug" constitute murder? Or is the *person* already dead? And, if you cannot murder the dead, is it nevertheless a crime of some sort because vegetative functions could have continued indefinitely?

2. Another patient is also comatose and unresponsive, but vegetative processes continue even in the absence of an elaborate life-support system. (An IV is in place, but there is no device to keep respiration going artificially.) Elsewhere in the hospital an organ transplant team is urgently seeking a kidney that might keep somebody else alive for many years. Ruling that the comatose patient is dead could liberate the kidney. The needed organ should be removed im-

mediately if the other patient is to have a chance at survival. The operation will probably be fatal for the comatose patient. Is this murder? Or a new type of life-taking crime? Or is it a valuable procedure that might help one person and cannot harm another because he or she is actually dead?

3. The vegetative functioning of a comatose, nonresponsive woman is being maintained by elaborate life-prolonging procedures. If a person in such a condition should be considered dead, then this woman is dead. However, there is a living fetus within. Without intervention the fetus will not survive. Would this constitute the death of a person? And what does it mean if society acts to keep a "dead" person "alive" long enough to improve the chances for the survival of an immature being whose claims to personhood are disputed within this same society? Would delivering the fetus safely result in a "second death" of the mother?

This leads to still another question. Clearly, the mother had been a person. This person seems to have died in some sense of the term. This death of a person may now be followed by the death of what still remained. How do these two types of death compare with the feared death of a fetus who, according to some members of society, was never a person in the first place?

Just how many deaths or ways of being dead can there be? Several possibilities have already been identified, all of which occur today:

- The *person* is dead. (He or she does not respond, communicate, or show any other characteristics associated with a distinctly human being.) Nevertheless, vegetative processes continue because of an elaborate life-support system.
- The same condition just described exists; however, vegetative processes continue without an elaborate life-support system.
- All vegetative functioning has ceased. (The body is dead.)
- The same condition just described exists; however, the dead organism had never been a person in the usual sense of the term.

Either the similarities or the differences among these conditions could be emphasized. How vital is the distinction between cessation of bodily processes and loss of the person as a person? What difference, if any, is there between the "deadness" of a body that continues to function on a vegetative level with or without an elaborate life-support system? Should the previous nature of the organism have anything to do with the present situation (who or what it was that no longer lives)?

These are some of the questions that confront health care professionals, legislators, and legal experts today. Philosophical and religious issues break to the surface in concrete situations, and important practical decisions must be made. The next section examines how the medical and legal communitites have attempted to respond to these philosophical and practical problems. (See also Chapter 11 for further examination of the problems raised here.)

Brain Death and the Harvard Criteria

The medical world was ready for the concept of brain death by 1959, when the French neurophysiologists Mollaret and Boulon reported their pioneering study of comatose patients whose breathing was being maintained by respiratory apparatus. Some of these patients were found to be "beyond coma": no electrophysiological activity could be detected from the brain (reflexes were also absent). Postmortem examinations eventually were performed on these patients. The investigators discovered extensive destruction of brain tissue consistent with the premortem evaluation of electrophysiological activity. The term *respirator brain* soon appeared. There was now some evidence to support the position that some patients connected to respiratory machines had lost their brain function—irreversibly—and therefore should be considered dead.

Another influential development occurred about a decade later, when a committee composed of Harvard Medical School faculty issued its opinion (Ad Hoc Committee . . . , 1968). Much of current policy and practice are derived from the *Harvard criteria* for determination of a permanently nonfunctioning (or dead) brain. The first three criteria (given below) would have come as no surprise to physicians of an earlier generation. It is the last two criteria, dependent on 20th century technology, that introduce a new consideration.

The Harvard Criteria

1. *Unreceptive and unresponsive.* No awareness is shown for external stimuli or inner need. The unresponsiveness is complete even under the application of stimuli that ordinarily would be extremely painful.
2. *No movements and no breathing.* There is a complete absence of spontaneous respiration and all other spontaneous muscular movement.
3. *No reflexes.* The usual reflexes that can be elicited in a neurophysiological examination are absent (e.g., when a light is shined in the eye, the pupil does not constrict).
4. *A flat EEG.* Electrodes attached to the scalp elicit a printout of electrical activity from the living brain. These are popularly known as *brain waves.* The respirator brain does not provide the usual pattern of peaks and valleys. Instead the moving automatic stylus records essentially a flat line. This is taken to demonstrate the lack of electrophysiological activity.
5. *No circulation to or within the brain.* Without the oxygen and nutrition provided to the brain by its blood supply, functioning will soon terminate. (Precisely how long the brain can retain its *viability,* the ability to survive, without circulation is a matter of much current investigation and varies somewhat with conditions.)

In many instances the first three criteria (the traditional ones) seem to be adequate. The Harvard report was not intended to require the use of the EEG in all cases, only those in which some

question remains. This is fortunate because EEG testing is not always feasible, and procedures for testing cerebral blood flow also require special provisions that may be difficult to arrange. The Harvard report was intended chiefly for application in problem situations in which the traditional criteria may not be enough. It was recommended that in such situations all the tests required for all the criteria be repeated about 24 hours later.

The Harvard report provides useful guidelines and has found widespread application. However, the definition of death and all its ramifications have remained a continuing source of concern. The situation was considered urgent enough to stimulate the activity of the President's Commission for the Study of Ethical Problems in Medicine and Biomedical and Behavioral Research (1981). This group produced its own monograph *Defining Death.* Reviewing the Harvard criteria after more than a decade of application, the Commission concluded:

> The "Harvard criteria" have been found to be quite reliable. Indeed, no case has yet been found that met these criteria and regained any brain functions despite continuation of respirator support. Criticisms of the criteria have been of five kinds. First, the phrase, "irreversible coma" is misleading as applied to the cases at hand. "Coma" is a condition of a living person, and a body without any brain functions is dead and thus *beyond* any coma. Second, the writers of these criteria did not realize that the spinal cord reflexes actually persist or return quite commonly after the brain has completely and permanently ceased functioning. Third, "unreceptivity" is not amenable to testing in an unresponsive body without consciousness. Next, the need adequately to test brainstem reflexes, especially apnea, and to exclude drug and metabolic intoxication as possible causes of the coma, are not made sufficiently explicit and precise. Finally, although all individuals that meet "Harvard criteria" are dead (irreversible cessation of all functions of the entire brain), there are many other individuals who are dead but do not maintain circulation long enough to have a 24-hour observation period. (p. 25)

Perhaps you have noticed something odd in this otherwise straightforward passage. It speaks of individuals who are "dead but do not maintain circulation long enough to have a 24-hour observation period." This quirky turn of thought alerts us again to the contemporary breakdown of the old, comfortably secure concept of *dead*. A Presidential Commission here seems almost to be rebuking some dead individuals for not maintaining their circulation. It may not yet have become a patriotic duty for the dead to make themselves available for all possible testing. Nevertheless, the message conveyed is that there are echelons among the dead—some appear to be "deader" than others. This is surely a departure from the usual conception of *dead* and *death* in Western society, although it would not have raised eyebrows in some other cultures.

Whole-Brain or Neocortical Death?

While the "deadness" of the body *per se* has not attracted much attention, there is a spirited controversy within the realm of brain death itself. The problem is suggested by the President's Commission in pointing out that spinal cord reflexes often persist or return even in the absence of brain waves.

Assume for the moment that it is only the brain that must be considered. *How much* of the brain must be included in the definition and assessment? Some attention to detail is needed to see the challenge. *Brain death* can refer to any of the following conditions:

- *Whole-brain death* is the irreversible destruction of all neural structures within the intracranial cavity. This includes both hemispheres and all tissue from the top (cerebral cortex) through the bottom (cerebellum and brainstem).
- *Cerebral death* is the irreversible destruction of both cerebral hemispheres, but excluding the lower centers in the cerebellum and brainstem.
- *Neocortical death* is the irreversible destruction of neural tissue in the cerebral cortex—the most highly differentiated brain cells, considered to be of critical importance for intellectual functioning.

Whole-brain death is the most frequently used biomedical definition today and the one that also appears most often in regulatory documents. It is a conservative definition; the certification of death is delayed as long as there is observable functioning in any subsystem of the brain. This conception has been challenged, however, notably by Robert Veatch (1975). He points out that (according to current biomedical knowledge) personhood depends on an intact neocortex. A flat (or *isographic*) EEG would tell us that the *person* is dead, and that is all we really need to know.

This is a position to consider carefully. It could resolve some of the questions already discussed. *Dead* would refer to the status of the *person*, regardless of any extraneous physiological processes that might still continue. Moreover, since there is a dependable measure of the death of the person (the flat EEG), the problem has been resolved at least in principle. If accepted, this solution would have a significant impact on the treatment and legal status of many individuals whose vegetative processes are being maintained by life-support systems (usually including respirators). So-called heroic measures with all their expense could be withheld or withdrawn.

The opposing view is well represented by Douglas N. Walton (1981–1982). He argues that although higher mental functions require a functioning cerebral cortex, there is still the possibility that "some form of experience or basic awareness might persist in the deeper centers of the brain" (p. 341). In some instances the lack of neocortical functioning might be caused by dysfunction in lower centers such as the reticular formation in the medulla and midbrain. Absence of consciousness and electrical activity of the neocortex could represent a potentially reversible situation: should the reticular formation regain its functioning, there might be a return to consciousness after even a rather long period of coma. Walton cannot estimate how often such a possibility might exist. His essential point is that it would be premature in light of present knowledge to treat the lack of neocortical functioning as synonymous with death. Walton reasons that we run the risk of error in two directions: treating a corpse as though a person, and treating a person as though a corpse. The first risk is the more acceptable one, he suggests.

If the medical and legal professions continue to prefer the whole-brain position, then there may also continue to be a felt obligation to maintain life in those who no longer show the ability to have conscious experiences or social interaction. And should advocacy develop for the intermediate concept of cerebral death, then implications for life support would again be altered. A consensus on what death is—or when deadness has been established—is necessary if society is to cope in an intelligent and coherent way with the many new problems that continue to arise in clinical medicine.

TOWARD A DEFINITION OF DEATH

A general definition such as *nonreversible cessation of life processes* may sound clear enough, but more precision is needed for practical decisionmaking. The quest for precision, however, generates controversy that may be with us for a long time. Some of this controversy concerns the technicalities of determining death and therefore may continue to take new turns as new methods of prolonging life and of assessing physiological functioning are introduced. Yet some of the controversy has implications beyond the biomedical sphere.

Consider just one set of problems that has made itself evident in this examination of current biomedical approaches. Can we agree upon what it is to be a person? Is personhood to be identified with an intact brain? How can we understand the relationship between person and body near the time of death unless we understand the nature of this relationship throughout life?

This is one way of expressing what is known in philosophy as the "mind-body" problem. The physician, the coroner, the legislator, and the judge cannot resolve this problem by signing their names to an official document. The mind-body problem goes well beyond technical expertise or current opinion in these fields. It is one of the classic problems in philosophy. Does the body run the mind? Is the mind only a secondary product of the body? Do mind and body carry out their own activities on separate, but parallel levels? Or are "mind" and "body" just two different ways of describing the same fundamental reality? These are among the positions that have been argued through the centuries and which will not be resolved by a vote taken in the state legislature (Ayer, 1973; Shaffer, 1967).

The main point here is that our beliefs about the nature of life, personhood, and the relationship between mind and body all are intimately related to the definition of death. These beliefs are being put to the test with every new legislative or medical initiative that affects our relationship to those who are somewhere in the borderlands between life and death. Philosophical and religious questions are raised rather than answered when the President's Commission (1981) observes that "brain-based criteria do not introduce a new 'kind of death,' but rather reinforce the concept of death as a single phenomenon—the collapse of psycho-physical integrity" (p. 58). This statement assumes rather than explains the nature of the "psycho-physical integrity" that existed before death. Perhaps we will never reach total agreement on this question, but we might at least show more awareness of the ambiguities and legitimate differences of opinion that exist.

In moving toward a definition of death it is useful to remember a few distinctions.

Viability Versus Deadness

An individual may have "only a precarious and burdensome existence," to use the language of some recent legislation. The precariousness translates into the low probability of survival for any extended time. This condition should be sharply distinguished from deadness in either the whole-brain or neocortical sense. A person with limited viability may still be quite alive and able to think, feel, and interact.

Absence Versus Alteration of Personhood

This distinction becomes relevant under conditions when vegetative functions are maintained, but with a complete absence of responsiveness, a prolonged inability to express thought or feeling. This is the state most often discussed. However, there are also instances in which elements of response or spontaneous action appear. My colleagues and I have worked with patients who occasionally demonstrate that something, or somebody, still exists, even though it is not the person who once flourished when the body was in its normal state (Kastenbaum, et al., 1981). Often such responses are fragmentary, transient, and seemingly unrelated to external events. Sometimes the behavior seems to be purposeful and responsive, even if fleeting and hard to replicate. Some examples follow:

• You have been holding the hand of a comatose person for some time and speaking about various things. Suddenly the limp hand squeezes your own. You had just mentioned the patient's favorite child. Is this a coincidence? This child (now an adult) is persuaded to sit by the bedside. She holds her mother's hand and speaks of old times they shared together. The daughter's hand is also squeezed—another coincidence? The possibility here (and it is only a possibility that we cannot confirm independently) is that the patient's personhood can still express itself, but in a very limited and fragmentary manner.

• A patient who has required total care and remained generally unresponsive for an extended period will occasionally speak or gesture in a childlike manner. There have been no observations to indicate persistence of an adult self. It appears that a more primitive type of personality organization is still present and can occasionally express itself.

• A woman now very old and impaired was known to have been a highly proper, mild-mannered person. She now oscillates between unresponsiveness and explosive flare-ups, using language she would once have recoiled from and denounced as unspeakably vulgar. To the dismay and confusion of others she shows little or no trace of the person she had been for most of her life—but somebody is doing all that cursing!

Total absence of personality should be distinguished from fragments, traces, and reversals that represent an altered and limited self. These expressions are more likely to occur when others take the time and show the sensitivity to maintain human contact. A comprehensive definition of death, then, should deal plausibly with the question of who is still alive when the previously integrated person has left the scene but some type of responsiveness or behavior remains.

Cessation Versus Permanent Cessation

This distinction is prompted by an underlying question that might seem very odd: how long does a person have to be dead to be really dead? It is relevant, however, because our customary idea of death includes two components that are not usually differentiated from each other: the idea of cessation and the idea of permanent cessation (Kastenbaum & Aisenberg, 1972). Assume that all the Harvard criteria prove applicable in a first set of observations. It might be logical to conclude that this person is now a corpse. Life functions have ceased. It would be consistent with this conclusion that a person was once alive if he or she were alive for an instant. Once a person has lived, if briefly, this fact cannot be erased by subsequent death. Similarly, once dead, could a "return to life" erase that fact? Bear in mind that a second set of observations made 24 hours later (as recommended by the Harvard committee) essentially would be no different from the first observations. The same criteria and methods would be used.

It might be a good idea to repeat the observations, perhaps even more often. This might occasionally lead to discovery of renewed functioning. From a definitional and theoretical standpoint, though, the issue is muddled. Do repeated observations simply protect the interests of everybody concerned, reducing the possibility of error? Or must deadness prove itself to be sufficiently persistent? (Actually proving it to be *permanent* would require a time scale of observations that is beyond human capacity.) Implications of this question include the status of people who believe they have returned from the dead (Chapter 13) and the availability of cadaver organ transplants. If we really mean to define death as the permanent or even the persistent cessation of function, then we may be placing an obstacle in the way of timely use of organs. Before the development of modern organ transplant techniques, physicians and family could simply wait a little longer if there were any question about the individual's status.

The distinction between cessation and permanent cessation is a peculiar and troublesome one that many would like to ignore. But it remains one of the problems to be resolved if we are ever to establish a firm and useful definition of death.

Event Versus State

We create some of our own difficulties by using the same word for two rather different though related ideas. Death is sometimes treated as though an event—that is, something that occurs in a specific way and at a specific time and place. When it is death as event that concerns us, it is often possible to be factual and precise. ("This is the room where the victim was found. There is the blunt instrument. The clock was toppled over and still shows the exact moment of this dastardly fatal act.")

Quite different is our use of the same word in referring to the state that follows the event. Life has ceased (death as event). What happens from now on? The answer to this question is much less accessible to ordinary sources of information. Some interpretations of death as state follow.

WHAT DOES DEATH MEAN?

What does death *mean*? What does it mean to be *dead*? These may seem to be foolish questions. Medicine and the law often define death as the nonreversible cessation of life processes. Is there anything else to say? Yes, a great deal. For centuries the human mind has constructed meanings for both life and death. These interpretations have influenced our actions as well as our thoughts and feelings. Newer concepts such as brain death are also becoming influential—in court decisions, legislation, medical practice, professional ethics, and many other spheres. In this chapter we draw upon both historical and current attempts to find meaning in death. Specifically, we will be looking at death as a state or condition. Here is one example to start with:

The soloist in Bach's haunting Cantata No. 53 sings:

Schlage doch, gewunschte Stunde,
brich doch an gewunschter Tag!
Strike, oh strike, awaited hour,
approach thou happy day!

The hour that is awaited eventually will be displayed upon the face of an ordinary clock. It belongs to public, shared, or mortal time. The hour and day of death will be entered into the community's vital statistics. What the devout singer anticipates, however, is entry into a new realm of being in which the time changes of terrestrial life no longer apply. The survivors will continue to measure their own lives by clock and calendar. They may remember that the deceased has been dead for six months, five years, and so on. But this conventional manner of marking time has no bearing upon the deceased. She will have entered heaven. The death event will have cleaved her from the community's shared time framework at the same instant that it transports her to eternity. The hour that strikes refers to death as event; the heavenly blessing that follows refers to death as state.

This, however, is only one interpretation of death as a state. There are a variety of meanings that have been given to the state of death.

INTERPRETATIONS OF THE DEATH STATE

Enfeebled Life

Young children often think of death as a less vigorous form of life. I have learned from preschool boys and girls that the people who "live" in the cemetery don't get hungry, except once in a while. They are tired, sad, bored, and don't have much to do. A three-year-old girl was saving her comic books for grandmother but was worried that she might have forgotten to take her bifocals with her to the grave. (Chapter 7 demonstrates that children's views of death are far from simple.)

The view of death as a diminished form of life is an ancient one. The little child of today who offers this interpretation is in a sense carrying forward the belief system common in Mesopotamia thousands of years ago. The deceased person is gradually submerged into the underworld. There he or she is transformed into a "grisly being" that retains no capacity for value or pleasure (Brandon, 1967). The mightiest ruler and the fairest maiden lose all power, all beauty. The dead become equal in their abysmally low estate.

Hebrews of the Old Testament period confronted the gloomy prospect of dwelling in *Sheol,* mere shadows and wretched remnants of what they once had been. This death state held special terror because it signaled isolation from the protective custody of *Yahweh,* or God. God was the creator and judge of *life.* He had no dominion over death. The despairing soul was consigned to a dark realm into which the illuminating and warming presence of God did not reach (Bultmann, 1965).

This decremental model of the death state prevailed throughout much of the ancient world. Abandonment, depletion, and endless misery were the lot of all mortals. The notion that the death state can be influenced by pious belief or moral conduct had not yet taken hold.

Continuation

Passage from the life familiar on earth has sometimes been interpreted as a transition to more of the same. This idea might seem odd today. We are accustomed to concepts of the afterlife involving a profound change, a transformation. Because death seems so extraordinary, it must also lead to something extraordinary. Even the decremental model recognized a significant change, if not a desirable one.

Yet a number of tribal societies have pictured the death state as one that has much in common with life as usual. Continuation after the death event does not guarantee immortality. The individual faces challenges and crises just as before. If some of the threat comes from what we would call a supernatural source, this is not a completely new situation. All through their lives on earth, members of the tribal society also have to contend with jealous and ill-willed spirits.

It is even possible for the dead person to be destroyed again. In discussing customs of various Borneo tribes at the turn of this century, for example, Robert Hertz (1960) declares for the Dayak:

> The soul does not enter the celestial city in order to enjoy an eternal rest there: immortality no more belongs to the inhabitants of the other world than it does to those of this. The soul stays in heaven for a period of seven generations, but each time it has reached the end of one existence it must die in order to be reborn. (p. 60)

The soul returns to earth after its seventh death and there enters a mushroom or fruit near the village. This returned soul invades the body of the woman who chances to eat the morsel, and soon is reborn. Or a buffalo, deer, or monkey might find this delicacy first, and the soul will then be reborn as an animal, losing its human identity in the process.

The cyclical model of the death state is mingled in this instance with the view of death as a continuation of life's hazardous journey. What is distinctive about this type of belief is the accompanying assumption that a person goes on through the death state with essentially the same personality, motives, and needs that characterized life before death. Yes, the death event makes a difference. No, it does not mean the person necessarily has become better or worse, more ennobled or more miserable.

Perpetual Development

Suppose that the universe itself is not completely determined, that all of existence is en route to making something else of itself. Suppose further that what we make of our lives is part of this universal process. What might be the death state in such a universe?

The answers to this question do not come from the ancient people of Mesopotamia or tribespeople maintaining their traditional customs against the encroachment of technology. Instead the answers come from prophets and philosophers of evolution, individual thinkers who either anticipate or build upon Darwin's discoveries in fashioning a different view of life and its place in the universe.

As a deaf old man whose long and handsome beard threatened to become entangled in the wheels of his bicycle, the British philosopher Samuel Alexander provided his neighbors with many an anxious moment. For the rest of us he has bequeathed a grand vision of the "in-process" universe (Alexander, 1920). In the beginning all that existed was a bare time-space manifold: no objects, no set rules. From this primitive state the other levels of existence emerged and continue to emerge. Life itself was one of the emergent qualities. Mind is a quality that has since emerged from life. And it is not only life and mind that bud out of space and time, but the universe itself is in the process of "flowering into diety." God is still being created. Similarly, the relationship between life and death continues to evolve. The basic law is continued development

for individual minds and for the universe at large. Lloyd Morgan (1923) and C. S. Pierce (1923) are among the other post-Darwin thinkers who constructed world views in which the idea of continued development was at the core.

For a vivid depiction of development through the death state itself, step back a few decades before Darwin to Gustav Theodor Fechner. In 1836 Fechner (1836/1904) proposed a model of the death state as perpetual development. He began by likening the death event to birth: transition to a freer mode of existence in which tremendous new possibilities can be found for spiritual growth. Translated into English as *The Little Book of Life After Death,* it might as appropriately be read as *The Little Book of Life Through Death.*

The so-called living and the so-called dead can interact on a spiritual level to advance universal development. Precisely what the death state *is* or *means* to the individual depends on the stage of spiritual development that had been attained up to the moment of the death event:

> This is the great justice of creation, that every one makes for himself the conditions of his future life. Deeds will not be requited to the man through exterior rewards or punishments; there is no heaven and no hell in the usual sense . . . after it has passed through the great transition, death, it unfolds itself according to the unalterable law of nature upon earth; steadily advancing step by step, and quietly approaching and entering into a higher existence. According as the man has been good or bad, has behaved nobly or basely, was industrious or idle, will find himself possessed of an organism, strong or weak, healthy or sick, beautiful or hateful.

In Fechner's view, the death state not only varies among different people, but the state itself is subject to change as the entire universe continues to evolve. In a sense, then, the death state provides everyone with at least the opportunity to become more alive than ever.

Waiting

What happens after the death event? We wait. In Western society this is often a triphasic conception that (1) begins with a sleeplike or suspended animation period that is (2) terminated by the dramatic Day of Judgment, after which (3) the soul proceeds to its ultimate destination or condition. "The sleeper awakens," receives judgment, and takes his or her place either for "eternity" or "for all time" (concepts that often are treated as though functionally equivalent, although philosophers hold them to be sharply different).

These phases may be given different priorities by particular individuals and societies. Some Christians, for example, emphasize the taking-a-good-long-rest phase. Others focus attention upon the critical moment of judgment. Still others contemplate that ultimate phase when sorrows and anxieties will have passed away, when the just are rewarded and everlasting radiance and peace prevail—sometimes further embellished by havoc wreaked upon their enemies. By contrast, in ancient Egypt the act of judgment seemed to occur more promptly after the death event (Leca, 1981). More emphasis was placed on the phases of judgment and final disposition than on waiting.

This general conception of the death state has been characterized as *waiting* to emphasize its implications for time, tension, and striving. A tension exists between the death event itself and the end state. The dead may seem to be at rest, but for those with particular religious views it is a watchful waiting. Judgment and final disposition are still to come. Furthermore, the sense of waiting cannot be contained on just one side of the grave. The aged and the critically ill are sometimes regarded as waiting for death. From a broader perspective, all the living, regardless of health status, are only putting in time until they too move through the event into the state of death. The waiting is not over until all souls have perished and awakened for judgment and final disposition. Not everybody shares this view of death and its relationship to deity, of course. But it embodies a sense of striving and tension that does not end with life but continues from the moment of life's cessation until a final outcome.

There has been an important corollary to the triphasic conception of death in both Egyptian and Christian belief systems. The prospect of surviving death gave the corpse an unusually high significance as compared with most other religions. Most Greek and Roman sects, for example, were outraged or amused by the early Christian claim of bodily resurrection (Wilkin, 1984). In an earlier era the Egyptians had already changed their collective mind on the subject. Moving from the depressing *death-as-enfeeblement* view to embrace conceptions of immortality, they also had to revise their system for managing the dead. The great eras of Egyptian mummification and tomb building followed in response to a new theology. The individual's *ka,* or life force, can enjoy the blessings of immortality, but only if there is an intact body. Many practical circumstances had to be altered to meet this new view, including the construction of larger burial vaults, provision of food and tools, and an elaborate code of moral conduct.

Cycling and Recycling

One of the most traditional and popular conceptions of the death state is also one of the most radical. Death comes and goes, wending in and out of life. This view is often expressed by children. After a person has been dead for a while, he or she will probably get up again and go home. Sure, the bird was dead Friday, but maybe it's been dead long enough. Some adults also have regarded death as a temporary condition that alternates with life and that represents a stage of transition between one form of life and another.

Death has been seen, for example, as one position on a constantly revolving wheel, the great wheel of life and death. Many examples are given in Philip Kapleau's (1971) *The Wheel of Death.* He points out that the wheel itself is one of the core symbols of Buddhism. Another important symbol is flame passing from lamp to candle. This indicates a rebirth that continues an ongoing process, not the simple transference of a substance. Kapleau also reminds us of the *phoenix,* "a mythical bird of great beauty who lived for five hundred years in the desert. It immolated itself on a funeral pyre and then rose from its own ashes in the freshness of youth, living another cycle of years" (p. viii). The phoenix represents both death and regeneration. As discussed in Chapter 9, the funeral process can also be regarded as a way of encouraging the regeneration or recycling of life through death.

Kapleau argues that the cyclical view of life and death is more rational than many people in Western society are willing to grant:

> The assertion that nothing precedes birth or follows death is largely taken for granted in the West, but however widely believed, it is still absurd from a Buddhist viewpoint. Such an assertion rests on the blind assumption—in its own way an act of faith—that life, of all things in the universe, operates in a vacuum. (p. xvii)

I cannot help but think of the all-too-bright ten-year-old who attended one of my classes with his mother. At the end of the session I asked him if there were anything he would like to say. He replied, "Just a little question. I mean, what are we *before* life and where are we or is it only nothing and would that be the same nothing we are after life or a different kind of nothing and . . ." I have grown more cautious in asking ten-year-olds for their questions.

The recycling of life through the death state is an article of faith for many peoples. A classic guide to this topic is *Wisdom of the Serpent* by Joseph L. Henderson and Maud Oakes (1971). It illustrates, for example, how people living at great distances from each other have somehow arrived at similar interpretations of cyclical phenomena, how life-and-death cycles readily become seen as a natural part of the rhythms of nature. The serpent slithering in the title of their book is itself just one of the many symbols of rebirth. Every agricultural society has watched anxiously for the renewal of springtime after the dead of winter, and the Egyptians were no less invested in rituals to promote fruitfulness and harvest than in those intended to secure immortality.

The name chosen for a newborn often reflects recycling (Kastenbaum, 1974). What is conveyed in this manner can be regarded as the family name-soul, something that long ago was considered too precious to lose (Kastenbaum, 1984). In some cultures the soul or spirit of a recently deceased person is thought to gain a new embodiment in this way. Philip Aries (1962) tells us that in French medieval art the soul often was depicted "as a little child who was naked and usually sexless . . . The dying man breathes the child out through his mouth in a symbolic representation of the soul's departure" (p. 36).

Nothing

Perhaps we are deceiving ourselves when we imagine death to be any kind of state at all. Dying is something. There are bodily changes with consequences for thought, feeling, and social interaction. The death event is something: the final cessation of life processes (although sometimes a complex and ambiguous sequence). But is death a state? Perhaps death should be seen instead as total absence: absence of life, absence of process, absence of qualities. The more we say about death, the more we deceive ourselves and use language to falsify.

This concept of death is repugnant to many people. It is felt to be much too barren and devoid of hope. Furthermore, it is simply difficult to cope with the concept of nothing. (Calling it *nothingness* is a useless exercise that essentially reifies a reification. We do not understand *nothing* any better by endowing it with the objective quality implied by *-ness*.) We know little if anything about *nothing*; our minds do not know what to do with themselves unless there is a little something to work with. Yet the difference between even *a little something* and the concept of *nothing* is enormous. Furthermore, we tend to become anxious when faced with formlessness, with experiences that do not fit into any of our fixed categories of thought.

Call death a void or a great emptiness. Does that really preserve the idea of death as a nonstate, or does it instead allow us slyly to construct images intended to conceal *nothing*? There are few people who seem to care for the definition of death as nonstate and fewer still who exercise the mental rigor it would require to adhere faithfully to this view. But as much as we ignore or reject *nothing,* it refuses to vanish into, well, nothingness.

Implications of the Ways in Which We Interpret Death

How we interpret the state of death can influence our thoughts, feelings, and actions. A person may refuse to touch or approach a corpse, even though it is that of a much beloved individual. The ancient Babylonians, Egyptians and Hebrews revered and attempted to comfort their aged. But who among them would want to be contaminated by a body that was beyond the pale of life? Who would dip a hand into the dark and dismal stream of *Sheol?* It is not only people of ancient times and distant lands who have avoided the dead, fearing great harm to themselves. There are both religious rituals and individual behavior patterns today that have as their purpose the avoidance of contact with the alien and contaminating aura of the human corpse.

By contrast, if death is waiting, and waiting is mostly a restful sleep, then the terminally ill person might agree with the late Stewart Alsop (1973) that "as the sleepy man needs to sleep, so the dying man needs to die." Yet the prospect of waiting is anything but tranquil for the person who is attuned to the moment of judgment instead of the interlude between death event and final state. Two people, good Christians both and both stricken with the same life-threatening ailment, might differ in their specific anticipations of death and therefore in their mood and behavior.

These are but a few of the implications of the varying interpretations of death as a state. It will mark some progress in our understanding if we simply become more aware of both our own interpretations and those of the people with whom we come in contact.

CONDITIONS THAT RESEMBLE DEATH

Sometimes we try to comprehend a strange phenomenon by comparing it to one that is more familiar. This happens frequently when we think and speak of death. It is a two-way process: we liken death to something else or we liken something else to death. Exploring death analogies will help not only in continuing the task of defining death, but will also lead us into certain problem areas that deserve sustained attention.

Inorganic and Unresponsive

Fire, lightning, flood waters, and other active natural phenomena have always impressed humankind. But you can also be impressed by the *lack* of activity in the world. This kind of perception sometimes contributes to a sense of comforting stability. Look at those everlasting mountains! They were here in the days of our ancestors and will continue to tower above our children's children. At other times, however, the inert, unresponsive character of a particular environment elicits a sense of deadness. "Stone cold dead in the marketplace" goes one old phrase. The parallel with the stiff form of a cadaver is obvious enough. "Stone cold" reinforces the deadness of the dead.

The hard, unyielding surface of a rock contrasts with our human flesh and spirit that can be wounded so easily. A suffering and vulnerable person may envy the durability of the rock. For a living person to liken him- or herself to stone suggests a subtle compromise: "I live, but to do so I must not experience life."

Stone as a representation of death is also familiar to us through a succession of mythological unfortunates who were transformed from flesh and blood into insensate rock by incident or unwise action—a glimpse of Medusa's terrifying visage or that backward glance upon leaving Hades.

We live in an invented as well as a natural world. The motor has died. Perhaps a dead battery is at fault. We age, and our machines wear out. We see death, and we scrap and abandon our failed machines. The family that lived close to the rhythms of earth had fire and stone to inspire representations of life and death. We have added the mechanical and electronic apparatus, from windmill to computer and beyond.

For example, stand at the bedside of a critically ill person with multiple lifelines to an external support system. Interpret, if you can, the situation in process. Is it a person living? Or is it a set of machines functioning? Or can it best be understood as an interwoven *psychobioelectromechanical* process in which the human and nonhuman components have merged to form a special system of their own? While you are considering this situation, it ends. But *what* has ended? Do we say the machines failed or the body?

Today the machine is more than a casual analogy to human life. It is routine for medical personnel to look upon the termination of human life as a sort of mechanical failure—machines have been integral to diagnosis and treatment, and the personnel have learned in their own training much that is conducive to a mechanical analogy.

Perhaps this is something more than an analogy. When we liken death to the hard, cold unresponsiveness of a stone we usually recognize that we are dealing in an evocative figure of speech. But the distinction between analogy and solid fact is often blurred in current treatment of the terminally ill. Failure of the machine can be seen as the failure of the machine that is the person as well. Unless alternative conceptions of the human person and of the death state are in evidence, the scene as the end of life approaches may come increasingly under the domination of a mechanical analogy that is not even recognized as analogy.

Sleep and Altered States of Consciousness

Sleep has long served as another natural analogy to death. The ancient Greeks pictured sleep (*Hypnos*) as twin brother to death (*Thanatos*). Herman Feifel (1949) reminds us that "many of our religious prayers entwine the ideas of sleep and death. Orthodox Jews, for example, on arising from sleep in the morning thank God for having restored them to life again" (p. 120).

Aries (1981) observes that the resemblance between sleep and death was long a mainstay both of the medical and the religious literature.

In many contemporary societies people replace the word *death* or *dead* with *sleep* as a less threatening way of speaking. However, when children are told that a deceased person is only sleeping, we may question what message is intended and what message is coming across. Does the parent intend to soften the impact of death somewhat or actually to lie to the child and deny that a death has occurred? The young child is not likely to have a firm grip on the distinction between sleep and death. The analogy, no matter how intended, may register as reality. Late in the evening a child is told, "Go to sleep!" Earlier the same day this child may have been told by the same parent that Grandmother is asleep or that death is a long sleep. It is not a surprise if the child has difficulty falling asleep that night. Indeed many children have nightmares in which death-related themes are prominent (Mack, 1970). Adults as well as children may experience insomnia as a symptom of disturbance when death has intruded in their lives. While working in a geriatric hospital, for example, experience taught me to expect insomnia and other nocturnal disturbances on a ward where a patient had died unexpectedly. An aged man or woman might speak matter-of-factly about the death and seem not to have been personally affected, then awaken in terror and confusion that night, seeking a living face and a comforting word.

Whether used wisely or foolishly, however, sleep remains one of the most universal, easily conveyed analogies to death. Myth and fairy tale abound in examples of characters who, believed dead, are actually in a deep (possibly enchanted) sleep. Snow White and Sleeping Beauty are among the examples best known to our children.

Altered states of consciousness occurring in sleep or resembling sleep have also been used as analogies to death. People dream they are dead and feel frozen, immobilized, powerless to act. Drug- and alcohol-induced states of mind sometimes are likened to death, whether as a joyful or a terrifying "trip." The now rarely employed technique of insulin coma therapy sometimes generated terrifying deathlike experiences for the psychiatric patients it was intended to help.

Normal sleep is not identical to the various other altered states of consciousness that can result from disease, trauma, drugs, alcohol, or other special influences. The coma of the seriously ill person, for example, is not likely to represent the same psychobiological state as normal sleep. The temporary loss of consciousness in some epileptic seizures has at times been interpreted as a deathlike state (e.g., Freud's [1961] commentary on the meaning of Dostoevsky's seizures). It is best, however, to distinguish the different types of altered states of consciousness from each other and from normal sleep.

Beings Who Resemble or Represent Death

In Homer's classic epic, Ulysses ties himself to the mast of his ship to protect himself from peril. Enormous birdlike creatures with the heads of women menace him and his crew. Some are perched on a rock, trying to lure them hither with sweet song; others are circling near the vessel. The hybrid bird-person has been a compelling figure in art and mythology for many centuries. Not all winged beings are associated with death, but such imagery is very common. In post-Homeric Greek times, *sirens* were distinguished from *harpies*. Both were rather nasty creatures: sirens brought death, and harpies had the special knack of obliterating memory. Death, then, might come with or without loss of memory, as represented by two different fabulous beings.

The winged hybrid at other times was depicted as a soul bird. This represented the spirit leaving the body at the time of death, suggesting resurrection. Later the bird-people were joined by a variety of fish-people many of whom are also associated with death. The hybrid death-beings usually are portrayed as females. Some historians hold that among ancient peoples there was a ten-

dency for peaceful death to be represented in masculine terms, whereas painful and violent death came through female agents. This characterization could hardly be less fair when you consider how many have died violently in man-made wars and been comforted in their terminal illnesses by woman. The *Muses*, arriving a bit later in history than the sirens and harpies, were females depicted in a somewhat more kindly light, their functions being to sing at funerals and guide departed souls on their journey through the underworld.

Orpheus was a being fabulous for his powers rather than his appearance. A master musician, Orpheus represented power over death. He could not only liberate Eurydice from Hades through his song but also bring rocks and trees to life. Orpheus is one of many personified symbols of resurrection that the human mind has created through the centuries.

The *skeleton* has also enjoyed a long career as an animate being. Examples can be found from scattered sources in the ancient world. Artifacts from the lost city of Pompeii include a rather modern-looking depiction of a skeleton boxed inside a black border, suggesting a symbolic depiction of death. The skeleton flourished particularly in medieval Europe, appearing in numerous works of art from approximately the 13th through the 15th centuries. We see the skeleton, for example, bearing a scythe on its shoulder and confronting young men with the world behind them and hell gaping opening underneath. This appears on the title page of one of many books of the time called *Ars Moriendi* (*The Art of Dying*). The skeleton is also a prominent figure in van Eyck's rendering of *The Last Judgment*.

The animate skeleton did not simply pose for pictures. It danced. One whirl with this dancer was enough for any mortal. Images of the Dance of Death flourished during the 14th and 15th centuries when the effects of the highly virulent bubonic plague, Black Death, were keenly felt.

Death was a quiet, almost sedate dancer; such was its power that extreme movements were not required. (This death-ridden period of human history is depicted powerfully in Ingmar Bergman's film, *The Seventh Seal.*)

We have not entirely forgotten this representative of death today. The skeleton still dangles from many a door on Halloween, and the image of skull and crossbones remains on bottles containing poisonous substances, highway safety brochures, and old Erroll Flynn pirate films. The skeleton is also conspicuous on the Mexican Day of the Dead (Green, 1972), often in the form of skull-shaped hunks of sugar or candy (perhaps not what the pious quite had in mind when singing "Come sweet death").

These are but a few of the shapes resembling and representing death that have formed themselves in the human mind. The next shape to consider is the human form itself.

Death Personified

"Man be my metaphor!" declared the Welsh poet Dylan Thomas. The human form has in fact served as a significant metaphor in the realm of death. Children's games through the centuries often have involved the participation of a character representing death (Opie & Opie, 1969). Here the focus is on the death personifications of adults in Western society.

My first study (Kastenbaum & Aisenberg, 1972) on this topic asked 240 mostly young adults the following questions. Answer these questions yourself before we look at the results:

> If Death were a person, what sort of a person would Death be? Think of this question until an image of death-as-a-human being forms in your mind. Then describe Death physically, what could Death *look* like . . . . Now, what would Death *be* like? What kind of personality would Death have? What age would Death appear to be, and what gender? (p. 155)

In a follow-up study another 421 people were asked to respond to a multiple-choice format:

> 1. In stories, plays, and movies, death is sometimes treated as though a human being. If you were

writing a story in which one character would represent Death, would you represent Death as:
> (a) A young man
> (b) An old man
> (c) A young woman
> (d) An old woman
> (e) If other, please specify.
> 2. Would death be
> (a) A cold, remote sort of person
> (b) A gentle, well-meaning sort of person
> (c) A grim, terrifying sort of person
> (d) If other, please specify

Four types of personification were offered most frequently by participants in the open-ended study. The *macabre* personification vividly depicted ugly, menacing, vicious, and repulsive characters. One undergraduate replied:

> I see Death as something I don't want to see at all. He or she—I guess it's a he, but I'm not sure—has jagged, sharp features. Everything about how he looks looks sharp and threatening, his bony fingers with something like claws on the end of all of them, even a sharp nose, long, sharp teeth, and eyes that seem as though they can tear and penetrate right into you. Yet all this sharpness is almost covered over by . . . hair, bloody, matted hair.

A young nurse had difficulty in personifying death at first and then said:

> I can imagine him, Death, being nearby. It makes me feel trembly and weak, so I don't want to take a good look at him. No look at him could be good, anyhow, if you know what I mean. I feel his presence more than actually see him. I think he would be strong, unbelievably strong, and powerful. It could make your heart sink if you really had to look at him. But if he wanted you, there wouldn't be anything you could do about it.

Macabre personifications sometimes included signs of physical deterioration as well as sheer unattractiveness. It was common for the respondents to express emotional reactions to their own creations—for example, "When I look at this person—don't think it isn't possible—a shivering and nausea overwhelms me" (p. 156). The macabre personification often was seen as an old person and almost always as a terrifying being who is the sworn enemy of life. The relationship between age and personification is not so simple, however, as the next image reveals.

The *gentle comforter* could hardly be more different. Although usually pictured as an aged person, there was little physical and no psychological resemblance to Mr. Macabre. The gentle comforter was the personification of serenity and welcome. People who gave this kind of personification generally were those who also found the task easiest and least threatening to do. A typical example is from a registered nurse:

> A fairly old man with long white hair and a long beard. A man who would resemble a biblical figure with a long robe which is clean but shabby. He would have very strong features and despite his age would appear to have strength. His eyes would be very penetrating and his hands would be large.
>
> Death would be calm, soothing, and comforting. His voice would be of an alluring nature and, although kind, would hold the tone of the mysterious. Therefore, in general, he would be kind and understanding and yet be very firm and sure of his actions and attitudes. (p. 157)

Although often seen as an aged person, the gentle comforter could also be seen as a younger individual, most often a male. Respondents were not always clear as to whether this was a male or female being. In general this personification seems to represent a powerful force quietly employed in a kindly way.

The *gay deceiver* is an image of death usually seen as a young and appealing or fascinating individual. This personification can be either male or female, often with sexual allure. The gay deceiver tends to be an elegant, knowing, worldly person who can guide you into a tempting adventure. But "one could not trust him. He would be elusive in his manners, hypocritical, a liar, persuasive. Death would first gain your confidence. Then you would learn who he really is, and it would be too late" (p. 160).

One young woman described death in the following manner:

> She is beautiful, but in a strange way. Dark eyes and long dark hair, but her skin is pale. She is slender and she is sophisticated looking. . . . I imagine her beckoning me to come with her. She will take me to a new circle of people and places, a lot fancier, more exotic than what I have in my own life. I feel sort of flattered that she would want my company, and I sort of want to go with her, to discover what I may have been missing. . . . But I am scared, too. How will this evening end?

The gay deceiver is unique for its mixture of allure, excitement, and danger. Death remains the outcome, but at least the getting there is interesting.

The *automaton* is relatively undistinguished in appearance. In fact, his physical hallmark is that you might pass him on the street or in almost any situation and not really notice him. The automaton tends to be dressed conservatively. There are no striking mannerisms. If there is any distinctive quality at all, it is a sort of matter-of-fact blandness or a vacant expression. One woman, for example, characterized him as:

> . . . Having no feeling of emotion about his job— either positive or negative. He simply does his job. He doesn't think about what he is doing, and there is no way to reason with him. There is no way to stop him or change his mind. When you look into his eyes you do not see a person. You see only death. (p. 159)

The automaton, then, appears in human guise but lacks human qualities. He does not lure, comfort, or terrify; he is merely an unresponsive employee or representative who is just doing his job. It has always seemed to me that there is something rather modern about this depersonalized personification, representing a quality of alienation in Western society.

On the multiple-choice version of this task, respondents were most likely to see death as "a gentle, well-meaning sort of person"; the "grim, terrifying" image was the least frequently selected. Death usually was personified as a relatively old person. Masculine personifications were given more frequently than feminine. In my more recent studies the percentage of feminine personifications has increased, but their masculine counterparts remain most common.

CONDITIONS THAT DEATH RESEMBLES

Between people we may observe spirited, intensive, and varied interactions. They are having a "lively" time together. We observe the other extreme as well: people sharing time and space but nothing else. "That was an awfully dead party," we might say, just as actors might remark when the final curtain drops, "Whew! What a dead house tonight!" Emphasis might also be on a particular individual instead of a group. "He has no life in him, just going through the motions." "She's dead on her feet."

There are still other ways in which deadness serves as an instructive way of acknowledging certain aspects of life.

Social Death

You are there, part of a situation, but nobody is paying attention to you. You might as well not be there at all.

Social death must be defined situationally. In particular it is a situation in which there is an absence of those behaviors we would expect to be directed toward a living person, and the presence of behaviors we would expect when dealing with a deceased or nonexistent person (Kastenbaum, 1969). Social death is read by observing how others treat or fail to treat people. The individuals themselves may be animated enough and potentially responsive. As a matter of fact, the person may be desperately seeking interaction. The concept of social death recognizes that a significant part of being a person is being a person in the eyes of others.

Some of the ways in which social death can be seen follow:

• A person has violated one of the taboos of the group. As a result he or she is "cut dead." This could be the West Point cadet who is given

the silent treatment or the child who married somebody of the "wrong" religion, race, or socioeconomic echelon.

• A taboo violation is considered so serious that the offending individual is ritualistically expelled, the equivalent (and in some circumstances the alternative) to being killed. The law may strip a person of the privileges of citizenship; the church may excommunicate. A more striking example is a bone-pointing ceremony. The tribal community officially certifies one of its errant members as dead. This public ritual does not harm a hair on the offender's head but has the effect of terminating his or her life as a group member. Property that once belonged to this person may be redistributed and the name itself discarded or assigned to somebody else after it has been decontaminated (Cannon, 1942).

• There is an intrinsic change in an individual that results in loss of "live person status." This phenomenon often can be observed in facilities for the impaired and vulnerable aged. This social transformation of living person into custodial object occurs in modern facilities with cheerful decor as well as grim and physically deteriorating institutions (Kastenbaum, 1983). Even the old person who lives independently in the community can be victim of the socially dead treatment (e.g., being passed over while trying to get the attention of a store clerk or being placed at the bottom of medical or educational priorities).

Exclusionary actions may also operate against people who have developed feared or unpopular diseases such as AIDS or who make others uncomfortable because of scars or physical infirmities. A person whose face has been severely burned in an accident, for example, may discover that others avert their eyes and keep a greater distance, sending out signals of unacceptance and unwelcome.

• The dying person may be treated as though already dead. An elaborate pattern of aversive and "person-denying" behavior may be generated around a living individual whose demise is anticipated. Particulars often include little or no eye contact, reluctance to touch, making decisions without consultations, and talking to others in the presence of the person as though he or she were not there.

What makes this kind of situation even more unfortunate is that the person taken for dead may still be very much alive, alert, and capable of meaningful interaction (Kastenbaum, 1983; Kastenbaum & Aisenberg, 1972).

Phenomenological Death

Concentrate now on what is taking place *inside* the person. Regardless of society's attitudes and actions, is the individual alive to himself or herself?

There are two types of *phenomenological death.* First, *part of the person may die in the mind of the surviving self.* Partial death can range in personal significance from trivial to profound. Two examples follow:

A young man undergoes surgery that saves his life but results in the loss of capacity to father children. In his own mind one part of his total self has died. He will never be a father. Although much else about his own self remains alive to him, there is now the mental and emotional challenge of working through the loss of one of his most valued potential roles and sources of satisfaction.

A young athlete is physically fit by most standards. But she has sustained an injury in athletic competition that is just disabling enough to end her career. She is a runner with bad knees. She was an accomplished athlete both in her mind and in the minds of others. Now she has to remake her identity, while still mourning privately for the athlete who has died.

The essence of phenomenological death in this first sense, then, is that there is a surviving self that recognizes the loss of one or more components of the total self. The person is alive enough to know that part of him or her has died. But there is an element of mourning—for a part of your own self.

Second, *the total self may take on a deadened tone.* The person does not experience life as freshly or intensely as in the past. Pleasures do not really please. Even pains may have become heavy, tedious burdens rather than sharp pangs.

Feeling dead to yourself is a quality of experience that can shade into depersonalization: "I have no body" or "This body is not mine." Some psychotic people present themselves as though dead, either in the sense that they have actually died or through the impression that they do not relate to their own bodies and biographies as though they belong to living persons. This may be accompanied by a depersonalized attitude toward other people as well. The person may be mute, slow moving, and given to maintaining a rigid posture for protracted periods. The self we expect to be associated with this body seems to be receiving and transmitting few messages.

The sense of inner deadness or fading out sometimes is experienced in conjunction with the use of alcohol or other drugs. It can also accompany a variety of other alterations in bodily state. However, there is reason to believe that it can be chiefly psychogenic as well. Whatever the cause, the circumstances, or the outcome, we must recognize a state of mind in which the person becomes as dead to himself.

Phenomenological death is a state that people sometimes appear to visit upon themselves. The pain of a life gone wrong may seem too much to bear. They subdue the pain with drink or drugs, find some way to reduce conscious experience. The resulting condition of temporary deadness is the price sometimes paid for reduction of pain. It may not be the only price. Inattentiveness and reduced coping ability are likely to accompany psychological deadness, and these make the person more vulnerable to a variety of life-threatening forces.

The relationship between aliveness and pain can also be observed:

Mrs. A. was a 62-year-old Puerto Rican who constantly refused to take any medicine, even when in great pain. Her rationale was similar to other Puerto Rican patients (with far advanced cancer) I met. Doctors don't know as much as they think they do about the person's body. Each body has a soul, and if the doctor cannot see the soul, then he cannot see the body. "I know, I know that my family does not want that I suffer . . . but suffering is part of life . . . and without it you are not a man. No medicine can help with any pain . . . or, sometimes it could help putting all your body asleep . . . like a baby . . . and then it takes away my pain . . . but it also takes away all that I feel and see. If I could feel the pain I also 'can feel my body . . . and then I know I am still alive." (Baider, 1975)

One person, perhaps in good physical health, reduces his or her sense of aliveness in an effort to avoid emotional pain. Another person, perhaps in extremely poor health, accepts intense physical pain as a link to life itself. These differences in our relationship to phenomenological aliveness and deadness are but two of the variations that must be acknowledged as exploration into the human encounter with death continues.

DEATH AS AN AGENT OF PERSONAL, POLITICAL, AND SOCIAL CHANGE

The meanings of death often can be felt in public as well as personal life. How we interpret death serves either to support the *status quo* or to hasten political and social change. Following are a few examples.

The Great Leveler

Human equality has seldom existed as a concrete fact in society. We have been sorting each other out by class, by caste, by sex, by race, by geography—by just about any imaginable criterion. Surprisingly, perhaps, death has at times been an effective force for human rights. On the eve of his execution in 1672, Peter Patrix wrote these lines:

I dreamt that, buried in my fellow clay,
Close by a common beggar's side I lay.
And, as so mean a neighbour shock'd my pride,
Thus, like a corpse of quality, I cried,
"Away! thou scoundrel! Henceforth touch me not;
More manners learn, and at a distance rot!"
"*Thou* scoundrel!" in a louder tone, cried he,
"Proud lump of dirt! I scorn thy word and thee.

We're equal now, I'll not an inch resign;
This is my dunghill, as the next is thine." (p. 292)

Shakespeare has *King Richard II* remind us that:

. . . Within the hollow crown
That rounds the mortal temples of a king,
Keeps Death his court; and there the antick sits,
Mocking his state, and grinning at his pomp;
Allowing him a breath, a little scene,
To monarchize, be fear'd, and kill with looks;
Infusing him with self and vain conceit—
As if this flesh, which walls about his life,
Were brass impregnable; and, humor'd thus,
Comes at the last, and with a little pin
Bores through his castle wall, and—farewell king!
(Act III, Scene 2)

Works of art commissioned during medieval times often displayed the theme of death as the great leveler. Gallant knights and beauteous maidens are greeted on their journeys by death, the skeleton (Gottlieb, 1959). Human skulls stare sightlessly from tables, shelves, and obscure corners of the room as scholars ponder their books or marriage rites are performed. In such ways did the elite remind themselves that pride and triumph are fragile commodities. Furthermore, the enormous toll of lives taken by the bubonic plague during its several major visitations had the secondary effect of temporarily unseating both the aristocracy and the church (Gottfried, 1983; Tuchman, 1978). Death did not seem impressed with the powers-that-be on earth; the peasants recognized this lesson and organized the first clumsy revolutions and reforms that many years later would eventually lead to a new and more equitable social order. As winds of social change swept through Europe, death the leveler had a distinctive role, emboldening the common person to resist the established social and political system. The democracy of the dead ("We're equal now, I'll not an inch resign; this is my dunghill, as the next is thine") suggested that perhaps rank and privilege was as inappropriate on one side of the grave as the other.

The Great Validator

Society can also use death to measure the value of its deceased members. Funereal splendor is perhaps the most obvious and traditional way of using death to demonstrate the worth of the individual (and his or her survivors). A Midwestern funeral director expressed the situation as he sees it.

I do what you want me to do. You come in here and say you want simple arrangements, and this is exactly what I will provide. You know what you want, and I am here to meet your needs. . . . But let me tell you why I sell some of the more expensive items—it's because the people themselves want it that way! . . . They are not satisfied until they feel they are getting the best funeral for their loved one that they can afford. . . . If everybody wanted bare-minimum funerals, that is what we would be providing. When you see a big, a magnificent funeral, you are seeing what the family felt it truly must have.

Interestingly, the tradition of a "big funeral" in which no expense is spared has roots in early American tradition. In colonial days, families sometimes spent themselves to the verge of poverty to publicly validate both their worth and that of the deceased (Stannard, 1975). The opportunity to validate worth through the funeral process (Chapter 9) has been seized throughout the centuries. The heroine in a Greek tragedy risks her own life by advocating the proper burial of her outcast brother (Sophocles). Decisions are made as to whether or not a deceased person of some distinction deserves to be buried in sacred soil. The cowboy implores, "Bury me not on the lone prairie."

Death Unites/Separates

Death can be seen either as the opportunity to rejoin others or as an act of separation from all hope of companionship. The common denominator is that death radically alters our relationships with others.

Occasionally death has been seen as a way of bringing friends and foes together. Alexander Pope wrote in the 17th century:

The grave united, where even the great find rest
And blended lie the oppressor and oppressed.

Two centuries later a British soldier and poet imagined his own death in battle—an event that soon thereafter actually happened. Wilfred Owen (1918/1959) made the theme of unity through death carry a fervent antiwar sentiment. The poem concludes with this poignant stanza:

I am the enemy you killed, my friend.
I knew you in this dark; for so you frowned
Yesterday through me as you jabbed and killed.
I parried; but my hands were loath and cold.
Let us sleep now.

Death may be seen as uniting the individual with God. The despairing or dying person who sees death as unity with the divine may yearn for this opportunity. This sentiment has gained expression in many hymns and carols. Typical is this brief piece from *The Original Sacred Heart* (1844):

Northfield
How long, dear Savior, O how long
Shall this bright hour delay?
Fly swift around, ye wheels of time,
And bring the promised day.

Mortal life on earth merely delays the promised hour. This promise, however, was not without its threatening aspect. The gravestone marker for Miss Polly Coombes of Bellingham, Massachusetts in 1795 takes a somber and challenging tone:

READER ATTEND: THIS STATE
WILL SOON BE THINE
BE THOU IN YOUTHFUL HEALTH
OR IN DECLINE
PREPARE TO MEET THY GOD.

The prospect of arriving at a secure, homelike heaven could be tempered, then, by doubts as to whether or not you were prepared for the judgment of God. A person might live in terror of that moment.

There is still another sense in which death has been regarded as the opportunity for union or reunion. The individual may look forward to being with loved ones again. An old woman dreams that she has become a little girl once again and is being welcomed by her father. A child wrestles privately with thoughts of suicide so that he can join the big brother he misses so much.

Although some of us may cherish the prospect of reunion with loved ones through death, the more obvious consequence is *separation*. The familiar face of someone who has died is not to be seen again. The pain of separation for the survivors can be overwhelming.

"I felt like part of me had been pulled apart. Like I wasn't a whole person any more. And then I went numb. Like I was in shock, with loss of blood, just like I had lost an arm or a leg or worse." This is the way a young woman felt when she learned that her husband had been killed in Vietnam. He had been alive to his loved ones until the message came, although in objective fact he had been dead for an indeterminate time. The moment that his wife learned of their final separation is the moment when the death event occurred for her. The moment we as survivors feel the shock and anguish of separation may be the most significant moment of death.

The sense of separation can occur in advance of the actual death and can also linger long afterward. Some families undergo the extreme stress of facing the probable death of their living children while still suffering from the loss of one or more who have already died.

> The family were still grieving Ann's death when Roy began to exhibit symptoms of the same disease. . . . The doctors confirmed her worst fears. Having lost one child the parents faced the situation once more. . . . Adam has a similar form of the same illness. . . . "We know it all now—we shall be left with nothing—no children—nothing." (Atkin, 1974, p. 66)

The children also experience the sorrow of separation from each other even if they do not fully understand the concept of death.

He had lost one sibling and was facing the experience a second time. His sister, in the latter stages of her illness, seemed unaware and unresponsive. Yet her little brother seemed to evoke some faint recognition. She appeared to smile with her eyes—a last window into the darkness. He said: "I don't mind if you don't talk to me. It's lonely without you. I can talk to you." He prattled on about his rabbit, his cars, and his wish to have a party on his birthday. (p. 69)

The difficulty in understanding death coupled with the strong need to continue the relationship can lead both children and adults to behave at times as though final separation had not really taken place (see also Chapters 7 and 10). Separation is one of the most universal of themes for those who are left to continue their lives on earth.

The Ultimate Problem or the Ultimate Solution?

Death is sometimes regarded as either the ultimate problem or the ultimate solution. In fact, we are complex enough to consider death as *both* the ultimate problem and ultimate solution in some circumstances.

A dark jest made the rounds in the aftermath of the French Revolution: "Come and see the wonderful new machine—a miracle! One treatment by the good Dr. Guillotine and—phoof!— never again a headache!" Indeed, Dr. Guillotine had intended his device as solution to more painful and lingering forms of public execution. But why have public executions in the first place? Obviously, many societies have considered execution the most appropriate solution to their problems.

Death as ultimate solution has been applied on a mass basis as well. History reveals many examples of one group of people slaughtering another to achieve what at the moment seemed to be an important objective. The 20th century alone has witnessed enormous slaughter on a mass scale (Eliot, 1972). Most notorious was Hitler's "final solution of the Jewish problem," which translated into the genocidal murder of more than six million men, women, and children. From a historical standpoint, however, this appalling action was exceptional only in its numbers and details. Mass death by human agency has erupted again and again throughout the centuries. Never mind history—we need only read today's news.

Self-destruction (Chapter 8) is still another familiar way of attempting to solve problems. Problems range from a sense of failure to the terrible anger you cannot bring yourself to express. Other solutions have failed; perhaps the ultimate solution is required.

Counterpoised against this theme is the conviction that death, far from being the final solution, is humankind's worst enemy and most profound problem. Death may be seen as the ultimate problem because it ends our opportunity to achieve—certainly a threat in a society in which the need to achieve is a dominant motive. ("I can't die just yet—I have so much to do!") Death may also be seen as the ultimate problem because it closes down the theater of inner experience—no more thoughts, no more feelings, no more consciousness. Still again, death may be seen as the ultimate problem because it defies understanding. Faith may take the place of understanding for some people, but for those who depend on science and logic, death has long been frustrating.

The Ultimate Meaningless Event

The ending of life often has been presented as though it is a supremely meaningful event. However, the facts of experience sometimes appear to contradict this view. Random, senseless death might be regarded as the ultimately meaningless event.

Two very different studies bear on this point. Kathlyn Ann Fritz (1975) found that the treatment of murder in British and American detective novels has changed with the times. In the 1930s the usual fictional homicide was presented as a rare event that interrupted the set ways of establishment life. The crimes had meaning, of-

ten deriving from complex relationships and attitudes. Now, however, murder seems to be "almost as much out of control in the novels as in life, with some killers evading detection or penalty" (p. 198). Death by murder has lost much of its special meanings. A life may be taken for no particular reason.

By contrast, aborigines in Australia's Northern Territory have held on to their conceptions of death meanings despite continuing interactions with technological culture. Anthropologist Janice C. Reid (1978) found that the aborigines continue to see illness and death as punishments for transgressions against social and religious law. Sorcerers and spirits do the punishing. What makes this finding particularly interesting is that many of the aborigines are well educated in Western ways and make use of modern health services. Ignorance or defiance of new ways cannot be cited as explanation for persistence of the old beliefs. What is the explanation then? Reid observes that the transgression-punishment theory has the advantage of providing "ultimate explanations for illness and death (that is, it explains why a certain person should be afflicted in a certain way at a given time)" (p. 137). In other words, the aborigine finds that the reasons for death are better understood by a time-honored view of the individual in the universe rather than by modern medical science. Death can be viewed within a meaningful context. Unlike many other people, the aborigine does not have to ask, "Why me?" Whatever other fear and stress might be aroused by the prospect of death, the loss of meaning does not have to be counted among them.

REFERENCES

Ad Hoc Committee of the Harvard Medical School to Examine the Definition of Brain Death. (1968). A definition of irreversible coma. *Journal of the American Medical Association, 205,* 337–340.

Alexander, S. (1920). *Space, time, and deity.* (Vols. 1–2). London: Macmillan & Co.

Alsop, S. (1973). *Stay of execution.* Philadelphia: J. B. Lippincott Co.

Aries, P. (1962). *Centuries of childhood.* New York: Alfred A. Knopf, Inc.

Aries, P. (1981). *The hour of our death.* New York: Alfred A. Knopf, Inc.

Atkin, M. (1974). The "doomed family": Observations on the lives of parents and children facing repeated child mortality. In L. Burton (Ed.), *Care of the child facing death.* London & Boston: Routledge & Kegan Paul, Ltd.

Ayer, A. J. (1973). *The central questions of philosophy.* New York: Holt, Rinehart, and Winston.

Baider, L. (1975). Private experience and public expectations on the cancer ward. *Omega, Journal of Death and Dying, 6,* 373–382.

Brandon, S. G. F. (1967). *The judgment of the dead.* New York: Charles Scribner's Sons.

Bultmann, R. (1965). *Life and death.* London: A. & C. Black, Ltd.

Cannon, W. B. (1942). Voodoo death. *American Anthropologist, 44,* 169–173.

Eliot, G. (1972). *Twentieth century book of the dead.* New York: Charles Scribner's Sons.

Fechner, G. T. (1904). *The little book of life after death.* Boston: Little, Brown & Co. (Original work published 1836)

Feifel, H. (1959). Attitudes toward death in some normal and mentally ill populations. In H. Feifel (Ed.), *The meaning of death.* New York: McGraw-Hill Book Co.

Frazer, J. (1959). *The new golden bough.* (rev. ed.) New York: Doubleday & Co., Inc.

Fritz, K. A. (1975). *Patterns and perceptions of homicide in detective novels.* Unpublished doctoral dissertation. New Haven: Yale University.

Gottfried, R. S. (1983). *The Black Death.* New York: The Free Press.

Green, J. S. (1972). The days of the dead in Oaxaca, Mexico. *Omega, Journal of Death and Dying, 3,* 245–262.

Henderson, J. O. L., & Oakes, M. (1971). *Wisdom of the serpent: The myths of death, rebirth, resurrection.* New York: Macmillan Publishing Co.

Hertz, R. (1960). *Death and the right hand.* Glencoe, IL: The Free Press.

Kapleau, P. (1971). *The wheel of death.* New York: Harper & Row, Publishers, Inc.

Kastenbaum, R. (1969). Psychological death. In L. Pearson (Ed.), *Death and dying.* Cleveland: Case Western University Press.

Kastenbaum, R. (1974). Fertility and the fear of death. *Journal of Social Issues, 30,* 63–78.

Kastenbaum, R. (1980). Habituation as a partial model of human aging. *International Journal of Aging & Human Development, 12,* 159–170.

Kastenbaum, R. (1983). Can the clinical milieu be therapeutic? In G. D. Rowles & R. J. Ohta (Eds.), *Aging and milieu.* New York: Academic Press.

Kastenbaum, R. (1984, May 18) Death, the child, and the family soul in modern society. Paper presented at the international conference, "Le mort, un probleme de civilisation," (Versailles).

Kastenbaum, R., & Aisenberg, R. B. (1972). *The psychology of death.* New York: Springer Publishing Co., Inc.

Kastenbaum, R., Barber, T. X., Wilson, S. G., Ryder, B. L., & Hathaway, L. B. (1981). *Old, sick and helpless: Where therapy begins.* Cambridge, Mass: Ballinger Publishing Co.

Korein, J. (1978). The problem of brain death: Development and history. *Annals of the New York Academy of Sciences, 315,* 1–10.

Leca, A. P. (1981). *The Egyptian way of death.* Garden City, New York: Doubleday & Co., Inc.

Mack, J. E. (1970). *Nightmares and human conflict.* Boston: Little, Brown & Co.

Mollaret, P., & Boulon, M. (1959). Le coma depasse. *Review of Neurology, 101,* 3–18.

Morgan, L. (1923). *Emergent evolution.* London: Williams & Norgate, Ltd.

Opie, I., & Opie, P. (1969). *Children's games in street and playground.* Oxford: Oxford University Press.

The original sacred harp. (Denson revision). Bremen, Ga.: Sacred Harp Publishing Co. (Original work published 1844)

Owen, W. (1959). Strange meeting. In E. Blunden (Ed.), *The poems of Wilfred Owen.* New York: New Directions Publishing Corp.

Patrix, P. In F. P. Weber (Ed.), *Aspects of death and correlated aspects of life in art, epigram, and poetry.* London: H. K. Lewis & Co., Ltd.

Peirce, C. S. (1923). *Chance, love, and logic.* New York: Harcourt, Brace, & Co.

President's Commission for the Study of Ethical Problems in Medicine and Biomedical and Behavioral Research. (1981). *Defining death.* Washington, D. C.: U.S. Government Printing Office.

Reid, J. C. (1978). *Sorcery and healing: The meaning of illness and death to an Australian aboriginal community.* Unpublished doctoral dissertation, Palo Alto: Stanford University.

Royal Humane Society. (1820). *Annual report of the Royal Humane Society for the recovery of persons apparently drowned or dead.* London: John Nichols and Son.

Shaffer, J. (1967). Mind-body problem. In P. Edwards (Ed.), *The encyclopedia of philosophy: Volumes 5 & 6* (pp. 336–346). New York: Collier-Macmillan.

Shrock, N. M. (1835). On the signs that distinguish real from apparent death. *Transylvanian Journal of Medicine, 13,* 210–220.

Sophocles. *Antigone.* Translated by R. E. Braun. New York: Oxford University Press, 1975.

Stannard, D. E. (1975). *Death in America.* Philadelphia: University of Pennsylvania Press.

Tuchman, B. (1978). *A distant mirror.* New York: Alfred A. Knopf.

Twain, M. (1972). *Life on the Mississippi.* Norwalk, Conn.: The Heritage Press. (Original work published 1883)

Veatch, R. M. (1975). The whole-brain-oriented concept of death: An outmoded philosophical formulation. *Journal of Thanatology, 3,* 13–30.

Walton, D. N. (1981–1982). Neocortical versus whole-brain conceptions of personal death. *Omega, Journal of Death and Dying, 12,* 339–344.

Whiter, J. (1819). *A dissertation on the disorder of death.* London: Hayes.

Wilkin, R. L. (1984). *The Christians as the Romans saw them.* New Haven: Yale University Press.

chapter 3

THE DEATH SYSTEM

This chapter describes the *death system*. Please take a few minutes right now to participate in a thought experiment that will help to demonstrate how a concept such as the death system can be useful.

A WORLD WITHOUT DEATH

Suppose that the world is just as we know it, with one exception. Death is no longer inevitable. Disease and aging have been conquered. Let us also suppose that air and water pollution have been much reduced through new technologies.

Take a few minutes to consider the implications and consequences. What will happen? How will people respond to this situation, individually and as a society? How will the quality of life change?

Think first of the effects of the no death scenario on the world at large. Write down the changes you think would be likely to happen in the top half of the box on this page.

Next think of how the no death scenario would influence *your own* thoughts, feelings, wishes, needs, beliefs, and actions. Describe some of the major ways the no death situation would be likely to influence you in the bottom half of the box. After you have completed this thought exercise, continue and see how your prophecies compare with those most often made by other students in classes such as this one.

GENERAL AND PERSONAL CONSEQUENCES OF A WORLD WITHOUT DEATH

Consequences for the World

_____

_____

_____

_____

Consequences for Me

_____

_____

_____

_____

None of us can know for sure what would actually happen in this hypothetical situation. Nevertheless, many plausible and interesting predictions can be offered. Compare your ideas with those that follow:

General Consequences
• Overcrowding would lead to infringements on privacy, mobility, and other individual liberties many of us now enjoy. ("Space would be incredibly precious." "People would develop new mental and physical habits to keep others at an emotional distance." "Turf mentality would be all-powerful." "After a while, nobody would feel comfortable being alone even if you could be." "I don't see how people could still be individuals.")

• Stringent birth control would be enforced, probably on the basis of highly selected criteria, "depending upon what the elite want (people) bred for."

• New laws would be needed because relationships between people will have changed so much. ("Inheritance might not mean anything any more. The younger generation couldn't expect anything from the older generation unless we cooked up new laws.")

• Society would become very conservative and slow to change its ways. ("Old people would outnumber young people so much that anything new would hardly have a chance." "The world wouldn't really have a future. There'd only be a terrific bias to keep things as they are or even to roll things back to the past.")

• The economic structure of society would change greatly, but in ways that are difficult to predict. ("Life insurance? Who would need it? And then, what would happen to not only life insurance salesmen but to that whole industry that handles so much money now?" "People wouldn't have to put money away for their funerals. In fact, there would be hardly any money to be made on the dead." "Doctors might not make as much money because there wouldn't be all this fear of death. But maybe they'd make even more money with plastic surgery and fancy ways to try to keep people looking young. Who knows?")

• Moral beliefs and priorities might change in many ways. ("That would be just about the end of marriage, and maybe of divorce, too, as we know it. People would think, hey, what's the point of being married to just one person forever and ever. Everybody'd either screw around a lot with everybody else or maybe just get tired of it after a couple of thousand years and play video games instead." "Religion is mostly getting people to shape up or go to Hell. If we're not going to die, then who's going to listen and what's going to happen to religion?" "Death has always been the enemy. Now it might be the biggest friend ever. If there's no natural death, we might hire people to kill us in some really decisive way, like blowing us to pieces. I think I would buy shares in the Mafia. Or maybe governments would arrange special wars only for the purpose of getting a lot of people killed." "I really don't think we can do without death psychologically. Society would find some way to make death possible, and this would be considered the right thing, not an evil thing.")

Personal Consequences
• "I don't know if I would have the same ambitions and make any progress on them. As it is now, about the only way I get anything done is when a deadline is staring me in the face, which happens all the time in my classes. If there's all the time in the world, there wouldn't be any pressure, and I might not ever get anything done."

• "I've always been afraid of death, really afraid. I don't know why. If I found out that there really and truly wasn't going to be any more death, I would feel light and free for the first time and I could really enjoy life. I hope I'm not kidding myself either, but even the thought of a no-death world makes me feel wonderfully free."

• "It's a crazy idea, but I like it and wish it would be true, then the people I care about would always be with me. Still, it would be a hard idea to get used to, especially with all that I have always believed as a Christian. I would want to keep my beliefs—I would have to—but it might make some difference, there not being natural death and therefore there not being eternity and heaven. Or would there still be? It could be confusing."

A world without death would differ in many ways from the world we know today. You may have thought of some general or personal consequences that go beyond those presented here, and the list certainly could be extended. The main point is that many of our societal and individual patterns of functioning are connected with death in one way or another. Death is never the only factor involved. Life insurance, for example, depends also on the profit motive, and the profit motive in turn arises from complex ideological and social conditions. Yet, as respondents have often observed, no death means no life insurance. Take as another example the relationship some respondents have predicted between the elimination of death and the establishment of stringent birth control measures. "If nobody dies, then nobody can get born."

Individual implications of our relationship to death cannot easily be separated from the more general consequences. Consider, for example, those who fear they would lose their drive for accomplishment if time were endless. This is certainly a personal matter. However, it is connected with a cultural ethos in which the achievement motive is highly valued. The pioneering social scientist Max Weber (1930) argued that one of the most powerful driving forces in Western society is the need to achieve a kind of salvation through achievement. We accumulate material goods and acquire status to demonstrate to ourselves and others that we are splendid souls deserving of whatever benefits the universe has to offer. (The more recently discovered "workaholic" pursues his quasi-spiritual quest with special intensity but otherwise is not much different from the rest of us.) Lessen the need to achieve and acquire and you begin to have a different relationship to time and death. The work- and achievement-oriented life-style is only one tradition within Western society and

has competition from the emerging enthusiasm for a leisure life-style. Whatever our individual life-style might be, however, each implies a certain relationship between what we do now and what will happen in the future. And the future, of course, is shaped in part by the expectations and realities of death. Whatever alters our expectations of death alters also our sense of self and futurity.

The thought experiment raises many questions that require the ability to think of society as well as the individual. The *death system* concept provides a way of doing so.

BASIC CHARACTERISTICS OF THE DEATH SYSTEM

A Working Definition

The concept of the death system invites attention to interconnections, to the subtle network of relationships and meanings through which one sphere of action influences another. We cannot fully comprehend our relationship to death by treating specific phenomena as though they exist in separate compartments.

It doesn't matter what names we give to these compartments. "Management of pain during the final illness," "suicide among adolescents," and "recovery from grief" may be the labels chosen for the compartments of particular interest. We can study these phenomena as carefully as possible; however, we will miss some of their most important determinants and consequences unless we recognize how artificial it is to keep them separated. We will remain unaware, for example, of the way in which management of pain during the final illness may depend on the unexamined value judgments of the physician, which in turn depend on many other factors. Concentrating exclusively on the suicide attempt of a particular adolescent may keep us from learning about the possible connection with the proportion of teenagers in the total population at a given time. Examining recovery from grief as a phenomenon in and of itself may lead us to ignore new developments in management-labor relations that are already influencing the behavior of bereaved persons. Furthermore, we may have failed to observe clues that relate an adolescent suicide attempt to difficulty in recovering from a never-shared grief for the pain suffered by a dying parent. These require connections, not compartments. Death is a network of relationships among diverse phenomena, not an isolated fact here and there—a network that behaves in a systematic manner.

It is useful to learn how to trace the remote and indirect as well as the more obvious relationships among the various types of social phenomena that bear upon our relationships to death. That requires a willingness to forgo quick and simple conclusions. Instead of being restricted to the focused-in, scaled-down approach that is often favored for purposes of instant research and education, the systematic approach makes it possible to accept society and human experience in its actual complexity. This text can only exemplify this approach. But perhaps it can do so just enough to encourage your own further explorations.

Now consider the *components* and *functions* of the death system: what the system is made of and the purposes it serves. Examples are drawn from the past as well as the present and from a variety of cultures because all societies have developed systematic relationships to mortality.

Components of the Death System

People

All people are potential components of the death system. Most phase in and out of the death system as circumstances and their own actions dictate. Others have a more continuous role even though they may not think of themselves as regular components of the death system. A smaller number serve as core participants in the death system, whose roles and identities cannot easily be separated from their functions in it.

The funeral director is an obvious example of a permanent and conspicuous participant in today's American death system. One funeral director described the typical situation members of this trade must contend with: "When I walk into a room, Death walks in with me. This is how people react to me." The fact that many of us find it difficult to think of a funeral director as a normal and distinct individual testifies to his or her embeddedness in the death system.

The agent who sells life insurance is also very much part of the death system. Not only does the agent participate, but so do all the clerks, adjusters, marketing people, and executives. The members of the custodial staff who clean up the highrise offices of MegaMoolah Insurance Company late in the evening are unlikely to reflect on their role in the death system, but their paychecks have their origin in somebody's decision to make a financial investment in anticipation of death. The premiums we pay to guarantee death benefits are part of a complex network of investments. The death money may be used to create new jobs or abolish old ones, support a local business or challenge it with a competitor, and so on. People associated with the insurance industry have a major role in the United States' economic status, and it is our reaction to the prospect of death that keeps much of this enterprise in motion.

The florist is also part of the death system. "Floral tributes" help flower growers and merchants stay in business. The lawyer is yet another person who is likely to be associated with the death system on a fairly regular basis. Take for just one example the lawyer's role in drawing up wills. This is one of the relatively few situations in which a healthy adult is likely to sit down and discuss personal death-related issues. Even so, many lawyers report that their clients usually prefer to delay will-making as long as possible because of the obvious connection with death. The lawyer often is on the scene after a death as well, helping to interpret and implement the provisions that have been made for distribution of the deceased's estate.

Clearly these connections are not simple or unidirectional. People working in a variety of occupations earn their livelihoods, in whole or part, from services they perform in connection with death. Although these people influence our lives, we also affect them by our own attitudes and actions. A consumer movement encouraging less elaborate funerals or memorialization will affect the funeral director, the florist, the cemetery association (and the local zoning board), and so on. A trend toward multiple marriages with "his, her, and our" children might complicate the inheritance process, while the growing popularity of life care retirement communities might reduce the amount of inheritances and therefore also the importance of will-making. (Life care retirement communities provide housing and a variety of personal services; those senior adults who choose to enroll in such a plan are required to sign over most of their financial resources to the management of the facility.) A change in one facet of our social or economic life, then, can show up as pressure or opportunity elsewhere. More often than we realize, our relationship to death is caught up in these changes.

There are many people whose association with the death system may not come so readily to mind. Think, for example of the big truck you saw pull up behind a supermarket the other day. It was filled with pet food, case after case. Every can in every case bears on the outside a picture of a contented dog or cat and on the inside some type of meat product. All that meat, of course, came from what once were living creatures. The truck driver, the person who shelves the cans, the assistant store manager who makes sure they are priced correctly, and the clerk at the checkout register are but a few of the people who participate in the death system through their processing of pet food. Those who raise, those who slaughter, and those who process a variety of living animals to become food for pets also should be included. The people in the canning factory should be included, as should the accountants, the executives, and the advertising agency. The cat who meows so convincingly for its favorite brand on television is also part of the death system. And if we purchase this product, are we not part of this complex network as well, a network that would not exist but for the fact of death?

This way of looking at people and death may seem peculiar, even outrageous. But it is a de-monstrable fact that the United States does boast major pet food industries, and that death is programmed right into them. In similar fashion you might turn from industry to industry and from occupation to occupation. What jobs have an important bearing on death and might not even exist otherwise? The list is in your hands to extend as you like.

The people in the death system represent a greater variety of life-styles than we might have thought at first. Still unmentioned are the health professionals and the clergy—all of whom have important roles in the death system. It would not do to leave out the scientists who are spending tax dollars to design lethal weapons, the legislators who vote budget appropriations for the weapons' production, and the armed services personnel who take the new devices into custody (assuming they are not sent to governments abroad that the United States is supporting at the moment).

It is difficult to determine how many people are the core participants in the death system. But all can be recruited as occasion demands. At any moment, you or I might become drawn actively into the death system, through a variety of paths. A friend unexpectedly reveals to us that she has a fatal illness. We are in an automobile accident in which somebody dies. A funeral procession interrupts our cruise down the street. Or perhaps it is the insurance agent inquiring in well-practiced tones if we have made adequate provision for the education of our children. The points of entry are numerous and do not always advertise themselves in advance.

Places

Certain places have become identified with death. The cemetery and the funeral home are obvious examples. There are other places whose associations with death are more variable, subtle, or dependent on the particular ideas and experiences we carry around with us. Consider the hospital, for example. Today people come and go from hospitals all the time. We have many different associations with the hospital—it is the place where babies are born, where minor surgical procedures are performed, where accident victims are treated, where clinics are available for outpatient care, and so on. It is also the place where people die sometimes, but this is only one facet of the modern medical center. People with long memories, however, give a different perspective. A spry woman of 93 explained:

> The doctor would say, "We're taking you to the hospital, Mike." And Mike he would directly close his eyes and turn his face to the wall. Then the doctor would say, "Now, now, Mike. Don't take on like that. We're going to make you well at the hospital." And Mike he wouldn't say a word. But when the doctor walked out the room, Mike he would say, "I'm a dead man." Everybody knew it. You went to the hospital to die. . . . And even to walk by the hospital, you would shudder right down to your shoes. And you'd walk a little faster.

Within the corridors of a modern hospital we find that death is given its small, isolated territory in return for promising to stay within those bounds. What makes a particular ward a death place is usually the fact that this is where the most seriously ill patients are housed. But any ward can suddenly become a death place for a time after an unexpected demise. I have seen how staff members and surviving patients respond to a raid by death on a ward that was thought to be safe. It can take months before the ward feels safe again. In the meantime, you can see a variety of decontamination rituals as those associated with the ward attempt to rid the environment of its newly acquired "deathness."

Similar measures have been taken in private homes as well: a bed may be given away because it is the one in which Uncle Otto "expired," and its continued presence somehow keeps "deathness" in the household atmosphere.

Historical battlefields may be thought of as death places for decades or even centuries. The royal murders said to have occurred in the Tower of London have added to the fame of this grim edifice by the banks of the Thames. The Ford Theater in Washington, D.C., is remembered as the place where Lincoln was assassinated. A pathway in the woods may be spoken of in hushed tones by the schoolchildren who discovered a human corpse while on a nature walk. Even a house across the street can be a death place in the minds of neighbors who now feel somewhat uncomfortable as they pass by. Whether famous historically or locally, once a place has become associated with death we no longer think and feel the same way about it. A newspaper report makes this very clear:

> San Diego—Workmen removed the trademark "Golden Arches" on Tuesday from the McDonald's restaurant in San Ysidro, Calif., where 21 people were killed by a beserk gunman, and the company announced it was tearing down the border-town eatery in response to community sentiment. Company executives said that the outlet will not reopen and that no decision has been made on whether to convert the site of last week's massacre into a memorial park, the goal of a local Hispanic movement. (United Press International, 1984)

"Community sentiment," "company executives," and "local Hispanic movement" do not have any intrinsic relationship to death but have in this instance become part of the death system. The golden arches, having taken on the aspect of a death place, could no longer serve their original purpose as a commercial trademark.

Times

Death also has its times or occasions. Memorial Day, for example, is a regularly occurring time set aside in the United States to honor those who have fallen in defense of the nation. Both the original purpose of Memorial Day and the way its meaning has changed through the years raise questions about the ways in which American society comes to terms with death. In some tribal cultures one or more days are devoted to communal mourning that honors all who have died during the preceding year. (Simpler burial rituals are held immediately after the deaths.) The Days of the Dead in Mexico can startle the unprepared visitor who expects death observances to be somber and restrained (Green, 1972). The carnival atmosphere that prevails is not as odd as it might seem. Many societies have established periodic occasions when death is granted dominance over everybody's thoughts and feelings.

Times devoted to death in American society do not begin and end with Memorial Day. Prayers for the dead are offered on regular occasions—for example, by Jewish and Japanese Americans who are keeping the faith—while Catholics celebrate Mass. December 29 is a date that some Native Americans observe in honor of the Sioux annihilated by the Seventh Cavalry at Wounded Knee, South Dakota, in 1890. The deaths of martyred individuals and groups throughout the world have often been perpetuated in memory by observations on the anniversaries of their demise. Recently, for example, a reported 100,000 Hungarians joined hands across Heroes' Square to honor Imre Nagy, a young man who had been executed more than thirty years ago for his role in an anti-Soviet revolt.

These examples of times and occasions set aside for the dead are embedded in society. It is also possible for a single individual to acknowledge a death time that has deep personal significance, even if it is not shared by others. This can take the form of what psychiatrists call an *anniversary reaction.* A year (or two years, five years, and so on) from the date of the death of a loved one, the survivor may suddenly fall ill, behave erratically, or suffer an accident.

The clock and the calendar treat each passing moment, each passing day with equal disinterest. For the individual and for society, however, certain times seem to fall under the particular auspices of death, and we tend to treat these times in a special manner.

Objects

Death has its objects and things as well as its people, places, and times. The hearse and the death certificate are among the conspicuous objects in the American death system. Death notices have their own separate section in the daily newspaper. The noose, the gallows, and the elec-

tric chair are also among our more obvious things of death, as are tombstones, shrouds and skull-and-crossbone labels on bottles, and a variety of other paraphernalia. The unexpected telegram often arouses concern. The little spraying device that "kills bugs dead" is an object in American society's death system; the same may be said of the nuclear devices aimed at potential enemies who aim nuclear devices back at us.

Objects whose intended uses have little to do with death may produce lethal effects through accidents or misuse. The continuing difficulties with the safety of nuclear plants and disposal of radioactive waste illustrate how objects intended for constructive purposes can come to arouse death-related thoughts and feelings. Critics of the automobile and of cigarettes have long spoken of these objects as instruments of death, although both were conceived as positive additions to the quality of life. Alcoholic beverages and many other pharmacological substances have also been viewed as death-related, although they are neither intended nor marketed for such a purpose.

Things, like people, places, and times, can be recruited into the death system, and when this happens their meanings are transformed, even though the objects themselves remain the same.

Symbols

Language and other symbols play a major role in Western culture's death system. The black armband tells a story. The black border around the card we receive in the mail signifies death and mourning. The funeral director generally provides black or other dark-hued limousines for the funeral procession and garbs himself in similar colors. Not all societies symbolize death with dark colors, but we soon learn to recognize those particular colors and other symbols meant to convey death-related messages in a given society or subculture.

In some neighborhoods, closing all the shutters has been a traditional signal of a death within, although this practice continues to fade. Administration of the priestly ritual for the sick is a highly symbolic interaction that is sometimes related to the prospect of death (although technically it is not regarded by the Catholic Church as "last rites," despite this common attribution given to the ceremony).

Death symbols tell us something about a culture's attitude toward death. The choice of music is one example. Slow, solemn music intoned on an organ suggests a different orientation from a simple folk song with guitar accompaniment and is different again from a brass band strutting down the street playing "When the Saints Go Marching In." A particular kind of music may seem either perfectly fitting or completely outrageous to us when brought into a death-related situation, indicating that we have a sense of what is "death appropriate," even if we cannot always put it into words.

The words we use and those we refrain from using also reveal much about the nature of the culture's death system. People "pass on," "expire," or "go to their reward" more often than they simply die. The occasional use of a synonym may not be important, but when we observe a consistent pattern of word substitution, then we might well wonder about the functions served by these evasions. I remember being puzzled about the frequent oral and written references to patients having been transferred to "Allen Street" when I served as a consultant to one of the nation's most prestigious hospitals. Inquiry revealed that this was a local euphemism for a morgue. This particular morgue and Allen Street itself had been out of existence for years, but the staff in this modern, state-of-the-art hospital remained more comfortable in expressing the fact of death through a quasi-secret code rather than with direct and honest language.

Although today more people discuss death openly than was the case some years ago, we still tend to cover the topic with indirect, symbolic, and sometimes downright evasive language. Take note of the next ten references to dying and death that you come across in conversation, reading, or elsewhere. What key words are used and why?

FUNCTIONS OF THE DEATH SYSTEM

The preceding pages have surveyed some of the main components of the death system. Now some of the functions served by the death system will be examined.

Warnings and Predictions

A core function of society is to protect its members. All societies issue warnings and predictions intended to stave off threats to life. These warnings and predictions can be based on folk customs, science, pseudo- or quasi-science, organized religion, or individual revelation. The threats that are forecast may be accurate, exaggerated, or completely imaginary. And society may choose either to respond to or ignore the alarms. Cassandra's plea to destroy the horse that the Greeks left as a gift at the gates of Troy is a classic example of a warning unheeded and its disastrous consequences. Often it is difficult to determine which warnings, if any, should be taken seriously. Although all cultures have had their share of warnings and predictions of danger, perhaps none have had such a profusion of alarms sounded as Western society. A central problem for our times, then, is how to navigate successfully between the extremes of constant hypervigilance and smug neglect.

Consider the following few examples of warnings and predictions in the death system. These were selected for what they suggest about the dynamics involved.

Californians repeatedly have been warned that they are literally standing on the edge of disaster, especially if they inhabit areas directly threatened by the San Andreas fault. Additional warnings have come directly from the earth itself, which has sent several substantial tremors through the area in recent years including the destructive quake that struck the San Francisco Bay area as the 1989 World Series was about to be played. Well-documented warnings and predictions do not necessarily lead people to evacuate the areas of danger.

Ecological disasters of various other types have also been predicted. One of the oldest such prophecies still being advanced is the possible danger of a new ice age, leading perhaps to a sudden and catastrophic shift of ice and snow as the overfrosted globe tilts to one side or another. Water and air pollution are other sources of threat for which the alarm has often sounded in our times. If we take all warnings seriously, it is difficult to know when to stop. Will it be the aerosol spray can that finally destroys civilization on earth by altering the atmospheric conditions crucial for human survival? Or will it be one of the thousands of rickety bridges that collapses while bearing the weight of dangerous cargo? The list of possibilities is extensive and open ended, with new candidates for catastrophe checking in almost every day.

Meanwhile the old, dependable sources of trouble remain with us. Both federal and local agencies provide predictions and warnings of storms and other natural conditions that could threaten life. "Small-craft warning" and "tornado watch" are familiar phrases in some parts of the United States. We expect to be advised of impending floods, blizzards, dust storms, avalanche conditions, and so on. More controversial are warnings about hazards associated with consumer goods. The complexity and power of the *system* in death system is demonstrated impressively every time a government agency attempts to toughen the cautionary language on cigarette packages or take a drug off the market. Business and industry must also respond when death-related warnings and predictions are hoisted.

The American death system provides warnings and predictions to specific individuals as well as to larger units of society. The physician is the most obvious example. "What do the x-ray film and laboratory reports mean? How serious is my condition?" Many others can also warn and predict: the mechanic who declares that your car is an accident waiting to happen unless you fix the brakes and replace the worn tires, the inspector who points out fire hazards in your home, and so on.

Societies can be compared on the basis of the warning and prediction components of their death systems. Who issues the warnings? What kind of warnings are taken most seriously? What kind of warnings are neglected? How accurate are the predictions? There is much to discover about the way warnings are given and heeded.

Preventing Death

All death systems have techniques intended to prevent death. For the prevention of death in Western society, we tend to think first of physicians, allied health professionals, and scientists. One of the great accomplishments of the past few generations has been the control of contagious diseases that once took a high toll, especially among the very young and the very old. Major efforts are currently being made to prevent other causes of death, such as cancer and heart disease, and continuing progress can be noted.

The treatment of acute and emergent conditions that threaten life has attracted particular interest. Specialists and advanced equipment are rushed to the bedside of a person suffering from a condition that almost surely would have been fatal in the past. Surgery on the most vital and delicate organs of the body has become increasingly sophisticated and successful. The number of pharmacological treatments also continues to expand.

Hard-won medical victories tend to create rising expectations. As one physician with more than 40 years of experience explained:

> People don't want much these days. All they expect is to live forever and, well, maybe to be young forever, too . . . I guess it's our fault for knocking off typhoid, scarlet fever, diphtheria, tuberculosis, and whatever. They expect us to cure everything now. I guess we almost expect it, too.

In many ways the United States is a culture with a strong investment in the preservation of life. This has been displayed more vividly in efforts to eradicate menaces to public health, such as virulent contagious disease, and in all-out intervention efforts during acute life-threatening disorders. We seem to enjoy the idea of "making war" on disease. Although the preventive function of the American death system has high priority, the system is also very selective and at times even contradictory in its efforts. Whether or not a particular individual will benefit from this general emphasis on prevention depends on a variety of personal and social factors, not the individual's physical status alone. *Whatever makes a person appear to have high social value in general also tends to make him or her a more favored candidate for death-prevention efforts.* "If you are going to have a heart attack, make sure you are wearing a good suit, and are in the right part of town—also, try to be young and white!" Cynical advice of this type unfortunately retains its core of truth even today.

Caring for the Dying

A staff member in one of the world's most sophisticated medical research centers was describing her work to me in a completely professional manner. Suddenly, tears of sorrow and frustration intruded as she tried to express what happens when a decision is made to shift from "cure" to "comfort" care:

> Sometimes the point comes when the doctors decide that's it. There's nothing we can do—or should do—all the cards have been played, and there's just no way we can really hope to arrest the illness. The brakes screech! We all have to come to a full and sudden stop. We may have been doing everything in the world to keep this person alive for months and now we have to stop all that and change what we do, but it is a lot harder to change how we feel about the patient and ourselves, about what we're doing. I don't think human thoughts and feelings were made for such sudden stops and starts!

The transition between trying to prevent death and providing care to a dying person is not always this drastic. Prevention and comfort-giving can be encompassed within the same philosophy and carried out by the same people in many situations. In practice, however, the med-

ical system's top priority is usually the treatment of acute conditions and the prevention of death and disability. Although this emphasis is understandable, too often it has led to gaps, discontinuities, and a pulling away of resources when death can no longer be averted.

How can various health professionals (each with specific talents, needs, and points of view), the family, and the life-threatened person achieve a continuing harmony if some of the people involved persist in the objective of prevention while others believe that comfort and relief from distressing symptoms should take precedence? Should prevention of death continue to be the overriding goal until the very end, or are there circumstances in which the emphasis should shift to comfort?

Advocates of both positions can be found in the ranks of all those associated with terminal care. There are physicians who take quite literally the never-say-die orientation—so long as life has any chance at all, it is the physician's responsibility to do all within his or her power to support this chance. But other physicians more readily accommodate their efforts to the signs of impending and inexorable death. This attitude sometimes seems old-fashioned, an approach more in keeping with earlier medical practices when the physician was inclined to see himself as Nature's junior assistant. Other staff members, as well as family, may also be divided on the cure-or-comfort approach for a variety of reasons, including the cost of continued treatment.

The hospice approach to terminal care (Chapter 5) represents an attempt to support dying people and their families in a holistic manner, offering as much skill and attention as is provided during the prevention phase. Chapter 4 illustrates how difficult it is for Western society to reconcile the caring-for-the-dying function with the need to either cure or deny.

Disposing of the Dead

"Disposing of the dead" is perhaps a harsh-sounding phrase, but it refers to a task all societies must perform. At the very minimum there is a need to dispose of the physical remains. Seldom, however, is a society content with the minimum. The funeral and memorialization process (Chapter 9) tells much about the stability and cohesiveness of a culture as well as what that particular society makes of death. Following are a few brief examples from American society:

> A minister dies unexpectedly. His wife and children are stunned, then grief stricken. Forced to think of funeral arrangements, they find themselves in perfect agreement. He had been a family-oriented person. He preferred the simple, the intimate, the natural. These same characteristics should be carried over to the funeral: no ostentation. Only the family and a few special friends should be involved; in this way they can most appropriately share their grief and support each other.
>
> But the congregation cannot abide this plan. A small, simple, private commemoration would fail to symbolize the deceased's significant place in the community. It would, in effect, diminish the status of the congregation itself. The congregation would also be deprived of this opportunity to express its respect for the departed spiritual leader. No, it just wouldn't be right to let this death pass without a conspicuous public ceremony.

This might appear to be the worst time for conflict between family and congregation, but that is precisely what happened. The power of the many prevailed in this instance. The disposal of this man's body and the accompanying ritual became essentially a public event. It was a "beautiful" funeral, with participation from community leaders as well as the congregation.

How did the family feel? They reacted as though not only the husband and father had been taken away from them but his death as well. What they experienced deeply as private loss and grief had become a public exhibit. And yet the community felt that it, too, had strong rights and needs. Just as much of this man's life had been devoted to the public sphere, so his death should be shared. This is one of many examples that could be given of the contest between private and public "ownership" of the deceased. Some

death systems emphasize one side, some the other, but the private-versus-public dialectic seems to exist in all:

> Two young men are pushing a stretcher through the corridors of a large modern hospital. This action has been planned to take as little time as possible and to attract little or no attention from others. Soon they have reached the service elevator and the door closes behind them.

The casual observer will have noticed only an empty stretcher. A more sophisticated observer knows or guesses that this is a false-bottomed stretcher designed expressly for disguised transportation of the dead. A society whose healthcare establishment goes out of its way to wrap a cloak of invisibility around the dead is telling us something about its fundamental attitudes toward the meaning of life. Do we think of the dead as fearful, disgusting, or dirty? Such an attitude is not difficult to read from some of the body disposal practices that can be observed:

> The old man has died. Family converge from everywhere. A funeral commands serious attention in this large and strongly ethnic family network. There is a problem, however. The oldest generation, including the widow, expect a strictly traditional observation of the death. All the time-honored rituals must be observed. The younger generations, however, are more Americanized and consider the old way too formal, too consuming of time and money, and generally not to their liking. The funeral director is caught squarely in the middle. The death of a respected family patriarch, then, threatens to bring a bitter intergenerational conflict to the surface.

These examples reveal several of the problems that can be associated with disposal of the dead: the conflict between public and private claims, negative attitudes toward the corpse, and the sparking of intergenerational and other conflicts in the ranks of the survivors.

In American society there remain several subgroups whose life-styles are rather distinctive. Kathleen Bryer's (1977) observations of "the Amish way of death" provide an illuminating contrast to what has already been described. There are approximately 80,000 Amish people in the United States, descendants of Swiss Anabaptists who were persecuted for their beliefs until granted refuge and religious liberty by William Penn in 1727. The Amish maintain a family-oriented society that emphasizes religious values, a simple agrarian life-style, separation from the non-Amish world, and a strong doctrine of mutual assistance. Marital separation and divorce are not sanctioned, and the infirm and the mentally ill are looked after in the community rather than in institutions. The Amish people function "at the same unhurried pace as . . . their forefathers, using horses instead of automobiles, windmills instead of electricity, and facing death with the same religious tenets and steadfast faith of their fathers" (p. 256).

The Amish way of life and its attitude toward death are clearly expressed in behavior associated with body disposal. The deceased is dressed in white garments by family members:

> It is only at her death that an Amish woman wears a white dress with the cape and apron which were put away by her for the occasion of her death. This is an example of the lifelong preparation for the facing of death, as sanctioned by Amish society. The wearing of all white clothes signifies the high ceremonial emphasis on the death event as the final rite of passage into a new and better life. (p. 254)

The funeral is very much a home-oriented event. A large room is cleared for the simple wooden coffin and the hundreds of friends, neighbors, and relatives who will soon fill it. The funeral service is held in the house or barn, a practice of the Amish for many generations. The grave itself is dug by neighbors on the preceding day and all watch in silent prayer as the coffin is lowered and the grave filled with earth. Other families see that the mourners are fed. The coffin is in the center of the room; there are no adornments or distractions from the core fact of death.

The problems and conflicts involved in body-disposal practices for American society at large have been avoided by the Amish. Their way of

life seems to involve a different way of death as well. This is expressed all through life (e.g., the old woman who carefully washes, starches, and irons her own funeral clothing so it will be ready when the time comes). A death may occasion grief and lead to various hardships for an Amish family like any other, but many of the doubts, tensions, and conflicts that have become commonplace in the larger death system seem to be absent for these people who have developed and maintained a life-style of their own.

Social Consolidation after Death

Death does not merely subtract one individual from society. It can also challenge society's ability to hold itself together, to assert its vitality and viability after death's raid. In small societies, the impact of *every* death challenges the integrity of the entire group. In a mass society this challenge usually becomes obvious only when death unexpectedly strikes down a powerful leader.

The assassinations of John F. Kennedy, Martin Luther King, Jr., and Robert Kennedy exemplify the types of death that shake even the largest and most powerful nations. Each of these men was highly visible, a part of American national consciousness. Each man also represented some form of power for action as well as something on a more personal and emotional level to millions of others. The manner of their deaths intensified the impact. The sudden, unexpected death of a significant person leaves us vulnerable for some time. The series of assassinations came too quickly to allow the development of a protective shield for our feelings. Our psychological defenses could not remain serenely in place as they sometimes seem to do for lesser threats.

Each death was not only sudden but violent. Had death come by natural causes, the nation might have been less alarmed. The impact of sudden violence and its resulting social disorganizations added to the force with which each death struck society. And this was not all. Each death was *intentional*. The chain reaction of fears and alarms that followed has not entirely disappeared today. People wondered how it could be that even the most powerful people among us were so vulnerable. What protection do any of us have? How safe are we as a nation when the life of a powerful leader can be so quickly destroyed. Conspiracy theories remain popular, perhaps fueled by the anxieties created when a powerful person dies suddenly.

One major function of the death system, then, is to meet the challenges posed to the individual and the group by loss of a member. This challenge may be of broad scope, as in the violent death of a powerful leader, or it can be as silent and personal as a death in the family:

> The realtor's illness didn't appear serious, but he died a day after entering the hospital, even before testing could be completed. From that point on the family hardly seemed to be a family anymore. They went their own ways, found things to do that kept them from being home at the same time, and seldom took a meal together. At first the 16-year-old son appeared to be the least affected. He continued his usual routines, although he did spend even more time behind the closed door of his room.
>
> Within a few months, though, it was obvious that the young man was really not doing so well after all. Most of the time he barely spoke, but then he would explode in anger without known reason and stalk away. An observant teacher noticed that the only time he mentioned his father he used the present tense, as though he were still alive.

This is an example of the temporary failure of social consolidation after a death. The family had fragmented, and for various reasons relatives, friends, and neighbors had also failed to provide useful support. Beverley Raphael (1983) apparently has observed many situations of this type in her work with bereavement outreach programs. She finds that adolescents have particular difficulty in participating in the reconstructive process after the death of a parent:

> The adolescent may feel helpless and frightened and wish to carry on as though nothing had happened. When a parent dies he may long to be a child again, to be protected from the death and all it may mean. His inner response is to wish to deny

it in every way. The adolescent, however, so sensitive to social cues and expectations, finds himself "expected" to behave in certain ways. He may be expected to be "grown up" and to comfort other family members, especially the surviving parent and his younger siblings. . . . But he may have great doubts about his ability to fulfill such needs when he feels so childlike and frightened himself. At other times he may be expected to be like a child and be treated as one; he may be excluded from what is happening; he may be told little about the terminal illness or death; and he may be kept from seeing the body or going to the funeral. He may bitterly resent this attitude, even though he secretly longs for the protection and security of childhood. Through all these expectations and his own fearful helplessness, his overwhelming experience is of bewilderment. (p. 151)

For contrast, consider again the Amish. Consistent with their general orientations toward life and death, the Amish provide direct and long-term support to those whose lives have been disrupted by the death of a loved one. It is not a case of many people coming by to express sympathy for a short period and subsequently disappearing; instead, vital functions in the home may be taken over for months by relatives or friends until the family can get back on its feet. Social consolidation after death is one more function of the death system that is closely related to the group's characteristic way of interpreting and coping with death, whether *group* means family, subculture, or society at large.

Making Sense of Death

Our efforts to explain death to each other represent another important function of the death system. Some explanations are handed down from generation to generation in the form of philosophical statement, poetic expressions, and commentaries on holy scriptures. There are also famous last words and scenes that have been attributed to heroes, leaders, and other celebrated people of the past.

Still other explanations are passed along informally within a particular subculture or family, or, again, through successive cohorts in the military service or schools of nursing or medicine. "This is what *we* say and this is what *we* think and this is what *we* do." Part of becoming a nurse, a physician, a funeral director, or even an executioner is becoming socialized to express the attitudes and explanations of death that come with the trade.

Sometimes it is not an actual explanation that we seek or receive. Rather, a need is felt to make sense of death. Laconic statements such as "Nobody lives forever!" and "When your number's up, it's up!" hardly qualify as explanations. Yet much of the wisdom we exchange on the subject of death is on this level. Perhaps such statements are of some comfort to the person who makes them, as a way of bridging what might otherwise be a tense and awkward silence. Perhaps hearing any words at all on the subject has some value to the recipient.

People often seem to feel a little better when they can exchange words at times of crisis and vulnerability. I spent several days in a hospital waiting area unobtrusively observing how visitors discuss the fact that the person they are about to see is terminally ill. Most of the conversation was usually on other matters, and most of the death-oriented talk was of the common, semi-explanatory type. ("She's been through so much." "I know." "Maybe it will be a blessing." "Maybe it will.") Apart from what the words mean or how adequately they address themselves to the problem at hand, it can be anxiety reducing just to hear the human voice intoning our language.

Consider the alternative. *Not* to have words spoken might confirm the fear that death truly is unspeakable. It would also be close to an admission that death is unthinkable as well. Such a conclusion probably would make us feel more helpless and alienated than ever. When we can at least go through the motions of exchanging words in this difficult situation, then we are showing the ability to function under stress. We are trying to make sense of death, and this activity itself helps keep us going.

At other times, however, we are not searching for just any words about death. We are looking for the most cogent and powerful understanding possible. The kind of explanation we seek cannot be separated, of course, from the particular questions we have in mind. These may be personal and highly specific, or they may relate to the meaning of life and the universe on the broadest level we can conceive. In comparing individuals or societies in their death explanations, we cannot ignore differences in the questions that seem most vital to each. Would the same explanation satisfy a person deeply rooted in Oriental tradition and one with equally strong roots in the Western world? Would a young child and an adult have the same questions and accept the same answers? What we are willing to take as an answer also tells much about the quality of our thought and character.

Killing

All death systems have another major function that has not yet been made explicit: *killing.* This function is carried out in many ways. Capital punishment is an obvious example. It is practiced by many, but not all cultures, with widely varying criteria for the conditions under which a person should be put to death. Ordinarily, only a few people have their lives ended by this mode. However, capital punishment conveys a mighty theme even when it is responsible for few deaths: this same society that on many occasions functions to protect and prolong life will on certain occasions act on behalf of death. Even if there were no other examples to cite, you would have to conclude that killing has been established as one of society's functions.

See Table 3–1 for some examples, and Chapter 8 for further consideration of murder and the death system.

But there are in fact many other examples to cite. Reference has already been made to the people who participate in the pet food industry. This component of the death system broadens even further when those who raise, slaughter,

TABLE 3–1

Crimes punishable by death in the USA: Some examples

State	Capital Offenses
Alabama	Murder during kidnapping, robbery, rape, sodomy, burglary, sexual assault, or arson; murder of peace officer, correctional officers, or public official; murder while under a life sentence; contract murder; murder by a defendant with a previous murder conviction; murder of a witness to a crime
Alaska	None (death penalty abolished 1957)
Arizona	First degree murder; multiple homicides during a first degree murder
Arkansas	Aggravated murder; treason; knowingly causing the death of a person 14 years of age or younger (child abuse)
California	First degree murder; treason; assault by life-term prisoner resulting in death; hindering preparation for war, causing death; omitting to note defects in articles of war, resulting in death; perjury, resulting in the death penalty; train wrecking, resulting in death
Hawaii	None (abolished, 1957)
Iowa	None (abolished, 1871; restored, 1878; abolished, 1965)
Maryland	First degree murder, either premeditated or during the commission of a felony
Missouri	Murder committed in the hijacking of public conveyances; murder of employees of correctional facilities
New Hampshire	Contract murder; murder of a law enforcement officer; murder of a kidnap victim
South Dakota	Murder; kidnapping when gross permanent physical injury is inflicted on victim
Vermont	Murder of a police officer or correctional officer; kidnapping for ransom
West Virginia	None (abolished, 1965)

Source: Information Aids: Capital Punishment: Cruel and Unusual? (1988). Information Aids, Inc: Wylie, Texas.

process, and consume "meat-bearing" animals are included. Even the casual fisherman kills ("drowning worms," as they say), whether or not an edible fish is landed for the family table. Any culture that is not thoroughly vegetarian is involved to some extent in killing for food. (And isn't pulling a turnip up by its roots a form of killing also?)

Living creatures may be killed for other reasons as well. The quest for fur and feathers has brought several species to the edge of extinction. The belief that the horn of the rhinoceros can bestow astounding sexual powers has led to the profitable slaughter of many a beast (by no means the only connection that can be drawn between death, sex, and money). Hunting may be pursued as an exercise in skill, a proof of "manhood," or just an excuse to be outdoors, among other reasons that are not related to bagging a meal.

Warfare has brought death to millions through the centuries. Our propensity for slaughtering each other raises fundamental questions about human nature. Are we killers at heart? Is there a deep-rooted aggressive instinct that must find expression in bloody triumphs? Or does making war arise from situational pressures that could be dispelled by improved knowledge, skills, and social organization? Does the commandment "Thou shalt not kill" represent our real moral position, or is it undermined by a more basic conviction that we have the right to take the lives of others? History provides contexts and examples that bear on these questions. (And doesn't history, at least as taught in American schools, often appear to be largely a procession of battles and wars?)

War has most often been considered a natural state of affairs. Every tribe, every city-state, and every dynasty expected armed conflict. It was taken for granted that one group would raid another's lands to steal the cattle and the valuables and that the other group would do the same as opportunities arose. Much of the routine fighting took the form of raids and skirmishes. Killing or being killed were possible outcomes but not necessarily the main objectives. It was so much the better if you could surprise and scatter someone else's forces and loot at leisure. However, there would also be raids of reprisal in which a previous death on one side must be avenged by killing somebody on the other side.

War held true as a normal fact of life for the most sophisticated civilizations of the time. The ancient Greek city-states were following the examples of their own gods when they took the field against the "barbarians" and even against each other. Had not their own deities triumphed over the Titans after the most awesome battles? A classic distinction did make itself known, however: anything goes when fighting outsiders, but certain rules of conduct should be observed when it is Greek against Greek. In practice, the concept of "honorable warfare" has often failed, both in ancient and modern times. The American war for independence eventually was marked by atrocities on both sides despite the sense of kinship (Wright, 1983), and the Civil War similarly had its episodes of savagery and inhumanity (Foote, 1983). Nevertheless, a theme of restraint and propriety has at times moderated the violence of warfare between people who have a sense of commonality. By harsh contrast, when the warring parties regard each other as totally alien, even nonhuman, there are often no limits to cruelty and bloodshed, such as the racist-tinged horrors of the Spanish conquest of Mexico (Todorov, 1984) and the agony of Vietnam (Karnow, 1984).

In its days of greatness Rome sent its legions on missions of conquest, and its successors, the Holy Roman Empire and the Byzantine Empire, both excelled in the military arts. Influential men of the cloth affirmed that war is not necessarily evil: the lawful authorities are certainly entitled to enforce their rights and claims through the use of deadly force (Northedge, 1967). Even in *Utopia* war is an accepted fact of life that is not intrinsically in conflict with religious principles—you must simply go about the business of killing in a well-planned, cost-effective manner (More, 1516).

There has been an unbroken continuation of warfare from ancient times to the modern era. Nevertheless, the emergence of major world re-

ligions has had many implications for the nature, scope, and meaning of war. This interpenetration of war and religion is by no means behind us. Consider, for example, Iran's present commitment to a *jihad* (holy war) and the so-called "Armageddon theologians" of the United States who assert that the Bible prophesies a nuclear catastrophe, a final killing ground centering in Israel's Jezreel Valley. Religion also figured mightily in one of the great confrontations of the past—the Crusades.

Christianity was divided and troubled as its second millenium dawned. Rome, "the eternal city," was a broken shell of its former glory, and the spiritual credentials of the Catholic Church were undermined by internal conflict. The conflict was symbolized by the fact that not one but two popes claimed authority, each backed by militant political factions. It was within this context that one of the competing popes called for a holy war of liberation. Urban II demanded that the Christians cease their internal fighting and unite to free the Holy Land from Moslem possession. The sepulchre of Christ and all the other sacred places and relics were to be restored to Christian hands. Urban told of the "people of the Persian kingdom, an accursed race, a race utterly alienated from God" that had conquered the Near East, defiled the holy places, and tormented Christian residents and pilgrims. (It was actually the Seljuk Turks that Urban meant, vigorous warriors whose invasion had destabilized the existing Moslem power structure.)

Urban's words, spoken in 1095, have come down to us through the years. To rouse the peoples of Europe to a common cause, he said:

> Christian warriors, who continually and vainly seek pretexts for war, rejoice, for you have today found a true pretext. You, who have so often been the terror of your fellow men, go and fight against the barbarians, go and fight for the deliverance of the holy places. You, who sell for vile pay the strength of your arms to the fury of others, armed with the sword of the Machabees, go and merit an eternal reward. If you triumph over your enemies, the kingdoms of the East will be your reward. If you are

conquered, you will have the glory of dying in the very same place as Jesus Christ, and God will never forget that he found you in the holy battalions. . . .

If you must have blood, bathe in the blood of the infidels. I speak to you with harshness because my ministry obliges me to do so. Soldiers of Hell, become soldiers of the living God! (Payne, 1984, pp. 34–35)

Urban succeeded in creating a unifying mission: death to the infidels for the glory of God! Soon the largest masses of fighting men ever assembled on earth would be pressing toward Jerusalem, their sins washed clean by this act of devotion.

The Crusade chronicles reveal in abundance every human quality taken to its extreme—high purpose and low scheming, extraordinary courage and frailty in the face of danger, merciless killing and loving compassion. One of the most stunning victories in history was inspired by the belief that God had come to the aid of the Crusaders by showing them a vision of where they could find a remnant of the lance that had pierced Jesus' body upon the cross. Inspired by this belief, the starving, poorly equipped troops of the first crusading host vanquished the strongest army ever assembled by the Moslem world. Other battles would be just as decisively lost, however, as when a personal point of honor led the Crusaders to walk into certain massacre at the Horns of Hattin.

From beginning to end, the Crusades expressed a complex and constantly changing relationship between religious faith and many other factors. In the name of Christianity, frenzied knights slaughtered women and children as they poured into Jerusalem. Yet on other occasions the same men in the name of the same religion would gently look after the pregnant women of their foe and treat the wounded with care and compassion.

What about their enemies, that "race utterly alienated from God"? The Moslems were in fact just as committed to their own religious beliefs, and it was in the service of Allah that they tried to put aside their own internal dissensions to combat the invading hosts. In historical retro-spect, the core beliefs and world views of 11th century Christians and Moslems had much in common (Finucane, 1984). Both worshipped one supreme being and tried to live by the principles and examples furnished by their holy men. They even agreed on some scriptures and considered some of the same places sacred. It is one of the deadly ironies of history that these true believers—Christian and Moslem—shed each other's blood generation after generation when, on other grounds, they had so much to offer each other. During the occasional interludes between open combat, Moslem and Christian showed a remarkable ability to appreciate and learn from each other. But when it was time for the Christian leader to sound his oliphant and the Moslem to strike his drums and cymbals, both sides pledged themselves to death. In 100 battles the men of Christ and the men of Muhammed sacrificed their lives, confident in the belief that by this pious action they would win eternity.

But what if all this killing was not "holy" after all? What if it was not even "just"? And what if it didn't even make any sense?

I didn't really speak the language. I could understand a few phrases, though. One day during a fire fight, for the first time in my life, I heard the cries of the Vietnamese wounded, and I understood them. When somebody gets wounded, they call out for their mothers, their wives, their girl friends. There I was listening to the VC cry for the same things. That's when the futility of the war really dawned on me. I thought, "Jesus Christ, what a fucking waste this whole thing is." (Baker, 1982, p. 216)

Despite what is often said, the Vietnamese War was not the first in which people came to doubt the purpose and value of mortal combat. Compare chronicles and diaries from the early and the late phases of almost any war and you will see questioning and disillusionment. Similarly, in the same war there is both a revulsion to killing and a lust to destroy.

By this time I have to admit that I was really into being a door gunner. I loved it. I loved flying. I liked shooting people as long as I wasn't too close.

Those little things on the ground were okay to kill. It was okay that they were shooting at me—that's part of the game. . . . I was a big, bad door gunner. . . . We were the tough guys. We were like brothers. It was a nice feeling. We were the heroes. . . . I was crazy. (Baker, 1982, p. 226)

I never saw so many guys cry as I did while I was in Vietnam. Some of the corpsmen and men from the field amazed me with how gentle they were with their buddies. One of the big fears the guys had was of dying alone. A lot of guys came into the hospital really badly hurt and they did die, but their buddies stayed with them. "Don't leave me, please don't leave me." And they didn't. (Baker, 1982, p. 242)

By the 18th century a great philosopher, Immanuel Kant (1795/1932), had become convinced that *Perpetual Peace* was an absolute necessity and could be achieved by international organization and cooperation. Years later, however, Karl von Clausewitz (1832/1984) could still persuade many that the capacity to make war is vital to the success of any nation. The "hawks" and "doves" of today are continuing a vigorous, sometimes bitter dialectic on the value of war as social policy.

The psychological dimensions of war were examined in a memorable exchange of correspondence between Albert Einstein and Sigmund Freud (1933/1953). The physicist believed that the most critical problem facing humanity was not the nature of the physical universe but our own nature—especially the so often demonstrated propensity for violence. The psychoanalyst agreed that what he called the aggressive instinct did exist and was not likely to be rooted out of human nature. We might, however, learn to love the other in ourselves and ourselves in the other person—in other words, to experience and respect our common humanity. Having survived the "war to end all wars," Freud believed that civilization had at least one chance left to transform its aggressive tendencies to more constructive use. A few years later he was an old man dying in a foreign land because the unthinkable second war had already flamed out from his own country to engulf the world.

There are examples that seem to prove almost any theory of war and human violence. Religious faith, for example, can be seen to provide visions of universal human kinship and perpetual harmony or incitement for the most relentless and fanatic slaughter. War is a rational instrument of state policy, or it is something we blunder into for any number of trivial reasons. Human nature itself has a warlike component that at best can only be diverted from its most destructive aims, or human nature becomes warlike only when so shaped by circumstances. No simple answer, however, encompasses all the themes, motives, and events that have issued from warfare.

There is at least one commonality among capital punishment, the killing of animals for food or other reasons, and warfare. These activities are carried out in an organized way, a *systematic* way. In fact, it has taken substantial advances in organizational skill to increase the range and extent of death. The development of the standing army made it possible to wage war in any season. The application of assembly-line tactics for raising livestock ensures that astounding numbers of chickens move from egg to fast food sandwich without ever seeing a barnyard. The high technology and high priority of night warfare have produced devices that further increase the hunter's advantage over his prey. Killing on behalf of society or some of its special interest groups is a function of the death system that thrives on organizational expertise.

The systematization of killing by the state can be seen in the careful specification of precisely how executions are to be conducted in relationship to the crime. Consider the following verdict passed on an Englishman in the 13th century (cited by Jankofsky, 1979):

Hugh (Hugh Dispenser the Younger) . . . you are found as a thief, and therefore shall be hanged; and are found as a traitor, and therefore shall be drawn and quartered; and for that you have been outlawed by the king, and . . . returned to the court without warrant, you shall be beheaded and for that you abetted and procured discord between the king and queen, and others of the realm, you shall be embowelled, and your bowels burnt. Withdraw, traitor, tyrant and so go take your judgment, attainted wicked traitor.

This example of "overkill" was not a random emotional outburst but a deliberate attempt to strengthen those in power. A respected individual who had merely taken the wrong side in a conflict or who was a member of the aristocracy might simply have his head severed. As a special privilege, the head of the executed might not be placed on a spike on one of the city's gates. Capital punishment could either inflict agony and heap disgrace on the condemned or be content with taking life but not reputation.

Killing by the death system (or, to put it another way, the social system turned killer) can take more subtle and indirect forms, and it is these forms that actually result in more deaths than capital punishment. Certain kinds of people routinely are deprived of nutritional and health resources that could enable them to enjoy a full life span. Infant mortality in America, for example, is higher in families who live below the poverty level: nonwhite subpopulations have an exceptionally higher risk, with respiratory illnesses being the most frequent specific cause of death (McMullen, 1983). Whether or not the term *kill* is used, the outcome of systematic deprivation may be premature death. There is often controversy on the particulars, but it is difficult to avoid the conclusion that the premature death of its own citizens is sometimes the effect of a society's own social policy and action.

Attitudes and behaviors related to killing can show in many ways. Consider some aspects of funeral practices in Madagascar. The Merina people, an ethnic group of Southeast Asian origin, are dominant in the Madagascar population. The massive megalithic tombs on this island have attracted much attention. Some anthropologists are particularly interested in the way that the Merina belief system *keeps the dead functional* within their social and political organization. Wise and influential people, now deceased, may be consulted at the cemetery when there are important decisions to be made, and also kept informed of current developments in the world of the living. Funerals play a major role in this process. At a certain point in the funeral preparations, a bull is teased by the men. In a game that is just as dangerous as it sounds, the bull is incited to rush around and around them. Later, a ceremony is enacted, and the bull is killed. The relationship between the funeral and killing goes beyond this. If the "wrong" bull was selected, or if it is killed at the "wrong time" or in the "wrong way," then there may be fatal results. Members of the village may actually die because of this error in conducting the rituals. According to Merina folklore, people who have died soon after a funeral were victims not of natural causes, but of errors made in selection or killing of the sacrificial bull (Bloch, 1971).

Teasing, challenging, and then killing bulls appears to be an activity that is relished by the Merinas despite or because of the risks it entails. The fact that killing bulls and risking people's lives should be an integral part of the funeral process may be surprising to us, but the Merinas might be equally astonished by some of the interweavings of killing in Western society's death system.

REFERENCES

Baker, M. (1982). *Nam.* New York: Quill Publishing Co.

Bloch, M. (1971). *Placing the dead.* New York: Seminar Press.

Bryer, K. B. (1977). The Amish way of death. *American Psychologist, 12,* 167–174.

Clausewitz, K. v. (1984). *On war.* Princeton, N.J.: Princeton University Press. (Original work published 1832)

Finucane, R. C. (1984). *Soldiers of the faith.* New York: St. Martin's Press.

Foote, S. (1983). *The Civil War: A narrative.* (3 vols.) New York: The History Book Club.

Freud, S. (1953). *Why war?* In C. James, and S. Grachen (Eds.) *Collected papers* (Vol. pp. 273–287). London: The Hogarth Press. (Original work published 1933)

Green, J. S. (1972). The days of the dead in Oaxaca, Mexico. *Omega, Journal of Death and Dying, 3,* 245–262.

Jankofsky, K. (1979). Public execution in England in the late middle ages: The indignity and dignity of death. *Omega, Journal of Death and Dying, 10,* 433–458.

Kant, I. (1932). *Perpetual peace.* Los Angeles: U.S. Library Associates, Inc. (Original work published 1795)

Karnow, S. (1984). *Vietnam: A history.* New York: Penguin Books.

McMullen, G. A. (1983). *Climatic variation in seasonal patterns of infant mortality.* Unpublished doctoral dissertation, Brown University, Providence, RI.

More, T. (1516). *Utopia.*

Northedge, F. S. (1967). Peace, war, and philosophy. In P. Edwards (Ed.) *The Encyclopedia of philosophy* (Vol. 6, pp. 63–67). New York: Macmillan Publishing Co., Inc.

Payne, R. (1984). *The dream and the tomb.* New York: Stein & Day, Inc.

Raphael, B. (1983). *The anatomy of bereavement.* New York: Basic Books, Inc.

Todorov, T. (1984). *The conquest of America* (R. Howard, Trans.). New York: Harper & Row.

United Press International. (1984, July 27). Massacre-site McDonald's is being dismantled. *The Arizona Republic.*

Weber, M. (1930). *The Protestant ethic and the spirit of capitalism* (T. Parsons and Sons, Trans.). New York: Scribner.

Wright, E. (Ed.) (1983). *The fire of liberty.* London: The Folio Society.

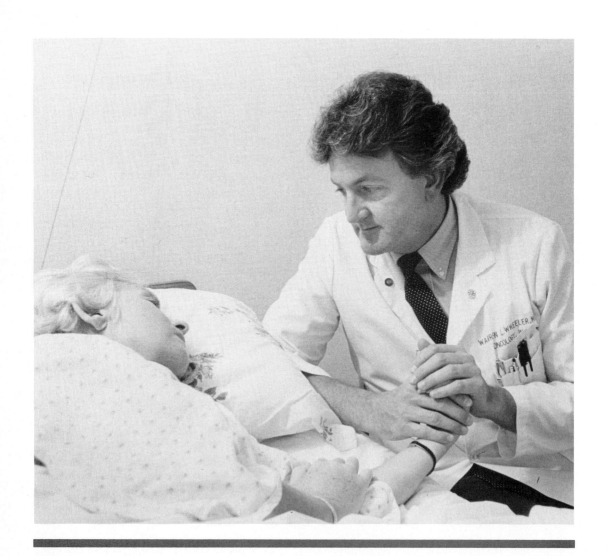

DYING

transition from life

Your first day of school should be . . . Your first date . . . Your first day on the job . . . The first time you hold your baby . . . Your first gray hair . . .

We all experience transitions in our lives. Some may have been long awaited ("At last, I'm old enough for a driver's license!"). Some may have been dreaded ("Do I actually have to support myself now?"). Many transitions are tinged with ambivalence ("I'm kinda ready to get married, sort of, but sort of not"). The transition from life itself is unique because the separation is so complete and so final. However, the dying process does have points in common with other types of transition: there are *interactions* that can either be upsetting or comforting, *communications* that can either inform or confuse, and *self-evaluations* that can either undermine or strengthen one's sense of identity. Perhaps most significantly, what the dying process *means* depends much upon the way that everybody involved thinks, feels, and behaves. It follows that the transition from life is unique for every individual. No two people bring the same thoughts, feelings, accomplishments, and relationships to their final illnesses, nor are the illness-related experiences ever identical.

In this chapter we develop an overview of the dying process. Attention is given first to the basic question of what dying is and when it begins. Next, we look at some of the different "trajectories" or forms the dying process can take. The

challenge of communicating well throughout the dying process is then considered. This is followed by an exploration of several models of the dying process, including two stage theories. The next two chapters also focus on the dying person. Chapter 5 concentrates on the philosophy and technique of care for dying people and their families, with special attention to the hospice approach. Chapter 6 looks at the person with AIDS from the perspectives of both individual care and social dynamics.

However, this is a good time to pause and consider dying from a very personal perspective. I suggest that you give your attention now to the thought exercise outlined in Box 4–1. Why not try this exercise right now? This exercise has proven helpful to other people who were also starting to study dying and terminal care. The questions raised in this exercise are taken up later in the text, and your instructor will have other observations to add.

WHAT IS DYING AND WHEN DOES IT BEGIN?

Individual and Interpersonal Responses

"What is dying?" and "When does it begin?" The knowledge that "I am dying" introduces many changes in the individual's view of self and world.

BOX 4–1
YOUR DEATHBED SCENE

A Thought Exercise

They are planning a movie about your life. This film is intended to be as faithful as possible to the facts. Help them plan the deathbed scene. Describe the ending of your life in as much detail as you can, based upon what you expect is most likely to happen. It would be best if this description is complete enough to help locate the setting, the time, who else might be on the scene, and anything else that is needed. (Yes, of course—they're giving you lots of money for your cooperation, but you are in control of planning this scene according to your best guess at what the future will bring.)

Please use a separate sheet of paper for this exercise.

A New England artist (Lesses, 1982–1983) who was terminally ill described the comfortable familiarity of her home:

I live with an oak coffee table
beside my bed where
my silver-framed clock ticks hard
through the night
like my cat when she purrs.

But this sense of comfort could not disguise the fact that her life had changed decisively:

I hate every morning
hating it
with my stomach jumping
before I've had a chance to think
of anything I awake non-thinking and I am
like a small animal backed into the corner
of a cage to escape from the hand clutching,
reaching through the wire door
I feel the power of the hand's grasp
and fear it
without knowing what the power is.

Other terminally ill people have different experiences to report, but the feeling that "How I

live now is not as I lived before" is hard to escape. The lives of close friends and relatives also change. Structured interviews were conducted with the significant others of cancer patients receiving chemotherapy in an ambulatory care setting (Hart, 1986–1987). Friends experienced a total stress level just as high as family members and responded to the stress in a similar manner. Feelings of helplessness, anger, and fear were the most stressful factors, according to both family members and friends. It is not just close family members, then, but also the larger interpersonal circle of the life-threatened person who undergo stressful change.

Family and friends of the chemotherapy patients had to contend with uncertainty. Was their friend or relation *really* dying? Some of the patients would recover, others would live for several years, and still others would die within a short period. The *possibility* and the *certainty* of dying both generate stress but tend to produce somewhat different responses. A pair of case examples illustrate this more clearly.

Greg was a college student who lived more than two years with the knowledge that he would *probably* die in the near future. He suffered from a form of leukemia that was unusually puzzling to his physicians. Greg recognized that the disease itself was his central problem, but often he was more concerned about the ways in which other people related to him:

I have had to develop almost a whole new set of friends. My good old buddies just felt awfully uncomfortable around me. They couldn't be themselves anymore. I realized they'd be relieved if I would just sort of drift away from them.

What seemed to disturb Greg's friends most was the discrepancy and ambiguity. Greg was a powerfully built young man who had been healthy and vigorous for most of his life. This appearance made it difficult to accept that he was in the grip of a life-threatening disease. None of the "good old buddies" could relate to *both* facts: that Greg looked healthy and functioned well and that he was also terminally ill. Most of his friends and family chose to relate to the healthy Greg.

> I guess it was my own fault. If I wanted to make things easier for everybody, I could have just shut up about my condition. But I didn't think I had to. I mean, you talk about important things with your best friends, don't you? I didn't go on and on about it. When something new happened, or I started feeling shaky about it, I would say something. Oh, man—they just couldn't handle it!

Greg posed a problem for his friends as well as his physicians. He touched on his illness often enough to make it hard for his friends to ignore it, but often he looked well enough. When he had an acute episode he would be in the hospital. Afterward he would keep to himself for a while. "I didn't like to show my face around when I felt rotten," he said. This pattern crossed his friends' expectations. Everybody knew that a dying person looks different, so Greg *should* have looked different. Similarly, it was assumed that dying was the last thing a dying person would want to talk about. A young man might be expected to be especially keen to preserve his "macho" image by concealing any signs of pain, weakness, or fear. Greg was a deviant, then, in behaving as a dying young man should not.

By contrast, Matilda D. was obviously depleted by many years of illness and seemed too frail to survive much longer (Kastenbaum, et al., 1981). She was admitted to a geriatric hospital at age 86 suffering from a painfully advanced rheumatoid arthritis condition, anemia, and difficulty in taking and utilizing nutrition. Attentive nursing care enabled her to remain relatively stable for several months, but Matilda's condition gradually worsened. Most of her time was spent sleeping or lying on her bed in considerable discomfort. At this point she was regarded as "failing" but not dying. This distinction was meaningful to staff members because it indicated to them what pattern of care would be most appropriate. They did not face the ambiguity that Greg's friends and the significant others in the chemotherapy study had to contend with. Furthermore,

the staff (and Matilda's daughter from the community) also exp and death would soon follow. This again contrasts with Greg and the chemotherapy patients for whom there was some hope of recovery or remission.

Matilda was officially considered a dying person when her lungs started to fill with fluid and her general condition weakened. Within the sociotechnical structure of the hospital, the next orthodox action was to relocate Matilda to the intensive care unit (ICU). Although the ICU is where some patients are treated successfully for a medical crisis, it also serves as the tacitly approved exit ward. Matilda's status change to a dying person meant that she would be moved to a death place. (One function of this maneuver is the effort to preserve the home ward as a non-death place.) Her new status could also be seen in an altered pattern of staff interactions. Basic care was still provided in a conscientious, professional manner, but the contacts were now briefer and more mechanical. The subtle change from a living to a dying person had taken place in the perceptions and actions of staff members. The certainty of her death made it easier for staff to shift their patterns.

Fortunately, Matilda's life did not end with the isolation and dehumanization that might have been suggested by this description. A therapeutic companion had formed a close relationship with Matilda just before the failing and dying sequences. There was a time to discover some of Matilda's distinctive personal qualities and values. The therapeutic companion and the daughter continued to relate to Matilda as a distinctive human being even when the old woman could no longer respond in words. Matilda's favorite music was sung and played to her and she died literally in touch with two people for whom she remained a distinctive and valued person.

Many studies have shown that we treat people differently when they are perceived as dying. One of the earliest studies of this type deserves mention because it has illustrated this fact so clearly.

Larry LeShan (Bowers, et al., 1964) recorded the amount of time that elapsed between a patient's call and a nurse's response. He found that nurses took a significantly longer time before going to the bedside of a dying patient as compared with other patients. This very obvious index of differential behavior toward dying people takes on further meaning when the nurses' reactions to the study are considered. When LeShan shared his findings, the nurses were surprised and upset. They had not been aware of this differential pattern of response. The nurses decided to make a special effort to respond more promptly to terminally ill patients. After a few weeks, however, the original pattern reinstated itself (LeShan, 1982). As much as they wanted to treat all patients equally, the nurses could not avoid being influenced by the attitude they share with the rest of society: dying people are different, and contacts should be kept to a minimum.

Onset of the Dying Process: Alternative Perspectives

When dying begins depends on the frame of reference that is used. Perhaps the most abstract perspective is the one that proposes we die from the moment we are born. This popular bit of philosophy reminds us that life is always related to death. This view can be useful in developing a personal philosophy of life. It does, however, encourage an attitude of denial. "We die from the moment we are born" accepts the general but trivializes the specific. The implicit message can be: "There is nothing really special here. Maybe you *are* dying, but *everybody* is dying, and isn't it a lovely day?" Often this abstract perspective is simply a way of reducing our own discomfort and anxiety.

This concept is also questionable as a direct statement of fact. It is true that there is a continual sequence of death among the cells that comprise our bodies. The outer layer of the skin, for example, is composed of dead cells that are replaced in turn by other dead cells. Certain forms of tissue death are programmed to occur at particular times in psychobiological development. The loss of the umbilical cord after birth is one of the clearest examples of a biological structure phasing itself out after its function has been served. The principle of programmed death as part of normal development is well established in biology (Hayflick, 1984).

Nevertheless, it would be misleading to insist that the normal turnover of cells and the atrophy of unnecessary structures constitute a process of dying for the organism as a whole. Should the term *dying* be used so loosely, we would simply have to find a new term to represent the very different processes observed when life actually is in jeopardy.

A more challenging concept has been with us for many years. Three centuries ago Jeremey Taylor (1651/1977), chaplain to King Charles I of England, likened aging to a form of terminal illness. In advanced age, to live is also to die. The concept of aging as dying has more impact than the proposition that dying begins with life. It is also interesting to consider Taylor's suggestion that aging might be regarded as slow dying and dying as fast aging. Nevertheless, there is not much point in linking dying with aging when we still have so much to learn about when aging begins (Hayflick, 1984; Kastenbaum, et al., 1981). Furthermore, elderly people cannot be described as dying without ignoring the vigor and vitality that many continue to express at an advanced age. It is also difficult to equate dying with aging pragmatically. A young person may die because of a specific bodily failure (e.g., an unexpected drug reaction or heart failure) although otherwise be in good health and not at all resemble an aged person.

There is a place for general and philosophical propositions. But more useful here is an in-depth view of the dying process. Dying usually begins as a psychosocial event. Organ systems fail, but it is in the realm of personal and social life that dying occurs. Now consider some of the contexts in which the onset of dying is discovered or certified.

1. *Dying begins when the facts are recognized.* The physician's office is visited by people with varying amounts of concern for their health. Included are essentially healthy people who have been convinced for years that they are dying and the person who has just come in for a routine checkup, yet the latter may be the one who actually has a life-threatening illness that is about to be discovered. Perhaps, then, the dying process begins when the physician observes it. However, the physician in turn is likely to rely on clinical and laboratory diagnostic procedures. From this perspective, the dying process begins when the physician has obtained and analyzed enough critical information to make such a judgment. The physician might suspect that the patient has been on a "terminal trajectory" for some time before the diagnostic evaluation was established. But this had not been "official" dying; it is only now that the person is considered a dying patient.

2. *Dying begins when the facts are communicated.* There is a big difference, however, between the physician's prognosis and the patient's awareness. Perhaps it makes more sense to date the onset of the dying process from the moment at which the physician informs the patient. This would give *two* possible beginning points of the dying process, not even counting that theoretical moment when bodily changes shift critically to a terminal course. It may seem peculiar to think of dying in this way. But the patient and the physician are different people with very different frameworks for interpreting the terminal process. Instead of jumbling together these two very different outlooks, it is useful to respect both frames of reference. When we ask, "Is this person dying?" it is important to bear in mind where the answer is coming from.

The actual situation is even more complicated. There is likely to be a time lag between the physician's determination of the prognosis and when it is shared with the patient. Physicians seldom break the news at the same instant they reach their conclusion. There may be a delay of days, weeks, or even months before the physician tells the patient precisely what has been found. Furthermore, sometimes the physician never does tell the patient. So we cannot entirely depend on the physician's communication as the definitive starting point of the process from the patient's standpoint. But even when the physician does share the findings with the patient, can this be taken unequivocally as the onset of the dying process?

3. *Dying begins when the patient realizes or accepts the facts.* More than one nurse has returned from the bedside of a patient almost bursting with anger at the physician. "Why hasn't he leveled with this patient? This man is dying, and nobody has told him what's going on!" At times this concern is well justified. The physician has not provided the terminally ill patient with a clear statement of the condition. But at other times the patient's apparent lack of knowledge cannot be laid at the physician's doorstep. The patient was told, but he or she "didn't stay told." Somehow the patient was able to forget or misinterpret the central facts. The patient was not psychologically ready to accept the news.

Note also that the physician's communication can be subtle or direct, couched in clear language or technical jargon. Or perhaps the physician said one thing with words and something else with facial expression and tone of voice.

The physician's ability to communicate can make a big difference in how quickly, accurately, and fully the message comes across. Howard G. Hogshead (1978) has compiled a succinct set of guidelines from his own experiences as well as those of other physicians. He recommends the following approach to breaking the news:

1. *Keep it simple.* Perhaps as a result of apprehension or uneasiness, there is a tendency to go into too many details and technicalities.
2. Ask yourself, *"What does this diagnosis mean to this patient?"* Many patients are simply unable to comprehend the nature of the diagnosis, in which case other methods must be found to gradually educate them.

3. *Meet on "cool ground" first.* It is very unpleasant to walk in to meet people you have never met before, knowing you have to give them a piece of really bad news. It is always easier to handle if you have some earlier relationship to the patient or his family, and have some notion of their background and possible reaction to the news.

4. *Don't deliver all the news at once.* . . . People have a marvelous way of letting you know how much they are able to handle. . . . This may mean that the full disclosure has to be spread out over two or three sessions.

5. *Wait for questions.* A long pause will allow the question that tells you where to go next.

6. *Do not argue with denial.* . . . This usually leads to loss of rapport. . . . In general, the patient will "hear" the message when he is ready to accept it.

7. *Ask questions yourself.* Ask the patient to tell you what you have told him or ask him what it means. Oftentimes, you will be surprised at the answer. Or, ask the patient what the doctors at such-and-such a hospital have told him.

8. *Do not destroy all hope.* There are a hundred ways of handling this, and it requires real tact and experience to acquire the necessary skill.

9. *Do not say anything that is not true.* This would be the cruelest blow of all.

There can be another time lag, then, between communication and realization of terminal illness that depends on many factors, including the physician's communication skills. A person is not *dying to himself or herself* until there is a clear and personal realization of the situation. In this sense the dying process cannot be dated from the medical prognosis nor the act of official communication, if there is one. We must be aware of the individual's thoughts and feelings. This often leads to disagreement as to whether or not a person knows. Disagreements can arise because some of us are better observers than others, and some of us are looking for clues to support a particular opinion. For example, a terminally ill person may talk about a relatively minor although distressing symptom. This may lead me to assume that the patient is not aware of the more critical situation that threatens life. But someone else may notice instead that this patient slips into the past tense when talking about family and occupational life, suggesting that she does not project herself far into the future. We come to different conclusions, based on different observations.

Disagreements may also arise because the terminally ill person, like anybody else, behaves differently depending on the situation. A different attitude toward the illness may be expressed to a member of the immediate family than to a physician, a colleague, or a stranger. Most of the health-care staff may be under the impression that the patient does not know, but one nurse may realize that he is keenly aware of the situation because he has selected that nurse with whom to share his most personal thoughts and feelings.

Additionally, the person's own estimation of his or her condition may shift from time to time. Avery D. Weisman (1972), an outstanding clinician and researcher, speaks of "middle knowledge." It is not a simple question of knowing or not knowing. The individual probably knows, suspects, or senses what is taking place in his or her body. But this awareness is not always on the same level of consciousness nor does the patient's overall interpretation of his or her condition remain constant. Depending on our relationship with the person and his or her total life situation at a particular time, we might come away either with or without the impression that the patient sees himself or herself as dying.

4. *Dying begins when nothing more can be done to preserve life.* This is a pragmatic definition that has important consequences for the care of very ill people. The physician may not have classified the person as dying despite the diagnostic signs because avenues of treatment remain open. The person was not doomed for certain. The physician would know that individuals with this particular condition have a certain probability of death within a particular range of time (e.g., six months, five years). Perhaps this patient could be one of the survivors. Furthermore, the probabilities themselves might shift as a new treatment model is introduced. The physician can fully appreciate the seriousness of a patient's condition

without having to classify her as dying, at least not until all treatment possibilities have been exhausted.

Even with this pragmatic approach, however, there is room for disagreement. The family physician may have a different opinion from the specialist—and one specialist from another. As long as there is one more procedure that might be tried to halt or reverse the pathological process, some members of the medical team may decline to think of the patient as terminally ill.

It should be obvious by now that determining the onset of dying is not always a simple matter. Disagreement and ambiguity are possible. This means that the practical consequences of classifying a person as dying are also affected. The judgment that a person is dying could be considered premature if it discourages actions that might have lead to recovery. As late as the 18th century in a city as sophisticated as London special efforts had to be made to persuade the establishment that victims of drowning could be restored by prompt treatment. By contrast, we might conclude that the classification of a person as dying has been delayed too long if painful and socially isolating treatments are continued beyond reasonable hope of success and therefore prevent the person from living his or her final days as he or she might have chosen. When to shift from "prevention of death" to "care of the dying" and how to accomplish this shift in an effective and human manner are questions that hinge in part upon our definition of *dying*.

TRAJECTORIES OF DYING: FROM BEGINNING TO END

So far we have been exploring the *onset* of the dying processes as interpreted by the various people involved. The *end* usually takes place in a hospital or nursing home. This was not always the case. Birth and death were both home-centered events in years gone by. Now it has become more common to think of birth and death as events that should be presided over by

experts in specialized environments. Important countertrends have been developing for both the entry and exit points, making it possible for people to have the advantage of modern knowledge and technology without surrendering personal values associated with birth and dying. The next chapter examines in detail the emerging hospice approach with its emphasis on the home and family. Here the emphasis is on what are still the most common pathways to death—those that conclude in a health-care facility.

A series of pioneering studies by Barney Glaser and Anselm Strauss (1966, 1968), Jeanne Quint Benoleil (1987–1988), and their colleagues was the first to clarify the variety of sequences and their distinctive characteristics. These researchers observed dying as a social phenomenon in six medical facilities in the San Francisco area. Keep in mind that the field researchers do not have the responsibility for patient care that occupies so much of the energies of the hospital staff. Furthermore, the researchers are not the husbands, wives, or children of a dying patient nor terminally ill themselves. This emotional distance gives field researchers a unique role. Their findings may strike you as too cold or aloof, but this does not necessarily mean that the researchers lack compassion any more than the physicians and nurses do. They are simply taking advantage of their distinctive viewpoints to see things the way that others with their more involved needs and functions cannot.

The San Francisco team organized many of their observations according to the concept of *dying trajectories*. All dying processes take time; all have a certain shape through time. The combination of duration and shape can be seen and even graphed as a trajectory. For one person the trajectory might best be represented as a straight downward line. For somebody else it might be represented more accurately as slowly fluctuating—going down, leveling off, declining again, climbing a little, and so on.

Dying trajectories themselves are perceived courses of dying rather than actual courses. This distinction is readily evident in the type of trajectory that involves a short reprieve from death. This reprieve represents an unexpected deferment of death. On the other hand, in a lingering death bystanders may expect a faster death than actually occurs. (Glaser & Strauss, 1968, p. 6)

Certainty and Time

According to the Glaser-Strauss team, staff members must answer two questions about every patient whose life is in jeopardy: "Will this patient die? If so, when?" These are the questions of *certainty* and *time*. The questions are important because the attitudes and actions of the health-care staff are based largely on the answers. In general it is easier for the staff to organize itself around the patient when the answers are clear. A hospital, like any other bureaucratic organization, relies heavily on standard operating procedures. It is uncomfortable and disrupting when a patient's condition does not lend itself to straightforward expectations such as "This man will recover" or "This woman will die, but not for some time."

The time framework can vary a great deal depending on circumstances. In the emergency room, the staff's uncertainty about a patient's recovery or death can change to certainty in just a few minutes. The fate of a premature baby may be determined in a few hours or a few days. But the outlook for a cancer patient may remain indeterminate for months.

Together, certainty and time yield four types of death expectations from the staff's viewpoint (which is not to say that all staff members necessarily have the same expectations):

1. Certain death at a known time
2. Certain death at an unknown time
3. Uncertain death but a known time when certainty will be established
4. Uncertain death and an unknown time when the question will be resolved

The Glaser-Strauss research team found that staff interaction with patients is closely related to the particular expectations they have formed about time and certainty of death. These expectations are important even when they are not correct because they form the basis for interactions among staff members as well as with patients and their families. Especially important are situations in which staff expectations change. One of the examples given is that of a physician's decision to discontinue any further blood transfusions. This is a clue to others that there is no hope for the patient's recovery. Yet the nurses may decline to take this hint and continue to do everything in their power to give the patient still another chance. This sequence has significant implications for patient and family no matter who (physician or nurse) has made the more accurate assessment of the objective condition in this instance. The subtle pattern of communication among staff in such a case affects everybody:

> Since the doctor had said nothing official, even nurses who believe the patient is dying can still give him an outside chance and stand ready to save him. They remain constantly alert to counterclues. "Everybody is simply waiting," said one nurse. If the doctor had indicated that the patient would die within the day, nurses would have ceased their constant watch for counterclues and reduced their efforts to save him, concentrating instead on giving comfort to the last, with no undue prolonging of life. (p. 11)

It is possible, then, for one member of the treatment team to come to a conclusion but still leave room for others to follow an alternative course. In the instance cited, the physician did not carelessly forget to instruct the nurses to alter their approach. It is more likely that the physician subtly but clearly indicated his opinion but, by putting nothing into words, allowed a little leeway for others to continue their efforts to maintain life despite the odds. The physician has decided that the *prevention* function of the death system cannot be achieved but has provided the nurses with some maneuvering room to maintain the possibility of a reprieve while devoting most of their efforts to the *caring and comforting* function.

Now consider three dying trajectories observed by the Glaser-Strauss research team: *lingering, expected quick trajectory, and unexpected quick trajectory.*

The Lingering Trajectory

The caregivers display a characteristic tempo and service pattern when a patient's life is fading slowly and gradually. Seldom is there a dramatic rescue scene. The staff tries to keep the patient comfortable and viable on a day-to-day basis. But when the patient is clearly failing, staff members are inclined to believe that they have already done "all that we can" and that the patient has earned death after a long downhill process. In the geriatric ward, for example, it would be unusual to find a team of specialists racing in to apply a battery of heroic measures. Many patients are "allowed" to die quietly. A quiet fading seems to be expected and accepted by the staff as a fit conclusion to the lingering trajectory.

Perhaps the death that terminates a lingering trajectory is more acceptable because the person may have been considered *socially dead* for some time. Even within the institution itself some patients may be considered more alive than others. Glaser and Strauss observed, as a number of others have also noted, that staff members become attached to some patients as they interact with them through the months. Yet, although the staff is likely to feel sorrow when the patients die, this reaction is held in check by the belief that their lives no longer had much value either to themselves or society. For every patient who has somehow attracted the special attention and sympathy of staff members, however, there are others whose distinctive human qualities have not been perceived by staff or reinforced by friends and relations.

Patients on a lingering trajectory seldom have much control over the management of their condition. Family members also seem to leave everything to the staff, especially as time goes by. In fact, the frequency and duration of visits from family members characteristically fall off when the lingering nature of the trajectory has become established. Furthermore, the slowly dying person usually does not speak of final things to family and friends. Glaser and Strauss pass along these last two observations with the clear awareness that what they have seen might not be all that transpires. My own work suggests that there is more awareness and communication than one might think, but it is often on either a symbolic or nonverbal level (see pp. 89–93).

In summary, the lingering trajectory most often does not produce obvious disruptions in the environment. Staff members tend to assume that the patient also moves rather gently toward death. Glaser and Strauss (1968) say:

> These patients drift out of the world, sometimes almost like imperceptibly melting snowflakes. The organization of work emphasizes comfort care and custodial routine, and is complemented by a sentimental order emphasizing patience and inevitability. (p. 64)

But the picture is not always so tranquil and orderly. Occasionally there is a patient, family member, or even a physician or nurse who does not accept the impending death. Glaser and Strauss also noticed incidents in which a patient's loved one would upset and confuse the staff by showing "too much emotion" after the patient died. Perhaps strong reactions to a patient's death challenged the staff's customary assumption that the social loss of a lingerer did not amount to much. By contrast, the patience of family and/or staff may be strained when a patient fails to die on schedule. My first experience with this phenomenon occurred many years ago when the daughter of one patient strode angrily back from his ward and said, "They said he was on the Death List, so I came here as soon as I could. And there he was—you can see for yourself! Sitting up in bed and playing cards. And winning!" (There had been a misunderstanding in this instance. The hospital actually had said that her father was on the "D.L.," meaning not "Death List" but "Danger List.") Nevertheless, the main problem was that the daughter did have reason to expect that her father was close to death and had organized her emotions accordingly. After a few minutes of cooling off and expressing her feelings, she made it clear that she did not really want her father dead, but that it was difficult to keep thinking of him as all-but-dead and waiting "for the other shoe to drop."

The lingering trajectory has the advantage of giving both the patient and the family *time* should they decide to use it—time to grow accustomed to the idea of dying, to make plans, to work through old conflicts and misunderstandings, to review the kind of life that has been lived, and so on. But this trajectory often also has the disadvantage of attenuating relationships and creating a situation in which the person is perceived as not quite alive and yet not securely dead. The lingering trajectory is not the image of dying that usually seizes the imagination of the media; however, it is becoming the most typical pattern in Western society in nursing homes as well as hospitals.

The Expected Quick Trajectory

Glaser and Strauss are among those who maintain that the American hospital system is best prepared to cope with emergencies. Human and technological resources are mustered most impressively when there is an acute life-or-death crisis. The emergency room (ER), the ICU, and the perpetual readiness of specialists to rush to the scene are life-saving resources that Americans have come to expect from the modern medical center.

Time truly is of the essence when a patient is defined as being on an expected quick trajectory. The staff organizes itself with precision to make the most effective use of the time that remains on the side of life. This contrasts vividly with the more leisurely, almost drifting pattern that surrounds the patient on a lingering trajectory. As staff members devote themselves to the patient's urgent needs, there may be a series of redefinitions in their minds—for example, "He is out of immediate danger but probably will not survive

very long" changes to "I think he has passed the crisis point and has the possibility of complete recovery."

Several types of expected quick trajectories were observed by Glaser and Strauss. Each involved a different pattern of interaction with the staff. In a *pointed trajectory* the patient is exposed to a very risky procedure, one that might either save his or her life or result in death. In this situation, the staff often has enough time in advance to organize itself properly. The patient may also have the opportunity to exercise some control and options (e.g., share some precious minutes with a loved one, see that certain personal matters are acted upon, and so on). By contrast, the *danger-period trajectory* requires more watching and waiting. The question is whether or not the patient will be able to survive a stressful experience such as high-risk surgery or a major heart attack. The patient may be unconscious or only partially aware of the surroundings as compared with the alert state a patient with a pointed trajectory might possess. The danger period can vary from hours to days. This is the type of situation in which the family may remain at bedside or in the corridor, with doctors, nurses, and monitoring devices maintaining close vigilance all the while.

The *crisis trajectory* imposes still another condition on both the patient and those concerned. The patient is not in acute danger at the moment, but his or her life might suddenly be threatened at any time. This creates an especially tense situation. It will persist until the patient's condition improves enough so that he or she is out of danger or until the crisis actually arrives and rescue efforts can be made.

Different from all of these is the *will-probably-die trajectory*. The staff believes that nothing effective can be done. The aim is to keep the patient as comfortable as possible and wait for the end to come, usually within hours or days. Glaser and Strauss give examples such as the person leaving the operating room after unsuccessful surgery, the accident victim who is beyond saving, and the individual whose suicide attempt failed to end life immediately but did result in a terminal course.

These are not the only types of expected quick trajectories, but they illustrate the range of experience and situations that exist among those who face death in the near future. There are also some common problems that arise in connection with the expected quick trajectory. The family, for example, is likely to be close by the patient. Glaser and Strauss emphasize the possible disrupting effects of this proximity based upon their direct observations. The presence of the family confronts the staff with more demand for interaction and communication. What should those people in the waiting room be told? Who should tell them? Is this the time to prepare them for the bad news, or can it be postponed a little longer? Should all the family be told at once, or is there one person in particular who should be relied on to grasp the situation first? The staff must somehow come to terms with the needs of the family while still carrying out treatment. Obviously, this is a situation to challenge the staff's judgment and interpersonal skills. In my experience, however, the presence of the family can also be helpful to the staff and, more importantly, to the patient as well. The presence of a familiar and supportive person can make a powerful difference to the patient.

The most salient features of the expected quick trajectory are time urgency; intense organization of treatment efforts; rapidly shifting expectations; and volatile, sensitive staff-family interactions. In the midst of this pressure errors can be made. Errors can include, as Glaser and Strauss note, attempts to save a patient from a disease he or she does not have. A person may arrive at the hospital in critical condition but with no readily available medical history to guide the staff. The pressure of time may then force medical personnel to proceed on the basis of educated guess rather than secure knowledge. This contrasts with the lingering trajectory, which provides the staff abundant time and opportunity to comprehend the patient's condition and anticipate possible crises.

Whether or not there is a chance to save the patient's life sometimes depends on the available resources in the particular hospital or even the particular ward. The lack of an oxygen tank on the ward or of a kidney machine in the hospital at times makes the difference between the will-probably-die trajectory and one with more hope. Even more significant, perhaps, is the observation that the *perceived social value* of the endangered person can spell the difference between an all-out rescue attempt and a do-nothing orientation. This is especially apt to happen when the medical team has pressing decisions to make about who will receive emergency treatment first or be given the benefit of life-support apparatus that is in short supply. "When a patient is not 'worth' having a chance," say Glaser and Strauss, "he may in effect be given none." When a prominent person enters the hospital on a quick trajectory or whose condition suddenly worsens in the hospital, the implicit definition that he or she is dying may be set aside in favor of an intensive campaign of heroic procedures. The person is considered too important to die. The psychosocial definition of dying, then, is no less critical at the end of the process than it is at the onset. This is also a reminder that social quirks that consider one person more important than another (whether on the basis of age, sex, race, economic status, or whatever) can play a direct role in the death system when quick decisions must be made about priority and extent of life-sustaining effort.

The Unexpected Quick Trajectory

The significance of the interpersonal setting in which dying takes place is emphasized again by the unexpected quick trajectory. Personnel in the emergency room, for example, expect to be called on for immediate life-or-death measures. The experienced ER team adjusts quickly to situations that might immobilize most other people. But in other areas of the same hospital the staff is likely to have a pattern of functioning and a belief system that is less attuned to a sudden turn of events: "The appearance of the unexpected quick trajectory constitutes crisis. On these wards there is no general preparation for quick dying trajectories—at least of certain kinds—and the work and sentimental orders of the ward "blow' up when they occur" (Glaser and Strauss, 1968, p. 121).

Perhaps the concept of "middle knowledge" (Weisman, 1972) should be applied to personnel as well as to terminally ill patients. The staff in nonemergency areas *know* but do not *believe* that a life-or-death situation might arise at any moment. It would be too stressful for them to function every day with that expectation in mind, an expectation that is also at variance with the kind of care they are called upon to deliver on a routine basis. In this sense, something really does blow up when a patient unexpectedly enters a crisis phase on the "wrong" ward—the staff's security-giving myth of an orderly and manageable universe is at least temporarily punctured.

Some unexpected deaths prove more disturbing than others to the staff. The "medically interesting case" is one of the most common examples. The staff is more likely to be taken aback and regret the death of a patient who presented unusual features to them. Personnel also tend to be affected more by the death of a patient whose life they had tried especially hard to save. They see their heavy investment in time and energy fading away. This is not the same as mourning the loss of a patient as a person. Instead it is the loss of the staff's effort that is felt as a blow. Glaser and Strauss report that it is the "poor physician who tried so hard" who receives the sympathy of other staff members rather than the patient. The patient may have never seemed like an individual being to the staff during the intensive life-saving efforts. The patient who dies for the wrong reasons also dismays and alarms the staff. Treatment may have been focused on one critical aspect of the patient's condition, while death was approaching through a different route.

The staff's need to shield itself against surprise is a major theme that runs through observations of the unexpected quick trajectory. Everybody in

a life-threatening situation has a need to exercise control—professional staff as well as patient and family. This need often leads both to an illusion of control and to persistent efforts to maintain the illusion (Kastenbaum, 1978). The well-practiced and institutionally supported defenses of the physician or nurse may become dangerously exaggerated or suddenly give way when reality punctures the illusion of control. Perhaps this makes it even more understandable that a turn for the worse in a patient's condition might disorganize a spouse, parent, child, or close friend. Not only is this loved one's relationship to the patient more intense and intimate, but the lay person may lack the professional's expertise in concealing vulnerability.

Unfortunately, the hospital itself at times precipitates an unexpected quick trajectory. Glaser and Strauss give examples such as confusion in the mobilization of treatment resources, the turning of attention away from other patients to concentrate on an urgent case, accidents attributable to carelessness or poor safety practices, and a variety of problems that can arise when a hospital is seriously understaffed.

The combination of time pressure and surprise can lead to what Glaser and Strauss term *institutional evasions*. There is not the time and opportunity to make the moves that are officially required in the situation, so available staff members must improvise a response or use an alternative approach that could expose them to reprimand or even to legal action. There may not be time to bring a physician to the scene, for example, and the ward nurses may have the skill to carry out the life-saving procedures themselves. If they carry out these procedures without direct medical supervision, then they have exposed themselves to the possibility of serious criticism; but if they do not act promptly, the patient may die before the physician arrives. There are many variations on this theme. Evasions of institutional rules may be minor or substantial. The institution itself may choose either to notice or to carefully ignore the infractions. One extra source of tension with the unexpected quick trajectory, then, is the conflict between immediately doing what seems to be best for the patient and strictly abiding by the regulations.

Life-or-Death Emergencies

There is another type of "quick trajectory" that can occur any time, any place. A person in good health may suddenly become victim of an automobile accident, a small child may fall into a swimming pool, an "unloaded gun" may discharge, a restaurant patron may choke, a person with a history of heart disease may suffer another attack. . . . These are just some emergency situations that can result in death.

Several types of problems are more likely to arise when there is a life-or-death emergency in a community setting as compared with a health care facility:

- Panic: "What's happening? What should we do?"
- Inappropriate action: "Let's get him on his feet. . . ."
- Misinterpreting the situation: "Stop whining and go back to bed!"
- Minimizing the danger: "I don't need a doctor. It's just a little indigestion."
- Preoccupied by own concerns: "I'd better clean this place up before I call anybody."

Fortunately, there have been many examples of prompt and competent response from family members, neighbors, colleagues, and passersby. Recently, for example, a man in his eighties had the presence of mind and the skill to perform cardiac pulmonary resuscitation (CPR) on a toddler who had fallen into the pool—an all too frequent occurrence in Arizona. This child recovered, but many have died or suffered severe and permanent injury. Errors and poor decisions can be made within health-care settings also, but the risk is greater in most community settings. A camper's friends, for example, may think they are doing the right thing by carrying out a snake bite remedy that has been passed along for years—but they would be doing more to save this person's life by rushing him to a poison control center.

The emergency technician and the paramedic are often called upon when life-endangering situations arise in the community. Trained specifically to provide society's front line response to emergent health crises, these men and women may have more encounters with disaster in two or three days than most people do in a lifetime. Surprisingly, relatively little attention has been given to their experiences by researchers and educators. Here is a fairly typical excerpt from a study of airborne paramedics that a small team of interested students and I have been conducting. The paramedic participating in this particular interview is a young married man who had started out as a firefighter. At this point in the interview he is reporting some of his first experiences:

> It was at a (community fraternal club). There was a dance going on—lots of loud music/dim lights. No one dancing. Everyone was just standing around. An elderly man had collapsed. . . . Communication was bad. We would give medicine then call a physician on the phone and tell him the situation and what we had done. The man had gone into ventricular fibrillation. I intubated him, and the RN with me tried to get an IV in him—it was hard for her because of the bad lighting.* He was a diabetic. IV was hooked up and we started defibrillation. There was that smell of burning hair associated with defib machines. We got a pulse and blood pressure back. Got an ambulance. The man was breathing fine so I took the tube out and we transported him to the hospital. He survived and was very thankful to us.

This man almost certainly would have died without the prompt and skillful intervention. Sometimes, however, no amount of skill and effort can prevent death, and it is not unusual for the paramedic to discover that there are one or more people already dead on the scene. Even though the paramedic knows that a person is beyond resuscitation, it may be necessary to carry

---

*Intubated: inserted a tube to facilitate breathing. IV: intravenous insertion of a tube through which fluids and medication can be added.

out CPR (cardiopulmonary resuscitation) and other procedures in order to conform with guidelines and regulations. At such times the paramedic is likely to feel—as this man did after responding to another call—that it is wrong to "go through all this trouble for a dead person, why not let her be at peace? I had lots of questions why we went through the whole routine when she was already dead."

There is another odd situation that can arise when a person dies suddenly in a community setting. Although paramedics or nurses on the scene may know that the person is dead, the legal declaration of death may not be made until the body has been transported to a medical facility (and, as already mentioned, useless resuscitation efforts may be continued during that time). This means that some of the deaths that are classified as having occurred in a hospital actually occurred elsewhere. Hospital physicians simply confirmed the emergency team's assessment that the patient was beyond resuscitation.

GUARDED FEELINGS, SUBTLE COMMUNICATIONS

Difficulties in Communication

Most of us exercise discretion in the way we communicate our thoughts and feelings. We do not say everything on our minds to whomever we happen to be with in every situation. Generally we will speak more openly with those we have learned to trust and who demonstrate understanding and good will. Furthermore, we take into account the other person's state of mind—should we alarm somebody who is already anxious or who has a difficult task to perform that requires complete concentration? And precisely how should we get a message across? Should we be as quick and direct about it as possible? Or should we work our way up, starting with something relatively neutral and gradually get to the point? Would a symbolic action or an allusion best communicate what we have in mind? Or must we lay out thoughts and feelings as though

making a formal presentation? How we communicate with another person depends on our own personality style, who that other person is, and the nature of the immediate situation.

We should not be surprised, then, to find feelings guarded and communications subtle among people faced with the prospect of death. One might conclude—erroneously—that the dying person either does not know what is happening or is unwilling to discuss it. Often clear communication has been made very difficult. One of my early studies (Kastenbaum, 1960), for example, found that hospital personnel usually responded to patients' direct communications about death in a style that quickly ended the interaction. The odds were about three to one against the staff member being willing to listen to what the patient had to say. Giving false reassurances ("Oh, you'll outlive me, Charlie!"), changing the subject, and a variety of other evasive responses were more common than an openness to what the dying person really wanted to communicate. My more recent field observations indicate that this attitude is still prevalent in many places. Aged patients on a lingering trajectory frequently were treated as socially dead and therefore denied even the opportunity to die as a person. Verbatim remarks made by staff members in the physical presence of the patients included:

> "This one, she can't talk. She doesn't know what you are saying."
>
> "You should have seen her when she first came here, but look at her now!"
>
> "The poor thing would be better off going in her sleep." (Kastenbaum, 1984, p. 6)

These remarks were not only degrading, but in error. In these three instances (and in many others) there was independent evidence that these patients, although vulnerable and failing, could hear and understand what was being said over their (socially) dead bodies. One example that I will always remember occurred during an official inspection visit to an extended care facility. This facility (operated by a public agency) had been under court orders to improve both its physical plant and its treatment program. The whistle had already been blown, time had been provided to improve care, and my visit as a consultant for the federal government was expected. However, there was no evidence of any improvement. Part of the explanation was that "These people don't understand anything anyhow."

I asked the staff members to show me the most impaired, uncomprehending patient on the ward. This request seemed to throw them into confusion, so I walked to the furthest corner of this large, dark, and filthy ward. An old, pale, scrunched-up woman was lying in bed, her hair tangled and untended, her body smelling of neglect. The charge nurse assured me that their patients were beyond being worth the effort. I asked for the patient's name and some information about her background: Did she have a husband, children, visitors? What had been her interests and achievements before she came here? and so on. All the staff knew was her name, the fact that her husband visited once in a great while, that she could not speak or understand anything, and probably did not have long to live. I then tried to engage the woman in some form of interaction, simply taking her hand and talking to her, and using the small bits of information I had been given. In less than a minute she had painfully faced around and squeezed my hand in return. In another few minutes she was speaking and moaning. I could not make out all the words, but there was no mistaking the fact she knew somebody was trying to communicate with her and that she had the need and the ability (although limited) to respond. The staff noted this interaction and retreated from it. But at the end of the inspection visit the charge nurse turned to me and muttered, "If you're going to write anything about this, I'd better tell you that this is not the patient I told you it was. I mixed the patients up somehow. That was Mrs. ____, not Mrs. ____."

This story was not told to criticize nurses or geriatric facilities in general. The situation on this particular ward was the outcome of systematic neglect of the frail elderly and of those who

try to provide care for them. Having their own sense of horror to contend with, the staff responded by psychologically depriving the patients of individuality and humanity. In the extreme circumstances I have mentioned, this woman had almost no opportunity to communicate to anybody about anything. Whatever she might be feeling about life and death would remain unknown. It is not simply that we often have difficulty communicating on "ultimate matters"; there are people close to death who are deprived of the opportunity for normal social interaction in general. And how unnecessary! My former therapeutic companion colleagues at Cushing Hospital are among those who have shown that social isolation can be overcome and meaningful communication can be developed even with people whose terminal phase of life is complicated by massive impairments (Kastenbaum, et al., 1981). Others around the world have also found it possible to reestablish the human connection by alert and sensitive care-giving.

Improving Communication

Some guidelines for improved communication have already been listed. Hogshead's suggestions for breaking the bad news are worth consideration by all of us, not just physicians. Also presented were illustrations of the way in which a poor attitudinal climate can threaten communication over time. Whatever improves self-respect, reduces fear, and encourages open communication in general is likely to have a positive impact on death-related communication as well. A few other suggestions will now be made with the aim of encouraging your own thoughts and observations rather than simply providing a textbook list.

First, *be alert to symbolic and indirect communications*. The following three examples are among those worth attention:

1. *Sharing dreams.* Some psychologists and psychiatrists (Greenberg & Blank, 1970) have come to the conclusion that people may prepare themselves for dying and death through their

dream work before conscious thoughts and direct interpersonal communications occur. A recent pilot study by Frederick L. Coolidge and Cynthia E. Fish (1983–1984) found a number of differences between dreams reported by terminally ill cancer patients and those of healthy older people. Among these differences was a greater frequency of death content in dreams, but it was usually somebody else who was dead in the dream. The dreamer often attempted to discover who was dead:

> I dreamt of a funeral and in the funeral was a little girl going to be buried. In her coffin I couldn't get to her so I tried to open it to see who it was and it was one of my daughters. Little Antonette. She was lying on her side and the lid was falling in the coffin . . . I went to fix the lid . . . I kept on doing things that would upset the coffin. I felt like a criminal that didn't belong there. (p. 3)

Some of the other dream characteristics of dying people were even more subtle. There was, for example, a tendency for their dreams to show more aggression, as Coolidge and Fish note:

> Although . . . aggression is not unique to the dreams of the dying, aggression may still serve as an ego-defense for dealing with death. It is hypothesized that when the dreamer is the object of the aggression, the dreamer might be comparing the dying experience to an act of aggression which is committed against the dreamer. When the dreamer is the source of the aggression, it is possible that the person is displacing aggressive feelings created by dying onto other characters or objects in the dream (pp. 4–5)

Listening to each other's dreams is generally a valuable way to supplement and enrich interpersonal communication.

2. *Symbolic language.* While dreams provide a treasury of symbolic language and actions, such characteristics can also appear in everyday speech. Following is an example that came to our attention during a research project (Weisman & Kastenbaum, 1968):

> The 75-year-old former stonemason had lost some of the vigor he had shown earlier in his hospital stay, but otherwise appeared to be in stable condition and doing well. One morning he asked for directions to a cemetery near his former home. Although he made the direct statement that he was expecting the undertaker, this was not taken up by the staff as a clue to impending death. It was just a statement that didn't make much sense. The next day, he told several people that his boss (going back many years, in reality) had called for him; he was supposed to help dig graves for eight people. The delusion now became persistent. He insisted on staying around the ward so he could be available to the people who would come to take him to the cemetery.
>
> Two days before he died, the patient had several teeth extracted (a procedure that was seen as having little risk because of his good condition). He then told staff that it was time to call his sisters—about whom he had never before said a word. His death came as a surprise to the staff although, apparently, not to himself. Cause of death was determined to be cerebral thrombosis. Despite all the clues this man had given, no notice had been taken. His "crazy talk" seemed even less crazy when a subsequent review indicated that the old stonemason had outlived seven siblings—his reference to digging a grave for eight people no longer seemed so arbitrary.

After a number of experiences such as this one, both our clinical and research staffs markedly improved their ability to identify patients whose death was more imminent than might have been expected and learned to pay close attention to what was said, whether in direct or symbolic language.

3. *Leave-taking actions.* Deeds as well as words can help to express the needs and intentions of people who are close to the end of their lives. My colleagues and I in both institutional and community settings have observed such behaviors as giving away small but prized possessions; sorting through possessions, organizing some and throwing others away; creating the occasion for one last interaction of a familiar kind, such as playing checkers or going fishing together; terminating mutual obligations and expectations (e.g., "Thanks for the loan of the bowling ball. I won't be needing it any more").

Most people who are aware of their terminal illness do hope to have the opportunity to bid farewell to the important people in their lives—

but not necessarily all in the same way (Kelleher & Lewin, 1988–1989). It is wise to take our cue from the dying person rather than impose a particular kind of farewell scene that happens to appeal to us.

As shown in the three examples, increasing our awareness of dreams, symbolic language, and leave-taking actions can make it easier for the dying person to convey messages that might not lend themselves as well to direct verbal expression. It also gives us more opportunity to express our own thoughts and feelings in return.

Second, *help to make competent and effective behavior possible.* Illness, fatigue, and reduced mobility make it difficult to continue functioning as a competent person. This is true whether or not the individual is suffering from a terminal condition. The progressive nature of terminal illness, however, tends to increase the individual's dependency on others and limits the range of spontaneous action. As Chapter 5 illustrates, the person attempting to cope with terminal illness often retains a strong need to be competent, effective, and useful to others. Family, friends, and other caregivers cannot only improve communication but also help to support the dying person's sense of self-esteem by striking a balance between meeting the realistic needs associated with dependency and creating an environment in which the person can continue to exercise some initiative and control. Timely and appropriate support is needed, not a total takeover of the dying person's life. Attentive listening and observing are required to match the style, level, and intensity of care with the individual's physical condition and psychosocial needs. By accomplishing one side of the communication process—listening and observing—it becomes more probable that the patient can maintain a core of competent and effective behavior and continue to communicate needs and intentions.

Third, *recognize that the dying person sets the pace.* The pioneering clinician and researcher Edwin S. Shneidman (1978) reminds us

Nothing *has* to be accomplished. The patient sets the pace. This includes, even, whether or not the topic of death is ever mentioned, although, if permitted, it usually will be. . . . Different individuals get in touch with their illnesses at various points of candor. Any one of these points is equally good, so long as it is comfortable for that person. (p. 212)

Fourth, *do not confuse the dying person's values and goals with our own.* Communication can be distorted or broken off when others project their own needs on the dying person or expect their goals to be achieved. Requiring the dying person to move along from one stage to another imposes an unnecessary and often unrealistic burden on everybody in the situation, as does requiring the person "to die in a state of psychoanalytic grace," as Shneidman puts it. Our own expectations, needs, and fantasies about how a life should end can interfere with discovering what particular dying people themselves think, feel and need.

It is seldom easy to separate our own needs and expectations from those of the dying person. It requires the ability to monitor our own thoughts and feelings as they bubble up inside as well as a general self-understanding and sense of discipline. Those who enter the scene with fixed ideas of what the dying person needs and what should be done would be better advised to listen, observe, and learn. And there is hardly anything that will arouse the psychological defenses of the dying person and damage communication so effectively as the approach of somebody who has "all the right answers" (most probably to all the wrong questions).

INDIVIDUALITY AND UNIVERSALITY IN THE EXPERIENCE OF DYING

Does everybody die in essentially the same way? If so, then it should be possible to discover general laws or regularities upon which care and management can be based. Or does everybody die in a unique way, depending upon many different factors? We are more likely to be good observers and useful caregivers if we prepare ourselves to understand the specifics of every situation. This can be exemplified by a survey of some of the factors that influence the nature and experience of dying. You will recognize that each of these factors has relevance to *any* person who is on a dying trajectory, but that the particular relevance and significance of these factors varies considerably from individual to individual. The discussion begins, then, with respect for both universal factors and individual dimensions of dying.

Factors that Influence the Experience of Dying

Age

Age by itself is an empty variable that exercises no direct influence. Nevertheless, chronological age serves as an index for a variety of factors that can make a significant difference throughout life, including the process of dying.

Comprehension of dying and death. Our intellectual grasp of death is related both to the level of development we have achieved and to the nature and extent of life experiences (see Chapter 7 for more detail). At one extreme is the young child who is keenly sensitive to separation but who may not yet comprehend the finality and irreversibility of death. At the other extreme is an aged adult who not only recognizes the central facts of death but has seen many close friends and relations die through the years. The same experience will be a rather different experience for people with widely varying life histories and cognitive structures.

Opportunity to exercise control over the situation. Children have fewer enfranchised rights than adults in general. Even the latest "natural death" acts passed by state legislatures do not propose to strengthen the child's position as a decision maker. In coping with the many life changes associated with serious illness, the child and the adult differ in the amount of control that is theirs to exercise, a difference in "social instrumentality" that affects personal experience in many ways.

Perception and treatment by others. Perceived social value differs with age. In practice this can influence not only the quality of the dying process but even the possibility of recovering from life-threatening illness, as the following examples show.

A 92-year-old woman returned to the nursing home after her second operation for a broken hip. Although the surgery itself was successful, she developed an infection that led to shock and coma. While in the comatose state she also was afflicted by aspiration pneumonia. Until this illness the woman had been in good spirits. Family members had been affectionate, attentive, and patient with her.

With the onset of the comatose state, however, the physician withdrew all drugs, stopped all feeding processes, and advised the nursing staff to "do nothing." He further stated, "This patient is better off dead than alive. Let her alone." The nursing staff, however, had become devoted to this patient during her long stay in the institution and voiced dissent with being committed to a "do-nothing" program and having been designated without consultation, as the agent of the death process. (Miller, 1976, p. 161)

The director of the nursing staff managed to persuade the physician to permit a treatment program that would give the woman at least a chance for survival. With restorative nursing the woman recovered and participated successfully in a rehabilitative nursing program.

In another instance the family of a confused and pain-ridden 86-year-old woman changed its attitude toward her when she stopped eating, slumped down whether placed in a chair or on her feet, and became incontinent. She admitted, after much questioning, that she wished to die but was afraid of death. The family repeatedly urged the staff to let the woman die. "Why not let her go? Isn't she vegetating?" The attending physician did nothing to institute a treatment regime that might restore her health and spirits. But again the nursing director helped to turn the situation about, calling on the institution's medical policy committee to take action. Permission was finally granted for restorative nursing. Social workers discovered the patient's self-destructive tendencies and their probable causes. The woman was assured that she was alive and was going to be helped to stay alive. The family was also told by the social workers that:

> . . . The patient had a right to live and that she was entitled to all the services and skills at the command of the rehabilitation team. In addition, the family was informed forthrightly that the institution and its staff members had a clear commitment to maintain life and had no obligation to be the agents of death for the patient, family, or physician. (p. 162)

This patient also recovered, became ambulatory again, and regained control over her bodily functions.

The reporter of these cases, Michael B. Miller (1976), observes that it is easy to assume that elderly people are ready to die, especially those who are seriously ill or who express self-destructive tendencies. Stereotyped ideas about the elderly can become life-threatening when *sick* or *depressed* hastily become translated into *dying* or *hopeless* in the minds of those whom the elderly rely on for care.

Misperceptions often occur at the other extreme of the age range as well. (Weisman & Worden, 1975):

> It is quite remarkable that for a long time it was believed by the medical profession that infants did not experience pain to the same extent as adults, and even in my lifetime I remember operations, such as the removal of tonsils and circumcision, being done on children without the use of anesthetic. From the result of a study I did . . . on the treatment of leukaemic children in hospital, it was obvious that this mistaken idea was still with us. Changing of dressing, taking of bone marrow samples and the insertion of needles into the spine are procedures which often cause a great deal of pain to children and yet they are still done without adequate analgesia. In a modern hospital there is no excuse for any child to suffer pain from such diagnostic or therapeutic measures. (p. 56)

Gender

Gender is intimately related to personal identity. Both biological nature and societal sex roles influence our lives and the way we meet death. The dying person remains either a male or a female. This means, for example, that a man with cancer of the prostate may be concerned with the threat of becoming impotent as well as with the risk to his life (although in practice, timely diagnosis and treatment can sharply reduce both risks). Cervical cancer may disturb a woman not only because of the life risk but also because one of the treatment possibilities—hysterectomy—would leave her unable to become pregnant. Both the man and the woman described may be troubled about the future of their intimate relationships even if the threat to their lives is lifted.

Some people interpret physical trauma affecting their sexual organs as punishment for real or imagined transgressions. Others become preoccupied with their physical condition in a way that interferes with affectionate and sexual relationships. "I'm no good anymore" may be a self-tormenting thought for either the man or the woman, each experiencing this in his or her own way. Even if the treatment is completely successful, there will have been a period during which concern about death was intensified by doubts as to the individual's intactness as a sexual being. These are not the only types of reactions that people express to cancer of the reproductive system; these simply illustrate some of the interactions between sex role and disease.

Serious illness of any type may pose different threats to men and women. This is most readily seen in families that operate within the traditional sex-role patterns of Western society: the husband goes off to work, the wife stays home and looks after children and home. Although important changes are occurring in sex-role patterns, it is useful to begin with the traditional pattern.

When the woman is faced with a life-threatening illness, she is likely to have concerns about the integrity and well-being of the family. Will the children eat well? Can her husband manage the household? What most troubles the woman-wife-mother may be the fate of her family more than her own.

The man-husband-father in this traditional family is likely to have distinctive concerns of his own. Has the illness destroyed his career prospects? Will he lose his job or his chance for advancement even if he makes a good recovery? Has he provided well enough for his family in case he doesn't pull through? Is he, in effect, a "good man" if he cannot work and bring in the money? There may be a crisis in self-esteem if he is confined to hospital or home for a protracted time, away from the work situations that support his sense of identity.

Gender differences in the dying patients may be important from the standpoint of professional caregivers as well as the patient. Direct care to the dying person is usually provided by women, often registered nurses, licensed practical nurses, or aides. Responsibility for the total care plan, however, is often in the hands of a male physician. The physician may be more time conscious and achievement oriented, characteristics that favor survival of the rigors of medical training. He may therefore be more persistent in cure-oriented treatments but also quicker to withdraw when death is in prospect. The nurse may be more sensitive to the patient's relationship with significant people in his life and less apt to regard impending death as a failure.

Changing patterns of sex roles in Western society can show up in adaptation to terminal illness. When one marital partner is disabled, the other may have more experience in the ailing one's sphere of responsibility and be better able to maintain the integrity of the family. It is more likely now than in past years, for example, that the wife is also a wage earner and familiar with financial management. Similarly, the husband of today may have had more time with the children and more responsibility for running the household than in the past. Furthermore, the healthy one may be more attuned to the needs and con-

cerns of the sick partner because there has been more commonality in their experiences.

It is likely that there will be many other effects of changing sex-roles on the management of terminal illness. For example:

- As more women enter or reenter the work force, the number of people available to serve as formal volunteers or informal helpers may decline—it remains to be seen whether the perceptible increase in male volunteers will compensate for the reduction in female volunteers. In addition to career-oriented interests, economic pressures for two paychecks in the family have prevented some women from giving time as volunteers in the terminal care situation.
- The traditional emphasis on home and family is being replaced for some women by career-related interests. The career-dominated single adult of either gender, for example, might be expected to have somewhat different concerns when facing death without spouse or children to worry about or to provide support for. Actually, however, almost nothing has yet been learned about possible differences in concerns, values, and feelings among terminally ill people whose life-styles diverge from what had formally been most normative in American society.
- Changing life-styles may be resulting in changing probabilities of death by various modalities. One of the clearest examples is the increased cigarette smoking by American women throughout the 20th century, with a resultant rise in related illnesses and fatality. The death rate from lung cancer among women has risen 239% over the past decade (Rubin, 1983). Certain pathways to death may become more frequent and others less frequent as both women and men move beyond traditional gender-linked life-styles.

Interpersonal Relationships

Interpersonal relationships are of great importance in the terminal phase of life. This is illustrated in a careful psychosocial study by Avery D. Weisman and J. William Worden

(1975). The investigators sought out patients who were likely to die within a short time (35 of the 46 patients did die one month to one year after entering the study). Weisman and Worden devised a *Survival Quotient* (SQ) to help determine if the quality of interpersonal relationships might be related to length of survival.

$$SQ = \frac{\text{Observed survival} - \text{Expected survival}}{\text{Standard error of estimated survival}}$$

This quotient was based on information collected on a much larger number of patients in Massachusetts by a tumor registry service. How long a particular person survived could be related to the average length of survival for the particular form of the illness as well as the patient's age and sex, type of treatments received, and so on.

One of the key findings was that patients who maintained active and mutually responsive relationships survived longer than those who brought poor social relationships with them into the terminal phase of life. Early separation from one or both parents during the patient's childhood and adolescence was associated with a shorter survival period. The patients who died rapidly also tended to have fewer friends, more distant relationships with their families, and more ambivalent relationships with colleagues and associates. Clearly, the quality of interpersonal relationships was one of the major differences between people who survived for long and short periods with the same type of terminal condition. Those who survive longer would sometimes express resentment and anger about their situation but are able to maintain intimacy with family and friends until the very last. "They ask for and receive much medical and emotional support. . . . They may be afraid of dying alone and untended, so they refuse to let others pull away without taking care of their needs" (p. 71). By contrast, those who die more rapidly "often talk about repeated mutually destructive relationships with people through the years. . . . Now, when treatment fails, depression deepens, and they become highly pessimistic about their progress.

They want to die—a finding that often reflects more conflict than acceptance."

In a subsequent report (Weisman & Worden, 1976) the same investigators observed that interpersonal difficulties were more frequent among those terminally ill patients who were experiencing the most distress. Not only the length of survival, then, but the quality of life was associated with the kind of interpersonal relationships enjoyed or suffered by the patient. To understand the experiences of the dying person, we must appreciate both the types of interpersonal relationships that have been developed through the years and the quality of these relationships in the immediate situation.

Disease, Treatment, and Environment

Disease, treatment, and environment together comprise another set of critical influences on the experience of dying. A person does not *just* die. A person dies *of something*—or of many things. And he or she dies in a particular place whose characteristics contribute to comfort, to misery, or to both. Similarly, the nature of the treatment also deserves consideration. Discussions of the dying process sometimes become so abstract and generalized that we neglect the specific medical problems involved. Think, for example, of the difference between a person whose likely cause of death will be kidney failure and its complications and a person suffering severe threats to respiratory function (perhaps a coal or uranium miner). The person with kidney failure may fade away as waste products accumulate in the body. Over time, she may become more lethargic and less able to sustain attention and intention. There may, however, be intermittent periods of better functioning when the patient seems more like her old self. The final hours or days may be spent in a comatose condition. (This is not the only possible sequence of experience with kidney failure, but it is a typical one.)

By contrast, a degenerative respiratory condition is apt to produce more alarming symptoms and experiences. Perhaps you have seen a person with advanced emphysema struggle for breath.

An episode of acute respiratory failure is frightening to the individual himself and likely to arouse the anxiety of those around him. Once a person has experienced this kind of distress, it is difficult to avoid apprehension about future episodes.

Some conditions are accompanied by persistent pain and discomfort unless very carefully managed. Other conditions can reach peaks of agony that test the limits both of the individual and the state of medical comfort giving. Nausea, weakness, and a more generalized sense of ill-being may be more dominant than pain for some terminally ill people. It is difficult to be serene when wracked by vomiting or diarrhea. All the possible symptoms of all the possible pathways of terminal decline need not be catalogued here. But the friend, relative, caregiver, and researcher should appreciate that the particular person is not dying in an abstract sense; there are specific impairments and symptoms that directly affect mood and thought.

Furthermore, different types of treatment may be carried out for the same condition, depending on characteristics of the patient and the hospital. Unfortunately, even today these can still include less adequate care for members of racial minorities and other disadvantaged groups (Barton, et al., 1979). State-of-the-art care, however, can also introduce its own problems. Some of the more advanced forms of treatment today use an environment specially designed for its freedom from possible contamination—a biologically nonliving environment. This is done, for example, when the patient has lost immune defenses and could not ward off even minor infections. Isolation as part of treatment is still isolation. At a time when the individual is much in need of support, interaction, and familiar faces, every effort is made to keep him or her in a sterile situation. In medical settings where the most advanced procedures are not available, the patient with the same condition may experience life rather differently. Note also that whether or not isolation and some other forms of heroic treatment are employed depends in part on how the person is defined by the physician in charge: "life-threatened," therefore requiring every action that might forestall death, or "dying," therefore requiring comfort-giving measures rather than aggressive medical practices.

It also makes a difference whether a person is suffering from a condition for which a standard regime has been well established or for which experimental treatments dominate. The fact that a treatment is experimental often means that the patient's life is controlled down to the smallest detail to permit careful evaluation of the results. The following instructions for patients were posted on a metabolic research ward (Fox, 1959):

> Patient can eat only what is given on his tray. Absolutely nothing else. He must eat every crumb of food on his diet, every grain of measured salt, if any, every bit of butter, sugar, bread, etc.
>
> Patient is to drink only the distilled water which is given to him in his carafe. He is not to drink water from the faucet or fountain.
>
> Repeat. Repeat. Repeat. Patient may have no candy, cake, fruit, soda or chewing gum which visitors might bring in. Only foods on the diet may be eaten.
>
> Patient may not use regular toothpaste because it contains calcium.
>
> Each patient has his own urinal and bedpan in the utility room marked with his name. . . . Remind patients to empty bladder when voiding. Urinal should be left on shelf in utility room with tag noting patient's name and time of voiding.
>
> **Special time for voiding:**
>
> a. Between 6–7 AM to complete 24-hour collection
> b. Between 9:30–10:30 PM (going to bed)
> c. Before defecating
> d. Before going to bath
> e. Before going off the ward for any reason
>
> **Procedure for defecating**
>
> a. Ambulatory patients void, then place a white enamel stool inside the commode. Can and lid are left on shelf in utility room and tagged with patient's name and time of defecation.

b. Bed patients void in urinal, then defecate in separate bedpan which has been lined with 2 layers of wax paper. (pp. 122–123)

This entire list has been reprinted to convey the extraordinary degree of control that may be exercised over a person's life for purposes of treatment and research. The individual would hardly dream up this kind of regimen if he or she were resolved to live out the final days in a manner consistent with previous personality and values. The example given here is fairly extreme but not altogether uncommon. It exemplifies a frequent trade-off—the person with a life-threatening illness surrenders options and control over much of his or her existence to receive the possible benefits of medical advances or to contribute to the eventual development of successful treatments.

The interactions among disease, treatment, and environment have been barely touched on here, but perhaps enough has been conveyed to call into question the lingering image of dying as either an abstract, generalized process or a brief dramatic episode.

Do We Die in Stages?

Two theoretical models of the dying process have been especially influential—although seldom to the same people. There is a basic similarity between these theories: both regard dying as a sequence of psychological or spiritual stages.

A Buddhist Perspective

The dying process has been given particularly close attention in the Buddhist tradition. Although some individuals in the Judeo-Christian tradition have meditated and commented on the dying process, it is in Buddhism that we find a systematic and detailed theoretical model. (Religious texts, of course, do not present their conceptions in the form of theoretical models, but we take the standpoint here of interested observers rather than faithful believers.)

His Holiness Tenzin Gyatso, the fourteenth Dalai Lama, has recently reviewed and commented on the Buddhist view of the dying process (1985). Long before contemporary studies of trajectories, Buddhists were well aware of individual differences in the way people die. A person might be killed instantly in an accident, or might have outlived his or her mental powers through a long period of decline. In such situations, there is no opportunity to progress through the stages. Furthermore, some people are anxious and beset by emotional conflict as death nears. For these people also, the transition from life to death is not likely to proceed through the stages of spiritual enlightenment. Buddhism does *not* assert that *all* people move through the stages as they die. One must have some time and be in a state of mind that is conducive to spiritual development. Those who have developed spiritual discipline throughout their lives are more likely to experience the entire cycle of stages.

For Buddhists, the relationship between mind and body is quite complex, involving "coarse," "subtle," and "very subtle" connections. At death, the coarse connections between mind and body are severed—but the very subtle connections continue. There is also a broad philosophical conception that is characteristic of Buddhism and which becomes especially significant as death approaches. As the Dalai Lama expresses it: ". . . when you are able to keep impermanence in mind—seeing that the very nature of things is that they disintegrate—most likely you will not be greatly shocked by death when it actually comes" (p. 170). The thoughtful Buddhist will have recognized that change and disintegration are inherent in the universe and that one's own death is a certainty. Therefore, it is wise to meditate on death and impermanence throughout one's life and to bring one's best qualities of mind and spirit to the dying process: "No matter what has happened in terms of good and bad within this particular lifetime, what happens right around the time of death is particularly powerful. Therefore, it is important to learn about the process of dying and prepare for it."

There are eight stages in the Buddhist journey toward death. Perhaps our first surprise is that these stages also occur in ordinary daily life as well. "In more subtle form, the eight transpire each time one goes in or out of sleep or dream, sneezes, faints, or has an orgasm" (p. 98). Only the sensitive and disciplined person is aware of these subtle forms of dying that occur in everyday life.

What are the fundamental changes that occur as one moves from the first to the final stage of dying?

Stage 1. Eyesight dims, but one begins to have mirage-like visions.

Stage 2. Hearing diminishes. There is a new internal vision: of smoke.

Stage 3. The sense of smell disappears, and there is now an internal vision "likened to fireflies in smoke." The dying person is no longer mindful of other people.

Stage 4. Sensation is lost from the tongue and the body. The dying person is no longer mindful of his or her own concerns. Breathing ceases. (At this point the person would be considered dead by a Western physician, but not so to the Buddhist.)

Stage 5. The first of the pure visionary stages. White moonlight is perceived.

Stage 6. Visions of red sunlight.

Stage 7. Visions of darkness. The dying person faints, and then awakens into the final stage.

Stage 8. **The clear light of death.** This unique state of consciousness persists until death.

The Buddhist stages, then, all focus on the experiential state or phenomenology of the dying person, and are divided equally into those that occur while the person is still alive by ordinary standards and those that occur when the person would appear to be dead to most observers.

This theoretical model of dying served as a guide to Buddhists for many centuries before the current death-awareness movement arose in Western society. (There is also a somewhat less elaborate stage theory of dying within the Islamic tradition [Kramer, 1988].) We turn now to the stage theory that, in recent years, has become most familiar to readers in the Americas and Western Europe.

The Five Stages

Five stages of dying were introduced by Elizabeth Kubler-Ross in her book *On Death and Dying* (1969). These stages are said to begin when the individual becomes aware of his or her terminal condition. The stages are presented as normal, or nonpathological, ways of responding to the prospect of death and the miseries of dying. The patient begins with a stage known as *denial* and moves through the remaining stages of *anger, bargaining, depression,* and *acceptance.* Some people do not make it all the way to acceptance. A person may become arrested at any stage along the way; furthermore, there can be some slipping back and forth between stages, and each individual has a distinctive tempo of movement through the stages. This conceptualization, then, emphasizes a universal process that allows for a certain amount of individual variation.

Stage 1. Denial is the first response to the bad news. "No, not me, it can't be true!" is the typical feeling that is communicated. The denial stage can be expressed in many ways, a reaction that is fueled by anxiety and usually runs its course in a short time. It could also be described as a "state of shock from which he recuperates gradually" (p. 37).

Stage 2. Anger wells up and may boil over after the initial shock and denial response has passed. "Why *me?*" is the characteristic feeling at this time. Rage and resentment can be expressed in many directions—God not excluded. The patient is likely to become more difficult to relate to at this time because of the struggle with frustration and fury.

Stage 3. Bargaining is said to be the middle stage. The dying person attempts to make some kind of deal with fate. He or she may ask for an extension of life, just long enough, say, to see a child graduate from high school or get married. The bargaining process may go on between the patient and caregivers, friends, or family or with God.

Stage 4. Depression eventually follows as the person experiences increasing weakness, discomfort, and physical deterioration. The person can see that he or she is not getting better. The symptoms are too obvious to ignore. Along with stress, strain, and feelings of guilt and unworthiness there may be explicit fear of dying at this stage. The person becomes less responsive and his or her thoughts and feelings are pervaded by a sense of great loss.

Stage 5. Acceptance, the final stage, represents the end of the struggle. The patient is letting go. Despite the name, it is not necessarily a happy or blissful state. "It is almost void of feelings. It is as if the pain had gone, the struggle is over, and there comes a time for 'the final rest before the long journey' as one patient phrased it" (p. 100).

Interwoven through all five stages is the strand of *hope.* Realistic acknowledgment of impending death may suddenly give way to hope for a miraculous recovery. Subtle though its expression may be, hope flickers back now and then throughout the whole sequence.

In addition to describing these stages Kubler-Ross indicates some of the typical problems that arise at each point and suggests ways of approaching them. She emphasizes, for example, the need to understand and tolerate the patient's anger during the second stage rather than to retaliate and punish him or her for it.

Evaluating the Stage Theory

The first set of points presented here concentrate on shortcomings of the stage theory; this is followed by observations that are more supportive of the theory.

First, *the existence of the stages as such has not been demonstrated.* This fact has remained constant through the years. There is no clear evidence for the establishment of stages in general, for the stages being five in number, or for the stages to be those specified. Dying people sometimes do use denial, become angry, try to bargain with fate, or lapse into depression or a depleted, beyond-the-struggle way of being. However, the reality of these moods or response sets has noth-

ing necessarily to do with stages. Dying people have many other moods and responses as well, such as expressions of the need to *control* what is happening or to *preserve a continuity* between themselves and those who survive them. These are just two of the many other dynamics that can be observed among dying people. Which dynamics are powerful and universal enough to be fixed as stages? What criteria and evidence should be used? Neither Kubler-Ross nor any subsequent observer has refined the stages clearly and completely and carried out competent research to test the theory. The available research (Metzger, 1979; Schulz & Aderman, 1974) does not support stage theory, and outstanding clinicians (Feigenberg, 1977; Shneidman, 1978) have found the five stages to be an inadequate model.

Second, *no evidence has been presented that people actually do move from Stage 1 through Stage 5.* In the original book examples of behavior said to comprise stages are given in the form of brief clinical descriptions involving various patients. But evidence that the *same* person goes through all the stages was not offered then and still has not been offered 20 years later. Clinical observations could be analyzed to evaluate the possibility of stages, but the theory won acceptance and continues to have its adherents despite the lack of data. This casual attitude regarding the factual basis of a theory suggests that it meets social or emotional needs very well indeed.

Third, *the limitations of the method have not been acknowledged.* The conclusion that there are five stages in the terminal process was based on psychiatric-type interviews conducted by one person and interpreted by the same person. This is a reasonable way to gather information, gain insights, and develop hypotheses to be tested within the structure of a formal research project—a potentially useful beginning. However, the research effort never moved past this beginning, and the inherent flaws and limitations of such an approach were never transcended. The interview method necessarily relies much on the particular experience, personality, and purpose of the interviewer and the type of relationship formed with the interviewee. The step from observation to interpretation is a critical one, but neither the basic observations nor the process of interpretation have been checked against the judgment of other qualified people. Furthermore, what the dying person says and does in the presence of a psychiatrist is only a small and highly selective sample of his or her behavior. The nurse who cares regularly for the patient's physical functioning often sees important aspects of the total functioning that do not show up in an interview, and the same may be said of the physician in charge and family members and friends. Behavioral studies might reveal a different perspective, as might a diary kept by the patient. In other words, one valuable but limited source of information about the experiences and needs of the dying patient has taken the place of extensive, multilevel, cross-validated approaches. Conclusions have been widely accepted without concern for the obvious limitations of methodology used for obtaining and analyzing the data. This would not be an acceptable practice in any other area of research and is not sound practice here.

Fourth, *the line is blurred between description and prescription.* Stage theories in general often fail to distinguish clearly between what happens and what *should* happen. Once a stage framework has been established, it is typical for people to attach positive values to timely movement from one stage to the next. Protests from Jean Piaget did not prevent some educators and developmentalists from devising programs to speed up the child's maturation. Kubler-Ross also has cautioned against trying to rush a patient through the stages. But the impulse often can be observed among caregivers or family who are acquainted with the basic idea of the stages. People may draw the implication that the patient should be moving "on schedule" from denial right through to acceptance, and that it is a mark of failure for everyone concerned if the timing is off. This expectation adds unnecessary pressure to the situation and enshrines the image of acceptance as the universally desired outcome of the dying person's ordeal. The concept of universal stages

lends itself to misuse by those who find their tasks simplified and anxieties reduced through a standardized approach to the dying person.

Fifth, *the totality of the person's life is neglected in favor of the supposed stages of dying.* The stage theory has tended to make the dying person seem very special. This has its positive aspects, yet it also engenders an attitude of hedging our relationships with the dying person around rules and expectations that are presumably specific to his or her situation. The supposed universality of the stages sometimes leads to the dying person being treated as a kind of specimen moving along predetermined paths rather than as a complete human being with a distinctive identity. But each dying individual is male or female, of one ethnic background or another, and at a particular point in his or her life. The nature of the disease, its symptoms, and its treatment can all have a profound effect on what the dying person experiences. Perhaps most important of all, *who the person is* deserves prime consideration in this situation as in any other. Even if the stage theory were clarified and proved, it is unlikely that it would account for nearly as much of the dying person's experience as has been widely assumed. We take the entire course of our lives with us into the final months and weeks. Emphasis on the still hypothetical stages of reaction to terminal illness tends to drain away individuality or at least our perception of it.

Finally, *the resources, pressures, and characteristics of the immediate environment can also make a tremendous difference.* There are still medical environments in which almost everybody denies death almost all of the time. There is abundant evidence, for example, that many physicians have difficulty in "breaking the bad news" to terminally ill patients (Benoleil, 1987–1988; Taylor, 1988). Some physicians give false or misleadingly incomplete information and then justify this deception to themselves with the assumption that they are doing it for the good of the patient. Nurses often characterize such physicians as "dancing around," referring to both their verbal and physical avoidance of encounters with a dying patient.

When the terminally ill person denies, it may be primarily an act of conformity to the implicit social rules of the situation rather than a manifestation of either individual personality or the hypothetical sequence of stages. Note that the same terminally ill person might respond quite differently in an Amish community or a hospice program (Chapter 5). Too much has been learned about environmental dynamics for us to treat these in a simple or neglectful manner when considering the experiences of the terminally ill person.

Nevertheless, several valuable contributions of Kubler-Ross' approach, including the stage theory, should be kept in mind.

The value of Kubler-Ross' work in awakening society's sensitivity to the needs of the dying person has not been called into question. Accepting the stage theory is not essential for appreciation of many of her useful observations and insights. Furthermore, it is not necessary that the stage theory be accepted or rejected in all its particulars. Careful and appropriate research is still welcome.

Some of the practical problems that have arisen in the wake of Kubler-Ross' presentations should be attributed to their hasty and uncritical application by others. With more death education courses now available and a growth of public awareness and sophistication in general, her work may receive more appropriate applications.

In summary, the need for a guide to the plight of the dying person—and the need to keep our own anxieties under control—led to a premature acceptance of the Kubler-Ross conceptualization as well as to simplistic and overly rigid uses of her observations. These range from the dismissal of a patient's legitimate complaints about poor treatment as "Just what you would expect in Stage 2" to the assumption that further research is not really important because the stages tell all. At the very least, however, the timely and charismatic presentations of Kubler-Ross have done much to heighten awareness of the dying person and his or her needs, making it possible for the dialogue to begin.

BOX 4–2
MY LAST DAYS OF LIFE

A Thought Exercise

The following questions were included in the National Hospice Demonstration Study (in a slightly different form). In the next chapter you will learn how terminally ill people responded to these questions and some of the implications for hospice care.

Now imagine yourself nearing the end of your life and give the answers that best describe your own thoughts and feelings. Write your answers on a separate piece of paper.

1. Describe the last three days of your life as you would like them to be. Include whatever aspects of the situation seem to be of greatest importance.

2. What will be your greatest sources of strength and support during these last days of your life?

Your Deathbed Scene

Perhaps you took a crack at the deathbed scene exercise suggested earlier in this chapter. Here is some information on the way that other people enrolled in death-related classes have depicted their own deaths (Kastenbaum & Normand, 1990). The typical respondent

- Expected to die in old age
- At home
- Quickly
- With the companionship of loved ones
- While remaining alert and
- Not experiencing pain or any other symptoms

What was the most common alternative response? Those who did not expect to die in the manner summarized above instead saw themselves as perishing in an accident, usually on the highway and while they were still young. In fact, those who thought their lives would end in a fatal accident tended to expect these accidents to occur in the near future. Almost all thought they would be alert and experience no pain or other symptoms as they neared death, whether death happened at home in old age or on the road in youth.

These deathbed scene expectations by mostly young college students will take on more meaning when we continue our exploration of the dying process in the next chapter with the focus on hospice care. You can enhance the personal meaning of the next chapter by pausing to answer the questions raised in Box 4–2, p. 103.

REFERENCES

Barton, S. N., Coombs, D. W., & Zakanycz, J. P. (1979). Rural cancer death. In J. Tache, H. Selye, & S. B. Day (Eds.), *Cancer, stress, and death* (pp. 146–160). New York: Plenum Medical Book Co.

Benoleil, J. Q. (1987–1988). Health care providers and dying patients: Critical issues in terminal care. *Omega, Journal of Death and Dying, 18,* 341–364.

Bowers, M., Jackson, E., Knight, J., & LeShan, L. (1964). *Counseling the dying.* New York: Thomas Nelson & Sons.

Coolidge, F. L., & Fish, C. E. (1983–1984). Dreams of the dying. *Omega, Journal of Death and Dying, 14,* 1–8.

Feigenberg, L. (1977). *Terminalvard.* Lund: Liber Laromedel.

Fox, R. C. (1959). *Experiment perilous.* Glencoe, Ill.: The Free Press.

Glaser, B. G., & Strauss, A. (1966). *Awareness of dying.* Chicago: Aldine Publishing Co.

Glaser, B. G., & Strauss, A. (1968). *Time for dying.* Chicago: Aldine Publishing Co.

Greenberg, H. R., & Blank, H. R. (1970). Dreams of a dying patient. *British Journal of Medical Psychology, 43,* 355–362.

Gyatos, Tenzin, the 14th Dalai Lama (1985). *Kindness, clarity, and insight.* (J. Hopkins Trans.) Ithaca: Snow Lions Productions.

Hart, K. (1986–1987). Stress encountered by significant others of cancer patients receiving chemotherapy. *Omega, Journal of Death and Dying, 17,* 151–168.

Hayflick, L. (1984). When does aging begin? *Research on Aging, 6,* 99–104.

Hogshead, H. P. (1978). The art of delivering bad news. In C. Garfield (Ed.), *Psychosocial care of the dying patient* (pp. 128–132). New York: McGraw-Hill Book Co.

Kastenbaum, R. (1960). Multiple perspectives on a geriatric "Death Valley." *Community Mental Health Journal, 22,* 456–466.

Kastenbaum, R. (1978). In control. In C. Garfield (Ed.), *Psychosocial care of the dying patient* (pp. 227–244). New York: McGraw-Hill Book Co.

Kastenbaum, R. (1983). Can the clinical milieu be therapeutic? In G. D. Rowles & R. J. Ohta (Eds.), *Aging and milieu* (pp. 3–16). New York: Academic Press, Inc.

Kastenbaum, R. (1984). When aging begins: A lifespan developmental approach. *Research in Aging, 6,* 105–118.

Kastenbaum, R., Barber, T., Wilson, S., Ryder, B., & Hathway, L. (1981). *Old, sick, and helpless.* Cambridge, Mass.: Ballinger Publishing Co.

Kastenbaum, R., & Normand, C. (1990). Deathbed scenes as expected by the young and experienced by the old. *Death Studies, 14,* 201–218.

Kelleher, A., & Lewin, T. (1988–1989). Farewells by the dying: A sociological study. *Omega, Journal of Death and Dying, 19,* 275–292.

Kramer, K. (1988). *The sacred art of dying.* New York: The Paulist Press.

Kubler-Ross, E. (1969). *On death and dying.* New York: Macmillan Publishing Co.

LeShan, L. (1982). Private communication.

Lesses, K. (1982–1983). How I live now. *Omega, Journal of Death and Dying, 13,* 75–78.

Metzger, A. M. (1979). A Q-methodological study of the Kubler-Ross stage theory. *Omega, Journal of Death and Dying, 10,* 291–302.

Miller, M. B. (1976). *The interdisciplinary role of the nursing home medical director.* Wakefield, Mass.: Contemporary Publishing, Inc.

Rubin, P. (1983). Statement of the clinical oncologic problem. In P. Rubin (Ed.), *Clinical oncology: A multidisciplinary approach* (6th ed.). Washington, D.C.: American Cancer Society, Inc.

Schulz, R., & Aderman, D. (1974). Clinical research and the stages of dying. *Omega, Journal of Death and Dying, 5,* 137–144.

Shneidman, E. S. (1978). Some aspects of psychotherapy with dying persons. In C. A. Garfield (Ed.), *Psychosocial care of the dying patient* (pp. 201–218). New York: McGraw-Hill Book Co.

Shneidman, E. S. (1980). *Voices of death.* New York: Harper & Row, Publishers, Inc.

Taylor, J. (1977). *Holy dying.* New York: Arno Press, Inc. (Original work published 1651)

Taylor, K. M. (1988). "Telling bad news": Physicians and the disclosure of undesirable information. *Sociology of Health & Illness, 10,* 109–131.

Weisman, A. D. (1972). *On death and denying.* New York: Behavioral Publications, Inc.

Weisman, A. D., & Kastenbaum, R. (1968). *The psychological autopsy: A study of the terminal phase of life.* New York: Behavioral Publications.

Weisman, A. D., & Worden, J. W. (1975). Psychosocial analysis of cancer deaths. *Omega, Journal of Death and Dying, 6,* 61–65.

Weisman, A. D., & Worden, J. W. (1976). The existential plight in cancer: Significance of the first 100 days. *International Journal of Psychiatry in Medicine, 7,* 1–16.

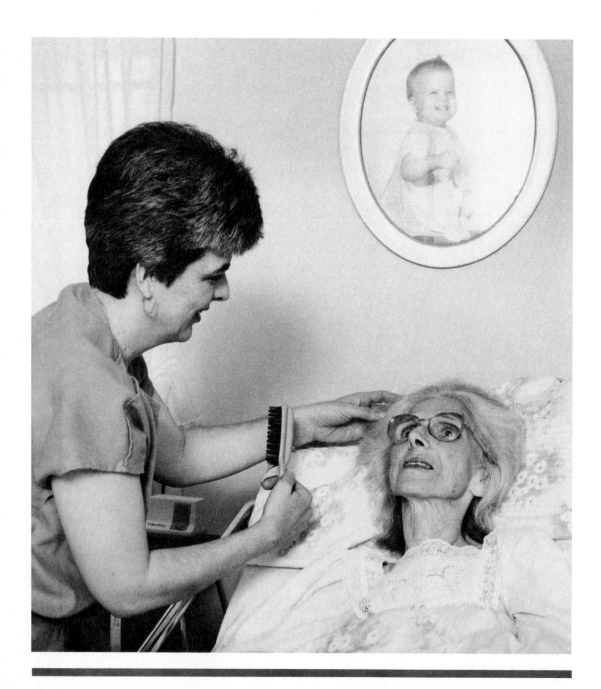

chapter 5

THE HOSPICE APPROACH TO
TERMINAL CARE

The American death system has made significant advances in the protection of life throughout the 20th century. Diseases such as tuberculosis, smallpox, and diphtheria had long been major threats to children and youth. One by one, major causes of debilitation and death have yielded to public health advances (i.e., in nutrition, sanitation, prenatal and postnatal care). Physicians became much more effective as they were given antibiotics and other new treatment techniques. The average life expectancy in the United States has increased by about a third during the 20th century (or, to put it a little differently, boys and girls born today are likely to live about 25 years longer than those who entered the world in 1900).

This remarkable increase in longevity has encouraged additional efforts to "defeat" death. The health care sciences organized themselves around the mission to prevent and cure all life-threatening illnesses. This has become a very expensive proposition as costs for diagnosis and treatment have skyrocketed with the development of new technologies and specialties. Furthermore, the focus on prevention and cure has had the unfortunate side-effect of neglecting the needs of the terminally ill person. Death has not been "defeated" after all by the "war" on illness. For all its energy and ingenuity in attempting to save jeopardized lives, the health-care establishment has shown relatively little skill or interest in caring for us as human beings when death is certain.

This is where hospice comes in. Although some wise and sensitive caregivers have been on the scene in every generation, it is only in the past few years that a systematic effort has been made to provide quality care for dying people and their families. In this chapter we will first examine the historical background of hospice care and how this approach was introduced to North America. We will then analyze the current state of hospice care, including its achievements, potential, and problems.

Hospice: A New Flowering from Ancient Roots

Temples of healing ministered to the psychological and physical ailments of the Greeks, and imperial Rome established hospitals for military personnel. You would probably recognize something of the modern bureaucratic style of organization in these early hospitals, and might be impressed by the holistic approach offered in the temples where music, positive imagery, bathing, massage, and walks in the countryside were all integral parts of the treatment plan. Neither the temple nor the hospital, however, was designed for the care of the dying person. The available information suggests that health care providers, then as now, were much more interested in working with those who had a chance of recovery.

And yet there is no reason to doubt that some compassionate people did provide comfort to the dying as best they could. It is likely that the earliest examples of hospice-type care did not leave documentary traces for the historian. Perhaps in the *ha-rem* of a Byzantine ruler there were women with special skill and sensitivity in caring for the dying; perhaps some wealthy families in Syria or Athens saw to it that the poor were treated well in their last days of life. The documentary trail becomes clearer with the advent of the Christian era. Public infirmaries (*nosocomeia*) were established in Greek-speaking areas of Christianity during the 4th century. These facilities provided care for those dying of epidemics as well as patients who were more likely to recover. Roman emperor Julian, an opponent of the upstart Christian movement, acknowledged that these hospices had made a very favorable impression on everybody "owing to the humanity evinced by Christians toward outsiders" (Phipps, 1988). He then resolved to establish his own hospices in every city although subsequent political events and his own death aborted this plan.

The hospice movement spread to western Europe near the end of the 4th century through the influence of Fabiola, a wealthy Roman widow who had been inspired by the care for the sick that she had witnessed in monasteries in the Holy Land (Phipps, 1988). Fabiola brought this concept back with her to Italy, not only supporting hospices financially but also serving as a nurse herself. St. Jerome knew Fabiola and honored her contributions, writing that "Often too she washed away the matter discharged from wounds which others, even though men, could not bear to behold . . . She gave food with her own hand and even when a patient was but a breathing corpse she would moisten his lips with liquid" (cited by Phipps, p. 93). And so Fabiola, this woman who lived and died about 1,600 years ago, may have given an enduring gift to humankind that in our own time has been renewed as the modern hospice.

The hospice became well established in the 5th century. Hospice derives from *hospitium*, a Latin term that has also given us such words as host and hostess. The medieval hospice was usually a house in which people in need could find food, shelter, and other comforts under Christian auspices. Those undertaking the arduous pilgrimage to the Holy Land and other travelers who were fatigued, ill, or dying would find welcome. Certain religious orders became especially known for their hospice care. Established by Benedictine monks in the 6th century, the Monte Cassino monastery was one of the most noted hospices—unfortunately this historic place was destroyed during World War II in a misguided military operation. Throughout the medieval period the hospice functioned as one of the purest expressions of Christian piety: here the hungry were fed, the thirsty given water, the naked clothed, the homeless sheltered, and the sick provided care and comfort. Medical treatment was minimal—probably just as well, considering how ineffective or even dangerous most "remedies" were at that time.

Obviously something went wrong between the time that the early hospices flourished and the time that the modern hospice movement started. In fact, during the intervening centuries the original hospice tradition clung to life in only a few scattered facilities. Phipps suggests that hospices became an innocent casualty of the Protestant Reformation and then were replaced by state-run institutions with different types of personnel and philosophies. Whatever the reasons, the religiously-oriented hospice and its mission of mercy for the dying faded away— although not completely—and bureaucratic, technology-oriented medicine took over the scene. Unfortunately, the newly emerging systems of health care took very little interest in dying people—now seen as disquieting reminders that "to all things there is a season."

The renewed hospice approach made its appearance in 1879 with the opening of Our Lady's Hospice in Dublin (Gilmore, 1989). Again, it was a woman who led the way, Sister Mary Aitkinhead. By 1905 a similar facility had been established in London, St. Joseph's Hospice. The hospice movement took its next major step forward when a medical officer at St. Joseph's Hospice began innovations in pain control for dying people. Dr. Cicely Saunders subsequently became the founder of St. Christopher's Hospice in London, which has served as an inspiration and model for many others. By the early 1970s it was clear that hospice care was a promising alternative to the "never-say-die," high-tech, impersonal approach increasingly dominant in Western medicine. Many questions and problems remained, however, including the establishment of standards of care and the challenge of establishing hospices in other nations, including the United States.

STANDARDS OF CARE FOR THE TERMINALLY ILL

Much and yet little had been accomplished by the time an international task force convened in 1975 to discuss issues in death and dying. The media had "discovered" death, largely through the charismatic efforts of Kubler-Ross, and many long-suppressed concerns were coming out into the open. Death education courses were starting to appear on some of the more adventurous American campuses, the clinical and research literature was becoming enriched with useful new contributions, and it was possible to find a hospital here or a support group there in which improved care for the terminally ill had become a priority. The hospice concept itself had become actualized in a few settings, most notably through Ciceley Saunder's leadership at St. Christopher's Hospice in London. Nevertheless, there was more talk than action. The International Work Group on Death and Dying (IWG) including Dr. Saunders and other pioneers existed (as it still does) but only as a forum, lacking the organizational and financial resources to establish new programs of care by direct means.

Despite these limitations, the IWG recognized that it had the opportunity to develop guidelines that might attract wider support. This is just what happened. Beatrice Kastenbaum and I led and summarized the sessions on standards of care. It was quickly agreed that no explicit standards of care existed in most places where people

passed their last months, weeks, days, and hours. The task force decided first to give expression to the *unwritten,* unofficial, but nevertheless quite influential assumptions and practices that governed the care of the terminally ill. As you read this list, please remember that these were *not* the standards that the task force intended to recommend—rather, it was our way of identifying the hidden standards that were implicit in the way that terminally ill people often were treated.

The items on the following list were seen as the typical pattern of a "good" or "successful" death from the perspective of the facility in which a terminally ill person spent his or her final days of life.

Hidden or Implicit Standards of Care

1. The successful death is quiet and uneventful. The death slips by with as little notice as possible; nobody is disturbed.
2. Few people are on the scene. There is, in effect, no scene. Staff is not required to adjust to the presence of family and other visitors who might have their own needs that would upset the well-routined equilibrium.
3. Leave-taking behavior is at a minimum.
4. The physician does not have to involve him- or herself intimately in terminal care, especially as the end approaches.
5. The staff makes few technical errors throughout the terminal care process and few mistakes in medical etiquette.
6. Strong emphasis is given to the body during the care-giving process. Little effort is wasted on the personality of the terminally ill individual.
7. The person dies at the right time, that is, after the full range of medical interventions has been tried out before the onset of an interminable period of lingering on.
8. The patient expresses gratitude for the excellent care received.
9. After the patient's death, the family expresses gratitude for the excellent care received.

10. The staff is able to conclude that "we did everything we could for this patient."
11. Physical remains of the patient are made available to the hospital for clinical, research, or administrative purposes (via autopsy permission or organ gifts).
12. A memorial (financial) gift is made to the hospital in the name of the deceased.
13. The total cost of the terminal care process is determined to have been low or moderate: money was not wasted on a person whose life was beyond saving (Kastenbaum, 1975).

The task force itself proposed a very different set of standards.

Proposed Standards Recommended by the International Task Force

- *Patients, family, and staff all have legitimate needs and interests.*
- *The terminally ill person's own preferences and life-style must be taken into account in all decision making.*

These were the two most general and basic guidelines from which the others were generated. The first proposition should help to promote honest interactions and reduce unnecessary conflicts and extremism of any type. Recognition that everybody in the situation is human and has legitimate needs and interests provides a valid starting point for care. The second proposition suggests that treatment should not be overly standardized. Each terminally ill individual's personality and life situation should be considered, even though this approach runs against the grain of medical system routine. The specific standards follow.

Patient-Oriented Standards

1. *Remission of symptoms is a treatment goal.* Terminal status, in other words, cannot be taken as a reason for neglect of medical or nursing efforts to reduce distressing symptoms. Even if it is expected that the person will die within hours or days, efforts should be continued to maintain functional capacity and relieve distress. A dying person should not be made to endure thirst, for example, or gasp for breath when a change of position might afford relief.

2. *Pain control is a treatment goal.* Although pain control is part of the larger task of symptom alleviation, it is specific and important enough to be counted as a standard in its own right. Uncontrolled pain not only intensifies the anguish of dying but also disturbs interpersonal relationships and can lead to demoralization. The patient's ability to maintain psychological equilibrium is severely tested by pain.

3. *The Living Will or similar document representing the patient's intentions will be respected as one of the determinants of the total pattern of care.* This does not mean that every expressed wish of the patient will automatically be granted. The rights and responsibilities of family, staff, and society as represented by the legal system, for example, must also be taken into account. The point is the willingness of family and health-care providers to take seriously any document that expresses the patient's own wishes, whatever their legal status as such might be. (See Chapter 11 for a detailed discussion of the living will.)

4. *The patient should have a sense of basic security and protection in his or her environment.* This standard is met when the dying person feels he or she can depend on the caregivers to perform their functions and maintain effective communication. The patient should feel *safe.* He or she should be able to count on the people responsible for care instead of living in apprehension of unexpected diagnostic or treatment procedures, brusque interactions, or breakdown in medication and meal routines. Most of all, the patient should feel safe emotionally, knowing that the people depended upon really do care.

5. *Opportunities should be provided for leave-takings with the people most important to the patient.* This requires flexible visiting hours and a more relaxed policy for admitting people who are often discriminated against by the rules (e.g., children). This standard also requires environmental adaptability for the needs of people who are see-

ing each other for perhaps the last time, such as a good place to sit, privacy, and freedom from interruption. The patient should also have the opportunity to take leave of other patients and staff members if desired.

6. *Opportunities should be provided for experiencing the final moments in a way that is meaningful to the patient.* For example, the patient should be afforded the opportunity to listen to music or poetry of his or her choice. Physical contact should be made possible if desired, unless there is some overwhelming contraindication (e.g., a highly contagious disease). This certainly includes a dying person being held in the arms of a spouse or other loved one if this is what they both want.

Family-Oriented Standards

1. *Families should have the opportunity to discuss dying, death, and related emotional needs with the staff.* It is not acceptable for the staff to disregard requests for information or expressions of the need to share feelings. Although this increases the time demands on staff, it helps the family maintain its own integration and thus to be of greater comfort to the patient.

2. *Family should have the opportunity for privacy with the dying person both while living and while newly dead.* This might include, in some family constellations, participation of close kin and friends in dressing the corpse and accompanying it to the funeral home. Or it might include simply being alone with the dead spouse, sibling, or parent for an hour or so without interruption by staff. Any automatic preparation and routing of the deceased for purposes of hospital convenience should give way to the family's need for opportunity to express their feelings in their own style and begin the difficult process of grief and recuperation.

Staff-Oriented Standards

1. *Caregivers should have adequate time to form and maintain personal relationships with the patient.* This is not a priority in most medical facilities. Implementation of this standard would require a new attitude toward the role responsibilities and

use of personnel. More attention might be given to the primary nursing system in which a particular staff member takes consistent responsibility for a particular patient. Better patient-staff relationships are desirable not only in themselves but also as a resource in treatment.

2. *A mutual support network should exist among the staff, encompassing both the technical and socioemotional dimensions of working with the terminally ill.* Care for the terminally ill can become a draining, depleting experience, especially in a situation in which there are frequent deaths. It is important that fellow workers be sensitive to each other's needs and limits and that they offer constructive suggestions and emotional support. Even the most humane and effective caregiver can lose perspective at a particular moment. The most buoyant spirit can require comfort and support from others. A medical facility in which there is little discussion of staff responses to care of the terminally ill and no place for the physician or nurse to turn with their own feelings would not be seen as functioning acceptably, despite whatever modern resources and skills the facility might offer.

ESTABLISHMENT OF HOSPICE PROGRAMS IN THE UNITED STATES

From Guidelines to Operational Programs

The standards proposed by the international task force have become well established in the hospice movement, as is evident from the following definition offered by the National Hospice Organization (NHO), created in 1978:

> A Hospice is a program of palliative and supportive services which provides physical, psychological, social, and spiritual care for dying persons and their families. Services are provided by a medically supervised interdisciplinary team of professionals and volunteers. Hospice services are available in both the home and an inpatient setting. Home care is provided on a part-time, intermittent, regularly

scheduled, and around-the-clock on-call basis. Bereavement services are available to the family. Admission to a Hospice program of care is on the basis of patient and family need. (Mor, 1987, p. 1)

This definition is typical in its (1) emphasis on care rather than cure, (2) support for family as well as patient, (3) inclusion of the home as a suitable environment, and (4) involvement of an interdisciplinary team including volunteers as well as professionals. The traditional medical-administrative model is replaced by a more flexible system in which many people make contributions.

The guidelines published both by NHO and the federal government (Health Care Financing Administration, 1983) capture the essence of the starting set of recommendations. Nevertheless, the hospice movement did not simply materialize from a list of proposed standards. Much effort was required from many individuals and agencies. Although the hospice principle had found its way into several existing health-care systems, it was the creation of the Connecticut Hospice in New Haven in 1974 that marked the first full-service program of its type in the United States. Like St. Christopher's, the Connecticut Hospice provides both inpatient and home-care services. Unlike St. Christopher's, however, the New Haven program started with home care and later added an inpatient facility when the National Cancer Institute agreed to provide start-up support. The founders of the Connecticut Hospice had to solve many organizational and financial problems that have also confronted most of the other programs that followed. The goals and methods of hospice care were often misunderstood; many physicians were reluctant to participate in the new approach, and secure sources of funding were difficult to find. It is a tribute to hospice leaders throughout the United States and to the flexibility of administrative and health-care agencies that significant progress has been made despite all the obstacles.

Today the Connecticut Hospice is far from alone. There are more than 1,700 in full or par-

tial operation. Hospice organizations take several forms in the United States and may even use different titles (e.g., palliative care unit). Some hospices are hospital-based; others are freestanding. St. Christopher's, the model for most hospice programs, was created as an independent organization, and this has set the pattern for most other hospices in Britain. In the United States economic considerations seem to have favored the hospital-based approach, if only because surplus hospital beds existed at the time that hospice care was introduced here (Russell, 1984). (This is but one more example of the way in which socioeconomic factors that have no direct relationship to death can exercise influence.) The hospice version might be interpreted somewhat differently within an existing medical facility than it is by an organization that was created specifically to care for terminally ill people and their families. (Some research bearing on differences between freestanding and hospital-based programs will be reviewed later in this chapter.)

Federal Standards for Hospice Care

Hospices also differ in the spectrum of services that are offered, and this difference has led to some problems and misunderstandings. At one extreme are those programs that limit themselves primarily to home visits in which a variety of comforting personal services are performed. A volunteer may take over for a few hours so the patient's family can attend to other responsibilities in addition to providing other simple but welcome services. It is unfortunate that this limited but helpful type of program is sometimes disparaged as mere "hand holding"—as though compassionate human contact were unimportant. Nevertheless, the friendly visiting type of program leaves much undone. It is the more comprehensive and the more professional and systematic type of hospice service that has won the support of the federal government. The National Hospice Reimbursement Act was enacted with a strong emphasis on the full-service and fully accountable hospice. In return for financial support a hospice must agree to such requirements as the following:

1. The hospice must have a *governing body* with clear authority and responsibility.
2. There must be a *medical director* with overall responsibility for patient care.
3. The hospice must ensure *continuity of care* and *professional management* at all times. (For example, if the patient transfers from home to hospital, the type of care provided at the hospital must be consistent with the agreed-upon hospice approach.)
4. A detailed *plan of care* must be established and maintained for each individual.
5. The hospice must *evaluate its quality of care and correct any problems that are identified.*
6. *The hospice must have an interdisciplinary team* including (at least) a physician, a registered nurse, a social worker, and a pastoral or other counselor.
7. The hospice must *comply with licensing regulations* in its state and locality.
8. Central *clinical records* must be maintained for each individual receiving hospice care.
9. The hospice must *provide all the core services* required by the individual.
10. *Additional services* must be provided as needed, including physical therapy, occupational therapy, speech-language pathology, home health aide and homemaker services, short-term inpatient care, and so on.
11. Essential hospice services must be available on a *24-hour, daily basis.*
12. An *in-service training program* must be in operation to maintain and improve the skills of staff and volunteers.

These are among the requirements laid down by the National Hospice Reimbursement Act. The government has insisted on the full-service model of hospice care and has built in many regulations (more than cited here) to see that the standards are met in practice.

Many hospice organizations that do offer the full range of services embodied in the legislation have *not* applied for reimbursement under the law. This nonparticipation is based primarily on concern that the reimbursement plan is not sufficient for survival of the hospice. A hospice can be of high quality and in compliance with the most essential features of the legislation and yet not be a participant in the current reimbursement program.

By the way, hospices have many expenses that are not reimbursed by the federal program. Many hospices conduct fund-raising programs and events and depend on community generosity to maintain their services.

For the patient, family, and physician alike it is important to become well acquainted with the local hospice services available. All should at least know whether partial or full services are offered. There are many other questions that can arise when deciding whether or not to select hospice care for a terminally ill person. Because of local differences in the nature and scope of hospice organizations and the possibility of continuing changes in national legislation and policy, you should discuss the current situation with representatives of the hospice organization(s) in your own area. You are almost certain to receive an attentive, frank, and useful response.

THE HOSPICE IN ACTION

Whether or not a particular hospice has enlisted in the national reimbursement program, it is likely to endorse the philosophy expressed in the legislation:

> Hospice care is an approach to treatment that recognizes that the impending death of an individual warrants a change in focus from curative care to palliative care. The goal of hospice care is to help terminally ill individuals continue life with minimal disruption in normal activities while remaining in the home environment. A hospice uses an interdisciplinary approach to deliver medical, social, psychological, emotional, and spiritual services through the use of a broad spectrum of professional and other caregivers with the goal of making the individual as physically and emotionally comfortable as

possible. (Health Care Financing Administration, 1983, p. 38146)

The following are a few examples of how a hospice actually works.

Entering St. Christopher's

The first example is an observation I had the opportunity to make during a visit to St. Christopher's.

> Word was received that a person was arriving for admission. A station wagon had just pulled up to an entrance facing the hospice's attractive garden plaza. The patient-to-be was a frail, emaciated woman who looked to be in her 60s. She was accompanied by a younger man. Dr. Saunders and the woman greeted each other as sunlight propitiously broke through the cloudy London skies. The woman smiled and said, "Well, I finally made it!" On her face there was the mark of physical ordeal but no indication of anxiety, anger, depression, or confusion. The patient was immediately introduced to the nurse who would be responsible for much of her care and then assisted to what would be her own bed (which had been transported by elevator to the ground-floor entrance). Just a few minutes later while touring the hospice we came on this woman again. She was already settled into her own place, sipping tea with the man who had driven her to the hospice. As it turned out, he was her husband. The woman was appreciably younger than her physical appearance had indicated because of the debilitating effects of advanced cancer.

This simple incident tells much about the aims and techniques of the hospice. The patient and her family had alread, een well acquainted with the hospice before time of admission. Consequently, there was a sense of having made the next logical stop on her journey through life rather than a jarring transition from home to an impersonal institution.

Much of St. Christopher's effort is devoted to a home-care program. This has become true of other hospices as well. With the guidance of hospice personnel, some families are able to provide high-quality care to their terminally ill members throughout the course of the illness. Patient and

family know that the inpatient facility is there when and if they need it. A hospice can be thought of more aptly as a process and a spirit of mutual concern rather than a place.

The sociophysical environment of the hospice or palliative care facility is designed for life as well as death. In the incident that has been described, for example, staff recognized the importance of the first few minutes of the admission process. Efficiency was improved by appropriate use of technology (such as having the patient's own bed ready to meet her). Many other up-to-date techniques are used throughout St. Christopher's when these are seen as beneficial to patient care. But perhaps more important was the affirmation of human contact by both the medical director and the nurse. The prompt welcoming of the husband through the tea service further signified the hospice's interest in encouraging the maintenance of interpersonal relationships and comforting habits. These are small details, but Saunders and her staff value the significance of details such as these as well as the more obviously important aspects of patient care.

The family of the terminally ill person is not merely tolerated at a hospice such as St. Christopher's. Instead the family is both a provider and a recipient of care. The philosophy of care encompasses the entire family unit. Many family members not only visit with their own kin but also befriend other patients. This permeability of the hospice much reduces the likelihood of social isolation for the patient and the sense of helplessness for the family. It does raise the possibility, however, that the family might spend so much time and effort at the inpatient facility that they do not look after their own needs adequately. To place a friendly limit on family involvement, St. Christopher's has established a weekly "family's day off." This allows the family a brief vacation without any sense of guilt attached.

Mother's Last Moments: A Daughter's Experience

The next example (this time from an American hospice) is a look at hospice care from the viewpoint of a family member—the young adult daughter of a woman who had been terminally ill for several months after a lifetime of good health. The woman was being cared for at home during what proved to be the final phase of her illness.

The next day I woke up and went in to see my mother. I noticed the difference immediately. She had this rattle in her throat. She kept trying to talk, but all her words were garbled by the mucus in her throat. . . . And I called the doctor, and he gave me a good idea of what was happening. It was very hard for me to believe that she was so close [*"to death" were the words implied but not spoken by the daughter*]. She looked so calm and serene. In her room and among all her things. She looked really OK. She didn't look like she was in distress. She looked like she was just *glowing*.

And my sister came over. She brought over a tape made by a priest on death and dying. We put it on and we let my mother listen to it; isn't that awful? And it was talking about acceptance of death and it seemed to be quite appropriate at the time. And then my sister went to the movies and I stayed around with Emma [*a housekeeper with some experience in caring for invalids, employed by the family to help out at this time*]. And my sister had left a picture of her little boy so my mother could see him. And it was just as if everything was in preparation.

I got out her make-up and lotion and started to make her up. Put lotion all over her skin. She did [*know what I was doing*], because she held out her arm like this, and moved a little here and there to make it easier to make her up. But I was afraid in touching her body—she was so *frail*, I was afraid her skin might break if I touched her too hard to hug her. Before this time she hadn't wanted to be touched, because it hurt. But now it didn't seem to hurt her at all; her pain had all diminished. I put blush on her face . . . and lipstick on . . . and I brushed her hair.

And then I explained to her that I was going out for a cup of tea, because Emma said, "Why don't you go out—you deserve a break, just take a small break. It's good for you to go out." OK, after I finished making her up, I told her I was going to go out for a cup of tea and I would be *right back*.

As I bent down to hug her, she—her body—I don't know how to describe it: she opened her mouth as I was holding her, and blood came out. And I thought at first, "What's wrong, what's hap-pening?" And Emma said, "It's OK, It's nothing. She's fine. She'll be OK." But it was hard for me to let go of her. A part of me felt like "that was *it*," but, oh, no, it couldn't have happened. When I looked at her again, she looked—beautiful.

She was glowing. She looked so smooth. She was just—beautiful. It was the only time I saw her look so beautiful during her whole illness.

And when I came back the hearse was in front of our house. And I said, "Oh, no! You're not going to take my mother away!" And my father was there. The people he had listed in his preparation. The people who were supposed to be there; the things that were supposed to happen . . . I resented it all. "They're not going to go into the room. I'm going into the room first!" I wanted to touch her. I wanted to be alone with her. I went in and closed the door. And I touched her all over, and took her all in. And then I realized, I realized . . . she had gone without a struggle. It was really right, it was all right, you know? She looked very good. *She looked as if it was right.* It wasn't painful. It was the right time, and she was ready to go.

This is part of just one person's experience with death. If it were to be enlarged further, it would include how the other family members were able to respond in their own distinctive ways to the situation. The father, for example, did much planning and managing—his way of coping with the impending loss. The other daughters had their own ways of relating to their mother and her illness. The daughter quoted had a very close relationship with her mother and was able to continue this relationship on an intimate basis not only up to but through the moment of death itself. Does an "appropriate death" (Weisman, 1972) perhaps include both an ending that allows loved ones to respond freely in their own distinctive ways and one that appears right for the dying person herself? It might have been much more difficult for all the family members as well as the terminally ill woman to have felt and acted like the distinctive people they were had they been constricted by a traditional hospital and a medically managed situation.

Other positive features are also obvious. The woman apparently died free of pain and suffering. The final impression that "*it was right*" could well be a valuable core around which the daughter integrates her mother's death into her own ongoing life. The daughter also took full advantage of the opportunity to relate with her dying mother. She will not have to live with regret, self-recrimination, or anger about her own actions. Would she have felt comfortable applying lotion and make up to her mother if they had been in a hospital? Would this even have been permitted? Would she have been allowed to stay to the very end or been shooed away by hospital staff? And would she have been allowed to return for a few minutes of privacy with her mother after death?

The hospice (in this instance, Hospice of Miami) was one important source of support for this family. It may have made the difference, but the strength obviously was in the family itself, the feelings that members of an intact and affectionate family had for each other. Perhaps the hospice offered just enough to help the family be itself through the entire period of crisis. This does not mean, however, that the relationship between hospice and family was smooth at all times. The family at first had some resistance to the hospice's approach because it confronted them with the realization that the mother and wife actually was terminally ill. Even now the daughter wonders what the *expectancy effect* might have been on the mother and the entire family. How was the mother's length of survival and her quality of life influenced by hospice care? This is a relevant question, but it also can be asked when terminal care is mediated through traditional medical systems. It is likely that different expectations are communicated. It should also be recognized that Emma was not a person carefully selected and trained by the hospice. How she behaved during the terminal crises differs in some aspects from the way that most hospices would prefer their staff and volunteers conduct themselves.

The experience reported here was not "successful" if the aim of terminal care is to keep everybody's feelings under control and maneuver the death event through with minimal impact. The

daughter's life had changed at the moment she first learned of her mother's terminal illness some months before. The circumstances of her mother's death and dying have influenced her much, and she is now pursuing a career that involves providing care and comfort to others. It is not "life as usual" for this woman; she regards both the fact of her mother's death and the particular circumstances under which it occurred as strong motivation for her own continued growth as a person. And it is very clear that she would not have wanted to be deprived of the opportunity to be with her mother to the end to appreciate the freedom and familiarity of their own house.

Helping Mrs. Doe: Excerpts from a Clinical Record

One additional example of a hospice experience comes from a detailed case history from the Palliative Care Service of Montreal's Royal Victoria Hospital (1980).

Before entering hospice (palliative) care, Mrs. Doe, a 47-year-old woman, had undergone extensive treatment for cancer of the breast that had spread to lungs and bones. Unfortunately, the treatments, including radical mastectomy, had not halted the progress of the illness. The time had come when she could no longer work or carry out most of her other activities, but she wanted to remain at home and be with her family. Members of the interdisciplinary team visited her regularly, looking after not only her medications but also trying to help in every other way possible. The following is an examination of the visit-by-visit reports:

1. At first contact Mrs. Doe said that she and her husband could talk about her situation, but she didn't want their children (aged 17 and 21) to know about it yet.
2. She was not afraid of death but was "scared of pain and really panicked when she suffered shortness of breath."
3. A "pleasant lady" who spoke openly about her condition, Mrs. Doe "cried when she talked about leaving her husband and children."

4. During a late visit Mrs. Doe said she felt "ugly and useless," because chemotherapy was causing her hair to fall out.
5. A new source of concern for Mrs. Doe was the behavior of her 17-year-old daughter who was starting to skip school and becoming "moody."

These were some of the wishes, feelings, and problems of the patient. The following are some of the services that the registered nurse representing this hospice, or palliative care, service provided to Mrs. Doe and her family:

1. The hospice nurse taught Mr. Doe how to give his wife good skin-care treatment. This not only contributed directly to her well-being but also enabled the husband to feel more competent and useful in this highly stressful situation.
2. The nurse contributed to Mrs. Doe's physical comfort in many specific ways, such as (1) consulting regularly with the physician to monitor the effect of the medications and make changes promptly whenever indicated, (2) bringing in a physiotherapist who taught breathing exercises to Mrs. Doe that helped to relieve some of her distress and increased her sense of control, (3) arranging for a hospital bed and portable oxygen set to be delivered to the home, (4) arranging for a volunteer to drive Mrs. Doe for her outpatient hospital checkups and, (5) sharing in updating the treatment plan through frequent consultations with the radiologist and other hospice specialists (one outcome of this interdisciplinary team approach was the decision to avoid subjecting the patient to treatments that would have weakened and distressed her without producing a remission).
3. The nurse also did much listening and when appropriate offered a few timely suggestions for the psychological well-being of Mrs. Doe and her family. Among the outcomes are (1) the Does became more comfortable with the idea of sharing the facts of her condition with the children. This immediately cleared up the tension that had been gathering, and the daughter resumed her normal school attendance and ended her moodiness. The daughter told the nurse how much it meant to her that her parents trusted her enough to tell her the truth, which she had suspected. (2) Mrs. Doe felt better about her physical appearance when the nurse showed her how to make and wear a turban and then provided her with an attractive wig. (3) Although her physical condition deteriorated as time went by, Mrs. Doe's pain was well controlled, giving her the peace of mind to relate to her family and remain herself. (4) Whenever Mrs. Doe wanted to discuss what would be happening to her next or to express a strong preference (such as remaining at home until the end), the nurse was available to listen, provide the most accurate information possible, and do what she could to support the patient's wishes.

These are but a few aspects of the total relationship between the Doe family and the hospice or palliative care unit that served them. Although this was a hospital-based organization, every reasonable effort was made to help Mrs. Doe remain at home in accordance with her wishes. Mrs. Doe did die, and she did suffer a variety of distressing symptoms despite the most attentive care. Yet it was clear that she and her family felt they had received sensitive and effective care that allowed them all to keep their lives together through this harrowing time. Not many years ago the medical system would have written off the treatment of Mrs. Doe as a failure because her illness could not be cured or stabilized. Today there are an increasing number of physicians, nurses, and other allied health professionals who realize that the limits of cure do not have to create a failure in caring and human response.

For other examples and information on hospice care in action you can consult a number of other recent and useful publications (DuBois, 1980; Gold, 1983; Munley, 1983; Zimmerman, 1981).

EVALUATING THE HOSPICE EXPERIMENT

There are many case examples throughout the United States to suggest that hospice care often does meet or at least approach its objectives. I have seen enough of hospice care in operation to be convinced that as a rule patients and families do benefit significantly from hospice services. Individual case histories and general impressions, however, do not substitute for thorough documentation. Following is a brief examination of the hospice experiment based upon recent studies.

Is Hospice Care Succeeding as a Health-Care Program?

The pioneers of hospice care were motivated to do all that is possible to protect the quality of life for terminally ill people and their families. Nevertheless, the future of the hospice movement does not depend entirely upon the achievement of clinical and psychosocial goals. Hospice services must also be seen as an acceptable and cost-efficient health-care program. If hospice care costs too much or reveals serious organizational flaws, then even a good record of patient and family care might not be enough to ensure its survival in Western society.

The Relative Cost of Hospice Care

Much of the existing evaluation and research effort has focused on the cost of hospice care in comparison with more traditional, hospital-oriented management. It is useful to remember that most terminally ill patients served by hospice services have some form of cancer, so all comparisons are between people with identical or similar diseases who have received either hospice or traditional care.

Several small studies have suggested that hospice care is less expensive (Amado, et al., 1979; Bloom & Kissick, 1980; New York State Committee on Aging, 1982). This is not a surprising conclusion, since hospice care might be expected to provide savings in categories such as number of days in the hospital, number of diagnostic procedures requiring special equipment and laboratory work, and so on. However, it became evident that a major study with tight controls was necessary. Such a project has now been completed. The National Hospice Demonstration Study (NHDS) was funded and supervised by the Health Care Finance Administration (HCFA). Although HCFA was interested primarily in the financial aspects, the NHDS also gave attention to clinical management and the responses of patients and families. The NHDS findings provide by far the largest collection of data on hospice care in the United States obtained under carefully supervised conditions. The data were collected in association with 31 hospice programs and eight hospitals throughout the United States. Only a few of the most relevant findings from this extensive study, drawn from the final technical report (Greer, et al., 1984) and a recent book, (Mor, et al., 1988) can be examined here.

In general, the NHDS supports the contention that hospice care tends to be less expensive than traditional hospital care for terminally ill cancer patients. As expected, conventional care patients more often received intensive medical interventions such as chemotherapy, radiation therapy, and surgery in the last few weeks of life as well as more diagnostic tests at every point of measurement before death. Also as expected, hospice patients spent more time at home and less in the hospital during the total course of their final illness. An important differential was found, however: the home-care hospices were less expensive than those based in hospitals. The cost pattern becomes more complicated than can be analyzed here when all combinations of factors are taken into account (such as age of patient, stage of disease, and specific services used). In some combinations of circumstances hospital-based care was less expensive, and patients being cared for at home used some services more than patients in the hospital.

A conservative conclusion would be that hospice care at least does not cost more than the traditional hospital-based approach that has been criticized so severely for overly aggressive and socially isolating practices. Nevertheless, for the most debilitated patients hospitalization often did seem more effective: "The case for hospital based hospice care . . . must rest on a determination that higher-cost institutional care may be appropriate for medically needy patients, rather than on the argument that hospice is less expensive than conventional care" (Greer, et al., 1984, p. V-48). It would be a mistake, then, to insist that all patients should remain at home under all conditions. There are circumstances in which special medical and nursing care is required when relief from distress cannot be accomplished in the home, and the higher cost should not be a deterrent.

The Operational Success of Hospice Care

Apart from the financial considerations, important as they are, there are many other components of a hospice operation that can make the difference between success and failure.

Attracting, training, and keeping qualified *volunteers* is one of the most important components for hospice care success. Most hospice directors well understand the value of the volunteer program and have developed high-quality screening and training programs (see Box 5–1). A hospice must work hard to establish and maintain the level of volunteer participation needed, but it is clear that many people from many walks of life are coming forth to accept this challenge. *Acceptance by the local professional community* is another major challenge for all hospices. Here the results, I believe, are mixed. Physicians and other health-care professionals have rallied to hospice care in some communities and backed off in others. Some hospices have faltered and some have failed because they were unable to attract enough support and collaboration in their locale. There are many reasons for this problem, including personality clashes, misunderstandings about the nature of the hospice, and competing financial interests. The continued proliferation of hospice programs in this country and their long-term future will depend to some extent on the

interest, trust, and good will of individual health professionals and agencies in every community.

The *administrative skills* of hospice directors and advisory boards also enter into success or failure. It is natural for the hospice staff to devote most of its energies to the primary challenge: care of terminally ill people and their families. However, should the hospice not give sufficient attention to complying with all manner of local, state, and federal regulations; should record keeping fall behind; should the endless paperwork pile up; then an otherwise effective hospice can be endangered. Care of the dying requires more than care of the dying—it requires administrative skill, good public relations, and the constant effort to keep a secure foundation under those who provide direct care.

Is Hospice Care Really Helping Terminally Ill People and Their Families?

Many personal experiences and clinical observations have indicated that hospice care has fulfilled its promise. But what conclusions can be drawn from systematic research?

Pain Control

Patients, family members, and hospice workers generally agree that pain control is a major, if not *the* major priority. The reasons are not difficult to identify:

- Pain is, by definition, a stressful experience.
- Pain reduces the ability to give attention to other matters, thereby isolating the sufferer and reducing his or her opportunity to reflect, interact, and accomplish.
- Pain can intensify other symptoms such as weight loss, insomnia, pressure sores, and nausea.
- Fear and anticipation of pain can also be demoralizing: "Will the pain return?" "Will it get worse?" "Will I be able to endure it?"
- Pain contributes much to anxiety about the dying process. There are people who assume that dying is "all pain" and unavoidably so. This expectation can lead to emotional distress,

BOX 5–1
SHOULD I BECOME A HOSPICE VOLUNTEER? A DIALOGUE

- *Does my local hospice need volunteers?*

  Probably so. A hospice usually has a director of volunteers and will welcome your call.

- *What should I expect when I meet the director of volunteers?*

  A friendly but "professional" interview. The hospice has responsibility for exercising good judgment in the selection of volunteers.

- *You mean they might not accept me?*

  This is a possibility. Has someone very close to you died recently? Many hospices ask people who have had a recent bereavement to wait a while before becoming a volunteer. Or the interviewer may judge that you have a disorganized life style. . . .

- *—hey, I'm going to get organized, starting tomorrow!*

  Fine! But the volunteer director will need to be convinced that you are a person who keeps appointments and does what needs to be done in a reliable manner. And should you come across like a person who needs to impose your own religious beliefs on others—or to use hospice in the service of your own fantasies and problems—then you might receive a polite but firm refusal.

- *That won't happen to me. I'm taking this great class on death and dying, and reading this really terrific textbook. So after I'm accepted as a volunteer, will they give me some guidance and supervision?*

  Definitely. You will be asked to attend a series of training sessions before you are activated as a volunteer. Most people find this is a valuable learning experience. You will receive guidance and supervision all the way along the line, and you will always have somebody to call if problems arise.

- *What kind of things would I do as a volunteer?*

  There are many possibilities. You might be a companion for a patient in his or her own home for a few hours so others in the household have the opportunity to shop or take care of business. You might drive the patient to an appointment or to visit an old friend. You might help the patient write letters. You might help prepare a meal when family or friends call. You might help the patient or a family member complete a special project. And at times you might just "be there." A hospice volunteer can wind up doing many different things, depending upon the needs of the individual families (Willis, 1989). But some volunteers devote themselves to keeping the hospice system going, rather than working with patients directly. They do office work, fund-raising, and other things that do not necessarily involve direct patient or family contact.

- *What are the other volunteers like?*

  I've been fortunate enough to know many hospice volunteers. As a rule, they are bright, mature, and neighborly people who have been rather successful in life. Many feel that through hospice they can give something back to other people. Some are health-care professionals who believe strongly in the hospice philosophy. . . .

- *Like nurses and medical social workers?*

  Yes, some volunteers are well-qualified professionals. Some have been very successful in other lines of work, but are new to health and social care. And you will find other students as well—looking for an opportunity to help others while acquiring valuable personal experience.

- *Anything else I should know?*

  Before you contact hospice, reflect on your own motivation: a passing curiosity or a firm resolve to help others? Are you going to be available to serve as a volunteer after you complete the course? Even though hospice may ask you to give only a few hours of your time per week, people will be counting on you to come through. If you have further questions at this time, you might ask your local hospice to put you into contact with several of their experienced volunteers.

- *See you at the hospice office!*

  Go easy on those donuts.

impaired communication, and, in some instances, to suicide ("I'd kill myself first!").

The very fact that pain control has now become a major priority in terminal care owes much to the hospice approach. Until recent years there was little dependable information available on the type and extent of pain experienced by dying people. Today there is renewed interest in assessing pain and providing relief. In his recent review of the literature, Michael H. Levy (1987–1988) concludes that pain is the most common symptom of terminally ill patients. Unless it is adequately controlled, pain is experienced by most patients with advanced cancer, and is present in many other types of terminal illness as well.

Levy's next conclusion—not unexpected by those familiar with general medical practice—is cause for alarm:

> Unfortunately, the pain of advanced cancer is all too often inadequately controlled, especially in the terminal period. This therapeutic deficiency is due more to improper application of current knowledge than to lack of adequate knowledge regarding the mechanisms of pain and the modalities available for its control.

Now comes the good news:

> In the highly controlled setting of free-standing hospices or palliative care units, pain can be controlled in 90 percent to 99 percent of patients. (p. 266)

Actually, not all studies show a clear reduction in pain with hospice care: the effects seem to be greatest when patients would otherwise suffer severe pain (Mor, 1987). Furthermore, it is very difficult to measure pain. Studies have used various approaches, including different types of self-reports and objective observations. No matter what method is employed, there is usually some room for doubt because states of mind are, by nature, subjective. There is another problem in comparing hospice with more traditional types of care: many individual physicians and community hospitals have started to learn and apply hospice techniques for pain control. This is a positive

development, of course, but it does complicate the attempt to compare the two approaches.

Nevertheless, it is clear that hospice physicians and nurses have become the state-of-the-art experts in pain control. How is this accomplished? Part of the hospice success in pain control derives from superior knowledge of available medications and their optimal use. But part of the success must be attributed to the hospice philosophy itself: a person *should* be as pain-free as possible as the end of life approaches, to allow them the opportunity to complete projects, engage in leave-takings, or just to find some enjoyment and meaning in each remaining day. This attitude translates into a refusal to "play the usual games" so often favored by physicians who would prefer not to associate themselves with dying patients at all. Hospice staff do not expect dying patients and their families to endure as long as possible until forced to "beg" for relief, nor do they harbor the bizarre fear that adequate medication would make a drug addict out of a person who may have only a few weeks to live. The hospice team is particularly expert in helping people cope with *unremitting* pain. In general, the medical profession has given more attention to relief of short-term or acute pain. Applying the same type of regime to a terminally ill cancer patient is a still-common mistake.

Hospice practice and research have demonstrated that most people can receive significant relief from pain throughout the dying process. There are exceptions, and therefore clinicians and researchers are continuing to look for improved techniques. Most of the failures in pain relief, however, are as Levy indicated, a failure to apply knowledge that has already become available.

Other Symptoms and Problems

Pain is not the only problem that can beset a dying person. Other types of symptoms may include

- Nausea
- Vomiting
- Respiratory difficulties

- Pressure sores
- Insomnia
- Incontinence
- Weakness
- Fatigue
- Confusion
- Depression

Effective care requires attention to the prevention or alleviation of all these problems. With the active participation of a family caregiver as well as the hospice professional staff and volunteers, it is often possible to relieve some or all of these symptoms—for a while. Despite the best care, however, the terminally ill person is likely to become weaker and more fatigued as the end approaches. It will also become increasingly difficult for the dying person to move about. Nevertheless, it has been found that hospice patients are somewhat less likely to be restricted to their beds until death is very close (Mor, 1987). But one must expect decline: "healthy dying" is something of a fantasy (Kastenbaum, 1979).

NHDS findings (Mor, Greer, & Kastenbaum, 1988) indicate that the *social quality of life* remained high for hospice patients during their final weeks and days. Despite the inescapable fact of continued physical deterioration, patients receiving hospice care maintained their intimate relationships and avoided the social isolation that has sometimes befallen the dying person. But the data also suggested that the personality and values of the person *before* becoming terminally ill also had a major influence on experiences during the last weeks of life. The difference between hospice and traditional types of care sometimes seemed to be less important than individual differences in personality and social support system. This finding can serve as a useful reminder that people as well as treatment approaches differ markedly.

There is some evidence that hospice patients were able to experience a situation close to their own preferences (given, of course, the severe problems associated with rapidly failing health). Recall the thought questions raised at the end of

Chapter 4. You were asked first to describe the last three days of your life as you would like them to be. This question, suggested by Beatrice Kastenbaum, was included in the NHDS. The data available to us at this time show that the following types of answers were most common (in order of frequency):

- I want certain people to be here with me.
- I want to be physically able to do things.
- I want to feel at peace.
- I want to be free from pain.
- I want the last three days of my life to be like any other days.

The support offered by hospice care makes it possible for many patients to be at home and enjoy the company of the "certain people" who mean the most to them. Similarly, with the advice and support of hospice volunteers and staff the patient could still control some activities of daily life (e.g., the type of help offered by Mrs. Doe's hospice nurse). Remaining in their environment provided a context for feeling at peace and having each day keep something of the feeling of a comforting routine. The patients' goals and the goals of hospice care were identical.

It is interesting to note some of the *least frequently* mentioned wishes for the last three days of life. Only about one person in 20 cared about "completing a task" or being "mentally alert." Even fewer hoped to "accept death," and fewer still wanted to "know when death is imminent," "be able to bear pain," or "live until a certain time or event." This collection of low-incidence items includes many of the most dramatic wishes that are sometimes attributed to the dying person. By far the greater number of terminally ill people simply wanted the comfort of familiar faces and the ability to continue to do a little for themselves and have a sense of peaceful routine. The goal of accepting death philosophically or demonstrating the ability to tolerate pain was seldom found. There is much that could be discussed in these findings. Simply note here that (1) what most people wanted was no more and no different from what hospice care tries to achieve and (2) it is wiser to learn from each individual what really matters than to attribute motives and themes picked up elsewhere.

The question on sources of strength was also included in the NHDS survey. Following are the most frequent responses given by a subsample of NHDS patients:

- Supportive family or friends
- Religion
- Being needed
- Confidence in self
- Satisfied with the help received

Again the hospice programs participating in the NHDS were designed to enable people to call upon just such sources of strength. Perhaps most important (at least the most frequently mentioned) was the one with which hospice had the most clearly documented success: helping the dying person remain with family and friends for much or all of the illness.

There appears to be a good match in general between what terminally ill cancer patients hope for (apart from recovery) and what hospice care is designed to achieve by its philosophy and method. Nevertheless, knowledge of hospice process and outcome needs to be improved and the current state of information should be considered as only preliminary and subject to expansion and revision.

Your Deathbed Scene, Revisited

Think about the personal deathbed scene you imagined while reading the preceding chapter. Now that you have read more about the dying process and terminal care, it might be instructive to review your own expectations. If your deathbed scene was similar to those of most students, you portrayed a rather sanitized image that does not have much in common with the way that most people actually die. This is true particularly with respect to pain and other symptoms. Most dying people have pain—although it may be controlled by competent physicians and nurses—and most dying people have a variety of other symp-

toms as well. Most college students portray themselves as dying without pain and without other symptoms (Kastenbaum & Normand, 1990). What does this discrepancy mean? At the least, it means that even those self-selected people who have chosen to enroll in a death-focused class have unrealistic ideas about their physical condition at the end of life. What else might this discrepancy mean? I will leave this question to your own reflections.

In some other respects, the typical deathbed scene expected by college students does have some relationship to the actual deathbed scenes experienced by many people who have received hospice care: elderly, at home, with family and other loved ones. But while many college students have made a point of indicating that they wanted to "go quickly" and would "go quickly," most people actually die over a longer period of time. To be sure, there are terminally ill people who do "slip away quietly" in their sleep, but this passage has usually been preceded by months of declining health and increased functional limitations. Realistically, most of us will live for some time with our final illness, and so will our loved ones. Each person must make his or her own decision about the desirable balance between wishful fantasy and reality.

ON THE FUTURE OF HOSPICE CARE

The hospice experiment has arisen from the deeply felt needs of many people, both professionals and the general public. Hospice care has already contributed to the psychological and physical well-being of terminally ill people and their families and seems to be stimulating a new wave of innovative and humanitarian approaches in the health-care field. Keep in mind the following points during the next few years:

- *Hospice care is an option, not a total solution.* The success of hospice care has been most evident for terminally ill cancer patients who have intact families. It remains to be seen how far current hospice techniques can be employed with a wider variety of life-threatening conditions and with people without families or close friends to share in the support.

- Hospital-based care may continue to be most effective and comforting for some people either because of the nature of their illness or social network or because they simply feel more secure in a medical facility.

- Your local hospice organization probably needs both financial support and a continued influx of capable volunteers. Economic survival is still not easy for most hospice organizations today, especially those that are home-based rather than hospital-based. Your help would be welcome.

- Although primarily intended to assist the terminally ill, hospice programs sometimes do serve other people as well (depending upon local circumstances) and have the potential to provide greater service to aged individuals, the physically disabled, and people experiencing an episode of unusual vulnerability and jeopardy. Those who learn from the current hospice efforts and go on to develop creative applications in other areas will be making a very significant contribution to the quality of life.

- The emergence of AIDS as a new life-threatening epidemic has created new challenges for hospice care and for our society in general. The dying person with AIDS and the response of hospice and society are considered in the next chapter.

REFERENCES

Amado, A., Cronk, B. A., & Mileo, R. (1979). Cost of terminal care: Home hospice vs. hospital. *Nursing Outlook, 27,* 522–526.

Bloom, B. S., & Kissick, P. D. (1980). Home and hospital cost of terminal illness. *Medical Care, 18,* 560–564.

Buckingham, R. W., & Lack, S. A. (1977). *Final report to National Cancer Institute.* Washington, D.C.: National Cancer Institute.

Du Bois, P. M. (1980). *The hospice way of death.* New York: Human Sciences Press, Inc.

Gilmore, A. J. J. (1989). Hospice development in the United Kingdom. In R. Kastenbaum & B. K. Kastenbaum (Eds.), *Encyclopedia of Death.* Phoenix: Oryx Press, pp. 149–152.

Gold, M. (1983). *Life support: What families say about hospital, hospice and home care for the fatally ill.* New York: Consumers Union Foundation, Inc.

Greer, D. S., and others. (1984). *Final report of the National Hospice Study.* Providence, R.I.: Brown University.

Health Care Financing Administration. (1983). Medicare program: Hospice care. *Federal Register, 48,* No. 163, 38146–38174.

Kastenbaum, R. (1975). Toward standards of care for the terminally ill. Part II: What standards exist today? *Omega, Journal of Death and Dying, 6,* 289–290.

Kastenbaum, R. (1979). "Healthy dying": A paradoxical quest continues. *Journal of Social Issues, 35,* 185–206.

Kastenbaum, R., & Normand, C. (1990). Deathbed scenes as expected by the young and experienced by the old. *Death Studies, 14,* 201–218.

Levy, M. H. (1988). Pain control research in terminal care. *Omega, 18,* 265–280.

Mor, V. (1987). *Hospice care systems.* New York: Springer.

Mor, V., Greer, D., & Kastenbaum, R. (1988). *The hospice experiment.* Baltimore: Johns Hopkins University Press.

Munley, A. (1983). *The hospice alternative.* New York: Basic Books, Inc., Publishers.

New York State Senate Committee on Aging (1982). *Hospice: Its concept and legislative development.* New York: State Senate of New York.

Palliative Care Service, Royal Victoria Hospital, Montreal. Case history. (1980). In M. Hamilton & H. Reid (Eds.), *A hospice handbook* (pp. 90–130). Grand Rapids: William B. Eerdmans Publishing Co.

Parkes, C. M. (1976). Home or hospital? Terminal care as seen by surviving spouses. *Journal of the Royal College of General Practitioners, 28,* 19–30.

Phipps, W. E. (1988). The Origin of Hospices/Hospitals. *Death Studies, 12,* 91–100.

Russell, G. M. (1984). *Hospice programs and the hospice movement: An investigation based on general systems theory.* Unpublished doctoral dissertation, University of Colorado, Boulder.

Saunders, C. M. (Ed.), (1978). *The management of terminal disease.* London: Edward Arnold, Ltd.

Twycross, R. G. (1979). Overview of analgesia. In J. J. Bonica & V. Ventafridda (Eds.), *International symposium on pain of advanced cancer* (pp. 617–634). New York: Raven Press.

Weisman, A. D. (1972). *On dying and denying.* New York: Behavioral Publications, Inc.

Willis, J. (1989). Hospice Volunteers. In R. Kastenbaum & B. K. Kastenbaum, (Eds.), *Encyclopedia of death* (pp. 147–149). Phoenix: The Oryx Press.

Worcester, A. (1961). *The care of the aged, the dying, and the dead.* Springfield, Ill.: Charles C. Thomas. (First printing 1935).

Zimmerman, J. M. (Ed.) (1981). *Hospice: Complete care for the terminally ill.* Baltimore: Urban & Schwarzenberg, Inc.

chapter 6

AIDS, SOCIETY, AND HUMAN EXPERIENCE

What is AIDS—really?

- Is it a disease that fascinates geneticists and medical researchers because of its unusual mode of operation?
- Is it an equally fascinating topic for epidemiologists who wonder where the disease originated and how it has become so pervasive in so short a time?
- Is it a source of extreme concern for governmental agencies and the health care providers because the AIDS epidemic is making major economic demands on an already precarious system?
- Is it a touchy moral and political issue that has divided many a community and intensified existing patterns of discrimination and distrust?
- Is it a menace that has affected sexual feelings, attitudes, and behaviors, leading to significant changes in how people approach some of their most intimate relationships?
- Is it a stimulus for confusion and panic as various stories about AIDS circulate throughout society and as people feel uncertain about risk factors?
- Is it an especially alarming disease because of the symptomatology, or because of some of the people who have fallen victim?
- Is it a cause of death that has received so much attention that the people themselves have sometimes been ignored?

As you have probably decided for yourself, the answer is "all of the above." Acquired immune deficiency syndrome (AIDS) was not described until 1981. Yet within a decade it has become a deadly reality to some people and a threat to many others. Furthermore the individual and societal reactions to AIDS have created a complex and ever-shifting image of the disease—an image that has itself become a kind of symbolic reality. To understand AIDS, society, and human experience we must attend to at least several of the ways in which this disease has entered our lives. The AIDS of the medical researcher is not the same as the AIDS of the person who is sitting by the bedside of a dying friend.

We begin here by focusing on the nature of AIDS as a cause of illness and death. This will be followed by explorations of the other topics that were mentioned so briefly in "all of the above": (1) the origin and spread of AIDS; (2) its impact on health and social care systems; (3) the moral and political response; (4) its influence on sexual relationships and behaviors; (5) explanations and rumors; (6) response to the victims of AIDS and their symptomatology, and (7) personal perspectives on the people themselves, as distinguished from the disease. We will draw some connections among these various concerns as we move along and conceptualize the overall issue of AIDS within the framework of the death system.

THE ACQUIRED IMMUNE DEFICIENCY SYNDROME

AIDS is a disease that is contagious under certain circumstances, but which produces its destructive effects in an unusual way. First, let's be clear about the modes of contagion:

1. Sexual intercourse with a person who has the AIDS virus
2. Use of contaminated needles for drug injection
3. Transfusion with contaminated blood or blood products
4. Passage from infected mother to fetus or newborn

Casual contact does not result in contagion. We can converse, dine, work, and play with people who have the AIDS virus without risk. Yes, we can touch and even hug another person without fear of contracting AIDS. A friendly little kiss on the cheek or lips is also considered to be a no-risk action by AIDS experts (e.g., Moffatt, et al., 1987). Unlike some other infectious diseases, AIDS shows its contagious character only when there is an exchange of body fluids: blood, semen, vaginal secretions, urine. AIDS is not transmitted by contact with toilet seats.

HIV is the name that has been given to the virus responsible for AIDS. This is simply the abbreviation for human immunodeficiency virus. Robert C. Gallo and Luc Montagnier are credited with first describing this virus and suggesting its link to the then-new disease. They recognized that this was a special kind of virus: one that invades genetic material within cells and then reverses the flow of information. In other words, HIV is a *retrovirus*. In a more recent article, Gallo and Montagnier (1989) summarize the basic facts about HIV:

> Like other viruses, retroviruses cannot replicate without taking over the biosynthetic apparatus of a cell and exploiting it for their own ends. What is unique about retroviruses is their capacity to reverse the ordinary flow of genetic information—from

DNA to RNA to proteins (which are the cell's structural and functional molecules). The genetic material of a retrovirus is RNA. In addition, the retrovirus carries an enzyme called reverse transcriptase, which can use the viral RNA as a template for making DNA. . . . Having made itself at home among the host's genes, the viral DNA remains latent until it is activated to make new virus particles. The latent DNA can also initiate the process that leads to tumor formation. (pp. 1–2)

HIV, then, is a clever invader that takes over critical aspects of the cell's command structure and proceeds to issue orders that benefit itself while undermining the host organism. Retroviruses had been discovered in several species of animals, but HIV was the first to be recognized in humans. It was already known that several retroviruses can disable the immune system in animals; feline leukemia, a leading cause of death among cats, is perhaps the most familiar example. Much has been learned about HIV since its discovery, information that might eventually contribute to effective means of prevention or treatment. HIV's own package of genetic instructions is a marvel of miniaturization—about 100,000 times smaller than the genetic information contained in a cell of the human body (Haseltine & Wong-Staal, 1989). Despite—or because—of its microminiaturized size, HIV reproduces itself very rapidly when it enters a host. Evidence of HIV infection first appears in the bloodstream and spinal cord, as well as in the fluids that surround the brain. The infected person is likely to become feverish and suffer from rashes and symptoms that resemble the flu. There may also be dizziness and other neurological symptoms. It is very difficult to recognize this combination of symptoms as the early stages of HIV infection unless laboratory studies are conducted of blood and/or cerebrospinal fluid.

This is only the first phase of the HIV's life cycle. After a few weeks, the HIV population in the blood and cerebrospinal fluid declines sharply. The flu-like symptoms disappear. Everything seems to be normal again. However, the

HIV has moved to its next phase of operations. It now has invaded some cells within the nervous system and intestines, and probably the bone marrow as well. Perhaps most ominously, the HIV will have found a new home within components of the immune system (such as the *T cells* that play an important role in the detection and destruction of infections). It is now known that HIV interacts in many different ways with different types of human cells. For example, HIV may remain dormant in T cells for months or years. But when the T cells receive a particular kind of stimulation (e.g., from an infection they are designed to combat), the hidden HIV "can destroy them in a burst of replication" (Haseltine & Wong-Stall, 1989, p. 13). The now-disabled immune system is unable to cope with the infection that triggered this reaction. This is one of AIDS' major lethal pathways: the retrovirus reduces the host organism's ability to fight off infections that ordinarily would have been attacked effectively. The person will die, then, not of AIDS directly, but of one or more "opportunistic infections." The same effect is achieved in a different way when HIV spares certain cells, but changes their function so that the host organism becomes less viable.

Another frequent consequence of the impaired immune response is the development of an external tumor known as *Kaposi's sarcoma* (KS). This condition resembles a bruise when it first appears, but it does not show the usual healing one expects after a week or two. KS is a cancerous condition that involves the walls of blood vessels. Prior to the AIDS epidemic, KS was found occasionally, usually in older men, and was seldom a life-threatening condition. However, KS both occurs frequently in association with AIDS, and is a more aggressive condition. KS was observed in many of the first AIDS patients, who were mostly homosexual men and who had some similarities in life-style. There is some evidence that KS has gradually become less common among AIDS patients as people of more diverse backgrounds and life-styles have developed this disease (Nichols, 1989). Another type of tumor—lymphoma—has also become part of the AIDS-related syndrome for some people. Some people are born with immune system deficiencies and therefore develop lymphomas, often in childhood. Adults whose immune systems are disabled by HIV can develop lymphomas for the same reason.

This brief overview cannot convey the complexity of the challenge that is faced by HIV researchers, nor can we keep up to the moment in the rapidly changing picture of basic findings and experimental therapies. A number of innovative strategies are being investigated, including the possibilities of destroying the "envelope" that protects HIV's own genetic information, or of somehow tricking HIV into destroying itself. Meanwhile, the health-care system, as yet unable to halt the destructive work of HIV itself, has developed more expertise in supporting what remains of the patient's own physical resources and in coping with pneumonia and opportunistic infections as they arise. We will return to the detection-prevention-therapy issue as we move through the other sectors of the AIDS problem.

AIDS as Epidemic: Origin and Spread

Epidemiology often seems to be a dry, statistic-obsessed branch of the public health. These numbers mean something, however. They can provide valuable clues to the success of prevention efforts, to the resurgence of diseases that once had been brought under control, and to many other vital questions. And perhaps epidemiology makes its greatest contributions when we are faced with a major threat to life whose nature and dimensions have not yet been tested by history. Bubonic plague, cholera, syphilis, influenza, malaria, and tuberculosis are among the life-threatening diseases that epidemiologists have learned a great deal about. What has been learned about the origin and spread of AIDS?

The remote origins of HIV and AIDS have not yet been firmly identified. We are limited to a working hypothesis that is based upon fragmentary information. This—not fully proven—scenario would have the following key components:

1. The HIV has existed for an unknown period of time in one or more relatively isolated areas of the world.
2. Possibly this virus was transmitted by contact with infected animals (e.g., through wounds); possibly an animal-seeking virus took advantage of convenient human hosts to develop a mutant form.
3. Advances in transportation and communication are rapidly incorporating even the most remote areas of the world into a "global village." One of the potential consequences is that a rare disease can suddenly make its appearance in populations far removed from its usual habitat.

A viral disease previously unknown to physicians and researchers suddenly appeared in Central Africa in the mid-1970s (Shilts, 1987). The new illness quickly proved lethal to half of those it infected. An emergency health care team was provided by the World Health Organization and the United States' Centers for Disease Control (CDC). This team discovered the pathway for contagion: body fluids—sexual intercourse and contaminated needles. It was also observed that the immune system (especially the lymph glands) of the stricken people had been severely damaged and that death seemed to be most immediately caused by suffocation through a seldom-encountered condition known as *Pneumocystis*.

There were striking resemblances to what would in a few years become known as AIDS, although the African outbreak seemed to take its victims very rapidly. The WHO/CDC team persuaded the residents (with some difficulty) to change their behaviors in ways that were likely to reduce the risk of contagion. For this reason or for reasons unknown, the new "Ebola River virus" soon disappeared. The health authorities believed that their quick intervention and the relative isolation of this region from world population centers may have spared humanity a frightening new

epidemic. This was a reasonable conclusion, but it would soon (although not soon enough) become clear that HIV had gained access to global distribution. Whether the virus had been picked up in Central Africa or in some other locale, it was already on its way to engendering the AIDS epidemic.

This is where *Patient Zero* comes in. And this is also where we can no longer limit our focus to the biomedical sphere. The life-styles of individuals, subgroups, and society in general would exercise a powerful influence over the course of the AIDS epidemic. Much of what follows here is based upon Randy Shilts' (1987) *And the Band Played On*. This is an extraordinarily comprehensive and well-detailed account of our society's first encounter with AIDS: read it! Subsequent contributions by other writers (cited below) have helped to bring us up to date as well as to add some alternative views.

By 1980 some health-care workers in the San Francisco area were well aware that promiscuous homosexual men were spreading several diseases among themselves. Hepatitis B, for example, had already infected about two out of every three homosexual men in San Francisco. A disorder that the medical journals called "Gay Bowel Syndrome" had increased in prevalence by an astonishing 8,000 percent in just a few years, a consequence of anal intercourse. And these were but two of many diseases. The situation added up to a major health problem, but one that was essentially unnoticed by the community at large—and also one that seemed to be of little concern to the victims themselves. Despite warnings from physicians, many men had their infections treated, and then repeatedly returned with new infections.

Why would so many people expose themselves to the very high risk of infection? Not all homosexual men in San Francisco (or elsewhere) took such chances. Some had long-standing monogamous relationships and would not think of visiting one of the bathhouses where casual sex and extremely high risk of disease were rampant. Shilts suggests that the sociopolitical climate of the 1970s had much to do with the behavior of those homosexual men who did engage in frequent, indiscriminate, and unprotected sexual contacts. "Promiscuity . . . was central to the raucous gay movement of the 1970s. [Furthermore] . . . commercialization of gay sex was all part of the scene. . . . The gay liberation movement of the 1970s had spawned a business of bathhouses and sex clubs" (p. 19). Excited about the opportunity to "come out of the closet," some homosexual men indulged in unrestrained sexual behavior and rejoiced in this proof of their liberation from mainstream political-moral disapproval. It should also be noted that use of recreational drugs was considered normal and the "in thing" to do among some subgroups of both homosexuals and heterosexuals. Every city had its core of drug addicts who lived from needle to needle. The man who was both a promiscuous homosexual and a drug user was in double jeopardy for a variety of infections. And then, into this scene entered Patient Zero and AIDS.

Gaetan Dugas was a handsome young Canadian, a former hairdresser whose job as an airline steward took him around much of the world. He was very active in his homosexual activities, easily attracting other men, having one night stands or other fleeting relationships and moving on to other men. Dugas especially enjoyed his visits to San Francisco. Proud of his good looks, Dugas did not like the fact that some rashy spots were appearing on his body and that physicians said there was no treatment for them. When he learned that there was a new condition appearing among some homosexual men—Kaposi's sarcoma—he made further efforts to find effective treatment. It became more difficult to keep his self-image as "the prettiest one" when his hair started to fall out as a result of chemotherapy and purple spots remained on his skin. Resourcefully, he shaved his head and confined his sexual adventures to bathhouses where the dim lighting made it difficult to see his "rash." Dugas continued to have about 250 sexual contacts a year; he estimated that he had about 2,500 sexual partners over a ten-year period.

It would be a while before public health experts discovered that Dugas had been a sex partner for many of the men who were coming down with KS and who were not responding to chemotherapy or other existing treatments. And it would be a while longer before medical detective work established that he was Patient Zero: the person who was most responsible for the spread of the disease that is now called AIDS. By 1982 the unusual syndrome that had been appearing with increasing frequency and was responsible for a growing number of deaths had been given the term GRID (Gay-Related Immune Deficiency). Doctors and patients, however, tended to speak of it as "gay cancer."

We now come to one of the critical junctures of medical, individual, and societal response. Some physicians and other public health authorities were keenly aware that a deadly new disease syndrome had appeared. Those who had the most contact with it knew that (1) there was no effective treatment; (2) in all probability, the disease had been developing within the infected individuals for several years, therefore (3) this was probably only the first wave of fatalities—many more of those already infected would die; (4) furthermore, new infections and fatalities were almost certain as a result of unrestrained sexual practices; and (5) there was no biomedical reason to believe that GRID would remain limited to homosexual men in major metropolitan areas.

These physicians and some other responsible citizens were ready—even desperate—to strengthen what we have described (Chapter 3) as the warning, predicting, and preventing functions of our society's death system. A vigorous program of health education might sharply reduce new infections. A thorough epidemiological analysis might help the nation—and the world—organize itself more effectively to control the new threat to life. A high-priority program of medical research might discover treatments that would halt the lethal course of the disease. At this point (early in 1982), the AIDS menace had been recognized by some physicians and community leaders. The next obvious step was to bring this concern to society at large and draw upon whatever resources were needed to halt the epidemic.

This next step did not succeed. The facts were presented clearly and in detail to Congress, to various agencies of the federal government, and to the media. The overall response bordered on indifference. Although some biomedical researchers in government agencies recognized that there was a potentially catastrophic epidemic in the making, they could only work within the totally inadequate budget made available to them. How could our death system fail to perceive and respond to the GRID/AIDS threat when the dangers had been so well documented?

Part of the answer is provided in a statement made by Congressman Henry Waxman who led the struggle for recognition of the new health crisis (quoted by Shilts, 1987, pp. 143–144):

I want to be especially blunt about the political aspects of Kaposi's sarcoma. This horrible disease afflicts members of one of the nation's most stigmatized and discriminated against minorities. The victims are not typical, Main Street Americans. They are gays, mainly from New York, Los Angeles, and San Francisco. There is no doubt in my mind that, if the same disease had appeared among Americans of Norwegian descent, or among tennis players, rather than gay males, the responses of both the government and the medical community would have been different. Legionnaire's disease hit a group of predominately white, heterosexual, middle-aged members of the American Legion. The respectability of the victims brought them a degree of attention and funding for research and treatment far greater than that made available so far to the victims of Kaposi's sarcoma . . . [although] Legionnaire's disease affected fewer people and proved less likely to be fatal. What society judged was not the severity of the disease but the social acceptability of the individuals affected with it. . . .

There has been no persuasive counterargument. Our society in general was slow, reluctant, and half-hearted in its response to the early phases of the AIDS epidemic—and part of the answer must be the perception that this was a disease that afflicted people who were not highly valued, who, in fact, seemed to reject the forms of predominantly middle-class, predominantly white American society. This was by no means a new phenomenon, nor one that was limited to the United States or the early 1980s. History provides abundant examples of death following the paths of existing prejudices, whether sexual, political, linguistic, religious, or racial, and whether the modality is disease, starvation, persecution, or outright massacre.

The total situation, however, was even more complicated. The Reagan Administration was determined to hold down spending on a broad variety of health, education, and social programs. The National Institutes of Health and the Centers for Disease Control were expected to operate on what amounted to reduced budgets. If the NIH and CDC wanted to play with this odd little epidemic, why, they would just have to take the money from some of their other programs. A broad policy agenda that gave low priority to nonmilitary research and development was not likely to be responsive to concerns about a disease that had appeared among "the wrong kind of people."

And just beneath the political agenda and the social stigma was the most implacable force of all: the wishful assumption that this "gay tumor" would remain a highly specialized killer, limiting itself to homosexual men who had chosen a lavishly promiscuous life-style. All the denial-like strategies described in Chapter 1 contributed to establishing and maintaining this assumption. Perhaps the most pervasive strategies were selective attention and compartmentalization. The media, for example, ignored the steady accumulation of evidence in favor of occasional articles or telenews documentaries that failed to indicate the overall picture. Moreover, as it became clear that AIDS was being transmitted by contaminated needles as well as by sexual intercourse, the media showed a strong tendency to choose their examples from those who were not "predominately white, heterosexual, middle-aged" members of society. Selective attention of this kind reinforced the belief that society in general was not at risk from AIDS. One thinks of Peter Ivanovich's reflection that Ivan Ilych was the sort of person who dies, therefore he, still alive, obviously was not the sort of person who dies (as discussed in Chapter 1). Compartmentalization was a mental and emotional trick that was practiced more often by government agencies and those health-care providers who had little direct experience with AIDS. Such people might be aware of many significant pieces of information, enough to complete the total picture of a widespread epidemic in the making. But these pieces would be kept in separate mental compartments. This made it possible to avoid drawing the conclusion that AIDS would surely spread throughout society, and that this process of dissemination must already be underway.

With these medical, sociopolitical, and psychological factors in mind, we now rejoin Patient Zero. By studying clusters of GRID/AIDS cases, public health experts had reached the conclusion that one person had been primarily responsible for transmitting the devastating new syndrome in major metropolitan areas throughout the United States. (However, it would not be accurate to conclude that he was the only source of infection.) This man was eventually identified as Gaetan Dugas, and it was known that he was still actively spreading the disease despite his own illness. A physician had a frank talk with him. How did Dugas respond?

> Though on leave . . . the thirty-year-old flight attendant still had the passes that allowed him to fly all over the world for virtually nothing . . . he decided to settle in San Francisco. It was around this time that rumors began on Castro Street about a strange guy at the Eighth and Howard bathhouse, a blond with a French accent. He would have sex with you, turn up the lights in the cubicle, and point out his Kaposi's sarcoma lesions. I've got "gay cancer," he'd say. "I'm going to die and so are you." (Shilts, 1987, p. 165)

Dugas reasoned that somebody had given him the "gay cancer," now he would take revenge by giving it to others. And he would make sure that the strangers he infected would realize that they now had the disease. Dugas still felt well, though not as abundantly healthy as before, and he took satisfaction in the fact that he had already lived longer than expected with his disease. When confronted with the fact that he was deliberately infecting others with a fatal disease by having sex with them, Patient Zero responded "It's none of your goddamn business. It's my right to do what I want to with my own body" (p. 200).

Attitudes toward sex and death can be related in many different ways. For example, society at large may become "hypersexed" for a while after there has been great loss of life (as through warfare); and, in their private lives, some couples may be motivated to "make babies" in order to overcome personal fears of death by reproductive fertility (Kastenbaum, 1974). To take another of many possible examples, the emotional state that some people experience after sexual intercourse has been characterized as "the little death" (*le petite mort*). Freud (1920/1948) even offered a major theory that asserted that an instinct representing death and oblivion (*Thanatos*) is in a constant dialectic with an instinct representing sex, growth, and increased stimulation (*Eros*). Given the circumstances, then, it was not unusual that Dugas should establish some connection in his mind between sex and death.

But why did he establish such an extreme and deadly connection, incorporating the mission of a remorseless killer into his ongoing activities as a roving lover? Did the act of killing (infecting) help him to keep the sense of being in control, as though he were saying, "I am the killer, I am death, so this proves that I am not the victim?" Had sex always been an activity that allowed him to express anger and exercise power over others, rather than primarily a way of giving and receiving sensual pleasure? If so, then it would not have required much attitudinal change to become a blatant "sex pistol" as his own stress increased. Had his interpersonal relationships been rather superficial all along, using people and being used for momentary needs, instead of developing meaningful and enduring friendships? If so, then infecting strangers with a lethal illness might have been just a different way of saying goodbye.

Patient Zero's state of mind is directly relevant to the still-continuing drama of AIDS, death and human society. The sexual transmission of AIDS involves the participants' thoughts, attitudes, feelings, and actions. A person chooses either to engage or not engage in high-risk sexual behavior. Dugas' state of mind—both before and after he became aware of his condition—was a critical factor in the early spread of AIDS. The decisions that many other people make today will also be critical in determining the future scope of the disease. Dugas made a choice that transformed him into the very image of the Gay Deceiver* (Chapter 2), the worldly, attractive personification of death who lures susceptible people to their doom with the promise of a good time. Fortunately, there are other self-images available, and far less lethal ways to cope with the threat of AIDS.

Efforts to Control the Spread of AIDS

The government and the health-care system at large took some time before recognizing the AIDS epidemic as a major threat to society. Some of the reasons for this delay have already been noted. Several other factors also contributed to the slow and hesitant response: (1) there was no effective treatment available, so the system could not simply gear up to apply existing knowledge; (2) health care providers were alarmed about the prospect of being exposed to infection, having already been put at risk for another serious contagious condition, hepatitis B; (3) the homosexual community was itself strongly divided on AIDS—some leaders urged intensive clinical, research, and educational efforts, but indifference, even apparent apathy,

was also encountered among those most at risk. A common denominator was *fear*—fear that no cure would be found, fear that the epidemic would expand until it became a universal catastrophe, fear that all social institutions (including the political and the medical) would prove to be as ineffective as were medieval institutions during the plague years.

But AIDS could not be ignored or denied for long, whether by politicians, health-care providers, or the increasing number of people at risk. Several initiatives were taken that seem to have been fairly effective:

1. The public bathhouses, primary breeding grounds for AIDS transmission, were finally closed down—although after much resistance and many delays: didn't the owners have the right to be in business and make money? Leaders of the antibathhouse measures were also verbally abused and subjected to death threats. Some continued to patronize bathhouses until their doors were locked, but many others had already decided that the risks were too great, and business declined significantly.

2. Eventually (again, after too much time had passed) it was acknowledged that HIV could be transmitted through blood transfusions under the existing system of blood collection and assessment. Additional steps were taken to protect the supply of blood and blood products. These procedures include improved screening of donors and a heat treatment that is applied to blood products. Health care officials believe that the blood supply is now safe (Moffatt, et al., 1987). However, there will continue to be new cases of AIDS from contaminated blood received in the past. Some people have become HIV-positive through transfusions received in the course of surgery or other major medical procedures. But perhaps the largest subpopulation at risk has been people with *hemophilia*. (Several varieties of this condition exist.) Many hemophiliacs have been able to lead normal lives with the use of blood products that improve the blood's ability

---

*The phrase, *Gay Deceiver*, originally had no association with sexual preference. It referred to a person(ification) who gave the appearance of being devoted to lighthearted pleasure, while actually intending to mislead others.

to form clots. When HIV entered the nation's blood resource network (about 1979) thousands of hemophiliacs were exposed to this virus.

3. The contaminated-needle pathway of AIDS transmission was recognized, and programs were started to provide sterile needles to intravenous drug addicts. These programs are subject to criticism and misunderstanding because they may seem to condone drug use; advocates take the position that it is simply being realistic to offer this form of safeguard, which may help to protect not only the addicts but others with whom they come into contact. Sterile-needle programs are effective when actually used, but not all addicts have taken advantage of them, nor are these programs equally available throughout the nation.

4. Education and training programs have been developed at many levels, especially for health care professionals and for media presentation to the general public. Some of these programs have been welcomed; others have faced either opposition or a mixture of indifference and denial-type attitudes. Effective educational efforts require a foundation of well-established facts. There are not only significant gaps in AIDS knowledge, but some of the facts and assumptions have already been changed. For example, it was first thought that the incubation period is a little under a year; now there is reason to believe that the HIV may lie dormant as long as ten years. Public education campaigns also have been confusing at times, especially when their quoted experts have offered different assessments of risk and different kinds of advice. Nevertheless, there is evidence that the public is becoming better informed about AIDS, and that education and training will continue to be important modalities for reducing future risks.

Who is at Risk for AIDS?

Although AIDS first came to attention as one of the risks taken by promiscuous homosexuals in San Francisco and a few other cities, it has become clear that many other people have been exposed, and that still larger and more diverse populations are endangered. Infants are being born with HIV, and there are many heterosexual adults among the growing list of persons with AIDS. We have already noted that some people have contracted HIV through blood products used in treating hemophilia or in connection with other medical problems; sexual preference and activity had nothing to do with this unfortunate circumstance. How many of the people who were infected with HIV through blood products will actually develop AIDS is not yet known, although there is some hopeful early evidence that the HIV-into-AIDS incidence may be appreciably lower than what was experienced in the first waves of "gay cancer" (Nichols, 1989).

The "most at risk" people are

1. *Prostitutes.* High rates of HIV infection have been reported in the United States, Europe, and Africa (Murphy, 1988).
2. *Babies of mothers with HIV.* It is no longer unusual to discover that a newborn infant has HIV antibodies, indicating that the infection has been transmitted from the mother. Lester (1989) estimates that pregnant women with HIV have more than a 50 percent chance of passing it to their babies. Some of the infants die within a short period of time; it is currently feared that most will not survive over an extended length of time, but only limited data are available. Women who contract AIDS are usually in their child-bearing years, so there is reason for concern that an increasing number of infants will be doomed by this lethal syndrome.
3. *Intravenous drug users.* The contaminated hypodermic needle remains a very high-risk instrument. Drug addiction itself is a major risk factor; sharing needles since the advent of AIDS is a behavior that might well be considered a form of suicide.
4. *People who engage in indiscriminate and unprotected sexual contacts.* It has already become

something of a cliche to say that when A has sex with B, each is also entering into an affair with all of the other person's past lovers. The more participants there have been in a "daisy chain" (or "sex network," to use the current jargon), the greater the chances that sexually transmitted diseases have been passed along. There was already an increase in a variety of sexually transmitted diseases before AIDS appeared. Each of these diseases has its own incubation period and may not be evident at the time of a particular sexual contact. Infection can occur even in the absence of obvious signs of the condition. Sex with multiple partners (even if these contacts have occurred over a period of several years) and sex without careful use of a condom-type device is now considered to be a highly significant risk factor for AIDS, whether one is heterosexual or homosexual. Condoms reduce but do not eliminate the risk of infection, as Surgeon General Koop (1988) and others have observed.

All of the above are direct risk factors: i.e., indiscriminate sexual contact greatly increases the risk of AIDS; it is the behavior that counts, not whether one is a prostitute or a sexually-active person with many partners. But some major indirect risk factors have also been identified. These are factors that increase the probability that a person will engage in high-risk behavior. There is nothing about being Haitian or Afro-American or Hispanic that directly affects the vulnerability to AIDS. Similarly there is nothing about living in poverty that directly increases the vulnerability to AIDS. Nevertheless, the statistical evidence is formidable that Haitians, Afro-Americans, and Hispanics who live in impoverished circumstances have much higher rates of AIDS infection than does the population at large (Nichols, 1989). Most of the "excess morbidity" occurs in just a few major metropolitan areas (in Florida, New Jersey, New York) where the populations at risk live in the midst of a drug- and crime-ridden subculture of despair. The risky sex-

ual behavior is part of a generally risky life-style in which, perhaps, many people feel that they do not have much to lose and must take whatever pleasures they can find when they can find them.

The Haitian connection requires a further word. AIDS did *not* originate in Haiti; rather, many foreigners were in the habit of visiting this nation to engage in sexual practices that are not acceptable in their homelands. It is most likely that some of these visitors brought AIDS with them, which then infected many residents of Haiti. People of Afro-American or Hispanic background are not especially vulnerable to AIDS—but the depressing life circumstances in which some clusters of racial and ethnic minorities have found themselves do increase the probability of engaging in high risk behaviors.

The Changing Pattern of AIDS Incidence and Mortality

More cases of AIDS have been reported in the United States than any other nation. The Centers for Disease Control have estimated that by the end of 1991 there will have been a total of more than 270,000 cases. Furthermore, a much larger number of Americans—about two million—are thought to have been infected with HIV. Of these, about half a million are expected to develop the actual AIDS syndrome within about five years (Fulton & Owen, 1988). In about a decade, the previously unknown syndrome has spread to all 50 states, the District of Columbia, and four United States territories. Even if no new HIV infections occurred, AIDS would be a major health concern for years to come. And, unfortunately, new infections occur every day.

It is understandable that Americans would be most concerned about AIDS in America. However, AIDS has become an international menace as well. The World Health Organization has learned of cases in 136 nations (Nichols, 1989). The rate of increase has been alarmingly swift in some nations. In Belgium and France, for example, there has been a threefold annual increase in the incidence of AIDS. The incidence throughout Africa is not known for certain, but it is invariably in the millions (five million, according to Fulton and Owen, 1988). Up to this point of time, the people of Asian nations, the Middle East, and Eastern Europe seem to have been spared epidemic-level outbreaks of AIDS. It is feared that this will be only a temporary reprieve.

AIDS seems to be essentially a single disease from the biomedical standpoint (although a second type of virus has been identified recently). Nevertheless, AIDS makes its way somewhat differently through different societies and subgroups. Perhaps a society as well as an individual can be thought of as being host to a disease. This can be illustrated through three geosocial patterns of AIDS transmission that have been identified by World Health Organization epidemiologists (reviewed by Nichols, 1988). These patterns are examined in Box 6–1.

We see that AIDS has reached epidemic proportions through two different geosocial patterns. One pattern was generated primarily by homosexual contact, the other by multipartner heterosexual contact and the use of contaminated needles. Ironically, it seems probable that many African children have been infected with HIV as an unforeseen side effect of inoculation and vaccination programs that were intended to protect them from other disease. The differences in patterns of geosocial transmission have implications for prevention and control. For example, infection through intravenous drug use remains a major source of AIDS in the United States and other Pattern One nations, but in Pattern Two nations, needle-borne infection occurs most often as part of medical practice or traditional rituals. Some types of prevention and control efforts obviously would be worth pursuing in all three patterns, notably the protection of the supply of blood and blood products.

It would also be valuable to learn more about nations, ethnic/racial subpopulations, and individuals who have remained at low risk for AIDS. What is the combination of attitudes, values, and life-style that has protected them—and is it

---

BOX 6–1
THREE GEOSOCIAL PATTERNS OF AIDS TRANSMISSION

Pattern One: Highly industrialized nations (e.g., Canada, United States, Western Europe, Australia, New Zealand).

Leading causes of infection: homosexual contact, intravenous drug abuse.

HIV infection exceeds 50% in the highest risk subgroups; less than 1% for population in general. Many more men than women are infected.

Pattern Two: Caribbean nations, and areas of central, eastern and southern Africa.

Leading causes of infection: multiple heterosexual contacts, including sex with prostitutes; contaminated blood and blood products and use of unsterilized needles and other instruments in medical practice or as part of tribal rituals; significant incidence of mother-to-baby transmission.

HIV infections have reached 25% of sexually-active people in some areas; in total population, estimated level is thought to exceed 1%. Men and women have roughly equal infection rates. Some evidence that the immune systems of African heterosexuals are in a chronically-activated state that increases their vulnerability to the HIV.

Pattern Three: Eastern Europe, Middle East, Asia, Pacific.

Leading causes of infection: sexual contact with foreign visitors and sexual contact when visiting nations that have the AIDS epidemic. To a lesser extent, imported blood or blood products.

HIV infection has increased to 16% in the highest risk groups. Thought to be much less than 1% for population in general. Male/female infection ratio has not been established.

possible to encourage this configuration of protective strategies in other groups of people?

SOME ATTITUDINAL, EMOTIONAL, AND SOCIAL RESPONSES TO AIDS

We will focus now on some of the ways that people have responded to both the reality and image of AIDS. Three areas of response will be explored: (1) attitudes toward the disease and its victims; (2) the related issues of trust and confidentiality; and (3) impact upon the way people manage their own lives.

Attitudes toward AIDS and Persons with AIDS

We do not find all potential causes of death to be equally disturbing. Throughout human history there has usually been a particular modality of death that has been especially feared (Kastenbaum, 1987). AIDS has emerged as a new image of catastrophic death that includes many features that had been associated with previously encountered fear-inspiring deaths. These include the death-through-sex connection of syphilis, the breath-stealing assault of tuberculosis, the blood connection associated with near-universal vampire legend, and the Black Death's invasion of the living body with visible signs of deterioration. Many people do not just fear dying—they fear dying of AIDS and its related complications. The overall image of AIDS as a new form of catastrophic death incorporates some bits and pieces of reality, because, in fact, a large variety of complications and symptoms may occur during the course of the illness. However, most illnesses are unpleasant, to say the least, and the terminal phase of AIDS is often a "lung death" characterized by increasing difficulties with respiration. This final pathway is very similar to that of people who are dying of lung disease that is related to the long-term use of cigarettes. The person who has contracted AIDS through sexual activity and the person who has smoked his or her way to death are likely to experience the same type of distress and confront the same decisions about the use of ventilator for life support in their last days. And yet, society has chosen to respond to AIDS as though it were a particularly horrifying disease, and lung cancer, emphysema, etc. as though they were almost natural ways for a person to die. This different response obviously has much to do with our attitudes and life-styles, not simply the diseases themselves.

AIDS is not only an actual disease syndrome but also an idea or construction that we have built in our minds. This assertion has been offered by a number of observers. For example, Paula Treichler (1988) reminds us that "the nature of the relationship between language and reality is highly problematic; and AIDS is not merely an invented label, provided to us by science and scientific naming practices, for a clear-cut disease caused by a virus. Rather, the very nature of AIDS is constructed through language . . ." (p. 31). Treichler found 38 different linguistic constructions of AIDS as she reviewed news stories, letters to the editor, scientific articles, religious tracts, etc. Each of these constructions refers to the same disease, but each advocates a distinctive way of interpreting AIDS and its meaning to us. Here are a few of the constructions she reports:

AIDS is

- A sign that the end of the world is at hand
- A plague stored in King Tut's tomb and unleashed when the Tut exhibit toured the United States (in 1976)
- The outcome of genetic mutations that were caused by "mixed marriages"
- A CIA plot to destroy subversives
- A Soviet plot to destroy capitalists
- A capitalist plot to create new markets for pharmaceutical products
- A fascist plot to destroy homosexuals
- An imperialist plot to destroy third-world nations
- The perfect emblem of our decadent civilization
- God's punishment of our weakness and sins
- Just another venereal disease

It is remarkable how the "same" medical syndrome can generate such a variety of interpretations or constructions. One of the lessons we can learn from this (partial) list is awareness of the ease with which our minds can depart from the basic facts of a situation and create lavish interpretations. This lesson has many applications. For example, several of the interpretations assign blame for the AIDS epidemic on some remote and powerful interests. People who become enthralled with the idea that King Tut (or "imperialists," "fascists," "communists," "capitalists") are responsible for AIDS are people who are not very likely to support practical efforts to prevent, control, alleviate, and cure the disease. Furthermore, if AIDS is to be interpreted as punishment for our collective sins, then the *person* with AIDS may also be viewed as an example of divine retribution, rather than as an unique man, woman, or child who is facing death. We are in a better position to understand and help the individuals who are directly affected by AIDS if we can free ourselves from the influence of linguistic constructions that reflect anxieties and dogmas more than the facts of the situation.

Prevailingly negative attitudes have been expressed toward persons with AIDS. Herek and Glunt (1988) observe that "Persons infected with HIV must bear the burden of societal hostility at a time when they are most in need of social support. Attempts to avoid such hostility may compromise individuals' health: Fear of being harassed, of facing job discrimination, and of losing insurance coverage, for example, deters individuals from being tested for HIV infection and seeking early treatment for symptoms" (p. 886). These authors share Treichler's view that AIDS-related stigma is a socially constructed reaction, but they add that it most often affects "groups that already were targets of prejudice." In short, "the American epidemic of AIDS has been socially defined as a disease of marginalized groups, especially gay men."

Persons with AIDS may then be regarded as in multiple jeopardy for social stigma: (1) "I have a disease that makes other people feel very anxious; (2) it is a fatal disease, so when people see

me they start to feel uncomfortable about their own deaths; and (3) middle-class, mainstream, heterosexual America never liked me in the first place, and now they have a new excuse to scorn and reject me."

Our society in general and each of us as individuals has the choice of participating in the stigmatizing of persons with AIDS or of developing a more compassionate orientation. In a recent small-scale study I found some indications that at least one subgroup within our society has declined the opportunity to stigmatize people with AIDS. As part of a larger questionnaire instrument, I asked 79 university students of nursing to suppose that they would be working and associating closely with another person on a project of mutual interest. This other person would be of the same sex and age. Three other characteristics of the other person were specified as variables: heterosexual or homosexual, tested positive or negative for the AIDS virus (HIV), and user or nonuser of illegal drugs. There was a strong preference expressed: the nursing students definitely did not want to work and associate with drug users. By contrast, they were not put off by the fact that a person was homosexual or had tested positive for HIV. Subsequent conversations with some of the respondents indicated that drug users were shunned because they were seen as having made a choice to break the law, damage their own mind and body, and encourage drug-related criminal activity. Homosexuality was regarded as a life-style that some people develop for reasons that are not entirely clear. They could see themselves trusting and respecting a colleague who happened to be homosexual, but not one who was drug dependent. Infection with the AIDS virus was regarded as a very serious health problem, but not as the basis for stigmatizing another person. As one advanced nursing student commented, "I chose nursing because I really want to help people. People with AIDS need help; it's as simple as that!"

Perhaps this small sample of student nurses represents a larger number of health care professionals and others whose philosophies of life guide them toward a more constructive and compassionate approach to people with AIDS.

Trust and Confidentiality

The related issues of trust and confidentiality have become salient ever since the AIDS-related syndrome has been recognized. There are both public and personal sides to these issues. The public side has been demonstrated with repeated denials that so-and-so (a well-known person) has died of AIDS. For several years it became routine practice for the dying person or a spokesperson to maintain that some other illness was involved. Usually the motivation was to protect the reputation of the dying or deceased person and sometimes to protect financial interests, as well as family and friends. Denial (in the sense of deception) and evasion would not have been necessary if society had been ready to "construct" AIDS as a life-threatening condition rather than as evidence of sinfulness, deviance, or some other negative quality. Eventually, the truth was told in some circumstances, and it was discovered that the public did have a capacity to accept the facts and mourn the death of a person it had admired. Many believe that one of the turning points in honest communication was when the cause of Rock Hudson's death was disclosed. Sorrow about his death seemed to take precedence over agitation about the cause.

Concerns about confidentiality of patient records remains a major issue in the public sphere. There have been many proposals to test certain subpopulations for possible HIV infection; some have even advocated universal testing. This has set up a confrontation between the right of the public to be protected from a life-threatening condition and the right of individuals to the privacy of their personal lives. Both rights are well entrenched in our tradition, but they have come into conflict in many situations. Health authorities have been trying to establish standards of confidentiality and disclosure that will respect both sets of concern. This has required taking a strong stand against extreme positions. For example, some people have advocated quarantine for people with the AIDS virus. This is a fairly popular theme in letters to the editor—but it would clearly violate the civil rights of individuals as well as introduce a major new socioeconomic problem. The informed public and health officials have repudiated this kind of overreaction. Nevertheless, it is recognized that other kinds of negative consequences could flow from the inappropriate release of information that identifies a particular person as having HIV or AIDS. Possible loss of employment is one of the most frequently mentioned of these consequences, but there is also the entire spectrum of harassment to be concerned about.

At present there are a variety of policies and procedures that affect the confidentiality-disclosure status of AIDS data. It would be a good idea to check with your local health department to be certain that you are up to date on the regulations. Overall, however, there is a trend toward establishing a responsible balance between the public's right to know and the individual's right to privacy. In Arizona, for example, people can be given a test for HIV infection through county health departments without fear of having their names reported. Unfortunately, according to a recent survey, most people in the highest risk group (homosexual men) did not realize that anonymous testing was available in the state (Arizona DHS, 1990). There are also federal guidelines intended to assure personal confidentiality in the collection of information on the AIDS epidemic (Turner, et al., 1989).

The personal side of the issue is very personal indeed. Can one lover trust another? Do people tell the truth about their sexual histories and health when they are hoping to begin a new sexual relationship? One recent study indicates that there is basis for concern (Cochran & Mays, 1990). More than 400 California college-students were asked about their honesty when discussing previous sexual experiences. About a third of the men and a tenth of the women said that they had told a lie at least once in order to have sex. The percentages rose precipitously when they were asked if they had ever been lied to. About 60% of the women and almost half the men reported that prospective sex partners had told them lies in order to ease the way to bed. And perhaps even more disturbing was the self-report that about 20% of the men would lie about having a negative HIV-antibody test in order to have sex. In interpreting the findings from their "Sex, Lies, and HIV" study, the researchers believe that deception may be even more frequent than the self-report data show, because people tend to underestimate the frequency and extent of their own lies. Trust in the intimate realm of sexual relations has always been an issue; today it is a more consequential issue than ever.

Has the AIDS Epidemic Affected the Way We Live?

Information can be made available and warnings can be issued—but the response cannot be taken for granted. This uneasy rule applies to many types of threat—people often have ignored emergency storm warnings, obvious fire hazards, evidence of hostile troops in the area, and, on the personal level, signs of cancer or heart trouble. With more refined methods of social research, it has been noticed that various subgroups in the overall population tend to respond differently to the same threat. It appears at the moment that the response to AIDS is following this differential pattern. Some people appear to be making significant changes in the way they manage their lives; others appear to be taking no account of the AIDS epidemic. The limited data now available suggest that the following pattern of response is taking place as the public becomes increasingly aware of AIDS information (from studies reviewed by Turner, et al., 1989 unless otherwise noted):

1. European data indicate that a substantial number of intravenous drug users will take advantage of sterile needle programs; these programs are not associated with an increase in the number of IV drug users.

2. There has been a marked reduction in high-risk behaviors by homosexual and bisexual men in the San Francisco area. It must be kept in mind that part of this reduction is attributable to the illness and death of those already infected with HIV. However, several studies indicate that safer sex practices are now more common than previously.

3. Throughout the nation there are also indications that more and more adults are becoming well informed about AIDS-related facts. In Arizona, for example, about 90% of the general adult population could correctly identify the high-risk behaviors for HIV infection and understood the role of condoms in preventing the spread of AIDS. Furthermore, about a third of the respondents indicated that they had already made some changes in their life-style. The most frequent change was to exercise more caution in "casual" sex contacts (Arizona DHS, 1990). Among homosexual respondents, the majority reported having fewer sexual partners and using condoms more often. This survey was somewhat biased in the direction of people with higher levels of education, and it did not adequately sample the spectrum of racial and ethnic minorities.

4. Despite these encouraging signs, there is still a large gap between knowledge and behavior. Essentially, almost all educated adults know the basic facts about AIDS transmission and prevention, and the majority use more safety precautions. But there are still many occasions on which they take a chance with their own lives and the lives of their partners.

5. There is no firm evidence that concern about AIDS has had much general effect on the sexual activity of teenagers. Most observations suggest that high school and college students seldom connect the AIDS menace to their own lives and actions. This compartmentalization strategy may have been strengthened by the media's tendency to depict AIDS as a disease of IV drug users or homosexual men. A typical attitude among youth—invulnerability—has probably also been heightened by the mistaken belief that venereal diseases have become rare and are easily

treated. Without doubt, there is an urgent need to create greater awareness among teenagers about the life-threatening risks they may be taking without much thought.

Psychological and Social Support for People with HIV/AIDS

To some extent this chapter has been reflecting society's primary concern with the prevention and cure of AIDS. The AIDS crisis is much more personal to some people, however: they *fear* that they may have been infected with HIV, they *know* they have the virus, they know they have actual AIDS-related *symptoms*, they know that their body's defenses are collapsing, that they are *dying,* or there is a *significant person in their lives* who is at one of these points of distress. Additionally, there are those many people who have already seen a friend, colleague, or family member die from AIDS-related complications. Grief is almost palpable, almost a component of the climate, in places where the AIDS death toll has been especially heavy. It is not unusual for a resident of the San Francisco area to name 40, 50, or more people on his or her personal list of people lost to AIDS. People who provide services to others have often been devastated by the illness and death of their clients or customers. Listen, for example, to Bay Area counselors, therapists, and social workers. See in their eyes the fatigue of grief superimposed upon grief, the anger, the confusion. The victims of HIV/AIDS include those who have shared their stress and those who mourn their deaths.

In succeeding chapters we will explore some of the ways people experience and attempt to cope with terminal illness and grief. Many of these facts and dynamics apply to AIDS-related dying, death, and grief. This is a useful point to keep in mind because there has been a tendency to portray living and dying with AIDS as a radically different type of experience. At the extreme, this has led to the assumption that a whole new approach is needed to understanding and support. There must be "AIDS dynamics," "AIDS counseling," "AIDS psychotherapy," etc. However, upon reflection most experienced caregivers will recognize that understanding and coping with AIDS has much in common with other critical situations. For example, it is not only when confronted by the possibility of an AIDS diagnosis that a person may delay medical testing. Similar dynamics have often been found in people who suspect that they might have cancer. And AIDS is not the only challenge that can severely test a person's basic philosophy and values; the death of a child has created a crisis of meaning for many parents. Furthermore, the response to AIDS has much to do with the individual's personality and life situation; the inarticulate loner and the person who thrives on social activity will cope somewhat differently with AIDS, just as they do with most other situations in their lives.

Nevertheless, there are some themes, conflicts, and stresses that are seen more frequently or in more intense form among persons with HIV/AIDS. These include

1. *Fear of losing one's most supportive relationships.* (Nichols, 1985). Men who have concealed their homosexuality or IV drug use from family members or colleagues are vulnerable to having these relationships disrupted when it is learned that they have the AIDS virus. Even those who have been open about their life-styles may have reason to fear that others will now withdraw from them. This means that it is not "just death" that a person must confront, but also the loss of their interpersonal ties. A friend, a chaplain, or a counselor can provide an exceedingly valuable service by helping people with HIV/AIDS to maintain and even strengthen their most important relationships.

2. *Confusion about treatment and prognosis.* AIDS is still a new condition. Physicians do not have many years of outcome studies and personal experience to answer the patient's questions. "How long will the virus remain dormant?" "Is there a way to prevent the virus from developing into the actual AIDS syndrome?" "What about that new treatment from Europe or Mexico that

I've been hearing about?" People with any life-threatening illness may become confused and anxious about the uncertainties of the situation and the mixed messages they hear from various sources. With AIDS, there is more basis for uncertainty than with many other conditions. The media frequently contributes to this problem by announcing "cures" that are based upon preliminary studies and may not prove substantial (Bazell, 1990). If the person with HIV/AIDS often has difficulty in interpreting and responding to the many and shifting pieces of information, so do the physician, the nurse, the researchers, and others with professional training.

3. *Thought and mood may be impaired by brain infection.* AIDS-related pathology and symptoms can take many forms. These include Kaposi's sarcoma, as already mentioned, and a variety of other neoplasms. The opportunistic infections that overwhelm the impaired immune system can affect any and all aspects of physical functioning. As the illness reaches its end phase, respiratory problems often become dominant and are likely to be identified as the most direct cause of death. Unfortunately, the individual's ability to cope with the illness and its impact on his or her life may also be undermined by brain pathology. The *AIDS dementia complex* (ADC) is usually caused by direct HIV infection of the brain, but it can also be a secondary effect of another AIDS-related condition (e.g., lymphoma or stroke). ADC is not easy to diagnose in its early phases: the unsteadiness in walking, the impairments of recent memory, etc. all could have other explanations. Eventually, however, many develop "a picture of profound global dementia associated with mutism, incontinence and eventual coma" (Fenton, 1987, p. 583). There may also be periods of delirium. It can be useful, then, to consider the possibility that changes in thought and mood may have an organic basis. Dementia syndromes sometimes do respond to medical intervention; furthermore, other practical actions might also prove helpful (e.g., providing assistance to the person with ADC when there are medical, financial or other decisions to be made).

We have briefly reviewed three of the most distinctive problems that confront people with HIV/AIDS. To these must be added the many other stresses and challenges that are likely to arise with any life-threatening condition. One can acknowledge that these are serious problems without surrendering to the attitude of therapeutic nihilism. People can and do bring comfort to each other even when faced with the most trying circumstances. Many metropolitan areas now have support groups that have the special purpose of comforting and counseling people with HIV/AIDS. Additionally, there are signs that many existing human service organizations, both professional and peer-volunteer, are becoming more responsive to the needs of people with HIV/AIDS. Whatever the caregiver knows about human nature in general and about counseling and therapy in particular is likely to prove useful here as well. This should surprise no one, for people with HIV/AIDS are people.

AIDS and the Death System: Some Implications and Questions

Human society repeatedly has been faced with major threats to life. The AIDS epidemic is not unique in every aspect, but its overall pattern is distinctive, and the times in which we live are also distinctive. We can draw some lessons from the past, but we would be limiting ourselves severely if we tried to understand, predict, and respond to AIDS as though it were a "standard plague." Here are a few of the implications and questions that come to attention as we observe AIDS in the contemporary death system of the United States.

1. *Can we find the balance between cure and comfort orientations?* Our energetic, aggressive, and action-oriented society has created a health care system that emphasizes the *warning, predicting,* and *preventing* functions (Chapter 3). The acute care model remains at the core of the system, even after many years of concern about rapidly growing needs of a chronic or long-term nature. The positive side of this picture is that,

after a delayed start, the United States is giving a relatively high priority to reducing the spread of AIDS and attempting to find a cure. The negative side is that the government and the health system in general remains less inclined to provide the best possible care for those who are already stricken with AIDS. General hospitals have not yet responded effectively to this need (Lyons, et al., 1989) and special interest groups are complaining about the cost of services to AIDS patients. If we hold true to form, most of the attention will be given to large-scale educational and research efforts, and relatively little to the actual HIV/AIDS patients and the grief of their survivors. What should we do? What will we do?

2. *Social integration or disintegration?* One of the basic functions of a death system is to encourage *social consolidation after death*. This is by no means a guaranteed outcome. Fresh in America's memory, for example, are the experiences of Vietnam War veterans and of the families who lost a loved one in that conflict. The war had become increasingly unpopular for reasons that are not difficult to understand. Unfortunately, though, this attitudinal rejection of the war also carried over in the form of the very limited emotional support offered to veterans and grieving families. In a different way, AIDS has also threatened to divide our society and lead to the emotional abandonment of many individuals. Will we reject the people because we don't like the disease? Or will we take this as an opportunity to strengthen the bonds within our society by overcoming some familiar biases and aversions?

3. *Do we still have a crisis of explanation?* One of the basic functions of any death system is the need to make *sense of death*. This is one of the reasons why "old age" is a relatively popular "cause" of death (although "old age" is an ambiguous term, and cannot really be said to "cause" anything). By contrast, AIDS has started out as a highly "unpopular" cause of death—partially because of its associations with deviant life-styles, but also because so many boisterous and contradictory explanations have been offered (e.g., Treichler's collection of linguistic constructions). This proliferation of explanations, many of them extreme and unfounded, suggests that our society has been unnerved by the AIDS epidemic. Will we continue to generate and pursue "explanations" that attempt to make scapegoats of various individuals, agencies, or groups, and imply that punitive actions should be taken? Or will we decide to stay close to the known facts and resist the temptation to use AIDS as a proving ground for our most fantastical theories?

These are but a few of the questions that AIDS poses for us as individuals and as a society. In the following set of chapters we expand our scope to explore the human response to dying and death across a much broader spectrum of situations.

REFERENCES

Arizona Department of Health Services (1990). Knowledge, Attitudes, and Beliefs (KAB) studies: Arizonans very knowledgeable about HIV transmission/AIDS. *Arizona Responds to AIDS, 1* (2). 1, 10–11.

Bazell, R. (1990). Medicine show. *The New Republic,* (January 22), pp. 16–19.

Cochran, S. D., & Mays, V. M. (1990) Sex, lies, and HIV. *New England Journal of Medicine, 322,* 774–775.

Fenton, T. W. (1987). AIDS-related psychiatric disorder. *British Journal of Psychiatry, 151,* 579–588.

Freud, S. (1920/1948). *Beyond the pleasure principle.* Standard edition. Volume 18. London: The Hogarth Press.

Fulton, R., & Owen, G. (1988). AIDS: Seventh rank absolute. In I. B. Corless & M. Pitmann-Lindeman (Eds.), *AIDS: Principles, practices, and politics* (pp. 237–250). New York: Hemisphere Publishing Corp.

Gallo, R. C., & Montagnier, L. (1989). The AIDS epidemic. In J. Piel (Ed.), *The science of AIDS* (pp. 1–12). New York: W. H. Freeman & Co.

Haseltine, W. A., & Wong-Staal, F. (1989). The molecular biology of the AIDS virus. In J. Piel (Ed.), *The science of AIDS* (pp. 13–26). New York: W. H. Freeman & Co.

Herek, G. M., & Glunt, E. K. (1988). An epidemic of stigma. Public reactions to AIDS. *American Psychologist, 43,* 886–891.

Kastenbaum, R. (1974). Fertility and the fear of death. *Journal of Social Issues, 30,* 63–78.

Kastenbaum, R. (1987). "Safe death" in the postmodern world. In A. Gilmore & S. Gilmore (Eds.), *A safer death* (pp. 3–14). New York & London: Plenum Press.

Koop, C. E., & Samuels, M. E. (1988). The Surgeon General's report on AIDS. In I. B. Corless & M. Pittman-Lindeman (Eds.), *AIDS: Principles, practices, and politics* (pp. 5–18). New York: Hemisphere Publishing Corp.

Lester, B. (1989). *Women and AIDS: A practical guide for those who help others.* New York: Continuum.

Lyons, J. S., Larson, D. B., Anderson, R. L., & Bilheimer, L. (1989). Psychosocial services for AIDS patients in the general hospital. *International Journal of Psychiatry in Medicine, 19,* 385–392.

Moffatt, B. C., Spiegel, J., Parrish, S., & Helquist, M. (Eds.) (1987). *Aids: A self-care manual.* Los Angeles: AIDS Project Los Angeles.

Murphy, J. S. (1988). Women with AIDS: Sexual ethics in an epidemic. In I. B. Corless & M. Pittman-Lindeman (Eds.), *AIDS: Principles, practices, and politics* (pp. 65–80). New York: Hemisphere Publishing Corporation.

Nichols, E. K. (1989). *Mobilizing against AIDS.* (Revised edition). New York: National Academy of Sciences.

Nichols, S. E. (1985). Psychosocial reactions of persons with the Acquired Immunodeficiency Syndrome. *Annals of Internal Medicine, 103,* 765–767.

Shilts, R. (1987). *And the band played on.* New York: St. Martin's Press.

Treichler, P. A. (1988). AIDS, Homophobia, and biomedical discourse: An epidemic of signification. In D. Crimp (Ed.), *AIDS: Cultural analysis, cultural activism* (pp. 31–70). Cambridge, MA: The MIT Press.

Turner, C. F., Miller, H. G., & Moses, L. E. (1989). *AIDS: Sexual behavior and intravenous drug use.* Washington, DC: National Academy Press.

Dear Grandmother

"Were did you Go, Will
you come back, Please
come back" F will Give
you a cake a car

as much as gold
as you want and
a Lot of house and
everything you want
are you in havin or
in your grave or
are you a ghost

If you are in
havin F will send
you a Letter to havin
If you are in
you grave F will
Put the Letter on
your grave and
If you are a ghost
F will be scerad

Dear Grandmother,

"Where did you go? Will
you come back? Please
come back." I will give
you a cake, a car
or as much gold
as you want and
a lot of house and
everything you want.
Are you in heaven or
in your grave or
are you a ghost?

If you are in
heaven, I will send
you a letter to heaven.
If you are in
your grave, I will
put the letter on
your grave and
if you are a ghost,
I will be scared.

—Letter written by an
  elementary-school child

chapter 7

DEATH IN THE WORLD OF CHILDHOOD

Childhood is the kingdom where nobody dies. (Millay, 1969)

Dear Grandmother:

Where did you go. Will you come back. Please come back. I will give you a cake a car as much gold as you want and a lot of house and everything you want. Are you in havin or in your grave or are you a ghost.

If you are in havin I will send a letter to havin. If you are in your grave I will put the letter on your grave and if you are a ghost I will be scerad. (Bertman, 1979–1980)

Most of us would like to believe that family life has always revolved about the child; that mother, father, and baby have constituted a domestic trinity as old as Western civilization itself; and that the nursery was always the most beloved and sanctified room in the family house. The reality is that until fairly modern times most children were either abandoned by their mothers or farmed out to other women shortly after birth and that, in fact, both the family and the family house as we know them today did not even exist until well into the 17th century. (Schorsch, 1979)

Is childhood really the kingdom where nobody dies? Much depends on how we answer this question. Adults who hold that children cannot comprehend death are likely to show a different pattern of interaction and decision-making than those who believe that children do grasp the meaning of death. A child may be commanded to "kiss Grandmother good-bye" or may be excluded from the funeral and memorial services altogether. A child may enter a room to find the adult conversation suddenly hushed or may be permitted to take part in a death-related discussion. Parents may provide the child with realistic-looking toy weapons or may try to limit the child's exposure to violent television shows and movies. There may be concern that a child has been emotionally devastated by the death of a person or a pet, or there may be confidence that he or she is too young to understand and remember. And should their child suffer a life-threatening illness, the parents may choose either to confront or avoid the topic of death in their interactions. These are some of the behaviors that are influenced by what adults assume that children know or don't know about death.

More than knowledge is involved, however. Adults may sense that a child has become aware of death, but may feel unsure about how they should respond. For example, a young child may suddenly ask a parent "Are you going to be dead?" Is it better to change the subject immediately? To walk away? To reply that "No, I'm not going to be dead!"? To firmly say, "That's not a nice thing to talk about"? Or is there a more effective response than any of the above?

This chapter helps to answer such questions by drawing upon a broad range of research and observation to examine the child's relationship to death. First, however, you are invited to review some of your own childhood experiences with death. (See the "Exploring Box," following.)

CHILDREN DO THINK ABOUT DEATH

The most basic fact has been well established: Children, even young children, do think about death. Evidence comes from many sources.

Historical Evidence

One of America's first distinguished psychologists, G. Stanley Hall (1922), was also among the first to study aging and death. Hall and his student, Colin Scott, asked adults to recall their earliest experiences with death. Most of their memories went back to their school years. These childhood experiences evidently had made a lasting impression because they were recalled in vivid detail.

> The child's exquisite temperature sense feels a chill where it formerly felt heat. Then comes the immobility of face and body where it used to find prompt

---

> ### EXPLORING YOUR EXPERIENCES WITH DEATH IN CHILDHOOD
>
> Write your answers on a separate sheet of paper.
>
> 1. How was the subject of death treated in your home when you were a child? What questions did you ask of your parents? What answers did you receive?
>
> 2. What most interested or puzzled you about death when you were a young child?
>
> 3. Do you remember the death of a pet or other animal at some time in your childhood? What were the circumstances? How did you feel about it? How did other people respond to your feelings?
>
> 4. Do you remember the death of a person at some time in your childhood? What were the circumstances? How did you feel about it? How did other people respond to your feelings?
>
> 5. Can you identify any ways in which childhood experiences with death may have influenced you to this day?
>
> 6. What do you now think is the best thing a parent could say to or do with a child in a death situation and why?
>
> 7. What do you now think is the worst thing a parent could say to or do with a child in a death situation and why?

---

movements of response. There is no answering kiss, pat, or smile. . . . Often the half-opened eyes are noticed with awe. The silence and tearfulness of friends are also impressive to the child, who often weeps reflexly or sympathetically. (p. 440)

Hall adds that funeral and burial scenes sometimes were the very earliest of all memories for the adults he studied. More recent studies (Tobin, 1972) also find death experiences common among adults' earliest memories, as I have also found in some of my own research. An Italian-American butcher recalled his earliest memory:

I was still in the old country. We all lived in a big old house, me, my family and all kinds of relatives. I remember it was just a few days after my fourth birthday, and there was grandmother laid out on a table in the front room. The room was full of women crying their eyes out. Hey, I didn't want any part of it, but somebody said grandmother was just sleeping. I doubted that very much. Grandmother never slept on a table in the front room with everybody crying their eyes out before. But what I really remember most is what I want to forget most. "Kiss your grandmother!" Yeah, that's right. They made me walk right up and kiss grandmother. I can still see her face. And I can still feel her face. Is that crazy? I mean, after all these years, I can still feel her cold dead face and my lips against it.

Although this man was the owner of a specialty meat shop and its chief butcher, he reported feeling panic on those few occasions when he has been in the presence of a human corpse. The early childhood experience with death had somehow become part of his adult personality.

Recently, the "earliest death-related memory" question was put to 163 college students in Kentucky (Dickinson, 1986). Most of the memories centered around the death of a person, whether relative (70%) or nonrelative (15%). By far the greatest number of death memories involved the loss of a grandparent (48%); parental death was reported by 6% of the respondents. Dogs were the pets whose deaths were most often recalled (7%), but the following reflections on another type of pet also illustrate that there may be long-term consequences of childhood experiences:

> As a young child, I would receive ducks and chickens as an Easter present. One of these chicks was able to survive the playing and was able to grow into a nice white hen. She was my pride and joy, following me and coming when I called. The hen stayed at my Grandmother's. One Sunday dinner the main course was "fried chicken." It took me several minutes to realize just what had happened. To say the least, I was devastated and do not eat chicken to this day." (p. 83)

The childhood loss and death theme was evident again in research interviews several students and I conducted with residents of Sun City and Sun City West (Arizona). These people were asked not for their earliest experiences with death, but for their earliest memories of any kind. The respondents went back at least sixty years and sometimes more than eighty for their memories. Many incidents were pleasant to recall; others were odd and hard to explain. However, more than one person in three reported an earliest memory that conveyed some encounter with death, loss, or separation:

- The green chair nobody sat in any more. I remember going into the room and out of the room and back into the room time after time. Maybe Grandfather would be sitting in his chair the next time I entered the room. I know I was four because I just had a birthday with four candles—on the cake.
- There were lots of people in the street, and there had been some kind of accident. I wanted to see what. A horse was on the ground and there was a twisted up, tipped over cart behind it. Somebody, a man, was saying they ought to shoot it. I got one look and then somebody pushed me away or led me away. I don't know what I thought about it at the time, but I can still see that horse.

Studies such as these indicate that the young child's experiences of death and loss may become life-long memories for the adult. Perhaps you found some death or loss-separation memories coming to mind when you answered the questions about your own childhood experiences. Some students have taken their early memories as the starting point for a little personal research. One young woman, for example, recalled having felt very much alone and frightened, "and there was something about the ocean and the beach in it." No other details came to mind from this memory that seemed to have taken place just before her kindergarten days. She decided to ask her parents what had actually happened. They were reluctant, but "then we had one of our best talks ever! Mom had had a miscarriage and the doctor had said she couldn't have any more babies

bies or she might die herself. It never occurred to them to say any of this to a little kid like me. But while we were talking I suddenly remembered them getting rid of baby things, a crib and all, giving them away, and my mother looking real strange and distant. And that was when they sent me to live with a family I didn't like much so they could also get away a few days, together, and try to feel normal again. I can understand that perfectly now. But then, it was like they were going to get rid of me, too! And in my little kid's mind, the beach and the ocean were part of it all. Maybe they were going to leave me all by myself on the beach, or maybe a big wave was going to come and get me!"

This student had developed a pattern of avoiding beaches and large bodies of water, although she was also attracted to these places. The long and frank conversation with her family not only helped her understand the unpleasant and unaccountable early memory, but also dissipated her anxieties about going to the beach. Many other students have found that it was possible to gain a better understanding of some of their ways of thinking simply by bringing early memories to mind. A graduate student of social work reported that "I think I know now why I'm so crazy about stuffed animals! I had my favorite kitten squashed by a truck, and then the mother cat, too, by some kind of vehicle. And then, all in the same short period of time, a coyote killed our old family dog. Stuffed animals have a much better life expectancy!"

Your childhood memories of death-related experiences may be quite different from these. It would be going much too far to say that a particular childhood experience "causes" us to behave or feel in a particular way in adult life. Nevertheless, it is clear that childhood experiences tinged with death, loss, or separation can become significant influences on the way we see life and cope with death.

Most of us carry in our memories our own personal historical evidence for childhood encounters with death. Cultural history provides examples of a broader scale. The "innocent" songs and games of childhood through the centuries have often centered on death themes. The familiar ring-around-the-rosie song and game achieved popularity during the peak years of the plague in 14th-century Europe. The "rosies" referred to one of the symptoms of the disease; the "all fall down" is self-explanatory. The children who recited and enacted this little drama were acutely aware that people all around them were falling victim. We can imagine the security they sought by joining hands. The ritual impersonated and in its limited and temporary way *mastered* death. The passivity and isolation of fear was converted into a group effort to actively master the threat. Today this game may seem quaint and innocuous. In its heyday, though, ring-around-the-rosie represented both an acknowledgment of the prevalence of uncontrolled death in the environment and the impulse to share and master death-related anxiety.

The death theme is explicit in many hide-and-seek and tag games. Even the adult most unwilling to admit children's awareness of death would have a difficult time dismissing the tag game known as "Dead Man Arise!" This type of game has many names and local variations. In Sicily, for example, children play "A Morsi Sanzuni."

> One child lay down pretending to be dead while his companions sang a dirge, occasionally going up to the body and lifting an arm or a leg to make sure the player was dead, and nearly stifling the child with parting kisses. Suddenly he would jump up, chase his mourners, and try to mount the back of one of them. . . . In Czechoslovakia . . . the recumbent player was covered with leaves, or had her frock held over her face. The players then made a circle and counted the chimes of the clock, but each time "Death" replied "I must still sleep." This continued until the clock struck twelve when, as in some other European games, the sleeping player sprung to life, and tried to catch someone. (Opie & Opie, 1969, p. 107)

In tag games the person who is "It" usually must not peek or move while the other players conceal themselves. The touch of "It" is both scary and thrilling—almost a training ground for future Count Draculas. Even the slightest touch has grave significance: The victim instantly is transformed from lively participant to death personified ("It"). Further resemblances to death are suggested in those variations in which the victim must freeze (enter suspended animation?) until rescued by one who is still free (alive?).

Historical observations strongly suggest that concern with death has been a common theme in children's play through the centuries, and I have not even spoken of all the zestful destruction games that have replaced each other over the years—zapping today's space invaders are the children of cops-and-robbers and the grandchildren of cowboys-and-Indians, whose more remote ancestors as children fought to the mock death as Saracens-and-Crusaders. History does not always tell us much about the lives of children, but when light does shine it often reveals that death-related games were well known to them.

Research and Clinical Evidence

That death is a familiar theme to children has been verified by studies conducted in various parts of the world and using a number of different research strategies. This basic fact emerges, whether it emerges from parents' diaries and children's story telling in England (Anthony, 1940/1972); children's responses to questions in Hungary (Nagy, 1969), Senegal (Vandewiele, 1983–1984), or the United States (Childers & Wimmer, 1971; Koocher, 1973); children's drawings in Canada (Lonetto, 1980); or children's interpretations of pictures in Taiwan (Lee, et al., 1983–1984). It is found in children who are perfectly healthy (Anthony, 1972; Childers & Wimmer, 1971; Koocher, 1973; Lonetto, 1980; Nagy, 1969; Vandewiele, 1983–1984; Wass, et al., 1983), who have a life-threatening illness (Lee, et al., 1983–1984; Spinetta, 1974; Wass, et al., 1983), and who are in psychotherapy for emotional problems (Lampl-de-Groot, 1976; Lopez & Kliman, 1979). It is the rule rather than

the exception for children to include death among their interests and concerns.

Following are a few examples from my collection of verified observations:

A boy, aged 16 months, was taken to a public garden by his father, an eminent biomedical scientist. This was a regular visit, one of their favorite expeditions together. The boy's attention was captured by a fuzzy caterpillar creeping along the sidewalk. Suddenly, large adult feet came into view, and the caterpillar was crushed (unwittingly) by another visitor to the garden. Immediately the boy showed an alarmed expression. He then bent over the remains, studying them intently. After a long moment, he stood up and informed his father, in a sad and resigned voice, "No more!"

"No more!" Can there be a more direct and concise comment?

Three children found a dead frog in a swampy area near their home. The boys, ages seven and eight, buried the frog and placed a marker on its grave. One of them announced the intention to open the grave later and see what there would be to see: "Maybe Mr. Frog will be alive again." The 3-year-old girl, perhaps miffed because she had not been allowed a major role in the burial project, took a scornful tone with them: "Don't be silly! Mr. Frog is dead, dead, dead, and when you're dead, dead, dead, you *stay* dead, dead, dead!"

There was no doubt in the minds of these children that death was something special that required special thoughts and actions. The burial as experiment provided a way to test their mixed ideas about the nature of death as well as a sense of mastery. What the little committee seemed to lack, however, was a patronizing adult voice, and this was readily provided by the junior member.

An eight-year-old boy was improvising—loudly—at the piano. His father approached him with the intention of asking him to cease and desist, but noticed that the pianist was in a mood of deep contemplation, not just idly banging away. "What are you playing?" the father asked. The boy replied, "A funeral song for Lovey" (the family cat, recently killed on the highway). As the boy continued his improvisations, he explained the meaning of each passage, "This is Lovey sharpening her claws on a tree . . . This is Lovey when she has just heard the can opener . . . This is Lovey curled up and purring. . . ."

Again, there can be no doubt that this child understood something of death's significance and, furthermore, felt the need and obligation to perform some ritual in honor of the deceased.

From direct observation, clinical experience, and systematic research there is ample evidence that children do think of death. It is good to keep this basic fact in mind, because the situation becomes more complicated as the specific nature of their death-related thoughts is considered in some detail.

RESEARCH CASE HISTORIES

Research findings usually are conveyed through statistics, and appropriately so. This custom, however, often fails to convey the reality of individual differences as well as the patterning of thoughts and actions within the individual. Three brief case histories drawn from my research (Kastenbaum, 1991) will enable you to glimpse individual and family patterns. A general review of research findings will follow. For the present purposes, this section concentrates upon data obtained in structured interviews with the mothers of schoolchildren.

Teresa

Teresa is a seven-year-old described by her mother as a quiet girl who enjoys her own company: "She's just a very nice girl, not afraid to express any emotions at all." Teresa is especially interested in plants and how they grow and is much involved in her family as a unit. The following is an interview with Teresa's mother.

INTERVIEWER: Has death come into Teresa's life?

MOTHER: My mother died, her grandmother, in January of this year . . . we all knew she was dying. I told Teresa and I told June [her sister] that she was dying. They wanted to know, "What is dying, where is she going to go, why is she going, why is she leaving me? She's my Grandma! I don't want her to die!" . . . And she was just very curious about the whole business of the wake and the funeral and "Why do we have to do this, why do we have to do that." The big thing was, "I don't want to see other people sad, because it makes me sad."

INTERVIEWER: How did Teresa respond to the death when it actually came?

MOTHER: She comforted me. She came to me. She would cry when I cried. She would put her arms around me and she would say, "Please don't cry; everything will be all right. Grandma isn't suffering anymore. Grandma is happy now."

The death was experienced as a major loss by everybody in the family. Grandma was 54 at the time of her death and had been very close to the whole family although not living with them. "My mother was my best friend and she was also my children's best friend," Teresa's mother said.

INTERVIEWER: What did Teresa understand about Grandma's death?

MOTHER: She understands that she [Grandma] was put in the ground in that cold outer casket, but Teresa realizes that she is not there. She's in spirit, beside her, watching and loving her always. And Teresa sees a bird—my mother was a bird freak—and she said, "I wonder if Grandma can see that bird?" You know, she's very much into, very aware that Grandma is around her, spiritually, not physically.

INTERVIEWER: What did Teresa *not* understand about this death?

MOTHER: She still doesn't understand . . . why. You know, why take her from us now, she wasn't old; she was a young woman. Why was she so sick, you know. What did she do? Did she do something bad?

INTERVIEWER: Does Teresa have any death concerns or fears?

MOTHER: I think she'd be very much afraid of losing me at this point because since my mother has died she's becoming extremely touchy with me; she gets a little bit upset when I have to go out, you know. "Please come back soon!" I think she relates it to losing me, to maybe her fears of losing her own mother.

INTERVIEWER: How have you answered her questions about death?

MOTHER: Well, as far as the religious, we don't get into it at my house, you know. I don't want to get into hell and heaven and that, because I don't want them to get hung up on it. . . . I really don't think we even discussed it, you know, before it actually hit us; we never really discussed it with the children. . . .

INTERVIEWER: Has it been difficult to discuss death with Teresa?

MOTHER: Not with Teresa, not at all. With June, yes, but not with Teresa.

INTERVIEWER: How do you feel in general about the way Teresa thinks about death?

MOTHER: I think she's got her head pretty well together. She's really probably done better than I have. . . . Two or three months after my mother died, I was sitting by myself, having my crying jag and getting it all out, and Teresa got up out of bed. You know, I was sitting in the dark. I just knew it was coming. I had put them to bed. So she got up, and she came beside me and she said, "Mama, I know why you're crying." And I said, "Why, Teresa?" And she said, "Because you miss your mother." And I said, "You're right." And Teresa said, "But you always have to remember, how good she was to us, remember she used to take us uptown and buy us ice cream and she used to sing us songs and remember when she bought me this bracelet."

And within a matter of, say three minutes, I felt so relieved, like, you know, tons had been lifted off me; from this seven-year-old child, you know, really laying it on me and telling me, come on, you know, you got to go on living . . . And the oldest one [June] will not discuss it at all. You know, it's too bad.

INTERVIEWER: Do you have any questions of your own about what to do with a child in things related to death?

MOTHER: There are things I don't know, and so I wouldn't know how to explain it to them. I don't know how to make it easier for them. . . . This is a society where everybody dies—why do you grieve then? Why is there a wake, why is there a funeral? There are things *I* don't understand so I'm sure they don't understand, you know, why the pain?

INTERVIEWER: Should parents and children discuss death together?

MOTHER: It's very important, so very important. I can remember my own first experience with death and how frightened I was of it. I think it's something that should be talked about in a family and . . . I'm having a hard time expressing myself, but I really think that when people die, that we love, we shouldn't have to grieve . . . why do they put us through the wakes, the funeral? This is what we saw when we were children; we saw grieving after death— and my children will grieve over death.

INTERVIEWER: What is the worst thing a parent could say or do with a child in a death situation?

MOTHER: I would hate to stifle emotions. I would hate to say, "Stop all that crying!" Or, the other thing is, "He's gone away for a vacation. He's left us, but he'll come back." That's a bunch of lies and children see through these things.

INTERVIEWER: What is the best thing a parent could say or do with a child in a death situation?

MOTHER: Let the children see what goes on. Let them be totally involved with the family, to be able to express with the family their own emotions and to be totally included in what goes on instead of shifted off to a friend's house.

INTERVIEWER: How curious about death were you when you were Teresa's age?

MOTHER: I wasn't at all . . . until I was about ten years old . . . I lost my cat and i remember, I cried all day upstairs in my room because I thought: This is death. I'm going to lose my mother. And I cried and cried and I was so scared and I had night-mares.

INTERVIEWER: How was death handled in your home when you were growing up?

MOTHER: It wasn't. I said to my mother once, "I'm so afraid that you were going to die." And she just said, "I'm not going to die." . . . And . . . she died. [These words were spoken very softly and sadly.]

INTERVIEWER: Was that the way she should have handled it, or what do you think she should have done instead?

MOTHER: I think that she should have drawn more out of me and really given me time that I needed, and maybe have said—well, I don't know what you can say to a child to make it any easier when there is a threat, a scare of losing a parent, but just be able to sit down and discuss it. . . .

INTERVIEWER: What are your thoughts and feelings about death now?

MOTHER: Since my first death was my mother, I think it was very hard. . . . I just accept the fact that she is dead and I will no longer see her, but I just hang on to the thought that she's not suffering and that she knew she was dying even though nobody told her . . . She said more with her eyes, more than anything else in the world. I feel very . . . I feel peace within myself.

INTERVIEWER: Did she tell you her thoughts or feelings at all?

MOTHER: No, she was aphasic . . . and paralyzed. She couldn't talk. The only thing she could do was move one arm and one hand and the night before she died, we went in there and they took her out of the special care unit and just took off the respirator and let her die and she just kept pointing up to heaven. She knew she was dying and she just . . . made us feel at ease. Because I was glad she knew, and she knew that I knew so we wouldn't have to play the game: "Okay, Ma, we'll get you out of here in a couple of weeks." It was kind of peace, you know, that we shared.

INTERVIEWER: Is there anything you would like to add?

MOTHER: I think we should teach children about death in schools. I don't mean we shouldn't teach them at home, but in school, too. Let people know what often happens in grief, so they won't be so surprised. . . . Should start early because it's like sex education, you know, you almost don't talk about it until it happens, until there is a problem.

Stanley

Stanley is another seven-year-old who is described by his mother as "just the nicest boy a mother could ever want. Does what you tell him to—most of the time . . . His life is pretty much centered around the family and his dog."

INTERVIEWER: What does Stanley understand about death?

MOTHER: That whoever would die they're not going to see again and that's about all. As far as feeling for the person, he hasn't come to that stage yet . . . We have a dog and if he died I wouldn't know what he would feel. I really don't. I would say he would be too little to think much about it.

INTERVIEWER: What does Stanley *not* understand about death?

MOTHER: What the purpose of death is. Why we were put on the earth for a reason and why we're going to die. Stanley is definitely too little to understand why somebody's laying in a casket. Especially if it is somebody young. Why is that person dead? You try to explain to him that God put him on this earth but He called him back. He wanted him back. I don't think he can comprehend that at all. . . . When a little boy dies, I tell him the little boy was very sick and God wanted him back.

INTERVIEWER: How have you answered Stanley's questions about death?

MOTHER: Sometimes I tell him that the person was very old and very sick. If it was a little boy, that the little boy was very sick and God wanted him back. . . . God put us here but He isn't going to let us stay here. We're all here temporarily and even though you boys are little doesn't mean you couldn't die tomorrow. Even Stanley, I told him, you could die tomorrow. I could die tomorrow. We don't know when. God doesn't tell us. It doesn't mean that just sick people die. Anybody can die—people get hit by cars.

INTERVIEWER: What is the worst thing a parent could say or do with a child in a death situation?

MOTHER: To hide it from them. If you want to cry, cry. That's the best thing. Make him experience it with you. Why not? They've got to be exposed to it the way it is.

INTERVIEWER: How was death handled in your home when you were growing up?

MOTHER: My parents shielded us from all of that. . . . We never got the answers we really wanted, so as a result we stopped asking. That was about anything, even about death. . . . But death can bring people together, it's just that in our family it didn't. Would have been nice if our parents had let us join in, instead of getting our relatives to babysit us while they went and did it all . . . going to the funerals and all of that . . . I would have liked to have been at their side.

INTERVIEWER: What are your thoughts and feelings about death now?

MOTHER: I'm very conscious about death now. It panics me, truthfully, it really panics me. I know we can't live forever. If I knew I was dying, I just wouldn't want to wake up in the morning, that's all. That's how I would want it to be for me and yet it's probably the easy way out. I'm not too happy about other people dying either. . . . Dead people are supposed to be with God. We're supposed to be happy but we still can't. Part of us says we are—part of us says we're *not!*

Brian

Brian is eight years old and "a bright boy with lots of curiosity. He's especially interested in rocks and minerals, gems, animals, underwater stories. He reads about them all the time, and talks about anything. But not death."

INTERVIEWER: What does Brian understand about death?

MOTHER: Oh, he understands it . . . I think. But he doesn't really like to talk about it. He doesn't like the idea that any of us will die. Like he said to me, "You'll never, never die, Mom." I tried to explain to him, well, that's not true, that I will die and so will Daddy, and when that time comes he must accept it because that's part of living. He understands what I'm saying. You can see that from the look in his eyes. But it makes him very, very sad, and he'll go, "I don't want to talk about that, I'd rather not—*please*, Mom!"

INTERVIEWER: What does Brian *not* understand about death?

MOTHER: Only one thing I can think of. His Daddy likes to hunt. He goes deer hunting and he killed, you know, a young deer. Brian couldn't quite understand that. He thought the deer was so beautiful and to kill him. . . . Well, we had to tell him *why* he killed the deer, and the deer hurt, and if he wasn't killed, if so many deer weren't killed a year, the balance of nature would be off.

INTERVIEWER: Does Brian have any death concerns or fears?

MOTHER: Losing one of us that he loves. He's very, *very* close to Cris [his sister] so, of course, he doesn't want her to leave the house. He's often said this. If she doesn't come home when she said she's supposed to come home he'll call me and say, "I'm awfully worried because she's out in the car, if she has an accident and gets killed, Mom, I don't know what I'll do." And I mean *upset.* I've seen him cry and tears going down his face and he'll say, "I would just die if my Crissy dies."

INTERVIEWER: What is the worst thing a parent could say or do with a child in a death situation?

MOTHER: Well, I'm going to say this from experience. I think the worst thing to do is not let the child grieve. To tell them they can't cry . . . bottling up these emotions does something to that person and carries on into their adult life. It does irreparable damage if you ask me, and I guess you did.

INTERVIEWER: How was death handled in your home when you were growing up?

MOTHER: Nobody prepared me for it, nobody answered my questions, nobody told me one thing or the other. "I don't want to talk about it," would be the answer, or, "I don't know why you ask me such foolish questions."

INTERVIEWER: What are your thoughts and feelings about death now?

MOTHER: Now, it's much different. I feel the more I think of it, the more at peace I feel with the fact that death is going to come. When I was younger I was hoping, oh, I'd never die, and now I know that I am, and the time comes I don't think I'll be afraid to die . . . I have more acceptance of the fact of death now than I did when I was—even ten years ago or even five years ago . . . I think it comes with time, you're more at peace with yourself. Even so, having children makes death more important in a way, too, your responsibility to them.

Reflections and Questions

Each person—child or adult—has a distinctive relationship with death that is based on the individuality he or she develops and the unique situations in which he or she participates. Young as they are, Teresa, Stanley, and Brian already differ in their experiences and concerns. A thorough analysis of their orientations toward death would need to take into account both their individual personalities and what they have in common as children of similar ages growing up at a particular time in history. Following are a few reflections and questions on these research case history excerpts:

1. Death has specific connotations to the child. It is not just death in general, but the death of particular people or animals that enlists the child's concern: Grandma for Teresa, Crissy and the deer for Brian. The possibility (Crissy) as well as the actuality (Grandma) of death can stimulate thought and feeling. Stanley, in fact, is confronted with specific death concerns by his mother (". . . you could die tomorrow. I could die tomorrow . . ."). As you will see, many of the studies focus on the question of the ability of the child to formulate abstract conceptions of death. Although this is a significant question, it

should not lead you to forget that thoughts of death most often arise around *specific* incidents and contexts. Children do not have to comprehend death in its most abstract aspects to recognize that it threatens their relationships with the people who are important to them.

2. Could we understand the differing death orientations of Teresa, Stanley, and Brian if we focused only on the children themselves? It is doubtful. By enlarging the focus to include the mother-child relationship, you see that experiences, attitudes, and ways of coping with death are part of the intimate flow of life between them. The influence can go in both directions. Brian's questions about the slain deer, for example, and his apparently exaggerated fear for Crissy's well-being present challenges for the parents' own attitudes toward death.

3. There may be several different orientations toward death within the same household. Teresa and June, for example, differ appreciably in their openness to discussion of death. A specific death may have varying effects on the children, depending upon their developmental phase, personality, and position in the family. It is important to become well acquainted with the entire family constellation if you want to understand the implications of one particular child's view of death. From other data it was clear that Brian, as the only boy in the family, wanted very much to be like his father—but does this mean he, too, will have to go deer hunting? If he were not first in the "line of succession," perhaps the slain deer would have taken on a different meaning.

4. Teresa's mother is a sensitive person who favors an open communication process and who reflects thoughtfully on her own behavior as well as her children's. This does not mean, however, that she has been able to cope with death-related problems to her own complete satisfaction. She has unresolved questions in some areas (the value of funerals and the grief process in particular). Although her own unresolved concerns lead to some difficulty in helping her children, Teresa's mother shows flexibility and the ability to learn from experience. By contrast, Stanley's

mother does not seem to have sorted out her own assumptions about life and death. When Stanley notices a death-related incident, his mother is not likely to use this as an occasion to reflect on her own thoughts and values or really share the experience with her son. Instead she relies upon passing along a received dogma that has been familiar to her since her own childhood—but never much thought about. The abstraction level and tone of her explanation was of doubtful help to Stanley. The parent who is not able to cope with a child's death-related curiosity on a simple, naturalistic level because of his or her own discomfort with the subject may be perpetuating the anxieties for still another generation. Imagine Stanley's thoughts after his mother's explanation: "God does not want healthy people? Is it wrong to want people to live? Is God the enemy who takes my friends away? Do I have to get very sick and die to be loved by God?" I have, in fact, heard reflections of this type from children whose curiosity about death was answered by an abstract theological patter that seemed to place the blame on God. On the topic of death, as on any other topic, it is useful to understand something of the child's frame of reference before unloading one of our "standard explanations."

5. Although Teresa's mother had a warm and loving home life in her own childhood, the topic of death had been glossed over by her parents. This has made it more difficult to cope both with the death of her mother (who had promised she was not going to die) and the feelings of her own daughters. Brian's and Stanley's mothers likewise grew up in homes where death was not to be discussed with the children. This background of death avoidance in the childhood home is typical for the mothers in our study (Kastenbaum, 1991). Today's young mothers in general seem to be more aware of the value of discussing death with their children as part of their general preparation for life. However, most often they have not benefited from such good examples in their own homes while growing up. It would seem, then, that we now have a transitional generation of parents who are trying to relate to their children in an area that was off-limits when they themselves were young. This leads to second-guessing of your own responses: "Did I say the right thing?" Eventually, however, the new openness should make death a less divisive topic between parent and child in generations to come.

It is not by accident or whim that the research case histories sampled here are based on the mothers' reports. Children have fathers, too, but they have been less willing to discuss this subject with me. Death education seems to be viewed as something for mothers to handle. This attitude certainly raises questions that deserve further exploration.

DEVELOPING AN UNDERSTANDING OF DEATH

It is clear that death has a place in the thoughts of children. But just what do children make of death? And how do their ideas develop from early childhood onward? The pattern of research findings now indicates that both maturation and specific life experiences play a role. A 12-year-old, for example, generally will show an understanding of death that is more accurate and complete than a four-year-old's. But is this because the older child has developed more advanced cognitive structures? Or is it simply because the older child has had another eight years of life experience from which to learn? Both maturation level and life experience do seem to make a difference, but their precise contributions to the child's understanding of death have not yet been established. This is similar to the general state of knowledge in developmental psychology. We know that individual maturation and the extent and nature of life experience both contribute to the child's pattern of growth as a person. The specific interplay between maturation and experience is difficult to establish, however, whether we are concerned with concepts of death or any other facet of the child's overall comprehension of reality.

This section begins with a selective review of research findings that emphasize maturational factors in the child's understanding of death and turns then to studies that give more attention to experiential and environmental factors.

Developmental Changes in the Child's Conception of Death

Two Pioneering Studies

Research in death-related topics was rare before the 1960s. Nevertheless, two important pioneering studies of children appeared before this time and still deserve attention.

Hungarian psychologist Maria Nagy (1948/1969) invited 378 children, ranging in age from three to ten years, to express their death-related thoughts and feelings. Nagy selected the children to be as representative as possible of the Hungarian population; they came from a variety of social and religious backgrounds, and there was an equal number of boys and girls. The older children were asked to draw pictures and to "write down everything that comes to your mind about death." Children of all ages were engaged in conversation on the subject. As she reviewed the children's words and pictures, Nagy found that three age-related stages could be established.

Stage 1. Stage 1 includes the youngest children, from the third until about the fifth year. In other words, it embraces the outlook of the post-toddler or preschool child. These very young children expressed the notion that death is a *continuation* of life but in a diminished form. The dead are simply less alive. They cannot see and hear—well, maybe they can, but not very well. They are not as hungry as the living. They do not do much. Being dead and being asleep are seen as similar conditions. The view of the Stage 1 child differs markedly from the adult conception that death is not the diminishment but the complete cessation of life.

The youngest children in this study differed from adults in another fundamental way also.

They thought of death as *temporary*. The dead might return, just as the sleeping might wake up. It was also clear that the theme of death as *departure* or *separation* was uppermost in the minds of many children. The dead person has gone away (e.g., to live in the cemetery) and would come back again some day, as people usually do after a trip.

Death, then, is partial and temporary—something like sleep—and reminded the children of other kinds of separations. But Nagy also noticed another characteristic of her young respondents' orientation. The preschoolers were very *curious*. They were full of questions about the details of the funeral, the coffin, the cemetery, and so on. This questioning fascination with the practical or concrete aspects of death has often been overlooked by other writers on the subject. Developmentalists have been quick to conclude from Nagy's study that very young children do not understand death as complete and final. However, they have been slow in appreciating *how active an effort* the children are making to achieve an understanding. This effort is related to another of Nagy's observations that has not received all the attention it deserves. Even though these very young children did not seem to understand death adequately by adult standards, what they did think about it was powerful enough to arouse negative feelings (Brian's anxiety comes to mind, as do the childhood experiences of all three mothers in the case history excerpts). For Nagy's respondents, death at the very least did not seem to be much fun—lying around in a coffin all day, and all night, too. The dead might be sleeping, which is acceptable but boring, or they might be scared and lonely, away from all their friends. The combination of what the young child knows and does not know about death can arouse anxiety. "He would like to come out, but the coffin is nailed down," one five-year-old told "Auntie Death," the name bestowed on the psychologist by the children. This comment suggests the fear of being buried alive that in some times and places has also been prevalent among adults (Kastenbaum, 1991). It also suggests that people are being cruel to the deceased by nailing down the coffin. The possibilities for further misinterpretations and ill feelings based on this limited conception of death are considerable, especially if the adults on the scene fail to understand how the child is likely to interpret death-related phenomena.

Stage 2. The next stage seems to begin at age five or six and persists until about the ninth year. A major advance in the understanding of death comes about during this time. The child now recognizes that death is *final*. The older the child within this age range, the more firm the conclusion. The dead do not return. When it's over, it's over.

Another new theme also emerged during this stage in Nagy's sample. Many of the children represented death as a person. Interestingly, *personification* is one of humankind's most ancient modes of expressing the relationship with death. One nine-year-old confided:

> Death is very dangerous. You never know what minute he is going to carry you off with him. Death is invisible, something nobody has ever seen in all the world. But at night he comes to everybody and carries them off with him. Death is like a skeleton. All the parts are made of bone. But then when it begins to be light, when it's morning, there's not a trace of him. It's that dangerous, death. (Nagy, 1948/1969, p. 11)

The association of death with darkness is, of course, also an ancient habit of mind, expressed by people in the earliest civilizations that have left us record. It is not unusual for the child's conception of death to include elements that once were the common property of adults.

The personification of death as a skeleton was fairly common in Nagy's sample of five- to nine-year-olds. As can be seen from the quoted passage, the anxiety associated with death may remain high even as the child grows older and is able to think in terms of finality. For Nagy's respondents, death personifications often were fearful, representing enormous if mysterious power.

Some Stage 2 children added threats or lethal wishes to their personifications. As Nagy reports, "Kill the death-man so we will not die" was a frequent comment. Some children also depicted death as a circus clown— supposedly the embodiment of mirth and good times. Other children saw dead people as representing death, while still others personified death in the form of angels. Even angelic death, however, did not remove the sting of fear. "The death angels are great enemies of people," declared a seven-year-old. "Death is the king of the angels. Death commands the angels. The angels work for death."

There is at least one more significant characteristic of Stage 2, according to Nagy. The realization of death's finality is accompanied by the belief that this fate might still be eluded. The clever or fortunate person might not be caught by the "death-man." This idea also shows up in specific modes of death. A child might be killed crossing the street, for example. But if children are very careful in crossing the street, they will not be run over, and therefore they will not die.

In other words, children in this age range tend to see death as an outside force or personified agent. "It's that dangerous, death." However, the saving grace is that you do not absolutely have to die. Death is not recognized as universal and personal. Stage 2, then, combines appreciation for one of death's most salient attributes—finality—with an escape hatch. Perhaps, just perhaps, you can be lucky or clever enough to elude it.

Stage 3. The final stage identified by Nagy began at about age nine or ten and was assumed to continue thereafter. By Stage 3 the child now understands death to be *personal, universal,* and *inevitable* as well as *final*. All that lives must die, including yourself. Discussion of death at this age has an adult quality: "Death is the termination of life. Death is destiny. We finish our earthly life. Death is the end of life on earth," declared one nine-year-old boy. A ten-year-old girl added a moral and poetic dimension: "It means the passing of the body. Death is a great squaring of accounts in our lives. It is a thing from which our bodies cannot be resurrected. It is like the withering of flowers."

This new awareness is compatible with belief in some form of afterlife, as with the nine-year-old boy who said, "Everyone has to die once, but the soul lives on." In fact, it might be argued that the child does not really have a grasp of afterlife concepts until death itself is appreciated as final and inevitable.

•   •   •

The other pioneering study was conducted in England on the brink of World War II. Sylvia Anthony (1940/1972) employed such a variety of techniques and reported such a variety of observations that the complexity and results of her research are not easy to summarize. This is probably the reason why even now her work has not been as well integrated into the field as Nagy's. Although there is no attempt to establish clear stages or sequences, Anthony's observations support several of Nagy's conclusions: The younger children she studied also tended to interpret death as sleep or a temporary departure. Anthony's differing methods also made it clear that almost all children have spontaneous death-related thoughts, even if they had not had close personal experiences with death nor understood the warfare that was coming closer to England's shores. One four-year-old girl, for example, was upset because her favorite flowers had died. In tears, she asked her mother, "Shall I die, too? Does everyone die?" When her mother replied that death does come to everybody, Jane "broke into really heartbreaking tears and kept on saying, 'But I don't want to die, I don't want to die' " (p. 139). The notion that children do not spontaneously think of death or take it seriously is contradicted time and again by Anthony's

findings. Notice also how difficult it is in this instance to separate developmental level from life experience. In most research projects Jane would have been classified as a child who had not had direct experience with death. How could the experimenter have known about her dead flowers or how she made a spontaneous connection between the withering of flowers and her own death?

What I find most interesting about Anthony's observations is the abundant evidence that children actively work on their understanding of death. Nagy noticed their curiosity. Anthony shows further that children will continue to deal with the challenge of death-related events, turning them over and over in their minds and invoking them in their play until a satisfying conclusion is reached. Even when the child seems to have forgotten the incident, it is likely that there is still mental processing in progress. Jane, for example, came to her mother a few days later in a very cheerful mood to show what she had just purchased—a poppy made of cloth sold in honor of armistice day. Flourishing the poppy, she announced, "You see *it* won't die!" There are also instructive examples of children who switch back and forth in their play between the role of the killer and the killed. By oscillating between different orientations toward death, the child gradually comes to a better understanding. It is also clear that children are not limited to any one cognitive response to death. If one conclusion does not satisfy, they will try another. Anthony's work suggests that it is our own thinking that is barren if we insist that children are simple and rigid in their attempts to comprehend death.

Recent Studies

There is now even more evidence indicating a relationship between concepts of death and the child's general level of maturation. Nagy's findings remain useful, although the tendency to personify death between ages five and nine has not appeared often in most follow-up studies. In my work with children, personifications of death have also been uncommon. Perhaps the world of childhood has changed enough from the time of Nagy's research to replace personification with more objective and scientific-sounding responses. ("Death is like the computer's down and you can't get it started again," one seven-year-old told his mother recently.) Superimposed on the child's basic structure of thought are the particular images and terminology of current society. And yet children given encouragement to draw death as a person seem to find this an absorbing task (Lonetto, 1980). Could it be that children today have developed a public response to death that has a fashionably scientific look but still have access to emotionally rich and evocative personifications?

The first studies grouped children's responses by chronological age. It is more useful, however, to obtain an independent measure of developmental level. At the same age some children are more advanced than others. Gerald Koocher (1973) respected this difference in 75 children who ranged from age 6 to 15 years. All the children were tested to determine their general level of cognitive functioning, using a set of tasks devised by Jean Piaget and his followers. This procedure enabled Koocher to divide the children into three categories based on the type of thought processes they had demonstrated rather than chronological age. These categories, starting from the lowest developmental level, are known as the *preoperational,* the *concrete-operational,* and the *formal-operational.* As might have been expected, there were more younger children at the lowest developmental level and more older children at the higher levels. But some of the youngest children showed a fairly advanced level of thinking, whereas some of the older children were functioning at less mature levels. So it would be a mistake to relate a child's conception of death to calendar age alone. Generalizations about how a child of a particular age thinks about death would be imprecise because of differences among children in their progress toward adult modes of thought—even if all children were within the normal intelligence range, as in Koocher's study.

Thoughts about death in Koocher's study were more closely related to the children's developmental levels than to their chronological age. Children at the higher developmental levels were more realistic and objective in their answers to a set of death-related questions. A preoperational child would explain "what makes things die," for example, with an answer such as, "By eating a dirty bug." A formal-operational child would speak instead of "physical deterioration." The level of the children's understanding of death was consistent with their overall way of understanding the world.

The groundbreaking Nagy study is confirmed in its general findings but modified in its details by Koocher's more recent investigation. Yes, there is a developmental progression in thoughts of death, but it is more accurate to relate this progression to direct measures of cognitive maturation than to chronological age. There were also two interesting "nonfindings." Koocher noticed that only 5% of the children discussed the possible effect of their own death on other people. Why would children fail to appreciate what their deaths might mean to others? This limitation is consistent with the general developmental principle advocated by Piaget and others, that a child must pass through an *egocentric* way of organizing the world before he or she attains a more mature outlook. Most children cannot yet see death both from the viewpoint of self and others. It is difficult for them to shift perspectives. This limitation might be useful to keep in mind when we interact with children on the subject of death. The other nonfinding was the absence of any personification-type responses.

Other recent studies are consistent with Koocher's findings but add other information as well. Kane (1973), for example, also found that death concepts become increasingly more abstract and adultlike as children move from preoperational to formal-operational modes of thought. However, she found that many children were reaching the more advanced levels of thought earlier than might have been expected. The typical eight-year-old in Kane's study showed an understanding of death that a previous generation of researchers would have believed possible only in adolescence. The notion that children today perhaps may be growing up faster than in the past has some indirect support here. Childers and Wimmer (1971) found that by age ten about 90% of the children had recognized the universality of death. However, children at all ages had more trouble grasping the idea of death as final. Individual differences were common on this point, and even by age ten more than a third of the children either denied that death was final or could not make up their minds. These findings should caution us against taking too simple an approach to the concept of death itself. There are several components to the death concept, and the child who has firmly grasped one aspect may not yet have come to terms with another.

Two other recent studies have made use of a new death concept questionnaire along with carefully selected measures of cognitive ability. Death concept scores were higher both for the older children and those with more advanced cognitive processes independent of age (Derry, 1979). It is not just general mental development, then, but verbal-conceptual development in particular that is closely related to the level of a child's understanding of death. Children with outstanding ability to acquire and use verbal information also expressed the most advanced concepts of death (Jenkins & Cavanaugh, 1985–1986). The developmental pattern of death concepts was similar for boys and girls.

It has been known for some time that younger children are more likely to attribute life to clouds, streams, and other natural phenomena that seem to move on their own. The child does not seem able to express adequate conceptions of death until he or she is able to make a clear distinction between animate and inanimate forms (Tallmer, et al., 1974). Safier (1964) has reported a three-stage progression in the child's understanding of life and death. The youngest children seemed to interpret both life and death as a constant "ongoingness," a *flux*. "Something goes, then it stops, then it goes on again"

(p. 285). At this stage of thought, death as well as life comes and goes. Next, there is an intermediate stage in which the dominant idea is of the *outside agent*. As Safier puts it, "Something makes it go, something makes it stop" (p. 286). An external force gives life and also takes it away. Her respondents (all boys) showed a strong interest in scientific explanation and expressed much curiosity about life and death. The highest stage embodies the principle of the *internal agent*. "Something goes by itself, something stops by itself" (p. 285).

Safier's study indicates a close relationship between thoughts of life and death at each of the three levels. It therefore tends to support some of the basic developmental principles of Piaget (1960) as well as the most general findings of Nagy. Death thoughts do not grow up all by themselves. They belong to a community of thoughts, all influenced by each other and by the individual's overall level of maturation.

Other useful information comes from a study that asked children to draw pictures about death and then talk about them (Lonetto, 1980). As in other studies, death was often seen as something that happens to old people (even if "old meant age 18 or 20"). The children were more specific about methods of separation (such as kidnapping and hiding) than about methods of dying (such as illness or violence). This at least suggests that it is the threat of separation that is foremost in the young child's view of death. "The happy smiles of the dead depicted by the younger children have all but faded away in the representations given by ten-year-olds, who show the dead with closed mouths and eyes" (p. 146). The older children were more likely to depict death as scary and horrible, and they also focus more on their own possible death as compared with others. By age 11 there was more use of abstract symbols in the drawings, indicating a new way of coping with death. They could hint at death and represent its meanings (e.g., a valentine with tears pouring down its face) without having to draw all the unpleasant details. Interestingly, the use of black as the only color became dominant among the older children. This also showed up in their verbal comments. Jenny, aged 11 years, 10 months, said:

> Death is blackness . . . like when you close your eyes. It's cold and when you die your body is cold. Frightening, I don't want to die . . . I wonder then, how I'm going to die . . . I feel scared and I try to forget it. When I feel like this, I try to forget it and just put something else into my mind. (p. 154)

A more high-spirited form of death denial was expressed by another girl at age five. She informed the interviewer that she had been in heaven before she was born, waiting for a replacement for her "other body," which had become "pretty old and dirty." After death she would come back in a new body. When the interviewer wondered if she would go any place besides heaven when she died, the girl assured him, "Any place you want to go, by just sliding and jumping up and down and saying, 'No, I'm not dead.' "

There are playful qualities in many of the young children's depictions and discussions of death, but these seem to be replaced by a more serious and troubled orientation in the older children, who perhaps know too much to allow themselves such indulgences.

Studies rich in vivid detail such as Anthony's and Lonetto's provide many examples of the child's ability to think of death in more than one way, to try out various thoughts and attitudes. Depending upon the particular situation and moment when we enter the child's thoughts on life and death, we may find an arbitrary and playful orientation, a demonic pleasure in zapping bugs or space invaders, or a solemn meditation such as this one by an eight-year-old boy in Lonetto's study:

> When my pet died I felt sorry for him. Because he was only a kitten. When my mom buried him he might be turned into bones. When people die they just turn into bones too. When you die you cannot talk, see, write or anything like that. When you die they bury you in a little yard. I think everybody will die. (p. 119)

Developmental studies and observations made in natural and clinical settings all indicate that children are aware of death from an early age. The child does not begin with the realization that death is inevitable, universal, and final but does quickly grasp the implications of separation and loss. It is likely that the questions posed to the child's mind by death stimulate the desire to learn more about the ways of the world and contribute to overall mental development. Chronological age is a rough indicator of the cognitive level of a child's view of death; independent measures of the child's verbal-conceptual development provide a more refined indicator.

What children emphasize most in their thoughts about death may depend upon cultural influences. For example, a recent study compared children's thinking about death in Sweden and the United States. Basically, the concepts of death were quite similar for Swedish and United States children who were in the same age range. However, United States children more often depicted violent causes of death, while Swedish children more often depicted chapels in cemeteries, tombstones, crosses on church steeples, caskets, and other cultural symbols. The researchers, Wenestam and Wass (1987), speculate that the much greater frequency of violence and death on United States television as compared with Swedish television may have a strong bearing on these differences in children's representations of death.

The role of religious beliefs and expectations is suggested by a recent study of Muslim girls, ages six through ten, in South Africa (Anthony & Bhana, 1988–1989). These children showed some basic similarities in their conceptions of death when compared with those in Western nations that generally follow the Christian tradition. There were, however, interesting differences as well. For example, the realization that death is universal and inevitable seemed to be grasped at an earlier age by Muslim children than by most of their Western/Christian peers. But this did not mean that they also accepted the irreversibility of death. "They believe that the dead come alive again under certain circumstances, such as when angels question them in the grave. It can, thus, be seen that the responses of the children are characteristic of their cultural and religious environments" (p. 225). The Muslim children were also more likely to believe in the importance of praying for the dead.

No doubt there are also many other variations in children's thinking about death as they respond to the ideas, actions, and symbols of their cultural backgrounds.

All the available studies share a common limitation that should be noted. They are cross-sectional (i.e., involve different children at different ages). This means that we do not have direct evidence on how the same children develop their concepts of death over a period of several years. It is not possible, then, to distinguish the effects of age or developmental status from possible cohort effects.

For example, children born in 1980 have been spared the daily television news coverage of the violent and brutalizing Vietnamese War. But they are also the generation that has heard about AIDS and whose sex-and-death education has become a matter of heightened controversy. Over a longer arch of time, children born before and after the conquest of fatal childhood diseases and the introduction of television might differ in their experiences and concepts of death. Every new generation of children brings somewhat distinctive experiences to its understanding of death-related issues.

Good longitudinal studies are needed, then, if we are to learn how the developmental process operates in the same child. Cross-sectional studies allow only approximate answers. There is one significant study, however, discussed later in this chapter that follows the same children over a period of months in a specific situation (Bluebond-Langner, 1975; Bluebond-Langner, 1977).

The Dying Child

Children sometimes think about death, loss, and separation even when there has been no obvious event to arouse their curiosity or concern. Writing about his own childhood, Spalding Gray (1986) recalls

. . . the time when I woke up in the middle of the night and saw my brother Rocky standing on his bed, blue in the face and gasping for air, crying out that he was dying. My mother and father were standing beside the bed trying to quiet him, and Mom said, "Calm down, dear, it's all in your mind." And after he calmed down, my father went back to bed, and my mother turned out the light and sat on the edge of Rocky's bed in the dark. . . . We were all there, very quiet, in the dark, and then Rocky would start in, "Mom, when I die, is it forever?" And she said, "Yes, dear." And then Rocky said, "Mom, when I die, is it forever, and ever, and ever?" and she said, "Uh-huh, dear." And he said, "Mom, when I die is it forever and ever and ever . . .?" I just went right off to this. (p. 14)

Many other healthy children also may have moments when they imagine themselves dying and worry about what it means to be dead. It should not be surprising, then, to learn that children who actually are afflicted with life-threatening illnesses are keenly aware of their predicaments.

Sometimes the failure to communicate adequately with dying children arises from a death taboo. This was documented in a study that compared children suffering from uncontrolled leukemia with other children who were hospitalized with orthopedic conditions that posed no threats to their lives. All the children were Chinese. Those with leukemia were more tense, detached, and guarded. Given projective tests, the life-threatened leukemic children also expressed stronger feelings of being isolated and abandoned, while at the same time tending to deny the seriousness of their illness. The authors, themselves Chinese, observed that in their ethnic group parents are especially reluctant to discuss death with their children (Lee, et al., 1983–1984). Death is a taboo subject in general and even more so when children are involved. The child, whether healthy or fatally ill, is left to develop and test death concepts with little or no adult guidance. Inadvertently, the parents convey the impression that they are rejecting their dying children—why else, wonder the children, would their parents spend so little time with them and seem to take so little interest in their illness? Wherever such a taboo prevails, both the dying child and the parents are likely to suffer additional anguish because of the communication barrier.

Fortunately, there are also many examples of sensitive communication within families that face the impending death of a child. Shira Putter, who died at the age of nine from a rare form of diabetes, has left a diary that offers the opportunity to learn how a child may interpret his or her own situation (Grollman, 1988). Problems in communication did arise along the way. At one point Shira was feeling that ". . . Daddy doesn't care about me. I know he comes to visit me practically every day, but once he comes he always seems so far away. It's like he can't wait to leave again." She was reluctant to share this concern with her mother because "I didn't want her to get upset." But she did tell her mother who then explained "that Daddy does love me and that was part of the problem. He loves me so much that it hurts him to see me sick and in pain. She asked me to please try to understand" (p. 12). This little episode put everybody more at ease, including Daddy, and restored the usual family pattern of warm and caring interactions.

It is not at all unusual for dying children to hesitate in sharing their concerns because of the fear that this will only make their parents feel even worse. On other occasions Shira did remain silent when she could see that her parents were upset by new complications in her condition. So, far from being unaware of the perils they face, children may take a kind of parental role themselves and try to protect adults from anxiety and sorrow.

A first-hand account of the child's experience of terminal illness is also valuable in reminding us that each day can bring some new threat or challenge. Shira, for example, had to cope with the fact that her favorite doctor took himself off her case because he was so upset by her continued physical decline. Shira responded, " 'Well, I'm not dead yet.' Then all of a sudden I got scared because if Dr. Frank could leave me, how do I know that the next doctor won't walk out,

too? Then maybe Mom and Grandma and Rachel will someday come up to me and say, 'Sorry, Shira. We can't deal with your illness anymore so you'll have to find someone else.' Who will take care of me then?" (p. 56). The fear of abandonment by the most important people in their lives is often a major concern of the dying child—and too often based upon the way that some adults do distance themselves from the child.

Shira and her family were able to maintain their closeness and mutual support until the very end. In one of her last diary entries, Shira writes of their Passover celebration. "In a way, it seemed like any other Passover. We said all the prayers. We sang all the songs. But when we were reciting the blessing, thanking God for letting us celebrate this special occasion, everyone started crying. Then, for about a minute, we all stood together quietly, holding hands. It was as if, without saying anything, I was telling everyone what was in my heart. That I loved them and wanted to be with them, but I couldn't make it much longer. That I wasn't afraid of dying anymore, so they had to let me go. They just had to" (p. 70).

Studies (e.g., Wachter, 1984) have confirmed the importance of keeping an open and honest line of communication with the dying child. This approach offers parents and other adults many opportunities to relieve the child of painful thoughts such as the fear that their illness is a punishment from God for some misbehavior or failure ("I sure used to talk a lot in class, sometimes"). Most significantly, open communication makes it less likely that the dying child and the distressed parents will retreat into their separate worlds of anguished isolation.

Myra Bluebond-Langner (1975, 1977) has provided the most systematic and detailed information on the dying child's thoughts and feelings. She spent many hours with hospitalized children, listening to them and observing their interactions with parents and staff. There was no question about the children's keen awareness of their total situation. One morning, for example, Jeffrey made a point of asking Bluebond-Langner to read to him from the classic children's book, *Charlotte's Web* (White, 1952). He wanted to hear again "the part where Charlotte dies." This chapter, "Last Day," offers a combination of humor, drama, and consolation. "Nothing can harm you now" is one of its thoughts. Another is: "No one was with her when she died." When Bluebond-Langner completed her reading of the chapter, Jeffrey dozed off. He died that afternoon.[3]

Many of the terminally ill children observed by Bluebond-Langner (1977) passed through five stages in the acquisition of information:

1. I have a serious illness.
2. I know what drugs I am receiving and what they are supposed to do.
3. I know the relationship between my symptoms and the kind of treatment I am getting.
4. I realize now that I am going through a cycle of feeling worse, getting better, then getting worse again. The medicines don't work all the time.
5. I know that this won't go on forever. There's an end to the remissions and the relapses and to the kind of medicine they have for me. When the drugs stop working, I will die pretty soon.

The children soon became sophisticated about hospital routines. They learned the names of all their drugs and how to tell one kind of staff member from another. Little escaped them. Staff members would have been astonished had they realized how much the children picked up on hospital processes and purposes. Most of all, perhaps, the children learned from each other. They would notice that they were now on the last drug that another child had received before his or her death or that people were now starting to treat them differently, meaning that something important had changed in their condition.

Recent studies such as these make it clear that seriously ill children work hard on understanding what is happening to them. They are aware of the possibility of death but must also give attention to the specific changes that are taking place in their bodies, the kind of treatment they are receiving, and how their family and friends are responding to them. A parent, teacher, physician, or nurse who assumes that a sick child is too young to understand anything is probably making a serious mistake.

We know less about the effect of other types of life experiences on children's death concepts, but it is probable that more relationships will be discovered as research in this area expands. Attention will need to be given to small, easily overlooked events such as the death of a pet as well as to more obvious experiences. Certainly, children among the "boat people" and others who have lived in high jeopardy can hardly fail to be influenced by what is happening around them. Death does not have to be fully appreciated in the abstract sense for a child to recognize real and present danger.

Care of the Dying Child

Along with emotional support and sensitive communication, the dying child is also likely to need a variety of medical, nursing, and other support services. In recent years the hospice approach to terminal care has been extended to include children. The basic philosophy is the same as with hospice care in general: to help the dying person enjoy the highest quality of life possible under the circumstances. This is accomplished by skillfully controlling pain and other symptoms, and by working with the family to support their own caregiving efforts. Although circumstances may arise in which a hospital stay seems to be necessary, the focus is usually on home care. Children as well as adults often feel most secure within their own homes. Because there can be situations in which neither the hospital nor the home seems to be the best place to care for the dying child, some hospice organizations have also established respite care facilities. These are usually small, home-like centers in which the child can receive care for a few days or weeks while the family copes with other problems.

Whether the child is at home, in a respite care center, or a hospital-based hospice service, the overall philosophy remains the same: give comfort, relieve distress, help the patient and family preserve their most basic values of life during this difficult time. At present, there are relatively few children's hospice programs, but a growing number of pediatric caregivers are applying hospice principles and techniques. Up-to-date information can be obtained by writing or calling Children's Hospice International (1101 King Street, Suite 131, Alexandria, VA 22314; (703) 684–0330). A useful reader, *Hospice Approaches to Pediatric Care*, has been compiled by Corr and Corr (1985).

Whether or not a hospice approach is used, the care of the dying child is likely to be enhanced by attention to the following needs:

1. The opportunity to express his or her concerns through conversation, play, drawing, writing, or whatever modality is most effective and natural for the particular child. Such creative activities as modeling clay figures or drawing pictures of the family may help to transform inner feelings into a tangible communication that can be shared with others. The very process of creative transformation—feelings into art—can itself have a therapeutic value. Resentment and anger may be expressed on occasion in the child's play or art; this is usually part of one's natural response to overwhelming circumstances and the opportunity to "get it out" often proves valuable.

2. Confirmation that he or she is still a normal and valuable person, despite the impairments and limitations imposed by illness. Sensitive parents and other caregivers will find ways to affirm and strengthen the child's basic sense of self. They will not allow "dyingness" to overshadow every interaction, every plan, every project. Instead, opportunities will be found for the child to do things that are still within his or her sphere of competence and to stay involved with roles and activities that have brought pleasure. One ten-year-old boy, for example, taught his younger siblings how to play chess while he was dying of leukemia; a girl, also ten, kept the statistics and figured the batting averages for her softball team after she herself could no longer play. With the availability of home computers, it is now also possible for children to enjoy computer-assisted learning programs, drawing, writing, and games with relatively little expenditure of energy.

3. Assurance that family members and other important people will not abandon the dying child, no matter what happens. Nonverbal behavior is a vital component of interaction that can either affirm or undermine the family's words of reassurance. As illustrated by Shira's diary, children are quite aware of discomfort, tension, and conflict on the part of the adults in their lives. By their every day actions as well as their words, parents and other caregivers must continue to convey their dedication to being with—to *staying* with—the dying child, come what may.

4. There is often a fear of being forgotten, of not being a part of what will happen in the family when he or she is no longer there. In some situations it may be useful to use mental imagery exercises to help the child prepare for impending separation and to participate in the future through imagination (LeBaron & Zeltner, 1985). The child may also come up with his or her own ways of feeling a part of the future, requiring of the adults only their sympathetic attention and cooperation. For example, a child may wish to give some favorite toys to a sibling or friend, or to make a cassette that can be listened to on birthdays or other special occasions.

In addition to these common needs and themes, each child with a life-threatening illness is almost certain to have distinctive ideas, hopes, and apprehensions. What special wish or secret fear is on the mind of this particular child? There is no substitute for careful listening and observation and for respecting the individuality of each child.

Siblings of the Dying Child

Anxiety and sorrow about the dying child can lead to neglect of other family needs. Parents may not give adequate attention to their own health, for example. The continuing stress can lead to a narrowing of attention, a concentration on "just what most needs to be done," and increased irritability and distraction even on the part of the most devoted parents. And, as recent findings suggest, the brothers and sisters of dying children may be at particular risk during this difficult period.

A leading researcher in this area has written that "The well siblings of terminally ill children live in houses of chronic sorrow. The signs of sorrow, illness, and death are everywhere, whether or not they are spoken of. The signs are written on parents' faces: 'My mother always looks tired now,' and 'Even my Dad's crying a lot.' The signs are there in hushed conversations: 'You learn everything by listening in on the (phone) extension . . ." (Bluebond-Langner, 1988, p. 9).

The healthy brothers and sisters often miss their parents' participation in their activities. Daddy doesn't watch them play basketball any more; Mom doesn't take them shopping. Enjoyable family plans, such as camping trips and other outings, may be suddenly cancelled. In fact, daily life is riddled with interruptions, disappointments and last-minute changes. The illness and needs of the dying child can intrude on virtually every aspect of the healthy sibling's life.

The following problems are among those observed in well siblings in the course of Bluebond-Langner's research (1985; 1988):

1. Confusion about what role they are supposed to play in the family. Should they try to be like the sick child? Should they try to become "assistant parents"? Or should they become invisible, "just blend into the woodwork and get out of the way"?
2. A feeling of being deceived or rejected by their parents: "They don't tell me the truth. . . . Nobody really cares about me any more. . . ."
3. Uncertainty about the future. "What's to become of all of us? . . . Does it do any good to have plans any more?"

4. Changes in the relationships among the siblings. For example, the illness and hospitalization of the sick child may deprive the well sister or brother of a very significant companion. "Siblings often find that they cannot give reciprocally to one another. . . . For example, while Jake lay dying, complaining of his back hurting him and not being able to breathe, his brothers offered to rub his back. He pushed them away saying, 'no, no, not you. Only Mommy now.' The ill child's alliances shift from a closeness to both the parent and the sibling to a closeness with the parent divorced from that of the sibling" (Bluebond-Langner, 1988, p. 13).
5. Feelings of guilt and ambivalence. The well siblings are distressed by the suffering of the sick child, but may also feel relieved—and feel guilty about feeling relieved—that they are not the ones who are dying.
6. Frustrated in not being able to express their feelings and fears to their parents who are so preoccupied with the dying child and with their own feelings.

Not all well siblings had all these reactions, nor did these feelings occur all the time. In some families few obvious problems developed until the sick child had become extremely frail and disabled. Until that time, the parents had managed to find some time and energy for the other children and keep a semblance of normal family life going. But the well siblings themselves often took account of changes in the sick child's condition and needs. They recognize that the sick child now requires a great deal of attention from the parents and they are less likely to feel rejected or in competition.

Well siblings may also express their distress in many other ways that are not so different from the way that anybody might respond in a prolonged stressful situation. There may be sleep disturbances, for example, or outbursts of anger. These are usually not serious problems in themselves, but, rather, symptoms of the stress that all members of the family are undergoing.

In my experience, families with strong and supportive patterns of communication prior to the terminal illness seem most likely to come through this ordeal with greater resilience, although not without sorrow and distress. Compassionate relatives, friends, neighbors, and teachers can lighten the burden by giving attention to the well siblings during and after the terminal process, and by unobtrusively helping the parents in coping with the responsibilities of everyday life. Furthermore, these good friends will be aware that episodes of forgetfulness, disorganization, irritability—even moments of rage or fantasies of escaping the situation—represent only the signs of distress in an emotionally devastating situation and need not be taken as indications either of animosity or "coming unraveled."

The family with a dying child certainly needs and deserves sensitive, understanding, and mature companionship from all the community.

SHARING THE CHILD'S DEATH CONCERNS: A FEW GUIDELINES

Childhood is not really "the kingdom where nobody dies." Adults may hope to shield children from death concerns, but it is in the child's own interests to identify and understand threats to his or her well-being. This has been all too true in situations in which children have been left to survive as they can with little assistance from the adult world (Schorsch, 1979). But it remains true even within the harbor of a loving family. Our children will encounter death in many forms—close and distant, imaginary and realistic. Many parents today received little guidance in death-related matters when they were young. It is not unusual, then, for adults to face inner struggles when called upon to respond to a child's questions.

This is not a "how-to" book, but it might be useful to present a few guidelines that have been helpful in relating to children on the subject of death.

1. *Be a good observer.* Notice how the child is behaving. Listen to what he or she is really saying. Do not rush in with explanations, reassurances, or diversions unless there is some overriding necessity to do so. You will be more helpful to the child if you are relaxed, patient, and attentive enough to learn what questions or needs the child actually is expressing rather than those you might assume to be there. For example, the child who suddenly asks a parent, "Are you going to be dead?" might have been thinking about something Grandmother said last week or any number of other happenings that aroused this concern. Taking a moment to learn how this question arose in the child's mind could also help to provide an appropriate response.

2. *Do not wait or plan for "one big tell-all."* Maintain a continuing dialogue with the children in your life as occasions present themselves. The death of pets, scenes in movies, newspaper articles, or television presentations—whatever brushes with mortality the children have—all can offer the opportunity for discussion. This does not mean, of course, that parents should remain poised to jump on a death dialogue opportunity. But it is more natural and effective to include death as one of the many topics that adults and children can discuss together. And we are more likely to be helpful when we are not ourselves caught up in the midst of a death situation. Combine a child who has been kept ignorant about death with an adult who is grief stricken or uptight and you have something less than the most desirable situation.

3. *Do not expect all of the child's responses to be obvious and immediate.* When a death has occurred or is impending, the child's total response is likely to unfold over time and to express itself in many ways. Changes in sleeping habits, mood, relationships with other children, and demands on adults may reflect part of the child's reaction to the death, even though the connection may not be obvious. Be patient; be available.

4. *Help the child remain secure as part of the family.* Sometimes adults have the panicked im-

pulse to remove children from the scene when death has come too close (e.g., sending them off to a relative or neighbor). Examine such impulses before acting on them. Whatever practical decisions you reach, consider what the children might learn from the opportunity to participate in the family's response and what lingering questions, misinterpretations, and fears might remain if they are excluded.

5. *Use simple and direct language.* This is much to be preferred over fanciful, sentimental, and symbolic meanderings. Too often what adults say to children becomes a sermon, peppered with words and concepts that mean little to them. Try to provide children with accurate information. See if they understand what you have said (e.g., by having them explain it back to you) and make sure that you have responded to what they really wanted to know in the first place.

6. *Be accessible.* The child's sense of comfort will be strengthened by the very fact that you are available to talk about death when the need arises. Your expression of feelings that are natural to the situation (worry, sorrow, perhaps even anger) are not likely to harm the child but rather will provide a basis for sorting out and expressing his or her own feelings.

7. *Be aware of all the children in the family.* In some situations one child may be central (e.g., the seriously or fatally ill). It may seem natural to concentrate the family's resources and attentions on that child. Other children in the family continue to need love and reassurance, however, and to participate somehow in the total process. Useful examples are offered by Kubler-Ross (1983).

8. *Don't break the relationship.* What a child feels or thinks about death at a particular moment might disturb or anger adults. We do not want to see or hear certain responses. Losing the closeness and support of important adults is a great danger to the child (Bluebond-Langner, 1975). This, in fact, is one of the reasons why children may not share their thoughts and feelings with us. We do not have to approve or agree with everything the child tells us about death, but we do have to maintain a supportive relationship.

REFERENCES

Anthony, S. (1972). *The discovery of death in childhood and after.* New York: Basic Books, Inc. (Revision of *The child's discovery of death.* New York: Harcourt Brace and World, 1940).

Anthony, Z., & Bhana, K. (1988–1989). An exploratory study of Muslim girls' understanding of death. *Omega, Journal of Death and Dying, 19,* 215–228.

Bertman, S. L. (1979–1980). The arts: A source of comfort and insight for children who are learning about death. *Omega, Journal of Death and Dying, 10,* 147–163.

Bluebond-Langner, M. (1975). *Awareness and communication in terminally ill children: Pattern, process, and pretense.* Unpublished doctoral dissertation, University of Illinois.

Bluebond-Langner, M. (1977). Meanings of death to children. In H. Feifel (Ed.), *New meanings of death.* New York: McGraw-Hill Book Co.

Bluebond-Langner, M. (1985). Living with cystic fibrosis: A family affair. In D. Schidlow (Ed.) *Cystic Fibrosis: Soma and Psyche* (pp. 9–24). New Jersey: McNeil Laboratories.

Bluebond-Langner, M. (1988). Worlds of dying children and their well siblings. *Death Studies, 13,* 1–16.

Childers, P., & Wimmer, M. (1971). The concept of death in early childhood. *Child Development, 42,* 705–715.

Corr, C. A., & Corr, D. M. (1985). (Eds.). *Hospice approaches to pediatric care.* New York: Springer Publishing Co., Inc.

Gray, S. (1986). *Sex and death to the age 14.* New York: Vintage Books.

Grollman, S. Shira. (1988). *A legacy of courage.* New York: Doubleday & Co.

Jenkins, R. A., & Cavanaugh, J. C. (1985–1986). Examining the relationship between the development of the concept of death and overall cognitive development. *Omega, Journal of Death and Dying, 16,* 193–200.

Kane, B. (1973). Children's concepts of death. *Journal of Genetic Psychology, 9,* 369–375.

Kastenbaum, R. (1991). *The psychology of death.* New York: Springer Publishing Co.

Katz, E. R., Kellerman, J., & Siegel, S. E. (1980). Behavioral distress in children with cancer undergoing medical procedures: Developmental considerations. *Journal of Consulting and Clinical Psychology, 48,* 356–365.

Koocher, G. (1973). Childhood, death, and cognitive development. *Developmental Psychology, 9,* 369–375.

Kubler-Ross, E. (1983). *On children and death.* New York: Macmillan Publishing.

Lampl-de-Groot, J. (1976). Mourning in a 6-year-old girl. In *The psychoanalytic study of the child, Vol. 31,* (pp. 273–282). New Haven: Yale University Press.

Lee, P. W. H., Lieh-Mak, F., Hung, B. K. M., & Luk, S. L. (1983–1984). Death anxiety in leukemic Chinese children. *International Journal of Psychiatry in Medicine, 13,* 281–290.

LeBaron, S., & Zeltner, L. K. (1985). The role of imagery in the treatment of dying children and adolescents. *Journal of Developmental Behavioral Pediatrics, 5,* 252–258.

Lonetto, R. (1980). *Children's conceptions of death.* New York: Springer Publishing Co.

Lopez, T., & Kliman, G. W. (1979). Memory, reconstruction, and mourning in the analysis of a 4-year-old child. In *The psychoanalytic study of the child: Vol. 34* (pp. 235–271). New Haven: Yale University Press.

Millay, E. S. (1969). The kingdom where nobody dies. In *Collected lyrics.* New York: Harper & Row.

Nagy, M. H. (1969). The child's theories concerning death. In H. Feifel (Ed.), *The meaning of death.* New York: McGraw-Hill Book Co. (Reprinted from *Journal of Genetic Psychology,* 1948, *73,* 3–27).

Opie, I., & Opie, R. (1969). *Children's games in street and playground.* London: Oxford University Press.

Piaget, J. (1960). *The child's conception of the world.* Patterson, N.J.: Littlefield, Adams & Co.

Safier, G. (1964). A study in relationships between the life and death concepts in children. *Journal of Genetic Psychology, 105,* 283–294.

Schorsch, A. (1979). *Images of childhood.* New York: Mayflower Books, Inc.

Spinetta, J. J. (1974). The dying child's awareness of death: A review. *Psychological Bulletin, 81,* 256–260.

Tallmer, M., Formanek, R., & Tallmer, J. (1974). Factors influencing children's concepts of death. *Journal of Clinical Child Psychology, 3,* 17–19.

Tobin, S. (1972). The earliest memory as data for research in aging. In D. P. Kent, R. Kastenbaum, & S. Sherwood (Eds.), *Research, planning, and action for the elderly.* New York: Behavioral Publications, Inc.

Vandewiele, M. (1983–1984). Attitudes of Senegalese secondary school students toward death. *Omega, Journal of Death and Dying, 14,* 329–334.

Waechter, E. H. (1984). Dying children: Patterns of coping. In H. L. Wass & C. A. Corr (Eds.), *Childhood and death* (pp. 51–68). New York: Hemisphere Publishing Co.

Wenestam, C-G., & Wass, H. (1987). Swedish and U.S. children's thinking about death: A qualitative study and cross-cultural comparison. *Death Studies, 11,* 99–122.

White, E. B. (1952). *Charlotte's web.* New York: Harper & Row.

chapter 8

SUICIDE, MURDER, TERRORISM: PEOPLE KILLING PEOPLE

Suicide . . . Murder . . . Terrorism

These are headline words. Page 1: Film Star Dead; Drug Overdose Suspected (two-column story with photo, continued inside). Page 2: Movie Patron Slain in Dispute over Popcorn (one-column story, three-paragraphs). Sunday feature section, page 1: Teenage Suicide on Rise (full page, with related stories). Page 1: Terrorist Seizes Wheel of Bus: 14 Die (two-column lead, one-column story).

It may be tempting to think that suicide, murder and terrorism are *only* headline words. Those who die by acts of violence are people we have never met who have gotten themselves into predicaments that we would never encounter. The facts are otherwise. Many people with "normal" life-styles have been touched by suicide, murder, or terrorism. I know a professor of history who will be grieving for the rest of his life because his son, a law student, was killed by a drug addict who wanted money for his next fix. I will never forget a charming and successful publishing executive who took his life when he was dismissed without explanation by his corporation's new ownership. The father of one of our students was murdered by terrorists in the Middle East. This only begins my list, and it does not include the troubled people I have met when

working as a clinical psychologist or hospital director.

It is not at all unusual for violent death to cross the lives of ordinary people—although, as we will see, some of us are more at risk than others. Furthermore, these actions affect all of us in many significant if indirect ways. We would not have Beethoven's greatest symphonies and string quartets had he followed the suicidal promptings he felt when he realized he was going deaf. We probably would have had much more music to cherish from Philip Heseltine (writing under the name, Peter Warlock) had he not killed himself. Suicide and murder have deprived the world of many people who might have provided parental guidance, friendship, creativity, craftsmanship, and other qualities beneficial to society.

In this chapter we explore first suicide, then murder and terrorism. All are vivid examples of people killing people. Some related topics such as assisted suicide and euthanasia are examined in Chapter 11.

SUICIDE

Suicide occurs at every age from childhood onward. The victims are males and females, the affluent and the impoverished, the seeming failures and the apparently successful. In rural Vermont and urban San Francisco, in crowded Tokyo and sparsely populated Lapland, the mortality rates are increased by acts of self-destruction. The scope of the problem is worldwide and not limited to any particular class of person (although some groups are more at risk than others).

The Statistical Profile

Suicide is consistently among the leading causes of death in the United States. When all deaths for a year are reviewed, suicide appears as the tenth most common cause. Experts in the field of suicide prevention have long been convinced that the actual toll is even greater than the approximately 30,000 certified suicides recorded in the United States each year. It is not unusual for a death to be classified in some other way (e.g., "accidental") if the suicidal component has not been established beyond a doubt. Furthermore, many people still find it difficult to believe that a child might be capable of committing suicide, so the reported statistics among the very young may not be reliable. "Accidental death" was the cause of death listed for one nine-year-old boy who arranged to drown himself in his bathtub after making sure that nobody was home. He was a more than capable swimmer who had been under stifling family pressure all his young life. At the other end of the age spectrum, I have seen the self-assisted death of ailing and socially isolated old men go into the records as arteriosclerosis or heart disease. Because insurance policies often have provisions prejudicial to suicide, sympathetic medical examiners have also been known to shade the facts when there is any ambiguity as to cause of death at any age. The statistical profile, then, tends to underrepresent the actual incidence of suicide.

Interpreting the reported suicide rate has also been made more difficult by changes in the classification procedures. Those responsible for determining the cause of death are obliged to use the International Classification of Diseases, Injuries, and Causes of Death (ICD). The ICD has been revised twice in ways that affect suicide statistics. In 1958 it was decided that all deaths associated with a self-inflicted injury would be classified as suicides unless there was a specific statement attesting to accidental factors. This resulted in an increase in the percentage of reported suicides. To someone who was not familiar with this change of procedure, it would look as though there had been about a 3% rise in suicide. In 1968 this procedure was again revised. It was decided that death associated with self-inflicted injury would not be classified as suicide unless the *intentionality* of the act was specified. Accordingly, this led to a drop in the percentage of official suicides of about 6% (National Center for Health Statistics, 1988). These shifts in classification procedure have nothing to do with the actual number of suicides and make it difficult to compare rates over time.

Still another problem becomes evident when we examine the technique used to calculate suicide rate. It is based on the following formula:

$$\text{Suicide rate:} \frac{\text{Number of suicides}}{\text{Population}} \times 100,000$$

A suicide rate of 15, for example, means that during a calendar year there were 15 suicidal deaths for every 100,000 people in the population. The accuracy of the reported rate will depend on the care with which population size has been estimated as well as the accuracy of cause-of-death classifications. Some populations tend to be undercounted in American society and probably in other societies also. Nonwhites, the young, and transients of any age are among those who are often underrepresented. Here, then, is one more source of possible error and confusion.

If suicide statistics are to be used appropriately, the suicide *rate* must be distinguished from the *total number* of suicides in a population. As the population increases into the 21st century, there is the likelihood of more deaths by suicide even if the rate remains constant. This consideration applies to smaller geographical regions as well. Has the development of a suicide prevention service actually reduced the rate in a particular city? The shifting population of the city (plus transients, minus youths away at college or in military service, and so on) can make it very difficult to answer this question. If all relevant information were available over a reasonable time period, it might be found that the true *rate* has declined; but, even so, the actual *number* of suicides might not be appreciably lower. This is one of the reasons why it is difficult to evaluate the effectiveness of suicide prevention services.

Finally, for many years population data were sorted crudely into "white" and "nonwhite" categories. Important differences within the "nonwhite" category tend to be merged and distorted, and it is, of course, dubious policy to define people by their "nonwhiteness." This practice is changing, but much of the available data are limited to this once-traditional distinction.

Recognizing all these difficulties, what messages do the suicide statistics have for us?

1. *Bad economic times are associated with an increase in suicide rates.* The overall rate of suicide in the United States reached a peak during the Great Depression of the 1930s and then declined (Diggory, 1976). A recent period of recession also seems to have led to another general rise in suicide. There is little reason to doubt that social and economic conditions can affect the suicide rate, but this effect may differ from one subgroup to another.

2. *Completed suicides come most frequently from the white male segment of the United States population.* (Oriental male suicide rates have also been reported as high, but the data base is less adequate for drawing conclusions.) At every age white males are at greater risk for suicide than white females or nonwhite males and females (with the possible exception of males of Oriental ancestry). The difference in suicide rates between white males and other groups is substantial. Suicide among white males has been more than twice as common at all ages over the past half century.

3. *The white male suicide rate increases with age, but females and nonwhites reach their peak vulnerability earlier in adult life* (see Table 8–1). Although the rate is highest among older white men, the actual number of suicidal deaths is higher for middle-aged men (because they are much more numerous, even a lower rate represents more fatalities).

4. *Suicide is increasing among youth, with males predominating.* Taking one's own life has become the third leading cause of death among people between 15 and 24 years old. Approximately a fifth of all suicides are committed by those under age 25. Furthermore, the increase in youth suicide has been observed in many other nations ever since dependable statistics have been collected.

5. *Other groups at greater risk for suicide include city dwellers, the divorced (of either sex), and those suffering from depression* (Farberow, 1980) *or cancer* (Marshall, et al., 1983). Some studies have identified other specific populations at risk, such as children who have lost a parent to death (Berlinsky & Biller, 1982) but the evidence seems to be clearest for the groups just mentioned.

Some recent trends in the prevalence of suicide in the United States are suggested by the data in Table 8–1. You will notice, for example, that the male suicide rate has been moving upward since 1950 for both whites and blacks. The female suicide rate follows a different pattern for these years. There was an upsurge of suicide among white females in and around 1970, but with this exception the rate has remained at the same level for 35 years. Suicide among black females also reached a peak around 1970. Although at this time suicide was still relatively infrequent among black females, their rate had nearly doubled within 20 years. Since circa 1970, the suicide rate for black females has declined, but never down to the earlier levels. These patterns indicate that men have become

TABLE 8–1

Suicide rates in the United States, 1950–1985

Race and Sex	15–24	25–34	35–44	45–54	55–64	65–74	75–84	85+	All
White Males									
1950	6.6	13.8	22.4	34.1	45.9	53.2	61.9	61.9	18.1
1960	8.6	14.9	21.9	33.7	40.2	42.0	55.7	61.3	17.5
1970	13.9	19.9	23.3	29.5	35.0	38.7	45.5	50.3	18.2
1980	21.4	25.6	23.5	24.2	25.8	32.5	45.5	52.8	18.9
1985	22.7	25.4	23.5	25.1	28.6	35.3	57.1	60.3	19.9
White Females									
1950	2.7	5.2	8.2	10.5	10.7	10.6	8.4	8.9	5.3
1960	2.3	5.8	8.1	10.9	10.9	8.8	9.2	6.1	5.3
1970	4.2	9.0	13.0	13.5	12.3	9.6	7.2	6.1	7.2
1980	4.6	7.5	9.1	10.2	9.1	7.0	5.7	5.8	5.7
1985	4.7	6.4	7.7	9.0	8.4	7.3	7.0	4.7	5.3
Black Males									
1950	4.9	9.3	10.4	10.4	16.5	10.0	*6.2	*6.2	7.0
1960	4.1	12.4	12.8	10.8	16.2	11.3	6.6	6.9	7.8
1970	10.5	19.2	12.6	13.8	10.6	8.7	8.9	10.3	9.9
1980	12.3	21.8	15.6	12.0	11.7	11.1	10.5	18.9	10.8
1985	13.3	19.6	14.9	13.5	11.5	15.8	15.6	7.7	11.3
Black Females									
1950	1.8	2.6	2.0	3.5	1.1	1.9	*2.4	*2.4	1.7
1960	1.3	3.0	3.0	3.1	3.0	2.3	1.3	—	1.9
1970	3.8	5.7	3.7	3.7	2.0	2.9	1.7	3.2	3.2
1980	2.3	4.1	4.6	2.8	2.3	1.7	1.4	—	2.4
1985	2.0	3.0	3.6	3.2	2.2	2.0	4.5	1.4	2.1

Sources: National Center for Health Statistics, (1988, March). *Vital Statistics of the United States. Vol. II, Mortality, Part A., 1950–1985.* DHHS Pub. No. (PHS) 8–1233. Hyattsville, Maryland.

*These age categories were not differentiated for statistical analysis.

increasingly vulnerable to suicide in recent decades, but that women have recovered from their higher rates of 1970. Gender differences seem to be more important than race as far as the general trend is concerned, but there are race-gender differences in the extent of the rate changes. What does all this mean? We don't really know! But it does look as though men and women in the United States continue to have different patterns of vulnerability to suicide, and are probably responding differently to societal changes.

The Human Side

The impact of suicide cannot be gauged by numbers alone. Even attempts at suicide can have an important effect. Family and friends are put on alert and may respond either by renewed efforts to help the individual or by further emotional isolation of the attempter because of their own heightened anxiety. The suicide attempt is sometimes viewed as a manipulative action and thereby arouses resentment and hostility—or it might win some temporary gains and concessions. I have observed a tremendous range of responses to suicide attempts. In one instance, colleagues became more sensitive to the individual's sense of despair and were able to provide valuable help both with emotional support and practical actions to change a frustrating situation. In another instance, however, the parents refused to be "impressed" by their adolescent daughter's near-fatal attempt and in effect challenged her to "finish the job." She did. A suicide attempt (or threat) is likely to alter interpersonal relationships as well as the individual's own feelings.

Completed suicide often leaves the survivors shaken. The guilt, for example, can be disabling. Furthermore, the survivors may feel they cannot speak openly about the death to others and therefore go into a period of deepening social isolation (Wallace, 1973). The social cost of suicide is high, although impossible to calculate precisely. Occasionally one suicide seems to encourage another as some vulnerable people identify with the deceased and see self-destruction as an acceptable means of solving their problems. When the suicide of a young celebrity is reported vividly by the media, there may be a short-term increase in suicide attempts and completions by some people who have identified with the star and who have been having problems of their own. The public at large, however, does not appear susceptible to "suicide by contagion."

The human side of suicide must also include children left without parents and therefore made more vulnerable to stress and self-doubts that can haunt them throughout their lives. Several studies have found that broken homes are more frequent in the background of suicidal adolescents (Cantor, 1972; Iga, 1976; Tishler, 1966). Obviously, suicide has a further disruptive effect on the family circle, and so the ripple effect of loss and distress continues to widen. Behind each number in the suicide statistics there are families, friends, and colleagues who will never be quite the same again.

FOUR PROBLEM AREAS

A more detailed look at suicide among youth, elderly persons, farmers, and native Americans will illustrate some of the many relationships between individual self-destruction and society.

Youth Suicide

The suicide rate among adolescents and young adults (15 to 24) has more than doubled since 1950. Furthermore, the director of the National

Institutes of Mental Health has estimated that about *half a million* serious attempts are made by American youths each year (Pardes, 1985). In a society that is often characterized as youth-oriented, it is enigmatic as well as alarming that completed and attempted suicide has become so prevalent among young people. Consider some of the additional facts:

1. The increase in completed suicides is clearly greater for males, although female suicide has also become more common. (More suicide *attempts* are made by young women.)

2. Both sexes now turn to firearms and explosives as the most common method of self-destruction (more frequent among males). Some form of poisoning or overdosing is the second most common method used by young women. Hanging and strangulation are also more frequent among young women (Frederick, 1985).

3. Studies consistently find that suicide rates are higher among college students than youth in general. Some of this difference, however, is related more to age than the college experience as such (Davis, 1983). Suicide rates generally increase with age, and the college student population tends to be older than the average person who is counted in the 15-to-24 age group. Furthermore, graduate students and others who are a little older than the overall college population are more at risk.

4. Academic pressure seems related to suicide among college students but not in a simple way. Seiden (1969) found that undergraduates who committed suicide actually had a higher grade point average than their peers. Objectively, they were doing well. Often, however, they had performed below their expectations on a recent test or paper. The typical college student victim of suicide had a respectable academic record but felt that he or she was not performing up to expectations. There were doubts about his or her ability to do well in college and to go on to an outstanding career.

5. Most of those who committed suicide expressed their despondency to others and often

made explicit comments about their intentions. Clinicians have long held that many suicidal people do issue a cry for help (Farberow & Schneidman, 1965). This seems to be true of many of the youths who see suicide as a possible solution to their problems. Every expression of suicidal intent provides an opportunity for a helpful intervention.

6. The immoderate use of alcohol and other drugs occurs more often with suicidal people than with the general population at all ages. Case studies suggest that a sudden change in drinking habits may be a particularly important factor and that the risk of suicide increases during periodic "jags." (Makela, 1983; Piokolainen, 1983). Alcohol and drug abuse have become important factors in the rising tide of youth suicide.

7. Past experiences of loss, rejection, and unworthiness make some youths more vulnerable to suicide when new interpersonal problems arise. Psychiatrist Herbert Hendin (1985) has worked with many college students who have "incorporated an emotional lifelessness that characterized their relationship with their parents. Most have learned to use school work in a defensive withdrawal from their families and from the world outside. This adaptation is often encouraged by their families, who find it easier to deal with the fewer demands of an emotionally muted child." It was not unusual for these people to have had depressed and suicidal thoughts for many years. The college experience, then, did not generate a suicidal impulse for the first time but may have provided an occasion for its expression.

Suicide among Elderly Persons

The elderly white man remains the person most vulnerable to suicide. Inspection of Table 8–1 will show that suicide rates among white men increase from middle age onward. There have been some recent changes, however. The oldest of the old (85 +) showed a marked reduction in their suicide rate in 1970 and held near this level in 1980. Some observers interpreted this change as a favorable result of improved health and fi-

nancial benefits for the aged. Just five years later, though, the suicide rate among the oldest of the old rebounded to a higher level. Again, some observers believe this is also an outcome of reduced benefits for aged people under a national policy that cut back on a variety of social programs. The suicide rate for the next oldest echelon (75–84) has also increased, even more markedly, in the most recent time period available for analysis.

However, despite this vulnerability, suicide among the elderly often fails to receive sufficient attention. The victim may have been socially isolated for some time before death, or the community may be less disturbed by the act than when a young person is involved. Nevertheless, suicide in later life not only represents the premature death of a fellow citizen but an implicit commentary on the place of the elderly in American society.

What would happen in your community if an elderly couple decided to make a suicide pact because they were both suffering from many physical problems and saw no reason to go on with life? Such a couple came to the attention of Mehta, Mathew, and Mehta (1978). At the last minute the wife felt unable to go through with the suicide and sought help instead. With only three weeks of inpatient psychotherapy and drug therapy, the couple rekindled its taste for life. Several years later they continued to do well, living independently in the community and free of suicidal thoughts. This is but one of many examples that could be brought forward to demonstrate that a suicidal crisis can be overcome in later life just as well as at earlier ages. The presence of physical illness and other negative realities does not necessarily make self-destruction the plan of choice. My colleagues and I have worked with many older people who had reason to despair and to prefer the prospect of death over the harsh realities of life. Often these people were able to draw upon their own personal resources and find the strength and will to live within a relatively short time. The key in some cases was a short reprieve from a stressful situation or objective changes to improve their quality of life; in other cases it was a therapeutic alliance and counseling. Stress and despair can be experienced at any age—and the same is true of recovery.

Several other findings about suicide in later life follow:

1. Most older people do *not* have suicidal thoughts (Robbins, et al., 1977).
2. When suicidal intentions do exist, the probability of a completed act of self-destruction is higher than at other ages; there is a smaller ratio of attempts to completed suicides (Maris, 1981).
3. The older person is less likely to reveal his or her suicidal intentions. This may be related to the social isolation experienced by some elderly people.
4. Suicidality is less frequent among older people who are married, stay in touch with their children and relatives, and have not had a suicide or suicide attempt in their family (Robbins, et al., 1977).
5. The suicidal older person tends not only to be less integrated socially than others of his or her age but is also more depressed and sees self-destruction as a more acceptable action in a variety of circumstances (Robbins, et al., 1977). There is also some evidence that those suffering from organic brain syndrome are more likely to attempt but less likely to complete suicide (Sendbuehler & Goldstein, 1977).
6. Although suicide is more common among older whites than nonwhites, the motivations and characteristics of those who take their lives are similar in both groups (Seiden, 1981).

Clearly social isolation is among the factors that increase the likelihood of suicide in later life. Age by itself does not *cause* suicidality; rather, we must attend to many specific conditions, personal and situational, that threaten to deprive the individual of hope and meaning. Perhaps the gradual decrease in suicide rates among the elderly is a sign that society has finally started to create more appropriate and useful roles for its older citizens.

Suicide among Farmers

For some years now there have been reports of a "declining farm economy" in the United States. Television coverage has brought the sorrow and stress of families seeing their farms being sold off at auction to the entire nation. Although some farmers have prospered and others have hung on, it is clear that many have been facing a crisis that threatens the stability and continuity of their lives. There are many ways of attempting to cope with economic pressures and anxieties. Has suicide become a more frequent alternative for farmers who feel they are being pressed to the wall?

During the Great Depression of the 1930s, suicides increased in Iowa and Minnesota as farm foreclosures also increased (Lunden, 1951). A more recent study found that suicides among male farmers went up substantially in Wisconsin as economic conditions worsened (Neshold, 1986). And now a more extensive study has looked at farmer suicide rates in 15 states between 1980 and 1985. John Ragland and Alan Berman (in press) found that the suicide rates of farmers were significantly related to their economic conditions: with higher debt and lower assets, a farmer was more likely to commit suicide. This relationship held true whether the farmer was white or black. It also held true for entire states: there were more suicides in those agricultural states that had a higher index of farmer indebtedness.

Overall, the suicide rate among male farmers was higher than for males in general in the United States. Take a moment to look again at Table 8–1. You will see that in 1980 and 1985 the overall suicide rate for white males was a little under 20 per 100,000; for black males the rates were much lower. By comparison, the suicide rate for farmers during the 1980–1985 period (in 15 states) was 44.9.

These studies all have limitations, as the researchers themselves observed, including the lack of intensive case studies for individual suicides. Nevertheless, Ragland and Berman draw a reasonable conclusion in suggesting that:

> . . . the economic stress found in the current farm crisis can be seen as both a predisposing and a precipitating factor for suicide. Chronic economic stress increases life stress, increases vulnerability, and predisposes the individual to a greater risk for suicide. The central issue is that not all economically distressed farmers . . . commit suicide . . . and that many farmers who do commit suicide may do so as a result of precipitating factors other than economic stress (e.g., bereavement over loss of a family member). The need to understand the dynamics of farmers who kill themselves necessitates a more intensive psychological analysis of individual farm suicides. The harvest we reap from such an understanding might help to reduce the tragic loss of life in America's heartland.

Suicide among Native Americans

The white man's conquest and development of the New World was catastrophic to the ancestors of many of those who are now known as native Americans. Although the infamous quotation "The only good Indian is a dead Indian" was in fact a misquote, there is no denying that American history expressed a genocidal component in some of its dealings with the nation's original inhabitants. It is equally unpleasant to think that the present high suicide rate among native Americans is a continuing part of that heritage. Whatever the actual connection might be, it is a matter of record that genocide has in fact been followed by high rates of suicide.

Two problems must be faced in considering suicide among native Americans. The statistical information usually is drawn from official United States government records whose adequacy in this regard is subject to serious question. As McIntosh (1983–1984) notes, it is probable that the number of reported suicides is well below the actual in many areas. And yet the rate of native American suicide may be overreported in other parts of the country because local suicide statistics on the general population are underreported. Furthermore, we must avoid the temptation to generalize about the characteristics and circumstances of native Americans. The tribal communities differ greatly (e.g., in geography, economic condition, folklore, and so on). Fortunately, the existing literature has been carefully reviewed by McIntosh (1983–1984) and McIntosh and Santos (1980–1981), whose work provides the major source for this section.

The basic facts about suicide among native Americans follow:

1. The rate is exceptionally high. Native Americans as a total group have the highest suicide rate of any ethnic or racial subpopulation.
2. Tribal differences in suicide rates are large and also vary over time.
3. While alcohol has an association with suicide for the general population as well, it appears to be an even more important factor for native Americans. Alcohol abuse has been related to high unemployment, prejudice, cultural conflict, and the loss of heritage, among other factors.
4. Unlike the general population, native Americans are more at risk for suicide in youth than in old age. Rates for elderly suicide are low; the peak occurs in the late teens and 20s.

If anything, suicide is an even greater problem among native Americans than in the general population. The average life expectancy remains relatively low for native Americans. This unfortunate fact contributes to a youth-oriented structure in the population, and it is the young native American who is most susceptible to overt self-destruction. (If a life foreshortened by alcoholism is to be regarded as a form of indirect suicide, then many older native Americans must also be counted as victims.)

•   •   •

Whether our primary interest is understanding or preventing suicide, it is obvious that we must keep a balance between individual and sociocultural factors. The realities of everyday life and prospects for the future may differ appreciably for a white, Anglo-Saxon, Protestant undergraduate; an elderly Afro-American widow; and a youth living on a poverty-stricken reservation. The same act of desperation can flow from many sources. Preventive and interventive efforts will be more effective in some circumstances if they are focused on the individual; in other circumstances a broader social policy approach may be necessary.

SOME CULTURAL MEANINGS OF SUICIDE

Now that some of the facts of suicide have been examined, let us consider the cultural and individual meanings.

Suicide as Sinful

One of our strongest cultural traditions regards suicide as sinful. This position has been held for centuries by defenders of the Judeo-Christian faiths. Catholics, Protestants, and Jews generally have been taught that suicide is morally wrong. Condemnation of suicide has been most emphasized by the Catholic Church, whose position was made firm as long ago as the 4th century.

But why? What about suicide is so appalling that it must be condemned and discouraged by all the authority that an organized religion can command? St. Augustine helped to establish the Catholic position by crystallizing two fundamental objections to suicide. The first depends upon articles of faith that are not shared by all followers of the Judeo-Christian tradition—namely, that suicide precludes the opportunity to repent of other sins. However, the other objection is based on the Sixth Commandment: "Thou shalt not kill." Suicide is not exempt from this commandment in St. Augustine's (426/1971) judgment.

In the 13th century St. Thomas Aquinas (1279/1971) reaffirmed Augustine's conclusion but added another objection. He argued that

God and only God has the power to grant life and death. Suicide is sinful because it represents a revolt against the ordained order of the universe. The self-murderer is engaging in a sin of pride, of self-assertion in a realm that is meant to be ruled by deity.

This point has also been advocated by a man whose ideas of human nature and society exerted great influence over the founding fathers of the United States. John Locke (1690/1971) refused to include self-destruction as one of the inherent liberties: "Every one . . . is bound to preserve himself, and not to quit his station willfully." A person who abandons his station thereby transgresses the law of nature (p. 26).

According to Locke, as the handiwork of God, we are possessions that are not at liberty to dispose of ourselves. This fierce moral condemnation of suicide allows few if any exceptions. Great suffering does not entitle a person to suspend the "law of nature" and take life into his or her own hands.

Reflect for a moment upon suicide as sinful. Notice that this interpretation of suicide need not be identified with the individual's personal motivation. The individual may commit suicide for a number of different reasons. The desire to be willful, rebellious, or prideful in the face of God may be far from his or her mind. But the suicidal action nevertheless will be *interpreted* as sinful by those who accept the religious dogma that has been sketched here. For an imperfect analogy, think of the motorist who drives through a red light. This act could be interpreted as disregard or defiance for law and order even if this was not the motorist's intention. This is one of the reasons why clergy reiterate the moral sanctions against suicide. The potential self-murderer should be advised how serious an act he or she is contemplating.

Individuals who accept the cultural tradition that views suicide as sinful might therefore be expected to have one or more lines of defense than others who are tempted to do away with themselves. There is more to lose by suicide. The survivors have more to lose as well. The suicide of a family member could bring a strong sense of shame as well as the feelings of loss and grief that accompany bereavement from death produced by other causes. Suicide, in other words, can be a moral stigma not only for the individual but for those who become contaminated with it by association.

Condemnation of suicide as a violation of the Sixth Commandment, however, is difficult to square with the tradition of warfare and violent death that has been not only condoned but at times actively pursued by those who see themselves as defenders of the faith. Religious wars and the persecution of heretics repeatedly have violated the edict, "Thou shalt not kill." As Jacques Choron (1972) observes, "during the Middle Ages, mass suicide was frequent among persecuted sects of Christian heretics and non-Christian minorities. . . . The category of non-Christians included Moslems and Jews, who refused to be converted to Christianity and preferred to commit suicide" (pp. 25–26). Violation of the Sixth Commandment therefore led directly to suicide. The persecuted victim might be regarded as a sinner for committing suicide, but the persecutors, acting in the name of their religion, would not be sinners if they either threatened the dissidents to the point of suicide or killed them outright.

The image of the crucifixion, so powerful in the Christian tradition, is a sacrifice of suffering unto death with strong suicidal connotations. Some of the early Christian thinkers, in fact, regarded the death as suicide (Alvarez, 1970), as did deeply reflecting Christians of later times, such as John Donne (1646/1977). Choron (1972) suggests that suicide through martyrdom became all too tempting to those who tried to follow along Christ's pathway. It was glorious to die as a martyr. The Church found it advisable to protect some true believers from themselves, to reduce the attractiveness of death now that immortality had been proclaimed, and to discourage widespread emulation of the early martyrs. Admiration of martyrdom has persisted, however, and so has the moral condemnation of suicide. (But keep in mind that martyrdom is not identical with suicide in general: it is a self-chosen death that occurs in a particular way in service of a particular cause or idea and requires the "cooperation" of others.) As both Alvarez and Choron remind us, the Old and New Testaments do not directly prohibit suicide, nor do they even seem to find this action particularly remarkable. This tends to support the idea that condemnation of suicide as a sin might function as an attempted safeguard against the allure of self-sacrifice in the Christian tradition.

Suicide as Criminal

Is suicide a sin or a *crime?* This distinction has not always been considered important. The intertwining of church and state once made it easy to regard suicide as both criminal and sinful. Even Locke with his radical ideas of equality and liberty spoke of the person who would lift his hand against himself as an "offender," one who is "dangerous to mankind" and commits "a trespass against the whole species." Certainly the sinful and the criminal interpretations of suicide have something in common. Both regard self-destruction as a willful violation of the basic ties that relate the individual to the universe.

Through the years, however, the civil and divine realms of authority have become more independent of each other. This has also strengthened the view that suicide is a crime and not necessarily a sin. Suicide as crime has been an influential tradition up to the present day, although it has always been accompanied by dissident voices. As Edwin Shneidman (1976) notes, the word *suicide* itself seems first to have entered use at about the middle of the 17th century. The earliest citation given by *The Oxford English Dictionary* attributes the following statement to Walter Charleton in 1651: "To vindicate ones self from . . . inevitable Calamity, by Sui-cide is not . . . a Crime."

When suicide is considered criminal as well as sinful, it is more apt to be punished by human authority. If it were a sin and only a sin, then perhaps answering to God would be quite a sufficient consequence. As a crime, however, suicide has occasionally brought severe punishment on top of the moral condemnation. This has included torture, defamation, and impoverishment. Surviving family members have sometimes been punished also by having their possessions confiscated by the state.

The interpretation of suicide as crime is waning. Criminal laws either have been erased from the books or are not vigorously enforced (Shneidman, 1976). Another indication of attitude change can be seen in life insurance policies. It was once common for insurance companies to treat suicide as though it were a special kind of crime—one intended to defraud the underwriters. It is now possible to have death benefits associated with suicide, although with certain limitations and restrictions built into the contract.

Decriminalization of suicide is based in part on the unworkability of most laws that have been enacted but also upon the realization that such penalties have not served as effective deterrents. It may also be in keeping with a social climate in which the meanings of life and death are being reevaluated in general. Law enforcement agencies have now become effective frontline resources for suicide prevention in some communities, liberated now from the legal responsibility of having to look upon the attempter as a criminal.

Suicide as Weakness or Madness

When a person commits suicide, it means that person has cracked. There is some flaw or limitation or deviation within him or her.

The fact is that some people who commit suicide can be classified as psychotic or severely disturbed, but some cannot. Individuals with diagnosed psychiatric conditions tend to have a higher suicide rate than the population at large. People diagnosed as depressive psychotics tend to have the highest rates of completed suicides. (Difficult as it is to be certain of the dependability of completed suicide statistics, it is even more

difficult to compare groups of people on suicide *attempts, threats, or preoccupations* because of various problems associated with the reporting of same.) If we are concerned with the probability of suicide in very large populations, then mental and emotional disorder is a relevant variable to consider—it will help us a little to identify people at risk and to make some predictions. However, psychiatric disorder is far from satisfactory as an explanation or predictor of suicide. Even when a psychopathological state is present, this itself does not explain, let alone motivate, the action. Many people go through disturbed periods without attempting suicide. And only through a distortion of the actual circumstances could someone claim *all* suicides are enacted in a spell of madness. It would be tempting to believe that a person has to be crazy to commit suicide, but this is simply not true.

What about the related explanation that suicide is the outcome of *weakness*? This view seems to have intensified as a result of the survival-of-the-fittest doctrine that has been with us for more than a century (Darwin, 1859/1971). During this time, many groups have interpreted Charles Darwin's theory of evolution in terms of their own values and only secondarily on the scientific evidence as such. Those who favor a rough-and-tumble, highly competitive struggle for power have tried to rationalize these tactics by analogy with the so-called survival of the fittest principle. This approach is meant to justify the raw pursuit and exploitation of power. Those who fall by the wayside just don't have "it." Seen in these terms, suicide is simply one of the ways in which a relatively weak member of society loses out in the junglelike struggle. Suicide is one of nature's ways to preserve the species by weeding out the less fit. (This interpretation is not necessarily one that would have been endorsed by Darwin himself, who had little control over how society chose to use or abuse his ideas.)

This position is not taken quite as openly today as in the heyday of rugged individualism and naive social applications of evolutionary theory. Nevertheless, we can still see it in operation.

"If you can't stand the heat, get out of the kitchen!" was one type of comment heard after a spectacular suicide in New York City. A ranking executive of a major international corporation leaped to his death from offices high above Manhattan. Media coverage emphasized the length of time that his fallen body tied up traffic and other circumstantial aspects of the death. Little attention was given then or later to his state of mind, the meaning of his suicide, or the impact upon survivors. Other executives around the nation commented off the record that some people just can't take the gaff. There was a note of pride in such comments: "I am strong enough to cope with adversity; that other fellow wasn't."

Both the weakness and the madness interpretations of suicide seem to have filled some of the gap left by decriminalization and by increasing dissidence about the sinful nature of self-destruction. The popularity of a psychiatrically-oriented view of human nature over the past several decades has been used for this purpose, just as Darwinism made do for earlier generations. To say that a person committed suicide because he or she was not right in the mind has the obvious effect of setting that person apart from the rest of us. It is his or her problem, not ours, the outcome of a flawed, deviant mind. The protective function of this cultural attitude—protection, that is, against any fear that suicide might be intimately related to our own life-style—suggests that we might think twice before endorsing it (Kastenbaum & Aisenberg, 1972).

Suicide as "The Great Death"

The Buddhist tradition in China and Japan includes the image of *daishi*, which translates roughly as "The Great Death." Through their own example, Zen masters have shown how a person might pass admirably from this life. The discipline and devotion of the master appealed to the warrior. The *samurai* would seek *daishi* on the battlefield. This influence remained strong enough through the centuries to enlist the self-sacrifices of *kamikaze* pilots in World War II (al-

though at least some of these young men still had their doubts about carrying through missions that meant almost certain death).

Suicide itself has been honored as a form of *daishi*. *Seppuku* is a traditional form of suicide in Japan, better known in the West as *hara-kiri*. The act itself consists of disembowelment, usually with a sword. In some situations this form of death has served as an honorable alternative to execution. A person condemned to death would be given the privilege of becoming his or her own executioner. Voluntary *seppuku*, by contrast, might flow from a number of different motives on the part of the individual (e.g., to follow a master into the great beyond or to protest an injustice). Placing your entire life at the disposal of an honorable or noble motive was a much admired action. In our own time the self-immolation of Buddhist monks in Southeast Asia to emphasize their religious and political protests has also made a deep impression on observers.

Ritualized, honorable suicide of this "Great Death" type seems to integrate various levels of existence. By opening his abdomen, the individual is showing the world that his center of being (thought to be located there) is pure and undefiled. The act therefore involves a network of physiological, individual, social, and religious referents. Specifically, the individual puts the sword to the *hara*, the (imagined) locus of breath control, and breath is regarded in many cultures as closely akin to both life itself and divinity (LaFleur, 1974).

Fascination with the Great Death theme remains potent today despite the many changes that have been taking place in tradition-oriented cultures such as China and Japan. Yet the precise significance of this theme must be understood in terms of the total life situation of the individual. This has been shown, for example, in the suicides of two celebrated Japanese writers, Yasunari Kawabata and Mukio Mishima. Kawabata, the 1968 Nobel Prize winner for literature, killed himself in 1972 at the age of 72 by inhalation of gas. In 1970 45-year-old Mishima, who had been a leading candidate for the Nobel Prize, delivered an impassioned speech to his followers on a political cause, then performed a traditional *samurai* ritual and, along with one of his admirers, committed *hara-kiri*. The lives and deaths of these two men have been carefully analyzed by Mamoru Iga (1976). He finds that although both writers drew upon the same tradition and both ended their lives with self-murder, there were sharp differences between them in the motivations and contexts of their deaths and the specific meaning death held for them. Iga, along with many other contemporary suicidologists, emphasizes that both individual and cultural factors must be considered in trying to understand why a particular person chooses suicide. The allure of the Great Death theme must be taken into account in some suicides, but this does not by itself adequately explain the individual's actions nor provide a sufficient basis for preventing suicide.

The association of suicide with desirable death has not been limited to the Orient. It was one of the characteristic themes of the ancient Greeks and Romans. As Alvarez (1970) comments, "the Romans looked on suicide with neither fear nor revulsion, but as a carefully considered and chosen validation of the way they had lived and the principles they had lived by" (p. 64). Suicide as an alternative to capture, defeat, and disgrace was considered laudable; it may even have been the expected course of action by a person of character.

Suicide as a Rational Alternative

The belief that suicide can bring a glorious death has a more subdued echo in another cultural tradition, also dating from ancient times. This is the attitude that suicide is an acceptable, rational alternative to continued existence. It is a view often conditioned by adverse circumstances. "Life is not always preferable to death" is the thought here. Individuals do not destroy themselves in hope of thereby achieving a noble postmortem reputation or a place among the eternally blessed. Instead they wish to subtract

themselves from a life whose quality seems a worse evil than death.

Renaissance thinkers often praised death as the place of refuge from the cruelties and disappointments of life. Erasmus (1509) is but one of the eminent humanists who observed what a distance there is between our aspirations for the human race and the failings discovered on every side in daily life. The newly-awakened spirit of hope and progress soon became shadowed by a sense of disappointment and resignation that, it sometimes seemed, only death could possibly swallow.

Much earlier in history there is also evidence that the harshness of life made suicide an appealing option to many. Alvarez (1970) contends that stoicism, a philosophical position that was enunciated in ancient Athens and Rome and has since become virtually a synonym for rational control, was in actuality

> A last defense against the murderous squalor of Rome itself. When those calm heroes looked around them they saw a life so unspeakable, cruel, wanton, corrupt, and apparently unvalued that they clung to their ideas of reason much as the Christian poor used to cling to their belief in Paradise and the goodness of God despite, or because of, this misery of their lives on this earth. Stoicism, in short, was a philosophy of despair; it was not a coincidence that Seneca, who was its most powerful and influential spokesman, was also the teacher of the most vicious of all Roman emperors, Nero. (p. 66)

Seneca himself died as an "honorable suicide." Maurice Faber (1978) has analyzed Seneca's death in much the same vein as Iga examined the deaths of Kawabata and Mishima. What made Seneca's suicide appear rational in its own context included his entire psychosexual developmental history and the nature of the specific circumstances of the time, not simply an abstract philosophical belief.

From ancient philosophers to contemporary existentialists, from victims of human cruelty and injustice to people whose lives just didn't seem to work out, a tradition has been maintained in which suicide is regarded as an option available to the reasonable person. Choron (1972) speaks of a German psychiatrist, Alfred Hoche, who proposed the following in 1919:

> The term *"Bilanz-Selbtsmord"*—"balance-sheet suicide"—to designate instances where supposedly mentally normal persons dispassionately take stock of their life situation, and, having found it unacceptable, if not intolerable, and not anticipating any change for the better, decide to put an end to their lives. (p. 96)

There have been many times in human history when misery was so general and the outlook so grim that it did not require any distinctive individual dynamics to think seriously of suicide. The horrors of the plague years, for example, intensified by warfare and general social disorganization, led many to question the value of continued life. "It's a sin!" "It's a crime!" "It's weakness!" "It's madness!" All these protests and admonitions can seem at times to be ways of discouraging a rational, balance-sheet view of life and death (see also Chapter 11).

The Judeo-Christian tradition has in general advocated life. There is intrinsic value in life. We should not dispose of life, no matter what the temptations. This message has been imperfectly delivered, and at times it has been contradicted by the actions of the true believers themselves. Nevertheless, enough of this spirit has come across to establish a most challenging issue for all of us: Is life to be valued and fostered under all conditions because it has primary and intrinsic value? Or is the value of life relative to the circumstances? This issue is confronted in many life-and-death situations today beyond the problem of suicide.

A SOCIOLOGICAL THEORY OF SUICIDE

The Importance of Social Integration

More than one meaning may exist in the same culture at a particular time, as is the case in the United States. But is there an overall relationship between culture and the individual? Emile Durkheim proposed a comprehensive sociological theory of self-destruction in 1897. *Le Suicide* (1897/1951) became a cornerstone for the then-new science of sociology and remains one of the most influential theories of suicide in particular. Durkheim realized that the study of an act so extreme as suicide was likely to reveal much about the general structure and function of society.

Durkheim's approach was audacious for its time. Suicide was not essentially a matter of intimate concern between the individual and God. Moral values were not the primary focus. Instead, suicide could be regarded best at a distance, and by a cool observer who was more interested in the overall pattern of self-destruction than in any particular life and death.

Rich and complex in its details, Durkheim's theory nevertheless can be reduced to several major propositions and a four-part classification of suicide "types." Why do people kill themselves? If we insisted upon a simple answer to this question, Durkheim would point toward society. Large-scale social dynamics determine the probability of individual self-destruction. The concept of *social integration* is important here. Every individual is more or less integrated into the structure of his or her culture. The suicide risk depends much upon the extent of social integration *between* individual and society. The culture itself shows more or less *social solidarity* or cohesiveness within itself. Social life may be stable, consistent, and supportive, or it may be falling apart under stress. *The individual, then, may be weakly or strongly integrated into a high- or a low-solidarity culture.*

The crucial index for suicide can be found in the interaction between integration and solidarity: How much does the culture *control* the individual? Both the weakly integrated person in a solid social structure and the person caught in a disorganized culture are in difficulty because there is not sufficient group control. And with lessened group control there is a heightened possibility of suicide. However, suicide can also result from too much control by society. Durkheim's theory, then, invites attention both to the cohesiveness of society and the social integration of any particular individual.

At least one other Durkheimian concept should be considered. Every culture is said to have its *collective representations.* These convey the spirit or personality of the culture as a whole, the guiding themes, moods, or emotional climate. Under certain circumstances this group spirit can turn morose and self-destructive. This means that the individual who is well integrated into the culture may be especially vulnerable. He or she somehow absorbs the dysphoric mood of the larger society and may act it out with fatal results. This aspect of Durkheim's theory suggests that the very forces that should hold a society together can take on the opposite character and lead to what we might call *sociocide.* The mass suicide and homicide in Guyana that resulted in the eradication of a unique community and more than 900 lives should prompt a reexamination of Durkheim's neglected concept.

Four Types of Suicide

Most of the attention to Durkheim today focuses on the four types of suicide he delineated. Each is thought to represent a distinctive relationship between individual and society.

The *egoistic* suicide is committed by people who do not have enough involvement with society. They are not under sufficient cultural control. The executive who literally fell from on high is one probable example. Individuals whose talents, inclinations, or stations in life place them in a special category, relatively immune from ordinary social restrictions, are especially vulnerable to egoistic suicide. The celebrity in the entertainment field, the creative artist who follows his or her own star, the person in a relatively distinct or unique role, all may go their own personal ways until they can no longer be reached effectively by cultural constraints. Intellectuals are common in this category. They are more likely than others to pick up those collec-

tive representations described as sociocidic. Sensitive to underlying currents of melancholy and despair in the culture and, in a sense, lost in their own thoughts, they have little outside themselves to grasp when the suicide impulse arises.

Very different indeed is the *altruistic* suicide. Already mentioned were such examples as the *seppuku* tradition and the *kamikaze* type of combat death. *Suttee,* (Sati) the now illegal Indian practice of a widow giving her life at her husband's funeral, is another dramatic example. According to Durkheim, the altruistic suicide occurs when the individual has an exaggerated or excessive concern for the community. This is usually the strongly integrated person in a high-solidarity culture. Altruistic suicides tend to be less common in Western societies but often are admired when they do occur.

Social breakdown is reflected most directly in the *anomic* suicide. Here it is less a question of the individual's integration with society and more a question of society's ability to function as it should. People are let down, cast adrift by the failure of social institutions. Unemployment is one pertinent example. The person thrown out of work has lost a significant tie to society and through society's doing, not his or her own. Bad times, unemployment, suicide—a predictable sequence. Similarly, a person who is forced to leave his or her occupation because of age may enter an anomic condition that leads to suicide. When the rupture between individual and society is sudden and unexpected, then the probability of suicide is thought to be especially high. This situation arises, for example, when the death of an important person drastically reduces the survivor's place in society.

For many years it was this set of three suicide types that dominated the picture. Recently, however, more attention has been given to a fourth type that Durkheim introduced but treated more as a curiosity. A person may experience too much control by society, he suggested. A culture that stifles and oppresses some of its members may thereby encourage *fatalistic* suicide. The individual sees all opportunities and prospects blocked. Durkheim spoke of slavery as a condition that engenders fatalistic suicide but thought that civilization had put this kind of oppression well into the past. Oppression and subjugation have not disappeared from the human condition, however, as totalitarian regimes continue to manifest themselves throughout the 20th century. Both the altruistic and the fatalistic suicide involve excessive control of the individual by society. In the former case the individuals appear to share wholeheartedly in the collective representations. They die *for* their people. In the latter case they die in despair of ever being able to actualize themselves in a culture that affords little opportunity for self-esteem and satisfaction. (I have had to import some psychologically-oriented concepts into the sociological framework here to help with the distinction.)

One recent study has taken an interesting new approach to Durkheim's concept of fatalistic suicide. Stack (1979) examined official suicide data from 45 nations, the best information available. To this information he applied a measure of *political totalitarianism* previously developed by Taylor and Hudson (1972). These include such sanctions against individual freedom as banning political rallies, exile, deportation, or arrest of those expressing opposition to the regime, censorship of the media, and so on. His study included other variables as well, but the relationship between suicide and totalitarian overregulation of the individual is most relevant here. A positive and statistically significant relationship was found between degree of totalitarian overregulation of the individual and suicide. This result was seen as consistent with Durkheim's observations on fatalistic suicide, although Stack notes that the complete explanation is likely to be more complex. In my view the data do not clearly support the conclusion that too much social control has in fact led to higher rates of fatalistic suicide. Nevertheless, this study was at least a promising attempt to test one of Durkheim's most challenging theses on a grand scale in our times.

Sociological approaches to suicide have attracted their share of criticism over the years, with Durkheim's theory, as the leading contender, receiving the sternest reexaminations. Clinicians complain that Durkheim's theoretical distinctions are difficult to apply in practice. Research psychologists complain that the neglect of individual dynamics leaves Durkheim's theory too incomplete to foster either understanding or prevention. Nevertheless, Durkheim was himself well aware of individual factors and his contributions continue to be of interest. Another recent study (Dangelis & Pope, 1979), for example, finds that sophisticated methods of data analysis that were not available in Durkheim's time support many of that pioneer's specific conclusions.

Durkheim and a number of sociologists after him have made a strong case for an intimate relationship between suicide and the social structure. The case for the individual's own thoughts, motives, and life-styles as factors in suicide will now be examined.

SOME INDIVIDUAL MEANINGS OF SUICIDE

Just as the preceding discussion did not exhaust all the cultural meanings of suicide, so this section can only sample some of the individual meanings. The intent is to convey something of the various states of mind with which people approach a suicidal action.

Suicide for Reunion

The loss of a loved one can be experienced as so unbearable that the survivor is tempted to "join" the deceased. Recently-bereaved people often experience the "presence" of the dead. Perhaps this helps mitigate the sense of abandonment. But desperate longing may impel a person to follow the dead all the way to the other side if the relationship has been marked by extreme dependency. "I can't go on without him." "I am not complete without her." "What's to become of me? I can't manage by myself." Many people have feelings of this kind. Sometimes these feelings are accompanied by suicidal thoughts. Reunion fantasies may have some temporary value while bereaved individuals reconstruct their lives, but they can also lead to suicidal actions.

Some components in American cultural tradition encourage suicidal fantasies and actions of this kind. Heaven is such a delightful place—and it is so miserable here. Death is not real; it is only a portal to eternal life. Insurance advertisements have even depicted a deceased husband gazing down with approval from the clouds. Messages of this type encourage a blurring of the distinction between the living and the dead.

Children are particularly vulnerable to reunion fantasies. They do not yet have a firm cognitive grasp of life and death (although they are more advanced in this respect than many adults believe). The child is still in the process of attempting to establish identity as an individual. The parent or older sibling who has "gone off to heaven" has left the survivor with painful feelings of incompleteness and yearning. Some adults remain relatively childlike in their dependency on others and feel very much the same way when separated by death. Suicide to achieve reunion seems most likely when the person lacks a fully developed sense of selfhood, whether because of developmental level or personality constellation, when death has removed a significant source of support, and when there are salient cultural messages that make death appear unreal and the afterlife inviting.

Suicide for Rest and Refuge

Worn down by tribulations, a person may long for a "good rest" or a "secure harbor." This motivation can have many outcomes other than suicide. A vacation far away from the grinding routine may restore energy and confidence. Somebody else may appear on the scene to share the load. Or the vexed and fatigued person may simply drop his or her responsibilities for a while.

Alternatives such as these may not work out, however. Life may be experienced as too unrelenting and burdensome. The miracle of an ordinary good night's sleep may seem out of reach as depression deepens. Under such circumstances the fantasy of a prolonged, uninterrupted sleep may take on a heightened allure. The sleep-death analogy is readily available in America as in most other cultures (Chapter 2). It is tempting to take a few more pills than usual and just drift away.

This attitude toward suicide is also encouraged by individual and cultural tendencies to blur the distinctions between life and death. It falls well within the established cultural style of solving problems by taking something into our mouths (puff on a cigarette; suck on a pipe; swallow pills for headaches, indigestion, any form of distress). People with oral or escapist tendencies dominant in their personalities might be expected to be especially vulnerable to these lures of suicide.

Suicide for Revenge

The lover is rejected. The employee is passed over for promotion. Another child is preferred and pampered. The particular situation is not as important as the feeling of burning resentment and hurt left inside. And it may not have been the first time. Some people repeatedly feel that they are treated unfairly. Their achievements never seem to be recognized. No matter how hard they try, love and appreciation are withheld. Others may not recognize the state of mind with which such a person approaches a situation and how intensely hope and doubt, anger and longing are intermingled.

> I felt crushed. Absolutely *crushed*. It was my first really good semester. No incompletes. No withdrawals. All A's and B's. And no "episodes." I kept myself going all semester. I really felt strong and independent. I knew I shouldn't expect too much when I went home, but I guess . . . I mean I *know* I expected a little appreciation. You know, like maybe Mother just smiling and saying, "Had a good

semester, didn't you? I'm happy for you" or "I'm proud of you," though she would never say *that.*

This young woman felt that her achievement passed without notice, that, in fact, the family hardly noticed that she had come back home. Hurt and angry, she decided to get back by making a suicide attempt. If her family would not pay attention when she did something right, maybe they would when she did something wrong. "I wanted to hurt them—and hurt me—just enough." She slashed away at her wrist and arm. The self-wounding seemed to release some of her despair. She had not injured herself seriously, so she wrapped the wounded area in a bulky bandage. Nobody seemed to notice. A few days later she removed the bandage, exposing the patchwork of fresh scars. There still was no obvious response from the family. Instead, they were enthusiastically anticipating the graduation and upcoming marriage of one of her cousins. She felt even more crushed and low when she was passed over in the wedding arrangements as well: "I couldn't even be part of somebody else's happiness . . . I knew that revenge was stupid. But I *felt* like doing something stupid. Listen everybody: you're 100% right! I *am* a stupid person. And here is something *really* stupid to prove it!" She hurled herself from a rooftop.

> I wanted to kill myself then. I *think* I did. But I also wanted to see the look on their faces when they saw that bloody mess on the sidewalk. I could see myself standing alongside the rest of them, looking at that bloody mess of myself on the sidewalk, and looking at their shocked looks . . . I *didn't* think what it would be like if I half-killed myself and had to live with a crushed body. Maybe that was the really stupid part of it.

She survived a suicide attempt that might have been fatal. She was also fortunate in that her injuries did not prove permanently crippling, although she was disabled for months. The physical pain and trauma relieved some of her emotional tension for awhile. Yet she felt that she might "have to" do it again, perhaps "next time

for keeps." She did not need a psychologist to suggest that her suicide attempts were efforts to punish others by punishing herself. She was also perfectly capable of pointing out that both attempts had been aimed at forcing either love or remorse from the people who had been letting her down for so long. (At last report, this woman was alive, well, and somehow a stronger person for the ordeals she had undergone.)

The particular example given here illustrates several other characteristics often shown by the person who is on a self-destructive footing. This woman's fantasy included witnessing the impact of her suicide. She had divided herself into murderer and victim. The revenge fantasy would have lost much of its appeal had she recognized that she would never be able to confirm or appreciate the hoped-for impact. People who attempt suicide for reasons other than revenge may also act upon the assumption that, in a sense, they will survive the death to benefit by its effect.

She also experienced some tension release through the self-destructive action itself. It is not unusual for the sight of one's own blood to relieve built-up emotional pressures, if only for a while. Another woman who had slashed her wrists on several occasions told me, "I felt as if I had done something finally. I wasn't paralyzed any more. I wasn't suffering helplessly. I took action into my own hands, and that felt good." Perhaps the experience of surviving this type of suicide attempt encourages the fantasy that one would still be around to feel better after a fatal attempt as well.

The low self-esteem of many suicide attempters is also evident in the instance given here. Having a very unfavorable opinion of yourself may be linked with a variety of other motivations in addition to the fantasy of revenge. The combination of the revenge fantasy and low self-esteem appears to be a particularly dangerous one, however.

Suicide as the Penalty for Failure

The victim of suicide may also be the victim of self-expectations that have not been fulfilled.

The sense of disappointment and frustration may have much in common with that experienced by the person who seeks revenge through suicide. But this kind of person essentially holds himself or herself to blame. The judgment "I have failed" is followed by the decision to enact a most severe penalty, one that will make further failures impossible. It is as though the person has been tried and found guilty of a capital offense in his or her own personal court. A completely unacceptable gap is felt between expectations and accomplishment. One person might take the alternative of lowering expectations to close the gap. Another might give a more flattering, benefit-of-the-doubt interpretation of his or her accomplishments. And somebody else might keep trying to bring performance up to self-expectations. However, for some people a critical moment arrives when the discrepancy is experienced as too glaring and painful to be tolerated. If something has to be sacrificed it may be themselves, not the perhaps excessively high standards by which the judgment has been made.

Warren Breed (1972) and his colleagues found that a sense of failure is prominent among many people who take their own lives. The conclusions are based upon intensive case studies of suicide in New Orleans and appear to be consistent with findings of other investigators as well (Miller, 1967). The significance of a failure experience first came to Breed's (1972) attention when he reviewed the cases of 103 white males, "many of whom had taken their lives after being fired, demoted, or passed over for promotion, or had suffered business reverses" (p. 6). He increased the size and variety of his study population and added interviews of people who had known the deceased. It was learned that suicidal women also failed "but in a different domain— that of the family. Young female suicides had endless troubles with men, not many became successful mothers, and older women fell into a general role atrophy." For women less than 50 years old, work failure did not seem to be nearly as common or important a factor in suicide as it did for men. Yet "very often there is multiple

failure—for example, the unemployed man whose wife leaves him."

Fortunately, not every person who experiences failure commits suicide. Breed and his colleagues discovered other factors that so intensified the failure experience as to produce a lethal suicide attempt. This has led to the concept of a *basic suicidal syndrome.* Failure plays a critical role but takes on more lethal potential because of its association with the other factors.

The syndrome includes *rigidity, commitment, shame,* and *isolation,* as well as *failure* itself. The individual tends to be rigid in that he or she cannot shift from one role or goal to another nor shift level of aspiration. There is only one goal, one level of expectation, and only one way to achieve it. There is also a strong sense of commitment—that is, an intense desire to succeed. The sense of *failure* involves more than having performed less adequately than the person had demanded of himself or herself; it also includes a sense of culpability, of self-blame. The feeling is likely to go beyond guilt. A person who has failed or erred still might have a chance for redemption. The suicidal syndrome is characterized by a generalized sense of *shame.* It is not just that the individual has failed at something—he or she feels totally worthless. "I am no good. Never will be. I am nothing." From all these interacting factors, the individual may develop a sense of isolation. "In his state of despair he is all too prone to believe that the others, too, are evaluating him negatively . . . a process of withdrawal often follows and the person becomes more and more isolated from other people" (p. 117). This syndrome has been found by Breed and his colleagues most conspicuously in white, middle-class adults, both men and women. It does not seem to hold for lower class black men who kill themselves.

It is going too far to speak of this as *the* basic suicidal syndrome. Breed himself readily acknowledged that there are other patterns associated with suicide. Several have already been sketched here. But the high-aspiration, shame-of-failure dynamics revealed by his research do come close to the meaning of suicide for many in American society today. It does not tell us, however, why one person with a basic suicidal syndrome commits suicide while another finds a different solution to his or her problems, nor does it explain how the syndrome develops in the first place. A sequence is at least suggested, though. An individual may not become suicidal all at once, but start leaning toward an eventual act of self-destruction from an initial rigid setting of high aspirations. This would be followed by failure, perhaps repeated failures to a shamed and despondent pattern of isolating himself or herself from others. Further understanding of this sequence could prove helpful in identifying people who are at particular suicidal risk and providing timely assistance to them.

Suicide as a Mistake

Death may be the intended outcome of an overdose or other self-destructive action, but the person might not die. A serious attempt may fall short of its objective for a number of reasons. An unexpected rescuer may appear on the scene, a determined self-mutilation may happen to miss a vital spot, the overdose may induce vomiting instead of coma, even a loaded gun may fail to fire. The victim may "betray" himself or herself, as in the case of the bridge jumper who survives the often-deadly fall and then swims desperately for life. Shneidman (1980) gives two particularly vivid examples of people who survived suicide attempts that ordinarily would have been lethal.

But there can be a discrepancy between intention and outcome in the other direction as well. Some people kill themselves even though there is good reason to believe that they had not meant to. The victim had counted on being rescued. The overdose was not supposed to be lethal. Some kind of control or precaution had been exercised to limit the effect, and yet the outcome was death.

We cannot automatically conclude that death was the intention any more than we can insist that a person did not intend to commit suicide because the attempt happened to abort. In suicide, as in most other actions, we do not always achieve the outcome we had in mind. The person may have wanted much to live, but a mood, a desperate maneuver, and a misjudgment brought life to a sudden close.

People who often work with the suicidal recognize that the individual contemplating a self-destructive act frequently is of two minds. This is the impression, for example, of volunteers who pick up the phone when a call is made to a suicide prevention hot line. The very fact that a person would reach out for human contact in this way suggests some continuing advocacy for life. We have no way of knowing if all people in a suicidal state of mind experience strong ambivalence. However, many people with suicide on their minds do go back and forth about it, experiencing conflicting life and death tugs even at the same time. A life-threatening act that emerges from a wavering or conflicting intention may itself show some apparent contradictions. Why would she have taken the overdose just a few minutes before her husband was due home if she was entirely of a mind to take her life? And yet she did take the pills, and if her husband happens to be delayed coming home this day, will this gesture have become indeed her final gesture?

Helping people to survive their own mistakes is an important part not only of suicide prevention but of public health safety in general. Access to lethal means of self-destruction could be made more difficult, for example, thereby placing some time and distance between a momentary intention and a permanent error. Seiden (1977) observes that suicide rates dropped significantly in England when coke gas was no longer widely available as an easily available mode of suicide in the home or when its toxicity was reduced. He has persistently advocated the construction of a lower-span sidewalk for the Golden Gate Bridge, a place that has become known widely as a "suicide shrine." Seiden followed up on more than 700 people who had approached either the Golden Gate or Bay bridge with suicidal intentions and who were intercepted by alert citizens or police before completing the action. Ninety-six percent of these people did not make subsequent fatal attempts, and all the survivors favored construction of a barrier. "If there had been a barrier every one of them reports they would have reconsidered" (p. 274). The suicidal intention had been strong but ambivalent. The attempters had given society a chance to catch them before making a fatal mistake. Seiden adds that "Considering the transitory nature of suicidal crises, the presence of a highly lethal and easily available means such as the bridge must be regarded as equivalent to a loaded gun around the house ready to be used in an impulsive outburst." Society could take a more active role in protecting people from those critical moments when the possibility of making a fatal mistake is on the horizon.

A Psychoanalytical Approach to Suicide

Since life seeks to preserve itself, how could a being actively pursue its own destruction? Freud's first explanation (1917/1959) was rather different from those that had been previously offered by others. It centered on the concept of the internalization of the wish to kill somebody else. Suicidal individuals turn a murderous wish against themselves. By destroying themselves, then, they symbolically destroy the other person. Suicide victims behave as though they are rooting out the inner representation of another person, a representation that might derive from early childhood when the distinction between self and other is incomplete.

Freud did not remain satisfied with this theory. Later (1923/1961) he offered a more philosophical concept. We do not have just one basic instinctual drive. Each of us possesses a pair of drives that have different goals. These are a life instinct, *Eros,* and a death instinct, *Thanatos.* These drives constantly interact in our lives. When Thanatos gains the upper hand, we may engage in a self-destructive action. One of the main departures from the earlier theory is that

self-destructive behavior no longer seems especially remarkable. Society has a way of frustrating all of us. We cannot pursue our personal pleasures unmindful of social demands and restrictions, nor can we express our antagonisms directly without incurring serious consequences. Vulnerability to suicide exists for all humans because there are so many obstacles in our pathway to gratification and because much of our aggression is forced inward. Furthermore, "the extreme helplessness of the human ego in infancy is never completely overcome so that there is always a readiness under conditions of great stress and conflict to regress back to more primitive ego states" (Litman, 1967, p. 75). The regressed ego may simply let itself die because it feels helpless and abandoned, or the suicidal action mayrepresent a desperate last stand against the sense of impending helplessness and abandonment.

This twin-instinct theory has not found much application in day-by-day interactions with people at suicidal risk, and researchers have yet to come up with convincing ways of testing the theory for its fit with the facts. However, the psychoanalytical approach does alert us to the long developmental career that precedes a self-destructive action. The young child, for example, may internalize the negative attitudes conveyed by cruel or thoughtless parents. This burdens the child with a superego that is excessively oriented toward criticism and self-destruction. Chaotic and inadequate parenting may also jeopardize the child by leaving him or her with a brittle ego that fragments and shatters under pressures that most other people are able to withstand. Many present-day clinicians and researchers have modified the early psychoanalytical approach to take sociocultural factors more into account. As we have seen, for example, some native Americans are at exceptionally high risk for suicide and other self-destructive actions. Research suggests that this seems to involve a sense of low self-esteem that is fostered by the subgroup's deprivation and discrimination against them in American society in general (Curlee, 1972). The child is in danger of growing up with a severe lack of confidence in his or her identity and worth as well as with a tendency to keep aggressive impulses locked up under high pressure until efforts at control fail. This is in contrast with the pride and satisfaction a child would have taken in being, for example, a Cheyenne in preceding generations when the people were independent and possessed a favorable group self-image. These dynamics of low self-esteem and self-directed aggression can lead to fatal outcomes other than suicide, as witnessed by the high alcohol-related death rates among older adults on the same reservation. The psychoanalytical approach, then, remains useful today, but it is not necessary to accept every interpretation nor to ignore other relevant data.

FACTS, MYTHS, AND GUIDELINES

Some of the major social and individual meanings of suicide have been considered. Now some of the *myths* that have grown around the subject over the years will be evaluated. It will then be possible to propose a few guidelines for your own relationship to self-destructive behaviors.

Popular Myths about Suicide

• *A person who talks about suicide will not actually take his or her own life.* There is abundant evidence to show that this statement is not true. Approximately three out of every four people who eventually kill themselves give some detectable hint ahead of time, whether by less serious attempts or by verbal statements (the latter are sometimes as direct as can be—e.g., "I'm going to blow my head off," "If things don't get better in a hurry, you'll be reading about me in the papers."). This is one of the most dangerous myths because it encourages us to ignore cries for help. The rejection of the communication itself can become the last straw.

• *Only a specific class of people commit suicide.* It is sometimes held that suicide is a particular risk of either the poor or the rich. The poor are

supposed to feel helpless and deprived, the rich to be bored and aimless. These simplifications fail to consider the complexity of the individual's relationship to society. People in all income brackets and social echelons commit suicide. An explanation limited to economic or class distinctions alone is not adequate and contributes to our blind spots in the identification of individuals at risk.

• *Suicide has simple causes that are easily established.* It would be closer to the truth to say that many of us are easily satisfied with hasty and superficial explanations. This chapter has emphasized *meanings* rather than *causes* of suicide, which are often far from simple.

• *Asking people about suicide will put that thought in their minds and encourage suicide attempts.* This is one of the most common of the mistaken assumptions. Many lives have been saved by opening communication on this topic.

• *Only depressed people commit suicide.* This misconception is held by some professionals as well as by the public. People with a psychiatric diagnosis of depression do have a higher suicide rate than those with other psychiatric syndromes or those without known syndromes. But suicide may occur in any type of psychiatric disorder. The person may not even seem to be especially unhappy immediately before the fatal action. It is dangerous, then, to overlook suicidal potential on the basis of the assumption that this is a risk only with the depressed person.

• *Only crazy or insane people commit suicide.* This mistaken proposition is related to the one just described. It remains difficult for some people to believe that a person in his or her right mind could commit suicide, but the cultural tradition of rational suicide has already been acknowledged. Psychiatrists disagree on how many suicides are associated with obvious mental disorder, but some of the most qualified researchers and clinicians find that suicide is not invariably related to psychosis.

• *Suicidal tendencies are inherited.* It is true that more than one person in the same family may commit suicide. Some families do have a suicidal tradition that seems to perpetuate itself. But there is no evidence for a hereditary basis, even in special studies made of identical twins. The explanation for suicide has to be sought elsewhere.

• *When a suicidal person shows improvement, the danger is over.* Experienced clinicians have learned that the period following an apparent improvement in overall condition is actually one of special danger. Sometimes this is because the client has improved enough to be discharged from a mental hospital and therefore has more opportunity to commit suicide. At other times, it seems related to a recovery of enough energy and volition to take action. Sensitivity and interpersonal support are especially needed when the person seems to be pulling out of a suicidal crisis.

• *People who are under a physician's care or who are hospitalized are not suicidal risks.* This is wishful thinking. Many people who commit suicide have received some form of medical or psychiatric attention within six months preceding the act. Suicides can and do occur in the hospital itself. Henry Davidson (1969) has detailed from case histories some of the ways in which hospitalization has failed to deter individuals from suicide and also notes that the dynamics of the institutional situation itself can at times contribute to anxiety, low self-esteem, and other conditions conducive to suicide.

• *Suicide can be prevented only by a psychiatrist or mental hospital.* Some of the most successful suicide prevention efforts are being made by a variety of people in the community who bring concern, stamina, and sensitivity to the task. The human resources of the entire community may hold more hope than the limited cadres of professionals or the institution. It is neither necessary nor realistic to pass all the responsibility to a few.

A Few Guidelines

Many suicides can be prevented. Perhaps you have already played a role in preventing suicide without realizing it. The companionship you offered a person during a crucial period or the confidence you displayed in a friend after he or she suffered a failure experience might have provided just enough support to dissolve a self-destructive pattern in the making. Whenever we bring sensitivity and a genuinely caring attitude to our relationships with other people, we may be decisively strengthening their life-affirming spirit.

When the suicide flag is up, there is a tendency among many of us to back off. Unfortunately, this includes some professional people as well as the general public. Pretending that we haven't heard suicidal messages or distancing ourselves from a person who is contemplating self-destruction can hardly be recommended as helpful approaches.

A formula approach to helping the suicidal person would be of limited value. How we are best to proceed depends upon who the suicidal person is, who we are, and what kind of relationship we have to go on together. A few general guidelines can be offered, however:

• *Take the suicidal concern seriously.* This does not mean panic or an exaggerated, unnatural response. But knowing as you do that thoughts, musings, and threats sometimes do end in fatal attempts, you have good reason to respect the concern.

• *Do not issue a provocation to suicide.* Strange though it may seem, people sometimes react to the suicidal person in such a way as to provoke or intensify the attempt. Do not be one of those "friends" who dares this person to make good his or her threat or who intimates that he or she is too "chicken" to do so. On a more subtle level, do not belittle his or her concern or troubled state of mind. A belittling response can intensify the need to do something desperate so that others will appreciate how bad he or she really feels.

• *Go easy on value judgments.* "You can't do that—it's wrong!" This is sometimes the exclamation that would come most readily to our lips, but it is seldom a useful one. In most situations it is not very helpful to inject value judgments when a troubled person is starting to confide self-destructive thoughts. Perhaps applying value judgments is our need, but receiving them at this moment is not likely to be perceived as helpful.

• *Do not get carried away by the "good reasons" a person has for suicide.* The interpersonal response to a suicidal individual sometimes involves much reading of our own thoughts and feelings into the other person's head. We may think, "If all of that were going wrong with *my* life, I'd want to kill myself too!" This conclusion might be attributed to the other person all too hastily. For every person who commits suicide when faced with realistically difficult problems, there are many others who find alternative solutions. It is possible to respect the reality factors in the suicidal individual's situation without lining up on the side of self-murder. This respectful, nonevaluative approach is taken by many of the people who pick up the phone when a crisis hot line call is put through.

• *Know what resources are available in the community.* Who else can help this person? What kind of help might this person find most acceptable? What services are available through local schools, religious groups, mental health centers? Does your community have a crisis intervention service? How does it operate? Learn about and if possible participate in your community's efforts to help those who are in periods of special vulnerability.

• *Listen.* This is the advice you will hear again and again from people who have devoted themselves to suicide prevention. It is good advice. Listening is not the passive activity it might seem to be. It is an intent, self-giving action that shows the troubled person that you are there. And it is an opportunity for the person to discharge at least some of the tensions that have brought him or her to a certain point of self-destructive intent and to sort out other possibilities. Other suggestions for preventing suicide have been offered by the contributors to *Youth Suicide* (Peck, et al., 1980–1981), Berent (1981), and Kastenbaum (1983).

INDIRECT SUICIDE AND OTHER RISK-TAKING BEHAVIORS

What about when people place their lives in jeopardy and yet are not clearly suicidal? The possibility that some deaths are "subintentioned" (Shneidman, 1963) has been much discussed by suicidologists in recent years. The individual places himself or herself in situations that markedly increase risk to life. If the risk does prove fatal, the official cause may be listed as homicide, accident, or illness (and in wartime as "action of the enemy"), when in actuality the victim contributed something significant to the probability of death. It is sensible to *be aware of the possibility* that some of our actions that increase risk to life may have a motivational component (as illustrated by the street-crossing study in Chapter 1).

MURDER

Overview

A person who takes the life of another has committed homicide. If a court rules that this killing was intentional and unlawful, then the act has been judged to be murder. All murders are homicides; some homicides are murders. You may have committed "justifiable homicide" if you used lethal force to protect your own life; or you may be guilty of "negligent homicide" if your carelessness resulted in the death of another person. Distinctions of this kind can be very important in the judicial process. For the purposes of this chapter, however, we will use the simplest and most direct word, murder.

The Statistical Picture

The United States has the highest murder rate in the world (of nations providing information to Interpol). The latest available international data are presented in Table 8–2.

It is difficult to escape the implication that there is something particularly "American" about this high rate. Neighboring Canada shares

TABLE 8–2

Homicide around the world

Nation	Homicide Rate*
Austria	1.3
Canada	2.7
Chile	5.6
Denmark	1.2
Egypt	1.0
England	1.1
Finland	1.8
Greece	1.0
Hungary	1.9
Ireland	0.8
Italy	2.1
Netherlands	1.2
New Zealand	1.7
Nigeria	1.5
Northern Ireland	4.9
Portugal	3.0
Sweden	1.4
Switzerland	1.1
United States	*7.9*

Data Source: Information Plus: *Gun Control* (1989), drawn from Interpol reports.

*Number of murders per 100,000 population.

the North American continent with us and is-comparable in many respects—yet has a murder rate nearly two-thirds lower. Western European nations, with whom we might also compare ourselves, generally have even lower murder rates than Canada. Politically troubled Northern Ireland is an exception, yet its 4.0 murder rate is only a little more than half as high as ours. And among the hard-pressed people of Chile, the relatively high murder rate is surpassed by the affluent and powerful United States. (Does the United States also have more murder *attempts* than other nations? International differences in reporting these data prevent drawing a firm conclusion.)

Who are the killers and who are the victims? Here are some of the major statistical findings:

• Approximately 20,000 Americans were known to have been murdered in 1985 (Foster, et al., 1989). The United States murder rate for

this year of 8.3 is higher than the rate shown in Table 8–2, where 1984 is the most recent year available for international comparisons.

• Men are most often both the killers and the victims. When a female is the victim, the murderer is a male in nine of ten cases. When the victim is male, the killer is a male in eight of ten cases. About three of every four murder victims is a male.

• People are most at risk to become a murder victim between the ages of 25 and 44. And only accidents claim more lives among those 15–24. Age is a factor, then, although people of all ages have become murder victims.

• Most murders (about 90%) are committed by killers who are of the same race as the victims. This fact is worth emphasizing because interracial murders often arouse more fear and anger. It has been observed that newspapers and other media give more attention to interracial murders and thereby "push the panic button" for many people.

• Murder rates are higher among blacks and nonwhites in general. In fact, "Homicide is currently the leading cause of death among black men and women aged 25 to 34" (Hawkins, 1986, p. 17). There are more similarities than differences between the murders committed by whites and blacks, apart from the higher rate among the latter. The most recent national data show a criminal homicide rate of 4.3 for whites and 31.6 for blacks (Foster, et al., 1989). The actual *number* of murders committed by whites and blacks is about the same (in the 8,000 range per year), although the *rate* is much higher for blacks. Murder continues to be among the higher risks of death for black men into old age.

• At least three of five murders are committed by people who are relatives, lovers, friends, neighbors, or colleagues of the victims. Again, the media tends to spotlight killings by strangers (e.g., in the course of a robbery, or a freeway sniping). But the fact remains that among both blacks and whites the killer and the victim usually were acquaintances if not relatives or intimate companions.

• Murders are most common in large cities—about three times more frequent than the national average.

• There is a major regional difference: Southern states continue to have murder rates about twice that of the next highest area, the Western region. (There is no such difference with respect to suicide.) The single most dangerous place is our nation's capital. Washington, D.C. has a murder rate of 42.66. The safest place is South Dakota with a rate of 0.72. Murder rates are at their lowest in predominately rural states such as Vermont and North Dakota.

• Handguns are the most often used weapons of murder. Firearms in general are involved in about three of five killings. Knives and other cutting or stabbing instruments are the next most common lethal weapons. Knives, however, are the weapons most frequently used in murders committed by those of Asian or native American heritage.

• One consistent finding has not been adequately explained. The highest black criminal homicide rates occur in states that have both the lowest proportion of blacks and the lowest crime rates (e.g., Maine, Nevada, Utah). Why?

• The overall trend in recent years has been for higher and higher murder rates in the United States. Most other causes of death have decreased during these same years, taking the 1940–1980 span as a convenient unit of analysis. Although the murder rate has occasionally dipped during this period of time, the overall trend has been for a marked increase.

Three Patterns of Murder in the United States

Murder, like suicide, is an action taken by an individual in a situation. The similarity in outcome—a person dead—is perhaps the most significant aspect of any murder, but the differences can also be remarkable. A man with a long criminal record ambushes and executes another criminal; this was his day's work. Another man nervously attempts his first hold-up. Something goes wrong and he fires his gun at the clerk, then flees in panic. After a bout of drinking, a rejected lover breaks in upon the woman, her children, and her new friend. Cursing them all, he sprays the room with bullets from a semiautomatic rifle. An emotionally fragile woman hears voices that tell her what to do in her predicament. Obeying the voices, she strangles her child and then attempts to take her own life.

These people and their situations are all quite different. It is obvious that there cannot be any one, all-encompassing explanation for murder. It becomes important, then, to look at some of the specific patterns that murder takes in the United States. Three such patterns are briefly examined here.

Domestic Violence: The Abused Woman Defends Herself

Law enforcement officers around the nation are well aware that they might encounter extreme violence when they respond to calls for a family situation. As already noted, most killings involve people who knew each other, often in very close relationships. The killer is usually a man, whether the murder grows out of a domestic or criminal situation. Women may also kill, however, especially when they have suffered humiliation, abuse, and injury at the hands of a man. The abused woman defending herself with lethal force will be our example of murder within the family circle.

Angela Browne (1987) has made an intensive study of battered women who eventually killed their husbands. Here is one typical incident that laid the foundation for homicide:

> Bella had gone to the movies with her sister. Isaac believed her place was at home, and had beaten her so badly in the past for going out that she usually never left the house. But this evening, he said he wanted her to go. Then he changed his mind while she was gone. He began telling the children that he was going to kill her when she returned, and they were all going to stay up and watch. The youngest

girl began to cry, and Isaac made her go up to the top of the stairs so she wouldn't give it away.

When Bella got back, Isaac began shouting, "Damn you, damn you. Who said you could go to the movies?" Bella tried to reason with him, saying, "You did, honey. You told me to go." But Isaac chased her toward the living room, yelling, "I'm going to kill you, you bitch. I'm going to kill you this night!" Bella ran from side to side in the room, but couldn't get to the door because Isaac had blocked it off. Isaac forced her into a corner, holding her up with a hand in her hair, and began hitting her repeatedly with his fist. Bella could hear the children screaming and kept crying to them to get help. She was sure Isaac would kill her if no one intervened. Then he began to bang her head against the wall. Bella was too dizzy to resist anymore, and just hung on. The attack ended a few minutes later when a relative stopped by and restrained him (pp. 61–62).

This violent episode is typical of many others experienced by the battered women in Browne's study. The rages were often sudden and unprovoked. The insults and accusations had little if any basis in anything the wife had done, and the attacks themselves were savage. Many battered women described their husbands as having become entirely different people during the assaults, e.g., "He'd get a look in his eyes and start to breathe differently. . . ." "It was like dealing with a stranger." Repeatedly the victim of a man who might become crazed with fury at almost any time, these women lived in fear for themselves and their children.

In Bella's case, she endured 20 years of severe abuse until one night Isaac went too far. He threatened to kill their oldest daughter when she came home. Isaac fell asleep first, however, and Bella and another daughter shot him and then set the house on fire. This removed one major threat from Bella's life but did not set her free. She was found guilty of murder in the first degree and sentenced to life imprisonment. Permanently disabled and in very poor health as a result of the repeated attacks from Isaac, she is considered to have a shortened life expectancy.

Browne offers several conclusions about the battered women who killed in desperation:

- American society perpetuates a tradition in which the male is considered to be supreme, and the female required to be submissive. The deeper levels of this tradition continue even though, technically, women have more rights than in previous generations. Physical abuse of women will not end until fundamental attitudes alter and true equality is achieved.

- Each year there are approximately one and a half million physical assaults upon women by their male partners. Many, but not all, of these men are in a drugged or intoxicated state at the time. It is the woman who usually suffers the injuries, sometimes of a serious and/or permanent nature. Severely battered women, by contrast, seldom have behaved violently toward their mates—until a few such as Bella try to end their ordeals through murder. Most often, the battered women tried to placate their husbands and did what they could to avoid such episodes.

- Legal protection and social support for battered women is still quite inadequate in most places. This means that more women (and children) will continue to suffer, and more will be provoked to take extreme measures.

- Early intervention is recommended when a pattern of abuse is detected. All too often, a bad situation worsens over time; it is not as likely to improve without some assistance. Isaac might be alive today, and a less dangerous person, and Bella would be free and healthy had somebody recognized the critical nature of their situation and arranged for effective help.

It is ironic that the United States with its commitment to preventing and treating life-threatening diseases and its support of hospice care has been so slow in protecting women from lethal attacks by their male partners. In a recent Arizona example, typical of many throughout the nation, a woman was repeatedly assaulted by her husband and the life of their infant daughter was placed in jeopardy. The health-care system looked after her injuries, but the judicial system turned the husband loose after each incident—until he did kill her. What our society will do to save a life varies greatly with the person at risk, the situation, and the attitudinal context.

The Mass Killer: Who Is He and Why Does He Do It?

Many killings appear to be understandable. An intruder picks the wrong home to burglarize and is shot dead. One drug dealer is ambushed by another in a turf dispute. A drunken brawl ends in death when one combatant goes for a knife. Whatever our attitude toward these acts of violence might be, we are not puzzled about the motivations; we can see how criminal activities and drunken disorder can lead to a killing. The mass killer represents something else, something that seems more remote from ordinary human experience. Who would kill one person after another, sometimes in bizarre and fiendish ways? Are they crazy or what? Is it possible to identify such people before they become so destructive? The mass killer is alarming to society both because of the lives he destroys and because his very existence appears to contradict our expectations of human feeling and conduct.

Some of the mass killers of recent years include:

- Albert De Salvo, "The Boston Strangler," killed 13 women in the Boston area after gaining entry to their homes and sexually molesting them.
- Dan Corll abducted, raped, and killed 27 boys in the Houston area.
- John Wayne Gacy abducted, raped, and killed 33 boys in the Chicago area.
- Angelo Buono raped and murdered ten girls and women in the Los Angeles area.
- David Berkowitz, "Son of Sam," killed six people and wounded nine others in the New York City area.
- Ted Bundy raped and murdered an unknown number of women—probably more than 20—in four states.

This is a very incomplete list, and new mass killers continue to come to public attention. There are some obvious commonalities among the killers mentioned above. All were men; all took the lives of people they had not previously known; sexual assault was involved in all cases except for Berkowitz; and all the murders occurred over a period of time. Some mass killers have taken all the lives in a single outburst of violence, and some have not shown any evident sexual motive. However, the male serial killer who sexually assaults his victims is among the most common types of mass murderer in the United States.

In their study of mass murderers, Jack Levin and James Alan Fox (1985) offer a composite profile:

> He is typically a white male in his late twenties or thirties. In the case of simultaneous mass murder, he kills people he knows with a handgun or rifle; in serial crimes, he murders strangers by beating or strangulation. His specific motivation depends on the circumstances leading up to the crime, but it generally deals directly with either money, expediency, jealousy, or lust. Rarely is the mass murderer a hardened criminal with a long criminal record, although a spotty history of property crime is common. The occurrence of mass murder often follows a spell of frustration when a particular event triggers sudden rage; yet, in other cases, the killer is coolly pursuing some goal he cannot otherwise attain. (p. 48)

But is the mass killer mentally deranged, crazy?

> . . . though the mass killer often may appear cold and show no remorse, and even deny responsibility for his crime, serious mental illness or psychosis is rarely present. Most unexpectedly, in background, in personality, and even in appearance, the mass murderer is *extraordinarily ordinary*. This may be the key to his extraordinary "talent" for murder: After all, who would ever suspect him?

This is a chilling conclusion. It would be comforting to know that the potential mass killer is an obviously crazed person. Most mass killers, however, had attracted little attention to them selves; some were considered "loners" or "a little odd" in retrospect, but others had been ordinary neighbors and colleagues. There is no telltale clue in appearance or behavior. As Levin and Fox add, "the mass killer typically is a white, middle-aged male who can look like anybody. At one extreme, Ted Bundy was noted for his attractiveness and charm; at the other extreme, Nazi cultist Frederick Cowan was balding, fat, and ugly. Edmund Emil Kemper III stood six feet nine inches; mass murderer Charles Starkweather was only five foot five."

How is the mass killer to be explained if he often passes for a "normal" person in society? No single explanation is adequate. For example, some received brutal treatment in their own childhoods; others organized their lives around bitter racism. These factors seemed to contribute to the violent crimes they eventually committed, but many other people who were abused as children or harbored racist hatreds did not become mass killers. However, there are a few special aspects about mass killers that are worth keeping in mind:

1. Mass killers do not draw their violence from the Southern tradition of homicide. Although murder is most common in the South—and often appears to be the outcome of a lethal response to a challenge—relatively few mass murders occur in the South, nor do they take the form of a direct confrontation. There is reason to believe that Southerners have continued to provide more support for each other through neighborhoods, churches, and other community organizations, thereby reducing the sense of alienation that can lead to violence against others. "Even an unemployed or divorced man in the rural South was far less likely to be alone. His kin, congregation, or lodge were there to help" (Humphrey & Palmer, 1986–1987).

2. Boom cities attract many people whose high hopes fail to be fulfilled. They become bitter, disillusioned, and ready to try something different to get rid of their frustrations and anger. This was the case, for example, with James Oliver Huberty, a 41-year-old man who thought he would have better career opportunities if he moved to the San Diego area. After he lost a job as security guard, he grew angry at the world, walked to the nearby McDonald's restaurant, and gunned down 40 people, 21 of whom died.

3. The age and race correlates of murder in general do not apply to the mass or serial killer. Most murders are committed by young adults, and, as already noted, with a higher rate among blacks. By contrast, most mass killers are white and more likely to be in their 30s and 40s.

4. Although only a few mass murderers prove to be psychotic there is another type of deviant personality that is well known to health professionals and law enforcement agencies. The person with an antisocial personality (also known as "sociopath" and "psychopath"; the "con man" is one type of antisocial personality) is not out of touch with reality in the usual sense of the word. He does not hear voices that order him to kill or show other symptoms of psychosis. Basically, the antisocial personality does not feel affection or empathy for other people. This is the person who invariably "uses" other people. Furthermore, the antisocial personality is likely to have a low toleration for frustration and to explode in rage when things don't go his or her way. According to one psychiatrist, "their main purpose in life is self-gratification . . . regardless of the cost to others . . . and the antisocial personality fails to benefit from experience or punishment" (Levin & Fox, p. 210).

5. The primary motivation of many mass murderers has been the need to dominate and control others. Rape is intended for revenge (even if the victim is a stranger) and the opportunity to humiliate and control another person. There is nothing unusual in a person enjoying power or dominance, but in the case of the mass murderer not only is this taken to a brutal extreme, but it is often based upon a defective sense of what it means to be a human being.

It is perhaps this type of menace, the antisocial personality, who has more than anybody else persuaded many people to become less trustful of others and to make special efforts to protect their children. A higher index of suspiciousness in everyday life is a fairly expensive price to pay for security, but the antisocial personality does exist and cannot be dismissed as a threat.

Political Murder:
Assassination in the United States

Abraham Lincoln . . . John F. Kennedy . . . Robert F. Kennedy . . . Martin Luther King, Jr. The assassination of these four leaders has become a disturbing part of American history. The murder of a political leader has both its private and its public side. A child loses a father, a wife her husband. The personal losses and distress caused by assassination should not be forgotten, but we will focus here on what makes this form of murder distinctive. The theories themselves— right or wrong—tell us something about our society's fears and needs.

A systematic examination of political assassinations in the United States has been conducted by James W. Clarke (1982) who researched the cases listed in Table 8–3. There has been a popular theory for many years that assassinations are the work of mentally unbalanced people. Some people take comfort in the view that a rational individual would not make an attempt on the life of a political figure. Attention has so often been given to the mental state of the assassin that one might conclude that this theory has been well established. Not necessarily. It is closer to the truth to conclude that the mental illness theory has been useful in protecting some of our beliefs and illusions, but does not account for all or even most of the assassination attempts.

Clarke found four types of assassins. These may be summarized as Type I: Political Extremists; Type II: Rejected and Misguided People; Type III: Antisocial Personalities; and Type IV: Psychotics. Three of these types were clearly in contact with reality and did not suffer from delusions, hallucinations or other cognitive distortions. This is not to say that the assassins were without personal problems. Social isolation or disturbances of interpersonal relationships were

TABLE 8–3

Political assassination attempts, United States

Year	Intended Victim	Assassin	Outcome
1835	Andrew Jackson	Richard Lawrence	Unharmed
1865	Abraham Lincoln	John Wilkes Booth	Killed
1881	James Garfield	Charles Guiteau	Killed
1901	William McKinley	Leon Czolgosz	Killed
1912	Theodore Roosevelt	John Schrank	Wounded
1933	Franklin Roosevelt	Giuseppe Zangara	Unharmed*
1935	Huey Long	Carl Weiss	Killed
1950	Harry S. Truman	Oscar Collazo & Griselio Torresola	Unharmed†
1963	John F. Kennedy	Lee Harvey Oswald	Killed
1968	Martin Luther King	James Earl Ray	Killed
1968	Robert Kennedy	Sirhan Sirhan	Killed
1972	George Wallace	Arthur Bremer	Wounded
1974	Richard Nixon	Samuel Byck	Unharmed‡
1975	Gerald Ford	Lynette Fromm	Unharmed
1975	Gerald Ford	Sara Moore	Unharmed

Source: James W. Clarke. *American Assassins.* Princeton: Princeton University Press, 1982.

*Chicago Mayor Anton Cermak was killed and four others were wounded in the volley of shots fired at President Roosevelt.

†Security guards Leslie Coffelt and Joseph Downs were wounded; Coffelt died as he returned fire and killed Torresola.

‡Killed two Delta pilots and wounded a cabin attendant in an aborted attempt to force the plane to crash into the White House.

characteristic of several types, and only one type was essentially free of emotional distortion in some form. They differed markedly in the primary motive for the assassination attempt. This can be most clearly seen when comparing the Type I and the Type IV assassin. The public stereotype of the crazed assassin is represented by the men who threatened the lives of Andrew Jackson, James Garfield, and Theodore Roosevelt. These people were delusional and, at times, incoherent. Almost anybody would have easily recognized their distortions of reality and need for treatment. In keeping with their defects in reality testing, Lawrence, Guiteau and Schrank were confused and idiosyncratic in their motivation. Guiteau, for example, had a friendly attitude toward Garfield, but convinced himself that the president must be killed to "save the Republic." He would later say that God had made him do it. It was clear that in this and in most other matters Guiteau had a grossly distorted view of himself and the world.

By contrast, the Type I assassins were motivated by political objectives: "rational extremists," as Clarke puts it (p. 262). These people have often been misrepresented as mentally ill, according to Clarke, because our society has so much difficulty in accepting the possibility that sane people might commit such an act. As we saw earlier, there has long been a parallel belief that people who take their own lives *must* be mentally ill, an assumption also not well supported by the evidence. Looking at Table 8–3, you will find five Type I assassins. Collazo, Torresola, and Sirhan were motivated by their identification with nationalistic aims. Booth's allegiance could almost be described as nationalistic as well, although sectionalistic or regionalistic might be more appropriate. Czolgosz thought that by killing McKinley he would be striking a blow for "the good working people," a class-oriented political motivation. None of these men was insane (legal framework) or psychotic (psychiatric).

The people Clarke classifies as Type III assassins will remind us of the antisocial personalities

who committed mass murders. These men, such as Bremer, Byck, and Zangara, hated the society they felt had rejected and frustrated them. Unable to express feelings other than helplessness or rage, they cast about for a target that would symbolically represent those aspects of society they most disliked. They did not have personal animosity toward the leaders they attacked. Like the mass murderers, the Type III assassins showed no remorse. Although neither the typical mass murderer nor the Type III assassin is "crazy," each has a fundamental character flaw in the ability to feel and express ordinary human feeling.

Up to this point we have seen that some assassins (Type III) have been the same kind of people who commit mass murders, and that a few others (Type IV) are, in fact, the psychotic killers celebrated in stereotypes, but that others (Type I) have been politically conscious people who took this extreme action thinking that it would further a cause to which they held allegiance. This leaves still another kind of assassin. Oswald, Byck, Fromm, and Moore were very anxious people who felt rejected and unable to cope with the demands of life. They wanted to be taken seriously by somebody and to prove themselves in some way. Although a Type II assassin might attach him- or herself to a political cause, the basic objective is personal: somehow to redeem one's own miserable life by a bold deed. As Clarke observes, the Type II assassins were misguided people, but not insane.

All this attention to the make-up of the individual assassin should not deter us entirely from more general factors. For example, the emergence of television has generated an unprecedented type and degree of coverage for spectacular events. How often do you want to see the stricken man crumple from the bullet? Would you like to see it in slow-motion? Split-screen? Reverse angle? Whether the potential assassin's motivation is primarily political or personal, over the past several decades there has been the added incentive of flashing this event before the eyes of many millions of people. Another point to consider is that some potential assassins have political grievances that are not in themselves irrational. We will encounter this problem again when we look at terrorism. To recognize that actual and significant political grievances can stimulate assassination attempts is not to condone such acts of violence. Instead, we may be better prepared as a society to prevent or respond to assassination attempts if we do not insist on believing that they are all the work of people who are mentally ill. A more general issue recurs here as it did when we considered mass murderers: can we continue to be an open and trusting society and still improve our ability to protect ourselves, our children, and our leaders from the killers?

No Theory of Murder

This statement is not true. There *are* theories of murder, some of which can be useful in particular circumstances. For example, psychoanalysts sometimes speak of people "acting out" impulses and "externalizing" their self-hatred. Sociologists are more likely to discuss such concepts as "relative deprivation" (having nothing to do, of course, with a shortage of uncles, aunts, sisters and cousins). Knowing that others in society drive expensive cars and live in high style, the young person trapped in a "subculture of exasperation" (Humphrey & Palmer, 1986–1987) may take extreme and violent actions to escape the unpleasant realities of everyday life and procure some of the goodies. Either of these explanations might be helpful in understanding a particular pattern of murder, but no explanation—or, at least, no simple explanation—accounts for the entire panorama of killing in the United States.

We have looked at a few of these patterns here and observed differences as well as similarities. There are no simple and adequate explanations for either suicide or murder. It is obvious that individual, situational, and large-scale sociocultural factors are all involved as we attempt to make the best of our lives, whether our ways of coping come down to working harder, trying to be more agreeable, changing our hair styles, placing faith in God, hoping for better luck, or, at the extreme, taking a life. And whatever explanations we prefer, there is no getting away from the fact that people killing people has established itself as part of our way of life.

TERRORISM

Overview

Who is the terrorist? A believer in the fundamentalist Shi'ite form of Islam who is prepared for his own death as he plans the massacre of others? Yes, sometimes. This was true, for example, of Raad Meftel Ajeel, the young man who crashed through the gates of the United States embassy in Kuwait, dying as his cargo of hexogen and butane exploded. The identity of the two Shi'ites whose earlier and similar suicidal attack resulted in the death of 241 American and 58 French servicemen in Beirut has never been determined. This new form of terrorism had been introduced a few months prior to these attacks, on April 18, 1983, when a truck loaded with explosives killed 45 people in Beirut. What was new about these attacks was the willingness of the terrorist to ensure the success of the mission by sacrificing his own life. Terrorism, in instances of this kind, combines murder with suicide and also resembles assassination in being motivated by a political or religious cause.

And yet terrorism itself is by no means either a recent development, nor a tactic used only by some Shi'ite extremists. Terrorism has had a long and diverse history. Some examples are listed in Table 8–4.

Terrorism was a force as early as the 11th century. The killers whose name is still invoked today—the Assassins—were members of a small but highly disciplined Middle Eastern religious sect that believed in the imminent beginning of a new millennium. Unable to establish themselves in the open and mistreated by those in control at the time (the Seljuks), the Assassins carried out lethal terrorist operations for about

TABLE 8–4
Some terrorist killers before the 20th century

Terrorist Organization	Time	Place	Usual Methods
The Assassins	11th–13th C	Persia-Syria	Dagger
Crusaders	11th C	Jerusalem	Burning alive
The Inquisition	13th–17th C	Western Europe	Burning alive
Tamerlane	14th C	Middle East	Burial alive
French Republic under Robespierre	1790s	Paris	Guillotine
The Thugs	19th C	India	Strangulation
Ku Klux Klan	1867–	USA	Guns, lynching, etc.
Molly Maguires	1870s	USA	Explosives, guns
Narodnaya Volya	1878–1881	Russia	Guns, explosives
The People's Will	1869–1885	Russia	Bomb-throwing
Anarchists (individuals)	1890s	Europe	Bomb-throwing

Sources: Dobson & Payne, 1987; Hofstadter & Wallace, 1971; Lacquer, 1987; Lea, 1906–1907; O'Brien, 1973; Raynor, 1987; Wakin, 1984.

two hundred years. Disguising themselves in various ways and choosing the dagger as their weapon, the Assassins killed a number of powerful leaders and succeeded in creating a climate of terror. Like some present-day Middle Eastern extremists, the Assassins expected to die as they completed their missions.

During part of this same period, Christian Crusaders fought for possession of the Holy Sepulchre (which actually no longer existed by that time). The Crusaders were not a terrorist organization, but they did abandon themselves to episodes of massacre and atrocity. The major example occurred when they broke through the defenses in Jerusalem and slaughtered many of the inhabitants, including women and children. The Jews of this city, who had played no particular role in the hostilities, were herded into a mosque and burned alive. Institutionalized terroristic killing as part of the Christian establishment awaited the formation of the Inquisition in 1231. The persecution of suspected heretics and dissidents spread through much of Western Europe. Thousands were burned alive, and many others died while being questioned and tortured. Conformity to church dogma and practice was to be achieved by fear, torture, and killing. The Inquisition proved that it is not only a small, harassed sect that might turn to terrorism: this

can also be the choice of a powerful establishment.

Many conquerors have utilized terror tactics not only to destroy enemies but also to undermine the will to resist. Tamerlane, for example, buried thousands of his victims alive. Terrorism has accompanied many other military campaigns throughout history (as distinguished from casualties inflicted in combat or deaths indirectly related to warfare).

For the word *terrorism* itself, we must turn to the French Revolution. The new government rounded up suspected "enemies of the people" and sent many of them (perhaps 30,000) to the newly invented guillotine. Robespierre seemed to believe that by making so many public examples of people guilty of unacceptable thoughts or conduct, he would create a new type of society where everybody lived in love and harmony. Like most other terrorist actions, the "reign of terror" failed to achieve its objectives, and Robespierre himself went to the guillotine.

Terrorism occurred in many places and circumstances throughout the 19th century, although the number of victims was relatively small by the murder and atrocity scale of our own 20th century. The Thugs (or Thuggees) of India robbed travelers who were unfortunate enough to come within their reach and strangled them with silk ties. The Thugs themselves regarded the killing as an honorable and sacred act of religious devotion. And, like many other murdering terrorists, Thugs professed to hold death in contempt. The terrorist tradition includes a pattern of belief and behavior in which there is no compunction about killing others and about meeting one's own death through violence.

The Ku Klux Klan (KKK) and the Molly Maguires exemplify terrorist groups that formed in the United States shortly before and after the War between the States. Started in 1867, at first the KKK attempted to protect Southern whites from some of the threats and abuses that followed their defeat. Before long, however, the KKK became a racist organization that used terrorist techniques in an effort to keep the freed Afro-Americans "in their place." Unlike some other terrorist operations (mainly in the 20th century), the KKK did not specialize in mass killing; instead, threats, beatings and property destruction were augmented by the occasional lynching. Perhaps the fact that the KKK often had the support of the local establishment (or actually *was* the local establishment under its robes) meant that the executions did not have to be numerous, but simply had to remind potential victims that "uppityness" would not be tolerated. The KKK as an official organization continued to change over the years, becoming a corporation, diversifying its interests, and going out of business in 1944 because of delinquent income taxes. Technically, the KKK no longer exists as a documented organization, though it is obvious that both its name and racist orientation persist.

The Molly Maguires first made themselves known in the 1860s as some Irish-Americans reacted to oppressive and dangerous circumstances. As one historian tells it:

> In Pennsylvania, the oppressors were mine owners who brutalized the miners and their families. The miners went down into the dangerous hell of the mines, often with their children along, digging up wealth for the owners and a marginal living for themselves. New waves of immigrants enabled the owners to keep wages low; workers were forced to live in company houses and buy at company stores in between periods of idleness when they earned nothing. Even while working, many a miner received, instead of his monthly pay, a "bobtail check" showing that he owed the company money. When workers tried to organize, the owners intimidated them, and when fledgling labor organizations protested or struck, they were crushed. (Wakin, 1984, p. 147)

The Molly Maguires threatened and beat mine owners, then used bombs to create an atmosphere of terror, killing several people they considered to be oppressors. This underground movement was effective in the sense that it did arouse fear and direct attention to the miners' predicaments, but, like so many other organizations that resorted to terror, it failed to achieve its basic objectives. Improved conditions for miners would still be a long time in coming—and clever detective work resulted in the conviction and hanging of 19 Molly Maguires: probably more men than the group had itself killed during its decade or so of activity.

Perhaps you have felt a twinge or two in reading about the KKK and the Molly Maguires. Their origins, aims, and actions developed right here in the United States, and not so very long ago. Some people today still have very strong feelings about these issues. Terrorism tends to breed continuing fear, distrust, and enmity through succeeding generations—and people tend to believe that their side was in the right and has been vilified by others. Terrorism can also be instructive: did the Molly Maguires perhaps learn something from the ruthless methods of their bosses, and did both management and labor in the forthcoming years teach each other new lessons in brutal force? And did the prolonged exposure to threat and violence suggest something to the 19th century Afro-American that is expressed in contemporary murder rates?

The United States gave relatively little attention to international affairs during the 19th century. However, reports of terrorism overseas occasionally penetrated the isolationist mood of the times. Two of the numerous Russian terrorist groups are noted in Table 8–4. Narodnaya Volya and The People's Will both attempted to improve the living conditions of the Russian people by assassinating their rulers. The czar was killed after several attempts, but both revolutionary movements were destroyed and failed to alter the basic status quo. It would be another generation before the Russian monarchy was overthrown and several new waves of terror were set in motion. Individual anarchists from various nations also resorted to terrorist killing—usually by throwing bombs—in the belief that the world would be better off without any government at all. The only lasting consequences of these actions, apart from the deaths they caused, has been introducing a new scare word—*anarchist*—to the international vocabulary of panic and hatred.

Twentieth Century Terrorism

The heightened concern about terrorism in recent years is based largely upon sporadic incidents, most of them occurring outside North America. The fatalities have been real enough, and, at times, alarming and shocking. There have been kidnappings, skyjackings, ambushes, hit-and-run shootings, and bombings. Some have chosen well known people as victims (e.g., Lord Mountbatten, killed by an Irish Republican Army bomb that was hidden in his fishing boat in 1979); others have taken "targets of opportunity" and murdered men, women, and children who had done no conceivable harm to the terrorists. Increasingly, terrorist attacks have taken place in crowded urban areas. It does not take many violent incidents in a major city—e.g., Belfast—to create the intended atmosphere of terror.

The terrorism that has dominated television and other media for several years *is* something to be concerned about. We cannot hope to have a comprehensive understanding of death, society, and human experience in our own times without taking contemporary urban terrorism into account. And nothing that will be said here is intended to minimize the grief and outrage that

terrorism has caused in recent years. But we have to look elsewhere for the unprecedented and almost unbelievable catastrophes that people have imposed upon other people in the 20th century.

Numbers can be numbing. We can grasp and respond to the death of one person, to the death of a family, perhaps to the death of all occupants of a jet liner. It is much harder to grasp both the individual and the mass tragedy when the victims are numbered in thousands . . . in millions. Table 8–5 looks much like any other table: some identifying information and a lot of numbers. But, for any thinking, feeling human being, there can be nothing "so what" about the horrors represented here.

There are survivors of all these campaigns of terror still among us who can recall their experiences with vivid immediacy. For example, there is an aged woman in Arizona who will never forget how her childhood and very nearly her life was destroyed when the Turks started their operation to eliminate the Armenian population. In her own neighborhood, the men were rounded up for "routine questioning" that turned out to be excruciating torture, followed by killing. As it became clear that this was only the beginning of the terror, she and her family barely managed to escape. If this had proved to be the only example of large-scale terrorism in the 20th century, then its memory might have been more firmly impressed upon society in general. Approximately 800,000 people slaughtered—not killed in combat, but slaughtered! There is nothing in the ordinary experience of most people that can serve as comparison. We know that thousands are killed in automobile accidents. We are aware of AIDS as a newly emerged life-threatening disease. We may have read the names on the Vietnam Memorial Wall. But years of highway fatalities, AIDS-related deaths, and Vietnam casualties are surpassed by what the armed forces of one nation did to the civilians of a differing ethnic group within a period of some months.

And this, in the eyes of some observers, was only a "sideshow" to World War I, and, as events would subsequently show, only one of numerous

TABLE 8–5

Examples of large-scale terrorism in the 20th century

Killers	*Victims*	*Date*	*Estimated Deaths*
Turks	Armenians	1915	800,000
Soviet Communist Party	Russian Peasants	1929–1932	11,000,000
Soviet Communist Party	Russians	1937–1938	500,000
Nazis	Jews	1933–1945	6,000,000
Muslims*	Hindus, Sikhs	1946 ⎱	1,000,000
Hindus, Sikhs*	Muslims	1946 ⎰	
Sudanese Muslims	Sudanese Africans	1955–1972	1,000,000
Indonesians	Communists	1965	600,000
Nigerians	Ibo	1966–1967	800,000
Tutsi/Hutu†	Hutu/Tutsi	1972–1975	100,000
Khmer Rouge	Cambodians	1975–1977	???

Sources: Amnesty International, 1984; Becker, 1986; Conquest, 1986; Grosscup, 1987; Gutteridge, 1986; Kuper, 1981; Laqueur, 1987; Morgan, 1989; Payne, 1973; Sterling, 1981.

*During the partition of India following War War II, Hindus and Sikhs moving east were slaughtered by Muslims, and Muslims moving west were slaughtered by Hindus and Sikhs.

†Terrorism, including massacre, was carried out both by the minority Tutsi and the majority Hutu peoples of Rwanda and Burundi.

reigns of terror that have marked the 20th century. The total number of estimated deaths from the various persecutions and massacres listed in Table 8–5 approaches 22 million men, women, and children. This number is larger, for example, than the populations of Finland and Holland combined, larger than the cities of Chicago, Los Angeles, Montreal, New York, Ottawa, and San Francisco combined. Without doubt, this total is also an underestimate. There is no really reliable estimate for the deaths suffered by Cambodians at the hands of the Khmer Rouge—in the hundreds of thousands, surely, perhaps more than a million. For the other totals, relatively conservative estimates have been selected. It could be argued that more than 30 million perished as the direct result of the various reigns of terror listed in Table 8–5—and this list is not intended to be complete.

It is not within the scope of this book to examine these events in detail. However, we can offer a few observations that are based securely upon the available documentary evidence.

1. Terror has often been unleashed against people who share the same land and many of the same experiences and tribulations, but who are *perceived as being different in some significant way.* Most German Jews, for example, were law-abiding and patriotic Germans—but when Hitler pushed the anti-Semitism button, Germans who also happened to be Jewish were ostracized, then slaughtered. Hindus, Sikhs, and Muslims alike had shared the hardships of drought, famine, and colonial subjugation, but the mutual perception that their religious differences were all-important led to widespread atrocities and killings during the partition of India and creation of Pakistan.

2. As in an example already given, killing is often preceded by ostracism, by *denying the other person's fundamental reality as a human being.* Our people are truly human. Those others are less than human. It would not really be killing a person to eradicate those vermin, waste those pigs. In this sense, the murder takes place first in the mind.

3. *Fear kills.* Reigns of terror have often been triggered or intensified because those in power have feared overthrow. The Stalinist purge of 1937–1938, for example, was directed almost exclusively at Soviet citizens who were suspected of harboring politically unreliable thoughts. An

alleged plot against the government of Indonesia aroused fear-driven hysteria of such magnitude that 600,000 fellow citizens were slaughtered in a short period of time; the slain included some actual Communists, but also many other people who seemed "suspicious" to somebody wielding a knife, sword, or gun.

4. *Cold-blooded "rationalism" kills.* There have been many episodes of terrorism in which the attackers have shown themselves as frenzied and brutal people, caught up and distorted by high passions. But some of the most destructive terrorist operations have been systematically planned as "rational" ways to achieve political objectives. Did 11 million Russians actually die at the hands of fellow Russians in 1929–1932? Yes, that is no misprint. Stalin (who would later kill another half million in a devastating purge) saw to it that millions of peasants died so that he could achieve his economic and political aims. Most died from planned starvation, but others were killed outright. (And this incredible destruction of his own countrymen did not achieve the "rational" objectives either; the Soviet economy is still trying to find its way.)

5. *Religious intolerance instigates and justifies terrorism.* Many people secure in their own religious beliefs have lived harmoniously with people of other faiths. Nevertheless, some of the bloodiest reigns of terror have been launched by people who were convinced both that they and they alone have the true religion and that they are therefore entitled to convert or destroy all others. The true believer becomes one of the most dangerous people alive when he or she turns killer. There is no hesitation, no reflection, little compassion. I have known several mental patients who heard voices or felt strong impulses that brought them to the edge of killing another person. They suffered terribly because they did not want to kill and yet they could not stand the pressure—so they sought help. I have yet to learn of a religious cult that asked for help to rid itself of murderous impulses.

6. *Terrorism fails.* Seldom has a terrorist organization or movement achieved its objectives by persecution and killing. The Nazi's "final solu-

tion," for example, was not only brutal and inhumane to the extreme, but it also contributed significantly to Germany's defeat. Many of that nation's leading scientists, physicians and other professionals were Jewish. *Germany without Jews* (Engelmann, 1984) was a weakened nation. In an earlier epoch, an arrogant and intolerant Spanish monarch banished the Moors from what had been their homeland for centuries. The conditions of this banishment were so harsh that more men, women, and children died than survived to move on elsewhere. This "purification" plan, carried out in a terroristic manner, dealt Spain a blow from which it has never recovered. Repeatedly, terrorism has failed to achieve lasting success; most often it has brought about violent discord among the terrorists themselves, retaliation from others, and the loss of opportunities for improving one's conditions by positive efforts.

Terrorism and the Death System Today

There have been several important structural aspects of terrorism in the 20th century. One of these involves the *direction* of terrorism: up or down? Upward-directed terrorism operations are conducted by people who consider themselves oppressed and disenfranchised. Violence and the threat of violence are selected as attempts to force the establishment to grant concessions or perhaps to recruit other supporters and overthrow the regime. Upward-directed terrorism— the terrorism of protest—usually takes episodic forms, claims some innocent victims, creates the desired climate of fear, and leads to violent reprisals, some of which also kill innocent victims. From ancient times to the present, women and children have been particularly vulnerable, caught between factional violence and reprisals.

Downward-directed terrorism is employed by the regimes themselves, seeking to maintain or extend their power. The more totalitarian the regime, the more terrorism. The terrorism of oppression is generally more efficient and far-reaching than the terrorism of protest. The entire apparatus of the government is available for this purpose, including paid spies and informers, controlled media, and military and paramilitary forces. Amnesty International continually reports on "disappearances," tortures, and killings that are still being carried out by many regimes today. There seem to be no limits to the brutality and violence that some governments will inflict on their own people.

Two facts stand out regarding upward-directed and downward-directed terrorism in the 20th century: (1) Totalitarian regimes have very few episodes of protest terrorism. The streets are safe—until the regime decides to launch one of its own reigns of terror. It is the open society that is more vulnerable to protest terrorism. (2) The death toll from terrorism has been much higher when the establishment itself has turned killer. Protest terrorists may kill dozens of people, even, on rare occasions, hundreds. Stalin's Soviet Communist Party systematically killed millions of Russian peasants.

Three other structural considerations are closely related: technology, media coverage, and financing. Terrorism of all types has become capable of causing more deaths and by a greater variety of methods through use of advanced technologies. It is no longer necessary to approach a victim with a dagger concealed under one's robe. Plastic explosives, remote detonation devices, and many other technological innovations have added to the lethal potential of terrorism. Mass media and terrorism have become an "odd couple." The media seems to feast on reports and rumors of terrorism, thereby augmenting the terrorists' own ability to create a climate of fear. Meanwhile, the controlled media of totalitarian regimes carefully avoids mentioning atrocities conducted by its own government. Financing is perhaps the least recognized major factor in terrorism today, especially on the international scene. Terrorism has become a fairly expensive proposition. Although some individual terrorists come from impoverished circumstances, the movements themselves are generally well financed and represent investments for which a substantial return is expected. The young

bomber, for example, may be giving his life for somebody else's dream of wealth and power.

What about the psychological side of terrorism? Here are several observations I would like to share with you:

1. The terrorist has often been portrayed or perceived as an alluring and powerful figure, a new kind of romantic. Thinking of the terrorist in this manner seems to meet some of our society's needs for heroic and romantic personages, and therefore strengthens the terrorist's cause while at the same time distorting the facts. Robin Morgan (1989) has even suggested that the terrorist has become a contemporary version of the Demon Lover:

> He evokes pity because he lives in death. He emanates sexual power because he represents obliteration. He excites with the thrill of fear. He is the essential challenge to tenderness. He is at once a hero of risk and an antihero of mortality. (p. 24)

From the standpoint of our own research, the image of the romantic and lethal terrorist seems to be another version of The Gay Deceiver—the worldly, strangely charming, sexy person who is willing to show us a good time, and then . . . ! Morgan also sees the terrorist as an example of unrelenting male aggressiveness that has victimized women in many ways throughout the centuries. Although this observation is worth reflecting upon, it is also a matter of documented fact that female terrorists have been every bit as deadly as the male.

2. It is useful to recognize that "one person's terrorist is another person's hero." The popular figure of William Tell represented a terrorist to the authorities of the time. You and I might find ourselves in sympathy with some people who have advocated or carried out terrorist activities against brutal regimes. In fact, the rebellious spirit has often been considered to be an American specialty, and the film industry has been supplying us for decades with heroes who saddle up against the forces of unjust authority. There is some danger, then, that the "terrorist" will be

whoever those in control of the media choose to portray in those terms. However, this relativistic view can be taken only so far. Do the victims really care if their torture and murder will be at the hands of "friends" or "enemies" of the people?

3. Some people clearly identify themselves with life. We may think of Mother Teresa, or the family who, despite its better judgment, keeps adopting stray kittens. Some people identify themselves with death. This was a characteristic of the Nazi self-image (Friedlander, 1984); it can also be observed in the dress, speech, and behavior of some "skinheads" today. The terrorist, lacking a positive self-image and filled with a generalized rage toward society (like some murderers), may be using the coping strategy of "identifying with the aggressor." Who is the aggressor? Death. Some terrorists may be attempting to disguise and transform their personal fear of annihilation by entering Death's service.

4. Freud's *death instinct* is a failed theory according to many critics, including probably the majority of psychoanalysts. Nevertheless, it is difficult to escape the idea that there is a propensity for destructiveness rooted in human nature. The terrorist—whether member of a furtive cult or a high-ranking government official—is a constant reminder that our death system does not represent only the caring, compassionate, and life-protecting passions of society. The killer has always been with us and, on some horrifying occasions, has been us.

REFERENCES

Alvarez, A. (1970). *The savage god*. New York: Random House, Inc.

Amnesty International. (1984). *Torture in the eighties*. London: Amnesty International Publications.

Becker, E. (1986). *When the war was over*. New York: Simon & Schuster.

Berent, I. (1981). *The algebra of suicide*. New York: Human Sciences Press.

Berlinsky, E. B., & Biller, H. B. (1982). *Parental death and psychological development*. Lexington, MA: D. C. Heath & Co., Lexington Books.

Breed, W. (1972). Five components of a basic suicide syndrome. *Life-Threatening Behavior, 3*, 3–18.

Browne, A. (1987). *When battered women kill*. New York: The Free Press.

Cantor, P. (1972). The adolescent attempter: Sex, sibling position, and family constellation. *Life-Threatening Behavior, 2*, 252–261.

Choron, J. (1972). *Suicide*. New York: Charles Scribner's Sons.

Clarke, J. W. (1982). *American assassins*. Princeton: Princeton University Press.

Conquest, R. (1986). *The harvest of sorrow*. New York: Oxford University Press.

Curlee, W. V. (1972). Suicide and self-destructive behavior on the Cheyenne Rivers Reservation. In B. Q. Hafen & E. J. Faux (Eds.), *Self-destructive behavior* (pp. 80–84). Minneapolis: Burgess Publishing Co.

Dangelis, N., & Pope, W. (1979). Durkheim's theory of suicide as applied to the family: An empirical test. *Social Forces, 57*, 1081–1106.

Darwin, C. (1971). *Origin of the species*. Cambridge: Harvard University Press. (Original work published 1859)

Davidson, H. (1969). Suicide in the hospital. *Hospitals, 43*, 55–59.

Davis, P. A. (1983). *Suicidal adolescents*. Springfield, IL: Charles C. Thomas, Publisher.

Diggory, J. C. (1976). United States suicide rates, 1933–1968: An analysis of some trends. In E. S. Shneidman (Ed.), *Suicidology: Contemporary Developments* (pp. 30–69). New York: Grune & Stratton, Inc.

Dobson, C., & Payne, R. (1987). *The never-ending war: Terrorism in the 80s*. New York: Facts on File, Inc.

Donne, J. (1977). *Biathanatos*. New York: Arno Press, Inc. (Original work published 1646)

Douglas, J. D. (1967). *The social meanings of suicide*. Princeton, NJ: Princeton University Press.

Dunne, E. J., McIntosh, J. L., & Dunne-Maxim, K. (Eds.), (1987). *Suicide and its aftermath*. New York: W. W. Norton Co., Inc.

Durkheim, E. (1951). *Suicide*. (J. A. Spaulding & G. Simpson, Trans.). New York: The Free Press. (Original work published 1897)

Engelmann, B. (1984). *Germany without Jews*. New York: Bantam.

Erasmus. *The praise of folly*. (Original work published 1509)

Faber, M. D. (1978). Seneca, self-destruction, and the creative act. *Omega, Journal of Death and Dying, 9*, 149–166.

Farberow, N. L. (Ed.) (1980). *The many faces of suicide*. New York: McGraw-Hill Book Co.

Farberow, N. L. (1983). Relationships between suicide and depression: An overview. *Psychiatria Fennica Supplementum, 14*, 9–19.

Farberow, N. L., & Shneidman, E. S. (Eds.). (1965). *The cry for help*. New York: McGraw-Hill Book Co.

Foster, C. D., Siegel, M. A., Plesser, D. R., & Jacobs, N. R. (Eds.) (1989). *Gun control.* Wylie, Texas: Information Plus.

Frederick, C. J. (1985). Youth suicide: An introduction and overview. In M. L. Peck, N. L. Farberow, & R. E. Litman (Eds.), *Youth suicide* (pp. 1–18). New York: Springer Publishing Co.

Friedlander, S. (1984). *Reflections of Nazism.* New York: Harper & Row.

Freud, S. (1959). Mourning and melancholia. *Collected papers, Vol. 4* (pp. 152–172). New York: Basic Books, Inc., Publishers. (Original work published 1917)

Freud, S. (1961). The ego and the id. New York: W. W. Norton Co., Inc. (Original work published 1923)

Grosscup, B. (1987). *The explosion of terrorism.* Far Hills, New Jersey: New Horizon Press.

Gutteridge, W. (1986). *Contemporary terrorism.* New York: Facts on File Publications.

Hawkins, D. F. (Ed.), (1986). *Homicide among black Americans.* Lanham, MD: University Press of America.

Hendin, H. (1985). Suicide among the young: Psychodynamics and demography. In M. L. Peck, N. L. Farberow, & R. E. Litman (Eds.), *Youth suicide* (pp. 19–38). New York: Springer Publishing Co., Inc.

Humphrey, J. A., & Palmer, S. (1986–1987). Stressful life events and criminal homicide. *Omega, Journal of Death and Dying, 17,* 299–308.

Hofstadter, R. & Wallace, M. (Eds.), (1971). *American violence: A documentary history.* New York: Random House.

Iga, M. (1976). Personal situation as a factor in suicide with reference to Yasunari Kawabata and Yukio Mishima. In B. B. Wolman (Ed.), *Between survival and suicide* (pp. 84–111). New York: Gardner Press, Inc.

Iga, M. (1981). Suicide of Japanese youth. *Suicide and Life-Threatening Behavior, 11,* 17–30.

Kastenbaum, R. (1983). Suicidality in the aged. In T. Crook and & G. D. Cohen (Eds.), *Physicians' guide to the diagnosis and treatment of depression in the elderly* (pp. 81–86). New Canaan, CT: Mark Powley Associates, Inc.

Kastenbaum, R., & Aisenberg, R. B. (1972). *The psychology of death.* New York: Springer Publishing Co., Inc.

Kuper, L. (1981). *Genocide.* New Haven & London: Yale University Press.

LaFleur, W. R. (1974). Japan. In F. H. Holck (Ed.), *Death and Eastern thought.* Nashville: Abingdon Press.

Laqueur, W. (1987). *The age of terrorism.* Boston: Little, Brown & Co.

Lea, H. C. (1906–1907). *A history of the Inquisition of Spain* (4 volumes). New York: Macmillan Co.

Lester, D. (1972). *Why people kill themselves.* Springfield, IL: Charles C. Thomas, Publisher.

Levin, J., & Fox, J. A. (1985). *Mass murder.* New York: Plenum.

Litman, R. (1967). Sigmund Freud on suicide. In E. S. Shneidman (Ed.), *Essays in self-destruction* (pp. 324–344). New York: Science House.

Locke, J. (1971). *Concerning the true original extent and end of civil government.* In R. M. Hutchins (Ed.), *Great books of the Western world* (Vol. 35). Chicago: Encyclopedia Britannica, Inc. (Original work published 1690)

Lunden, W. A. (1951). *Suicides in Iowa and Minnesota and farm foreclosure in the United States: 1924–1940.* Unpublished manuscript, Iowa State University.

Makela, R. (1983). Alcohol and self-poisoning. *Psychiatria Fennica Supplementum, 14,* 85–92, Helsinki, Finland.

Maris, R. W. (1981). *Pathways to suicide.* Baltimore: Johns Hopkins University Press.

Marshall, J. R., Burnett, W., & Brasure, J. (1983). On precipitating factors: Cancer as a cause of suicide. *Suicide and Life-Threatening Behavior, 13,* 15–27.

McIntosh, J. L. (1983–1984) Suicide among native Americans: Further tribal data and considerations. *Omega, Journal of Death and Dying, 14,* 303–316.

McIntosh, J. S. (1989). Suicide: Native-American. In R. Kastenbaum & B. K. Kastenbaum (Eds.), *The encyclopedia of death* (pp. 238–239). Phoenix: The Oryx Press.

McIntosh, J. L. & Santos, J. F. (1980–1981). Suicide among native Americans: A compilation of findings. *Omega, Journal of Death and Dying, 11,* 303–316.

Mehta, D., Mathew, P., & Mehta, S. (1978). Suicide pact in a depressed elderly couple: Case report. *Journal of the American Geriatrics Society, 26,* 136–138.

Miller, D. H. (1967). Suicidal careers: Toward a symbolic interaction theory of suicide. Unpublished doctoral dissertation. School of Social Welfare, University of California at Berkeley.

Morgan, R. (1989). *The demon lover. On the sexuality of terrorism.* New York: W. W. Norton Co., Inc.

Neshold, R. D. (1986). *Changing farm and nonfarm suicide rates: Wisconsin, 1961–1985.* Paper presented at annual meeting of the American Public Health Association, Las Vegas.

National Center for Health Statistics. (1988, March). *Vital statistics of the United States. Vol. II, Mortality, Part A., 1950–1985.* DHHS Pub. No. (PHS) 8–1233. Hyattsville, MD.

O'Brien, J. (1973). *The Inquisition.* New York: Macmillan Co.

Payne, R. (1973). *Massacre.* New York: Macmillan Co.

Pardres, H., Preface In M. L. Peck, N. L. Farberow, & R. E. Litman (Eds.), (1985). *Youth suicide.* New York: Springer Publishing Co., Inc.

Peck, D. L. (1980–1981). Towards a theory of suicide: The case for modern fatalism. *Omega, Journal of Death and Dying, 12,* 1–14.

Piokolaninen, K. (1983). Heavy alcohol use and seasonal variation of suicide rates. *Psychiatria Fennica Supplementum, 93–96,* Helsinki, Finland.

Ragland, J. D., & Berman, A. L. (In press). Farm crisis and suicide: Dying on the vine? *Omega, Journal of Death and Dying.*

Raynor, T. P. (1987). *Terrorism: Past, present, future.* Rev. edition. New York: Franklin Watts.

Robbins, L. N., West, P. A., & Murphy, G. E. (1977). The high rate of suicide in older white men: A study testing ten hypotheses. *Social Psychiatry, 12,* 1–20.

St. Augustine. (1971). *The city of God.* In R. M. Hutchins (Ed.), *Great books of the Western world* (Vol. 18). Chicago: Encyclopedia Brittanica, Inc. (Original work published 426)

St. Thomas Aquinas. (1971). *Summa theologica.* In R. M. Hutchins (Ed.), *Great books of the Western world* (Vol. 19). Chicago: Encyclopedia Brittanica, Inc., (Original work published 1279).

Seiden, R. H. (1969, December). Suicide among youth: A literature review, 1900–1967. *Bulletin of Suicidology* (supplement).

Seiden, R. H. (1977). Suicide prevention: A public health/public policy approach. *Omega, Journal of Death and Dying, 8,* 267–276.

Seiden, R. H. (1981). Mellowing with age: Factors influencing the nonwhite suicide rate. *Omega, Journal of Death and Dying, 13,* 265–281.

Sendbuehler, J. M., & Goldstein, S. (1977). Attempted suicide among the aged. *Journal of the American Geriatrics Society, 25,* 245–248.

Shneidman, E. S. (1963). Orientations toward death. In R. White (Ed.), *The study of lives* (pp. 201–227). New York: Atherton Press, 1963.

Shneidman, E. S. (1976). Current over-view of suicide. In E. S. Shneidman (Ed.), *Suicidology: Contemporary developments* (pp. 1–21). New York: Grune & Stratton.

Shneidman, E. S. (1980). *Voices of death.* New York: Harper & Row.

Stack, S. (1979). Durkheim's theory of fatalistic suicide: A cross-national approach. *Journal of Social Psychology, 107,* 161–168.

Sterling, C. (1981). *The terror network.* New York: Reader's Digest Press.

Swanson, W. C., & Breed, W. (1976). Black suicide in New Orleans. In E. S. Shneidman (Ed.), *Suicidology: Contemporary developments* (pp. 99–128). New York: Grune & Stratton.

Tabachnick, N. (Ed.). (1973). *Accident or suicide?* Springfield, IL: Charles C. Thomas Publishers.

Taylor, C., & Hudson, M. C. (1972). *World handbook of political and social indicators.* New Haven, CT: Yale University Press.

Tishler, C. L., McHenry, P. C., & Morgan, K. C. (1966). Adolescents who attempt suicide: Preliminary findings. *American Journal of Psychiatry, 122,* 1248–1257.

Wakin, E. (1984). *Enter the Irish-American.* New York: Thomas V. Crowell.

Wallace, S. E. (1973). *After suicide.* New York: Wiley-Interscience.

chapter 9

THE FUNERAL PROCESS

Why have funerals? This is one of the most common questions raised in death education classes. The question itself is perhaps almost as interesting as any answer that can be given. For most societies through the centuries, the funeral process has been considered a vital function. It would have been almost unthinkable to question or challenge its significance. In the United States of the late 20th century, however, questions and challenges do arise. We no longer take for granted something that was at the core of human experience for a great many years. Before us, then, is the task of understanding the nature and implications of this shift in the American death system as well as our own attitudes toward the funeral process.

And what are your thoughts and feelings about the funeral process? I suggest you begin by answering the questions in Box 9–1 on p. 216.

FROM DEAD BODY TO LIVING MEMORY: A PROCESS APPROACH

It may be common to think of the funeral as the major observance of a death. Usually, however, there is a more extensive process involved, starting before and continuing beyond the graveside rites. This process has many dimensions, ranging from the legal, technical, and financial to the personal and the symbolic. When the total exit process functions well, the survivors succeed in converting what has become a dead body into a living memory integrated into their ongoing

lives. When the process aborts or fails, it is not only the immediate survivors but also society that tends to suffer.

Common Elements of the Funeral Process

Although specific customs differ tremendously, certain basic elements often can be found.

Premortem Preparations

When a person is expected to die, it is common for a kind of alert to be issued and a variety of practical actions to be readied. The law recognizes that actions taken in contemplation of death comprise a unique situation. Gifts made under the shadow of death, for example, sometimes are regulated and taxed more severely. Premortem preparations may be initiated by the dying person (e.g., specific instructions for cremation or burial, disposal of personal property, and so on) as well as by family, colleagues, and health-care professionals. A family member may start to contact family and friends so they can make plans to visit the dying person or at least attend the funeral. Colleagues may have a different type of preparation to make, such as replacing the coworker who will not be coming back to the job. The physician might be interested in removing an organ for transplant or in conducting an autopsy to determine the precise cause of death, and therefore must decide how best to obtain permission. A mortician may have already been consulted and carried out preliminary arrangements to see that the wishes of the

---

BOX 9–1
THE FUNERAL PROCESS: A SELF-EXAMINATION OF ATTITUDES AND FEELINGS

1. Funerals are a waste of time.
   Agree _____
   Tend to agree _____
   Tend to disagree _____
   Disagree _____

2. Bodies should be donated for scientific use.
   Agree _____
   Tend to agree _____
   Tend to disagree _____
   Disagree _____

3. Funerals are a comfort to the next of kin.
   Agree _____
   Tend to agree _____
   Tend to disagree _____
   Disagree _____

4. People often are too emotional at funerals.
   Agree _____
   Tend to agree _____
   Tend to disagree _____
   Disagree _____

5. The death of a family member should be published in the newspaper.
   Agree _____
   Tend to agree _____
   Tend to disagree _____
   Disagree _____

6. All things considered, most funerals are not excessively costly.
   Agree _____
   Tend to agree _____
   Tend to disagree _____
   Disagree _____

7. People often do not show enough emotion at funerals.
   Agree _____
   Tend to agree _____
   Tend to disagree _____
   Disagree _____

8. The size, length, and expense of a funeral should depend on the importance of the deceased person.
   Agree _____
   Tend to agree _____
   Tend to disagree _____
   Disagree _____

9. Allowing for some exceptions, cemeteries waste valuable space and should be diverted to other uses.
   Agree _____
   Tend to agree _____
   Tend to disagree _____
   Disagree _____

10. It would be preferable to be cremated.
    Agree _____
    Tend to agree _____
    Tend to disagree _____
    Disagree _____

11. It would be preferable to be buried in a cemetery.
    Agree _____
    Tend to agree _____
    Tend to disagree _____
    Disagree _____

12. A funeral director should be required to give a summary of laws stating what is and what is *not* required before the bereaved purchase a funeral.
    Agree _____
    Tend to agree _____
    Tend to disagree _____
    Disagree _____

13. My idea of the perfect funeral process is the following: _____

14. For me the best or most useful aspects of a funeral are: _____

15. For me the worst or most distressing aspects of a funeral are: _____

These questions will be discussed at the end of the chapter.

family are carried out. The extent and nature of premortem preparations vary greatly, but often the exit process has started before the individual's death.

Immediate Postdeath Activities

The death becomes official when it is certified by a physician. Certificates vary slightly from state to state but, as seen in Figure 9–1, always require information on time, place, and cause of death. One immediate postdeath activity, then, is to convert the person into a statistic or, more accurately, to complete the record keeping that started with the certificate of birth. Another immediate action is to contact next of kin, should they not already be on the scene. It is common for the body to be cleaned and wrapped in a shroud (these days, usually a plastic sheet). If the death occurred in a hospital, the body will either be kept in the same room or transferred to some available nearby room pending the arrival of the next of kin. If a hospital is pressed for space, the decision may be made to remove the body to the morgue after a short time.

Preparations for Burial or Cremation

In most societies and under most conditions there is a period between death and the final disposal of the body. Often there are both practical and symbolic or psychological reasons for the delay. One of the most common practical reasons is to allow time for distant friends and relatives to gather for the funeral. Some deaths also raise questions that require action in the public interest. Was this death caused by negligence, suicide, murder? Was the deceased the victim of a disease that poses a hazard to the general population? When such questions exist, it is usually the medical examiner (or coroner) who must decide whether or not a full investigation is needed. A particular death, then, can initiate a sequence of investigative and public health actions. An autopsy may be ordered by the medical examiner (under usual circumstances the autopsy is an optional procedure that requires consent of the next of kin). When special public health problems exist, a person whose

death has certain characteristics may become the focus of investigation. This has happened when swine flue and Legionnaire's disease became problems in the 1970s, for example. Learning whether or not a particular condition has been associated with a particular death can provide important information for protecting others.

Burial or cremation may also have to await the clarification of financial arrangements. Did the deceased have an insurance policy with funeral benefits? Precisely who is prepared to spend how much for the funeral? Financial and legal matters and the family's need to arrive at a consensus may require a certain amount of time before final arrangements can be made.

Problems can arise in less bureaucratic societies as well. Was there sorcery at work in this death? And, if so, was it a personal enemy within the tribe who must confess and make amends, or was it caused by another tribe as part of a traditional animosity? Again and again, circumstances may arise that require resolution before the proper final arrangements can be made.

The time interval also allows many symbolic and psychological needs to be met. Among some ethnic and religious groups the survivors have specific tasks to perform after death. These tasks help the survivors to express their affection for the deceased and to demonstrate their ability to support each other during a period of loss or crisis. Carrying out these responsibilities is also felt to be an act of piety. If someone neglected to prepare special foods or create special objects to be placed in the grave, he or she would lose esteem in the group.

The process of preparing the body varies greatly from society to society. Embalming by a mortician is now a widespread practice in the United States, although it is not always required by law (Editors of *Consumer Reports*, 1977). In some circumstances this practice serves emotional and symbolic needs. For example, each year Arizona ships more than 3,000 bodies back to the hometowns of those people who had left to spend their retirement in Arizona (Rowles, 1984). Presumably, other Sun Belt states could report a high rate of "postmortem emigration" as

FIGURE 9–1

Death certificate in use in Arizona.

BOX 9–2
FLASHES AND DISAPPEARANCES IN THE WORLD OF ADOLESCENCE

In my high school days there were occasional reminders of mortality that intruded into our daily realm of classes, sports, and dating. These reminders usually were set aside after the moment had passed. Two classmates were sons of the local mortician and occasionally were seen in dark, expensive suits for a funeral service. We were impressed by their seriousness on such occasions but also amused to see them decked out so elegantly. Later in my life I would encounter teenagers who felt they had to joke and fool around whenever some aspect of death presented itself. In our rather new and small town, however, the mortician's establishment had a solid and accepted place. There was no question where death was to be found—on Eastern Avenue in the vicinity of J.G. Allen's Funeral Home. We probably derived some comfort from knowing precisely where death kept itself. Furthermore, we did not have to think much about it because death was obviously in good hands: the Allen boys were pretty much like the rest of us (although with more advanced social skills; they could talk to grownups with greater ease and security), and their father was always good for an advertisement in the yearbook. The long black hearse was "normal" then and an indication that people were doing what needed to be done without impinging closely on our own feelings.

Death most often took the form of flashes and disappearances. News that somebody known to us had died would circulate with the force of an electrical current. There was no comparison between the slow procession of vehicles leaving J.G. Allen's for the cemetery with the body of somebody we had never known and the sudden, incredible news that a recent graduate had just been killed in an automobile accident. We had difficulty in connecting ourselves personally to either event. The funeral arrangements in the first case were abundantly clear but had no bearing on our lives. By contrast, our lives were touched by the flash of sudden death and the resultant disappearance of a person who had been one of us; and yet this same flash and disappearance made it difficult to realize fully what had happened. It seemed easier to talk about the visible funeral arrangements for a person not close to us—these simply confirmed that death is something that happens to other people. We had a much harder time when death subtracted one of our own number and we generally kept our confused thoughts and feelings to ourselves.

Looking back, it is not difficult to see that part of our difficulty in *realizing* death was related to the degree of personal threat. A funeral procession for an older person we did not know was much less threatening than the news that one of us had died. But this was not the only difficulty. Often we had only a fleeting and incomplete relationship to the death. We were not part of what might be called the total exit process. It was hard to comprehend that a person alive not long ago now was gone forever if all we had to work with was a brief notification of death. This was the unfortunate situation, for example, when a quiet and attractive girl who had recently moved into town stopped coming to class. Nothing was said for a while, then a teacher let us know that she had died of a brain tumor. None of us had known of her condition, seen her during her illness, or attended whatever funeral services there might have been. She had become just an empty chair, through a mysterious and unsettling process.

Similarly, merely participating in funeral rites did not necessarily make the death completely "real" from a survivor's standpoint. As a college student I served as pallbearer for the elaborate Catholic funeral of a young man I had once worked with. I had not seen or heard from him for almost two years when I learned of his death through the funeral invitation. Certainly his death was becoming real to me as I helped shoulder the casket. That was my only place, however, in the entire sequence of events that had started with an accident that was to prove fatal and continued within the family circle after the funeral itself. It was not easy to grasp the whole from any one of its parts.

well. Although embalming and shipping a body does increase the interval between death and final disposition, it also may serve the expressed needs of the deceased or their families. And the cost of shipping a body back home may be considerably less than the expense of many family and friends traveling to a distant funeral.

In some societies attempts to embellish as well as preserve the body have taken considerable time, effort, and art. The ancient Egyptians' creation of mummies is perhaps the most famous example (Hamilton-Paterson & Andrews, 1979), but it is by no means the only one. Some rich and powerful people in various Western nations have also demanded and received extensive post-mortem treatment before burial. The wife of Louis XVI's minister "ordered her body to be preserved in alcohol, like an embryo" so that her widowed spouse could spend the rest of his life gazing at her beautiful face (Aries, 1981, p. 386). The distinguished social philosopher Jeremy Bentham, principal founder of the University of London, still has a place on the faculty although he died in 1832, represented by his embalmed corpse. Millions have stood in line to see Lenin's carefully preserved body, and the physical remains of other political or symbolic leaders around the world have also been prepared for display. Whether the deceased was a famous and powerful person or one whose life passed with less notice, there often are symbolic and psychological as well as practical reasons for interposing delay between death and disposal.

The Funeral Service

The funeral service itself is usually the centerpiece of the entire process. Two major purposes are achieved by the funeral service: final placement of the remains and society's public recognition that one of its members has made the transition from life to death. There are many variations of funeral services, both in American society and in different cultures. Perhaps the most familiar form is the church funeral service, in which respects are paid to the deceased in a church or funeral home, then mourners gather in the cemetery to hear eulogies and witness the casket being placed in grave. Most often the arrangements for the service are carried out by the funeral director—ordering flowers, providing the hearse and possibly other vehicles, and so on. A member of the clergy usually presides over the commemorative services (whenever possible, a clergy member who has known the deceased and the family for several years).

These basic functions can be almost obscured by other events and details that crowd into the service. Different factions of the family, for example, may collide because of long-standing grievances and hidden resentments. The ensuing tension can distract from the central purpose of the funeral services. A very elaborate funeral can also attract so much attention (positive or negative) to itself that it is difficult to keep a focus on the deceased. A lack of consensus among the mourners can also be a source of distraction. One common example is the decision to have either an open or closed casket. These two choices are of almost equal popularity (Doka, 1984–1985). This virtually guarantees that some visitors will be displeased with whatever choice is made. And even those who prefer an open casket may disagree on the way it has been accomplished. Should Louise's visage be restored into a semblance of the robust person she once had been or presented with the lines of exhaustion that developed during her last illness? Should Harry be displayed in his favorite old sloppy clothes or in an elegant dark suit that he would literally never have been caught dead in? For a variety of reasons the mourner can be distracted or disturbed by details of the funeral service. Nevertheless, the underlying purposes remain: to make a final disposition of the body and to use this occasion as a way of acknowledging that a life has passed from among us.

Memorializing the Deceased

Most societies under most conditions attempt to fix the deceased in memory. In the United States a death notice is often (but not always) published in a local newspaper. An obituary may also appear, especially if requested by the family. Traditional burial is almost always requested by the family. Traditional burial is almost always accompanied by a grave marker, whether simple or elaborate. This identified site provides the opportunity for those who wish to return and pay homage to the deceased in the future. Some survivors have experienced great distress when circumstances (such as war or catastrophe) make it impossible to know precisely which grave is that of a relative or dear friend. Tens of thousands of unidentified soldiers lie buried in foreign lands, their graves usually marked by simple crosses. Many American families visited World War I burial grounds such as Flanders Field so they could at least be close to the place where their loved ones were probably interred. Survivors often experience the need to know precisely where the body has been placed and to have some type of appropriate marking. Memorialization can take many other forms, including the lighting of a candle on the deceased's birthday or the anniversary of the death, saying prayers, or making sacrifices or gifts in the name of the deceased.

Starting the Process of Continuing and Renewing Life

Much of the funeral process is devoted to completing society's obligations to the deceased and supporting the survivors in their grief. Often, however, the process takes another direction after the physical remains have been accommodated. Attention now turns to helping the immediate survivors and society in general to go on with their lives. The "life must go on" motif often takes the form of a festive occasion. Family, neighbors, and best friends gather to eat, drink, and share lively conversation. In former generations the food was usually prepared by family members with great skill and care, representing a gift in the service of life. It was a mark of pride to offer the fine ethnic delicacies in abundance, along with the beverages most favored by the guests. The prevailing mood would be much different from the previous phases of the funeral process. The guests were now expected to enjoy

themselves, to be vital and frisky. There might be dancing and, as the feasting proceeds, even some romancing.

This type of festivity started to give way as society became more impersonal, mobile, and technologically oriented (Lofland, 1978) and as efforts were made to banish death from public awareness (Fulton, et al., 1982). A cup of coffee with a few family members and friends has sometimes replaced the elaborate proceedings of earlier generations. Although the size and splendor of the postfuneral gathering may differ greatly, the underlying function is the same—to help everybody concerned begin to direct his or her attention to the continuation and renewal of life. This is why conversation may seem unnaturally lively and why people may seem to eat, drink, and laugh too much considering the recent death of an intimate. If you happen to walk in while a risqué story is being told, it is easy to be offended and think that insensitivity and disrespect is afoot. Usually, however, lively and lusty behaviors after a funeral represent a partial release from tension and the compelling need to show each other that life can and should go on—"Harry (or Louise) would have wanted it that way!"

MAKING DEATH "LEGAL"

Society's claim on the individual is demonstrated clearly both at the points of entry and of exit. Well before the development of social statistics, births and deaths were recorded at the neighborhood church. Demands of the faith required that each soul be entered into the books and therefore subject to the expectations of God and the state. A written notice was also required as the soul was released to join its maker—proof that the clergyman was carefully watching over his flock. These records would be consulted if questions arose about kinship rights and obligations. Even centuries later the surviving records continue to be of social value. Historians seeking to understand the effects of a harsh winter in rural England in the 17th century or migration patterns in northern Italy 100 years later are almost certain to consult entries preserved at the local parish.

The certificates of death (Figures 9–1 and 9–2) and birth (Figure 9–3) familiar to us today serve similar functions in a more secular society. The newborn and the deceased are now listed as citizens beginning or ending their active roles in society. Church records now provide supplementary rather than official documentation. Despite all the changes that have occurred through the years, governing authorities still insist on "keeping the book" on the individual. This may seem a peculiar insistence—that you must not only be alive but have proof of birth, that you must not only be deceased but have proof of death! It represents, however, the Western world's view of the social contract. No matter what we care to think, society acts as though none of us belong entirely to ourselves but are subject to these "legalizations" both coming and going.

This section examines some of the major features of making death legal as part of the contemporary funeral process.

Establishing the Facts of Death

A death is real but not official until certified. Today it is usually a physician who is called upon to perform this task, but less adequate systems can still be found in some areas of the United States. It is the responsibility of the physician to establish the principal facts of the death and to initiate an investigation if serious questions arise.

Cause of death raises the most obvious question. As Figure 9–1 shows, the physician has the opportunity to indicate something of the complex sequence of events that led to death. This provision recognizes the fact that life often comes to an end through an interaction of jeopardizing conditions. Some examples are:

- "Cardiovascular accident, secondary to hypertension"
- "Pneumonia, secondary to lung cancer"
- "Hemorrhage, secondary to cancer of the larynx"
- "Septicemia, secondary to extensive third degree burns"

Nevertheless, the actual situation may be even more complicated than the death certificate can express. A woman in her 80s suffers from heart and urinary tract disorders in addition to a loss of bone mass and resiliency (osteoporosis). One day while she is simply ascending a staircase, the brittle bones give way. She falls. Both hips are broken. Her already impaired cardiovascular system is subjected to further stress. Internal bleeding proves hard to control. Confined to bed and fitted with a catheter, she develops an infection that further saps her strength. Medical and nursing management becomes very difficult because treatments that might improve one condition can worsen another. Her lungs soon fill with fluid, and she dies. But what is *the* cause? Or what is the precise relationship among the many interacting factors that lead to death? The physician may or may not be able to give a secure answer. What the physician will attempt to do, however, is specify the two or three major contributing causes. The death certificate often cannot provide all the information relevant to cause. As a source of research data, then, the death certificate has its limits. Even so, the information it does provide can be quite useful. For example, the fact that this elderly woman suffered a fall adds to a growing body of data that emphasizes the need for better understanding and clinical and environmental management.

The physician may have a sufficient understanding of a particular death to sign the certificate even though some of the factors and their interaction are not entirely clear. Under some circumstances, however, the question of cause requires further investigation. Although certifying death is one of the routine functions that some physicians are required to perform, it is always a matter of importance, emphasized by laws and statutes that must be obeyed.

The cause of death is often the most salient item of information required on the certificate, but the other entries are also of potential significance. Who is the next of kin? Was the death related to occupational hazard or stress? Has there been an unusually high rate of death from the same cause in this geographical area in the

THIS IS A PERMANENT RECORD AND REQUIRED FOR FETAL DEATHS OF 20 WEEKS OR OVER GESTATION.

USE TYPEWRITER WITH FRESH BLACK RIBBON. ALL SIGNATURES MUST BE IN BLACK OR NEAR BLACK INK.
SEE MANUAL FOR COMPLETION INSTRUCTIONS.

STATE OF ARIZONA
DEPARTMENT OF HEALTH SERVICES · VITAL RECORDS SECTION
CERTIFICATE OF FETAL DEATH

ORIGINAL
STATE COPY

FETAL DEATH NO.
FD 102-

IDENTIFICATION OF CHILD AND PLACE OF BIRTH

(IF UNNAMED LIST SURNAME ONLY)

14

PARENTS

15

16

RESIDENCE OF
17 MOTHER

'ERMANT

(ITEM 18)
MEDICAL CAUSE OF DEATH
CODE ___
18

19

CERTIFICATIONS
ATTENDANT

* MED. EXAMINER

DISPOSITION AND REGISTRATION DATA
20

21

FATHER

22

23

MOTHER

* - OR TRIBAL LAW ENFORCEMENT AUTHORITY

24

25

26

27

FIGURE 9–2
Fetal death certificate.

THIS IS A PERMANENT RECORD. USE TYPEWRITER WITH FRESH BLACK RIBBON.
ALL SIGNATURES MUST BE IN BLACK OR NEAR BLACK INK. SEE MANUAL FOR COMPLETION INSTRUCTIONS.

STATE OF ARIZONA
DEPARTMENT OF HEALTH SERVICES - VITAL RECORDS SECTION
CERTIFICATE OF LIVE BIRTH

BIRTH NO.

B 102-

19. ORIGINAL STATE COPY.

CHILD

NAME OF CHILD   A. First   B. Middle   C. Last

SEX   TYPE OF BIRTH (Single, twin, triplet, etc.) SPECIFY: IF MULTIPLE BIRTH (Born first, second, etc.) SPECIFY: DATE OF BIRTH   Month Day Year   Hour

PLACE OF BIRTH   A. County   B. Town or City   C. Hospital or Clinic (if home birth, give street address)

PARENTS

FATHER'S NAME   A. First   B. Middle   C. Last   DATE OF BIRTH   Month Day Year   PLACE OF BIRTH   State or Country

MOTHER'S MAIDEN NAME   A. First   B. Middle   C. Last   DATE OF BIRTH   Month Day Year   PLACE OF BIRTH   State or Country

RESIDENCE OF MOTHER

MOTHER'S USUAL RESIDENCE   A. State   B. County   C. Town or City   D. Zip Code

STREET ADDRESS OR R.F.D.   IN CITY LIMITS? YES NO   MOTHER'S MAILING ADDRESS (If different from item 12)

CERTIFICATIONS:
PARENT

14. THE INFORMATION LISTED IN ITEMS 1-13 IS TRUE AND CORRECT TO THE BEST OF MY KNOWLEDGE.   PARENT OR INFORMANT'S SIGNATURE   RELATIONSHIP TO CHILD   DATE SIGNED

ATTENDANT

17. I ATTENDED THE BIRTH OF THIS CHILD WHO WAS BORN ALIVE AT THE PLACE, TIME, AND DATE ENTERED ABOVE.   ATTENDANT'S SIGNATURE (Type name below line)   TITLE ☐ M.D. ☐ D.O. ☐ OTHER (specify)   DATE SIGNED

FOR STATE REGISTRAR'S USE ONLY

SUPPLEMENTARY ENTRIES

REGISTRAR'S CERTIFICATION

DATE REGISTERED   REG. FILE NO.   REGISTRAR'S SIGNATURE   REG. DISTRICT   DATE RECV'D. IN STATE OFFICE

MEDICAL AND HEALTH DATA SECTION — PLEASE COMPLETE ALL ITEMS BELOW

26. RACE OR COLOR   27. SPANISH ORIGIN - PARENTS   28 EDUCATION - HIGHEST GRADE COMPLETED   41 PREGNANCY HISTORY (Complete each section)

FATHER

SPECIFY WHITE, BLACK, AM. INDIAN, ETC.   YES NO   IF YES, SPECIFY MEXICAN, CUBAN, PUERTO RICAN, ETC.   ELEMENTARY-SECONDARY (0-12)   COLLEGE (1-4 or 5)

MOTHER

SPECIFY WHITE, BLACK, AM. INDIAN, ETC.   YES NO   IF YES, SPECIFY MEXICAN, CUBAN, PUERTO RICAN, ETC.   ELEMENTARY-SECONDARY (0-12)   COLLEGE (1-4 or 5)

	LIVE BIRTHS (Do not include this child)		OTHER TERMINATION (Spontaneous and induced)	
	A. NOW LIVING	B. NOW DEAD	D. BEFORE 20 WEEKS	E. 20 WEEKS OR MORE
	NUMBER	NUMBER	NUMBER	NUMBER
	NONE	NONE	NONE	NONE

SEROLOGY ON MOTHER? YES, NO, UNKNOWN-SPECIFY: DROPS IN BABY'S EYES? YES, NO, UNKNOWN. SPECIFY: BIRTH WEIGHT   32. APGAR SCORE 1 min. 5 min.

DATE LAST NORMAL MENSES BEGAN (Month, day, year)   MONTH OF PREGNANCY PRENATAL CARE BEGAN (First, second, etc.) SPECIFY   PRENATAL VISITS - TOTAL NUMBER (If none, so state)   IS MOTHER MARRIED? (SPECIFY YES OR NO)

COMPLICATIONS OF PREGNANCY (Describe or write "none")

CONCURRENT ILLNESSES OR CONDITIONS AFFECTING THE PREGNANCY (Describe or write "none")

DEATH UNDER ONE YEAR OF AGE. ENTER STATE FILE NO. OF DEATH CERTIFICATE FOR THIS CHILD.

COMPLICATIONS OF LABOR AND/OR DELIVERY (Describe or write "none")   DATE OF LAST LIVE BIRTH (Month, year)

CONGENITAL MALFORMATIONS OR ANOMALIES OF CHILD (Describe or write "none")   DATE OF LAST OTHER TERMINATION (As indicated in d or e above (Month, year)

VS-1 (Rev. 3-80)

FIGURE 9–3
Birth certificate.

past few years? Questions such as these can have many implications for the well-being of surviving individuals.

The Medical Examiner and the Autopsy

The legalization of death at times requires the intervention of the coroner or medical examiner. Funeral arrangements will be suspended until the investigation is completed or the coroner decides that it is unnecessary. This additional procedure can inconvenience and distress the survivors, but it can also serve important purposes. It is possible, for example, that the death may have been caused by a condition that poses a continuing danger to the populace. What has become known as Legionnaire's disease was not well understood when it was first encountered in 1976. Public health authorities had no way of knowing if this life-threatening affliction had resulted from some unusual combination of circumstances or if it represented a new threat of major proportions. A decade later, autopsies again became vital sources of information as another essentially unknown condition began to claim its victims: AIDS. In both instances, public health authorities had to determine whether they were dealing with a limited or with an extensive and uncontrolled threat to life. Physicians would have been remiss if they certified the deaths in a routine manner, as would public health authorities if they did not immediately examine both living and deceased victims. Certain diseases trigger automatic reports to the coroner's office when discovered by a physician in a living patient or during an autopsy. In the Southwestern states, for example, physicians must report cases suggestive of plague. Such cases are very rare, almost always involving contact with disease-bearing fleas on dead or dying wild animals. Nevertheless, history has taught us to beware of any possible outbreak.

Suspicion that the death was "unnatural" can also lead to postmortem medical examination. The possibility of homicide is perhaps the most frequent instigation, especially when other possibilities also exist (e.g., accident or suicide). Even when the likelihood that death was caused by homicide has already been well established by circumstances, there may be reasons for investigating the alleged crime in more detail. Did the victim die instantly? Was death caused directly by the injuries suffered or by subsequent events? In building a case, the authorities may need all the evidence they can find.

Inquests will also be ordered when there is reason to suspect that the death was the outcome of negligence or error. Was this patient given the wrong medication? Had this prisoner been held too long in an unheated jail cell? Did nursing home personnel fail to provide adequate nourishment to a "difficult" resident? It is obvious from all these examples that the interests of society can be served on occasion by requiring an investigation after death.

The examination itself can vary in scope and effort. In some instances it may be sufficient to look for one or two telltale signs (e.g., the trace of certain substances in the lungs or intestines, the presence or absence of cerebral hemorrhage). In other instances a more comprehensive examination may be required. Dissection and examination of the body may be considered necessary, along with a variety of laboratory tests, including bacteriological and toxicological.

The *autopsy*, or postmortem examination, often is conducted for other reasons as well. There may be no suspicion of foul play or negligence and no serious question about cause of death. Nevertheless, either the family or the medical facility may decide that there is something to be gained by an autopsy. Had this person lived for many years with a certain physical problem that had been suspected but never demonstrated? Was the slowly deteriorating mental condition of that person accompanied by brain changes such as might be caused by Alzheimer's disease? Answering questions such as these case by case can build up useful knowledge and develop implications for future research and treatment. Autopsies have also been considered for many years a source of valuable learning experiences for medical personnel, and in this way indirectly contribute to improved health care.

Autopsies cannot be performed legally without permission from the next of kin. Usually there are further regulations that surround the permission process in an attempt to ensure that undue pressure is not placed on the family. In my experience the decision whether or not to grant autopsy permission often depends on situational factors—the state of mind of the next of kin, for example, and that person's relationship to the deceased and to the physician. The request for autopsy permission can be difficult for all parties. The physician may hesitate to make this request so soon after the death, and the next of kin may have conflicting thoughts and fluctuating feelings. Effective communication and mutual trust are very important.

Body, Property, and the Law

Knowledge of current laws and statutes (Editors of *Consumer Reports*, 1977) is important if the survivors are to avoid unnecessary conflicts, delays, and litigations. Attention must be given to insurance provisions and options and the often-revised probate laws that regulate the inheritance of estates. The advantages and limitations of drawing up a will should be understood, and this document should be supplemented by a letter of instructions that is readily available in time of need.

Organ or total body donation has emerged in recent years as an important option. After some years of dispute and uncertainty, "anatomical gifts" now have a firm legal foundation. The clearest way to exercise this option is for individuals to sign a simple legal instrument that offers any part of or all of their body for medical humanitarian purposes upon death. The provisions of the Uniform Anatomical Gift Act are satisfied by a brief statement of intention, signed by the individual and cosigned by two witnesses. Typically, such donor cards provide the following choice:

I give ___ any needed organ or parts
I give ___ only the following organs or parts ___

Your physician or a local hospital can provide an approved legal anatomical donor card; some states also include this form as part of the driver's license.

The willingness to donate your body or some of its parts does not always lead to fulfillment of this intention. Those responsible for the body upon death may not know that a donor card has been completed, or family members may oppose the anatomical gift (in which case the hospital or other medical organization may decline to become involved in the family dispute and turn down the gift). There have also been examples of mix-ups and miscommunications within the medical network that have thwarted the donor's purpose. Furthermore, in some instances, the organs or tissues are not in condition for safe and effective transplantation.

Even greater difficulties have arisen for those who have attempted to exercise the option of *cryonic suspension*. This controversial procedure differs from all other forms of body disposal in one critical respect: the "deceased to be" intends to use his or her own body again! The hope encouraged by cryonicists is that bodies preserved at low temperatures (not quite freezing) can later be restored to life and treated successfully when cures are developed for the previously fatal illness. There have been no such restorations, but some individuals have requested this form of internment, and the bodies of a few have actually been placed in cryonic chambers. Frequently, however, the expressed written wishes of people who have requested cryonic internment have not been honored at the critical moment. Discomfort, disbelief, and hostility on the part of the medical establishment have taken precedence over the patient's wishes, no matter how clearly expressed.

The first human known to have been placed in cryonic suspension was Dr. William H. Bedford (January, 1967). His body was perfused with dimethylsulfide (DMSO) and packed in dry ice, then transferred to long-term storage in a chamber filled with liquid nitrogen. I know from my own research at the time when cryonic suspension was introduced that the typical response of nonbelievers was disapproval shading into anger. Furthermore, legal aspects of cryonic suspension have not been established as clearly as the more familiar alternatives for body disposal. The very concept of cryonic suspension arouses anxious hostility. At present American society is much more receptive to organ gifts than to the prospect of terminally ill people choosing the cryonic option.

WHAT DOES THE FUNERAL PROCESS ACCOMPLISH?

The funeral process would not have become so important to so many societies unless it served or attempted to serve significant needs and values. A few of the meanings have already been noted. This section will consider a broader range of funeral observations and memorializations that will reveal even more about death system dynamics and the values that are at stake.

When Great People Die

The Silent Army of Ch'in Shih-huang-ti

Every life and thus every death should perhaps be considered of equal importance. In practice, however, societies consider some people more crucial than others. The loss of a great person in a particular society often triggers a massive response. The question, "Who does this society consider really important?" can be answered by observing the nature and magnitude of the funeral process. But it can be observed from another perspective as well: Given that a great person has died, what is it that society feels it must accomplish through the funeral (and memorialization) process? A few examples will illustrate the dynamics and principles involved. Other ex-

amples will probably come to your mind as you read.

Ch'in Shih-huang-ti was one of the most powerful and influential monarchs who ever appeared in either the East or the West. He unified the peoples of an enormous and diversified region into nationhood and stimulated the development of a vigorous and distinctive culture. It was Ch'in, as the first Emperor of China, who built the Great Wall more than two centuries before the birth of Christ.

In 1974 Ch'in's tomb was discovered. Although the work is not complete, it is obvious that it is one of the most incredible archeological finds of all time. The tomb is encased within a large mound whose location was selected through the ancient Chinese practice of *feng-shui,* an occult art intended to deter evil spirits from disturbing either the deceased or the living. To call the site a tomb is an understatement—it answers better to the name of palace. There are a variety of funerary buildings, each with a specific purpose to serve; additionally, there had once been a set of double walls to protect the complex and housing for guards and attendants. Ch'in's tomb was built near the graves of earlier rulers and was clearly designed to surpass them all.

Four huge underground chambers have been excavated. Pit No. 1, for example, is a rectangle approximately 700 by 200 feet. It is divided into 11 parallel corridors, with the entire structure skillfully constructed by a combination of rammed earth, bricks, and timber crossbeams. In this pit excavators found an entire army! Arthur Cotterell (1981) describes the scene:

> The chambers are arranged in the battle order of an infantry regiment, which faces eastwards. Altogether it is estimated that there are 3,210 terracotta foot soldiers. They do not wear helmets; only Ch'in officers have these. But most of the infantry soldiers wear armour. These armoured men are divided into forty files; they stand four abreast in the nine wide corridors, and form two files in each of the narrow ones. The head of the regiment in the eastern gallery comprises a vanguard of unarmoured bowmen

and crossmen, nearly 200 sharpshooters, drawn up in three north-south ranks. Their clothing is light cotton because they are fast moving, long-range fighters—the ancient equivalent of artillery. They would have fired their arrows from a distance, keeping away from hand-to-hand engagements, once contact was made with the enemy. The three ranks would have taken turns at firing, so as to keep a continuous stream of arrows. The majority carried crossbows with a 200-metre (650-foot) shooting range.

Between these sharpshooters and the armoured infantry are six chariots and three unarmoured infantry squads. Each chariot is pulled by four terracotta horses and manned by a charioteer and one or two soldiers. The guards would have wielded long flexible lances, possibly bamboos measuring as much as six metres (20 feet), in order to stop enemy soldiers from cutting off the heads of the horses. (pp. 22–23)

You cannot help but be impressed by the artistic craftsmanship devoted to the creation of this subterranean army and by the enormous economic resources poured into the enterprise. And yet if you can step back from the size and splendor of the palatial tomb, it is possible to wonder "Why?" What purpose was served by such a vast expenditure of labor and resources?

I will propose a set of interlocking answers to this question based upon historical materials, although we must always recognize the difficulties in trying to understand motivation from such a distance. Ch'in's motivation may well have included the following components:

1. To support his claims as the greatest of all monarchs
2. To impress the deities and ensure his place among the immortals
3. To confound his enemies and secure a continuation of his royal succession and regime.

Ch'in made history, but he also made enemies. During the last years of his reign in particular Ch'in placed enormous strains on the economy through his military adventures. He was also stern in the administration of justice. Scholars who displeased him were buried alive. Those who did not hew to the party line in every particular were in danger for their lives, and books that displeased him were consigned to the flames. Revolution was held back only by Ch'in's might and vigilance. Construction of a monumental tomb was one way, then, to display his ability to defend his regime even from the grave. The terracotta army originally was provided with real weapons, although enemies later were able to make off with them. Ch'in, then, continued to brandish his power as long as he could and for the same purposes that had guided his life. Like many another ruler, the first Emperor of China craved immortality and sought every opportunity to gain this advantage for himself in both life and death. The fantastic tomb at Mount Li represents a continuation and culmination of his self-aggrandizing life-style. Just as he literally required his subjects to sing his praises throughout his life, so he established a mute army to protect his afterlife from both earthly and spiritual foe. Despite all the effort and expense, however, the endeavor failed. A fierce peasant revolution soon toppled the regime, and it is only in our own time that China has been able to recover detailed knowledge about its first Emperor.

Death Makes a Hero

Dynamics of a very different sort produced one of the most elaborate funeral processes of the 19th century. England's Prince Consort had died unexpectedly after a short illness at the age of 42. *Prince Albert* of Saxe Coburg-Gotha had married the illustrious Queen Victoria in 1840. Those in a position to know him well had admired Albert both for his personal qualities and his service to his adopted nation. The British public had been rather cool to him, however, because of his foreign origins. We might have expected some pomp and circumstance in his funeral and memorialization process. What actually happened, however, far exceeded the demands of a respectful tribute. Darby and Smith (1983) characterize the response as nothing less than the development of a cult for the Prince Consort.

Some of the evidence remains available for inspection today. Simply examine the monuments and portraits throughout the British Isles—Balmoral, Aberdeen, Edinburgh, Nottinghamshire, South Kensington, Whippingham, Frogmore, Manchester, and so on. Among the physical tributes in London alone there is a memorial chapel in Windsor Castle and the Albert Memorial, which itself is only part of the impressive Victoria and Albert Museum. Existing parks and facilities were renamed in his memory. Many small statues and other items were manufactured and sold as memorabilia. One could purchase Prince Albert belt clasps, lamps, pencil cases, and stationery. Eventually his handsome likeness would be put on packages and cans of tobacco. Alfred Lord Tennyson wrote one of his most famous poems to honor him (*Idylls of the King*). The late Prince Consort had quickly become the most popular image and topic in the land and also something of an industry.

Albert's widow, the Queen of England, demonstrated a worshipful attitude toward her late husband and would not allow people to speak of him in the past tense. His private rooms at three favorite residences were preserved just as they had been during his life. A nobleman who visited the Queen observed:

> She talked upon all sorts of subjects as usual and referred to the sayings and doings of the Prince as if he was in the next room. It was difficult to believe that he was not, but in his own room where she received me everything was set out on his table and the pen and his blotting-book, his handkerchief on the sofa, his watch going, fresh flowers in the glass, etc., etc., as I had always been accustomed to see them, and as if he might come in at any moment. (Darby & Smith, 1983, p. 4)

The observant Lord Clarendon noted an implicit contradiction in the arrangements. On the one hand, there were the fresh clothes, jug of hot water, and clean towels laid out for the use of the Prince, yet a tinted photograph of his corpse hung by the side of his bed. Obviously, the Queen was having difficulty in reconciling her conflicting needs to acknowledge reality and to preserve the illusion that her beloved was still with her.

What purposes were achieved by the funeral and memorialization process for Prince Albert? I suggest the following:

1. The elaborate memorialization process served the function of *symbolically incorporating* Albert into the British Empire. In effect, he became an Englishman after his death. This was both a gesture of support for their highly esteemed Queen and a way of grafting Albert's attributes onto the national self-image. His handsome figure would always stand at alert attention or gracefully sit astride a beautiful horse. The alternative was to lose for the national consciousness one of the more picturesque and talented men of the day, whose qualities were not generally appreciated until a death that was felt to be both unexpected and premature. The memorialization also served as a sort of postmortem compensation for their cool attitude toward Albert while he was alive. The need to incorporate and preserve what were now seen as his heroic attributes, however, was probably more powerful than the gesture of reconciliation.

2. Albert's death provided an excellent opportunity to express current sentiment and belief. In a sense Victorian England seemed to have been waiting for the chance to make a definitive demonstration of attitudes that had been developing through the years. This was a period in which manifestations of mourning had become increasingly elaborate. There was implicit competition to see who could express bereavement most impressively through clothing ("widow's weeds"), idealization and memorialization of the deceased, and withdrawal from customary social activities and responsibilities. Linked with these customs were affirmations of belief in the certainty and blessings of immortal life. Queen

Victoria and Prince Albert appeared to share the prevailing faith. The Victorians' own public self-image emphasized faith and propriety, although skeptics in the society were abundant enough and wondered what other motives were being served or disguised by ostentatious mourning. It was the Victorian age, after all, that provided Sigmund Freud and other pioneering psychoanalysts with the raw material for their exploration of hidden motives and thwarted impulses (Gay, 1984). Albert's death provided a most attractive occasion for expressing private fears, doubts, and hopes in public guise.

The postmortem cult of the Prince Consort would not have developed had not the spirit of the times been so conducive. Albert could easily be seen as an ideal representation of almost every quality his generation would have liked to claim for its own. A further point should be noted. Once the man was dead, his memory could be elaborated upon and fixed for posterity without the danger of competition from his ongoing life. It is often easier to admire dead heroes. They are less likely to turn around and do something that would force us to alter our judgment. The British public eventually came to resent the Queen's continued attachment because it seemed to distract her from more pressing responsibilities. By contrast, Ch'in's vigorously defended image of warrior-emperor was rejected almost immediately after the entombed palace closed around his mortal remains.

Hiding the Illustrious Dead

Many more examples could be given of elaborate funeral and memorialization processes for illustrious people. We would find both common and distinctive purposes underlying the practices. A common feature, for example, is the slow, stately tempo favored for the funeral procession itself and for the arrangements in general. This provides more time for the realization of the death and its meanings to sink in. By contrast, the final arrangements for an obscure person not especially valued by society may take the most efficient form available. (Robert Frost's poem "Departmental" describes just such a smooth and unruffled process among ants.) Distinctive purposes relate to the social standing of the person at the time of death, the mode of death (illness or violence, expected or unexpected, and so on), and the moods and themes prevalent in society. Prince Albert's life-style and achievement represented the highest aspirations of the people of his time; Elvis Presley, also the subject of a postmortem industry, may continue to "earn" as much as 50 million dollars a year for those who have gained control of his name and properties.

Instead of multiplying such examples, however, it will be more instructive to explore a deviant case, one in which the usual rules seem to be suspended. Why would an illustrious person *not* be honored with an impressive funeral and memorialization process? Considering how important these rites and rituals appear to be in most societies, we should be on alert when the death of a powerful or celebrated person somehow passes with little notice. One major example will serve to make this clear.

Although he has been dead almost 200 years, Mozart's music is performed and recorded more frequently than ever, and the "Mostly Mozart" series has proved to be one of the most popular concerts in music-rich New York City. However, the circumstances of his death remain subject to controversy to this day.

The bare facts are that Mozart died at 5 minutes before 1 A.M. on December 5, 1791, in his 35th year of life. He had been ill for about two weeks. The story of his funeral has often been retold. As a matter of fact, there have been two stories. The first and most popular version is that Mozart was buried by a few friends in an unmarked pauper's grave during a snowstorm. This version is usually accompanied by statements that Mozart was no longer appreciated by the fickle Viennese and had been living in poverty. The traditional account of Mozart's death, then, has been used as a sad commentary of the way society treats its most creative people. Occasionally this version of the story is embroidered by the rumor that he had been fatally poisoned by a jealous rival composer, Antonio Salieri. This rumor incorporated the known facts that Salieri had said some envious things about his younger rival, and that Mozart at least once expressed the belief he had been poisoned. The Oscar-winning movie, *Amadeus,* presented this thoroughly discredited version of his death, but the most probable explanation is even more dramatic.

The day of Mozart's burial was in reality calm and mild. That his body was placed in a mass grave, according to at least one authority, was "in accordance with contemporary Viennese custom" (Carr, 1984). The common supposition that Mozart was not held in high esteem by his contemporaries also fails to hold up. One had but to read the obituary notices that, without exception, acknowledged his greatness. By this time, also, Salieri's innocence of homicidal intent or action had also been well established.

These different stories of Mozart's death and burial also represent different relationships between the creative artist and society. And yet it may be that neither of these versions conveys the true picture of Mozart's demise. Historian Francis Carr has recently amassed evidence that supports the homicide-by-poisoning theory of Mozart's death (Carr, 1984). Although Mozart and his wife had what appeared in many ways to be a successful marriage, Amadeus and Constanze each were involved in a serious affair with another person. Constanze's lover was Mozart's pupil Frances Xaver Suessmayr who, ironically, later completed the Requiem Mozart had not had the opportunity to finish. Mozart was enamored with Magdalena Hofdemel, the beautiful and talented wife of one of his friends. New evidence discovered by Carr now points clearly to Hofdemel, the jilted and distraught husband, as the murderer of Mozart, by use of the specific poison Mozart had suspected (a hard-to-detect blend of lead oxide, antimony, and white arsenic). Hofdemel killed himself the day after Mozart's death and very nearly killed his pregnant wife as well.

Adding other information unearthed by Carr, the facts now finally fall into place. Near the end of his short life, Mozart had been held in high regard by his contemporaries and was not in desperate financial circumstances. The funeral rituals and burial were deliberately conducted in an obscure fashion to prevent inquiry and autopsy. Friends of Mozart and the Hofdemels (including at least one high government official) knew the true cause of his death and saw no point in making a tragic situation worse by bringing it to public attention. There is evidence that the apparently hasty and disrespectful funeral arrangements were actually the result of careful planning and included evasionary actions to reduce the possibility of being discovered. Compassion for Magdalena, who had lost both husband and lover and was herself recovering from a dangerous assault, led to another deception. By the custom of the times, a person who committed suicide was to be sewn into a cow's hide and thrown into an unmarked pit. Although it was obvious that Hofdemel's death was indeed suicidal, the attending physician falsified the record and even changed the date of death so that Magdalena might at least be spared this ignominy.

How society chooses to respond to the death of its most illustrious members is not only a fascinating subject but one that provides many opportunities to discover the implicit purposes that all funeral processes are intended to achieve. Do the members of the society want to model themselves after the deceased? Do they simply want to remember the deceased with honor and affection? Or would they rather forget that he or she ever existed? What people do and don't do when somebody dies tells us something important about society's attitude toward the deceased.

Balancing the Claims of the Living and the Dead

Another major function of the funeral and memorialization process is to achieve a balance between the competing rights or claims of the living and the dead. This may sound like a strange idea. We often hear it said that funerals are for the living. In truth, however, the need to honor the claims of the dead is also a common and well-entrenched component of most death systems. It is expressed most clearly in funeral processes that are rooted in long-standing cultural traditions. Some of these traditions have been assaulted and eroded by changing social conditions. Nevertheless, even in a society as mobile and technological as American society, the need to balance the claims of the dead and the living can still be discovered if you look beneath the surface. First consider how this process expresses itself in a traditional context.

Potamia is a village in Northern Greece not far from Mount Olympus. The 600 people who live there remain in close physical and symbolic contact with the dead. The small cemetery is crowded with 20 or more grave markers that memorialize villagers who have died in the past few years. Anthropologist Alexander Tsiaras (1982) entered a building in the corner of the cemetery:

> Although I knew what I would find inside, I was still not fully prepared for the sight that confronted me when I opened the door. Beyond a small floor-space a ladder led down to a dark, musty-smelling area filled with the bones of many generations of villagers. Near the top of the huge pile the remains of each person were bound up separately in a white cloth. Toward the bottom of the pile the bones—skulls, pelvises, ribs, the long bones of countless arms, and legs—lay in tangled disarray, having lost all trace of belonging to distinct individuals with the disintegration of the cloth wrappings. Stacked in one corner of the building were metal boxes and small suitcases with names, dates, and photographs identifying the people whose bones lay securely within. (pp. 10–11)

By local custom, bodies remain in the grave-yard for five years and then are removed to the bone house. During this temporary burial the survivors have ample time to visit their lost loved ones. The survivors' feelings often become expressed with great intensity as the time nears to exhume and transfer the body. Tsiaras recorded a mother's lament:

> Eleni, Eleni, you died far from home with no one near you. I've shouted and cried for five years,

Eleni, my unlucky one, but you haven't heard me. I don't have the courage to shout any more. Eleni, Eleni, my lost soul. You were a young plant, but they didn't let you blossom. You've been here for five years. Soon you'll leave. Then where will I go? What will I do? Five years ago I put a beautiful bird into the ground, a beautiful partridge. But now what will I take out? What will I find? (p. 15)

In contrast to many cemeteries in the United States, the little graveyard in Potamia is often filled with mourners, usually women. They come not only to express their sorrows through song, speech, and prayer but also to tend the graves. Candles are kept burning at the foot of each grave, and the grounds are tended with scrupulous care. When the grave-tending activities have been completed for the day, the women sit and talk to their dead and to each other. The conversation may center on death, and one mourner may seek to comfort another. But the conversation may also include other events and concerns. An important aspect of the village's communal life is mediated through their role as survivors of the dead. For the women especially, the graveyard provides an opportunity to express their *ponos* (the pain of grief). The men find a variety of outlets, but the women are usually expected to be at home and to keep their feelings to themselves. "A woman performs the necessary rites of passage and cares for the graves of the dead 'in order to get everything out of her system' " (p. 144).

It is again the Greek women in particular who attempt through their graveside laments and rituals to achieve a balance between the dead and the living. The custom of temporary burial has an important role in this process. The deceased can still be treated as an individual and as a member of the community, somebody who retains the right of love, respect, and comfort. In effect, the deceased suffers a second and final death when the grave is destroyed and the physical remains are deposited with the bones of the anonymous dead. It is easier to cope with the symbolic claims of the dead when a definite time limit has been set—in this case a rather generous five-year period. Although the memory of the deceased will continue to be honored, removal of the remains to the bone house represents the reemergence of the life-oriented needs of the survivors.

The survivors are *obliged* to tend the graves and carry out other responsibilities to the deceased. As Tsiaras points out, this process involves a symbolic interaction and continuation between the living and the dead. The dead have the right to expect it, just as those who are now among the living can expect their survivors to honor their postmortem rights when the time comes. In Potamia and in many other communities where traditional value systems remain in place, the obligations of the living to the dead are clear, specific, and well known.

Peoples as different as the Kotas of Southern India and the Orthodox Jews dispersed throughout the world continue to carry out extensive rituals to ensure that both the dead and the living receive their due. Their observations differ greatly in detail. The Kotas, who cremate their dead:

> Believe that death is contaminating and all who come into contact with death are defiled. Through the rituals of two funerals, the Green Funeral and the Dry Funeral, the spirit of the deceased is assisted in departing to the "Motherland" and the survivors are thereby cleansed so that they might resume their normal life within the society. Since the concept of an afterlife is not clear to most Kotas, the adherence to ritual is seen more as a cleansing process for the survivors, than for the attainment of existence in another world for the deceased. (Goldberg, 1981–1982, p. 119)

Orthodox Jews obey strict laws and rituals that exclude embalming and cremation and require that funeral arrangements be simple and standard no matter what the family's financial status. Goldberg notes, "It is believed that only the soul of the deceased is judged, nothing else" (p. 122). The *Burial Kaddish* prayer affirms faith in God; *Shiva*, the seven days of mourning, unites the family in grief. Interestingly, the ritual action of washing your hands before sitting at *Shiva* has its parallel in the more elaborate purification rites of the Kotas. The Kota, the Orthodox Jew, the rural Greek villager, and many others with long ethnic traditions must fulfill obligations to the dead up to a certain point in time. When these obligations have at last been faithfully performed, however, it is time for the living to again turn their full attention to life.

There are still pockets of traditional symbolic interaction with the dead in American cities. While interviewing older people in small industrial cities, I often heard reference to the neighborhood cemetery. Although the cemetery may have been surrounded by deteriorating industrial buildings, it still remained the focal point of continuity. One octogenarian, for example, said:

> I know I should get out of this neighborhood. Hell, it isn't even a neighborhood any more, not like the old days. But how can I sell this house? It's where my mother and father lived and died. And who'd look after them? . . . Oh, sure, I'm out there every Sunday at least to keep things as nice as I can. It's not their fault what's happened to this neighborhood. Me and a few others I still meet there, we keep up the graves. And it's not just my parents. Just about everybody else is there, too, I mean, six feet under. I keep them company. They keep me company.

This man, by the way, was not at all of morbid disposition. He had an active and well-integrated life-style but drew some of his strength and self-esteem from the knowledge that he was continuing to fulfill his obligations to the dead.

There are many other examples of continued bonding or symbolic transactions between the living and the dead that are often but not always associated with the funeral and memorialization process. Even in bustling, urban America survivors often select images, materials, and objects connected with the deceased to somehow keep the beloved alive as part of themselves. Salient or treasured aspects of the deceased's personality become part of the survivor's life-style, and therefore the memorialization process continues well beyond the funeral (Unruh, 1983).

Memories of Our People: Ethnic Cemeteries in the United States

The shores of the United States have attracted millions of people who sought to make new lives for themselves and their children. Others were brought here involuntarily, wrenched from their homelands and sold into slavery. Still other people lived freely in forests and plains until they encountered the aggressive newcomers who would eventually transform a wilderness into a powerful industry-driven nation. Memories of this incredible variety of people remain with us in many forms. Poet Stephen Vincent Benet (1942) reflects on this heritage:

I have fallen in love with American names,
The sharp names that never get fat,
The snakeskin-titles of mining-claims,
The plumed war-bonnet of Medicine Hat,
Tucson and Deadwood and Lost Mule flat. . . .
I will remember Carquinez Straits,
Little French Lick and Lundy's Lane,
The Yankee ships and the Yankee dates
And the bullet-towns of Calamity Jane.
I will remember Skunktown Plain. . . .
I shall not rest quiet in Montparnasse.
I shall not lie easy at Winchelsea.
You may bury my body in Sussex grass,
You may bury my tongue at Champmedy.
I shall not be there. I shall rise and pass.
Bury my heart at Wounded Knee.

The land also remembers. Ethnic cemeteries, often overlooked by society at large, still affirm that "our people" lived their own distinctive lives here and contributed to the nation's history. Here are a few examples of cemeteries whose responsibility is to preserve not physical remains, but memories and symbols of those who have gone before us.

• *Afro-American Section, The Common Burying Ground, Newport, Rhode Island.* This colonial cemetery dates from 1650. More than 8,000 people were buried here until it became an historical site. Only a few years ago, a visitor appeared who realized that this was probably the only remaining burial site of Afro-Americans in colonial New England. Ann Tashjian and her husband, Dickran Tashjian (1989), photographed and transcribed the gravestones and researched the history. Many of the gravemarkers described the

deceased as "servant," which is thought to have been a euphemism for "slave" (a term considered too harsh, even though accurate, in New England households of the time). Some of the gravestones are elaborate in design and execution, suggesting that the deceased had been held in high regard by the white families they served. Do the gravestones or burial sites show any trace of the cultures and belief systems that the Afro-Americans had left behind when they were brought to the American colonies? Not a trace. Whatever beliefs and practices these people may have continued to cherish from their own tradition, upon their deaths it was the dominant white American culture of the time that prevailed. If you visit this cemetery, make your way to the northern edge and you will see those Afro-American gravemarkers that have survived the vicissitudes of time. You will see that they are similar to the other gravemarkers of the same time periods. Cherubs, for example, were popular adornments, and these appear alike on white and Afro-American gravemarkers. The cemetery itself, then, tells us something about the subordinate place of Afro-Americans in colonial New England; in death as in life, their own culture was denied expression. The Tashjians found that a Free African Union Society, active in the 18th century, had encouraged Afro-Americans "to assume a dignified public appearance (at funerals) to protect the integrity of private grief" (p. 192). Along with other evidence, this suggests that the occasion of death was seen as having potential for racial tension, with the dominant white society seeking to maintain its control over the funeral services and burial. The longing to be free, so often expressed in gospel song, takes on added significance here. In death an Afro-American would become free of servitude, but the public memory of his existence would still be under the control of the dominant society.

• *Navajo and Mormon companions, Ramah Cemetery, Ramah, New Mexico.* Members of The Church of the Latter-day Saints (often referred to as Mormons) established a community in Ramah, New Mexico in 1876. The Ramah people of the Navajo Nation had previously taken up residence in this area. The same graveyard serves families of both cultures, although their beliefs and practices differ markedly. The cemetery was established by the Mormons on a knoll surrounded by farm and ranch land. There are no large memorial statues, and the ground is covered by the native grasses and weeds. The Navajo section includes 71 graves that could be positively identified. A few recent graves have commercially manufactured gravestones. A few others are decorated with artificial flowers, but most are undecorated. "There is no indication of any attempt to bury family members side by side or close together. All the graves are approximately the same distance apart and are laid out in what is basically a straight line. The headstone or other marker and the grave are placed so that the main side of the marker and the head of the deceased point toward the West, and the deceased would face East if sitting or standing" (Cunningham, 1989, p. 204). This description tells only part of the story, however. Beneath the earth, the Navajo culture expresses itself through valued objects that are placed with the dead. Turquoise jewelry is thought to have special powers, attributed both to the gemstones themselves and to the spirituality transmitted by the artists. In burying this jewelry with the deceased, the family both speeds its spirit on its journey to the afterlife and confuses and thwarts any *ch'iidii* (evil ghosts) that might covet these powerful objects.

The Mormon section (209 graves) has numerous markers, some of them homemade by family members. There is a large variety of style and materials represented by these markers, in contrast with the simple metal markers that identify the Navajo graves. The Mormon markers include examples of folk art revival (e.g., in red sandstone carvings) and such others as "an actual picture of the deceased as a part of their design and contemporary sand-blasted stones which allow very intricate and exact representations of floral motifs and even recognizable representations of Mormon temples at Mesa, Arizona, and Salt Lake City, Utah." The Mormon graves also

differ from the Navajo in their spatial arrangement: they are usually grouped according to family relationships, including some joint stones for husband and wife. The memorial stones also provide more information about the deceased.

The Navajo and Mormon dead in New Mexico appear to be more companionable than the Afro-Americans and colonial whites in Newport. The cemetery itself blends easily into its surroundings, the "landscaping" for both Navajo and Mormon left up to nature. The family-oriented Mormons have preserved this orientation in the arrangement of graves and markers, but have not imposed their beliefs and practices upon their native American neighbors, nor objected to the jewelry burials. For their part, some Navajos have chosen to become Mormon—or "semi-Mormon"—and have expressed the thought that the worst of the evil spirits have departed from the burial grounds because of the Mormons' presence. Ironically, perhaps, the Mormons feel this cemetery meets their needs because it pays respect to the dead in an appropriate manner, while the traditional Navajos find it satisfactory as a place that keeps the dead (and the dangerous ghosts they attract) away from the living. Navajo and Mormon appear to have respected and learned from each other in life and to have shared the land in a manner acceptable to both. And now, in death, they can lie under the same ground without requiring one faith to bow to the wishes of the other.

• *Mexican-Americans in San Antonio's San Fernando Cemetery.* The standardization of American life extends to many urban cemeteries: this one does not look much different from that one. Lynn Gosnell and Suzanne Gott (1989) describe some of the activity at a cemetery that has retained its special character:

Throughout the year, but especially during religious and secular holidays, including Halloween, All Souls' Day, Christmas, Valentine's Day, Easter, Mother's Day, and Father's Day, the visitor to San Fernando takes part in an energetic practice of grave decoration and visual display. During these days, cars and trucks jam the narrow traffic lanes which provide access to each block of this ninety-three acre cemetery. Relatives crowd the burial grounds, bringing with them gardening tools, flowers, and other decorative materials. . . . Some people busily tend to a gravesite, while others take time to chat and remark on a particularly well-decorated grave site. Still others stand quietly, singly or in groups, near the grave of a loved one. Grave decorating days within San Fernando Cemetery are therefore marked by a lively social interaction between the living and a heightened interaction between families and their deceased loved ones. (p. 218)

The visitors are Mexican-Americans who follow Roman Catholic beliefs and practices. How important is this cemetery to them? Each family could continue to remember and honor its own dead privately. But having a cemetery to share with other people who hold similar beliefs and values adds several major dimensions to the memorial process. The dead have their special place which the living can visit (just like one living person might visit another). Furthermore, when one arrives at the gravesite, there are things to do for the loved ones (again, reminiscent of what one living family member might do for another). No less important is the vista: "We are not the only people to have lost a loved one. It is the human condition. We are, all of us, together in our respect for the dead and our celebration of life." Finally, after the trip, the decorating, the interaction, the family returns home and is able to separate, for a while, from the dead. Some outsiders might be puzzled or even annoyed by all this activity at a cemetery—have they never felt isolated by a loss, and never carried a death around with them, unable to set it down even for a moment?

These are but three examples of the ethnic cemetery in the United States today. Can you find examples in your own area? And can you read the stories they tell?

THE PLACE OF THE DEAD IN SOCIETY YESTERDAY AND TODAY

Society today places a strong emphasis on curing illness and preventing death. This emphasis expresses itself in many realms, from expenditures for finding new ways of treating life-threatening illnesses to the sometimes overzealous efforts of the medical profession in employing aggressive instead of comfort-giving procedures to dying people. By contrast, most death systems in the past gave more emphasis than Americans currently do to relationships with the dead. On the basis of available evidence, the following points are worth attention:

1. *The dead are more secure in past-oriented societies.* They maintain a role in the symbolic continuity for people with shared language and cultural values who have lived in the same place for many generations, perhaps even for centuries. If the past is known, valued, and seen as relevant to daily life, then the dead are likely to be respected. In future-oriented societies the past is often seen as something to be transcended and improved upon. Technological knowledge, ever-changing, is more valued than the wisdom and values of the dead past.

2. *Geographical detachment from the dead will cause distress to the living, especially in past-oriented societies.* Vietnamese families who were relocated by the American military during "pacification" efforts expressed great anguish in having to depart from the land where the spirits of their remote and recent ancestors held sway. Native Americans were subject to the same kind of stress and loss for many years, and there are still active cases in which tribes are being pressured to move from their sacred ancestral lands. When we have all become ancestors (if current trends continue), there will be even considerably less concern for the dead because fewer people will have formed deep, long-term attachments to particular places.

3. *The dead will be remembered and "used" more often in societies in which children are highly valued as continuing the family soul over the gap created by death.* Preliminary research suggests that young Americans today in general do not regard children as important for this purpose (Kastenbaum, 1974). Each individual (and each

generation) is seen as having its own moment in the sun, free to pursue its own pleasures and values, but not linked inexorably together as was often the case in the past.

4. *The combination of longer life expectancy and low vested power of the elderly tends to make the dead less important.* In earlier times many people died at an age we would now consider premature. Such deaths often are especially painful and disruptive to the survivors. The incomplete lives are therefore more likely to be carried forth in memory, propelled by their unfinishedness. Today more people live to an advanced age, and the survivors do not have a sense of incompleteness that needs to be compensated for by memorialization. Furthermore, in today's youth-oriented world the older person does not as often control property and wealth and therefore is less powerful and less in need of being honored or placated. Older people also seem to be losing some of the special status once enjoyed when they were thought of as close to the gods and ancestral spirits.

5. *A society lacking unifying and transcending themes will assimilate the funeral and memorialization process into its utilitarian motives.* The rural Greek villager, the Kota, and the Orthodox Jew will all in their different ways persist in treating the dead in a manner intended to bestow honor and respect as well as eventually to free the survivor for renewal of life. The time, expense, and inconvenience of this process do not discourage them, nor do the misunderstanding, ridicule, and hostility that they might on occasion receive from others. When a society does *not* have strong shared values of a unifying and transcending type, then the funeral process loses its special status. The cost of the funeral may become the most salient concern (Editors of *Consumer Reports,* 1977). If the living no longer attach importance to the dead, then the funeral might as well be as inexpensive as possible. Similarly, not too much time should be "wasted" on funeral rituals. (Even in the slower paced, rural South I have heard mourners complain that a funeral was "dragged on too long. One flower girl wasn't

enough! They had to have three, and all of them took their own sweet time!") For the dead to be useful they will have to be functional, just like everybody else, and earn their place. If public recognition of the dead continues to diminish (Fulton, et al., 1982), then donating organs may be one of the few ways in which the dead can remain a part of society.

6. *Societies that live close to nature need the assistance of the dead to promote fertility and regeneration.* This thesis is implicit in the work of anthropologist Maurice Bloch (1982). The Merian of Madagascar, for example, make sure that the female element (the body) has thoroughly decomposed so that the male element (the bleached bones) can emerge purified and ensure that both the people and their harvests are fertile. The decomposition process is thought to be dangerous, but it is also very important. A Merina cannot shrink from the reality of decay as people tend to do at Western funeral services because it is from decay that the miracle of regeneration is wrought. Bloch sees one of the major functions of the Merina funeral process as transforming death into life. The dead are very important because it is literally from their breath and bones that the species regenerates itself.

In general, the dead are losing status and importance in the United States, and this may be true in other nations as well. It is not necessarily the case, however, that this trend will continue indefinitely. Circumstances may arise in which we feel that we need all the help we can get—from the dead as well as the living.

"You Were the Best Dog Ever": The Pet Cemetery

I have turned over the rocky ground of Massachusetts and the dry sands of Arizona to bury several very important cats. When the dog of the family died quietly in his basket-bed, none of us could regard his body as only the dead body of an animal. Millions of other people have had close attachments to their pets—or to animals they have worked with, the horse who drew the milkman's wagon, the dog who guided its visually impaired owner, etc. This attachment does not automatically end at death, whether the loss be that of another human or of an animal companion.

The pet cemetery is one instructive example of the way in which some people attempt to cope with the death of an animal companion. The modern version of the pet cemetery seems to have started in France around the turn of the 20th century. Not only dogs and cats, but also horses, monkeys, rabbits, birds (and a lioness) have been buried there. Perhaps the most famous "resident" is Rin-Tin-Tin, once the reigning animal star of Hollywood. However, the impulse to honor the memory of an animal companion through a funeral and burial process has been expressed throughout history. There are examples among the ancient Greeks and in the early years of our own nation. In the United States there are presently 145 pet cemeteries that are affiliated with the organization that attempts to set professional standards and provide public information (International Association of Pet Cemeteries). It is estimated that there are perhaps another 250 that have not affiliated themselves.

In looking at pet cemeteries in the United States we seem to be viewing some of the same mixed and changing attitudes toward death that characterize our society in general. For an example, consider Pet Rest Memorial Mortuary and Cemetery. Located just up the road from Arizona State University (Tempe), Pet Rest provided the opportunity for a recent study by Vivian Spiegelman and myself (1989–1990). If you visit Pet Rest you will find that it resembles many another small cemetery, a fenced-in, park-like space with a variety of grave markers. Some graves are decorated with plastic flowers; some markers include a photographic or sculptured representation of the deceased. Ceramic cats play inside a white picket fence at one gravesite. But you will also notice that the burialground is not well cared for. Some monuments have already fallen into the weedy grass, and there is a general impression of neglect. What has happened?

Pet Rest has become a "dead cemetery," i.e., no more burials are allowed, and nobody has accepted the responsibility for maintenance. If there is a villain to this piece, it is the pressure of urban development. The continuing influx of people into Arizona, the change from an agricultural to a residential community, the transformation of a small college into one of the nation's largest universities—these are among the factors that have contributed to the decline and eventual destruction of Pet Rest. Developers see the land as too valuable now to be "wasted" on dead animals, and also are uncomfortable with having death on display while attempting to "upscale" commercial properties in the area. Meanwhile, those who cared enough for their pets to purchase a "final resting place" are both distressed about the present circumstances and fearful about the future. In this sense, Pet Rest is proving vulnerable to pressures of economic and social change that also affect many "regular" cemeteries across the nation. Other pet cemeteries have been forced to relocate the physical remains when the land was literally sold from over them, and there are reports that in some instances the remains were simply carted away and dumped.

Those who see the pet cemetery as a meaningful way of remembering animal companions may have to confront some painful economic and political realities. However, many other people have found it consoling to conduct their own memorial services upon the death of a pet, and to satisfy themselves with photographs in the family album—and, perhaps, a trip to the local animal shelter to save a life that might otherwise be lost.

Pet cemeteries have invited parody and mockery on occasion (Waugh, 1948/1977). And people have sometimes behaved oddly after the death of a four-footed (or feathered) friend. Nevertheless, those who understand and value the bonds of affection that can form between one creature and another may judge that "too much" love is not the worst thing that might be said of a person.

IMPROVING THE FUNERAL PROCESS

This chapter began with the question "Why have funerals?" A set of questions was provided to help your personal attitudes surface. Now please review these questions and your attitudes in light of the material you have been considering, with emphasis on the implications for improving the funeral process.

The questionnaire provided opportunities to express negative attitudes and feelings. Funerals might have been seen as a waste of time and land, as costing too much, and as providing the occasion for too much emotionalism. These are common criticisms today. At the extreme, some hold that funerals are obsolete and unnecessary. However, most people do appreciate that the funeral process does serve important human needs. Many of the purposes underlying funeral processes have already been noted. Perhaps the most basic need of all is to help the survivors achieve the emotional realization that one of their fellow mortals has in fact died and that they must find a way to go on in this person's absence. Nevertheless, many are convinced that the traditional commercial funeral process does not always meet these needs adequately and that alternatives should be explored.

The usual suggested alternative is for a swift, simple, and inexpensive form of body disposal rather than a more elaborate, public process. One recent study, for example, found that even people with a traditional and conservative religious orientation felt that funerals often are too expensive and elaborate (Bergen & Williams, 1981–1982). These small town, Midwestern Protestants, however, also believed that the funeral and memorialization process provides an important source of support for the survivors. They preferred an alternative type of funeral in which there is less formal ritual and more opportunity for the entire congregation to participate actively and comfort the bereaved. This approach is in line with Doka's (1984–1985) findings that active participation in some aspect of

the funeral process is likely to be of value to the survivors. Much of the material presented by the Consumers' Union report of funeral practices also advocates modifications and alternatives (Editors of *Consumer Reports*, 1977). This book, *Funerals: Consumers' Last Rights*, is a valuable source of information on current funeral and cemetery practices, although it is now becoming slightly dated.

Perhaps even more useful is a publication of the American Association of Retired Persons. *It's Your Choice* (Nelson, 1983) offers information on many of the choices that can be made regarding funeral services and costs. This book also lists local memorial societies throughout the United States and Canada. (For the most current information on local memorial societies, write to: Continental Association of Funeral and Memorial Societies, Inc., 1828 L Street, N. W., Suite 1100, Washington, DC 20036 or Memorial Society Association of Canada, Box 96, Station A, Weston, Ontario M9N 3M6, Canada.)

It is certainly easier to take an active and effective role in planning a funeral if you are well informed on legal, financial, and other matters and aware of the full spectrum of possible alternatives.

Interestingly, a number of funeral directors—especially the leaders—encourage greater participation on the part of the community and the survivors and welcome a more individual approach to funeral planning. Keith Royal (1976, 1983), for example, believes that the death awareness movement has improved the ability of both the survivors and the funeral director to respond to the specific situation rather than to rely upon a standardized ritual and service. The nature and the scope of the funeral arrangements can be designed through the collaboration of the survivors and the funeral director. At times the dying person will also be willing and able to specify important details. In answering the open-ended questions at the beginning of this chapter you may have come up with some valuable ideas for alternative funeral arrangements. An attitudinal climate is now developing in which it is becoming easier to consider alternatives. This requires more open communication among the survivors and between the survivors and the funeral director than what has often taken place.

Although the specific ceremonies may change and become more diversified, it is likely that most funeral services will continue to have a ritualistic quality. Margaret Mead (1972) has defined *ritual* as the "ability of the known form to reinvoke past emotion, to bind the individual to his own past experience, and to bring the members of the group together in a shared experience . . . (giving) people access to intensity of feelings at times when responsiveness is muted." Facing death is certainly one of those situations that challenges our individual integrity and group feeling and that therefore seems to issue a call for ritual. But in our own times it is not always easy to tolerate rituals. Mead continues, "Contemporary American celebrations suffer from our objections to anything we can classify as ritualistic, repetitive, or even familiar." Other observers, such as Toffler (1970), believe that we may need ritual more than ever, our protestations to the contrary notwithstanding. We are faced with so many changes in our lives and have such a difficult time in relating ourselves simultaneously to past, present, and future that rituals can serve the vital function of confirming our bonds with people and symbols beyond the moment.

All the questions on the self-examination bear upon the type of funeral and memorialization process that you consider to be appropriate. Many people are more comfortable discussing the questions pertaining to objective facts (e.g., funeral cost) than to the emotional and value issues involved. The likelihood of developing funeral processes more adequate for our needs would be increased if we could face the emotional issues more directly. An alternative funeral can serve to obscure or deny death-related feelings just as well as the traditional funeral. The outward forms are not really our only concern. It may be our own unresolved problems that lead us to judge that somebody is expressing either "too much" or "not enough" emotion at a funeral. We may criticize the expense of the fu-

neral because that is one of the few elements we feel comfortable in discussing. Our anger may flare at some person or event associated with the funeral process even though the source of our agitation lies elsewhere. Discomfort with a traditional funeral may derive from a more general conflict or tension between the attitudes of an older, more ethnic generation and the younger generation. In other words, not all of the anxiety, anger, and distress accompanying the funeral process are directly associated with the death. The funeral process sometimes provides an occasion for many unresolved problems and competing points of view to collide. The death system, after all, is but a part of our larger pattern of individual and social life.

Some Common Questions about the Funeral Process

Here are some of the questions that are most frequently raised about the funeral and memorialization process, along with answers that you might find useful.

Q: *Do we need to have the body embalmed?*
A: Laws may differ, but usually embalming is required only when the body is to be transported, or when there are specific health-related reasons. However, many families find embalming useful when the body is to be held for several days to allow distant friends and relatives to attend the funeral.

Q: *If there is an autopsy—or removal of organs to donate for transplantation—does this mean we can't have an open-casket funeral service?*
A: Not necessarily. Many open-casket services have been held after these procedures, especially with improved techniques in postmortem exams. It is a good idea to inform the physician and the funeral director in advance that an open-casket service is planned; in many, but not all, circumstances, they should be able to carry out their procedures without disturbing the final appearance of the body.

Q: *What becomes of the ashes after cremation?*
A: This depends entirely upon the family's wishes. Please be sure to give clear instructions to the funeral director—there are thousands of "cremains" still in storage in funeral homes because next of kin have not returned for them, nor left instructions.

There are few restrictions on where the remains may be scattered. Bear in mind, however, that the so-called "ashes" actually consist of small fragments of bone and may not have the smooth, sand-like appearance that some people envision.

Q: *Could we have cremation, but also ground burial and a service at the graveside?*

A: Yes, and this is a choice that an increasing number of people seem to be making.

Q: *Is it a good idea to contract for a "prearranged" funeral?*

A: This option may be appealing to people who prefer to plan ahead in general, and to those who want to reduce the amount of decision-making that is needed at time of death. On the negative side, there have been some deceptive dealings by unscrupulous funeral directors: know the reputation of the establishment you select. And remember that it is possible to make advance arrangements *without* advance payment, even though the more aggressive funeral directors tend to present advance payment plans.

Q: *This funeral director kept asking us if we were sure, really sure that we didn't want to view the body. Why did he keep after us that way—it was really irritating!*

A: Probably from experience with people who didn't think they wanted a viewing, but regretted the lost opportunity when it was too late. Not everybody does want a viewing, but it's wise to think about this decision carefully.

Q: *I don't like to bring up the subject of money at such an emotional time. . . .*

A: Being level-headed about cost doesn't take anything away from your respect for the deceased. You have the legal right to receive full and accurate information about every aspect of funeral cost, and a reputable funeral director will have no problem in discussing these matters with you and carrying out your wishes.

Q: *Should children go to the funeral?*

A: Most people who have had experience with this issue agree that it is usually appropriate for children to take some part in the funeral proceedings *if* the children themselves want to do so. This means that there needs to be adequate communication so the children will have a reasonable idea about the purpose of the services and what will take place. Often it is also a good idea to arrange for children (especially the youngest) to spend only a short time at the services and then be given the opportunity to go off and play, rather than have to endure what might be too long a test of "good behavior." Most parents who include their children as part of the funeral process later believe they did the right thing. Be sensitive to individual differences among children, however, and be available to the child should questions or problems arise afterward.

Q: *What are funeral directors really like?*

A: It's a family business for many of them. They tend to be somewhat conservative "mainstream" type people who want to be acceptable to the entire community; therefore, they must have good reputations as individuals as well as corporations. At times, all this "model citizenry" may be felt as a burden, so they welcome the opportunity to relax and "be like everybody else." As a businessperson, the local funeral director today worries about competition from large national corporations and the complexity of governmental regulations with which his operation must be in compliance. As an expert in the preparation of bodies for viewing, transportation, and final disposal, the funeral director is concerned about such challenges as restorative care for victims of disfiguring accidents and the possibility of contamination through contact with the victims of AIDS, hepatitis, and a number of other conditions. (Precautionary measures are now in common use.) As a human being, the funeral director may be emotionally devastated by the death of a child, or moved by the words spoken at graveside.

REFERENCES

Aries, P. (1981). *The hour of our death.* New York: Alfred A. Knopf, Inc.

Benet, S. V. (1942). American Names. In *Poetry of Stephen Vincent Benet* (pp. 367–368). New York: Farrar & Rinehart.

Bergen, M. B., & Williams, R. R. (1981–1982). Alternative funerals: An exploratory study. *Omega, Journal of Death and Dying, 12,* 71–78.

Bloch, M. (1982). Death, women and power. In M. Bloch & J. Parry (Eds.), *Death and the regeneration of life* (pp. 1–44). Cambridge: Cambridge University Press.

Carr, F. (1984). Mozart's mysterious death: A new interpretation. *Ovation, 5,* 19–27.

Cunningham, K. (1989). Navajo, Mormon, Zuni graves: Navajo, Mormon, Zuni ways. In R. E. Meyer (Ed.), *Cemeteries and gravemarkers* (pp. 197–216). Ann Arbor: U. M. I. Research Press.

Editors of *Consumer Reports.* (1977). *Funerals: Consumers' last rights.* Mt. Vernon, NY: Consumers' Union.

Cotterell, A. (1981). *The first emperor of China.* New York: Holt, Rinehart & Winston.

Darby, E., & Smith, N. (1983). *The cult of the Prince Consort.* New Haven: Yale University Press.

Doka, K. J. (1984–1985). Expectation of death, participation in funeral arrangements and grief adjustment. *Omega, Journal of Death and Dying, 15,* 119–130.

Durkheim, E. (1951). *Le Suicide* (J. A. Spaulding & G. Simpson, Trans.). New York: The Free Press. (Original work published 1897)

Editorial committee (1980). Mozart. In S. Sadie (Ed.), *The new Grove dictionary of music and musicians: Vol. 12* (pp. 680–752). London: Macmillan Publishers, Ltd.

Fulton, R., Gottesman, D. J., & Owen, G. M. (1982). Loss, social change, and the prospect of mourning. *Death Education, 6,* 137–154.

Gay, P. (1984). *Education of the senses.* New York: Oxford University Press.

Goldberg, H. S. (1981–1982). Funeral and bereavement rituals of Kota Indians and Orthodox Jews. *Omega, Journal of Death and Dying, 12,* 117–128.

Gosnell, L., & Gott, S. (1989). San Fernando Cemetery: Decorations of loss in a Mexican-American community. In R. E. Meyer (Ed.), *Cemeteries and gravemarkers* (pp. 217–236). Ann Arbor: U. M. I. Research Press.

Hamilton-Paterson, J., & Andrews, C. (1979). *Mummies: Death and life in ancient Egypt.* New York: The Viking Press.

Kastenbaum, R. (1974). Fertility and the fear of death. *Journal of Social Issues, 30,* 63–78.

Keith, R. (1976). Some observations on grief and the funeral. In V. R. Pine, et al. (Eds.), *Acute grief and the funeral.* Springfield, IL: Charles C. Thomas, Publisher.

Keith, R. (1983). Lecture, Arizona State University, Tempe.

Lofland, L. (1978). *The craft of dying.* Beverly Hills: Sage Publications, Inc.

Mead, M. (1972). *Twentieth century faith, hope, and survival.* New York: Harper & Row, Publishers, Inc.

Nelson, T. C. (1983). *It's your choice.* Glenview, IL: AARP, Scott, Foresman & Co.

Rowles, G. (1984). Private communication.

Spiegelman, V., & Kastenbaum, R. (1990). Pet Rest Cemetery: Is eternity running out of time? *Omega, Journal of Death and Dying, 21,* 1–13.

Tashjian, A., & Tashjian, D. (1989). The Afro-American section of Newport, Rhode Island's common burying ground. In R. E. Meyer (Ed.), *Cemeteries and gravemarkers* (pp. 163–196). Ann Arbor: U. M. I. Research Press.

Toffler, A. (1970). *Future shock.* New York: Random House, Inc.

Tsiarias, A. (1982). *The death rituals of rural Greece.* Princeton: Princeton University Press.

Unruh, D. R. (1983). Death and personal history: Strategies of identity preservation. *Social Problems, 30,* 340–351.

Waugh, E. (1977). *The loved one.* London: Chapman & Hall. (Original work published 1948)

10

BEREAVEMENT, GRIEF, AND MOURNING

What will I do without her? I mean, after all these years, what is life without her?

I just can't stop thinking about him. I even talk to him. And sometimes, to tell the truth, I just know he's right here with me. I must be going crazy or something.

It's a relief. The axe finally fell. Know what I mean? Or do I sound cold and heartless?

These are among the many ways that we may react when death has deprived us of a significant human relationship. The loss of an animal companion can also hit us hard: "The house is so empty without Ruffy. I could cry. I guess I do cry." We may question our ability or our desire to go on without the person we have lost. The familiar routines of everyday life may seem distant and meaningless: "I saw everything that was going on around me, but I couldn't touch it or feel it. It was as though there was a wall of glass between myself and the rest of the world." Our attention, concentration, and memory may falter. Friends, finding us preoccupied and unresponsive, may decide to leave us alone with our own thoughts. On the other hand, friends may marvel at "how well" we are doing, "how strong" we are; little do they realize the doubts

and anxieties we are concealing through "acting normal." Furthermore, our physical health may be in jeopardy. Perhaps we are sleeping poorly, failing to take adequate nourishment, and neglecting our own well-being. Some of us may be on the verge of a drinking problem, while others may be developing suicidal ideation— risks that the people around us may or may not recognize.

Bereavement, grief, and mourning have been universal human experiences throughout history. Few people escape the sorrow and stress of loss. Individual grief has not been abolished by mass communication, computers, and all the technological innovations of the 20th century. In this chapter, then, we examine one of our strongest links with the whole procession of the human race on earth: the capacity to suffer deeply and yet to renew our commitment to life when separated by death from a beloved person.

Attention will first be given to clarifying the basic concepts of bereavement, grief, and mourning. How people cope with loss in childhood and in adult life will then be examined in some detail. Although we will discover common patterns and themes, we will also become aware of great individual differences and of the role played by sociocultural expectations. Finally, we will build upon these observations to improve our ability to recognize and respond helpfully to the grief experience, whether in ourselves or others.

INNER AND OUTER EXPRESSIONS OF LOSS

Bereavement, grief, mourning—the words are not adequate to convey the transformation a death can bring upon the survivors. But let us at least begin with these words and see how they can best be understood.

Bereavement: An Objective Fact

Bereavement is an objective fact. We are bereaved when a person close to us dies. It is also a change in status. The child may have become an orphan, the spouse a widower or widow. The *experience* and *consequences* of bereavement can take many forms. The fact itself, however, is simple: a person close to us has died. Bereavement status can only suggest what the survivors might be experiencing and how they have adapted to the loss. It is a clue to possible psychological distress, then, as well as an objective fact.

Shifting from individual to death-system perspective, bereavement can also be seen as an outcome of large-scale social phenomena. Widowhood and orphanhood are major consequences of war. The effects of war are to be gauged not only in territories seized or relinquished but also in the short- and long-range effects of bereavement. British, French, and German observers who lamented that the cream of their youth was de-

stroyed in World War I, for example, could not be accused of exaggeration. The social consequences from the deaths of young men by the tens of thousands defy calculation. Each nation was not only deprived of the talents and energies of these men but was left with a population of survivors who could not be expected to pick up their lives as usual when the war ended. How much of human history since World War I has been affected by the slaughter and bereavement of that one major conflict alone? And what has been the effect of other wars before and after? There is no way of answering these questions satisfactorily, but the consequences of individual bereavements massing together within the same society at the same time must surely exert strong influences on the quality of life for many years thereafter.

War is just one of the more obvious large-scale events that influence who is bereaved when. Bereavement points to many other social phenomena as well. The number of widows in American society, for example, has been increasing in recent decades. The increase in adults who have outlived their mates is one of the reasons why *loneliness* has become such an important topic for research and intervention. Studies often find that widowed people are more likely to be socially isolated than others (Clayton et al., 1968). And social isolation in turn tends to be associated with low morale and difficulties in coping (Lopata, 1988). Although bereavement by itself is only a bare objective fact, it is also a fact that tends to generate increased vulnerability and stress.

Grief: A Painful Response

Grief is a response to bereavement; it is how the survivor feels. It is also how the survivor thinks, eats, sleeps, and makes it through the day. The term itself does not explain anything. Rather, when we say that a person is grief-stricken, we are only directing attention to the way in which his or her total way of being has been affected by the loss. Grief requires careful understanding on a person-by-person basis; it is not a word that can be taken as a simple and automatic explanation of what is being experienced and why.

Furthermore, grief is not the only possible response to bereavement. There may be anger or indifference, for example. Some individuals show what psychiatrists term a *dissociative flight* from the impact of death—a pattern of denial that can become so extreme that it forms the core of a psychotic reaction. Some people clearly recognize their loss but appear unable or unwilling to grieve. We cannot assume, then, that a bereaved person is experiencing grief at a particular point in time. Nevertheless, the grief response is so frequent and so painful that it is of primary importance for those who wish to understand and comfort the bereaved.

In his pioneering clinical study Erich Lindemann (1944) described the physical symptoms of grief:

> The picture shown by people in acute grief is remarkably uniform. Common to all is the following syndrome: sensations of somatic distress occurring in waves lasting from 20 minutes to an hour at a time, a feeling of tightness in the throat, choking with shortness of breath, need for sighing, an empty feeling in the abdomen, lack of muscular power, and an intensive subjective distress described as tension or pain. (p. 145)

Other symptoms also commonly seen were insomnia, absentmindedness, problems in concentrating, failures of memory, and the tendency to do the same things over and over again.

This classic description by Lindemann should be seen in context. He was working with people who had been stunned by the sudden death of loved ones in the Cocoanut Grove fire (in Boston, 1942) in which 400 people perished in less than 15 minutes and others died later of severe burns and smoke inhalation. Subsequent experience indicates that the total symptom picture seen by Lindemann may not be expressed by every person who has an acute grief reaction, but

his description still conveys a vivid sense of what it is like to be overwhelmed by grief.

Grief can affect all spheres of life. The grieving person's body doesn't work very well. Some clinicians and researchers believe that the physical side of grief is so severe that it can properly be considered a disease process. George Engel (1963) suggested that an intensive or sustained grief reaction can precipitate serious illness, even death, in bereaved individuals who have underlying physical problems. The biochemical and physiological concomitants of grief place additional strain on the weak links in the bereaved person's physical systems, with the particular type of somatic reaction that develops depending on the particular weak link or defect that pre-existed in the bereaved. Jerome K. Frederick (1976) has proposed a specific pathway by which the grief reaction might trigger serious physical disorder. He cites a variety of studies indicating that the incidence of infections and neoplastic conditions (cancer) increases in the weeks and months directly following a major bereavement.

Several more recent studies find that infant monkeys show significant immunological and other physiological changes when they are separated from their mothers for even a short time. Laudenslager (1988) has made additional observations that could be important for understanding the human response to loss as well. He has noticed, for example, that the behavior shown by the young monkeys was closely related to the magnitude of the physiological changes taking place within their bodies. Those infant monkeys who were most agitated, slouching, and withdrawn were also those whose immune systems were most affected by the stress of separation. However, when the mother and infant are reunited, the young monkey's immune system returns to normal. (It would be interesting to know what is happening to the mother's immune system during this time as well!) Furthermore, the young monkeys show less behavioral and physiological stress during maternal separation if they are kept in a familiar environment and can see their peers. Familiar surroundings seem to have some value in buffering the effects of the loss experience. From other studies it has also been found that when the young of various species have had a history of being held and petted they are somewhat less vulnerable to the effects of stress, and they seem to have a more effective immune system.

Although it would be foolhardy to assume that the psychobiological response to loss is identical in humans, there is reason to believe that there are some instructive similarities with grief-of-separation response in primates. Frederick's (1976) theoretical model of the loss experience might apply to both humans and primates. He suggests that the following sequence occurs when a person undergoes a loss experience:

1. The pituitary releases more ACTH (adreno-cortico-tropic hormone) as part of the body's reaction to stress.
2. This leads to stimulation of the adrenal cortex, which then either activates or releases corticosteroids.
3. The corticosteroids act to depress the body's immune mechanism.
4. If this response pattern continues (as it might with continuing psychological stress), the high activity of corticosteroids suppresses more and more of the immune responses that protect our bodies both from infection and the development of neoplastic disorders.
5. Disease processes themselves (infectious or neoplastic) become evident, generate new stress, and threaten the bereaved individual's own life.

It should be noted that this is not the only possible pathway through which an interpersonal event (death of a loved one) might lead to the jeopardized health of the survivor, nor has Frederick's theory been conclusively proved. However, it is clear by now that survivors are themselves at increased physical risk and that grief can be regarded at least partially as a generalized stress reaction that has potential for major physical change even though it seems to begin on a

psychological level. The telephone call, the knock on the door, and the look in the doctor's eyes convey meanings, and somehow these meanings are rapidly converted into a pattern of biochemical and physical as well as phenomenological events.

Physical aspects of distress can be intensified by what the person does or fails to do in response to the loss. Going without proper nutrition and rest and general neglect of self-care is one characteristic pattern that sometimes accompanies the grief syndrome described by Lindemann and others. Both behavioral and physiological responses to the stress of loss, then, can place the bereaved person at heightened risk.

The mind of the grieving person may not work very well either. The concentration and memory problems already mentioned increase the person's risk to others as well as himself or herself—as an inattentive driver, for example, or as a parent who fails to notice household hazards, or as a worker who becomes careless on the job.

It is the emotional side of grief that often besets the survivor with the greatest distress, however. The person may be tossed between opposite extremes of reaction.

> When I got home from the morgue, I was just out for the rest of the day. I just couldn't help myself. I thought I would have a nervous breakdown, and my heart was going so fast. The man at the morgue said, "Well, if you don't stop crying, you're going to have a nervous breakdown." But all I could do was cry. That's all I could do. And I told him, "If I don't cry, God, my heart will burst." I had to cry, because he wasn't going to be back no more. (Glick et al., 1974, p. 17)

This woman had just found herself transformed from wife to widow. She first experienced shock, could not feel or think at all. And then she could not stop herself from feeling and crying. Her alarm built up further as she feared for her self-control and sanity. It is not uncommon for people in acute grief to feel that they are "going crazy," that they will keep "getting worse and worse and then just fall all apart." This is one reason why people who have previously experienced grief and have since found their way back can be very helpful to those who are in the midst of such experiences.

Distress does not end with the first wave of shock and grief. After the realization that a loved one is dead, there often is the later realization that life is supposed to go on. Depending on the individual and the situation at the time of the death, there are likely to be further waves of confusion, anxiety, rage, and other painful inner states. The sense of numbness can also return, sometimes to linger as though it would never go away.

That grief can return in wave after wave of distress was discovered in a recent investigation of 19th century American diaries. During this era (before the telephone and other modes of mass communication) many people confided both their joys and sorrows to the pages of a diary. Paul C. Rosenblatt (1983) found that recurring experiences of grief were common to the bereaved:

> It [grief] does not seem, in the thoughts and feelings of the typical diarist, to wane gradually but to be absent some of the time and present some of the time. The diary data show that, rather than grief or thoughts of the lost person becoming steadily weakened, times of remembering alternate with times of no mention of the lost person. (p. 21)

People who felt they had recovered completely from the pangs of grief might be engulfed in a wave of distress months or years later. Some of the diary entries expressed a more profound sense of grief years after the loss than they had at the time.

> I think of Ma so much, & the horror of her taking never leaves me. Why should that condition come to her. Why should she keep it secret so long. What would have prevented it.

This entry was written two and one-half years after the death of this man's wife. He had expressed no sense of grief for her in some time.

Many occasions could renew the sense of grief:

> I think of Henry every time I sit at table and see his place is vacant.

> [Sitting again] in our old pew, I could not help thinking of my dear parents and before I could stop myself was crying bitterly. . . .

Places that rekindle a memory, people who remind you of the lost person, and anniversaries all have the power to start a new wave of grief long after the death. Grief, then, is not only a formidable emotional state, but one that may return at various points in time. The grieving person suffers. Make no mistake about that.

Mourning: A Signal of Distress

Mourning is the culturally patterned expression of the bereaved person's thoughts and feelings. Geoffrey Gorer (1977) observed striking changes in mourning behavior within the same culture during his own lifetime. When his father died aboard the *Lusitania*, capsized by a torpedo in 1915, his mother became "a tragic, almost a frightening figure in the full panoply of widow's weeds and unrelieved black, a crepe veil shrouding her . . . so that she was visibly withdrawn from the world." But within a few months the death toll from World War I had become visibly represented throughout all of England: "Widows in mourning became increasingly frequent in the streets, so that Mother no longer stood out in the crowd." Eventually, signs of mourning were modified, reduced. Too many people were being touched too closely by death. The functioning of society as a whole would have been impaired had every bereaved person pursued every step of the traditional mourning ritual, which included a long period of withdrawal from everyday life. The previous tradition of mourning maintained its place so long as death was occasional; a new pattern had to be developed when death was rampant in everybody's neighborhood almost all the time.

There are times when the bereavement and grief of individuals find clear expression, even in a heterogeneous society such as the United

States. The gold star in the window of many a home in the United States during World War II indicated that a very particular life had been lost. But that particular death represented part of a national, shared cause. Each gold star mother had her special bereavement, but collectively they signified a loss felt by the entire nation. Where are the "gold star mothers" for Americans who died in Vietnam? Acknowledgment, sympathy, and support for families grieving for loved ones killed in Vietnam have been much less in evidence than in most previous military engagements. By the time American armed forces had withdrawn from Vietnam, the war had lost much of its sense of being a national, shared cause. Social support for individual grief, then, can either be heightened or diminished by the general spirit of the times, even though the agent of death (e.g., war) may be the same.

In American society and most others, there are also occasions when the death of a prominent and respected person is expressed through forms of general mourning. The flag stands at half-mast. The train bearing the coffin rumbles slowly across the nation, observed by silent crowds. The city swarms with people as the old leader who for so long has been a part of the national identity (e.g., Churchill, deGaulle, Franco) is given a historic funeral.

Mourning occurs on a smaller and more personal scale for most of us in private life. Still, the ways in which we express the recognition of death reflect the attitudes and customs of society. Nations as varied as the United States offer many patterns of mourning—compare those of Americans who are of African, Chinese, Italian, or Central European-Jewish heritage, for example. Furthermore, most traditions of mourning constantly change, some more rapidly than others. There are reasons to be concerned about the expression of mourning in American society today and the support that is available for the bereaved in general. (This problem will be examined later in this chapter.)

We have expectations that the bereaved person will experience grief and that the grieving person will mourn. These expectations are often confirmed. However, any and all of these expectations may be confounded in a particular instance. Here is a person who experiences no grief. Nevertheless he or she engages in the culturally patterned expressions of mourning, perhaps out of courtesy for others who are grieving or from fear of being thought insensitive. And here is another bereaved person who grieves deeply but does not mourn, perhaps because he or she has become alienated from subcultural patterns in general and feels it inappropriate to conform now or because the patterns require a network of others who share the same approach to mourning and who are not available. The fact that the bereavement-grief-mourning sequence is subject to such variation suggests that the specific sense of each of these terms should be kept well in mind.

There is some evidence (Clayton et al., 1968; Hobson, 1964; Yamamoto et al., 1969) that the core experience of grief is much the same throughout the world. Expressions of mourning, however, may be specific to a particular culture. It is therefore possible for people in one culture to conclude that people elsewhere do not feel deeply when they are bereaved when the fact is that the others simply express their grief differently. The notion that life is cheap in the Orient, for example, has been fostered by misinterpretations of culturally expressed modes of mourning. Our difficulties in comprehending what another person is experiencing when bereaved often are compounded by cultural differences, but there is also a lack of understanding within our own culture about what the bereaved person goes through.

Pulitzer Prize winning poet and novelist Alice Walker (1988) has described some of her own personal experiences that help to illuminate both what is universal and what is distinctive about a particular culture's response to grief. In a book written primarily for children—*To Hell with Dying*—Walker tells of her love for an old man by the name of Mr. Sweet. He was not the usual type of elderly person who would be invited to be the main character in a children's story: "Mr. Sweet was a diabetic and an alcoholic and a guitar player and lived down the road from us on a neglected cotton farm" (p. 1). Nevertheless, he was a continual source of delight and instruction for Walker and her older brothers and sisters. One of Mr. Sweet's specialties was dying. He seemed very close to death on several occasions, but was rescued by the Walker children who, on a signal from their father, would "come crowding around the bed and throw themselves on the covers, and whoever was the smallest at the time would kiss him all over his wrinkled brown face and begin to tickle him so that he would laugh all down in his stomach, and his moustache, which was long and sort of straggly, would shake like Spanish moss and was also that color."

As told by the adult Alice Walker, Mr. Sweet had long ago learned that the careers he wanted for himself—doctor, lawyer, or sailor—were at that time out of reach for a poor black boy. In this sense, he might have been living in grief all his life, having lost his childhood vision of an exciting and rewarding career. However, he had in fact developed a very individualistic career of bringing joy to the children in his rural neighborhood. Alice Walker, belonging to a new generation, moved away for the college education that eventually contributed to her notable career as a writer. And, using these writing skills, she has given us a portrait of love and grief during a period of time in American history when many people of African heritage were denied equal access to opportunity, while others were crossing into the mainstream, though not without stress and pain. The smiles and tears of *To Hell with Dying* have universal resonance—but the *particulars* of the experiences shared by Mr. Sweet and the Walker family reflect the unique patterns of life in a rural black community during a recent period of our own society. An outsider, for example, would have no way of knowing that the old guitar in a young black woman's hands was a tangible expression of both loss and continuity, grief and love. Perhaps you have a cherished possession that reminds you of a person who is no longer with you. And perhaps, like Alice Walker, the memories represented by this object or picture help to nourish your sense of personal identity across all the years of your life. Getting rid of Mr. Sweet's old guitar might seem like a good idea—we wouldn't have to look at it and have our sorrows rekindled. But this might also deprive us of a precious link to the past and those who have meant much to us.

WHEN A SPOUSE DIES

The Early Response to Bereavement

An even more common source of grief is the death of a spouse. We turn now to one of the best and most useful studies ever conducted of responses to the death of a husband or wife. The Harvard Bereavement Study concentrated on the experiences of relatively young men and women who lost a spouse through death. This is only one type of bereavement, but the limited focus makes it possible to obtain in-depth knowledge. The material presented here is drawn from *The First Year of Bereavement,* an important book-length report by Ira Glick, Robert Weiss, and C. Murray Parkes (1974), and from Parkes and Weiss' (1983) follow-up study, *Recovery from Bereavement.*

The participants were 49 widows and 19 widowers, none of whom were more than 45 years old. They were contacted by project staff while they were still newly bereaved. Those willing to participate were given a series of informal, open-ended interviews that were tape recorded and transcribed. The ethnic, racial, and religious composition of the widows and widowers in this study reflected that of the Boston area in general—there were more Irish-Catholic widows (31%) than might have been found in other metropolitan areas. Newly bereaved black women were somewhat more willing to participate in this study than their white counterparts. Men and women whose spouses had died of cancer seemed especially willing to participate.

The Immediate Impact of Bereavement

The response to bereavement is best considered separately for men and women, although there are some important similarities.

Most of the widows had known for some time that their husbands were seriously ill. But approximately one in five experienced a completely unexpected bereavement (by accident or sudden heart attack, for example). Another one in five knew that her husband was not in good health but did not think his life was in immediate danger.

These varied expectations made a difference when bereavement actually occurred, but in a complex way. Most women who had been expecting their husbands' deaths felt that they had been grieving *before* the event actually came to pass. This is a phenomenon that Lindemann called *anticipatory grief* and has been discussed increasingly in the past few years. Often a woman expressed relief that her husband's long period of suffering had ended. However, the anticipatory grief did not eliminate the impact of the actual death; the wife felt pained and desolate when the end did come. Those who found themselves suddenly transformed into widows did tend to suffer more intensively, however, feeling overwhelmed, anguished, as though there were no limits to the catastrophe that had befallen them. The newly and suddenly bereaved woman might feel so numb that she feared she would never again move, act, or think, or she might cry as though she would never be able to stop. Both states might alternate in the same person soon after she had learned the news. Although these reactions were not limited to the women who experienced sudden bereavement, usually they were more intense under these circumstances.

An independent study by Justine Ball (1976) has since come up with findings consistent with the Harvard study: grief reactions are common among all newly bereaved women, but those for whom the death has come with little or no warning tend to have the most severe reactions. However, neither study supports the idea that you can somehow pay the emotional price of loss in advance—anticipation may help keep the response within certain bounds, but the husband's death still has a strong impact when it comes.

Some of the wives had been told explicitly that their husbands were dying. However, few used this information as the basis for making plans for life as a widow:

> Most widows, although they consciously believed that it would be good for them to have plans, could not bring themselves to make them. They may have feared that planning would somehow hasten the spouse's death or indicate that they wanted it; or they may have been unable to deal with the pain they felt when they considered their own widowhood. Or they may simply have been unaccustomed, after years of marriage, to planning for themselves. (Glick et al., 1974, p. 32)

The husband who became a widower usually responded to the impact of the death very much as the widow did. The men differed, however, in how they interpreted their feelings and related the death to their entire life patterns. Although the women often emphasized a sense of abandonment, the men reported feeling a sort of *dismemberment*. The women would speak of being left alone, deprived of a comforting and protecting person. The men were more likely to feel "like both my arms were being cut off." The authors suggest that these different emphases are related to what marriage had meant for widow and widower. Marriage had sustained the man's capacity to work. For the woman, marriage had provided a sphere of interpersonal engagement. This meant that the newly widowed woman could more readily find some expression of her interpersonal needs by going to work, whereas the man was more likely to become disorganized in his existing work patterns.

Emotional and Physical Reactions Soon after Bereavement

Bewilderment and despair often continued beyond the first impact of loss. There were still periods of weeping, although widowers were more apt than widows to feel choked up rather than to express themselves through tears. Many physical symptoms appeared and sometimes lingered for weeks or months. Aches and pains, poor appetite, loss of stamina, headaches, dizziness, and menstrual irregularities were reported by many. Sleep disturbances were especially common and distressful. A widow would go to bed hoping to forget her cares for a while and to wake up the next morning with more energy and a brighter outlook. Often, however, she would wake up instead in the middle of the night and remain tormented by grief and the reality of her partner's absence. Instead of offering temporary relief from sorrow, the night often held anxieties of its own. Some women tried to knock themselves out by working hard and staying up late. Others turned to sleeping medications. The dread and emptiness of facing the night alone were relieved for some of the bereaved by having close friends or relatives who could listen to them and keep them company until sleep finally took over.

Most of the widows tried hard to maintain emotional control. This was a difficult effort. Often the newly bereaved woman would long for somebody else to take over and organize life for her. Although some widows expressed this need directly, most attempted to resist it. The typical widow doubted her ability to meet the challenges but still assumed a stance of responsibility and competence. Each woman had to find her own balance between the desire to receive help and the fear of becoming dependent on others. Most women avoided a state of general collapse during the first few weeks after bereavement. However, some had increasing difficulty later. "The failure to begin to reorganize satisfactorily may not display itself until several weeks or months have passed" (Glick et al., 1974, p. 67).

The widowers were more likely than the widows to be uncomfortable with direct emotional expression of their distress. The typical widower attempted to maintain control over his feelings because he considered it unmanly, a weakness, to

let go. The men also tended to emphasize realism more prominently. Such statements as "It's not fair!" were seldom made by men, although fairly often by women. The men seemed to require more rational justification for their reactions to bereavement. Although less troubled by anger than the widow, the widower did have difficulty with guilt. He was more likely to blame himself for what he did or did not do about his wife's death: "I wasn't sensitive enough to her," "I should have made things easier." When a wife died during childbirth, the widower sometimes felt guilty about his responsibility for the pregnancy. The widower's guilt reaction, however, tended to subside fairly soon, although the need for rational control over all responses to the death persisted.

Leave-Taking Ceremonies

The realities of daily life continue during the process of grief and recuperation. One of the major demands of the period soon after bereavement is the necessity to bid farewell to the lost spouse through some type of funeral process. The leave-taking ceremonies went well for most of the bereaved in this study. They often found it helpful to hear from others that they had done their part to ensure a proper farewell. This bolstered their sense of confidence in managing difficult affairs despite their shock and suffering. The widows were usually seen as the central and responsible individuals even though they were provided with significant assistance. The widow was seen by all as the final authority on what should be done, regardless of different wishes that, for example, the husband's family might have. In this way the widow began to gain public acceptance as the new head of the family, a transition not usually involved when the bereaved person was the husband.

The frequently heard criticisms of funerals and funeral directors were *not* in evidence in this study. "These ceremonies were of great emotional importance for all respondents; there was nothing of empty ritual in widows' participation"

(p. 102). The widows often felt that in arranging the ceremonies they were able to continue the expression of their love, devotion, and attachment. "And those widows who felt their marriages had been only too deficient in these respects saw in the ceremonies of leave-taking a last chance to repair the lack" (p. 201).

The funeral directors usually were seen as supportive rather than as obtrusive businessmen. Nevertheless, there were painful moments despite all the support available. Some widows suddenly felt the full pangs of their late husband's death at a particular point during the funeral process, such as the last viewing of the body. The funeral in this sense emphasized the reality of the death, cutting through the haze of unreality in which many of the newly bereaved functioned despite their outward control and competence. The complete realization of the death, however, did not seem to dawn upon the bereaved at any one moment in time, although some of the moments were critical steps toward this realization.

The role of the clergy in the leave-taking ceremonies was not as prominent as might have been expected, at least from the widow's perspective. Most widows seemed to be operating on very limited emotional energy. They neither sought out nor took in what the clergy might have had to say. Understandably, the widows tended to be absorbed in their own feelings. Many of the widows were religious, however, and seemed to find some comfort in clergymen's repetitions of traditional beliefs about the continuation of soul or spirit after death.

The leave-taking ceremonies did not seem to be quite as important to most of the widowers in this study. They gave less attention to the details and did not express as much gratitude toward the funeral directors. They were also more likely to feel that the cost of the funeral was too high. The emotional significance of the funeral itself may have been relatively less important for the men because they were primarily concerned with how they would manage in the months to come. The funeral and all that it involved was something that they had to "get through" rather than the milestone it represented for many widows. These differences of emphasis should not obscure the fact that the leave-taking ceremonies were important to all the bereaved, whether men or women.

Grief and Recovery: The First Year

And after the funeral? The study found what many have observed in their own lives: community, colleagues, neighbors, and relatives are all inclined to turn back quickly to their ordinary concerns. This has the effect of a turning away from the bereaved person. For a short time there is concentrated attention upon the needs of the bereaved. But the deceased spouse remains dead and the bereaved person's emotional and pragmatic problems continue day after day. The long months after the funeral often seem to be the most difficult ones for both widow and widower.

The widows in this study were left with the realization that they had to reorganize their lives, but now they lacked the clustering of help that had been available to them in the first days after bereavement. Most did not show much mourning behavior during this period but continued to grieve almost constantly. Typically, they would withdraw somewhat from ordinary social life to signify their mourning status but seldom did anything conspicuous to emphasize it. From this study it was not possible to determine how aware others were of the anguish that the widows continued to feel. The widows seemed to feel that they should not burden others with their sorrow. Here was another situation, then, in which the widows had to balance two impulses: to express their feelings outwardly and to avoid the impression of asking for sympathy. They felt that a "decent" amount of time had to pass before they could reenter ordinary life and yet did not feel comfortable with a full-blown expression of mourning such as is customary in some societies. The widow's rather quick departure from the role of mourner is further explored later in this chapter.

Some features of the internal process remained intense even though the outward and formal signs of expression quickly diminished. Many widows engaged in *obsessional review*. Events surrounding the husband's death were relived over and over. The women often realized that this process was taking up much of their time and energy. They wanted to turn off the obsessional review but often could not. The review seemed to perform a vital function for them. As Glick and his colleagues suggest, it may help the widow to integrate the realities of her loss into her ongoing life. Mulling over the death may not be a useless exercise but part of the recuperation process. This interpretation has similarities to Freud's (1919/1959) analysis of *grief work*. Freud believed that the bereaved person must slowly and systematically detach his or her intense feelings from everything that linked him or her with the deceased. This takes time and repeated effort. Although the concepts of obsessional review and grief work are not the same, both suggest that we should be more tolerant of the time required for a bereaved person to recuperate.

The obsessional reviews described in this study often were concerned with what *might* have happened instead of what actually did happen. How could the accident have been avoided? How might it all have turned out differently? In this way the review provided an outlet for temporary escape through fantasy but came back with renewed realization that there was in reality no way to undo the past.

Additionally, the widows frequently searched for meaning through these reviews. *Why* had their husband been taken away? This was more of a philosophical than a pragmatic quest. It was not the name of the disease or the technical reason for the accident that concerned the widow but the need to make sense of the death. If "Why me?" is the question some people ask when they learn of their own terminal illness, "Why *him*?" seems to be the survivor's parallel question. It is also one of the questions that a society's death system attempts to answer in general. It does not appear that American society at present offers much support to the individual who is trying to fathom either the "Why me?" or the "Why him?" question nor for that matter the more abstract "Why death—and why life?"

The passage of time and the psychosocial processes that accompany it often relieved these questions of some of their original intensity. The question of meaning may linger indefinitely, however. There did not seem to be any indication in this study that persuasive answers were found by the bereaved, at least within the time period encompassed.

Throughout the first year of grief and recovery most widows paid close attention to their own reactions. Although they could not overcome sorrow or put their lives back together simply by monitoring their feelings, this was a way of checking to see if they were making progress. About two months after the death, for example, many women judged that they were coming back from the earlier shock and turmoil. This sense of revitalization helped to reassure them as they continued to struggle with both the emotional and pragmatic consequences of bereavement.

Frequently, the widows were immersed in memories of their husbands. These were usually comforting thoughts. Although it remained painful to review the events leading up to the death, memories of the husband himself and of shared experiences generally were positive. This was especially true in the early weeks and months. A tendency to *idealize* the lost spouse was observed here as it has been in many other studies. The deceased husband was the best man who ever lived, a wonderful husband, a marvelous father—he had no faults whatsoever. Later a more balanced view usually emerged. The widow would still think about him frequently and positively, but now some of his quirks and imperfections gained recognition as well.

Surges of anger—sometimes very intense—occasionally broke in between the early tendency to idealize and the later, more balanced view. The widow might find herself suddenly angry at the husband, for example, for leaving her with the children to raise by herself. Some women then became even more upset when they caught themselves with harsh feelings toward the dead spouse and reacted with guilt or confusion. In general, however, these invasions of negative feelings into the idealized memories seemed to be part of the long process of developing a realistic attitude that the widow could live with through the years.

Often the widow's feelings about her husband went beyond vivid memories. She might have a strong sense that he was still there with her. This impression would make itself felt soon after the death or a few weeks later. Once the widow developed the experience of her husband's presence, it was likely to remain with her off and on for a long time. This sense of remaining in the presence of a significant person who has died has been observed by many other clinicians and researchers as well. The current study adds the finding that the sense of presence was especially persistent for women whose bereavement came without advance notice. The sudden loss of a spouse, allowing no opportunity for emotional preparation, seemed to lead to more extensive haunting experiences. For most of the widows it was comforting to feel that the husband was still there somehow. But even when the sense of his presence had all the vividness of hallucination, the widow knew the difference. She knew that her husband was really dead, even though her sense of his presence was also real in its own way. It was neither unusual nor crazy for a widow to feel this sense of presence.

During the first year of the widow's bereavement there was a gradual movement away from absorption in the loss and toward reconstruction of her life. This was not a smooth process by any means. By the end of a year, though, most of the widows had found more energy to channel into the obligations and opportunities of daily life. They might still experience episodes of anguish known only to themselves (e.g., when a situation reminded them poignantly of what they had lost). There was seldom a decisive severing of thoughts and feelings about the past. Instead, the widow continued to feel a sense of attachment to her deceased spouse but had called back

enough emotional energy to cope more adequately with her current life situation.

Widows with children at home usually recognized their responsibilities clearly and felt that the need to provide parental care helped to keep them from becoming lost in their own grief. They attempted to help the children feel that the world was still a good place, that life could and would go on. Often there was a new resolve to be a good mother. These efforts were complicated by conflicting needs and values: the widows felt the need to be straightforward and realistic with the children yet to shelter and protect them and keep their spirits up. The conflict would become acute in some situations, such as in trying to tell the children what had happened to their father and why. Often unable to answer that question themselves or to keep themselves from asking it, the widows were in a difficult position in trying to provide answers to their children. That the children were at various ages and levels of cognitive development also complicated the communication process.

The widowers in this study seemed to accept the reality of the death more rapidly and completely. Although the bereaved man was almost as likely to feel the presence of his wife soon after the bereavement, as time went by this phenomenon became much less common than it was for the widows. The man's need for control and realism expressed itself also in the tendency to cut off obsessional review after just a few weeks. The widower did not seem as tolerant of his impulse to dwell upon the past; he pushed himself right back to immediate realities, although, like the widow, he too felt a desire to replay the circumstances of the death.

What has often been noticed about the attitudes of men in American society showed up in the aftermath of bereavement as well. The widowers were not only control and reality oriented but also less likely to speak openly about their feelings. They did not usually seek out the opportunity to share either the events themselves or their personal reactions, although most men would respond to direct questions by the interviewers. Despite this more limited reaching out to others, the widowers did receive assistance from friends and kin. But their perceptions of sex-role differences confounded the problem. Instead of trying to help the widower with his sorrow or anxiety, the people who rallied around him emphasized practical deeds that would help him to manage the house and the children. In short, society responded to the widower by trying to replace some of the practical support he had received rather than providing him with an emotional outlet. Women most often were the providers of this kind of assistance.

Widowers expressed more independence and more sense of confidence in recovering from the loss by themselves, although they often did make use of the practical assistance offered to them. And when widows and widowers were compared at the same points in their bereavement, it usually *seemed* that the men were making a more rapid adjustment. However, the researchers had reason to doubt that the widowers were actually recovering more rapidly. It was true that they did return more quickly to their previous roles and functions; they were also even less likely than the widows to go through a period of conspicuous mourning. The typical widower gave no outward sign of his grief. Yet a close look at the quality of the widower's personal life, including the occupational sphere, indicated a decrease in energy, competence, and satisfaction. This was especially true when comparisons were made with nonbereaved men. The researchers were led to make a strong distinction between *emotional* and *social* recovery. The widower usually made a more rapid *social* recovery than the widow, but the evidence suggests that *emotional* recovery was slower for the men. The widower usually started to date again earlier than the widow, and the same was true of eventual remarriage. But this did not mean that he had worked through either his attachment to his former wife or the feelings stirred up since her death. The widower who had not sought female companionship a year after his wife's death was much more likely than the widow to feel lonely and depressed.

Types of Recovery from the Impact of Marital Bereavement

There were differences in the type of recovery made other than the gender differences already described. For example, although the death of a spouse made a strong impact whether or not the survivor had known it was imminent, the absence of an opportunity to prepare emotionally for marital bereavement had a major effect on the intensity and duration of the trauma. In his independent analysis of data from this study C. M. Parkes (1972) found that lack of preparation for the loss, especially in cases of death through accident or coronary thrombosis, was associated with poor recovery. After slightly more than a year had passed, the spouse who had experienced sudden, unexpected bereavement was more socially withdrawn than the person who had known in advance that the spouse would die. He or she remained more preoccupied with the details of the death, had more difficulty in accepting the reality of the loss, and in general was experiencing more disorganization in daily life. Such a person was likely to be anxious and have a pessimistic future outlook. Virtually every index of adjustment showed that lack of emotional preparation for marital bereavement was related to poor outcome.

From findings such as these it is obvious that much attention should be given to the situation of a man or woman who suffers sudden marital bereavement. The effects of bereavement per se are intensified by the shock of the unexpected. Furthermore, we cannot rely upon the passage of time by itself to facilitate good recuperation from the trauma. To acknowledge this is not to be fatalistic. Instead, we are in a better position to try to understand and help the person whose life is wrenched apart by the sudden death of a spouse. A study by Raymond G. Carey (1979), for example, provided further evidence that men and women whose spouses died with little or no advance warning had more difficulty in adjusting not only at the moment but also during the next year. This study added the finding, however, that follow-up visits by clergy and physicians were decidedly helpful to the survivors. Respondents in the Carey study further indicated that the help of neighbors had been very welcome in the early days after bereavement and would have continued to be welcome (the neighbors in this case, as in other studies, mostly withdrew from the scene after a short period of expressed concern).

Parkes also found that the response to early bereavement provides useful clues as to how the individual will respond as the months go by. Those who were most disturbed a few weeks after the death usually were the ones who continued to be disturbed a year later. The person who had strong feelings that the death was unreal and who tried to behave as though the spouse were still alive also was likely to have more difficulty than others over an extended time.

The death of a spouse by cancer often was associated with more rapid and less distress-ridden recovery of the survivor. This may be, as Parkes notes, because incurable cancer is a condition that provides time for both the terminally ill individual and the family to adjust to the prospect of death. (It should be understood that we are speaking here only of those people whose cancer proved fatal; it is erroneous to equate "cancer" in general with "terminal illness.")

The quality of the marital relationship had some bearing on the course of the grief and recovery process. When the partners had very mixed feelings toward each other, the experiences associated with bereavement often were more disturbing. Similarly, it was harder for the survivor to adjust if the relationship had been based on a clinging dependence. If soon after bereavement the surviving spouse felt cast adrift, empty, and helpless because the mate was no longer around to make life run properly, then difficulties in adjustment were likely to be more prolonged.

Recovery or Continued Despair?

The latest report from the Harvard Bereavement Study (Parkes & Weiss, 1983) includes follow-up interviews ranging from two to four years after the death of the spouse as well as a more extensive analysis of all the available data. The focus here will be on one of the central questions of the investigation: Why do some people make a strong recovery, while others continue to experience stress and difficulties in coping with life over a prolonged period? (And such difficulties, of course, can persist long beyond the four-year period encompassed by this study.)

Of the many questions asked of the participants, ten items proved most useful. The following areas were tapped by the ten most useful and productive questions:

1. Using tranquilizers
2. Smoking more heavily
3. Drinking more heavily
4. Considering it risky to fall in love
5. Wondering whether anything is worthwhile any more
6. Having sought help for emotional problems
7. Feeling that life is a strain
8. Feeling depressed
9. Feeling a lack of happiness
10. Wanting to change the way life is going now

Bereaved people as a group gave more responses in the direction of increased smoking and drinking, depression, and so on than comparison groups of the nonbereaved did. Furthermore, bereaved people with a preponderance of responses indicative of heightened stress or depression were considered to be having a more difficult time recovering.

One of the most important findings was that those who were making a strong recovery within a year of the loss were also those who were doing best several years later. This confirms earlier data from the study and suggests that efforts to provide assistance for those with particularly stressful responses to bereavement should begin rather soon.

The people who made a strong recovery generally had arrived at a clear understanding of what had happened and were therefore able to go on more easily with their lives. The arduous pro-

cess of reviewing events associated with the death of the spouse had finally been completed (or nearly so). People who were coping well had also made progress in achieving a revised identity. All of the bereaved people in this study had to face the question of who they are now, having lost part of their identities with the loss of their spouses. By contrast, those still in despair had not formed a conception of the death that they found coherent and acceptable, nor were they able to modify their self-images in preparation for a new life without the husband or wife.

But this differential pattern does not resolve the original question. Parkes and Weiss (1983) could discern a number of differences between those who had reintegrated their lives and those who had not. There was still the underlying question of why some people fell into one pattern and some into the other. Careful study of individual case histories led the investigators to the concept of *unresolved grief*. Parkes and Weiss found three syndromes, or types, of unresolved grief.

The *unexpected grief syndrome* occurs in some people when the spouse dies without warning; therefore they do not have the opportunity to prepare themselves for the overwhelming loss. Disbelief and intense anxiety often became not only the first but the continued response.

The *conflicted grief syndrome* can occur when death ends a relationship that had been rather troubled, often one in which separation or divorce had been contemplated. Some of the marriages in the study had been to alcoholic men whose behavior had created a climate of fear and disorder. Other marriages leading to the conflicted grief syndrome had been marked by depression and the withdrawal of the survivor. The unresolved grief experienced by survivors of a troubled marriage appears in a sense to be a continuation of the frustrations and disappointments that had characterized the relationship while the spouse was alive.

The *chronic grief syndrome* is marked by the survivor's strong feelings of dependency. Although some distress may be experienced around the time of the death, the more compelling and lasting response is a deep sense of yearning for the lost one. Yearning for the deceased is often a part of any grief experience, but for people with this syndrome it becomes predominant. Parkes and Weiss conclude that the type of intractable distress suggested by the term *chronic grief syndrome* arises from the survivor's unusually powerful dependence on the deceased spouse. The survivor does not feel personally capable of taking on the responsibilities of life with his or her partner gone.

Awareness of the nature of the marriage relationship that has been sundered by death and by the circumstances of the death itself (sudden or anticipated) could, then, improve our ability to identify those who are at particular risk for intense and prolonged distress.

Whatever the particular circumstances of the death, however, the grief process can be so disabling that the bereaved person is essentially out of commission for an extended time. Suicide attempts and severe depressive reactions requiring psychiatric treatment are among the risks. There is a need to distinguish between "normal" bereavement—enough of an ordeal itself—and responses that are exceptionally intense, debilitating, or prolonged. Most of the bereaved men and women in the Harvard study made their way through their distress without reaching extremes of despair or self-destructiveness. But there are others whose vulnerability increased so much that the concept of grief as disease appeared applicable. Parkes (1972) elaborates on this concept from a social perspective:

> Illnesses are characterized by the discomfort and the disturbance of function that they produce. Grief may not produce physical pain but it is very unpleasant and it usually disturbs function. Thus a newly bereaved person is often treated by society in much the same way as a sick person. Employers expect him to miss work, he stays at home, and relatives visit and talk in hushed tones. . . . On the whole, grief resembles a physical injury more closely than any other type of illness. The loss may be spoken of as a "blow." As in the case of a physical

injury the "wound" gradually heals; at least, it usually does. But occasionally complications set in, healing is delayed, or a further injury reopens a healing wound. In such cases abnormal forms arise, which may even be complicated by the onset of other types of illness. Sometimes . . . the outcome may be fatal.

In many respects, then, grief can be regarded as an illness. But it can also bring strength. Just as broken bones may end up stronger than unbroken bones, so the experience of grieving can strengthen and bring maturity to those who have previously been protected from misfortune. The pain of grief is just as much a part of life as the joy of love; it is, perhaps, the price we pay for love, the cost of commitment. To ignore this fact, or to pretend that it is not so, is to put on emotional blinkers which leave us unprepared for the losses that will inevitably occur in our own lives and unprepared to help others to cope with the losses in theirs. (pp. 5–6)

BEREAVEMENT AND THE CHILD

We have just examined in some detail how adults grieve and attempt to reintegrate their lives after the death of a spouse. Death does not spare children, either. How do children respond to the death of a parent or sibling? And how does the family respond when it is a child who has died? We begin with the situation of the child who has lost a family member through death.

The Bereaved Child

A death in the family can draw attention and energy away from the needs of the children. When one parent dies, for example, the surviving parent's grief can interfere with the ability to care for the emotional or even the physical needs of the children. While some newly bereaved women try to make their relationships with the children a core around which their lives can be steadied and reorganized, often it is difficult for lone parents to manage both their own sorrow and the needs of their children.

Sometimes it is a sibling who dies. In this situation the parents may be so involved in the plight of the dying child that other children are neglected. The surviving child is apt to face two sources of stress. First, he or she may be deprived of some of the normal support expected from the parents because of their own involvement in the bereavement. (He or she may not be as well protected from accidents, for example, or given sufficient access to a loving, receptive parent.) Second, the child has his or her own bereavement response to suffer through. The child may feel isolated in his or her own distress if the adults in the situation fail to appreciate his or her level of understanding or to read his or her bereavement response accurately. The sensitive adult will take into account both the child's developmental level and the role that the deceased person had played in the child's life. What did this child understand about separation and death? Was he or she in a transitional period of thinking in which the difference between permanent and temporary loss by death was still elusive? Or had the child recently discovered that death is final and universal? The developmental considerations explored in Chapter 7 are also relevant. The specific meaning of the loss must also be understood. Was the deceased person an older sibling whom the child had looked up to? Was the deceased a younger sibling whom the child had resented as a competitor for parental attention?

Furthermore, the quality of the child's personal and family situation before the bereavement deserves consideration. Had this been a tightly knit family and did the child have a strong sense of love and security? Was it a broken or bent family characterized by anxiety and insecurity? These are among the questions that are worth examining in every individual situation. The impact of bereavement depends to some extent upon the child's developmental level, the specific loss that has been experienced, and the previous pattern of family security and affection.

The bereaved child may express distress in ways that do not seem closely associated with the loss. Serious problems in school may appear for the first time. The child may turn on playmates with sudden anger. Fear of the dark or of being alone may reappear. There are many ways in which the child's life pattern can show the effect of bereavement without an obvious show of sorrow. In fact, when the surviving parent tells the children they should be "brave" and keeps his or her own tears hidden from them, they may find it difficult to express their feelings openly.

Studies of bereaved children who have lost a parent have found some types of response that might often be overlooked. Erna Furman and her colleagues (1974), for example, have observed that young children tend to express their memories of a lost parent through specific activities that were associated with him or her. An adult can preserve a valued relationship by replaying memories in private or sharing them with others. But a two-year-old boy who loses his father is more likely to express his longing and sadness over the death through actions.

> For weeks he spent much of his time repeating the daily play activities that had constituted the essence of his relationship with his father. He also insisted, over and over, on taking the walks he had taken with his father, stopping at the stores where his father had shopped and recalled specific items. (p. 55)

The toddler's need added to the mother's emotional pain, but she recognized that it was the best way he had to adjust to the loss.

The memory of children is more likely to be focused on a relatively few strong images, in contrast to the bereaved spouse who has many recollections from all the years of marriage. The young child carries much of the remembrance of the lost parent in the form of highly cathected (emotionally invested) scenes and activities. Years after the death the child may suddenly be overwhelmed with sadness when he or she encounters a situation that touches off a now precious memory.

Furman and her colleagues were surprised to learn how long bereaved children were capable of experiencing and bearing up under their emotional suffering. The mental image of the lost parent remained with them. This is important to

keep in mind. Adults sometimes make it easier on themselves by assuming that a child forgets easily, forgets even a significant death. The child may contribute to this assumption by his or her own apparent lack of grief and mourning by adult standards. The child goes back to watching television, a behavior that suggests to the adult that he or she probably doesn't understand what has happened. This assumption is contradicted by most clinicians and researchers who have observed childhood bereavement in detail. Although "some children could bear an astonishing amount of pain alone . . . most needed a loved person who could either share their grief or empathize with them and support their tolerance and expression of affect" (p. 57). The silent sadness of the bereaved child can be painful for the adult to share. But how are we to support and comfort unless we can accept the reality of the child's suffering?

It can be even more difficult to accept the child's response when it includes anger at the deceased. The surviving parent may be horrified to hear criticisms of the deceased parent coming from the children. This may happen precisely at the time the widowed spouse is at the peak of idealizing the lost husband or wife. And yet such expressions may be a necessary part of the child's adaptation to the loss. They do not mean that the child does not love and miss the lost parent—quite the opposite. One of the reasons some adults find it very painful to accept the child's expression of mixed feelings toward the deceased is that these feelings are within them as well. Whoever helps a bereaved spouse express grief openly and begin the long process of recovery is also helping the children by returning the strength and sensitivity of their remaining parent.

Most studies of children's parental bereavement have concentrated on the loss of the father, limiting the conclusions that can be drawn. A careful review of the research literature has found several consistent differences in the behavior of children who have suffered paternal bereavement as compared with children with both parents living (Berlinsky & Biller, 1982). The bereaved children tended to be more submissive, dependent, and introverted. As a group they showed a higher frequency of maladjustment and emotional disturbance, including suicidality. They were also somewhat more likely to display delinquent and criminal behavior. To make a bad situation worse, the bereaved children also tended to perform less adequately in school and on tests of cognitive functioning.

Age at time of bereavement has been shown to be an important variable. Younger children (seven years old and younger) tend to have more difficulties adjusting after bereavement, perhaps in part because at that early developmental phase they do not have a clear understanding of death.

This general pattern does not mean that all bereaved children will experience the difficulties mentioned. The surviving parent and other social supports can help to insulate the child, as can the personal resources the child has already developed. Nevertheless, bereavement from a parent's death must be regarded as a potential problem in many areas of a child's life.

The effects of childhood bereavement are not limited to childhood. Loss of a significant person in childhood can have an important effect on subsequent development. Major physical and mental illnesses occur more often in the adult lives of those who were bereaved as children.

Robert Bendiksen and Robert Fulton (1975) followed up on 256 men and women who had participated in a study more than 30 years before. Children whose parents had divorced when the children were young showed many of the problems usually characteristic of those bereaved in childhood. Both groups had experienced more difficulties than those who grew up in intact homes. In some ways the children of divorced parents seemed to have had a worse time. They were described by Bendiksen and Fulton as "double victims." In addition to the loss of normal family interactions and support, they were exposed to issues of guilt and blame and to a separation and desertion that lacked the conclusive end and explanation of death. This study is a reminder that bereavement is not the only form

of significant loss nor in every instance the most devastating. Nevertheless, evidence continues to accumulate that the child who suffers loss by death of one or more parents is likely to be more vulnerable to emotional and physical problems throughout all of adult life than the child who does not.

Many clinicians have observed that the effect of bereavement sometimes shows up most strikingly at a particular point in adult life that harks back to the time of the bereavement. The little girl whose mother dies may become depressed, suicidal, and desperate when she has reached the point of becoming the mother of a little girl herself (Moriarty, 1967). Josephine Hilgard and her colleagues studied such *anniversary reactions* in adults who had suffered either paternal or sibling bereavement when young (Hilgard, 1969; Hilgard & Newman, 1959). Enough examples of this phenomenon were discovered to merit continued alertness to the long-delayed as well as the quickly seen effects of bereavement.

One of the examples concerned a distinguished lawyer. When Matthew was 12 years old, his brother died suddenly and unexpectedly of encephalitis. The older brother had been a brilliant student who conformed to adult expectations and wishes, whereas Matthew had barely passed his classes and showed a belligerent attitude. The mother of these boys placed great emphasis on education. With the older son gone, she took special interest in Matthew. Psychological testing revealed that he was much brighter than people had been assuming. He went on to an outstanding career that was still on its way up until he poisoned himself on the day after *his* boy, Matthew, Jr., celebrated his 12th birthday. Later it was learned that the suicide victim had told people he felt guilty because his success came only as a result of his brother's death. Had his brother lived, then Matthew would have been a failure, perhaps a criminal. Instead he became a criminal lawyer, a career choice that might easily be interpreted as a defense against his own early antisocial tendencies (Hilgard, 1969). The whole story, then, is not told in the first few weeks or months after bereavement.

Darwin: Child and Man

A story with a very different outcome provides a contrast. All his life Charles Darwin retained the memory of his mother's deathbed, her black velvet gown, and the worktable but hardly anything of her appearance and his conversations with her. His memory of his mother's death when he was eight years old was vivid but fragmentary: he remembered being sent for, going into her room, being greeted by his father, crying afterward. Yet Darwin had much more detailed recollections of the funeral of a soldier that he attended a few weeks later.

Ralph Colp, Jr. (1975), one of many who have examined the role of developmental influences on Darwin's personality and career, was struck by the apparent repression of many of his memories of his mother and her death when details of the soldier's death remained fresh in Darwin's mind. Colp finds that death-related themes were closely interwoven with Darwin's work throughout his life. Even Darwin's dreams and his notes in the margins of books have been analyzed as part of the psychological detective work. One of the major themes disclosed was a "keen instinct against death." Colp and others believe there is a connection between Darwin's ardent advocacy of life and his fascination with the generation of new life forms (evolution). Darwin's own observations confronted him with a challenge both on the personal and the scientific level. His growing perception that there might be a process of *natural selection* in which entire species became extinguished—a form of mass slaughter—resonated with the feelings he still carried from the time of his mother's death (and other early life bereavements). At about the middle of his life he expressed fear of sudden death and regarded his theory as an indirect form of continued personal survival. Darwin had more bereavements to suffer in his adult life, notably the death of his much-loved daughter, Annie.

Above all, Darwin's personal experiences with death and his scientific perspective on the destruction of entire species contributed to an ardent love of life. Unable to believe in any doctrine of survival of death, Darwin had to bear with his own "intolerable vision of slow and cold death—death irrevocably, and finally, ascendant over all life" (p. 200). Yet he also had the example of his father to inspire him. The elder Darwin had lived to age 83 with a lively mind right up to the end; vivid memories of a father admirable throughout a long life seemed to help sustain him during the course of a life's work that was so burdened with death-related experiences and observations.

Near the end of his life Darwin felt too ill to pursue major research, but he returned to the first creatures that interested him as a young boy—worms. As a child he enjoyed fishing and had mixed feelings about sacrificing worms. As an elderly man Darwin did little studies on the feeding of worms. In Colp's words, "Thus, the old man, who as a boy had killed worms, now, 'night after night,' observed how he would soon be eaten by worms" (p. 200). This line of thinking was not as unrelievedly morbid as it might sound. It was after all a continuation of Darwin's incessant fascination with life and death. Scientist Darwin respected worms as coinhabitants of planet Earth, who in fact have a key role in maintaining the living ecology by literally passing the earth through themselves. That he, too, Charles Darwin, would become part of the worm and part of the earth again was not a cliché or a horror story but an acceptable part of the natural functioning of the world.

• • •

Ten thousand examples would provide ten thousand different stories of the direct and indirect ways in which childhood bereavement influences the entire life course. One person cannot shake off unresolved feelings of guilt about the death of a sibling during childhood and commits suicide (thereby passing a tremendous burden on to his surviving son); another young boy goes on to make scientific contributions of the first magnitude based in part on feelings engendered by the loss of his mother in his childhood. The impact of childhood bereavement should not be interpreted in a simplistic manner, but neither should it be neglected for both its short- and long-range influence on the developing individual.

THE FAMILY THAT HAS LOST A CHILD

Beyond Endurance is the title Ronald J. Knapp (1986) selected for his book on the death of children. Many would agree that losing a child to death is one of the most painful of all human experiences. The immediate anguish may be followed by many years of sorrow. Acquaintances of grieving family members are almost certain to observe the powerful impact that follows soon after a child's death. What neighbors and colleagues might not realize, however, is that the distress continues long beyond this acute phase and that the lives of the grieving family members may be altered in many ways.

When the emotional response to a loss remains a dominant aspect of a person's life over a long period of time it is sometimes referred to as "chronic grief." This is a useful term from the descriptive standpoint. It does differentiate between the intense immediate response (acute grief) and the variety of continuing and changing responses that sometimes can persist throughout the remainder of the person's life. Unfortunately, however, "chronic" is often taken to mean that a condition is unalterable and permanent. It might then seem that a family suffering prolonged grief after the death of a child is destined to remain in this painful state forever. But this is not necessarily true. There is no reason to rule out in advance the possibility that chronic grief can be relieved and the survivors once again find meaning and pleasure in life—although never forgetting their loss and never being quite the same.

The sorrow of a child's death often seems to follow a family like a shadow. After observing the reactions of mothers who had lost a baby before or soon after birth, Peppers and Knapp (1980) introduced the term, *shadow grief*. Years after the death, many of the mothers were still feeling the anguish. In a later study, Knapp (1986) found the same phenomenon among parents who had lost older children to death. They were no longer completely dominated by grief, but the shadow or cloud had a way of making itself known as they moved through life. Knapp offers a description of this state of mind:

> Shadow grief does not manifest itself overtly; it does not debilitate; no effort is required to cope with it. On the surface most observers would say that the "grief work" has been accomplished. But this is not the case. Shadow grief reveals itself more in the form of an emotional "dullness," where the person is unable to respond fully and completely to outer stimulation and where normal activity is moderately inhibited. It is characterized as a dull ache in the background of one's feelings that remains fairly constant and that, under certain circumstances and on certain occasions, comes bubbling to the surface, sometimes in the form of tears, sometimes not, but always accompanied by a feeling of sadness and a mild sense of anxiety. . . . (pp. 40–41)

Knapp's findings are consistent with the observations that many others have made; parents who have lost a child often feel that their own lives also changed at that moment. Furthermore, they may not want to relinquish the grief. The pain is part of the memory—and the memory is precious. Few people would choose to experience the intense anguish of acute grief. But the twinge of sorrow and the sharp but passing pain of memory may be something that both the individual and the family need to keep their lives whole (or as whole as they can be) following the loss of a child.

It is significant that shadow grief was first recognized in a study of mothers who had lost newborn infants. The death of so young a child is often given relatively little attention by society. The lack of communal recognition and support tends to leave the parents (especially the mother) alone in their grief. Some newspapers even prohibit publication of newborn death notices and there are no sympathy cards on the market for this specific loss (Nichols, 1989). It is difficult to reconcile society's pattern of neglect of *perinatal death* with both the intensity of the parents' grief and the number of people who suffer such loss. This term, perinatal death, refers to infants who die at any point from the 20th week after conception through the first month after birth. Premature birth is still the most common cause of perinatal death, although advances in medical and nursing techniques have saved some neonates who otherwise would have died. Deaths also occur for a variety of other reasons (e.g., a genetic defect or a prenatal infection), and sometimes for reasons that are never clearly determined. We cannot exclude socioeconomic causes, either. Even in the United States—a technologically advanced society whose resources are the envy of much of the world— many pregnant women do not have access to perinatal health services. Others do not seem to realize that such services are available and could improve the odds in favor of a healthy mother and a healthy baby. State and local health agencies often are underfunded for perinatal health services, another indication of society's lagging recognition or concern for death and grief at the very beginning of life.

Grief over a perinatal death is similar in many respects to grief over any loss. There are, however, some circumstances and consequences that are more likely to be present. For example, the mother may still be sedated or exhausted at the time she learns of her child's death. She is also likely to be ready to mother her baby, both physically and emotionally. This total readiness, including lactation to provide breast milk, now has no opportunity to express itself directly. Another significant problem can arise in families that have other children. As Nichols observes:

> The cliche "you have your other children" suggests that the other children are a source of comfort and perhaps could even take the place of the one who has died. Frequently nothing could be further from the truth for grieving parents. No other child replaces the one who died. Further, children can intrude upon the grief of parents simply because they are naturally being themselves. In addition, many parents do not know how to tell their children about the baby's illness or death, nor do they know how to help the children. (p. 120)

Sensitive caregivers have learned that their first step is to recognize that a significant loss has occurred (or is about to occur, if the infant is still alive but not expected to survive). It is difficult if not impossible to be helpful to the parents and siblings unless caregivers and friends are themselves able to comprehend the meaning of this loss. There have been particularly effective responses by some nurses and physicians in situations where the mother and baby are still in the hospital, but the baby is almost certain to die soon. The family is encouraged to interact with the infant in a natural and loving way. Photographs may be taken of parents holding the baby, and various memorabilia (such as the child's first footprints or a lock of hair) given to them. It is encouraging to report that some physicians have taken leadership in developing "bereavement protocols" that help to prepare the entire staff to provide emotional support for family members (Weinfeld, 1990).

At whatever age it occurs, the death of a child not only brings the direct emotional pain associated with this loss, but can also unsettle the parents' overall philosophy of life. It is not unusual for religious people to wonder why God would allow such a thing to happen, and to follow this with anger or doubt. The perceived link between past, present, and future may also be disturbed. We usually expect "the next generation" to be just that. In some cultures, one of the strongest motivations for having children in the first place is to project the "family soul" ahead into future generations and thereby alleviate the parental generation's own death anxiety (Kastenbaum, 1974). If issues of this kind remain unsettled they can generate additional tension within the family, sometimes contributing to separation or divorce.

There are now a number of useful readings available for those who wish to be sensitive caregivers and friends to people who have suffered the death of a child. *Parental Grief. Solace and Resolution* (Klass, 1988) discusses the contributions of The Compassionate Friends, a self-help group that has chapters in many parts of the United States. *Disenfranchised Grief* (Doka,

1989) devotes several valuable chapters to the loss of a child. *A Child Dies. A Portrait of Family Grief* (Arnold & Gemma, 1983) offers many illuminating excerpts from grieving families as well as the authors' own observations. These readings and many others make it clear that there are many ways in which the community can be helpful to the family that is grieving the loss of a child. It might be said that we would not really be a community at all if families were isolated and abandoned during this harrowing time.

BEREAVEMENT IN LATER LIFE

Sorrow upon Sorrow, Loss upon Loss

Older adults often experience as much life satisfaction (and sometimes more) than their juniors (Schaie & Geiwitz, 1982). It is a careless error to perpetuate the myth that usefulness and the enjoyment of life end at a certain age. Nevertheless, it is also true that the longer a person lives and forms loving attachments, the more there is to lose. This is the concept of *bereavement overload* (Kastenbaum, 1969).

Elderly men and women are more likely to develop a condition in which sorrow has been heaped upon sorrow, loss upon loss. The long-lived person is more apt to have survived many people to whom he or she was deeply attached. Furthermore, there are personally significant losses other than death that can lead to grief responses. Loss of physical abilities, employment, social respect, and familiar environments are all life changes that can trigger responses similar to what occurs when an interpersonal relationship is terminated by death. Elderly people tend to accumulate such losses, one on top of the other.

It is possible that many of the dysphoric and maladaptive behavior patterns sometimes associated with old age have much more to do with bereavement overload than with biological changes intrinsic to old age as such.

What changes would we expect in a person (of any age) who has been forced to contend with too many losses in too short a period of time? He might attempt to reconstitute his personal world by replacing the losses. This process often requires a great deal of time even under the best of circumstances. And if there were *no* appropriate replacements available (as in the death of a life-long friend), then his response would have to take another form. One might lose himself in work or other engrossing activities, at least until the burden has lightened. But this alternative often is closed to the elderly. What now? The person may simply take these emotional blows "on the chin." I am referring here to the process of developing bodily symptoms when grief cannot be handled adequately by the psychological structure. The person becomes increasingly preoccupied with bodily functions, often is in a state of discomfort, seldom has free energy to invest in new activities or relationships. Furthermore, the experience of multiple losses may lead to a sense of extreme caution. "I had better not care about anybody or anything else. Sooner or later I will lose these people and things as well. And I just cannot bear to lose and mourn again." (Kastenbaum, 1969, pp. 48–49)

The whole constellation of "old behaviors," then, could develop from multiple, unbearable bereavement. Suicide attempts, both direct and indirect, might well be generated from such a psychological state. The individual may give up when stricken by a relatively minor ailment and allow the condition to worsen or reduce his or her activities so drastically that both body and mind are in poor tone to respond to any kind of stress. Such considerations suggest that bereavement in old age is a condition deserving careful and systematic attention.

Loss, Loneliness, Illness

Loneliness is possibly the most critical problem for the bereaved adult. Many elderly people experience loneliness from a variety of circumstances (e.g., less opportunity to stay in contact with people important to them because of financial or transportation factors). Additional bereavement in old age can intensify the existing sense of loneliness and contribute further to the exacerbation of many physical problems.

The older person is vulnerable to deaths of many kinds—not only the death of the spouse, but siblings, adult children, grandchildren, and even parents. I have stood at the side of a 74-year-old man as tears ran down his cheeks because his 97-year-old father was dead. The outsider might rush to the conclusion that the death of a very old parent should not mean so much to a child also advanced in years. Consider, however, how long this relationship had to develop and flourish and what a blow it now was to go on without the father he had known for three quarters of a century. Parent-child bonds may continue strongly for many decades. When death severs the pair, the grief can be sharp and devastating. Not to be overlooked is the death of (or forced separation from) a beloved pet. On several occasions I have discovered that an elderly patient with whom I was working first sank into a depressed, no-point-in-living state following the death of a pet.

Depressive states in later life can develop for a variety of reasons, and bereavement is certainly among them. Clinicians and all those who work with the elderly are well advised to be aware of the connection between bereavement, depression, illness, and suicidal tendencies in later life (Andreasen, 1983; Kastenbaum, 1983; Richards & McCallum, 1979; Salzman, 1983).

However, the overall picture is not entirely negative. Many elderly men and women have proven themselves quite resilient when tested by loss. This impression is supported by a number of studies. For example, Lund (1989) has found in his own research that older widowed persons often have effective coping abilities that help them to get on with their lives even though they regard the death of their spouse as having been the most stressful event they have ever experienced. This is consistent with the results of several other studies that have followed the same people throughout their adult lives. After several months of considerable stress after the death of their spouse, many elderly persons are able to restore order and hope to their lives. An additional finding is of particular interest. Practical problems of day-by-day functioning are apt to be especially difficult for the older bereaved person; assistance with home repairs, financial transactions, transportation and other "little things" can make the difference between staying at home and living independently or being forced into a more dependent lifestyle.

The elderly bereaved person often has a wealth of experience and skills that can not only be applied to reintegrating his or her own life, but also to enrich the lives of others. Often this person needs only positive human companionship and a little help with some of the details of everyday life in order to continue as a resourceful and well integrated member of society.

THE INDIVIDUAL, THE SITUATION, AND GRIEF

The individual and the situation should be considered in any attempt to understand the response to bereavement. Recent studies and clinical observations have contributed to this understanding.

Individual Differences in Response to Bereavement

Freud (1919/1959) and other psychoanalysts have suggested that grief and mourning can become severe enough to be considered psychopathological. The individual is overwhelmed and debilitated, unable to function. Furthermore, time does not bring relief. The period of intense mourning continues for years and does not move toward resolution. Buy why?

As already shown, the nature of the relationship between the survivor and the deceased can generate some of the difficulty (Parkes & Weiss, 1983). Horowitz and his colleagues (1980) found that "a major cause of pathological grief appears to be the reemergence of earlier self-images and role relationship models . . . News of the loss activates these usually dormant organizers of mental life" (p. 1159). Negative thoughts and feelings that usually remain in the realm of the

unconscious now break into awareness and interfere with daily life. In other words, some people
carry with them an unusually strong predisposition to become "frighteningly sad." The bereavement experience strikes a deep chord of fear
within them. The survivor feels as helpless and
dependent as a lost child. This extra measure of
vulnerability derives from insecurities and conflicts in earlier relationships, usually with the
parents. The new loss, then, arouses preexisting
anxieties. It impels the survivor to think that he
or she really is as worthless or helpless as once
seemed to be the case many years before. Because
this sense of helplessness is so disturbing, the
individual may engage in periodic episodes of intense rage. The alternation between a sense of
worthlessness and explosive rage makes progress
through grief and mourning very difficult indeed.
Fortunately, both traditional and cognitively oriented psychotherapy (Beck, 1976) can prove
helpful in restoring the individual's sense of
worth and competence.

Extremes of physical and psychosocial distress
after bereavement can usually be identified
clearly, but there remains a range of individual
differences that is too often obscured by generalizations. One of the most useful attempts to
examine this question freshly is provided in recent and continuing work by Catherine M.
Sanders (1977; 1979). She notes:

> [There is] a tendency to think in such terms as
> "good grief," "bad grief," "pathological grief," even
> "sick grief." The use of these expressions suggests
> that bereavement itself is a malady, from which the
> bereaved person must be extricated or cured. And
> the sooner the better. This stereotypic notion of the
> way people experiencing grief should behave places
> unrealistic limitations on the need to cope in their
> own characteristic ways. This notion also presup-
> poses, quite erroneously, that all persons possess
> equal quantities of those elements which go into
> individual personalities—elements such as ego
> strength, optimism, frustration tolerance, and emo-
> tionality." (Sanders, 1977, p. 14)

Sanders' research involved interviews with
men and women who had lost a spouse, parent,

or child within the previous three months. The
Minnesota Multiphasic Personality Inventory
(MMPI) was used to help classify respondents'
general coping styles, and a Grief Experience Inventory was used to assess specific feelings and
behaviors since bereavement. The participants
were seen again between 18 and 24 months after
bereavement. Sanders found four distinct types
of bereavement patterns: (1) a disturbed group,
(2) a depressed, high-grief group, (3) a denial
group, and (4) a normal, grief-controlled group.
The latter group, it should be emphasized, was
not made up of emotionally cold or bland
people—they had strong feelings of loss and sorrow also but were able both to express their feelings and move ahead with their lives. Each of
these groups showed a relationship between general style of coping with life problems and the
way in which they tried to cope with bereavement in particular. Furthermore, each group
showed a characteristic pattern of response to
grief over time. Some people, for example,
showed a general pattern of trying to maintain a
"stiff upper lip," covering up any signs of weakness, shortcomings, or distress (based on MMPI
scores). Those who used these denying types of
coping strategies were of particular interest because of the assumption that people will break
down if they fail to talk about their grief or ven-
tilate their emotions. This danger did not seem
to materialize. Most of the "stiff upper lippers"
had their grief responses under reasonable control both at the time of initial contact and two
years later. The normal group showed reductions
in level of grief intensity over the two-year period, whereas most of the disturbed group remained almost as anxious as they had been soon
after bereavement. The depressed participants
were also still experiencing symptoms usually associated with acute grief after two years had passed
but were making some progress. Many of these
people were beset by continued or new forms of
stress that made it particularly difficult for them
to work through the grief experience itself.

Another provocative finding by Sanders was
that the type of person seemed to be more

important than the type of bereavement. How the individual coped with stress in his or her life in general proved to be more closely related to bereavement outcome 24 months later than did the specific nature of the bereavement (the death of a child, parent, or spouse).

In general this study indicates that it can be quite misleading to set a time limit for grief and expect all people to be at a certain level of recovery at a particular point. Individual life-styles must be respected and taken carefully into account. This has implications not only for the distinction between so-called normal and pathological grief but also for our general interventions and expectations. Not everybody, for example, seems to have a powerful need to open up and discharge feelings generated by bereavement, even though the need is strong for many people. It might, then, be as inappropriate to try to force certain people to open up and express their grief directly as it is to demand that other people keep their feelings under tight control. While continued research refines our understanding in this area, it remains for each of us to be sensitive to the unique personalities of the particular bereaved people we encounter rather than to apply a rigid, formulated approach.

The prevailing social climate seems to favor the denying type of response more than the expressive. The widower is reducing his colleagues' anxieties when he goes right back to work and gives no indication that he expects special concern. "I am OK," he is saying in effect, "I am not mourning." The widow releases others from the more obvious forms of obligation by refraining from displays of mourning. "She's a strong woman," her friends say with admiration. The bereaved person among us tends to be more socially acceptable if signs of mourning are set aside. But the absence of mourning behaviors too easily gives the illusion that the person is "over" the grief action. This may be one of the reasons why some bereaved people have fears of going crazy. All of the anxiety and confusion, all the depths of feeling, seem to be on the inside. The rest of the world continues to move along in its

usual way. With little social recognition or tolerance for grieving, the individual can be made to feel as though his or her responses were abnormal or pathological.

Situational Differences in Bereavement Response

It has been thought for some time that a sudden death creates more distress for the survivor. Another study by Sanders (1982–1983) supports this observation. She interviewed and administered the MMPI to people who had experienced bereavement under one of three circumstances: sudden death, long-term chronic illness, and short-term chronic illness. Those experiencing the sudden death of a loved one seemed to carry an extra burden of physical stress over a prolonged time. They reported more symptoms indicating an "anger-in," or self-punishing, orientation than did survivors of those who died of long-term or short-term illnesses. High blood pressure, colds, influenza, arthritis, infections, chest pain, and skin allergies were among the physical conditions that afflicted survivors of sudden death more frequently.

Those who had lost a loved one after a long illness expressed an "anger-out," or hostile, response. After 18 months many of them were still dejected, frustrated, and lonely, but they no longer felt physical signs of stress and strain. Those whose bereavement came after a short-term illness at first held themselves together in an attempt to maintain socially acceptable behavior. Nevertheless, they did encounter difficulties later as the realization of the death set in more forcefully. It was not unusual for these bereaved people to lose some of their coping abilities while struggling with their feelings. Despite their problems, however, those who had experienced the death of a loved one through a short-term chronic illness generally showed the greatest degree of recovery after 18 months. The side effects of stress had diminished appreciably. Sanders believes one reason for their relatively strong recovery was because "the short time between onset of illness and death had not been so long that friends had drifted away" (p. 237).

Much remains to be learned about both individual and situational factors in bereavement, and both must be given careful consideration.

SUPPORT FOR THE BEREAVED

American Society's Discomfort with Grief and Mourning

One test of how well a culture's death system is functioning can be made by examining the support it provides for the bereaved. There are some signs that American society at present does not pass this test.

The men in the Harvard Bereavement Study did little to show the world that they were suffering the impact of a spouse's death. This seems to be in keeping with a mass, efficiency-oriented society. Mourning gets in the way. It may not seem to serve any real purpose. Pressures have been increasing against the expression of loss in many forms. There are still places in the United States where people will stop what they are doing when a funeral procession goes by. Pedestrians stand in respectful silence and motorists wait patiently, whether or not they know the identity of the deceased. But the funeral procession is a target of efficiency practitioners in many metropolitan areas. Abolition or restriction of this practice has been urged because it slows traffic. Similarly, there are pressures against the use of land for cemeteries. In some parts of the United States it is now almost impossible to open new cemeteries, and existing cemeteries have been criticized as wasteful and out of step with the times.

Memorialization of the dead and support for the bereaved have fallen relatively low on the list of priorities of the American death system. People still gather around for the funeral—often with reluctance—and for a short period of ritual and visiting. After that, however, the bereaved is frequently left alone. How long do colleagues sympathize with somebody who has suffered a significant loss? How long are relatives and neighbors prepared to be sensitive and support-

ive? I have noticed an increasing impatience with grief. The mourner is supposed to shape up after a short time and let others get on with their lives. In this cultural context it is not surprising to come across a doctoral dissertation featuring a "prescribed degriefing intervention method (DIM)" that requires but a single treatment session! (DiMeo, 1978) DIM, indeed! Quicker is cheaper, better, more cost-effective. But are we really prepared to line up for "degriefing" when overcome by profound sorrow and loss?

The potential conflict between the individual's need and society's demands can express itself in the very practical question: "How much time should a person be allowed to grieve before returning to work?" We live in a society that emphasizes time rather relentlessly. The invention of the clock made it possible to measure time precisely and divide it into units of standard length. The Catholic Church was quick to use the clock to reinforce the discipline of monastery life. The belfry clock symbolized the subordination of the individual to higher authority. The subsequent rise of industrialization and science resulted in the further refinement of time and the heightened general emphasis on schedules and deadlines (O'Malley, 1990). Soon we had "efficiency experts" among us. They measured the worker's effectiveness in carrying out a specified task and then tried to find ways to increase productivity per unit of time. Charlie Chaplin's experience with the wonderful new feeding machine in his classic film *Modern Times* illustrates the depersonalizing effects of industrialized time. An often bitter and sometimes violent succession of labor-management confrontations was required before the workday and workweek were reduced to their present dimensions. We still are influenced by our heritage of conflict regarding "company time" and "personal time."

What does all this have to do with death? Sociologist Lois Pratt (1981) has herself studied "grief by negotiation" in 40 large companies and has also drawn upon other sources of information on more than 600 other companies. She finds that there had once been a tradition of management granting bereavement leave as a matter of judgment and discretion. The new trend, however, is to specify bereavement leave as part of the formal agreements between management and labor. This means that how much time off a person will be allowed for bereavement depends largely on the monetary value computed for this time. Pratt reports, "Although bereavement leave is a minor cost item in the overall benefits structure, it is handled in the same way as all benefits—within a cost framework" (p. 322).

Suppose now there is a death in the family. The grieving survivor will have distinctive personal feelings about the loss and may also have distinctive responsibilities to perform in the immediate period after the death. These personal matters, however, do not figure into the union-management agreement. What does count is the monetary equivalent of the time to which the survivor is entitled. And so we now have an answer to our question: it is acceptable to grieve for three days after the death of specified people. The standard policy is for leave to begin after the death, not while the dying person is still alive. "Sorry Dad—I'll be back when you're dead." Some contracts have become very specific about the arrangements. For example, if the death occurs on a Saturday, be back to work on Tuesday. It may be a better plan for the death to occur on Tuesday; the survivor is not expected back until the next Monday.

Strictly speaking, it is the social recognition of bereavement rather than the state of grief that is regulated by the current generation of management-union agreements. The negotiation of bereavement leave, however, conveys the message that our public reaction to death should be brief and standardized. Our personal reaction is anything but brief and standardized, so a wedge is driven between the public recognition of bereavement and the private experience of grief.

Perhaps even more crucial is the question of who an employee is entitled to mourn. A person who was very important to us might not be on the list of those for whom a full three-day leave is granted. There are some signs that bereavement leave provisions are becoming a little more flexible to take into account the changing configuration of interpersonal relationships in our society.

Perhaps our impatience with grief is one of the reasons why so much attention is given to the question of how long grief is supposed to endure. It is one of the questions most frequently raised by the public and bruited about by professionals. The sense of chronic time urgency that characterizes the type A personality also seems to characterize much of American society in general. We are reluctant to pause for death, and thinking about the dead is regarded as a waste of time.

My impression is that the term *abnormal* could be applied more appropriately to American society's withdrawal of support from the bereaved. In some religious and ethnic groups there remains a sense of closeness, of reconfirming bonds with each other. This may even include a legitimized relationship with the dead. The survivors may have prayers to say, offerings to make, vigils to keep. Within such a context there is time and opportunity for personal grief to find expression in a socially approved form. The newly dead can remain as an important person during a critical period of psychological adjustment to the loss. The bereaved need not pretend that the funeral marks the end of the relationship with the parent, spouse, sibling, child, or friend. It is possible to have thoughts and feelings about the deceased, even to sense the presence vividly, without violating social norms. In this sense societies that have functioned with less technological sophistication often have embodied more insights into the psychological needs of the bereaved. As a society, Americans may be uncomfortable with the seeming irrationality or inefficiency of grief. If so, this says rather more about dominant values in the United States than about the realities of core human experience.

Helping Interventions

Fortunately, there are signs that both mutual support and professional care are being made more available for the bereaved. The Compassionate Friends, already mentioned, is a self-help group that has proved valuable in helping those who suffer the severe grief after the death of a child. As a participant-observer, Dennis Klass (1988) found that bereaved parents could help themselves by reaching out to comfort others who had lost a child. Many of the parents had to overcome emotional obstacles within themselves to open themselves to others on this most painful topic. The fact that the other group members had been through a similar experience, however, made a big difference:

> My friends didn't understand and I felt lonely. I felt I needed somebody or something but I didn't know what. I wanted to talk to someone who had gone through what I had gone through. . . . Finally, though, out of sheer desperation I had to do something. I couldn't survive the way I was going. I had lost 15 to 20 pounds, and the doctor was angry that I wouldn't take any medication. I simply couldn't function when I attempted to take the tranquilizers, so I told him, "I've dealt with things my own way for too long to begin dealing with them your way. I'll survive." He said, "I don't think you will."

Although many people seem to have found comfort in peer support groups of various types, there are hazards here as well. Julie Wambach (1983) also conducted a series of participant-observer contacts with self-help bereavement groups, in this case several widow-to-widow programs. She observed a rigid and constrictive philosophy that assumed widows should go through a sequence of stages of mourning in a prescribed time period. This rigid timetable and the concept of stages had no adequate basis in fact. Nevertheless, this view had the force of social reality and worked to the disadvantage of many widows who could not adjust to the demands of the timetable. Discrimination against the older widows was also observed. As Wambach also notes, there are probably many important differences in the nature and functioning of self-help bereavement groups, so that a reasonable degree of caution is recommended.

Professional help is also variable in style and quality and often is not necessary in the first place. When the response to bereavement is especially painful, debilitating, or prolonged, how-

ever, it is clear that alert and sensitive professional interventions can be useful. Frederick (1982–1983) suggests that some physical ailments following bereavement might be prevented by bolstering the body's immune system. Several other biochemical approaches to the prevention or reduction of bereavement-related stress may emerge from ongoing research.

The importance of *timely* emotional support is underscored by the results of the Harvard Bereavement Study. Parkes and Weiss (1983) identify the need for improved sensitivity in breaking the news when death occurs unexpectedly and for being available to the bereaved person both immediately and for an extended time period. A suicide attempt and other extreme responses are sometimes real possibilities. Therefore Parkes and Weiss suggest:

> A contract for ending therapy should be drawn up and agreed to. From the very beginning, the patient should be aware that the aim of therapy is the achievement of autonomy. . . . Inevitably, the dependent patient will have a hard time after therapy has ended and may need brief help from another therapist at this time. It may sound strange to suggest that one should use psychotherapy to treat the end of psychotherapy but a short-term intervention of this kind may well help someone get through the severe grief that can follow termination of a therapy on which he or she has become heavily dependent. (p. 256)

Timely emotional support can sometimes be offered at a much earlier point, when a person realizes that a loved one is terminally ill. It is not unusual to experience "anticipatory grief" while the friend or family member is still alive. There may be an impulse to devote much attention and feeling to the person while he or she is still with us, but at the same time experience an impulse to begin the process of distancing ourselves and becoming accustomed to life without our companion (Rando, 1986, 1989). Sensitive friends and caregivers can help the individual balance the conflicting emotional states and attitudes that are likely to arise when we grieve in advance of the loss.

In some of my own work I have found that a helping relationship can sometimes liberate a person from years of accumulated depression and rage stemming from unresolved problems in their mental, social, and physical status after a therapist has broken through the barriers of isolation (Kastenbaum et al., 1981). Having somebody to *mourn with* can be the critical factor. Whether we are concerned with children or the aged, attention to grief and mourning must include both the immediate situation and the individual's previous life history.

REFERENCES

Andreasen, N. (1983). Diagnosis of depression in the elderly. In T. Crook & G. D. Cohen (Eds.), *Physician's guide to the diagnosis and treatment of depression in the elderly* (pp. 1–8). New Canaan, CT: Mark Powley Associates, Inc.

Arnold, J. H., & Gemma, P. B. (1983). *A child dies. A portrait of family grief.* Rockville, MD: Aspens Systems Corporation.

Ball, J. F. (1976). Widow's grief: The impact of age and mode of death. *Omega, Journal of Death and Dying, 7,* 303–333.

Beck, A. T. (1976). *Cognitive therapy and emotional disorders.* New York: International Universities Press.

Bendiksen, R., & Fulton, R. (1975). Death and the child: An anterospective test of the childhood bereavement and later behavior disorder hypothesis. *Omega, Journal of Death and Dying, 6,* 45–60.

Berlinsky, I., & Biller, E. (1982). *Parental death and psychological development.* Lexington, MA: Lexington Books.

Calvert, P., Northeast, J., & Dax, E. C. (1977). Death in a country area and its effects on the health of relatives. *Medical Journal of Australia, 2,* 635–636.

Carey, R. G. (1979). Weathering widowhood: Problems and adjustment of the widowed during the first year. *Omega, Journal of Death and Dying, 10,* 163–174.

Clayton, P., Desmarais, L., & Winkokur, G. (1968). A study of normal bereavement. *American Journal of Psychiatry, 125,* 168–178.

Colp, R., Jr., (1975). The evolution of Charles Darwin's thoughts about death. *Journal of Thanatology, 3,* 191–206.

DiMeo, V. V. (1978). *Mourning and melancholia: A prescribed degriefing intervention method (DIM) for the reduction of depression and/or belated grief.* Unpublished doctoral dissertation, United States International University, San Diego, CA.

Doka, K. J. (Ed.) (1989). *Disenfranchised grief.* Lexington, MA: Lexington Books.

Engel, G. L. (1963). A unified concept of health and disease. In D. Ingele (Ed.), *Life and disease* (pp. 7–24). New York: Basic Books, Inc., Publishers.

Fischer, C. S., & Phillips, S. L. (1982). Who is alone? Social characteristics of people with small networks. In L. A. Peplau & D. Perlman (Eds.), *Loneliness. A sourcebook of current theory, research and therapy* (pp. 21–39) New York: John Wiley & Sons, Inc.

Frederick, J. K. (1976). Grief as a disease process. *Omega, Journal of Death and Dying, 7,* 297–306.

Frederick, J. F. (1982–1983). The biochemistry of bereavement: Possible basis for chemotherapy? *Omega, Journal of Death and Dying, 13:* 295–304.

Freud, S. (1959). Mourning and melancholia. *Collected papers,* (Vol. 4). New York: Basic Books, Inc., Publishers. (Original work published 1919)

Furman, E. F. (1974). *A child's parent dies.* New Haven: Yale University Press.

Glick, I. O., Weiss, R. S., & Parkes, C. M. (1974). *The first year of bereavement.* New York: John Wiley & Sons, Inc.

Gorer, G. D. (1977). *Grief and mourning.* New York: Arno Press.

Hilgard, J. R. (1969). Depressive and psychotic states as anniversaries to sibling death in childhood. *International Psychiatry Clinics, 6,* 197–211.

Hilgard, J. R., & Newman, M. F. (1959). Anniversaries in mental illness. *Psychiatry, 22:* 113–128.

Hobson, C. J. (1964, September 13). Widows of Blakton, *New Society,* (pp. 5–12).

Horowitz, M. J., Wilner, N., Marmar, C., & Krupnick, J. (1980). Pathological grief and the activation of latent self-images. *American Journal of Psychiatry, 137,* 1157–1162.

Kastenbaum, R. (1969). Death and bereavement in later life. In A. H. Kutscher (Ed.), *Death and bereavement* (pp. 27–54). Springfield, IL: Charles C. Thomas, Publisher.

Kastenbaum, R. (1974). Fertility and the fear of death. *Journal of Social Issues, 30,* 63–79.

Kastenbaum, R. (1983). Suicidality in the aged. In T. Crook & G. D. Cohen (Eds.), *Physicians' guide to the diagnosis and treatment of depression in the elderly,* (pp. 81–86). New York: Canaan, CT: Mark Powley Associates, Inc.

Kastenbaum, R., Barber, T. X., Wilson, C., Ryder, B. L., & Hathaway, L. B. (1981). *Old, sick and helpless: Where therapy begins.* Cambridge, MA: Ballinger Publishing.

Klass, D. (1984–1985). Bereaved parents and the Compassionate Friends: Affiliation and healing. *Omega, Journal of Death and Dying, 15,* 353–373.

Klass, D. (1988). *Parental grief. Solace and resolution.* New York: Springer Publishing Company, Inc.

Knapp, R. J. (1986). *Beyond endurance.* New York: Schocken Books.

Laudenslager, M. K. (1988). The psychology of loss: Lessons from humans and nonhuman primates. *Journal of Social Issues, 44,* 19–36.

Levy, R. I. (1984). The emotions in comparative perspective. In K. R. Scherer & P. Ekman (Eds.), *Approaches to emotion* (pp. 49–66). Hillsdale, NJ: Erlbaum.

Lindemann, E. (1944). The symptomatology and management of acute grief. *American Journal of Psychiatry, 101,* 141–148.

Lopata, H. Z. (1988). Support systems of American urban widowhood. *Journal of Social Issues, 44,* 113–128.

Lund, D. A. (1989). *Older bereaved spouses.* New York: Hemisphere Publishing Company.

Moriarty, D. M. (Ed.) (1967). *The loss of loved ones.* Springfield, IL: Charles C. Thomas, Publisher.

O'Malley, M. (1990). *Keeping watch.* New York: Viking.

Nichols, J. A. (1989). Perinatal death. In K. J. Doka (Ed.), *Disenfranchised grief* (pp. 117–126) Lexington, MA: Lexington Books.

Parkes, C. M. (1972). *Bereavement.* New York: International Universities Press.

Parkes, C. M., & Weiss, R. S. (1983). *Recovery from bereavement.* New York: Basic Books, Inc., Publishers.

Peppers, L. G., & Knapp, R. J. (1980). *Motherhood and mourning: Perinatal death.* New York: Praeger Special Studies.

Pratt, L. (1981). Business temporal norms and bereavement behavior. *American Sociological Review, 46,* 317–333.

Rando, T. A. (1986). *Loss and anticipatory grief.* Lexington, MA: Lexington Books.

Rando, T. A. (1989). Anticipatory grief. In R. Kastenbaum & B. K. Kastenbaum (Eds.), *Encyclopedia of death* (pp. 12–15). Phoenix: The Oryx Press.

Richards, J. G., & McCallum, J. (1979). Bereavement in the elderly. *New Zealand Medical Journal, 89,* 201–204.

Rosenblatt, P. C. (1983). *Bitter, bitter tears.* Minneapolis: University of Minnesota Press.

Salzman, C. (1983). Depression and physical disease. In T. Crook & G. D. Cohen (Eds.), *Physician's guide to the diagnosis and treatment of depression in the elderly* (pp. 9–18) New Canaan, CT: Mark Powley Associates, Inc.

Sanders, C. M. (1977). *Typologies and symptoms of adult bereavement.* Unpublished doctoral dissertation, University of South Florida, Tampa.

Sanders, C. M. (1979). The use of the MMPI in assessing bereavement outcome. In C. S. Newmark (Ed.), *MMPI: Current clinical and research trends* (pp. 122–146). New York: Praeger Publishers.

Sanders, C. M. (1982–1983). Effects of sudden vs. chronic illness and death on bereavement outcome. *Omega, Journal of Death and Dying, 13,* 227–242.

Schaie, K. W., & Geiwitz, J. (1982). *Adult development and aging.* Boston: Little, Brown & Co.

Walker, A. (1988). *To hell with dying.* San Diego: Harcourt Brace Jovanovich.

Wambach, J. A. (1983). *Timetables for grief and mourning with and without support groups.* Unpublished doctoral dissertation, Arizona State University.

Weinfield, I. J. (1990). An expanded perinatal bereavement support committee. *Death Studies, 4,* 241–252.

Yamamoto, J., Ohonogi, K., Iwasaki, T., & Yoshimura, S. (1969). Mourning in Japan. *American Journal of Psychiatry, 126,* 74–82.

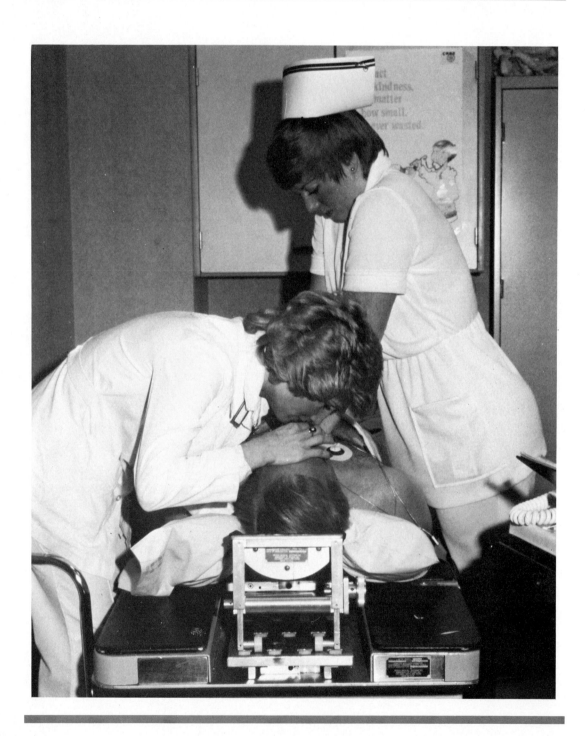

chapter 11

A RIGHT TO DIE?

ethical issues and tough decisions

Life-or-death decisions are not new to human experience. Should we offer a blood sacrifice to the gods in order to assure a bountiful harvest? And, if so, *whose* blood? If starvation threatens, who should be allowed to perish—newborns or the aged? When a medieval city falls to the conquerors after a long seige, which of the inhabitants should be put to the sword—why not all of them? If the astoundingly expensive, high-tech medical procedure might save a person's life, who should be given the chance—the rich man's or the poor man's child?

Most of the tough questions have been of this type; they have centered around the right to *live*. This type of question is still very much with us. The continuing controversy over abortion is a major example. Capital punishment is another. But a new type of question has become increasingly dominant over the years. Is there a right to *die*? If so, where does this right come from? To what circumstances does it apply? How would death on demand affect our society at large? And who should actually make the decisions? These are among the leading questions of the day. We can seek the answers by consulting law, philosophy, religion, or science. Or we can cast our lot with the pragmatists: "I'll do what seems to work best in this situation."

Either of these approaches might alleviate our anxiety for the moment, but neither measures up to the challenge. Ideally, each of us would develop an informed and coherent perspective that can guide our decisions when we encounter each unique life-or-death situation. We would not be prisoners of a theory or dogma, unable to cope realistically with actual people in actual situations. And we would not be a frantic crew, trapped by the situation and intensifying each other's anxiety as we try to do the "least wrong" thing. Instead, we would know how to bridge concept and reality: we would *be* the bridge. The core purpose of this chapter, then, is to provide an introduction to the issues, views, and facts that must be taken into consideration by those of us who want to prepare our own minds and hearts for the life-and-death decisions that may await us. Although our focus will be on the right-to-die issue, we will also be exploring some related problems, especially those affecting interpersonal communication.

KEY TERMS AND CONCEPTS

Several key terms and concepts are often encountered in discussions of the right-to-die issue. The following brief survey will help us to find our way through the maze of facts and assertions.

Euthanasia: This term has undergone a significant transformation over the years. A direct translation would be something like: happy (*eu*) death (*thanasia*). However, it would be more accurate to understand this original usage as "dying without pain and suffering." (We do not have to assume that dying is a great pleasure.)

Furthermore, this concept did not necessarily involve actions taken to shorten a life. Some people pass from life to death with little or no evidence of suffering. Today, the term euthanasia retains something of its original meaning, a peaceful, painless exit from life. But it has taken on another meaning as well: the deliberate foreshortening of a person's life to relieve suffering (or indignity, or some other undesirable condition).

Active and Passive Euthanasia: In recent years many people have emphasized the distinction between a death that is advanced by doing something and a death that is advanced by deciding *not* to do something. The outcome is the same: death. The moral, psychosocial, and legal aspects might be quite different, however. The same procedure can illustrate both types of euthanasia. The ventilator is one of the most familiar pieces of equipment in the intensive care unit, frequently used in life-support situations. Suppose that a patient has been attached to a ventilator for weeks or even months. Family and hospital staff agree that this patient has no chance for recovery and is receiving no quality-of-life benefit from being connected to a life-support system. One day or one night, somebody pulls the plug. In a little while, the patient is dead. This would be an example of active euthanasia. But suppose instead that a person has just been brought to the hospital after a massive stroke or severe injuries from an accident. It is obvious to the health-care team that the higher brain centers have been destroyed and that death will soon occur unless the unresponsive body is hooked up to a life-support system. The decision is made against using a ventilator and other apparatus. The patient is soon certified as dead. The physician who ruled against using the ventilator in the first place might possibly face a malpractice suit. But a greater risk is faced by the person who pulled the plug—there could be a murder charge. How much importance do you attach to the difference between active and passive euthanasia? Are both methods equally moral/acceptable or immoral/unacceptable? And what if it was up to you to hasten a death—would

pulling the plug be no more difficult than deciding not to connect the plug in the first place? The question of active vs. passive euthanasia is central to the right to die controversy, and we will be returning to it later.

Assisted Suicide: This term has started to replace the more dramatic—and more frequently criticized—phrase, "mercy killing." We must first remind ourselves why there has often been a strong outcry against the idea of mercy killing. There are still many people among us who remember how the political, medical, economic, and military forces of a modern nation all collaborated in the murder of millions of people. The holocaust that eventually claimed millions of lives was preceded by Hitler's policy of *Vernichtun lebensunwerten Lebens* that was directed at thousands of German citizens (Lauter & Meyer, 1984). In the Nazi's "extermination of valueless life," they asserted that they were putting these people out of their misery . . . for their own good and to save the country the cost of feeding and housing them. Perhaps the most alarming part of this prolonged episode was the fact that many German physicians participated in the killing without protest (Lifton, 1986). Discovering that he could induce physicians, lawyers, and other responsible people to engage in "mercy killing," Hitler moved on to his large-scale genocidal assaults against Jews and Gypsies. "Mercy killing," then, is a term that arouses horror and anger in many people who know their 20th century history. "Assisted suicide" is a term with fewer emotional associations and is therefore preferred by most writers today. How does it differ from euthanasia? There can be a blurring of boundaries between active euthanasia and assisted suicide. However, there is a principle that is always involved in an authentic assisted suicide and which may or may not be involved in euthanasia. This is the principle of request and informed consent on the part of the person whose death is at issue. "I want to die—help me!" is the key message in assisted suicide. By contrast, a decision in favor of active or passive euthanasia might be made by others when the affected individual is not able to express his or her own wishes. Precisely what actions constitute assisted suicide is the subject of lively controversy today and, of course, so is the question of whether or not this procedure should be legitimatized.

Slippery Slope: We use the "slippery slope" argument when we acknowledge that one particular instance of euthanasia or assisted suicide might be justifiable in itself—but that it could lead to widespread abuse in other instances. "I can understand and I can sympathize with this person's request to be put out of her suffering," we might say. "But if society consents to 'mercy killing' in this instance, then tomorrow we will be asked to consent in a case where the right to die is not quite so clear. And so it will go, until we slide all the way down the slope." What do we fear discovering at the bottom of the slope? Perhaps many people would give up too soon when confronted not only with a terminal illness but with other crises. Suicide might become too easy an alternative, or even what is expected of a person. Perhaps the role of the physician will be undermined by his or her participation in assisted suicide. And perhaps "mercy killing" will be abused as the Nazis once did, serving as a linguistic cover-up for murder. Most people who are involved in the right-to-die controversy do have some concern about the possible abuse of this concept, but there are sharp disagreements regarding the applicability of the slippery slope argument to a particular decision.

Living Will: There is a class of documents known as "advanced directives." These are instructions concerning actions to be taken should certain events occur in the future. The living will is an advanced directive that was introduced in 1968 by a nonprofit educational organization that is now known as Concern for Dying (Weingarten, 1989). This document has become important not only for its specific function but also as a stimulus to discussion of right-to-die issues. Let us begin by reviewing the current version of the living will (Box 11–1).

The living will has played a valuable role in stimulating both public and professional aware-

ness of death-related issues. People have had to examine their own thoughts, feelings, and assumptions. Communication has increased somewhat between individuals and their families, physicians, nurses, ministers, and lawyers. "What do you think of the living will?" "What do they mean by 'heroic measures'?" Questions such as these have made it easier to open up dialogues on death and dying with the important people in our lives. Over the years, there has been a growing consensus in favor of the living will, even among people who have not completed one themselves ("I just haven't gotten around to it, I guess").

We will return to the living will later in this chapter to see how it works in practice and what the next steps might be. However, it is important at this point to emphasize that the living will does *not* include provisions for assisted suicide. There is a movement that advocates legislation favorable to assisted suicide, with The Hemlock Society being especially active in this effort. A measure favoring assisted suicide was recently introduced into one state legislature, but rejected. There are almost certain to be continuing efforts in this direction. However, many people who support the living will as an instrument that expresses an individual's preferences (Scofield, 1989) do not support assisted suicide.

One sentence in the living will does walk the boundary between passive euthanasia and active euthanasia/assisted suicide: "I do, however, ask that medication be mercifully administered to me to alleviate suffering even though this may shorten my remaining life." Suppose that you are a physician. The patient you are attending at this moment has previously entrusted you with a signed copy of her living will. She is dying. She is also in physical and emotional distress. "I want to die," she tells you. It had been your intention to give her morphine to relieve her distress. A larger dose would not only relieve her distress but also hasten an easy death. Would this subtle but effective action be justified because it is consistent with the advance directive (". . . even though this may shorten my remaining life")?

BOX 11–1
MY LIVING WILL

To My Family, My Physician, My Lawyer and All Others Whom It May Concern

Death is as much a reality as birth, growth, maturity, and old age—it is the one certainty of life. If the time comes when I can no longer take part in decisions for my own future, let this statement stand as an expression of my wishes and directions, while I am still of sound mind.

If at such a time the situation should arise in which there is no reasonable expectation of my recovery from extreme physical or mental disability, I direct that I be allowed to die and not be kept alive by medications, artificial means or "heroic measures." I do, however, ask that medication be mercifully administered to me to alleviate suffering even though this may shorten my remaining life.

This statement is made after careful consideration and is in accordance with my strong convictions and beliefs. I want the wishes and directions here expressed carried out to the extent permitted by law. Insofar as they are not legally enforceable, I hope that those to whom this Will is addressed will regard themselves as morally bound by these provisions.

DURABLE POWER OF ATTORNEY
(optional)

I hereby designate _____attorney for the purpose of making medical treatment decisions. This power of attorney shall remain effective in the event that I become incompetent or otherwise unable to make such decisions for myself.

Signed _____
Optional Notarization: Date _____
"Sworn and subscribed to Witness _____
before me this _____ day Address _____ of _____ ,
19 _____ ," Witness _____
Notary Public Seal Address _____
Copies of this request have been given to _____
_____

(Optional) My Living Will is registered with Concern for Dying (No. _____).

Copies of this form may be obtained without charge from:
  Concern for Dying, Room 831
  250 West 57th Street
  New York, NY 10107
This form may also be reproduced, as a courtesy of Concern for Dying.

Or, when it comes right down to it, would this be assisted suicide or even murder?

The living will, then, valuable instrument that it is, does not answer all the questions for us, and may indeed continue to raise new questions.

OUR CHANGING ATTITUDES TOWARD A RIGHT TO DIE

Attitudes toward the right to die issue have changed appreciably in recent years. We will track this pattern with the help of a nationwide poll that has just been completed by the Times Mirror Center for the People and the Press (1990). The fact that a poll of this kind was given high priority by a major news organization is itself testament to the growing public concern about death-related issues. Before turning to the poll results, we should be clear about three points:

1. Survey findings should not be used to answer basic questions of science or morality. A ten to one vote against the law of gravity would not prevent unsupported objects from falling. A hypothetical medieval survey would have found a preponderance of believers in witchcraft, and a hypothetical 19th century survey would have found that most physicians believed washing their hands to be an unnecessary and ridiculous idea. There is good reason to pay attention to survey results, but these do not free us of responsibility for informed and critical thinking.
2. Attitudes toward the right to die and related topics will not remain where they are today. There will be continuing changes, and some may be quite substantial. This means we must update our information on a regular basis.
3. Attitudes influence decisions and actions. Does the spouse of a critically injured accident victim have the nerve to ask the physician to discontinue treatment? Does the physician have the nerve to honor this request? Does a terminally ill person feel secure enough to discuss his or her suicidal thoughts with a friend? Does a minister judge that the congregation is ready to hear his most searching thoughts on the moral significance of suicide soon after one of the members has taken his own life? The attitudinal climate does not directly "cause" decisions and behaviors, but it does affect the expectancies and probabilities. This is perhaps the most practical reason for attending to survey results: what do they tell us about the kind of life-and-death decisions that are likely to be made in the master bedroom, the emergency room, the nursing home, and many other venues across the land?

Survey Findings

Now let's look at the major findings of the Times Mirror survey. First we will review the most general and clear-cut results.

1. *There are circumstances in which a person should be allowed to die.* About eight in ten Americans agree with this statement.
2. *People do have the right to make their own decisions about receiving life-sustaining treatment.* There is a six to one majority in favor of this statement.
3. *Doctors and nurses do not pay "a lot of attention" to the instructions they receive from patients about wanting or not wanting life-sustaining treatment.* Only one in five believed that physicians give their instructions careful consideration.
4. *The closest family member should be able to decide whether or not to continue medical treatment for a person with terminal illness who is unable to communicate and who has not made his wishes known in advance.* About 75% of the respondents agree with this statement.
5. *It is sometimes justified for a person to kill his/her spouse because he/she was suffering terrible pain from a terminal disease.* This statement wins the support of seven of ten people.
6. *Most people (71%) know about the living will, but relatively few (14%) have actually made living wills for themselves.*
7. *If suffering great physical pain or unable to function in daily activities because of an incurable disease, most people would ask their doctors to stop treatment* rather than do everything possible to save their lives. About two out of three people agreed with this statement, excluding those with "don't know" responses.
8. *Right-to-die legislation*—allowing medical treatment for a terminally ill patient to be withdrawn or withheld, if that is what the patient wishes—*is approved by about eight people in ten.*

This first set of findings reveals a fairly strong consensus in favor of the individual's right to make decisions about life-sustaining treatment. Furthermore, it indicates a continuing movement toward the acceptance of suicide in certain circumstances, notably in the advanced stages of terminal illness. Broadly speaking, the public seems to be marching in step with the action of state legislatures across the nation that have passed measures supportive of the living will. But the public may also be somewhat ahead of existing legislation in its willingness to consider suicide and assisted suicide as acceptable options.

It would be mistaken to assume that the public has reached a consensus on all right-to-die questions. Here are several questions that elicited a more divided response from the national sample:

9. *Parents have the right to refuse medical treatment for an infant that is born with a severe handicap.* About half the respondents *disagreed* with this view, a third agreed, and the rest were divided between no opinion and "it depends." Although more people select the "should receive most treatment possible" alternative than any other, there is a substantial number who do not endorse this view.

10. *The hospital or doctor should be held responsible if a patient's instruction to withhold life-sustaining treatment is ignored and the patient survives, but with severe disability.* Those who had clear opinions were divided six to five in favor of holding the hospital or physician responsible. Evidently, we are a long way from having a consensus on what should be done in such a situation.

11. *A person has the moral right to end his or her own life if afflicted with an incurable disease.* Again, the public is closely divided on this question, with a seven to six edge for those who agree that there is a moral right to suicide under this circumstance (but see the findings in numbers 12 and 13 below).

12. *A person has the moral right to end his or her own life if he/she is an extremely heavy burden on the family, or living has become a burden to*

the person him/herself. These were separate questions on the survey, but the responses were very similar: about two out of three respondents disagreed. They held that there is no moral right to end one's life because it has become burdensome either to one's self or family.

13. *A person has the moral right to end his or her own life if suffering great pain with no hope of improvement.* Given this circumstance, most people agreed that there was a moral right to end one's own life. The eight to five margin in favor indicated that the public makes a sharp differentiation between pain and the sense of being a burden as justification for ending one's life.

14. *I would tell my doctor to do everything possible to save my life if I had a disease with no hope of improvement that made it hard for me to function in my day-to-day activities.* This statement found the public almost equally divided in its response, with a very slight tendency toward disagreement. The differential (52% to 48%) is small enough to have arisen as a sampling artifact or error. The main point here is that "save life" and "stop treatment" attitudes are about equally current today.

The set of findings we have just reviewed (numbers 9–14) suggests a fairly complex pattern of attitudes toward the right to die in various situations. The public does not support a sweeping, generalized approach. Instead, people recognize that circumstances differ and their approval or disapproval of a right to die depends much upon these circumstances. This differentiated approach might be discomforting to policy-makers: it would be easier for them if a strong public consensus existed. However, there is reason to be encouraged by the fact that many people do take the specific circumstances into account. This suggests that the public has become more aware of death-related issues and is willing to think carefully about the personal and medical realities involved, instead of relying upon broad generalizations.

Finally, let us consider a third set of findings that attempt to analyze public attitudes in a little more detail. Does the respondent's age, sex, race, or religious beliefs make a difference in attitudes toward a right to die?

15. Overall (combining results from all relevant questions), there is somewhat less support for the right-to-die position among people age 65 and older, nonwhites, and those who report themselves as being very religious. Age makes a particularly strong difference with respect to the moral right to commit suicide; people under the age of 30 are much more likely to hold that such a right exists. It should be added, however, that most people in the subgroups just mentioned do support many of the right-to-die options, but this support is not as widespread as it is in the population in general.

16. Born-again Christians and others who describe themselves as very religious are strongly opposed to parental decision-making when a severely handicapped infant is born. There are no differences between Protestants and Catholics with respect to parental decision-making; the differences are found between individuals who either see their religion as very relevant or not very relevant to practical decision-making in their lives.

17. Family communication about death-related issues follows at least two different patterns. Daughters were more likely to have discussed their mothers' preferences with them than sons were. Few adults, sons or daughters, have discussed these matters with their fathers.

18. The data also suggest that adults can be classified into those who seldom communicate about right to die and other death-related issues and those who communicate with many of the important people in their lives. Women, people in the higher economic brackets, and those who have had significant personal experiences with death are more likely to discuss death with others.

The *Times Mirror* survey results indicate that the American public has become somewhat more open and knowledgeable about death-related issues over the past several decades. Perhaps this change owes something to the death education and counseling movement (Chapter 12). It certainly owes something to the changing character of medical treatment and its associated psychological, social, and economic challenges. More specifically, there is a general trend toward rejecting the view that every possible effort must be made to sustain life under all circumstances. The other side of this coin is that an increasing number of people believe that individuals should have the opportunity to state their preferences and participate in making the life-and-death decisions that directly affect them. There is consensus on some right-to-die choices, but not on others. The individual's age, sex, race, religiosity, and prior experience with death have some bearing on right-to-die attitudes.

THE RIGHT-TO-DIE DILEMMA: CASE EXAMPLES

Having brought ourselves up to date on changing public attitudes toward right-to-die issues, we can now look at several case examples. Statistics are, after all, just statistics. The actual decisions must be made about actual circumstances in which people face some of the most difficult situations of their lives, often while under great stress. Each example will enrich our understanding of the right-to-die issue in its real-life contexts.

The Ethics of Withholding Treatment: A Landmark Case

A young woman became the center of national attention and controversy when she lapsed into a coma after a birthday party. One friend applied mouth-to-mouth resuscitation while another called the police, who also attempted resuscitation and took her to a hospital. She started to breathe again, but Karen Ann Quinlan did not return to consciousness. Traces of valium and quinine were found in her blood, leading to a preliminary diagnosis of drug-induced coma. This diagnosis was later disputed and has never been fully clarified. Whatever the precipitating cause of her condition, Quinlan had suffered severe and irreversible brain damage from a period of oxygen deprivation.

Weeks and then months passed. Quinlan remained in the hospital; her body maintained on a ventilator, with intravenous tubes providing fluids and nutrition. Her body gradually wasted away. After a few months, the once attractive and vital young woman had become a 60-pound shriveled form, curled into a fetal position. Talk of recovery and a miraculous return to life became less frequent as time went by, and the hospital expenses continued to mount every day.

Karen Ann was the adopted child of deeply religious parents. Joseph Quinlan maintained hope for nearly half a year, until finally persuaded by his priest that extraordinary means are not morally required to prolong life. This communication did not resolve the moral issue, however; it simply expanded it into other spheres. The Quinlans asked two physicians to turn off the ventilator. They declined to do so. The physicians were not sure of the moral and legal implications of such an action, nor did they wish to expose themselves to possible malpractice charges. What were the Quinlans to do? They pursued their request through the courts. The time-consuming legal process provided the opportunity for many opinions to be aired in the media and in professional circles as well as in the courts. Some confusion was also generated, for example, there was a tendency to speak of Karen Ann as though she were already dead. The fact was that EEG tracings still showed weak electrical activity in the brain. A neurologist described her condition as a "persistent vegetative state." An attorney for New Jersey described a brief visit to her room:

Her face is all distorted and she is sweating. Her eyes are open and blinking about twice a minute. She's sort of gasping. I'd never seen anything like that. . . . I was there for seven minutes and it seemed like seven hours. (Kron, 1973, p. 22)

Medical testimony was given that Karen Ann would die within a short time if removed from the ventilator.

The court ruled against the Quinlans' request, rejecting a religious freedom argument. This decision was appealed to the New Jersey Supreme Court. Here, for the first time, a court ruled that a ventilator could be turned off. However, a condition was imposed; physicians must agree that Karen Ann had no reasonable chance of regaining consciousness. The New Jersey Attorney General decided not to challenge this decision. This meant that the United States Supreme Court was not asked at that time to make a decision that would have set an important precedent for the entire nation.

Finally, 14 months after she had lapsed into a nonresponsive state, Karen Ann was disconnected from the ventilator. But this proved not to be "finally" after all. She was transferred to the skilled care section of a nursing home and there she remained alive—in her very persistent vegetative state—for more than ten years until she succumbed to pneumonia in 1985.

Karen Ann's predicament was not the first example of its kind but it became the starting place not only for discussion but also for efforts to develop due process for right-to-die issues. There have now been many cases that brought the "pull the plug" issue into the courts. Judges and attorneys today can consult a number of previous legal opinions and decisions, which makes their task at least a little less daunting. There have also been many other experiences with people who have entered persistent vegetative states (PVS) and been maintained on life-support systems. It is rare that a person recovers from a PVS. Nevertheless, even the occasional recovery of a person who appears to be suspended indefinitely between life and death can provide a basis for hope. (One striking example of recovery involved another young woman, Carold Dusald Rogman, who remained comatose for several months after suffering injuries to her brainstem in an automobile accident. She was nonresponsive during this time, and experienced physical deterioration similar to that of Karen Ann Quinlan. Carold made a full recovery, however (*Boston Globe*, 1976).

Perhaps because of such rare instances or simply because of the family's wish to believe in the possibility of recovery, the survivors may continue to be "afflicted with hope" for a long time. By "afflicted," I mean that the family cannot fully grieve the loss and reorganize their lives while their loved one is viewed as not quite alive but also not quite dead. Hope may sustain people, but it can also be a burden and a source of stress as well. Furthermore, it may be difficult for the community to provide personal and ritualistic support to the family when there has been no official death or funeral process to signal the loss.

"It's Over, Debbie": Compassion or Murder?

The Quinlan case was characterized by a long period of consultations, discussions, and legal proceedings. Many people participated in the decision-making, and many facts were brought forward for public as well as family and professional scrutiny. More recently a very different case was reported in a leading medical journal. No author's name was attributed to "It's Over, Debbie," when this brief report was published in the *Journal of the American Medical Association* (Anon, 1988). The article was offered as a personal experience and consisted of only three paragraphs. This is what the story told:

A presumably young physician—a resident in gynecology—was on duty when aroused by a call in the middle of the night. The request came from a nurse on the gynecologic-oncology (cancer) unit. This was not the physician's usual duty station. The doctor "trudged along, bumping sleepily against walls and corners and not believing I was up again." Upon reaching the unit, the physician picked up the patient's chart and was

given some "hurried details" by the nurse. A 20-year-old patient named Debbie was dying of ovarian cancer. An attempt had been made to sedate her by using an alcohol drip, but this had led her to vomit "unrelentingly."

Entering the patient's room, the resident saw that she was emaciated and appeared much older than her actual age. "She was receiving nasal oxygen, had an IV, and was sitting in bed suffering from what was obviously severe air hunger." There was another woman in the room who stood by the bed, holding the patient's hand. The physician had the impression that "The room seemed filled with the patient's desperate effort to survive." The physician also observed that the patient was breathing with great difficulty. The report also states that the patient had not eaten or slept in two days nor had she responded to chemotherapy. Presumably this information had been obtained from the doctor's quick glance through the patient's chart. Trying to take in the whole situation, the resident felt that it was a "gallows scene, a cruel mockery of her youth and unfulfilled potential. Her only words to me were, 'Let's get this over with.' "

At this point, the physician returned to the nurse's station to think over the situation. There the physician decided that he or she would "give her rest." The nurse was asked to draw morphine sulfate into a syringe, " 'Enough,' I thought, 'to do the job'." The physician returned to the patient's room and told the two women that he was going to give Debbie "something that would let her rest and to say good-bye." Within seconds of the intravenous injection, the patient's breathing slowed, her eyes closed, and her distress seemed to be at an end. The other woman stroked Debbie's hair as she slept. The doctor "waited for the inevitable next effect of depressing the respiratory drive." Four minutes later, the breathing slowed further, sputtered, and came to an end. "The dark-haired woman stood erect and seemed relieved. It's over, Debbie."

This brief report raised a furor among the readers of this well-known medical journal, and, picked up by the media, generated public controversy as well. The response was divided, but critical reactions dominated. Let's try to identify the most salient problems and issues involved in this now famous or infamous case. As we do so, consult your own personal thoughts and feelings, but do not lose sight of the facts and assumptions inherent in the specific episode that is under review.

1. The physician had no prior acquaintance with the patient or her companion. This means that the life-and-death decision was made—and carried out—by a stranger.
2. The decision was also made very quickly and without consultation.
3. The physician was under the influence of fatigue and his or her emotional reaction to a scene that was painful to observe.
4. The patient's distress had been intensified by a procedure (the alcohol drip) that had produced new symptoms without alleviating the existing symptoms.
5. The "gallows" and "cruel mockery" images were those that stirred in the doctor's own mind.
6. The nurse was ordered to prepare a lethal injection.
7. Debbie spoke only one sentence to the doctor. Did the doctor try to converse with her or her companion? Was any effort made to have a dialogue with Debbie, even a few more words, before making the decision to end her life?
8. Did the doctor give any consideration either to other people who might have been in Debbie's life or to legal and religious principles that might have bearing on the decision?

These concerns and questions add up to an episode that raises the warning flag, especially for those who already have some doubts and fears about possible adverse consequences of the right-to-die movement. At the risk of losing textbookish neutrality, I want to share my thoughts with you as directly as possible:

A tired and probably overworked physician found him- or herself in a stressful situation that neither medical training nor personal experience had equipped him or her to master. The physician's own insulation from dying and death was pierced momentarily by seeing another young person in such a painful and vulnerable condition. As a compassionate individual, the physician recognized Debbie's anguish and wanted very much to relieve it—after all, this is one of the traditional motivations for entering the medical profession. Almost immediately, the physician was feeling the stress not only of the patient's anguish, but also of his or her own sense of personal vulnerability and the inability of modern medicine to treat Debbie effectively. At this point the physician must have felt an urgent need to resolve the situation, that is, to reduce both Debbie's anguish and his or her own.

The physician had several options. These included taking other measures to relieve the patient's distress (and discontinuing those that were adding to her distress), and consulting with others—the nurses as well as more experienced physicians. Certainly, the physician could have made more effort to learn who Debbie was and what she wanted. It is not unusual for a person to wish themselves dead when experiencing acute distress—but to be grateful later that another alternative had been found. But all the options required time and patience—and time is not what this tired, poorly prepared, anxious, and overmatched physician could afford. The decision to end Debbie's life was to some important extent influenced by the physician's urgent need to terminate a situation in which he or she felt powerless, vulnerable, and distressed. The needs and feelings of other people were barely considered, nor did the physician feel any obligation to think of the philosophical, legal, sociopsychological and religious factors that might lead one to hesitate before taking another person's life.

Much of the critical response also called attention to the physician's disregard of standards and due procedure. Other doctors were quite aware that their own image and reputation were endangered by such episodes. The ease with which one young physician disposed of Debbie's problems by disposing of Debbie in the middle of the night seems to be a prime example of how slippery the slope can be. We should keep in mind, however, that the anxieties of doctors or other caregivers can lead to the opposite outcome as well: bodies being maintained on life-support systems despite the obvious futility of this procedure and despite the family's and even the patient's own expressed wishes. The legal justice system in our society, for all its flaws, does at least allow time and does require evidence. Decisions hastily made in the middle of the night by doctors who are poorly trained in interpersonal communication afford few if any safeguards.

You have no obligation to agree with the way I have reconstructed Debbie's death based upon the limited information available. But you will be serving your own educational interests more effectively if your alternative scenario is also based upon the known facts. (The *Journal of the American Medical Association* has declined to provide additional information.)

Does a Person Have to Be Dying in order to Have the Right to Die?

This odd phrase brings us to one of the issues that has not yet been fully discussed but which is likely to become increasingly important as time goes on. Much of the right-to-die controversy has centered around people such as Karen Ann Quinlan (unresponsive, locked into a persistent vegetative state) and Debbie (alert, responsive, but with little time left to live). As we have seen, there is increasing public support for the right to terminate life-sustaining procedures when a person is in either of these conditions. But what are we to think about a case such as the following? As you read about this case, consider what decision you would have recommended at each point—and why. Test your own decision-making skills and tendencies.

A 26-year-old woman has earned a degree in social work and is seeking employment. Her husband leaves her. She becomes depressed and anxious. If she also becomes suicidal, would you recommend:

__ Everything possible should be done to prevent her from committing suicide.
__ Somebody should listen to her, offer support and advice, but not otherwise intervene.
__ Some other course of action should be taken, namely _____
_____
__ Why did you make this particular recommendation?_____
_____
_____

Now we add some further information. This woman is also afflicted with cerebral palsy. She retains just enough muscular control to operate an electrically-powered wheelchair, to speak, and to chew and swallow food when someone feeds her. Suppose that she expresses a strong wish to end her life—what course of action would you recommend?

__ Everything possible should be done to prevent her from committing suicide.
__ Somebody should listen to her, offer support and advice, but not otherwise intervene.
__ Some other course of action should be taken, namely_____
_____
__ Why did you make this particular recommendation?_____
_____
_____

There is a new development. The state will no longer provide assistance in transportation. This makes it almost certain that she will not be able to find and keep a job. Deprived of the opportunity to pursue the career for which she prepared herself and the chance to support herself, she expresses a strong wish to end her life at this point. What course of action do you recommend?

___ Everything possible should be done to prevent her from committing suicide.

___ Somebody should listen to her, offer support and advice, but not otherwise intervene.

___ Some other course of action should be taken, namely_____

_____

_____

In desperation the woman arranges to have herself admitted to a hospital so she would "just be left alone and not bothered by friends or family or anyone else, and to ultimately starve to death" (Annas, 1984, p. 20). Attempts are made to change her mind, but her purpose holds firm. At this point, what course of action would you recommend?

___ Force her to take nourishment against her wishes.

___ Allow her to carry through her plan, while also providing her with companionship and the opportunity to discuss and reconsider her options if she so chooses.

___ Some other course of action should be taken, namely_____

_____

___ Why did you make this particular recommendation?_____

_____

_____

Now let's see what actually happened in this case. Riverside (California) General Hospital refused to accept Elizabeth Bouvia's plan and brought the issue to court. The judge declared that Ms. Bouvia was fully competent and had made a decision that was both competent and sincere. Nevertheless, he decided in favor of the hospital's position:

> The decisive point was that Ms. Bouvia was "not terminal" but "had a life expectancy of 15 to 20 years." He concluded, "The established ethics of the medical profession clearly outweigh . . . her own rights of self-determination." Therefore, "forced feeding, however invasive, would be ad-

ministered for the purpose of saving the life of an otherwise non-terminal patient and should be permitted. There is no reasonable option." (Annas, p. 20)

George Annas, a professor of health law, argues that this was a poor decision that gave legal force to "brutal behavior." His key point is that medical care requires consent and is really no care at all when it is imposed against the patient's wishes. He reports that "four or more 'attendants' wrestle her from her bed in the morning and restrain her while a nasogastric tube is rudely forced through her nose and into her stomach" (p. 24). The hospital's position was that its staff should not be asked to become accessories to a suicide. (The impasse was resolved, in a way, when Ms. Bouvia checked herself out of the hospital and was admitted to a nursing home that promised not to force food upon her.)

Ms. Bouvia's predicament—and the predicament of all who became involved with the situation—illustrates what can happen when various rights come into conflict. Here are some of the rights that were involved or implied:

1. The right to end one's own life—for any reason that seems significant to that person.
2. The right to end one's own life when not terminally ill, but facing years of infirmity and isolation.
3. The right to ask or require other people to help end one's own life.
4. The right of society to oppose the wish of a person to end his or her life.
5. The right of "experts" (physicians, lawyers, judges) to do what they think is best for a person even if it directly contradicts what that person seeks for him- or herself.

No judicial decision can resolve all the issues raised by competing claims of rights in matters of life and death. Some of these issues are linked with our deepest personal values and beliefs and may therefore be highly resistant to change as per court order. In this instance, many people were outraged by the court's support of physical intervention to force Ms. Bouvia to take nourishment. The basic sense of fair play and compassion seemed to be violated when a disabled individual, innocent of any crime, could be so abused by the system, and with a judge's consent. In situations such as these, judicial rulings might be "proper" on their own terms, but are more likely to create than solve problems because they run counter to society's view of how people should treat each other.

Reflect a moment on the recommendations you made at various points in the development of Ms. Bouvia's predicament. What perspective did you take? Were you placing yourself in Ms. Bouvia's situation, trying to see the situation from her standpoint? Or did you see yourself instead as a hospital administrator or as the nurse responsible for her care? The priorities and pressures of the situation take on a different pattern as we shift perspective. It is a constant challenge to put ourselves in the position of all the various people who may be involved in a life-and-death predicament. Even the question of "which right is the rightest" may be answered in a different way, depending upon our particular involvement and stake in the situation.

Ms. Bouvia's experience leaves us with three fundamental problems that neither society at large nor medical and legal experts have fully resolved: (a) If we do have a "right to die," must this be limited to terminal illness and, if so, why?; (b) are there any limits to the power the state can legitimately exercise over an individual who wishes to die?; and (c) is it acceptable to ask others to help us die? We might try to force a solution by simply declaring that such-and-such is (or is not) a right. However, if we seek a more rooted and enduring solution, we will have to pursue the questions through careful observation and open dialogue.

Competent to Decide? The Retarded Man and the Bright Child

Unlike Elizabeth Bouvia, some people who become enmeshed in life-and-death situations are not able to make informed decisions. This places the total burden of judgment upon society. Moreover, before the actual decision is made, there must be agreement regarding who should be allowed or required to make the decision. We will briefly review two cases in which the question of competency was involved. It will quickly become obvious that there are great differences within this realm and, again, some disturbing questions that have not yet been adequately answered.

A Mentally Retarded Adult

Joseph Saikewicz was a 67-year-old resident of the Belchertown State School (Massachusetts). He was considered profoundly mentally retarded with a mental age of less than three years. Saikewicz was robust, ambulatory, and usually enjoyed good health. However, he was able to make his wishes known only through gestures and grunts. He had adjusted fairly well to the sheltered institutional environment but was vulnerable and disoriented in any other setting.

The need for decision-making arose when Saikewicz was diagnosed as suffering from acute myeloblastic monocytic leukemia, a form of the disease that is considered to be incurable. Chemotherapy produces a remission in some patients (between 30% and 50%), but this usually lasts only for several months, and the course of treatment can produce serious side effects. According to the medical testimony, "a patient in Saikewicz's condition would live for a matter of weeks, or perhaps, several months. . . . A decision to allow the disease to run its natural course would not result in pain for the patient, and death would probably come without discomfort" (Robbins, 1983, p. 38).

If Joseph Saikewicz had been capable of comprehending his condition he would have been able to decide whether or not he wanted chemotherapy with its prospect of extending survival for several months but also making him feel sicker. Because he was not capable of making this decision, it fell to the medical and administrative officials and eventually the courts. In this instance a Massachusetts probate judge ordered that all reasonable and necessary supportive measures should be provided to Saikewicz but that he was *not* to be subjected to chemotherapy. This decision was based on the consideration that the state had no applicable interests or claims that outweighed Saikewicz's right to be spared the discomfort of a treatment that could not save his life. The patient remained in his familiar institutional home until he died of pneumonia, a complication of the leukemia. Reportedly, he died without pain or discomfort.

Unlike the judicial decision that gave precedence to social institutions over the individual's own wishes, this ruling supports the position that the state does not necessarily have the right or obligation to subject a person to treatment simply because the treatment is available. Each new case that comes up for judicial review will have its own distinctive features. This means that even when competency or incompetency has been clearly established, the ruling may be affected by other factors. Even if we have kept track of previous judicial decisions, we cannot be sure how a judge will interpret the next case that comes along.

The dying patient's right to decide about or at least to influence the course of his or her treatment is often determined by the health-care system rather than the courts. Both social institutions have a tradition of regarding children as incompetent to make significant decisions for themselves. Even a very bright young child, then, is likely to be considered "incompetent" for no reason other than the fact that he or she *is* a child.

Marie: A Ghostlike Seven-Year-Old

This brings us to Marie. She was seven years old and dying. Marie understood that she was very sick. She also felt mutilated, frightened, abandoned, and in physical pain.

> Several months before she died, Marie, a ghostlike seven-year-old, awaited her fourth cadaveric kidney transplant. Due to both her kidney disease and steroid therapy, Marie's stature was that of a four-year-

old child. Her wisp of golden-white hair was thinning and light; her complexion was wan and pale. Marie appeared very old and fragile as she hobbled along, dragging a cumbersome, plastic right leg that never seemed to belong to her. Marie suffered from a mindless, indifferent fluke of nature: cystinosis, a rare, fatal genetic disease. . . . During Marie's short life, she experienced numerous hospitalizations and separations from her family, who eventually abandoned her. . . . Marie's lonely, monotonous hospital days were interrupted only by traumatic episodes, which affected her both physically and emotionally. For example, Marie scratched her wounds constantly, and they did not heal. One day . . . she scratched her incision line fully open. Terrified, she watched the contents of her body ooze forth. Panicky nurses doused her with sterile compresses as hospital staff frantically rushed her to the O.R. for repair. (Meagher & Leff, 1989–1990, p. 178)

A recurring ordeal in Marie's life was the hemodialysis treatment that she had to endure twice a week. These treatment episodes, which required her to be placed in a restrained position, seemed to take from Marie one of the last vestiges of her sense of control. She would try to prepare herself for the treatment and would also try to reverse roles by pretending to be the hemodialysis technician. But the hemodialysis sessions continued to torment her and "Marie's mother would not be waiting for her after the ordeal had ended."

Marie sought comfort, companionship, security, and freedom from pain. The health-care system, however, wanted to do everything it could to keep her alive. "Despite Marie's pain, mutilation, and longing for home, the single-minded, technical battle against death raged on and assumed a form and momentum of its own" (Meagher & Leff, pp. 180–181). And so Marie spent her days in a crib or a treatment room, often stuffed with pumps, tubes, needles and catheters. The stark medico-technical atmosphere had done much to scare away her parents. She was basically alone.

The aggressive medical treatment plan was part of a belief system that abandoned Marie to unrelieved suffering. When she asked for medicine to relieve her pain or help her to sleep, the staff practiced a policy of deceit. She was given placebos instead of actual medications. Physicians would sometimes make it a point to mislead her. For example, "The pediatricians showed Marie the small bottle of Valium, prepared a syringe, and pretended to inject the medication into Marie's tubing. Why was Marie still crying? The child-life worker was fooled, but Marie was not. When she asked the pediatricians why Marie had not responded, they explained that they had injected the syringe into Marie's mattress" (p. 180).

This peculiar behavior on the part of the staff was based upon the fear of turning Marie into a "drug addict." This fear—unrealistic and highly inappropriate to the circumstances—was given precedence over the young girl's obvious need for relief from pain and anxiety. Unfortunately, this is not an unusual assumption. It has (mis)guided many a physician in the past and still occurs today, although apparently not as often. There was a huge gap, then, between the girl's wish for comfort and the system's intention to concentrate upon a rescue mission that it knew was almost certain to fail.

Again, the competition between "rights" looks somewhat different depending upon the perspective we choose. Suppose yourself to be part of the health-care team. You are an adult, therefore competent. Marie is only a child, therefore not competent to make such decisions. You were trained in a school of medicine or nursing. Marie would just be a grade-schooler, if she could go to school. You represent a major social institution, the health-care system. She doesn't represent anybody. You have a critical responsibility: the exercise of professional judgment. She is just supposed to be a good patient. Suppose, though, that you are Marie. You know that you have lost practically everything: the opportunity to live at home, to go to school and play like other children, to be with your parents, and to do things for yourself. You hardly dare to ask to have all of this returned to you (already one

leg has been amputated). But you do wish the pain would stop. You do wish they would stop doing all those things to you. You want to go home.

Unfortunately, there was never a clear chance to evaluate these conflicting claims and perhaps soften the discrepancy between these conflicting perspectives. It was unthinkable that Marie should present her case for official judgment because of the presumption that young children do not have the competency, therefore they do not have the right to participate in making treatment decisions. Furthermore, Meagher and Leff raise the question of who will protect the child's best interest when the parents are not available to do so (for whatever reason). They suggest that such a person should be on the scene and provided the opportunity to advocate on behalf of the child. Perhaps the traditional concept of "informed consent" needs to be modified when children are involved; a concept such as "assent" might be developed instead.

It is difficult to disagree with Meagher and Leff's conclusion that "Marie has the right to expect considerate care. She has the right to expect that she will be treated with the dignity and respect afforded any other person. Marie has the absolute right to expect that any procedure or course of treatment will be in her best interest" (p. 183). And relief of her suffering, both physical and emotional, should certainly be regarded as in her best interest. But we are left with the reminder that our society's death system is rooted in its overall view of life. If we are not inclined to take the child's mind and feelings seriously in other circumstances, then we are not very likely to do so in critical situations either. The ongoing movement to formulate and respect the rights of children must still struggle against centuries of habit through which adults have assumed that all the knowledge and power belongs in their own hands.

These are but two examples of the "incompetency" issue as applied to the right to die. Coping with this issue as it arises in a variety of real-life situations requires a great deal of competency on the part of all those persons who may be called upon to make decisions.

A SUPREME COURT RULING: THE NANCY CRUZAN CASE

The Supreme Court of the United States has recently (June 25, 1990) issued its first ruling that focuses on the right to die. The specific case before the court centered on Nancy Cruzan, a young woman who was critically injured in an automobile accident in 1983. She has been in a persistent vegetative state since that time. The court heard testimony that Cruzan might exist in this condition for many more years if she continues to be nourished through a feeding tube. From 1983 to the present, Cruzan has shown no signs of awareness and no ability to respond. After four years of the persistent vegetative state her parents sought permission to withdraw the feeding tube and let her die. Her family and friends testified that Nancy Cruzan had said she would not want to live as a "vegetable" on life-support systems. The Missouri Supreme Court denied this request, observing that she had not made a living will nor was there any other "clear and convincing evidence that the patient would want to die in her current circumstance."

This judgment was upheld by the Supreme Court. It was ruled that states can prohibit families from discontinuing life-support procedures from loved ones who are in persistent vegetative states and who have not made their wishes known in a clear and convincing manner. In writing the majority opinion, Chief Justice William Rehnquist said:

> Close family members may have a strong feeling—a feeling not at all ignoble or unworthy, but not entirely disinterested either—that they do not wish to witness the continuation of the life of a loved one which they regard as hopeless, meaningless and even degrading. But there is no automatic assurance that the view of close family members will necessarily be the same as the patient's would have been had she been confronted with her situation while competent.

The minority opinion, as summarized by William Brennan, held that:

> The testimony of close friends and family members often may be the best evidence available of what the patient's choice would be. Nancy Cruzan is entitled to choose to die with dignity.

The Supreme Court decision had two facets: (a) It gave each state broad powers to keep comatose patients on life-support systems and deny requests to withdraw these supports; (b) It affirmed the right of individuals to make advance directives—such as the living will—while they are competent and alert. The strong implication is that the Supreme Court would have affirmed Nancy Cruzan's right to die if she had made a living will.

The decision was as close as possible (five to four). This means that one of the most significant death-related issues of our time has been "decided" by a single vote. Sharp disagreements have already been expressed. There is no doubt that sharp disagreements also would have been expressed had one vote changed and the decision been made in the opposite direction.

The Supreme Court decision has now been followed by a County Probate judge's ruling that the feeding tube could be removed. Judge Teel stated that there was "clear and convincing evidence that Nancy Cruzan would want to die." The tube was subsequently removed by her physician and, at the time of this writing, it was expected that Miss Cruzan would die within a few days.

The right-to-die controversy will continue to be with us. The Supreme Court's decision will be very influential, but it would be unrealistic to expect family members, friends, and caregivers to easily surrender their own feelings, values, and stakes in the situation. Perhaps the greatest difficulties will arise where the patient is in a persistent vegetative state, no living will exists, and the family and health-care team share the view that life-sustaining procedures should be withdrawn. Perhaps the most useful outcome of the decision will be to encourage more people to think about their own values and wishes and specify these in an advance directive.

SOME GUIDELINES FOR UNDERSTANDING AND ACTION

Each of us brings our unique experiences and personality to situations that are themselves unique. It would be naive to expect us all to think and feel the same way about euthanasia-type issues. Furthermore, we are probably all better off if we continue to be stimulated by an interchange of viewpoints. This chapter concludes, then, not with a formula that is intended to apply to all persons in all situations, but with a few general guidelines for understanding and action that each of us can use in our own way.

1. Be cautious in asserting or accepting claims that there is a "right" to do such-and-such. The term "right" implies that a firm and indisputable principle rules the situation. Misunderstandings are likely to arise when this term is used in a loose and indiscriminate manner. It is not unusual for people to support or attack a "right to die" without having much idea about where rights come from nor their philosophical, moral, religious, or legal status. Over the years I have learned to translate "right" into "claim" until the speaker or writer has made a persuasive case for the former. In emotion-laden discussions people may simply use "right" as a way of emphasizing their dedication to a certain position. No matter how loud the war of words may become, a "right" is not a "right" until it has passed stringent critical tests.

2. Clarify the details. We might find ourselves in apparent disagreement because we are using terms differently or because we are really talking about different situations. For example, a discussion of the incompetency issue might quickly go off the rails if one of us has been influenced chiefly by a Saikewicz-type case and the other by the plight of a child like Marie.

3. Be aware of our own personal feelings and concerns. The self-monitoring attitude invento-

ries you completed earlier in this book can be useful in this regard. Conversations with family members and good friends can also help us to discover the assumptions, doubts, fears, and hopes that influence our own attitudes and beliefs. We are more prepared to understand right-to-die predicaments involving other people when we have examined and refined our own thoughts.

4. Try to see things from the other person's perspective, even if you disapprove of that person's ideas or actions—*especially* if you disapprove! We can learn much from our disagreements.

5. Stay in touch with continuing developments that affect attitudes and behavior. The emergence of the AIDS epidemic, for example, is leading to increasing public awareness of suicidal thoughts among terminally ill people. An association between terminal illness and suicidality existed long before AIDS appeared; many people have had passing thoughts of taking their own lives when they learned that they had a progressive and incurable disease. AIDS, however, gives new dimensions to this problem because it is a new and devastating illness many of whose victims had expected to have long lives ahead of them. Changes in health-care financing, the continuing "graying of America," and the periodic development of new experimental treatments for a variety of life-threatening conditions—all these factors and more will influence the euthanasia controversy for many years to come.

6. Cultivate your own network of supportive and resourceful people instead of relying entirely upon institutionalized safeguards. This guideline can be illustrated by returning to the best known and most influential "tool" of the right-to-die movement, the living will. Completing and filing a living will does not guarantee that your instructions will be followed. In an emergency situation, for example, paramedics and other personnel might be much too busy responding to the immediate demands, or there might not be an authenticated copy of the living will readily

available. In another scenario, your regular physician is away, and a doctor new to the situation (perhaps Debbie's exhausted and anxious resident) is faced with the need to make a quick decision, and opts for a life-support system. It is even possible that a physician or hospice administrator will deliberately go against the instructions because they conflict with his or her personal views. Whatever we can do to promote a frank exchange of views and build mutual respect will increase our chances of having our living will understood and acted upon when the occasion arrives. This includes discussions with our family and close friends, with health-care personnel and with other relevant people in our lives, such as the clergyperson and lawyer we most respect. We can also improve our chances of having an effective living will by making its provisions more comprehensive and specific. The standard living will now in common usage leaves a number of questions that may arise unanswered. For example, do you want to have fluids and nutrition discontinued? This is a practical decision that is not addressed by the usual living will. By developing a more effective living will instrument (Culver & Gert, 1990) and building a strong network of interpersonal communication and support we are more likely to have our wishes respected.

Most people are not yet aware that the living will can be modified to express our own wishes more clearly and reduce the possibility of misunderstandings. How is the public to become informed? And who is qualified to provide advice, counseling, and, when necessary, therapy for death-related problems? Next chapter, please. . . .

REFERENCES

Annas, G. J. (1984). When suicide prevention becomes brutality: The case of Elizabeth Bouvia. *The Hastings Center Report, 13,* 20–21, 46.

Anonymous. (1988). It's over, Debbie. *Journal of the American Medical Association, 259,* 272.

Boston Globe. (1976, April 1). Former "medical vegetable" is now a mother. *Boston Globe.*

Culver, C. M., & Gert, B. (1990). Beyond the Living Will: Making advance directives more useful. *Omega, Journal of Death and Dying, 21* (4).

Kron, J. (1973, Oct. 6). The girl in the coma. *New York Magazine,* pp. 17–24.

Lauter, H., & Meyer, J. E. (1984). Active euthanasia without consent: Historical comments on a current debate. *Death Education, 8,* 89–98.

Lifton, R. J. (1986). *The Nazi doctors.* New York: Basic Books.

Meagher, D. K., & Leff, P. T. (1989–1990). In Marie's memory: The rights of the child with life-threatening or terminal illness. *Omega, Journal of Death and Dying, 20,* 177–191.

Robbins, D. A. (1983). *Legal and ethical issues in cancer care in the United States.* Springfield, IL: Charles C. Thomas, Publisher.

Rollin, B. (1985). *Last wish.* New York: Linden Press/Simon and Schuster.

Scofield, G. (1989). (The) Living will. In R. Kastenbaum & B. Kastenbaum, (Eds.), *Encyclopedia of death* (pp. 175–176). Phoenix: The Oryx Press.

Times Mirror Center for the People and the Press. (1990). *Reflections of the times: The right to die.* Washington, D.C.: *Times Mirror* Center for the People and the Press.

Weingarten, P. B. (1989). Concern for dying. In R. Kastenbaum & B. Kastenbaum, (Eds.), *Encyclopedia of death* (pp. 56–57). Phoenix: The Oryx Press.

chapter 12

HOW CAN WE HELP?

the promise of death education and counseling

Learn about death? Help somebody to die? It was not many years ago that an expression of interest in death education and counseling would have met with widespread puzzlement and uneasiness. People who have been active in these related fields for a while have many stories to tell. Among anecdotes that can be quickly told, here are two of my own favorites: The assistant program director of a major city television station was a brisk, no-nonsense kind of person. He approached a colleague and me with a commanding "I've-seen-it-all" attitude. Aware that we were to be among the guests on a talk show, he snapped: "What are you here for?" "Death," I said, "and dying," added my colleague Ronald Koenig. Our host froze, blinked his eyes once, took an awkward step backward—and fell thuddingly upon his backside. "Terrific," we assured him, "Will you do that for us on camera, too?" Years later the United States electronic and print media had become much more accustomed to death-related communications. It was a new and unsettling experience, however, for the radio newsman who was about to broadcast from West Germany's first conference on death and dying. "Doctor, tell us this," he said, thrusting his microphone toward me as though it were a weapon, "how do you make people die with smiles on their faces? That is what you do, yes?" "Friend," I lied, "you have

probably just horrified several million men, women, and children. What you have imagined certainly horrifies me. Do you want to know what we really do and why?" (He really didn't: he just wanted to get this uncomfortable interview over and done with.)

There is still a mixed reception. Some people have difficulty in understanding how death can be studied or taught. Others are fearful that strangers under the guise of educators and counselors will invade the sanctity of their innermost beliefs and attempt to force some kind of unwelcome change upon them. Different questions are sometimes raised by fellow researchers, educators, and counselors in other fields. Is there a solid basis for this field, or does death education purvey only untested assumptions and fancies? What do people derive from death education and counseling? And what *should* people derive? Furthermore, anybody might well be curious about the kind of person who steps forward to become a caregiver or educator in this area. Who is attracted to this field and for what reason? And how do they cope with the stress?

We begin our exploration with a brief historical introduction, then examine the current scene in death education and counseling, and conclude with some observations about future prospects and challenges.

DEATH EDUCATION IN HISTORICAL PERSPECTIVE

From Ancient Times

The term "death education" itself and the field to which it refers did not become a recognizable part of our society until the 1960s. In the broader sense, however, we have never been without some form of instruction and guidance. Ancient documents from Tibet and dynastic Egypt offer detailed accounts of what becomes of the soul after death and what preparations can be made ahead of time to improve one's chances for a safe passage. These documents have become known in the Western world as "books of the dead." Their emphasis is heavily weighted toward funeral and memorial practices and the fate of the soul after death. For example, it helps if one knows the names of the underworld demons and deities and the challenges they will put to the spirits of the deceased.

By contrast, much of contemporary death education focuses on people attempting to cope with death in the midst of life, e.g., the hospice nurse, the grieving family member, the individual who has just learned that he or she has a life-threatening disease. It might seem a little odd to us that some cultures would emphasize education for the dead and the mourners. The ancient Egyptian or Tibetan, however, might also have difficulty with our priorities and preoccupations: e.g., the mass of regulations that surround eligibility and reimbursement for hospice care could appear as formidable as the priestly injunctions for funeral rituals or postmortem behavior in the underworld.

Down through the centuries, many religious leaders, philosophers, and creative artists have offered a variety of images and ideas about our relationship to death. One of the most basic and common themes has been the fleeting nature of life. Job (13:12) laments: "Man that is born of a woman is of few days, and full of trouble. He cometh forth like a flower, and is cut down: he fleeth also as a shadow, and continueth not." The *Old Testament* repeatedly compares human life with the grass that withers and is blown away by the whirlwind. The evanescence of life is linked with the limits of human knowledge and power. Do we suppose ourselves to be lordly beings? Proverbs (27:1) quickly deflates us: "Boast not thyself of tomorrow; for thou knowest not what a day may bring forth." If we cannot even be sure of having a tomorrow, how can we claim knowledge and power?

It is not only the Judeo-Christian tradition that has attempted to bring awareness of our mortality to the fore. The collection of stories known as *The Arabian Nights* is best known for the celebration of sensuality that can be found on many pages. But death is also given eloquent attention. The following passage demonstrates how awareness of our mortality might provide the basis for a mature philosophy of life:

> O sons of men,
> Turn quickly and you will see death
> Behind your shoulder.
> Adam saw him,
> Nimrod saw him
> Who wound his horn in the forest,
> The masters of Persia saw him.
> Alexander, who wrestled with the world
> And threw the world,
> Turned quickly and saw death
> Behind his shoulder. . . .
> O sons of men,
> When you give yourselves to the sweet trap of life
> Leave one limb free for God.
> The fear of death is the beginning of wisdom
> And the fair things you do
> Shall blow and smell like flowers
> On the red and fiery day.
> (Mathers, 1972, pp. 300–301)

Notice the similarities as well as the differences between the perspectives offered by the *Old Testament* and *The Arabian Nights*. Both emphasize the brevity of human life and the possibility of sudden death at any time. Both suggest that for these very reasons it would be foolish to allow ourselves to be carried away by our own triumphs and ambitions. Both contrast the power of God with the powerlessness of the mortal person. But the emotional tone is not at all the same. The troubled, fleeting shadow portrayed in the *Old Testament* seems to find neither pleasure nor solace. By contrast, the readers of Scheherazade's tales of one thousand and one nights are expected to give themselves to "the sweet trap of life." What are we to do, then? Should we spend our lives lamenting and "eating worms" before the worms eat us? Or should we enjoy the sweet trap while we can, knowing full well that our pleasures and triumphs will not endure because *we* will not endure?

It is worth keeping this divergence in mind. Death education and counseling today carry forward the awareness that death is a central fact of life. Once we have the basic facts in mind, however, we still have a choice of what attitudes we will take toward these facts, what lessons we intend to draw from them. At one extreme we might crawl into a box and wait for the end; at the other, we might attempt to live in a feverish quest for thrills. Perhaps "the fear of death is the beginning of wisdom," but it may be only the beginning. We still have the challenge of developing a coherent and meaningful life based upon our awareness that "all flesh is as grass."

The *New Testament* introduced a radically different perspective: "Whoso eateth my flesh, and drinketh my blood, hath eternal life; and I will raise him up at the last day" (John 6:54). "And this is the promise that he hath promised us, even eternal life" (John 3:15). "And the sea gave up the dead which were in it; and death and hell delivered up the dead which were in them: and they were judged every man according to their works. And death and hell were cast into the lake of fire" (Revelation 20:13–14). In centuries to come, Christians would differ among themselves on many death-related issues (e.g., is it faith, good works, or predestination that will ensure the triumph over death?). Right from the start, however, it was clear that at the core of

Christianity was its bold contention that man had been redeemed from death through Jesus.

The Christian "death education lesson" differed markedly from those of the *Old Testament* and the *Arabian Nights*. We do not have to go through life in sorrow and lament, nor surrender to the "sweet trap" with the bittersweet knowledge that it will soon snap shut upon us. Instead, we should feel joyful about the life to come after this brief and unsatisfactory sojourn on earth is completed. This rousing lesson did not escape change through time, however. As the Christian faith grew larger and its membership became more diverse, other themes became increasingly significant. Three related themes remain influential today, although all have been challenged within as well as outside of the Christian orbit:

1. Death is punishment for all humans because of Adam and Eve's disobedience in seeking forbidden knowledge (original sin doctrine);
2. Death is a test that will separate the worthy from the unworthy: the final exam of all final exams.
3. Life on earth is just something we must endure; its pleasures are insubstantial, if not deceptive. Death, therefore, is a blessed release.

Not all Christians subscribe to these views. However, they have the cumulative weight of centuries behind them and are still influential today. Death educators and counselors would have to be very naive to ignore this powerful and complex heritage. For example, the fact that the Christian tradition includes images of death both as punishment and as blessing should alert us to the many possible implications. "I am eager to fulfill myself through death" can be a compelling wish that competes with the equally compelling fear, "What if I am judged to have lived a sinful and unworthy life?" To take another example: a born-again minister paid an unexpected and unrequested visit to a woman hospitalized with a terminal illness. He burst into her room with these words: "God knows what a sinner you are! Prepare yourself for the moment of judgment!"

The astonished woman quietly replied, "God and I have never given each other any trouble." Undeterred, he made repeated attempts to bully the exhausted woman into confessing her sins and placing her life into his hands. Upon learning of this incident, the official hospital chaplain was even more distressed than the woman who had fallen victim to this brutal "educational" or "counseling" intervention. Unfortunately, there is a potential for harming people at vulnerable points in their lives by attempting to impose one's own beliefs upon them. Responsible death educators and counselors hold a variety of religious beliefs themselves, but they also are aware and respectful of the traditions that influence their students and clients.

Those with a sense of history will have the further realization that traditional ways of communicating about death might not be entirely appropriate or effective in the world of the late 20th century. These traditions developed in societies that differed from ours in many ways. In medieval times, for example, most people lived in small, agrarian communities. They had little education, little contact with people outside their own circle. The concepts of having "inalienable" human rights, holding one's own political and religious opinions, and being free to pursue unlimited personal interests and ambitions were known to few people. They lived in a low-technology society that was fairly stable from generation to generation and which offered little protection against the forces of nature and the disasters encountered in everyday life. When darkness fell at night, few would venture out of doors where both real and fantasy terrors lurked. Little faith could be placed in the wrong-headed "medical" treatments of the time which frequently caused as much suffering as the diseases themselves. Many newborn babies failed to survive into adulthood. Infections associated with childbirth, wounds, and injuries often proved fatal to adults, and epidemics periodically decimated the population.

Some of the most vivid and forceful traditions reached their peak and faded away before our own era. The dance of death (*danse macabre*), for example, was a compelling image that was introduced by poets, artists, and performers in the 13th century, if not earlier. The living and the dead are portrayed as engaging in a slow and solemn dance together. The danse macabre theme often depicted Death as a skeletal figure who laid claim to all mortal souls, whether low or high born (Kastenbaum, 1989a). "We all look the same to Death: kings, bishops or peasants, we are all mortal beings" was part of the core message. And a powerful message this was— bearing in mind that society was highly stratified at the time, with a few "high and mighty" people lording it over the masses. The zing of this message gradually decreased as the ruling classes became destabilized by social and technological changes that continue into our own time. Nevertheless, some 20th century artists have still found powerful uses for dance of death imagery, and millions of viewers have watched Woody Allen trip the light fantastic with a shrouded companion in the final moments of *Love and Death*.

Another significant tradition arose in the 15th century: Christian guidebooks for priests and others who might be in the position to help people in their last days and hours of life (Kastenbaum, 1989b). This has become known to historians as the *Ars moriendi* tradition—literally, the art of dying well. These guidebooks differ in many ways from the writings on dying and death that have appeared in our own time. For example, most of the guidebooks limited themselves to describing rituals that should be performed as part of the deathbed scene. Two themes already mentioned—death as punishment and as a test of the soul's worthiness—tended to dominate. People were never more at risk than at the moment of death. The priest tried to help the dying person resist the assaults and temptations of the demons who hoped to consign the soul to the flames of hell. As we will see below, there might be a subtle link between the priestly soul-saver and at least one image of the modern death educator/counselor.

Despite these differences, however, the *Ars moriendi* guidebooks were motivated by some beliefs and concerns that have reappeared in our own death awareness movement. These include: (a) the view that *how* a person dies is a significant matter; therefore (b) some deaths are better than others; so (c) a "good death" is a real achievement, and (d) flows more readily from a life that has been lived in the recognition of mortality, with (e) the support of caring people who have also prepared themselves properly for the encounter with death.

The capstone of the *Ars moriendi* tradition was reached in 1651 with the publication of Jeremy Taylor's *The Rules and Exercises of Holy Dying* (1651/1977). In dedicating the book to his friend, The Earl of Carbery, Taylor enunciated the key principle:

> My Lord, it is a great art to die well, and to be learnt by men in health, by them that can discourse and consider, by those whose understanding and acts of reason are not abated with fear or pains: and as the greatest part of death is passed by the preceding years of our life, so also in those years are the greatest preparations to it; and he that prepares not for death before his last sickness, is like him that begins to study philosophy when he is going to dispute publicly in the faculty. All that a sick and dying man can do is but to exercise those virtues which he before acquired, and to perfect that repentance which has begun more early. (Taylor, p. iv)

Death education and counseling did not really begin in the 1960s, as we have seen from this brief historical survey. But death education and counseling had to begin anew. Let's see why.

Beginnings of the Modern Death Awareness Movement

Death became a casualty of massive social and technological change with the rise of commercial interests, individualism, nationalism, and science (to mention only a few of the major developments). To be more precise: it was *the willingness to confront death and dying* that became a casualty. People were remaking the basic conditions of their lives. Increasingly, there was less appeal to enduring deprivation and hoping for a better life after death. Instead there was a heightened sense of energy and opportunity to make something of life on earth. Technological innovations began to appear in dizzying profusion: the printing press, the steam-powered locomotive, electric lights to blaze through the darkness of night, the telephone, and on and on.

The image of a person dying became overshadowed by a new concept: the failed machine. Medieval injunctions to think steadily about our deaths seemed out of place in the excitement of early industrial development. The "action" had moved decisively into the sphere of scientific and technological advances. These advances included the biological sciences as well. The body seemed to be only a rather complicated machine. Some independent thinkers suggested that the mind was also a kind of mechanism— and society itself perhaps a larger, clattering contrivance whose many moving parts could be manipulated by technicians. There was less talk of souls and demons, more of inventions and opportunities.

As we entered the 1960s, some of the bloom had already departed from the technological vision. Despite all the innovations, there was still hunger, tension, and fear in the world. Furthermore, technology itself had become a menace; proliferation of nuclear and biological weapons, pollution, and environmental deterioration were already of concern to observant people. There was also a growing dissatisfaction with the emphasis on materialism and mechanistic thinking. Such marvels as color television and space exploration did not really seem to meet society's needs for a sense of purpose and meaning.

This uneasy feeling became especially intense as people faced their own death or the death of loved ones. By this time we had entered a new era in medical care. The positive side was very impressive. One disease after another had been tamed. The media led us to expect a new medical miracle every day. Some people who would have died young now lived long and active lives. But the negative side could not be entirely ignored. The personal relationship between doctor and patient was being replaced by a complex system that already seemed to be eluding anybody's control. It was one thing to put up with the stress and depersonalization of this system when there was realistic hope for successful treatment. It was quite another thing, however, to be caught up in an aggressive and mechanistically-oriented treatment system when one's death was in close prospect.

Conditions were ripe, then, for a new approach. The old guidebooks for dying had long been forgotten and were out of sync with modern times, while the new face of medicine appeared to be that of an aloof and aggressive technician who was intent upon achieving his own aims. It was—and it remains—the challenge of the death education and counseling movement to draw upon both past values and present realities to offer an effective alternative.

Sociologist Vanderlyn Pine (1977) reports that most of the first teachers and scholars were males who ranged in age from 25 to 40 and had "distinctively academic orientations." Few were medical doctors; few came to this subject with an "overriding global view of the issues involved." The teachers and scholars hoped to learn from their direct observations, rather than to prove some preexisting theory. I find something paradoxical in this historical note. Why did men so predominate among the teachers, scholars, and writers when—then and now—women predominate among those who provide direct services to dying persons and their families? And why have so few physicians, relatively speaking, come forward when they might be expected to have an unusually strong stake in the situation as well as extensive experience? (I will leave these questions for your own reflections.)

Writings on death and dying started to appear in the late 1950s, and series of lectures and formal courses soon followed. There was very little solid information available on many topics, but now it had at least become acceptable to discuss our death-related thoughts, doubts, hopes, and experiences. And the discussions frequently were stimulating and broad ranging. The participants came from a variety of fields, e.g., psychology, sociology, nursing, social work, and theology. A typical course on death and dying would include observations and ideas from many fields. The rigid boundaries between one field and another did not hold up as participants quickly saw the value in learning the other person's viewpoint and making use of all the relevant information. This interdisciplinary approach showed up in many research projects as well. The psychological autopsy procedure, for example, required extensive communication among physicians, nurses, psychologists, social workers, clergy, occupational and physical therapists, etc. (Weisman & Kastenbaum, 1968; Weisman, 1974). It would be some years before hospice care established itself, but already some caregivers, researchers, and educators were learning how to work together with mutual respect and trust.

By the mid-1960s death courses had entered the curriculum in a number of colleges and universities, and soon thereafter the first multidisciplinary centers for education and research were established (at Wayne State University and the University of Minnesota). The demand for courses rapidly increased. With the appearance of Kubler-Ross' (1969) book *On Death and Dying,* there was a further surge of interest which now extended to nurses, social workers, clergy, and the general public. As the 1970s ended, death education had become a recognized component of college and university curricula and had also radiated out to some elementary schools, high schools, and some schools of medicine. Seminars and workshops on death became commonplace, as did media coverage of death-related issues. The field now had two scientific journals of its own (*Omega,* and *Death Education,* later renamed *Death Studies*). Death-related articles also became more welcome in a variety of other scientific and professional journals, and the list of death books continued to grow rapidly.

The rapid growth of death education and counseling brought with it the related questions of purpose, responsibility, and quality control. Writing in 1977, Pine classified death educators into three distinct groups. The "old school" (not that old, actually!) "have a thorough knowledge of the field and extensive research and writing experience. Unfortunately, too many have not seriously considered the educational aspects of their material." The "new school" was showing "a deep interest and commitment to death education, (but) many do not possess research or writing experience or extensive practice knowledge of the field." In other words: they were not very well prepared for the challenges they had taken on and would have to work hard to gain expertise. Of most concern to Pine was "the upcoming horde or the 'nouveau arrivé.' These teachers present a serious problem for death education because many are joining the field primarily because of its popularity . . . through the perspectives of 'pop death' " (Pine, p. 73).

Pine raised several other concerns. Should it be the intention of death education to change attitudes? Should death education be used to persuade people to accept a particular view that is favored by the instructor or a special interest group? Will "bad death education" drive out "good death education" through "poorly conceived courses" and "publications which are ill-conceived, nonscholarly . . . weak, and diluted"? He also raised the more subtle concern that "death education may actually be used for denial of death . . . it is possible for courses in dying and death to be so abstract or lacking in a humanistic perspective that the courses themselves become a means of denying. Alternatively, by believing that death education can insulate against the pain of loss and grief, some teachers and students may use such a course for purposes of denying" (p. 79).

These were all realistic concerns when death education had become something of a fad. Now, just a few years later, much of the "fizz" has evaporated. Death education is well established in many contexts, but it is no longer the latest wonder and scandal. With Pine's concerns still in mind, let us examine death education today.

DEATH EDUCATION: THE CURRENT SCENE

We can gain a quick view of the changed scene by looking at an organization known as Association for Death Education and Counseling (ADEC). This nonprofit organization was incorporated in 1976 with the express purpose of improving the quality of death education and death-related counseling (Leviton, 1989). In pursuing these goals, ADEC has introduced national training workshops and a certification procedure for death educators and counselors. If you attend one of ADEC's national conferences you will probably be impressed with the combination of maturity and receptivity to new knowledge. What you will not see is the person who has read one book and attended one workshop and is ready to impose his or her ignorance upon the world. The "pop death" people have pretty much come and gone. Fortunately, the most valuable elements of the early death education movement have continued to flourish. The typical participant is a person who is well aware of his or her own death-related feelings and who has had direct experience in one or more areas of real life concern (e.g., supporting families after the death of a child, counseling people who have tested positive for the AIDS virus, training hospice volunteers, etc.). You will probably find this person to be compassionate, realistic, welcoming of newcomers, and blessed with a resilient sense of humor. For weird people who are committed to bizarre projects, we will have to look elsewhere.

Some people may still put themselves forward as death educators or counselors without possessing either the personal or experiential qualifications. The minister who burst into the dying woman's hospital room was motivated by his personal agenda, not by the expressed needs of a person he had never met. The teacher who does not even know that journals such as *Death Studies* and *Omega* exist will be lecturing from assumptions and limited personal observations that are often at variance with the facts. There are still places where unqualified people can function in the role of death educators or counselors, but with increasing professional and public sophistication, these opportunities are diminishing.

What we should expect from death education and the death educator is a question that has not yet been fully resolved. Perhaps there will never be a definitive answer because people come to this topic with a variety of needs and expectations. Students in my classes, for example, often enroll with the purpose of adding to their competencies as nurses, paramedics, social workers, or psychologists. Others have had personal experiences, such as the death of a parent or the serious illness of a spouse, that give the topic special urgency. Still others are keenly interested in working with the dying or the bereaved; others have become curious about some particular facet of death (e.g., funerals, the near-death experience, etc.). All these expectations can be addressed in a death education course, but it is difficult to give them all equal attention. Although the classroom situation is flexible enough to permit a mix of thought and feeling, structure and openness, it may not be able to meet all the students' needs.

Clinical skills are probably developed best in clinical situations. Classroom examples can be helpful, but case experience and supervision is also needed. "Deep learning"—an experience that is emotional as well as intellectual—can be achieved at times in the classroom, but this more often requires a series of in-depth and intimate discussions that are not always possible within academic constraints. It is useful, then, for all participants to recognize what can and should be accomplished in a particular death education course, conference, or workshop and what must be achieved in other settings. A particular death education course is not likely to meet all the expectations of all students, although it can have some value for everyone.

The role of the death educator is often ambiguous. When it is not clear what death educators should expect of themselves, then students may also encounter difficulties. Richard A. Kalish (1980–1981) observes that the death educator

came along at a time when two of society's most important traditional roles have undergone significant change. According to Kalish's analysis, the priest was once the dominant person who mediated our relationship to death. ("Priest" is used here in the generic sense.) The physician has gained increasing importance, however, as society shifted its orientation from hopes of a better life after death to a longer and healthier life on earth. Both the priest and the physician have had to complete formal studies and apprenticeships, and both are set apart from the rest of society in a number of ways. The relationship among priest, physician, and society has continued to change, however, and in ways that affect our perception of the death educator. According to Kalish:

> . . . lengthened survival was seen as leading to the spectre of slow deterioration in nursing homes, of living out lives of loneliness, and of turning control of one's fate over to an impersonal technician standing behind an impersonal machine. The knowledge, machines, power, buildings, rituals, in effect, the magic of the new priesthood (physicians) was clearly inadequate. (p. 75)

The death educator entered the scene, then, when society was no longer as enthusiastic about accepting an afterlife as substitute for a long and fulfilling life on earth—but also at a time when society had judged that the physician did not have the "magic" either. This situation led Kalish to portray death educators as "deacons who will never become priests." The priest and the physician both possess a kind of vested power and authority that is not shared by the death educator (who may, however, also *be* a priest or physician!). Death educators or "deacons" can come into conflicts with priests and physicians by venturing into their turfs in ways that are considered unwelcome or competitive. Death educators can also seem to be promising too much and thereby set themselves up for failure.

> Death educators and counselors are treading sacred ground, and must expect to be attacked for their errors, their vanities, any signs of greed or lust or

need of power. Just as they attack the old and new priesthoods. These attacks have begun. The media, which only recently carried nothing but laudatory articles on the death awareness movement, is now publishing subtle and not-so-subtle digs. . . . (p. 83)

Kalish's point that death educators and counselors must be aware of their role relationships with other professionals is well taken, as is the caution that they should refrain from creating unrealistic expectations on the part of students or clients. Furthermore, skill in teaching or learning about death does not fully equip a person for therapeutic interventions outside the classroom. Social pressures may also encourage the death educator to deliver a "comforting product rather than a searching encounter." The result of sugar-coated superficialities in the name of death education can be an *illusion of understanding and control.* Death is not just one more fact of life to be placed alongside another. However, once a course number has been assigned and all the academic niceties have been observed, there may be the unearned assumption that "we covered death today" (Kastenbaum, 1977).

Leviton and Wendt (1983) enunciate a potentially important goal of death education that has not yet found widespread application. The study of death might—just might—enhance the quality of civilized life in general.

> From the death educator's perspective we find it necessary to remind our students of the horrors of Nazi concentration camps, and our own actions in Vietnam. We have long been aware of how quickly the generations forget. Students in their second decade know little of the atrocities of World War II; they know only slightly more about Vietnam. Thus, we read first person accounts of their experiences during such times. We guide our students through . . . mental imagery. . . . The tears come. But students learn. . . . As death educators we can indeed work toward improving the quality of civilized life. (pp. 384–385)

This is a controversial position. Many death educators continue to limit their mission to the "classic" topics of dying and grief, with perhaps

some attention to suicide as well. Once the decision is made to move into the larger sphere of social criticism and change, then the "deacon" is likely to stir up dissension and, possibly, wander beyond his or her range of competency. The death educator who chooses to include war, terrorism, environmental catastrophe, and other large-scale topics should also be prepared to cope with the ensuing controversy and to bring in-depth knowledge to this expanded coverage. In just the past few years there has been an increasing trend toward politicization of death education and counseling as society struggles with such divisive issues as abortion, assisted suicide, capital punishment, and the right to die. Death educators who ignore the larger sociopolitical context of their work may be dismayed to find themselves caught in the crossfire between mutually antagonistic vested interests. Along with the Delphic oracle's advice to "know thyself," the death educator will also need to know his or her society and its pressure points.

Finally, it should be noted that death educators do not constitute a distinctive discipline of their own. Rather, effective death educators come from a variety of established fields, such as psychology, psychiatry, medical ethics, nursing, sociology, and the ministry. It is valuable to have a solid grounding in one or more substantive fields as well as particular competency in death-related topics.

How Effective Is Death Education?

It is to the credit of this new interdisciplinary field that many attempts have been made to study its effectiveness rather than simply to assume that death education classes are achieving their goals. Attention will be given here to some of the studies that have illuminated the process or outcome of death education or that have raised the most interesting questions for further research.

Channon (1984) explored a question relevant to death education in general: How much personal experience with death do students bring with them? Her respondents were 454 preclinical medical students in Sidney, Australia. Most had a friend or relative (usually a grandparent) who had died. Deaths among their own generation were uncommon (2%), and only about 1 respondent in 12 had actually been present when somebody died. The most typical experience with death was in the cadaver room as part of their medical training. Channon concludes, "Very few respondents had seen a dead body other than in a medical context. The relatively low number who had seen a dead family member at home or at the funeral again underlines the tendency in our society to keep knowledge of death and dying away from our awareness" (p. 234).

Fortunately, a number of death educators have found ways to help medical students overcome their anxieties about relating to the dying and the dead. Marks and Bertman (1980) developed techniques to provide emotional support for first-year students in their traditional assignment to dissect a cadaver. In a more recent study, Wear (1989) invited several medical students to express the thoughts and feelings they experienced working with cadavers: before dissection, after the first cut, and at the conclusion. It was clear that the cadaver experience aroused a variety of strong feelings—and also that the students found it valuable to have the opportunity to formulate and share their thoughts rather than have to keep them "under wraps." One of the main themes that emerged were the students' difficulties in coping at the same time with the physical reality of the cadaver and the humanity of the deceased person. For example, one student started to think about the life that her own cadaver left behind: "It grew up, *just like me* . . . it's more than a body . . . it's a person! I guess you have to put those feelings aside" (Wear, p. 382). Although this small study could yield no statistical findings, it does provide many entry points for discussion and guidance. This kind of qualitatively oriented study can enrich death education courses by identifying fears, doubts, and conflicts and exploring ways to resolve them.

One practical way to evaluate the effects of death education for health care professionals would be to determine what trends exist within the curriculum. There is fierce competition for the opportunity to offer specialized classes in schools of nursing, medicine, and pharmacy. So much technical material must be covered that instructors often have to campaign vigorously to win time for a lecture or two on a topic of particular interest to them. Within this context, then, death education courses might seem to be of peripheral interest, academic luxuries that cannot be afforded. In fact, however, death education courses are now doing fairly well in these traditional and highly competitive environments.

A research team surveyed 126 medical schools, 396 baccalaureate nursing schools and 72 pharmacy colleges throughout the United States to determine the extent of their death education offerings (Dickinson, Sumner, & Durand, 1987). They found a marked increase in the number of such offerings when compared with the situation even ten years previously. Almost all medical and nursing schools include some death education content in their curriculum. Usually, this material is integrated into other courses. Medical and nursing schools are much more likely to provide the opportunity for discussion; colleges of pharmacy tend to rely entirely on lectures. The researchers note that most of the reported death education content has been added to the curriculum in just the last few years. This is taken as an encouraging sign that death education is regarded as contributing to professional preparation in the health-care fields, even though the coverage is limited by severe pressures on available time in the curriculum.

The scope of death education is gradually expanding to include a greater variety of people who are responsible for human services. This steady and successful expansion suggests that the programs are effective in meeting needs. For example, Air Force mortuary officers report that death education has provided valuable guidance, assistance, and emotional support for their difficult task of informing and working with bereaved families (Rosenbaum & Ballard, 1990). There is, however, a significant exception to the continued growth of death education. A survey of 423 public schools has found that there is still relatively little death education being offered in the entire range from prekindergarten through the 12th grade (Wass, Miller, & Thornton, 1990). Only about one school in ten reported having any kind of death education program. The possibility of providing occasional death education at the "teachable moment" by discussing recent death-related events is seldom utilized. It is possible that many teachers do not feel secure in opening discussions on such emotion-laden topics as the death of a teacher or student. Survey results show that the teachers are being offered very few opportunities to develop their own expertise in this area. Suicide prevention/intervention programs were no longer quite as rare, though, with about one in every four schools reporting some kind of effort in this area. The authors suggest that "public attitudes toward death may not have changed as dramatically as we would like, and the 'death avoidance' previously observed by social scientists may still be prevalent today" (p. 262).

Another way to evaluate the effects of death education programs is to explore their possible effect not only on the direct participants but on other people as well. There is some evidence to indicate that "ripple effects" do occur. One study found that a three-week university symposium not only had positive value for the student and faculty participants, but also affected the thoughts and feelings of other people on the campus who had not taken the course themselves (Cook, et al., 1984–1985). They were stimulated by what they had heard about the symposium and engaged in more conversations about death-related matters. It is likely that ripple effects occur in many other death education situations as well. For example, I have had several contacts with adults who had been unable to share their concerns about death until the sub-

ject had been brought up in their children's classroom. In another recent instance, I had spoken about sudden death situations to an introductory class in human communication. One of the students had survived an automobile accident in which a friend had been killed. The driver was now this student's roommate, and had never said a word about the accident and the death. The communication student decided it was time to do something about this situation, and over the next few days he and his roommate talked—and wept—about the tragedy. Later he reported, "We both have grown up a lot, I think—and _____ doesn't have those screaming nightmares any more." My experience is probably typical of many other death educators whose students report that their friends and family express curiosity and use the course as an occasion to bring up their own thoughts and feelings. There are probably some disturbing incidents as well when an enthusiastic student runs up against a friend or family member who is appalled at the idea of discussing death.

The informal side of death education programs is also emphasized by the results of a study by Waldman and Davidshofer (1983–1984). Their participants experienced a significant decline in their level of death anxiety because they had had the opportunity to discuss their thoughts and feelings. The formal program had provided useful information, but it also brought people together and gave them the license to discuss death-related topics. It might be that formal and informal presentations serve different functions. A lecture, for example, can dispel misinformation and provide useful new knowledge. However, the release of tension, the growth of emotional understanding, and the modification of personal attitudes may occur most effectively in an informal setting.

There is one school of thought which holds that death education courses *should* reduce death anxiety. I hesitate to endorse this view. As we have seen (Chapter 1), there is little solid information available on what constitutes the "right" level of death anxiety. Furthermore, most people express only a moderate level of death anxiety most of the time, if the most commonly used assessment techniques are to be believed. In addition, the term "death anxiety" is often used in a vague way. Precisely what are we trying to reduce? Furthermore, anxiety is a valuable signal; it tells us that something is disturbing our peace of mind. Perhaps we should respond to death anxiety as a clue and see where it leads us, rather than moving swiftly to dull or displace the symptom. There will be circumstances in which the reduction of death anxiety could be an appropriate and perhaps even an urgent goal of educational efforts. However, I do not think it would be wise to conceive of death education primarily as an instrument for reducing death anxiety.

The question of whether or not death education actually does reduce anxiety has been answered in various ways by various studies. For example, a recent study finds that emergency medical technician trainees who did *not* have an instructional module on death and dying later showed less reluctance to confront death than those who did have the module (Coleman, in press). Those who had been exposed to the death education module seemed to have become more aware of the emotional and spiritual issues involved—and apparently did not have the opportunity to integrate this heightened awareness into their pattern of thoughts, feelings, and attitudes.

We should not leave this topic with the impression that death education itself is a standardized product that can be prescribed and administered in precise dosages. It is a complex process that depends much upon the interacting personalities of instructor and students and upon much else as well—for example, the scholarly and professional qualifications of all participants, the specific purpose of the course, the amount of time that can be devoted to this enterprise. This is well illustrated by an unusual experiment in death education conceived by Prunkl and Berry (1988). Fourteen college students agreed to

spend an entire week pretending that they were dying. The participants were free to choose "how, where, with whom, and at what hour they were to die" (p. 4), and were required to keep a daily record or journal of their feelings and behaviors. The experiment was developed as part of an ongoing course, and it was offered to the students as an alternative to writing a conventional term paper. What took place was rather complicated, often unexpected, and not easily summarized. This simulation experiment is reported in detail in *Death Week* and is recommended for those with a keen interest in death education and its evaluation. The point for us to remember is that death education can and does take various forms and can have more than one outcome. Even the "same" experience can affect participants in markedly different ways.

COUNSELING AND THE COUNSELORS

Although our emphasis here is on counseling and psychotherapy, we will also look at the experiences of other people who provide direct services to terminally ill patients, their families, the grieving, or the suicidal. These include the many nurses, social workers, clergy, and hospice volunteers who sometimes enter into close personal relationships with people who are confronting death. Counseling, like education, can occur under informal circumstances or as part of a systematic program. The boundary between counseling and education can also be crossed easily from either side. A classroom discussion, for example, may become transformed into an advice-sharing session to help a student decide whether or not to continue his or her practice of avoiding funerals. Similarly, a priest who is counseling the spouse of a dying person may be able to reduce anxiety by providing specific information about church beliefs and practices. In exploring counseling and the counselors, then, we are not entirely forgetting death education.

Characteristics of Professionals in the Death System

In the fields of counseling and psychotherapy it is an article of faith that people who would help others must not only be adequately trained from the academic and clinical standpoints, but must also be well aware of their own personalities and in control of their own conflicts. This requirement seems applicable to all caregivers who accept responsibility in death-related situations, whether ministers or social workers, psychiatrists or hospice volunteers.

It is useful, then, to examine the death concerns of mental health professionals as Morrison, et al. (1981–1982) have done. They found that professionals representing five different fields were neither more nor less anxious than a comparison population. However, those who had never been married and those with a serious medical illness expressed higher levels of death concern. It may be reassuring, then, to learn that mental health specialists are as "normal" as everybody else in their self-reported death attitudes. However, the unexpected finding that never-married mental health professionals express a higher level of death concern merits further investigation. Perhaps more attention should be given to the interaction between a caregiver's personal life and his or her orientation toward death.

Another approach has been taken by Neimeyer and colleagues (1983) who asked medical residents in pediatrics to provide autobiographical information and to complete the Death Threat Index, a more sophisticated instrument than the usual death anxiety scale. Additionally, the residents were asked to respond to a pair of case history vignettes. They were to imagine themselves as being the attending physician in each case and to make several ratings. Further information was obtained by asking a group of more advanced medical residents to rate each of the study participants on their actual effectiveness in helping patients and their families cope with death. Here,

then, is one of the few studies that not only obtains in-depth information on the respondents, but also attempts to compare self-reports with information from an external source. The researchers found that, yes, there was a relationship between personal feelings and style of interacting with dying patients. The medical residents who felt most strongly threatened by death were also those who most often used avoidance strategies when caring for a dying patient. These were the young physicians who busied themselves in reviewing charts and finding other things to do instead of meeting their patients' needs for personal contact, information, guidance, and emotional support. We might well expect similar findings among other health-care specialists when personal death anxiety leads to the avoidance of meaningful interactions with patients and their families.

The most extensive study of caregivers' response to working with dying people has been conducted by Mary L. S. Vachon (1987), who herself had extensive experience as a helping person. She interviewed about 600 professional caregivers from hospitals, palliative care facilities, chronic care institutions, and voluntary agencies. The caregivers included Australians and Europeans as well as Canadians and Americans. As might be expected, most of the caregivers were women, and most of the men in her sample were physicians. Vachon placed the problem in the broad perspective of occupational stress. What was the basic source of stress for physicians, nurses, and others who care for dying patients? And how did they cope with this stress?

Her answer might be surprising—especially to those who have not worked in a health-care setting. The findings are crisply expressed in one of her chapter titles: "Dying Patients Are Not the Real Problem." The caregivers reported they were most stressed by their work environment and occupational roles, not by their direct work with dying patients and their families. They had many specific stresses to report, e.g., poor communication within the health care facility, conflicts between one unit and another, lack of continuity as employees come and go, etc. Many of the specific stresses were continuous or recurring and showed themselves through inadequate patterns of communication. As Vachon noted, it is possible that underlying death anxiety contributed to the stress and communication difficulties, but the overall evidence points to the significance of environmental variables.

Vachon's findings ring true. Tense, anxious, frustrated, and exhausted caregivers have difficulty bringing their best selves to dying patients and their families. For example, we do not have to assume that a nurse who withdraws from a dying person is motivated by her own excessive death anxieties. It is perhaps even more likely that she is caught in a role conflict (between technical expert and humane caregiver), a time bind, and an ambiguous situation created by poor interstaff communications. And those professional caregivers who do have intense death-related fears are not likely to find much opportunity to reduce or resolve them on the job. This makes it tempting for them to "go with the flow" and perpetuate a brisk, distant, noninteractive strategy of making it through the day.

Whatever improves communication among caregivers is likely to reduce frustration and anxiety. Delving into the caregiver's personal anxieties may not always be the most useful place to begin. Instead, we might help the caregiver to be more helpful with terminally ill people and their families by preventing or reducing the systematic stresses they encounter in their workplace. There is a growing research literature that identifies specific sources of stress (e.g., Yancik, 1984). It has also been found that burnout and staff turnover are relatively low among hospice nurses (Turnipseed, 1987) suggesting that some of the principles and practices of a well functioning hospice might be applied to other health care settings as well.

Careful selection, effective training, and a supportive work environment should be given high priority whether we are dealing with professional or volunteer caregivers in death-related situations. For our nation's health-care systems in general, we have a long way to go if we are to achieve these goals.

Counseling and Psychotherapy

People do not necessarily need counseling or psychotherapy when death enters their lives. Sometimes the needed strength can be drawn from love, friendship, a familiar environment, and one's own beliefs, values, and coping resources. Financial security and competent nursing and medical care are also likely to help see the person through. Before considering counseling or therapy, then, it is usually wise to assess the total situation. Perhaps what this man needs is a more effective pain management regime; perhaps what this woman needs is the opportunity to spend some time with the sister or brother she has not seen for years. Counseling and therapy are options that may be worth considering, but not to the neglect of the many other factors that could provide comfort and peace of mind.

What approach should be taken when counseling or therapy seem to be indicated? The Rev. Edgar N. Jackson (1977), a pioneer in counseling with the dying, believes that one of the most important goals of the helping person should be the facilitation of the client's ability to summon up his or her own inner strengths. A sense of helplessness can reduce an individual's ability to cope with illness not only physically but also psychologically. The counselor can help to restore self-confidence, relaxation, and a renewed sense of still being a valuable and lovable person. This more positive psychological state is thought to have a favorable effect on bodily response, e.g., through improved cardiovascular circulation or more vigorous functioning of the immune system.

The success of this healing-oriented approach depends much upon the caregiver's personality. Jackson's own "technique" is difficult to separate from his well-centered personality and firm but gentle manner. It is difficult to imagine a nervous, time-conscious and hard-driving personality achieving the same results.

There is more than one pathway to effective counseling or psychotherapy with the dying patient. The German psychiatrist Hilarion G. Petzold (1982) operates within the framework of Gestalt therapy and uses guided imagery, shared fantasy, and creative media such as clay, poetry, and colors. In attempting to help the person in crisis recover a sense of wholeness, Petzold does not hesitate to reveal his own feelings of frustration, anger, and insecurity. He enters into frank and personal dialogues with the patient rather than remaining in a more traditional therapeutic role. Note the give-and-take quality of this excerpt from one of Petzold's transcripts:

LUTZ: . . . And that's what makes me so angry. So furiously angry, that I am dying so unnaturally, not a normal death: cancer.

HILARION: What do you feel when you say it like that?

LUTZ: Offended, a horrible feeling of being wronged. Of mischief, of destruction, and somehow degradation. Everything here is degrading. You are degrading, how you watch me die. Let me just die.

HILARION: It makes you angry, that I am alive and well. I can understand these feelings, too. It's not fun to watch what is happening to you, and sometimes I feel almost guilty for being healthy.

LUTZ: And why do you do this then? Why do you come here then, and why are you writing all this down and keeping a record of it?

HILARION: I've often asked that myself. Not only with you. I've sat through it with others. . . . Mostly old people. Maybe that's my way of dealing with my fear of dying. Be as close to it as possible; then a person knows how to handle it when it's his turn. . . .

LUTZ: Then I'm probably the wrong subject to study. I guess.

HILARION: Dammit, your cynicism is really getting on my nerves! Why are you so offensive? Sure, now you're the one who's been hit, but it will get me, too, just like everybody—you can be *dead* sure of it.

LUTZ: Sorry. Sometimes I can't come to grips with it any other way. I think it's good that you are writing all this down. Really. You are documenting it for me. I sure can't do it anymore. (p. 256)

Petzold's method is intense and requires both the ability to disclose his own feelings as well as to explore those of the patient. Furthermore, he operates within a strong conceptual framework. This approach is not likely to work for a therapist who fears self-disclosure, hesitates to confront clients, or lacks a coherent theory. The excerpt given above does not demonstrate gentle support from a patient counselor. But it does demonstrate an unabashed interaction in which the therapist asserts his own rights ("Why are you so offensive?"), thereby giving the client permission to respond as a whole person rather than as a role-trapped dying man. This approach can be very effective in some therapist/client match-ups. It can also be disturbing and destructive if the therapist is not sufficiently aware of his or her own feelings and uses Gestalt (or any other approach) as an outlet for personal anxiety and anger.

Those who would provide counseling or psychotherapy in death-related situations would be wise to select an approach that is in harmony with their own personalities as well as one that is well grounded in the knowledge of human nature.

Two other and very different examples support this point. At one extreme is what might be termed the healing care approach, represented by Jackson, but also by an entire team of therapists who have worked with severely impaired and terminally ill geriatric patients (Kastenbaum, et al., 1981). Therapeutic touch, singing together, and interpreting each other's dreams and fantasies are among the untraditional modalities that are used in addition to dialogue. Conveniences such as carefully scheduled sessions and a formal setting are put aside. The therapists make themselves available when needed at any hour of the day or night. Not all caregivers would find this approach acceptable or possible, but it may at times be the treatment of choice when a person is at risk of dying alone and in despair.

At the other extreme is the behavior modification approach (Sobel, 1981). Some behavioral principles were used by the healing care therapists, and have been incorporated into a variety of other approaches. However, when the overall approach is behavior modification there is more of a "rational" as contrasted with an emotion-intensive framework. One does not have to be an exceptionally intuitive person to conduct successful behavior modification. In fact, spontaneity at the wrong time might interfere with the treatment plan. The behavior modification approach may be taken not only with the dying patients themselves, but also with the professional and personal support network. For example, a systematic desensitization technique might help reduce some of the anxieties of the dying person's spouse and thereby also reduce the anxiety in their interactions.

There is no definitive list of counseling and therapeutic approaches that can be effective in death-related situations, nor is there compelling evidence to demonstrate that one approach is generally superior to another. Furthermore, there is no reason to suppose that all dying people require such interventions. Counseling and therapy does have a place, however, in the total spectrum of services that should be available when appropriate.

REFERENCES

Channon, L. D. (1984). Death and the preclinical medical student. Part I. Experiences with death. *Death Education, 8*, 231–236.

Coleman, T. (In press). The effect of an instructional module on death and dying on the death anxiety of emergency medical technician trainees. *Omega, Journal of Death and Dying.*

Cook, A. S., Oljenbruns, K. A., & Lagoni, I. (1984–1985). The "ripple effects" of a university sponsored death and dying symposium. *Omega, Journal of Death and Dying, 15*, 185–190.

Dickinson, G. E., Sumner, E. D., & Durand, R. P. (1987). Death education in U.S. professional colleges: Medical, nursing, and pharmacy. *Death Studies, 11*, 57–62.

Jackson, E. (1977). Counseling the dying. *Death Education, 1*, 27–40.

Kalish, R. A. (1980–1981). Death educator as deacon. *Omega, Journal of Death and Dying, 11*, 75–85.

Kastenbaum, R. (1977). We covered death today. *Death Education, 1*, 85–92.

Kastenbaum, R., Barber, T. X., Wilson, S. G., Ryder, B. L., & Hathaway, L. B. (1981). *Old, sick and helpless: Where therapy begins.* Cambridge, MA: Ballinger Publishing Co.

Kastenbaum, R. (1989a). Dance of death. In R. Kastenbaum & B. K. Kastenbaum (Eds.), *Encyclopedia of death* (pp. 67–70). Phoenix: The Oryx Press.

Kastenbaum, R. (1989b). Ars Moriendi. In R. Kastenbaum & B. K. Kastenbaum (Eds.), *Encyclopedia of death* (pp. 17–19). Phoenix: The Oryx Press.

Kincade, J. E. (1982–1983). Attitudes of physicians, housestaff, and nurses on care for the terminally ill. *Omega, Journal of Death and Dying, 13*, 333–344.

Leviton, D. (1984). Association for death education and counseling. In R. Kastenbaum & B. K. Kastenbaum (Eds.), *Encyclopedia of Death* (p. 19). Phoenix: The Oryx Press.

Leviton, D., & Wendt, W. (1983). Death education: Toward individual and global well-being. *Death Education, 7*, 369–384.

Marks, S., & Bertman, S. (1980). Experiences with learning about death and dying in the undergraduate anatomy curriculum. *Journal of Medical Education, 55*, 48–52.

Mathers, P. (1974). (Translator). *The book of the thousand nights and one night.* Volume 2. New York: St. Martin's Press.

Morrison, J. K., Vanderwyst, D. Cocozza, J. J., & Dowling, S. (1981–1982). Death concerns among mental health workers. *Omega, Journal of Death and Dying, 12*, 179–190.

Neimeyer, C. J., Behnke, M., & Reiss, J. (1983). Constructs and coping: Physicians' responses to patient death. *Death Education, 7*, 245–266.

Petzold, H. (1982). Gestalt therapy with dying patients: Integrative work using clay, poetry, therapy, and creative media. *Death Education, 6*, 249–264.

Pine, V. R. (1977). A socio-historical portrait of death education. *Death Education, 1*, 57–84.

Prunkl, P. R., & Berry, R. L. (1988). *Death week.* New York: Hemisphere Publishing Corporation.

Rosenbaum, S. D., & Ballard, J. A. (1990). Educating Air Force mortuary officers. *Death Studies, 14*, 135–146.

Sobel, H. J. (Ed.) (1981). *Behavior therapy in terminal care.* Cambridge, MA: Ballinger Publishing Co.

Taylor, J. (1977). *The rules and exercises of holy dying.* New York: Arno Press. (Original work published 1651)

Turnipseed, D. J., Jr. (1987). Burnout among hospice nurses: An empirical assessment. *Hospice Journal, 3*, 105–119.

Vachon, M. L. S. (1987). *Occupational stress in the care of the critically ill, the dying, and the bereaved.* Washington: Hemisphere Publishing Corporation.

Waldman, D. A., & Davidshofer, C. (1983–1984). Death anxiety reduction as a result of exposure to a death and dying symposium. *Omega, Journal of Death and Dying, 14,* 323–328.

Wass, H., Miller, M. D., & Thornton, G. (1990). Death education and grief/suicide intervention in the public schools. *Death Studies, 14,* 253–268.

Wear, D. (1989). Cadaver talk: Medical students' accounts of their year-long experience. *Death Studies, 13,* 379–391.

Weisman, A. D. (1974). *The realization of death.* New York: Jason Aronson.

Weisman, A. D., and Kastenbaum, R. (1968). *The psychological autopsy: A study of the terminal phase of life.* New York: Behavioral Publications.

Yancik, R. (1984). Sources of work stress for hospice staff. *Journal of Psychosocial Oncology, 2,* 21–31.

chapter 13

DO WE SURVIVE DEATH?

Survival of death is a question for some people, an answer for others. These differences have persisted to the moment of death. Adam Smith, the famed economist, quipped to his friends, "I believe we must adjourn this meeting to some other place." Poet John Milton said farewell with the words, "Death is the great key that opens the palace of eternity." Others have died with their doubts and questions still intact. One of the most often discussed remarks was offered by writer Gertrude Stein on her deathbed. Raising her head from the pillow, she whispered, "What is the answer?" Stein then closed her eyes and let her head fall back. After a moment's silence she opened her eyes again, laughed, and added, "What's the question?" A tough-minded New England farmer, in his 90th year and within a day of his death, shared his thoughts with me. "Everybody I know's dead has stayed dead. Stubborn damn bunch, they get something in their mind!" (What are *your* plans?) "I'll rise at rosey-damn dawn with wings on my ass or I'll just—(laughs-coughs)—I'll go on rotting like I been rotting. Ask me tomorrow!"

Belief, disbelief, or uncertainty about survival of death may be important to a person throughout life. Some people have periods in their lives when their most intense motivation is to find the answer, or to develop more confidence in the answer they have in mind. This quest can occur at any time of life: e.g., a 13-year-old's first questions about the meaning of life, a 50-year-old's sudden anxiety after the death of a loved one, a 90-year-old's need to take stock of the assumptions that have guided him or her this far.

Evidence that bears upon survival of death may be of particular interest to people who have not quite made up their minds or who are open to the challenge of reviewing their existing beliefs. However, even those who are firm in their beliefs/disbeliefs might find it useful to examine the evidence that has been put forth to support or challenge the prospect of following this life with another. There are still other reasons to give careful consideration to this topic: If there is survival, what *form* does it take? A variety of alternative images have been offered, some of them quite different from the most familiar Christian conception. How has the *idea* of survival been used and abused? And what should the prospects of cessation or survival *mean* to us?

These are the major questions that will be considered here. First, however, please complete the self-quiz in Box 13–1. This will give you the opportunity to bring some of your own attitudes and beliefs to the surface and to compare them with what others have reported.

NEAR-DEATH EXPERIENCES: NEW EVIDENCE FOR SURVIVAL?

The Primary, or Moody-Type, Near-Death Experience

Renewed attention has been given to the survival question since the publication of a book

---

BOX 13–1
SURVIVAL OF DEATH? A SELF-QUIZ

1. I believe in some form of life after death.
   ____Yes ____No

2. I have the following degree of confidence that my answer is correct.
   ____Completely sure   ____ Very sure
   ____Somewhat sure   ____ Not sure at all

3. If you *believe* in some form of afterlife, describe on a separate sheet of paper precisely how you picture or understand the nature of life after death. If you *do not believe* in life after death, describe what you think it would be like *if* it were true.

4. Suppose that you really wanted to persuade somebody that there is *not* life after death. What evidence, experiences, or line of reasoning would you use? Be as specific as possible and put your heart into it, as though you wanted very much to convince a person that there is no afterlife and had to call upon the strongest objections to this belief.

5. Suppose now that you wanted to persuade somebody that there *is* life after death. What evidence, experiences, or line of reasoning would you use? Again, be specific and put your best efforts into it.

6. You have already stated your own ideas and beliefs. What kind of experience, evidence, or logic could persuade you to change your mind? It does not matter if you consider the contrary evidence or experience to be very unlikely. What might lead you to change your mind if it did happen or were true?

7. Suppose that you actually have changed your mind. You have discovered that your present belief is mistaken. *What difference would it make in your life?* In what ways and to what extent would your life be different if you had to accept the opposite of your present belief about life after death?

8. What influence has your *actual* belief or disbelief had upon the way you live? What decisions has it influenced and in what way?

9. What do you think would be the best thing about life after death (whether or not you are a believer)?

10. What could be the worst thing about life after death?

11. How did you come to your present belief or disbelief about life after death?

12. What would you tell a child who asks what happens when a person dies?

Place your answers in an imaginary sealed envelope for consideration after the clinical and research dimensions of the survival question have been examined in this chapter.

---

entitled *Life After Life* in 1975. Author Raymond A. Moody, Jr. listened to the experiences of men and women who had recovered after coming close to death. Some of these people had suffered cardiac arrest; all had been in serious peril. Moody's report and discussion of these near-death experiences (NDEs) became a surprise best seller. Almost immediately, additional NDE reports appeared from many sources. Some people had had such experiences years before but were reluctant to speak about them until Moody's book brought the phenomenon into the open. The same was true for some physicians and other allied health workers who had encountered occasional NDEs in their practice and now felt more comfortable about sharing them. Although Moody's NDE collection was not based on a controlled research effort (nor did he claim it to be), it did stimulate studies by a variety of medical and sociobehavioral scientists.

Moody selected 50 cases from his collection for analysis. Some of these people were said to have been pronounced dead by a physician; all appeared to have been close to the end. Examining his interview notes, Moody found 15 elements that occurred frequently (but not necessarily all elements occurred in each interview). A typical experience follows:

> I was hospitalized for a severe kidney condition, and I was in a coma for approximately a week. My doctors were extremely uncertain as to whether I would live. During this period when I was unconscious, I felt as though I were lifted right up, just as though I didn't have a physical body at all. A brilliant white light appeared to me. The light was so bright that I could not see through it, but going into its presence was so calming and so wonderful. There is just no experience on earth like it. In the presence of the light, the thoughts or words came into my mind: "Do you want to die?" And I replied that I didn't know since I knew nothing about death. Then the white light said, "Come over this line and you will learn." I felt that I knew where the line was in front of me, although I could not actually see it. As I went across the line, the most wonderful feelings came over me—feelings of peace, tranquility, a vanishing of all worries. (p. 56)

This report illustrates some of the major features of the primary NDE. Instead of panic or despair there is a sense of serenity and well-being. The sensation of being "lifted right up" is also one of the most striking characteristics. Known popularly as the "out-of-body experience," this state has a more technical name as well: the *autoscopic* experience. (This scholarly term, however, does not really add anything to the explanation.) Rising and floating are also common experiences reported, as well as a sense of journey, a going toward something. A "brilliant white light" may be discovered as the journey continues. Furthermore, there is often a turning-point encounter. The individual reports feeling as though he or she had a choice about death at this time. Moody comments:

The most common feelings reported in the first few moments following death are a desperate desire to get back into the body and an intense regret over one's demise. However, once the dying person reaches a certain depth in his experience, he does not want to come back, and he may even resist the return to the body. This is especially the case for those who have gotten so far as to encounter the being of light. As one man put it most emphatically, "I *never* wanted to leave the presence of this being." (p. 11)

Soon clinical researchers came up with additional cases of NDE (Sabom & Kreutziger, 1977). Historians pointed out ancient examples from religious experiences, especially in the Eastern tradition (Holck, 1978). The type of experience confided to Moody was not limited to the survivors who had happened to come his way.

The question now arose: How is this remarkable experience to be explained? It is here that we enter the realm of continuing controversy. Does the primary NDE constitute proof for survival of death?

Evidence Favoring the NDE as Proof of Survival

Moody at first did not claim that the reports he had collected were evidence for survival. "In my opinion anyone who claims that near death experiences prove or give scientific evidence of an afterlife is only betraying his ignorance of what terms like evidence or proof mean" (Moody, 1980). More recently, however, Moody (1988) has reversed this position. He now supports the survival hypothesis.

What has been learned from systematic research? Psychologist Kenneth Ring took the lead in establishing research procedures for the study of NDEs (1978; 1980; 1984). He developed a scale to assess the depth of intensity of an NDE and therefore made it possible to study the phenomenon in more adequate detail. The components of this scale are summarized in Box 13–2. A very intense NDE would include all these

---

BOX 13–2

COMPONENTS OF A
NEAR-DEATH EXPERIENCE*

I felt as though I were dead.
I felt at peace; a pleasant experience; no suffering.
I was separated from my body.
I entered a dark region.
I heard a voice . . . I encountered a kind of "presence."
I could see this spiritual being . . . I spoke with the spirit.
I reviewed my whole life.
I saw lights ahead of me. . . . lights all around me. . . .
I actually entered into the light.
I saw the most beautiful colors.

*Based upon the Near-Death Experience Scale introduced by Ring (1980) and further developed by Greyson (1983).

---

possible components, some of which are also rated according to their vividness or depth.

Ring found that age, sex, economic status, and the type of near-death experience (e.g., automobile accident, surgery, etc.) did not seem to make a difference. The NDE occurs in many types of situations and among many kinds of people. In a recent summary of all available research in the field, Ring now (1989) estimates that the NDE occurs in about one of every three cases that have been studied. Although this means that two of every three people who have survived a brush with death did *not* report an NDE, the number of those now on record is in the thousands. How many have had NDEs without coming to the attention of researchers? "It seems reasonable to assume that there must be many millions who have and, because of modern cardiopulmonary resuscitation measures, many more who will" (Ring, p. 194).

According to Ring's studies, the NDE seems to have a powerful effect on many survivors. After a brush with death, people often have a renewed sense of purpose in life. Daily life also becomes more precious to them. And what about the fear of death? Many survivors report that they have become much less concerned about dying and death; there was something very comforting and reassuring about their close encounter. These changes in perception and attitude were seldom found among people who had near-death episodes without near-death experiences. The differences were greatest between people who had deep or intense NDEs and those who reported no NDE at all. People who could recall intense NDEs were much more likely to think of these as spiritual experiences that had changed their lives, whether or not religion had played an important role for them before these experiences. It would appear, then, that the renewed purpose, appreciation of life and sense of spirituality are closely associated with the *experience* rather than simply the fact of a life-threatening encounter.

In Ring's opinion the NDE does provide evidence for survival. He believes that the individual has attained an altered state in which the mind is free—temporarily—from the limitations imposed by the physical body. No longer bound by physical make-up, the individual is granted a direct perception of the universe. The perception of some form of radiant light at the end of a tunnel might represent a glimpse of astral reality, according to Ring. In attempting to provide a scientific rationale for this view, Ring refers to Karl Pribham's (1977) neurobiological theory, which suggests that the human brain functions in a holographic manner: We are biologically equipped to interpret the complex frequencies that comprise the universe and to translate these into usable sensory experience.

As a behavioral scientist, Ring attempts to keep his conclusions within the limits of his data, so he does not make the flat statement that the NDE proves survival of death. Nevertheless, he marshals his evidence and speculations in this direction and appears to be personally convinced of survival himself.

Cardiologist Michael B. Sabom (1982) was among the earliest contributors to NDE research and has now reported his investigations in some detail. His findings for the most part are consistent with those of Ring and other researchers. The NDE is frequently reported as a beautiful experience, accompanied by a sense of serenity and freedom rather than anxiety or depression. Again, no relationship was found between the NDE and characteristics of the individual or of the life-threatening condition. Among Sabom's many useful examples are several that illustrate the individual's attempt to make contact with others while in the NDE state. A Vietnam veteran, for example, immediately experienced the split-self state when a mine explosion left him close to death. He continued to watch his body and what was happening to it all the way to the surgical table in the field hospital:

SUBJECT: I'm trying to stop them (the doctors). I really did try to grab a hold of them and stop them, because I really felt happy where I was . . . I actually remember grabbing the doctor. . . .

AUTHOR: What happened?

SUBJECT: Nothing. Absolutely nothing. It was almost like he wasn't there. I grabbed and he wasn't there or either I just went through him or whatever. (p. 33)

The sense of being separate from your own body comes across strongly in many of Sabom's cases, whether drawn from the battlefield, domestic accidents, or critical illness.

What gives the work of Sabom and his colleagues particular distinction is the effort to compare the survivor's subjective reports with the information available in hospital records and retrievable from staff members. This is important because it provides an opportunity to determine whether or not the person in the midst of an NDE actually does make observations that could not have been possible if trapped within a horizontal, impaired, and endangered body. Sabom is aware that people who have not been adequately anesthetized occasionally show a memory for events that happened during their surgery. Could

the NDE be the same sort of occurrence? He concludes it is not likely. The NDE bears "no resemblance to the nightmarish experiences reported by inadequately anesthetized patients. *Visual* details of an operation are not later retrievable by hypnosis from the subconscious minds of patients who had been anesthetized, although *spoken* words can sometimes be recalled" (p. 80).

Furthermore, Sabom at times was able to establish a positive correspondence between what the patient "saw" and what did in fact take place during a life-and-death medical procedure (in his study this was usually the emergency procedure for reversing cardiac arrest). In a preliminary study he was able to establish what kind of educated guesses people tend to make about cardiopulmonary resuscitation (CPR) so that he would not credit a survivor with a specific and accurate description unless it was well justified by the evidence. Sabom eventually had a set of 32 people whose NDEs included visual impressions of what had taken place during the peak of their crisis. Most of their descriptions included statements that correspond to what had actually happened but were not highly specific. The key information was derived from a smaller set of six survivors who had recalled specific details of their near-death crisis. In each of these cases the individual recalled having seen one or more specific events and developments that could not have been obtained through guesswork or prior knowledge of CPR. In other words, there was objective evidence that some individuals who reported an NDE did in fact gain information consistent with out-of-the-body status.

Sabom does not rush to the conclusion that his findings constitute evidence for survival of death. Nevertheless, after considering several alternative hypotheses, he judges that the autoscopic phenomenon may be authentic, that some type of split between mind and body can occur during points of crisis, and that during this altered state a person can make accurate observations of immediate reality as well as enter into the mystical state of being often reported for NDEs. Sabom's work is highly recommended for further reading on all counts: as a human document, as an application of careful methodology in a difficult situation, and as a thoughtful assessment of alternative explanations.

Another research approach lends some indirect support to the claim that the NDE should be considered as evidence for survival. Why accept the survival interpretation if there are simpler explanations available? Scientists usually prefer explanations that stick closely to the observed facts and do not require bringing in additional assumptions and speculations. If only certain kinds of people or certain kinds of situations produced NDEs, then the survival interpretation could be criticized as an extravagant flight of fancy. We have seen that Ring's early studies found otherwise; the NDE seemed to occur to many different people in many different situations. A number of questions were left unanswered by these studies, however, and have since been examined carefully by Glen Gabbard and Stuart Twemlow (1984). Here are some of their most important findings:

1. NDEs are not caused by nor are they necessarily symptoms of mental illness. Very few people who reported NDEs showed signs of psychopathology.
2. NDEs are not related to level of education. Therefore, it cannot be said that the NDE is either something that is "imagined" by people with little formal education, or "created" by people with perhaps too much education.
3. There is no evidence that NDEs occur mostly among people who had already been fascinated by mystic or other unusual phenomena. (*After* the NDE, however, people often did become more interested in spiritual phenomena.)
4. The NDE does not have much similarity to dreams. In comparing their NDE reports with studies of normal dreams, Gabbard and Twemlow observed more differences than similarities. Therefore, it cannot be said that the survivors "dreamed" their experiences, if we are to use the term "dream" in its usual sense.

As we will see, there are other Gabbard and Twemlow findings that are not so favorable to the survival interpretation. Nevertheless, the results that have just been reviewed do suggest that some of the more conservative interpretations (e.g., mental illness, dreaming) are not well supported. However, the poor showing of these alternative interpretations does not prove the survival hypothesis. There are other alternative hypotheses still to consider, as well as some problems with the data and logic of the survival interpretation.

Evidence and Logic Against the Near-Death Experience as Evidence for Survival

There are a number of logical as well as empirical objections to interpreting NDEs as evidence for survival:

1. Some people who return from a close encounter with death do *not* have experiences of the primary NDE (Pelletier & Garfield, 1976). They have no memories at all or only vague and dreamlike fragments to recall. This argues against the universality of the NDE and therefore weakens the NDE. Since death is universal, how could the NDE be otherwise if it is truly a visit to the other side?
2. Some survivors return with nightmarish experiences that neither increase their spirituality nor decrease their fear of death. Although Sabom apparently did not come across such examples, the equally careful research of Garfield (1979) did, and I have collected both positive and negative reports myself (Box 13–3), p. 322.
3. The primary, or Moody-type, NDE occurs sometimes in situations in which the individual is in no bodily peril of death, therefore it should not be considered as distinctively related to death (LaBarre, 1972). The out-of-the-body component of the NDE has also been reported frequently—and sometimes even created experimentally—apart from any death peril (Brent, 1979; Myers, 1975).

4. Careful research of medical records shows that many people who report NDEs actually had *not* come close to death. The most recent such study found only about half of the NDE reporters had survived a life-threatening illness or injury. Nevertheless, it was common for people to believe that they had been dead or very near death even if they had not been in serious danger. Some patients had decided for themselves that they had been "dead" or "clinically dead." Others (mis)interpreted what they had been told by doctors or nurses. The researchers comment that "having had the NDE itself may have led some people to believe retrospectively that their condition must have been worse than it otherwise seemed" (Stevenson, et al., 1989–1990, p. 52).

5. The fact that many kinds of people report NDEs in many kinds of situations has weakened such alternative explanations as mental illness or a strong predisposition toward fantasy. However, there are also findings that do suggest relationships between the specific circumstances and the specific nature of the NDE. Gabbard and Twemlow, for example, found that people who had been in severe pain were more likely than others to experience a sense of distance from their bodies. They note that, "In hypnotic pain experiments, it is a common suggestion to dissociate the painful part from the body so that it is treated as 'not self'" (Gabbard & Twemlow, 1984). Furthermore, patients who had been under anesthesia were especially likely to see brilliant lights and hear unusual sounds. These effects are known to occur with many people who have been anesthetized, whether or not their conditions were life-threatening. Results such as these indicate that the overall picture is not that simple. The specific type of NDE that one experiences seems to be influenced by a number of circumstances, even though NDEs, as a class of phenomena, may occur to many kinds of people under many kinds of stress.

6. We hear NDEs only from the survivors. There is no evidence that what happens when a person really dies "and stays dead" has any relationship to the experiences reported by those who have recovered from a life-threatening episode. In fact, it is difficult to imagine how there could ever be such evidence; the very fact that a person has recovered disqualifies their report of "permanent death." There is always an observing self that categorizes the observed self as inert or dead. This split consciousness may result in the opinion that "I was dead," but there was always another "I" lively and perceptive enough to make that judgment.

Several explanations have been offered as alternatives to the conclusion that NDE survivors have actually returned from the dead. These explanations do not deny the experiences as such, nor the emotional significance and meanings that might be drawn from them. The alternative explanations, however, do attempt to provide interpretations that are plausible and that remain within the framework of basic clinical and research knowledge.

What are these alternative explanations? Psychiatrist Russell Noyes, Jr. and his colleagues conducted a series of studies (Noyes & Kletti, 1976; 1976; 1977) with people who survived a variety of life-threatening crises. He and his colleagues found a set of common features in these reports. Three major factors emerged from the statistical analyses: mystical, depersonalization, and hyperalertness.

The *mystical* dimension of experiences close to death includes:

Feeling of great understanding
Images sharp or vivid
Revival of memories
Sense of harmony, unity
Feeling of joy
Revelation
Feeling of being controlled by outside force
Colors or visions
Strange bodily sensations

The *depersonalization* dimension includes:

Loss of emotion
Body apart from self
Self strange or unreal

BOX 13–3
SOME FRIGHTENING NEAR-DEATH EXPERIENCES*

- *There were so many pews on each side, and each pew was filled with people wearing black robes with hoods. I couldn't see their faces but if I turned my eyes I could see the inside of the hoods were lined with red . . . I stood there wondering where I was and what I was doing there, when a door opened to the right of the altar and out came the devil. . . . I saw that what he was pouring from the jug was fire, and I screamed, dropped the goblet, and started to run. . . .* (Irwin & Bramwell, 1988, p. 42)
- *I was thrilled to meet this person or was it an angel—and then all at once I saw that she or it was truly horrible. Where the eyes were supposed to be were slits and kind of blue-green flames flickered through them, through the eye-places. I can still see this demon, this whatever-it-was. With my eyes wide open, I can still see it.*
- *She told me to go back. I didn't want to. I said I was so happy being where I was, not that I knew where I was. I thought she was being mean to make me go back into that bloody, wrecked body. I could feel myself shaking and crying. I didn't feel good any more.*

*Told to the author by survivors of motor vehicle accidents.

Objects small, far away
Detachment from body
World strange or unreal
Wall between self and emotions
Detachment from world
Body changed in shape or size
Strange sounds
Altered passage of time

The *hyperalertness* dimension includes:

Thoughts sharp or vivid
Thoughts speeded up
Vision and hearing sharper
Thoughts blurred or dull
Altered passage of time
Thoughts and movements mechanical

With these findings Noyes attempts to explain the primary NDE. He believes it is important to consider both physiological and psychological levels. Hyperalertness and depersonalization are interpreted as part of the same neural mechanism. The function of this hypothetical mechanism is to help the human organism react to dangerous circumstances. Drawing upon earlier observations of Roth and Harper (1962), Noyes suggests that this is an adaptive mechanism that combines opposing reaction tendencies, "the

one serving to intensify alertness and the other to dampen potentially disorganizing emotion" (Noyes, 1979, p. 78). When this mechanism is working properly, a person is able to cope exceptionally well (cooly, calmly, objectively) in the midst of a crisis. Noyes writes:

> On a *psychological* level depersonalization may be interpreted as a defense against the threat of death. Not only did people in the studies . . . find themselves calm in otherwise frightening situations but they also felt detached from what was happening. . . . *The depersonalized state is one that mimics death* [italics added]. In it a person experiences himself as empty, lifeless, and unfamiliar. In a sense he creates psychologically the very situation that environmental circumstances threaten to impose. In so doing he escapes death, for what has already happened cannot happen again; he cannot die, because he is already dead. (p. 79)

This is a cogent and powerful explanation because it is in contact with NDE data and with the broader realm of psychobiological dynamics.

The dimension of mystical consciousness is seen by Noyes as being somewhat apart from the depersonalization-hyperalertness mechanism. This feature occurs most often with people who are dying from physical disease. Noyes suggests that the physiological changes associated with terminal illness may induce altered states of consciousness in which experiences of a mystical type are more likely to appear. Noyes' theoretical analysis, with many points of reference to clinical data, is richer than what can be presented here. (If you have a serious interest in this topic, you should become familiar with Noyes' work in more detail.)

I have suggested a related possible explanation with two components (Kastenbaum, 1981). First, you might expect that those who are closest to death—in the most perilous physical condition—should be the most likely to have intense NDEs. The available evidence, however, finds just the opposite (Greyson, 1981). Survivors who had been very close to death reported fewer experiences of any kind than those who had been less jeopardized. This weakens the assumed connection between the NDE and death. It also highlights a question that has been somewhat neglected: Precisely when does the NDE occur? There is no firm answer. Quite possibly, the NDE is a memory created *on the way back.* In other words, it is not necessarily what the person experiences at the peak of the crisis but rather represents an attempt to make sense of the profound and confusing events that have transpired. The greatly impaired physical function close to the point of death does not allow much in the way of either perception or thought. On the way back, however, some people may be able to integrate their extraordinary but chaotic experiences through a memory story whose content and texture is drawn from the psychobiological response itself as well as individual and cultural factors.

A second component of the NDE might arise from the specific nature of the life-threatening condition. It is true that several studies have failed to find a relationship between the nature of the death threat and the production of an NDE. Such a relationship is more likely to be observed, however, if you attend to the individual's role in the crisis. A driver faced with an impending collision is much more likely to make an emergency

maneuver than to split off into an autoscopic experience. In general, we engage in instrumental actions—we do something—when the circumstances permit. This is a survival mechanism: action to avoid catastrophe. The NDE is more likely to occur when the jeopardized person has no instrumental action available. In such a situation the NDE serves a quieting, energy-conserving function. The sense of serenity implies the activation of self-produced brain opiates (endorphins). This altered state enables body functions to continue at a basic level with minimum expenditure of energy and is represented at the psychic level by comforting imagery. The imagery becomes more coherent as the individual recovers, although in retrospect it is attributed to an earlier phase of the crisis.

Still another explanation has been offered by psychologist Ronald K. Siegel (1980). He emphasizes the hallucinatory nature of NDEs (and the deathbed visions described later), drawing in particular upon the work of Grof and Halifax (1977):

The specific content of complex hallucinatory imagery is determined largely by set (expectations and attitudes) and setting (physical and psychological environments). For many dying and near-death experiences, the sets (fear of approaching death, changes in body and mental functioning, etc.) and settings (hospital wards, accident scenes, etc.) can influence specific eschatological thoughts and images. Grof and Halifax suggest that the universal themes of this imagery may be related to stored memories of biological events which are activated in the brain. Accordingly . . . the feelings of peace and quiet may be related to the original state of intrauterine existence when there is complete biological equilibrium with the environment. The experience of moving down a dark tunnel may be associated with the clinical stage of delivery in which the cervix is open and there is a gradual propulsion through the birth canal . . . the dying or near-death experience triggers a flashback or retrieval of an equally dramatic and emotional memory of the birth experience. . . . To the extent that this reasoning is correct, the experience of dying and rebirth in the afterlife may be a special case of state-dependent recall of birth itself. (Siegel, 1980, p. 920)

Why the hallucinations in the first place? Siegel suggests (as others have) that the sensory world of the terminally ill person is likely to be drastically reduced. Not much of sensory input is getting through from the outside. This lack of external stimulation encourages the release or escape of stored memories. These memories reenter conscious awareness as though they were perceptions. The result is that experiential state known as the hallucination.

There is one more way of looking at NDEs that deserves our attention. Carol Zaleski, an expert in religious studies, examines what she calls *Otherworld Journeys* (1987) that have been reported from ancient times to the present. Here is one of her examples:

> Four days ago, I died and was taken by two angels to the height of heaven. And it was just as though I rose above not only this squalid earth, but even the sun and moon, the clouds and stars. Then I went through a gate that was brighter than normal daylight, into a place where the entire floor shone like gold and silver. The light was indescribable, and I can't tell you how vast it was. (p. 58)

This quotation is from a deeply religious man by the name of Salvius who had been left for dead one evening on a funeral bier. He was said to have revived and, inspired by his vision, became a bishop. Zaleski's perceptive review of "otherworldy journeys" offers some interesting comments along with the wealth of examples. She concludes that there is "a fundamental kinship" between these visions (or NDEs) and the imaginative powers that we use in everyday life:

> . . . we are all, in a sense, otherworld travelers. Otherworld visions are products of the same imaginative power that is active in our ordinary ways of visualizing death; our tendency to portray ideas in concrete, embodied, and dramatic forms; the capacity of our inner states to transfigure our perception of outer landscapes; our need to internalize the cultural map of the physical universe, and our drive to experience that universe as a moral and spiritual cosmos in which we belong and have a purpose . . .

we are able to grant the validity of near-death testimony as one way in which the religious imagination mediates the search for ultimate truth. (p. 205)

On this view, then, the NDE is one particularly interesting form that has been taken by the human mind in attempting to explain itself *to* itself. Science takes one path; imagination and intuition take another. Why choose only one path and dismiss the other? Zaleski's approach does not necessarily reduce the fascination and significance of NDEs, but it does attempt to show their continuity with the quest for meaning and purpose that many people have undertaken from ancient times to the present. Nevertheless, in common with the other alternative explanations that have been presented here, Zaleski's does not support the interpretation of the NDE as the report of a literal return from the dead.

The NDE clearly is of interest as a remarkable human experience. But were the survivors really dead? Do such reports provide evidence for survival of death? These questions remain controversial. In my judgment the case for the NDE as proof of survival has too many logical and empirical flaws to accept, despite the fact that some worthwhile research has been done. But what are we to make of Sabom's six survivors with demonstrably specific and accurate recollections? There may yet be important new developments in this field.

OTHER TYPES OF POSSIBLE EVIDENCE FOR SURVIVAL

Deathbed Escorts

People have searched for proofs of survival for many centuries, long before the health sciences enabled people to survive close calls with death and thereby increased the frequency of the NDE. Mythology and folklore provide many examples of a guide who is said to escort the living across the border to death. This guide often takes a form very similar to the "gentle comforter" personification of death that was discussed in an earlier chapter.

Such stories have come from a number of specific locations. One of the most famous series of alleged occurrences involves a "gray lady" who started to appear to dying patients in a London hospital many years ago. When a modern physician decided to examine this legend, he discovered that new instances were still being reported (Turner, 1959). Dying patients insisted that the gray lady visited them often and even filled their water jugs. The reports were always of a gray uniform, but the staff nurses actually wore blue. These patients had not known that gray was the color of the nurses' uniforms when the hospital had been new. For other examples, Sir William Barrett's recently reprinted *Deathbed Visions* (1926/1986) might be consulted.

An adventuresome research team has examined the deathbed escort phenomenon both in the United States and India. Karlis Osis and his colleagues (Osis, 1961; Osis & Haraldsson, 1977) eventually collected observations from more than 2,000 physicians and nurses, many of whom had multiple observations to share. Their major findings follow:

1. Patients at times were observed to be interacting with a visitor or apparition that others could not see. These patients were clear of mind and in possession of their mental faculties, not drugged, confused, or delusional.
2. The visitations usually come to people who were known to be dying, but there were also instances in which the deathbed escort appeared to a person who was not thought to be gravely ill—and that person did pass away shortly afterward.
3. The visitations were not always welcome. It sometimes appeared as though the escort had to convince the patient that the time was near.
4. The escorts were varied. Some people saw the apparition of one of their parents; others believed they were interacting with an angel or messenger of God.
5. Occasionally something happened that the physicians or nurses themselves could witness:

    In the room where he was lying, there was a staircase leading to the second floor. Suddenly he ex-

claimed: "See, the angels are coming down the stairs. The glass has fallen and broken." All of us in the room looked toward the staircase where a drinking glass had been placed on one of the steps. As we looked, we saw the glass break into a thousand pieces without any apparent cause. It did not fall; it simply exploded. The angels, of course, we did not see. A happy and peaceful expression came over the patient's face and the next moment he expired. Even after his death the serene, peaceful expression remained on his face. (Osis & Haraldsson, 1977, p. 42)

In general, the deathbed visions had similar features in the United States and India, despite the substantial cultural differences. The visions could be distinguished easily from ordinary hallucinations, and many had received no sedation.

Do these reports provide evidence for survival? The critical response (Kastenbaum, 1984) points out that the data were retrospective and difficult to verify, depending upon the vagaries of the respondents' memory. Furthermore, many if not all of the deathbed visitors may have been wish-fulfilling fantasies. Such fantasies, deriving from the special needs of the dying person, could differ appreciably from the hallucinations of the mentally disturbed but be hallucinations nevertheless. The escorts may well have been created by the dying person's own unconscious and projected into the outer world. One part of the dying person's self would therefore be able to communicate with another part through the hallucination, thereby overcoming the internal barriers within the personality. It is also noted that although reports of deathbed visions can be collected when the effort is made, it still remains a fairly unusual occurrence. Why doesn't every dying person have an escort? The answer is easier to find if the deathbed vision is regarded as a wish fulfillment based on overwhelming psychological and physical needs than if we make the speculative leap to literal belief in a messenger from the beyond.

Again, I do not find the evidence here nearly strong enough to stand as proof of survival. And yet I have witnessed several deathbed vision scenes and continue to wonder.

Communicating with the Dead?

There is a sizable older literature that explores the survival hypothesis through still another approach. A *medium* is a person who is thought by some to have an unusual sensitivity to communications from the deceased. Interest in "spiritism" ran high from the middle of the 19th century onward. Although in decline during recent decades, interest in reputed communications with the dead has not completely disappeared. Because more detailed accounts of mediumship and its vicissitudes are readily available (Evans-Wentz, 1960; Garrett, 1968; Ring, 1978), this section will concentrate on only a few points of particular relevance.

First, it is important to distinguish between a "high road" and a "low road." There have been repeated exposures of bogus mediums; indeed, "spook sleuths" have enjoyed themselves mightily in uncovering both the out-and-out frauds and the self-deceived (Proskauer, 1928). The stereotype of the charlatan has gained wide distribution: the unprincipled phony who preys upon the sorrows and hopes of the bereaved and the uncritical innocence of the curious. This stereotype is well justified. It does not encompass all the phenomena in this area, however. The focus here is on the "high road"—efforts made by people who appeared to have both integrity and critical intelligence.

Interest in alleged communication with the dead was stimulated by a challenge to the prevailing belief that the universe was safe in God's hands and humankind's place secure. The rise of technology and science led to an alternative conception that many felt to be alien and threatening. The doctrine of an afterlife seemed in particular jeopardy. Some people fought against the inroads of science with the weapons of emotion and scripture. Others decided to bend science's methods to their own use. People of both types joined in the establishment of the British Society of Psychical Research (SPR) in 1882 (still quite alive). The scholars and scientists in this group are of particular interest. F.W.H. Myers was a man of prodigious learning in the classics and up to date in his comprehension of the very new depth psychology movement. A number of others in the SPR charter group were also learned people with rigorous criteria for evidence. These people differed among themselves in their attitude toward survival, but all were keenly interested in trying to come up with a conclusive answer.

They tried every method that came to mind. A Census of Hallucinations was taken (one of the first major public surveys). Personal observations suggestive of communications with the deceased were critically examined, and most were discarded. This left a core of incidents that they believed deserved to be taken more seriously. F.W.H. Myers (1903/1975) presented and discussed many of these in his monumental two-volume work, *Human Personality and Its Survival of Bodily Death*. In attempting to explain these phenomena, Myers weighed many alternative possibilities. The books are still a treasure-trove for those who seek a starting point in this area. A "spirit photography" approach became popular for a while but was rather quickly deflated by the prick of multiple criticisms. Of more promise were the relatively new phenomena of automatic writing and trance reception. Automatic writing seemed to be a dissociative state. A person would write rapidly—sometimes amazingly so—and scarcely be aware of this activity either then or later. The thoughts seemed to write themselves down, as messages from some other person, whether living or deceased. Later more phenomena of the trance type appeared. The individual would appear to go into what these days would be called an altered state of consciousness. In this state there were sometimes the intrusion of thoughts and personalities that appeared alien to the individual.

Serious investigators of the survival hypothesis were fascinated with these phenomena. Here was an improved opportunity to check out possible cases of communication. Automatic writing provided a written text that could be examined at leisure and checked against external data.

Trance states could be witnessed and monitored. They could and did devise strategies to detect fraud, self-deceit, and other possible influences. The "sensitive" or "medium" became the star—and in a real sense the defendant—in survival research proceedings. The life of more than one impressive medium was made miserable by the controls and invasions of privacy demanded by skeptical investigators. A very few of these mediums seemed to survive scrutiny, although criticism was not lacking even in these instances. (The names of Mrs. Leonard and Mrs. Piper are among those that most often are mentioned when you look for the strongest exemplars of the mediumistic tradition.) You could choose to be persuaded by the evidence or reject it on the basis either of flaws actually noted or flaws that might have thus far escaped detection.

There was a particularly interesting variation of the medium studies that still has not been satisfactorily resolved. Soon after the death of Myers there appeared a series of communications in the form of scattered and coded messages—sense could be made only when the various partial messages were collated. Furthermore, the messages seemed to be highly distinctive and specialized. The impression grew that Myers had himself made a postmortem innovation: a research method that would make it clear beyond reasonable doubt that he had communicated to the living. The cross correspondences started in this manner but became even more complex as various people tried to "interview" Myers and as the range of both transmitters and receivers increased somewhat over the years. Saltmarsh (1938/1975) has given a fascinating account of the cross-correspondence phenomena up to about half a century ago. It is practically impossible to develop a definitive evaluation of the cross-correspondence material that has accumulated, although perhaps computer analysis would prove useful. Other investigators have been suggesting methodologies that embody a similar logic (e.g., a lock whose combination can be solved only through communications from the dead to the living [Gauld, 1977]).

The central question, "Is there survival of death?" was not decisively answered by the first generation of professional researchers nor by their successors. The material they have gathered has enriched our general understanding of psychosocial dynamics, and some of their side observations (e.g., the sensing of "presences" soon after bereavement) have become part of established knowledge. Can the central question *ever* be answered? *Ever* is a long time. The inability to answer the question definitely today on the basis of available knowledge and methodology tells us little about the prospects tomorrow.

Reincarnation

The ancient belief in reincarnation until recently had little place in the death awareness movement. Attention to NDEs has encouraged, perhaps "licensed," renewed attention to phenomena suggestive of reincarnation. This phrase itself, "suggestive of reincarnation," has been made familiar by the systematic research of psychiatrist Ian Stevenson. His work in this area started well before the current increase of interest and provides the most substantial and systematic body of information from a clinical research standpoint. His *Twenty Cases Suggestive of Reincarnation* (1974) is perhaps the classic book in this field, but he has contributed many other articles and books as well (1975; 1977; 1978).

A hallmark of Stevenson's approach is intensive case-by-case analysis. These case histories often are presented in considerable detail. Readers are left to draw their own conclusions. It is a method that combines some of the art of the researcher and the detective. Stevenson's work is lucid, systematic, and detailed. His series of case histories is a model of its kind. The reader, therefore, has no easy way out. You can simply refuse to examine evidence suggestive of reincarnation because the idea itself appears incredible. If you do examine the evidence, however, it becomes difficult to make a quick and decisive judgment.

Stevenson characterizes the typical case as one that starts early in childhood, usually between ages two and four years. The child starts to describe details of a previous life.

> The child often begins talking about this previous life as soon as he gains any ability to speak, and sometimes before his capacity for verbal expression matches his need to communicate. . . . The subjects . . . vary greatly both in the quantity of their utterances and in the richness of the memories. . . . Some children make only three or four different statements about a previous life, but others may be credited with 60 or 70 separate items pertaining to different details in the life remembered. . . . In most cases the volume and clarity of the child's statements increase until at the age of between five and six he usually starts to forget the memories; or, if he does not forget them, he begins to talk about them less. Spontaneous remarks about the previous life have usually ceased by the time the child has reached the age of eight and often before. Unexpected behavior . . . nearly always accompanies the statements the child makes about the previous life he claims to remember, or occurs contemporary with them. This behavior is unusual for a child of the subject's family, but concordant with what he says concerning the previous life, and in most instances it is found to correspond with what other informants say concerning the behavior of the deceased person about whom the subject has been talking, if such a person is traced. (Stevenson, 1974, p. 324)

Attention has been given here to only a few characteristics of the suggestive cases; many other characteristics are described by Stevenson.

The possibility of fraud is considered highly unlikely by Stevenson because of the large number of witnesses in many of the cases and the lack of opportunity or motivation for deception. Suppose for sake of further discussion that fraud could be ruled out decisively. Are there alternative explanations of these phenomena that require assumptions less radical than reincarnation? Perhaps the most obvious alternative is what has become known as the "super ESP hypothesis" (Gauld, 1961). The child who acts as though a reincarnated spirit may instead be an exceptionally adept recipient of psychic communications from others. You might well protest

that this alternative does not have much advantage over the reincarnation thesis. Many remain skeptical of "ordinary" ESP and are even less inclined to accept the "super" variety. This alternative, although itself quite controversial, does seem a shade more parsimonious. The "messages" are thought to be some form of communication from one living being to another. In this view it is not necessary to assume any direct connection between a deceased and a living person. The super ESP hypothesis has problems of its own and, though more conservative than the reincarnation interpretation, can offer little positive evidence in its favor. The patterns of thought and action reported in reincarnation-type cases have not yet proved amenable to solid explanation.

Additional questions rather than answers come forth when evidence for reincarnation is sought through hypnosis. This approach has the advantage of introducing an experimental condition under circumstances that are more or less within the researcher's control. You can go "reincarnation hunting" with specified respondents and standard procedures instead of waiting for spontaneous cases to appear wherever and whenever they choose. Helen Wambach (1979) has prepared a nontechnical report of her explorations with hypnosis. *Life Before Life* offers statistical information and brief case examples from her work with 750 people. The material obtained from her respondents often dealt with experiences they believed were associated with birth. Some of the recollections elicited in the hypnotic state, however, concerned supposed previous existences—including one or more death experiences. These cases, as presented, do not include the extensive detective-like verification process that characterizes Stevenson's work. We have less reason, then, to accept these reincarnation accounts as having strong ties with objective reality. There is also the question of how we are inclined to interpret the hypnotic state. Commercial hypnotists have encouraged a mystique that portrays it as a very special state of the organism in which almost anything can happen.

Some leading researchers, however, favor a different conception (Barber, 1969). Hypnosis is seen to be more of an interactive process, a collaborative effort, not the passive response of one person to the influence of the other. It is reasonably clear that the hypnotic process can help some individuals recall events that do not seem to have been available to them under ordinary circumstances. The limits of this recollection have not been definitively established. The claim for recalling actual birth or reincarnation experiences is an extreme one.

Of the many questions that might be asked about available data suggestive of reincarnation, there is one that appears especially salient to me. How could *anybody* be reincarnated unless *everybody* is reincarnated? The test of universality was applied earlier in this chapter to NDEs, which were found clearly lacking in this respect. The true incidence of reincarnation experiences is not known. From the voluminous files of Stevenson and from other cases that have been described, it would seem that this is not as rare a phenomenon as once believed. Yet these cases do remain unusual, which is one of the reasons they have generated such interest. You might argue that everybody *does* become reincarnated, but that only a few have conscious awareness. This possible explanation would be difficult to put to the test, although refinements of the Wambach approach might be useful. There is an even more radical possibility: *Death may not be the same for everybody.* Of all the possibilities considered in this chapter, the prospect of *pluralistic death* might well be the most extreme. It could be the possibility that would most challenge our basic assumptions about the nature of life and the universe. There is survival of death, or there is not survival. The rational mind may find either of these alternatives more acceptable, more probable than the possibility that death may be not an immutable certainty but a variable. It may be important to recognize this possibility since conventional views of death do not seem quite able to encompass all the phenomena that have been described in this book.

SHOULD WE SURVIVE DEATH?

"Should we survive death?" may seem to be a peculiar question. The quest for prolongation of life is among the most ancient of human themes. We find it expressed in the *Epic of Gilgamesh,* which has somehow managed to come down to us from the Sumerian people who lived more than 3,000 years before the Christian era (Heidel, 1970). The elaborate Tibetan (Evans-Wentz, 1960) and Egyptian (Gardiner, 1935) rituals governing our relationship to the next life are perhaps the best known of their kind, but anthropologists have routinely discovered and historians have frequently reconstructed many other examples (Frazer, 1977; Wunderlich, 1974). Most of the world's great religions have generated images of an afterlife, often powerful enough to influence the everyday functioning of individual and society (Choron, 1963). Furthermore, scientific endeavor often has been motivated by the hope of achieving victory over death, whether we scan as far back as the medieval alchemist (Gruman, 1977) or examine the current scene (Harrington, 1969).

And yet not everybody takes comfort in the survival doctrine. The person who fears an eternity of torture and damnation is one obvious exception. This is by no means the only basis for hesitation about the desirability of an afterlife. Consider these comments from college students to item 3 in the self-quiz that started this chapter. These respondents believe in life after death and attempted to describe it:

I really can't answer that question. That's funny, isn't it? Here I am, a good Christian and I believe in heaven and all that, but I can't get what it's all about clear in my mind. I think my problem is in the idea of a literal heaven, a Sunday school fairytale. I can't really accept that any more, but I don't have anything to replace it.

You tell me! I imagine eternity as a state of perfection. No more worries, no more problems. Best of all, no more deadlines and exams! But then what? All I can imagine is God and all the rest of us posing forever for our portrait with this transcendental smile on our faces. I think I'd go crazy! I need to worry and rush around and fight against time or I'm not really myself.

It will be beautiful and peaceful. More beautiful and peaceful than anything we can know on earth. Maybe the closest would be a long and relaxed Sunday afternoon. What makes a Sunday afternoon so great, though, is that it comes after one hectic week and before another. I don't know how I would do if there was only Sunday afternoon. This is probably a dumb way to think about heaven, but it's the best I can do.

Perhaps the difficulty these people confronted in forming a conception of the afterlife is what the Rumanian essayist E. M. Corian (1963) had in mind when he asked, "If Sunday afternoons were extended for months, where would humanity get to . . . ?" He answered his question, "The universe transformed into a Sunday afternoon . . . is the very definition of ennui, and the end of the universe . . . Take away the curse [of mortality] hanging over History and it immediately vanishes . . . in absolute vacancy. How kill this time which no longer passes?" (pp. 22–23).

Some conceptions of the afterlife involve continuing activity, change, risk, and danger. The loves, hates, hopes, and fears of earthly life persist, while we meet new perils that can even result in a second and permanent death (Amore, 1974). It is not difficult to imagine a new form of life that preserves so much of what you have already experienced. For Christians, however, the afterlife has often been portrayed in rather static terms, as a final and unchanging state of bliss. The hyperintellectual and the mystic may have ways of sensing a Christian afterlife that is neither literal nor dull. Some believers, however, are uncomfortable with a heaven that seems just too heavenly and therefore remote from their own lives and thoughts.

A more radical orientation can also be taken toward the desirability of survival. There are two main components here: (1) we do not deserve survival, and (2) the prospect of survival encourages the worst side of human nature.

The first part of the negative case would be supported by all the cruelty, stupidity, greed, and pettiness that can be found in the lives of individuals and societies through the centuries. Make your own list. How many examples of genocide will you include? How many examples of fortunes being made by inflicting suffering on others? How many examples of wanton destruction, of royal whim or bureaucratic arrogance? History and literature (not to mention the daily news) provide more examples than we can use. Whatever items we may choose for our list, the conclusion might be the same: *Homo sapiens* has by no means earned the right for survival beyond the grave.

We might also count against ourselves the way we often waste time and therefore life. Should eternal life be granted to those who have no ideas, motives, or ability to use the hours and days of earthly life? If much of our discretionary time is merely filled or killed, what claim do we have on immortality?

The second facet of the negative case is no less complimentary to the human race. One of the arguments here is that the prospect of eternal life has been used repeatedly to manipulate believers in the service of power and greed and at times raging fanaticism. The toll in lives and brutalization is high enough if we count only violence within and between religious establishments. The guarantee of immortal blessing for those who die while slaughtering designated enemies has led to some of history's most ferocious battles. The toll rises when we consider all the other manifestations of intolerance that can draw strength from belief in a life everlasting.

The moral case against survival, then, is that we might be forced to become better people and learn to make more constructive use of our time on earth if we did not have the prospect of an afterlife as either an all-dominating or fail-safe goal.

Of course, this is controversial. A thorough consideration of Eastern thought and practice would add still other dimensions. The way of the Buddah, for example, differs greatly from the

Christian conception of life-death-afterlife (Lee, 1974). "Death," in effect, disappears if you can attain a heightened spiritual development in which birth and beginnings, cravings and ambitions also dissolve. The character of the Buddhist survival doctrine is distinctive in both its internal features and its implications for individual and social action. Militant violence against others, for example, does not flow readily from this tradition. Nevertheless, arguments can still be advanced against the desirability of this survival doctrine as well.

Consider a single example: The Buddhist philosophy encourages inwardness, the cultivation of the inner self. This can be regarded as a valuable, even as an indispensable orientation. The turning inward, however, with its cosmic agenda, can lead to neglect of pressing concerns on the worldly plane. A holy person pursuing the ultimate spiritual development inadvertently may contribute to the persistence of poverty, suffering, and inequity that could have been modified by vigorous action in the world. In this sense a doctrine pointed toward spiritual transcendence of life and death might work against the improvement of conditions on earth.

Neither the Buddhist nor the Christian *necessarily* ignores the everyday human condition. Certainly, there have always been activists who envision their own mission as both individual and social-humanitarian. The point can always be raised, however: Does a dominating vision of the afterlife divert and obstruct attention from flesh-and-blood realities here and now?

BUT WHAT KIND OF SURVIVAL?

Suppose that there *is* survival after death. I can imagine a roomful of people who are in agreement with this statement—yet each of these people might have a very different conception of the afterlife. Here is what they might tell us:

• "Survival? Yes, as a burst of pure energy. The person dies, and at the last moment of life there is a discharge of electromagnetic radiation.

Does this *death flash* continue in some form, and does it encode and preserve the individual's identity? Perhaps. This we do not know yet. But the burst of electromagnetic radiation can be documented."

• "Have you seen a ghost? Most apparitions, or ghosts if you will, seem rather lost and slow-witted, not like the real people they once were, more like shadows or representations. What happens after death—at least in some circumstances—is that a temporary trace of the person remains in the locale. You might call this a force-field. When you encounter this 'person-shaped' force-field you have encountered something that exists in nature; but it does not exist for long and it is not the survived person, but his or her energy traces, and these will fade before long."

• "Fading, that is just what happens, but not in the way that you have proposed. When people die they move from the realm of light to the realm of darkness. There is survival here, in this underworld, but it is a sad survival, a slow fading away to blank, characterless beings who lose all that made them passionate and knowing individuals. The Greeks called them *shades.* Poor lost souls, poor wandering creatures in a cosmic nightmare."

• "These quaint ideas miss the real point. There is true immortality—but not for everybody. Like much else in life, survival of death is *conditional.* What is it conditional *on?* This surpasses our understanding at present—but it might well be that people who develop great spiritual strength will not perish along with their bodies. The soul does not possess immortality, rather it may have the potential for immortality. And so, the lives of many of us may end when we think they do, at physical death, but the lives of some people may continue because they have become *real* in a different way."

• "Survival? How can you avoid it? We are born but to die, and die but to be reborn. Not only those of us who are at the moment human beings, but all living things (and perhaps 'inanimate' things as well) go through cycle after cycle of existence. There are so many beginnings and so many ends: but, for most of us, no Beginning and no End."

- "We live. We die. We are judged. We are damned or we are granted salvation through the mercy of the Lord. The righteous dwell forever with the Lord; those who live in ignorance or defiance will know the fires of hell."

- "Human life is—or should be—a progression toward enlightenment, toward spiritual development. This does not have much to do with the external forms of religion, but rather with each person's journey from ignorance to understanding, from concern with individuality and materiality to becoming part of a more universal consciousness. The passage from life to death is but one transition in this long journey, and what the person brings to death—and takes from death—depends upon his or her level of spiritual development at that point."

- "What crazy people! The juice of the silly-berry has made you see things as they are not and fail to see things as they are. A person dies, of course. This always happens. And then that person just goes on with his life or with her life. This always happens, too. The next life is much like this one. There are pleasures. There are troubles. One can say the wrong thing or touch the wrong person and get one's self killed again, too. What else is a person to do in the next life but those things this person has always known and has always tried to do? These strange stories I hear from you—well I do not like them very much, but maybe I will like them better if you have saved some of that powerful silly-berry juice for me!"

All the views paraphrased above have been expressed at various times. The concept of the next life being essentially a continuation of the present life has been held by many tribal peoples over the centuries. By contrast, the "death flash" theory is a recent proposal that is based upon experiments on electromagnetic radiation in living tissues (Slawinski, 1987), and the "trace-field" theory was proposed by a leading psychic researcher around the turn of the century (Myers, 1903/1975), while "conditional immortality" was suggested by one of the few 20th century philosophers who took the question of survival as a serious intellectual issue (Hocking, 1957). What attitude should be taken toward these competing views? All speak of survival in some form, yet the forms differ markedly from each other. We can decide not to trouble ourselves with the less familiar or more disturbing concepts, and stick with whatever ideas we brought with us to the beginning of this chapter. Or we can pause for at least a moment to acknowledge that humankind has imagined more than one kind of survival and may have still other versions to discover. Even (or especially) those concepts that most trouble us might be valuable in what they suggest about the nature of the minds that dare to think beyond the limits of everyday experience.

YOUR THOUGHTS ON SURVIVAL: A REVIEW

Your thoughts on survival of death were invited at the beginning of this chapter. Now compare your responses with those of health professionals and other college students. Following are some of the findings:

1. Most health-care professionals and college students who have answered these questions do believe in some form of life after death (ranging from 71% to 87% in various samples).
2. Almost half (48%) of the believers across the samples report themselves "completely sure." About one believer in seven (14%) is "not sure at all."
3. Although belief in survival is somewhat more frequent and confident among females and among the older health-care professionals, believers outnumber nonbelievers for both sexes at all ages studied.

4. The New Testament and accepted tradition are most often cited as sources that would be used to convince others of survival. The next most common answer is that we need faith in God and immortality to make it through the tribulations of life.

5. Some believers (from 28% to 45%) were unable or unwilling to indicate how they would try to persuade a believer to the opposite conclusion (item 4). The most commonly used approach by both believers and nonbelievers is that the body does stop functioning, the mind depends on the body, and the dead do not actually come back to us.

6. Believers seldom were able or willing to specify any possible evidence, event, or experience that might lead them to change their opinion about survival, whereas almost all nonbelievers could think of something (a general "scientific breakthrough," for example, or "a powerful personal experience, like really having a dead person I knew very well come back to me in some kind of vision and say things that made me realize I wasn't making it up myself.") Highly confident believers were even less likely to imagine anything that could lead them to change their minds.

7. There is a great deal of variability among both believers and nonbelievers in regard to the way that their views of survival may be affecting their lives. Believers tended to say that they drew strength from the prospect of survival but did not often specify examples.

8. Beliefs were formed early in childhood, according to almost all respondents, but the nonbelievers were more likely to have reconsidered this topic in recent years.

9. What to tell a child proved to be most difficult for those who were not very sure of their position on survival, whether believers or nonbelievers. Nonbelievers more frequently expressed some conflict or uncertainty in what to say, but wavering believers also had their difficulties. Responding to a child's questions can test our own belief system. (Review Chapter 7 for suggestions on discussing death with children.)

This overview of the way other people have responded to questions about survival suggests that believers are less open to possible negative evidence than nonbelievers are to positive evidence.

But what of national data? Surveys indicate that about seven of ten people in the United States believe in an afterlife (Klenow & Bolin, 1989–1990). Those in the 18–29 age range are somewhat less likely to believe in an afterlife when compared with those in the 30–59 range. Although it is often assumed that belief in afterlife is especially common among old people, surveys find that those over 60 are actually a little *less* likely to hold this belief when compared with middle-aged people. Another interesting finding is that Afro–Americans have a lower incidence of belief in an afterlife (about 55%) than whites (about 71%). Believers are slightly more common among women than men (72% to 67%). Strong beliefs in afterlife are expressed most often by Protestants (86%). Most Catholics (74%) also report confidence in their beliefs, but relatively few Jews (8%) indicated that they had firm beliefs in an afterlife.

Statistics such as these have some value as a way of monitoring the beliefs of the American public. However, the questions associated with survival of death cannot really be settled by survey results, nor by insisting more loudly than the other person that our views are the only views that matter.

REFERENCES

Amore, R. C. (1974). The heterodox philosophical systems. In F. H. Holck (Ed.), *Death and Eastern thought* (pp. 114–163). Nashville: Abingdon Press.

Barber, T. X. (1969). *Hypnosis: A scientific approach.* New York: Van Nostrand Reinhold Co., Inc.

Barrett, W. (1986). *Death-bed visions.* Northampton: The Aquarian Press. (Original work published 1926)

Brent, S. (1979). Deliberately induced, premortem out-of-the-body experiences: An experimental and theoretical approach. In R. Kastenbaum (Ed.), *Between life and death* (pp. 89–123). New York: Springer Publishing Co., Inc.

Choron, J. (1963). *Death and Western thought.* New York: Collier Books.

Cioran, E. M. (1975). *A short history of decay* (R. Howard, Trans.) New York: The Viking Press.

Douglas, A. (1977). *Extra-sensory powers: A century of psychical research.* Woodstock, N.Y.: The Overlook Press.

Evans-Wentz, W.Y. (Ed. & Trans.). (1960). *Bardo Thodol, the Tibetan book of the dead.* Oxford, England: Oxford University Press.

Frazer, J. G. (1977). *The fear of the dead in primitive religion.* New York: Arno Press. (Original work published in 3 volumes in 1933)

Gabbard, G. O., & Twemlow, S. W. (1984). *With the eyes of the mind.* New York: Praeger.

Gardiner, A. (1935). *The attitude of ancient Egyptians to death and the dead.* Cambridge, England: Cambridge University Press.

Garfield, C. (1979). The dying patient's concern with "life after death." In R. Kastenbaum (Ed.), *Between life and death* (pp. 45–60). New York: Springer Publishing Co., Inc.

Garrett, E. J. (1968). *Many voices: The autobiography of a medium.* New York: The Putnam Publishing Group.

Gauld, A. (1961). The "super-ESP" hypothesis. *Proceedings of the Society for Psychical Research, 53,* 226–246.

Gauld, A. (1977). Discarnate survival. In B. Wolman (Ed.), *Handbook of parapsychology* (pp. 557–630). New York: Van Nostrand Reinhold Co., Inc.

Greyson, B. (1981). Empirical evidence bearing on the interpretation of NDE among suicide attempters. Paper presented at the annual meeting of the American Psychological Association, Los Angeles.

Greyson, B. (1983). The Near-Death Experience Scale: Construction, reliability, and validity. *Journal of Nervous & Mental Diseases, 171,* 967–969.

Grof, S., & Halifax, J. (1977). *The human encounter with death.* New York: Dutton.

Gruman, G. J. (1977). *A history of ideas about the prolongation of life.* New York: Arno Press.

Harrington, A. (1969). *The immortalist.* New York: Random House, Inc.

Heidel, A. (1970). The *Gilgamesh epic and Old Testament parallels.* Chicago: The University of Chicago Press.

Hocking, W. E. (1957). *The meaning of immortality in human experience.* New York: Harper.

Holck, F. H. (1978). Life revisited (parallels in death experiences). *Omega, Journal of Death and Dying, 9,* 1–12.

Irwin, H. J., & Bramwell, B. A. (1988). The Devil in Heaven: A near-death experience with both positive and negative facets. *Journal of Near-Death Experiences, 7,* 38–43.

Kastenbaum, R. (1981). Recent studies of the NDE: A critical appraisal. Paper presented at the annual meeting of the American Psychological Association, Los Angeles.

Kastenbaum, R. (1984). *Is there life after death?* London: Unwin.

Klenow, D. J., & Bolin, C. (1989–1990). Belief in an afterlife: A national survey. *Omega, 20,* 63–74.

La Barre, W. (1972). *The ghost dance: The origins of religion.* New York: Dell Publishing Co., Inc.

Lee, J. R. (1974). *Death and beyond in the Eastern perspective.* New York: Gordon & Brezch, Science Publishers, Inc.

Monroe, R. A. (1971). *Journeys out of the body.* Garden City, New York: Doubleday & Co., Inc.

Moody, R. A., Jr. (1975). *Life after life.* Atlanta: Mockingbird Books.

Moody, R. A., Jr. (1980). Commentary on "The reality of death experiences: A personal perspective" by Ernst Rodin. *Journal of Nervous and Mental Disease, 168,* 265.

Moody, R. A., Jr. (1988). *The light beyond.* New York: Bantam.

Myers, F. W. H. (1975). *Human personality and its survival of bodily death* (Vols. 1–2). New York: Arno Press. (Original work published 1903)

Noyes, R., Jr. (1979). Near-death experiences: Their interpretation. In R. Kastenbaum (Ed.), *Between life and death* (pp. 73–88). New York: Springer Publishing Co., Inc.

Noyes, R., Jr., & Kletti, R. (1976). Depersonalization in the face of life-threatening danger: A description. *Psychiatry, 39,* 19–27.

Noyes, R., Jr., & Kletti, R. (1976). Depersonalization in the face of life-threatening danger: An interpretation. *Omega, Journal of Death and Dying, 7,* 103–114.

Noyes, R., Jr. & Kletti, R. (1977). Panoramic memory: A response to the threat of death. *Omega, Journal of Death and Dying, 8,* 181–194.

Osis, K. (1961). *Deathbed observations by physicians and nurses.* New York: Parapsychology Foundation.

Osis, K., & Haraldsson, E. (1977). *At the hour of death.* New York: Avon Books.

Pelletier, K., & Garfield, C. (1976). *Consciousness: East and West.* New York: Harper & Row, Publishers, Inc.

Piper, A. L. (1929). *The life and work of Mrs. Piper.* London: Kegan Paul.

Pribham, K. H. (1977). Holonomy and structure in the organization of perception. In U.M. Nicholas (Ed.), *Images, perception and knowledge* (pp. 19–35). Dordrecht: D. Reidel.

Proskauer, J. (1928). *Spook crooks.* London: Selwyn & Blount.

Ring, K. (1978). Some determinants of the prototypic near death experience. Paper presented at the annual meeting of the American Psychological Association, Los Angeles.

Ring, K. (1980). *Life at death.* New York: Coward, McCann & Geoghegan.

Ring, K. (1984). *Heading toward Omega.* New York: William Morrow & Co.

Ring, K. (1989). Near-death experiences. In R. Kastenbaum & B. K. Kastenbaum (Eds.), *Encyclopedia of death* (pp. 193–196). Phoenix: Oryx Press.

Roth, M., & Harper, M. (1962). Temporal lobe epilepsy and the phobic anxiety-depersonalization syndrome. Part II: Practical and theoretical considerations. *Comprehensive Psychiatry, 3,* 215–226.

Sabom, M. B. (1982). *Recollections of death.* New York: Simon & Schuster.

Sabom, M. B., & Kreutziger, S. (1977). The experience of near death. *Death Education, 2,* 195–204.

Saltmarsh, H. F. (1975). *Evidence of personal survival from cross correspondences.* New York: Arno Press. (Originally published in 1938.)

Siegel, R. K. (1980). The psychology of life after death. *American Psychologist, 35,* 911–931.

Slawinski, J. (1987). Electrometic radiation and the afterlife. *Journal of Near-Death Studies, 6,* 79–94.

Stevenson, I. (1974). *Twenty cases suggestive of reincarnation* (rev. ed.). Charlottesville, Va.: University Press of Virginia.

Stevenson, I. (1975). *Cases of the reincarnation type: Vol. 1. Ten cases in India.* Charlottesville, Va.: University Press of Virginia.

Stevenson, I. (1977). Reincarnation: Field studies and theoretical issues. In B. B. Wolman (Ed.), *Handbook of parapsychology* (pp. 631–666). New York: Van Nostrand Reinhold Co., Inc.

Stevenson, I. (1978). *Cases of the reincarnation type. Vol. 2. Ten cases in Sri Lanka.* Charlottesville, Va.: University Press of Virginia.

Stevenson, I., Cook, C. W., & McClean-Rice, N. (1989–1990). Are persons reporting "near-death experiences" really near death? A study of medical records. *Omega, 20,* 45–54.

Thomas, L. E., Cooper, P. E., & Suscovich, D. J. (1982–1983). Incidence of near-death and intense spiritual experiences in an intergenerational sample: An interpretation. *Omega, Journal of Death and Dying, 13,* 35–42.

Turner, P. (1959). "The grey lady": A study of psychic phenomena in the dying. *Journal of the Society for Psychic Research, 40,* 124–129.

Wambach, H. (1979). *Life before life.* New York: Bantam Books, Inc.

Wunderlich, H. G. (1974). *The secret of Crete.* New York: Macmillan, Inc.

Zaleski, C. (1987). *Otherworld journeys.* New York: Oxford Press.

INDEX